New Frontiers in Regional Sci
Asian Perspectives

Volume 42

New Frontiers in Regional Science: Asian Perspectives

This series is a constellation of works by scholars in the field of regional science and in related disciplines specifically focusing on dynamism in Asia.

Asia is the most dynamic part of the world. Japan, Korea, Taiwan, and Singapore experienced rapid and miracle economic growth in the 1970s. Malaysia, Indonesia, and Thailand followed in the 1980s. China, India, and Vietnam are now rising countries in Asia and are even leading the world economy. Due to their rapid economic development and growth, Asian countries continue to face a variety of urgent issues including regional and institutional unbalanced growth, environmental problems, poverty amidst prosperity, an ageing society, the collapse of the bubble economy, and deflation, among others.

Asian countries are diversified as they have their own cultural, historical, and geographical as well as political conditions. Due to this fact, scholars specializing in regional science as an inter- and multi-discipline have taken leading roles in providing mitigating policy proposals based on robust interdisciplinary analysis of multifaceted regional issues and subjects in Asia. This series not only will present unique research results from Asia that are unfamiliar in other parts of the world because of language barriers, but also will publish advanced research results from those regions that have focused on regional and urban issues in Asia from different perspectives.

The series aims to expand the frontiers of regional science through diffusion of intrinsically developed and advanced modern regional science methodologies in Asia and other areas of the world. Readers will be inspired to realize that regional and urban issues in the world are so vast that their established methodologies still have space for development and refinement, and to understand the importance of the interdisciplinary and multidisciplinary approach that is inherent in regional science for analyzing and resolving urgent regional and urban issues in Asia.

Topics under consideration in this series include the theory of social cost and benefit analysis and criteria of public investments, socio-economic vulnerability against disasters, food security and policy, agro-food systems in China, industrial clustering in Asia, comprehensive management of water environment and resources in a river basin, the international trade bloc and food security, migration and labor market in Asia, land policy and local property tax, Information and Communication Technology planning, consumer “shop-around” movements, and regeneration of downtowns, among others.

Researchers who are interested in publishing their books in this Series should obtain a proposal form from Yoshiro Higano (Editor in Chief, higano@jsrsai.jp) and return the completed form to him.

More information about this series at http://www.springer.com/series/13039

Zhenhua Chen • William M. Bowen
Dale Whittington
Editors

Development Studies in Regional Science

Essays in Honor of Kingsley E. Haynes

Springer

Editors
Zhenhua Chen
Knowlton School of Architecture
City and Regional Planning
The Ohio State University
Columbus, OH, USA

William M. Bowen
Department of Urban Studies
Levin College of Urban Affairs
Cleveland State University
Cleveland, OH, USA

Dale Whittington
University of North Carolina at Chapel Hill
Chapel Hill, NC, USA

University of Manchester
Manchester, UK

ISSN 2199-5974 ISSN 2199-5982 (electronic)
New Frontiers in Regional Science: Asian Perspectives
ISBN 978-981-15-1434-0 ISBN 978-981-15-1435-7 (eBook)
https://doi.org/10.1007/978-981-15-1435-7

This Springer imprint is published by the registered company Springer Nature Singapore Pte Ltd.
The registered company address is: 152 Beach Road, #21-01/04 Gateway East, Singapore 189721, Singapore

Endorsement

Kingsley Haynes is a wise and insightful leader of the field of regional economics. He has contributed significantly to research, policy making, and the creation of enduring academic institutions. This book is a fitting tribute by his friends and students that combines rich scholarship and much gratitude for all that Kingsley has accomplished. It is full of sparkling essays that capture the range of areas in which Kingsley has left his mark.

Harvard University
Cambridge, MA, USA

Edward Glaeser

Contents

Chapter 1
Introduction

William M. Bowen, Zhenhua Chen, and Dale Whittington

Abstract This chapter introduces and describes several selected aspects of Professor Kingsley E. Haynes' background and orientation. These include his many academic accomplishments, deeply thoughtful scientific perspectives, and tremendous personal relationships with numerous students and colleagues. It gives an overview of each of the chapters and describes their organization throughout the book.

Keywords Extraordinary record of research and scholarship · Administrative appointments · Perspectives and impacts on regional science · Influence on students and colleagues · Overview of chapters in book

The Festschrift is a largely European academic tradition in which the contributions of an eminent scholar are honored and celebrated by colleagues who contribute original works to a volume dedicated to that scholar. Festschrifts are usually oriented around a prominent theme in the honoree's work and are usually written toward the end of the honoree's career. In this case, the honoree is Kingsley E. Haynes, and the theme is development studies in regional science.

W. M. Bowen
Department of Urban Studies, Levin College of Urban Affairs, Cleveland State University, Cleveland, OH, USA
e-mail: w.bowen@csuohio.edu

Z. Chen (✉)
Knowlton School of Architecture, City and Regional Planning, The Ohio State University, Columbus, OH, USA
e-mail: chen.7172@osu.edu

D. Whittington
University of North Carolina at Chapel Hill, Chapel Hill, NC, USA

University of Manchester, Manchester, UK

Z. Chen et al. (eds.), *Development Studies in Regional Science*,
New Frontiers in Regional Science: Asian Perspectives 42,
https://doi.org/10.1007/978-981-15-1435-7_1

The challenge of reducing Kingsley Haynes' wide-ranging body of extraordinary scholarship to this one theme was daunting. For nearly 50 years, Kingsley has tirelessly dedicated himself to building and advancing knowledge in applied geography and regional science. He has worked and published widely not only in development studies but also in areas including transportation and telecommunication infrastructure investment, regional economic development, and analytic modeling for decision support. He has been an active participant and source of financial support for a wide range of conferences. He has engaged in one way or another with an exceptionally large number of students, including the three of us, challenging us and encouraging us to prepare research for presentation at conferences. When his students have successfully risen to his challenges, he has sent them to the conferences to present. In this way he has formed bonds and maintained his relationships with his students for years after graduation and on in to our professional and academic lives. In this and other ways, thankfully, he has developed such a large number of devoted students, colleagues, and friends that the task of finding willing contributors to a volume honoring him and his work turned out to be surprisingly easy.

Kingsley began to develop an interest in geography starting in his high school years in Canada (Haynes 2007). From there, his odyssey as a student unfolded from Western Michigan University, to Rutgers University, to Johns Hopkins University where he learned geographical and regional scientific theory, analytic methods, and statistics, and he learned to apply them, first in predicting migration behavior and spatial interaction. As a Ph.D. student, he studied economics, demography, sociology, operations research, as well as game theory and neural networks. This multidisciplinary academic background led to a lifelong interest in transportation and urban development patterns. He worked in the Middle East as the Director of the Ford Foundation's Office of Resources and Environment. While there he focused his research upon the management of the Nile River, the development of operating rules for the Aswan High Dam, capacity building in water quality monitoring and management, and assessment of the Jonglei Canal project in the southern Sudan. By the time he returned to the United States, he had started his career-long characteristic behavior pattern of seeking and securing academic and governmental grants on one hand and at the same time using the resources from those grants to work on a wide range of applied problems, such as simulation models for airport design, airport development, university location decisions, and the regional effects of school district consolidation on the other. He developed interests in energy and pollution management through his research in the Ohio River Basin and energy expansion and water resource management in the Yellowstone Basis. He developed expertise in environmental analysis, infrastructure, investment and financing, decision support, GIS, public management, and public policy. Throughout his research and applied activities in these many areas, he has always kept a core focus upon the interaction of theory and practice within the context of real-world problem-solving.

To say that Kingsley's contribution to research and scholarship has been extraordinary is, in many respects, an understatement. In the course of his career, he has held faculty and various administrative appointments at McGill University, the University of Texas, Indiana University, Boston University, and George Mason University. In 1990, after serving as the Chair of the Department of Geography at

Boston University, he became the founding Director of the Institute of Public Policy at George Mason University. In 2000, after having grown the Institute into a School of Public Policy, he became the Founding Dean. He then led the young School's growth to the point of having over 75 faculty members, 150 PhD students, and 850 MA students in five programs, with a total of 350 staff members. For his many accomplishments, he has earned numerous honors and awards including the James R. Anderson Medal for Applied Research in Geography, the North American Regional Science Conferences' Boyce Distinguished Service Award, Fellow of the Regional Science Association International, and Fellow of the National Academy of Public Administration. Along the way he has been the principal investigator, co-principal investigator, or researcher on approximately 90 grants and contracts worth over $66,000,000.00 from sources such as the National Science Foundation, the National Atmospheric and Space Administration, and the US Departments of Transportation, Defense, Energy, and State. And he published over 220 peer-reviewed and academic publications with over 120 separate co-authors.

The limits on time, energy, and attention faced in introducing a Festschrift for Professor Haynes do not allow us to fully describe the impact he has had on knowledge in regional science and applied geography nationally and internationally. We could not say it better than Peter Nijkamp, Emeritus Professor of Regional Economics and Economic Geography at the Vrije Universiteit in the Netherlands:

> Kingsley Haynes has a long standing career in the area of regional science. He belongs to the second generation of regional scientists who have built on the scientific inheritance of founding fathers, such as Walter Isard, Charles Tiebout and Bill Alonso on the American side and Leo Klaassen and Torsten Hagerstrand on the European side. Kingsley has been for decades a great ambassador of regional science. His pioneering and seminal work covers a wide range of regional science topics, ranging from metropolitan areas to developing countries. He is one of those surprising scholars who can be found at many meetings all over the world. That also explains his great international reputation: he is a typical travelling salesman for regional science, always accompanied by his inspiring wife Susan.
>
> Kingsley Haynes has been very influential in the quantitative orientation in regional science. His interesting research is always characterized by advanced modelling and statistical techniques. In this way he has been very influential in shaping the next generation of regional science researchers.
>
> In addition to his great scholarship, he has also played an important role in leading functions in the Regional Science Association International (RSAI). His admirable administrative skills have also made him a core person in regional science, not only domestic but also international.

The core intellectual content in much of Kingsley's work is simply fascinating, which is one of the reasons some of his students are so devoted to him. He consistently takes a distinctly theoretical, quantitative, and analytical approach to problem-solving. His is not an approach to research based upon deducing actual regional phenomena from theory and mathematics. Rather, in the approach he taught to us, the actual phenomenon is to provide inductive verification of the general principles from which regional scientific theory and mathematics starts. All of the empirical observations and data are to retain their full evidential value. Insofar as possible, the observations and data confirm (or disconfirm) not merely a particular theory but also the general conceptual or mathematical foundations from which the deductive chain of reasoning starts. The theory and concepts as well as the data provide insight and guidance for finding the solutions to problems. Thus, he has never fallen prey to the all-too-common tendency to emphasize the theoretical and mathematical dimensions of research at the expense of the empirical dimensions or vice versa. Rather he has been able to consistently find and apply the interconnection between them all. Despite the significance of so much regional scientific and other theory and of all of the associated deductive mathematical constructions, Kingsley has consistently kept empirical investigation and real-world problem-solving of paramount importance.

But perhaps above all of Kingsley's contributions in importance is the impact he has had on his many colleagues and students. To characterize the sorts of relationships he has built and maintained, which of the three of us are privileged to share, we asked Dr. Fred Phillips to comment:

> Meeting Kingsley Haynes in 1974 was a fortuitous turning point in my education. Further, it was a meeting that grew into a lifelong friendship. As a graduate student in operations research I had little opportunity to engage my personal interest in places, especially in the lure of faraway ones. My PhD advisor, Abe Charnes, wisely saw how these could connect with O.R. He encouraged me to work with Kingsley, who was then a young professor in UT-Austin's geography department, about to move to UT's LBJ School of Public Affairs.
>
> Our first work together, with geography grad student Jerry White, was the Texas coastal planning project. It involved much productive writing of papers and questionably productive consumption of beer. I think it's fair to say that Kingsley in those years was primarily an impresario of research. At first I wondered why he would take this path, but I came to realize that this stance, bringing him into contact with many researchers in many fields, was Kingsley's deliberate learning strategy. Watching it was one of the ways I learned how to learn. In my later positions, I put it to good use.
>
> Though I'm now known as the Flying Professor, I have not matched Kingsley's amazing record of travel and adventure. I keep trying – often encountering Kingsley and Susan in exotic locales.
>
> I'm glad to have this chance to say, "Kingsley my friend, many thanks!"

With only slightly further effort we could undoubtedly have obtained literally dozens of such statements from former students all around the world.

The chapters in this volume span a wide range of issues and use many different methodological approaches, but the chapters are tied together by three attributes of Kingsley's professional work that have influenced his friends and colleagues. First, Kingsley works on important problems that have real consequences of human well-being. Academic minutiae and theoretical niceties have never drawn his attention. Throughout his career, Kingsley has been engaged with questions about economic and social development, in both low-income, middle-income, and high-income countries. His focus on research that can improve human well-being and promote development is reflected throughout this volume but especially his interests in the roles of infrastructure and the management of natural resources in regional development.

Second, Kingsley's research incorporates the practical realities of complex problems. He studies the complexities of the world as it is, not as a theoretical abstraction. He has used a wide array of systems tools and quantitative methods to characterize these complexities. Indeed, it would not be an exaggeration to say that only a handful of scholars in the world are as skilled and proficient in so many quantitative methods. But systems analysis and quantitative methods were never an end in themselves; his objective was always to use these techniques to develop a more realistic, sophisticated, nuanced assessment of complex problems.

Third, Kingsley's work has been profoundly interdisciplinary. He is at home in the disciplines of geography, regional science, economics, planning, decision science, and public policy analysis. As a public policy analyst par excellence, he was never caught up in the current preoccupation of the economics profession with the identification of causal relationships, which often limits the analyst to working on minor development problems. Kingsley Haynes' work and interests were never restricted by what a discipline defined as an acceptable problem or by what a particular method was able to do.

So, his work has been important, practical, rigorous, and interdisciplinary. And it was all done with an infectious joie de vivre that has inspired both students and colleagues.

He was on the faculty at four leading universities: University of Texas-Austin; Indiana University; Boston University, and George Mason University. We represent his former students from three of those universities and are very honored to have been invited to be Editors of this volume.

1.1 Overview of the Book

The book is organized in three parts. Part I concentrates on clarifying fundamental issues pertaining to development studies and regional science. In Chap. 2, Antoine Bailly and Lay Gibson uncover potentials to expand the content of regional science without disturbing its established character. It also discusses the need to minimize risks to the content while gathering the benefits of expanding the discipline into new content areas.

In Chap. 3, Kenneth Button provides a novel perspective by addressing a fundamental question: is there any substantial intellectual difference between regional science and other economic subjects, such as regional economics? Through a thorough review of regional science-related journals, the chapter explores the general patterns of specialization in economics. It then discusses the driving factors and moves to review the development trends of spatial economics and recently debated problems in applied economics.

Chapter 4, written by Alan Murray, discusses essential microscale thinking for bringing about change in order to mitigate the negative impacts of human-induced growth and development. The use of spatial analytical approaches, such as geographic information systems, spatial optimization, and spatial statistics, is considered. Central themes of microscale thinking and their applications for decision-making are reviewed, and their importance for achieving long-term sustainability and resilience are highlighted.

In Chap. 5, Richard Wright explores some of the core issues of social equity in development studies from the perspective of residency, race, and public employment. Using a case study in cluster towns in Northern New Jersey as an example, the analysis reveals that residency requirements designed to be inclusive can operate to be exclusive at the same time.

Chapter 6 was contributed by Mustafa Dinc. It explores the challenges of conflict in humanitarian local and regional economic development. Through a thorough examination of the conflict and related issues in the information age, the chapter provides insightful implications for future developments in information and communication technologies.

In Chap. 7 Laurie Schintler uncovers the new opportunities and challenges for regional policy analysis in the era of spatial big data. She further discusses the suitability of various methods and techniques, such as Data Envelopment Analysis, shift-share analysis, and spatial econometrics and statistical models, for the assessment of spatial big data. The chapter suggests that for spatial big data to achieve its full potential, a multidisciplinary approach, such as an integration of machine learning models with traditional nonparametric methods and econometrics models, may ultimately augment all stages of policy analysis. Such an approach will also contribute to the formulation and implementation of policies that support livable and sustainable regions.

In Chap. 8 Zheng Wang focuses on exploring some of the technical aspects of spatial modeling, which itself has a potential to advance the understanding of spatial interactions in the process of social and economic development. The chapter extends the spatial interaction model from the pioneering work done by Wilson (1970) by applying statistical mechanics of physics with an aim to improve the applicability of the model. The modeling framework provides new insights for the understanding of interactions of various agents, such as people, goods, and financial resource in space.

Computable general equilibrium (CGE) analysis, as the state-of-the-art method for economic impact analysis, has been widely adopted in development studies. However, the results of CGE analysis are generally reported based on macroeconomic indicators, such as GDP and employment, whereas less attention has been paid to economic welfare. James Giesecke and John Madden in Chap. 9 evaluate factors that affect the net social benefits of an economy using CGE. The chapter demonstrates that the most commonly adopted indicator for measuring the outcome (GDP) turns out to be a poor proxy for the effect on economic welfare. Instead, CGE modelers should focus on economic welfare indicators.

Part II of this volume introduces various cases that address challenges and opportunities in the process of development through the lens of Asian countries. Specifically, Chap. 10, authored by Barry Solomon and Fei Li, addresses environmental (in)equity in the patterns of toxic chemical releases vs. residential location. Using nuclear waste repository siting as an example, the chapter analyzes this issue through four case studies in Japan, South Korea, China, and Taiwan following unified equity principles. Their study reveals that governments in all of the cases need to work more diligently to maintain environmental equity for nuclear waste repository siting.

In Chap. 11, Inácio Araújo, William M. Bowen, Randall Jackson, and Amir Neto provide new insights to understanding the proximate causes of the change of CO_2 emissions and how its influence on economic development varies among different megaregions in Japan, the United States, Europe, China, India, and Russia. Through applying structural decomposition analysis to the World Input-Output Database, their analysis confirms that the patterns of emission vary substantially between developing and developed nations. In addition, their chapter reveals that increased consumption levels are the major driver for the increase of CO_2 emissions, which implies the unlikely but nevertheless logically and empirically justified conclusion that future policies need to emphasize eliminating ever-greater consumption.

Chapter 12 is contributed by Syed Hasnath. The chapter analyzes uneven development patterns in Bangladesh with a focus on income equality. The chapter suggests that moving and allocating resources to less developed regions for industries, infrastructure, and social overhead would help to increase income levels.

While most Asian countries are still in the development stage, the rapid economic development in China over the past decades has also strengthened its role in the regional economic systems in Asia and beyond. One of the salient examples is the implementation of the One Belt and One Road (OBOR) Initiative, also known as Belt and Road Initiative (BRI). In Chap. 13, Kailai Wang and Zhenhua Chen evaluate the role of infrastructure investment and regional economic growth with a focus on 65 OBOR countries. A dynamic shift-share method is adopted to decompose the employment changes into various effects, such as regional share, industry mix, and local shift. The analysis shows that the variation of employment is substantial among different sectors and countries. Hence, future infrastructure development strategies should be prioritized in accordance with regional competitiveness of different countries.

In Chap. 14, Francis Fukuyama and his colleagues further discuss the different approaches of infrastructure development between China and the Western world, using the BRI as an example. The analysis starts with an introduction of the origin of Chinese policy for development. Through a careful comparison of the Western and Chinese infrastructure investment strategies in terms of planning, financing, and deployment, the chapter provides important insights on infrastructure development that should be useful in future decision-making for both the Chinese government and Western development institutions.

In Chap. 15, Serdar Yilmaz and Robert Ebel extend the discussion of development challenges that East Asian countries face from the perspectives of governance, infrastructure, and public finance. The chapter begins with a review of recent literature on infrastructure deficit and the link between infrastructure services, economic growth, and development. It then discusses the function and goal of the intergovernmental organizational and institutional arrangements. The chapter concludes with a discussion of the risks related to debt financing by subnational governments.

Chapter 16, by Yang Zhou and Jean-Claude Thill, develops a new approach to identifying socioeconomic communities through a regionalization of urban structure based on transportation network data. Using taxi data with detailed information from the city of Wuhan, China, as an example, the study reveals that a new approach based on big data analytics is able to capture the socioeconomic characteristics through flow data. Such a finding also provides critical implications for urban planning and development. For instance, the efficiency and effectiveness of spatial configurations of the built environment and local communities may be improved through a better understanding of urban flow and urban structure.

Some of the development challenges, such as the lack of a sufficient infrastructure system and problems with social and economic inequality, are especially important in developing countries. Other problems, such as how human societies might adequately deal with the scarcity of critical resources such as water and how regions might attract and maintain high-skill labor to support sustainable growth, are more generic and are important in both developing and developed countries. Part III examines some of these development problems and issues from a global perspective. It is intended to provide readers with a holistic view of various ideas and approaches that may help us find solutions.

In Chap. 17, Joseph Cook and his colleagues provide an evaluation of customer assistance programs (CAPs), a strategy to address waster scarcity through implementing full cost recovery tariffs for water and sanitation services. Such programs are designed to help ensure that poor households have access to piped water and sanitation services, while water utilities implement price reforms to address revenue generation and water conservation objectives. Based on a comprehensive review of CAPs from industrialized countries and low- and middle-income countries, the chapter provides public agencies both in developed and developing countries with guidance for considering the effectiveness of their water subsidy programs.

Haifeng Qian in Chap. 18, addresses a fundamental question related to entrepreneurship and the geography of intergenerational economic mobility: why do young people born in some cities demonstrate a greater probability of moving up the income ladder than those born in others? The empirical analysis confirms that intergenerational upward mobility does have a positive statistical association with entrepreneurship activity. The empirical evidence, although preliminary, provides important insights for policy makers to better understand the benefits of entrepreneurship.

In Chap. 19, T.R. Lakshmanan and William Anderson discuss the nature and scope of the economic structural evolution in the dynamic settlement corridor stretching from Boston to Washington, D.C. in the United States. Through a review of the classical work by Jean Gottmann and an analysis of the urban development patterns in the I-95 corridor for a period of over a half-century, the chapter indicates that the economic dynamism along that corridor over recent decades has interdependent consequences for newly emerging transport and communication systems. The development of new technologies facilitates the rise of the global economy, and further promotes the emergence of new knowledge in the manufacturing and service economies.

Chapter 20, contributed by Bob Stimson and Alistair Robson, investigates factors that explain the spatial variation of endogenous regional employment performance in Australia. An integrated method of both shift-share analysis and regression modeling is applied to data that cover the period 1996–2016. The results confirm that factors such as population size, industrial structure, and the degree of concentration play major positive roles in the growth of endogenous regional employment.

However, the association between population and employment can also be different in other countries. In Chap. 21, Gordon Mulligan and Helena Nilsson analyze recent population and employment change in 381 US metropolitan areas. Using the simple but fundamental adjustment model, the chapter reveals that the changes of population and employment can be quite distinctive. In addition, the results further indicate that employment growth in many small US cities does not necessarily follow the traditional pattern of demand-induced growth (where people follow jobs). Overall, the chapter suggests that future development policies need to be developed more cautiously with a consideration of the size of the targeted metropolitan area.

Adam Rose, Zhenhua Chen, and Dan Wei evaluate the benefits of US antidumping (AD)/countervailing duty (CVD) enforcement in Chap. 22. This issue has become particularly relevant for economic sustainability given that global trade tension is on the rise due to the influence from the Trump Administration. Using the Global Trade Analysis Project (GTAP) Model, a multicountry computable general equilibrium (CGE) model, the research finds a positive impact of AD/CVD duties on the US economy. The chapter suggests that what at first might be viewed as an impediment to international trade actually benefits the US economy in a small way. Also, some sectors, such as electronic equipment, gain more than others.

In Chap. 23, Umut Turk and his colleagues examine the impact of job accessibility on social capital with a focus on rural areas in both Turkey and Italy using a quantile regression model based on a data at the NUTS3 level. The study reveals that social capital in response to accessibility and rurality in Turkey and Italy varies substantially, which could be mainly explained by their different levels of spatial accessibilities.

Chapter 24, contributed by Marco Alderighi and his colleagues, analyzes the issue of price discrimination and inter-group externalities in airline routes between European cities. The chapter provides some important empirical evidence that might help to improve air travel service through optimizing airline pricing.

In Chap. 25, Fred Phillips and Nasir Sheikh provide practitioners of economic development with a new perspective to understand the factors affecting business relocation incentive decisions. A multi-criteria decision framework called STEEP (Social, Technological, Economic, Environmental, Political) is adopted for the assessment. Based on a detailed analysis of survey results from economic development professionals, the chapter reveals that although the economic perspective is the key factor for business relocation decision-making, other factors in STEEP may also be important.

Last but certainly not least, in Chap. 26 Richard Florida and Charlotta Mellander examine the relationship between human capital and cross-national innovation and economic performance. The novel aspect of their work is that innovation and economic performance are measured by three indicators, all of which are associated with a new measure of human capital that focuses on the creative class. The results confirm that the occupation-based creative class measure is associated closely with all three measures of innovative and economic performance.

Overall, although this volume is the product of the contributions of a wide range of people, including scholars who are experts in development studies and regional science and practitioners who work at various organizations, all of them have been directly or indirectly influenced intellectually by Kingsley Haynes. Scholars and students who are interested in development studies and regional science will greatly benefit from the multidisciplinary analyses of the variety of case studies in the book. Planners and policymakers who are interested in obtaining new insights about regional economic development will also find the diverse perspectives captured in this volume valuable for their development practices.

References

Haynes KE (2007) The evolution of an applied geographer: a personal Odyssey. Res Geogr Educ 9(1):55–60

Wilson AG (1970) Inter-regional commodity flows: entropy-maximizing approaches. Geogr Anal 2:255–282

Part I
Fundamental Issues

Chapter 2
Expanding the Content of Regional Science: Risks and Rewards, an Essay

Antoine S. Bailly and Lay James Gibson

Abstract Regional Science has developed as a rigorous science with a strong foundation in economics and geography. There is no apparent reason for regional science to seek an entirely new orientation, but there is an argument for it to expand its horizons and reach by exploring opportunities for incorporating other disciplines. The idea here is not to dramatically shift the focus of regional science but rather to encourage the incorporation of new content and to expand the participant base by scientists and scholars who benefit from incorporating their fields with the approaches offered by regional science. The potential rewards are substantial but there are risks too. One obvious reward for disciplines and professional fields that elect to work within a regional science framework includes viewing problems through a new lens. The risks might include the dilution of the distinctiveness of the regional science approach as it seems to try to be all things to all people. This paper explores potentials to expand the content of regional science without disturbing its established character. And it discusses the need to minimize risks to the content while gathering the benefits of expanding the discipline into new content areas.

Keywords Epistemology of regional science · Pluridisciplinarity · Future of regional science · Social and economic sciences

> We need to pry into the space-economy with welfare considerations in mind to relate spatial structures to social well-being and to introduce political variables and policy decisions.... (Isard 1956:287)

A. S. Bailly (✉)
University of Geneva, Geneva, Switzerland
e-mail: antoine.bailly@unige.ch

L. J. Gibson
University of Arizona, Tucson, AZ, USA
e-mail: ljgibson@comcast.net

Z. Chen et al. (eds.), *Development Studies in Regional Science*,
New Frontiers in Regional Science: Asian Perspectives 42,
https://doi.org/10.1007/978-981-15-1435-7_2

2.1 Introduction

Scholars interested in strengthening regional science usually want to encourage its growth by promoting its application to a variety of research questions in a number of different settings. This was certainly an issue approached by the founder of regional science, Walter Isard, in a number of different settings including conferences, keynote addresses to colleagues, and publications. Isard saw the regional science perspective being of value to researchers in a host of different disciplines and professional fields. Isard's "Fused Framework" (Isard 1960:685) (Fig. 2.1) illustrates the complexities of dealing with political, social, and economic systems when cultural context comes up against efficiency and equity goals in cultures with different values.

We share Isard's enthusiasm for spreading the word, but we are also cautious realizing that a possible downside is that regional science might spread itself too thin and dilute its real power by trying to be too many things to too many research problems.

What we are proposing is not new, but we think that it does deserve another look given the growth in publication outlets and regional science conferences in recent years. Most disciplines want to grow and extend their reach and regional science is no exception. We want our conferences attended by an ever-increasing number of appropriate scholars; we want conference programs populated by challenging

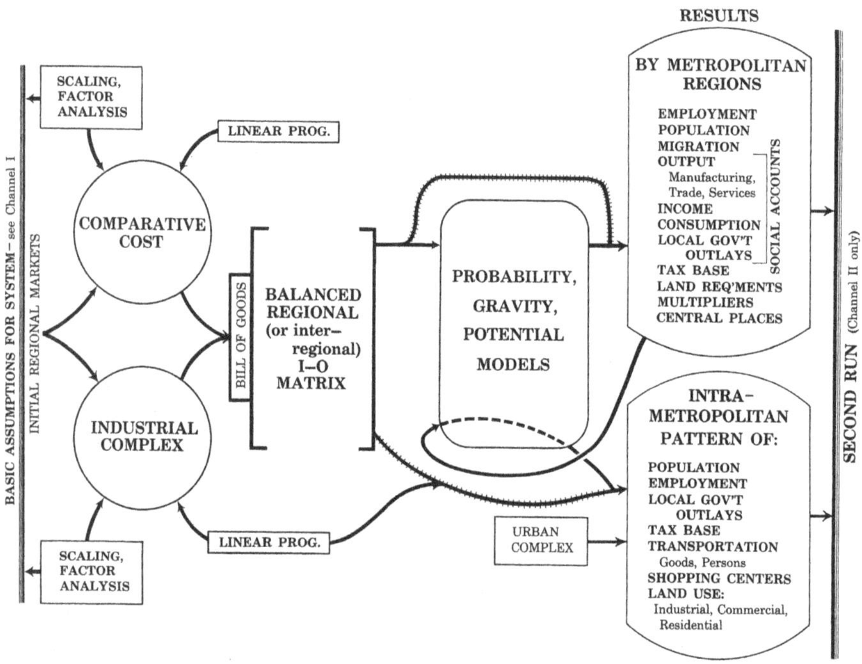

Fig. 2.1 Fused framework (Isard 1960:685)

quality papers that are competitive for program time. In the 2018 Goa RSAI World Congress, the focal theme is a common pursuit of a sustainable future, by a better understanding of the region as a spatial unit (not only physical and social spaces but shared space). The sub-themes show the necessity of a change: water management; smart cities; territorial governance; walled territories; regional cooperation; climate changes; rural transformation; leisure, tourism, mobility; citizenship and regional planning; conflict-migration; disaster management; globalization – regionalism, gender – social justice; innovation, entrepreneurship. The same is true of regional science publications. But we don't simply think that bigger is necessarily better. We want content that complements, and perhaps even extends the core concepts and approaches of regional science. We want to continue to do what we do, but we are willing to do even more if it is consistent with the fundamental notion of space science.

2.2 Academic Influences: Past and Possible

As we review a few of the academic influences on regional science, it is fair to make note of the disciplines and techniques that have been much in evidence since the second half of the 1950s and those which seem to have potential to emerge and grow in the near future. The definitive list of academic influences would be long; regional science is a discipline that has an almost endless capacity to incorporate ideas and approaches from other fields both theoretical and applied. For purposes of discussion here, we will limit our discussion to just nine academic disciplines and professional fields.

1. Economics

This is certainly the major influence on regional science today and over the past 60 or 70 years too. The founder of regional science, Walter Isard, was trained as an economist and brought this training to the emerging discipline of regional science which drew heavily on the field of location theory. Much of Isard's early work drew on economics, was quantitative, and stressed rigorous analysis. These have become hallmarks of regional science and, perhaps, limiting features of regional science too. When looking at potentials for expanding regional science, an obvious potential constraint is the issue of rigorous analysis. In other words how soft is too soft? Is there room for a softer and more subjective approach to regional science? Our hunch is that regional science will be very tolerant of other perspectives, especially at the margins. We wrote in 1994 (Bailly and Coffey 1994:13) "In making these observations, we are not advocating the abandonment of either basic research in regional science, or research on economic activities. Rather, what we are advocating is a more balanced approach" to reevaluate the foundations and the goals of regional science. But it is difficult to imagine a regional science that is not at its center quantitative and rigorous. Economics has been, and we are sure will continue to be, a lynchpin of the regional science discipline.

Supporting these assertions is the fact that Isard himself was eager to explore the connections between regional science and a number of other disciplines, especially geography but also sociology, psychology, city planning, and political science. He also founded the Peace Research Society. Isard saw regional science as being a "big tent," and this implies that regional science should be sympathetic to efforts to expand its reach by being tolerant of new perspectives and new approaches.

2. Geography

> Unlike geography, regional science is much more confined to scientific analysis of social processes. (Isard 2003:188)

This discipline, especially the quantitative and analytical approaches favored in the second half of the twentieth century, is also a major influence and is compatible with the location theory approach so much in evidence in the early years of regional science (Berry 1967). Hopefully this will be the case for years to come although Professor Arthur Getis suggests that quantitative and analytical approaches in geography may be on the decline (Paper presented at the 56th Annual Meeting of the Western Regional Science Association, February 2018). Ideally even an evolved form of quantitative and analytical geography will have something to offer regional science as we know it now and as it too grows and evolves in the future. Especially in urban studies (Glaeser 2011), and in the field of geo-political approaches to regional

Table 2.1 Geographical questions and concepts

Questions	Concepts	Extensions
Where?	Place	Latitude and longitude Site
How far?	Location Territory Environment	Limit Frontier Natural hazard Topophilia Political implications
How much?	Quantity Measurement	Distance Scale Density Flow Population Duration
Who and to whom?	Identification	Strategy Human risk Demography Interaction
How?	Representation	Development Information Quality of life
Why?	Understanding Analysis Explanation	Socioeconomic and spatial explanations

questions, such as identities, regional freedom, migrations... Geographical questions can be useful for regional science (Table 2.1) (Bailly 1995:787).

3. Sociology

> Regional science is primarily a social science. It is concerned with the study of man and spatial forms. (Isard 2003:188)

This discipline has attributes including a tradition of rigorous quantitative analysis that gives it the potential to have a strong influence on regional science. But some might argue that thus far sociology has not realized its potential. Perhaps sociology is a bit like geography inasmuch as both of these disciplines have been distracted by so-called social theory and have wandered off from a trajectory that would be sympathetic to the core of traditional regional science. However, it is clear that Isard saw sociology with its focus on the functioning, development, and structure of human communities, and its concern with social problems would be an ideal partner in a larger and more fully developed regional science. Sociology has not been quick to take its place near the front of the pack in an expanded regional science, but it would certainly be welcome especially in an applied regional science which focuses on regional problem-solving, especially on territorial identities.

Demography has traditionally been recognized as an important part of sociology, geography, and economics too and might be considered separately or as a part of any one of these three sciences. In a time when we expect new world migrations and changes in the demography, demography could likely be a major branch of regional science in the years ahead.

4. Environmental Science

This field might be thought of as a stand-alone discipline or perhaps as a subfield of geography and natural sciences. It certainly has not risen to the top among regional science conference topics and journal submissions despite its popularity in academic circles and in public policy discussions. Professor Isard saw environmental issues as a future "growth industry" and to stake out this turf for regional science published a book on "Ecological-economic analysis for regional development" in 1973. Whereas it is fairly easy to see how environmental science and regional science can join forces, less clear is the question of who exactly might champion the merger. One proven partnership is that of environmental engineering and regional science (Kahn 2006). Similarly physical and environmental geography and regional science show evidence of being comfortable as cooperating disciplines, often now in the same departments which focus on climate change, pollution, and environmental risks.

5. Management

Both business and public sector management have boomed in importance as academic subjects for 50 years or more. Unfortunately the link between regional science and regional management appears to be less robust than regional scientists might prefer at this time. Perhaps as regional science continues to grow as an applied science, the skills and understandings that it offers will be more obvious to those building curriculum in schools of business management and public policy and public management (Haynes and Nijkamp 2006). Ideally additional graduate programs in these fields will join those in the United States, Canada, Japan, France, and several other European and Asian nations which are already firmly committed to regional science perspectives in management solutions to public and private sector issues. Many management schools (such as ESSEC in France) have regional science professors to prepare students with regional management skills.

6. GIS: Geographic Information Systems

GIS has terrific potentials for use when dealing with a variety of applied regional science problems. Early on two things slowed the adaption of GIS. First, the technical and hardware requirements for GIS put it beyond the reach of some geographers and regional scientists. Second, there was an argument that GIS was "simply" a technique and not a legitimate focus for scholarly research. Both of these one-time barriers have been pushed aside over time, probably, by the simple force of GIS as a problem-solving tool. Today it is so widespread that it is difficult to imagine regional science without GIS. It is a popular component in many regional science research designs, and it is a stand-alone focus for both public and private sector applications. Looking back it is hard to imagine why it has taken so long for GIS to gain prominence in regional science research. Today it has arrived and is expected to be even more prominent in the future.

We are reminded of W. Tobler's work (1970) to develop a basic law in geography and regional science. In his classic 1970 article where he offhandedly penned the first law of geography, in defending the parsimony of his model of urban population growth, he noted: "The model I describe, for example, recognizes that people die, are born, and migrate. It does not explain why people die, are born, and migrate. Some would insist that I should incorporate more behavioral notions, but then it should be necessary to discuss the psychology of urban growth; to do this properly requires a treatise on the biochemistry of perception, which in turn requires discussion of the physics of ion interchange, and so on" (1970:234). The first law of geography is succinctly stated as: "everything is related to everything else, but near things are more related than distant things."

7. Human Ecology

It is easy to make a case for human ecology being a natural field of interest for regional scientists. It explores the relationship between humans and their cultural (social, political, and economic), natural, and built environments. The reasons for only limited interest in the regional science community are not totally clear, but a lack of quantitative analysis might leave some regional scientists with the idea that human ecology is "too soft." In the first one-half of the twentieth century, there was reason to believe that human ecology might dominate the "Chicago School of Sociology." In the mid-twentieth century, advances in planning and architecture incorporated human ecology, but it does not seem as though much of this has rubbed off on regional science. It certainly could, and perhaps should, but it hasn't, despite the useful results of factor-analysis on metropolitan regions. For K. Donaghy (2014),

Isard was thinking that economic theory did not explain the behavior observed in the real-world and wanted to introduce culture and quality of life in his models.

8. Planning

The link between regional science and planning is strong and appropriate (Rodwin and Hollister 1984). Planning is a professional field that draws on regional science and geography, among others, for its theory. The relationship is by no means exclusive, but it is well established and strong. Planning of course covers the waterfront, but city and regional planning are both good examples of types of planning where regional science perspectives and techniques are especially useful. There is also often a significant connection between public management and policy and planning, especially in countries where planning is considered as necessary for a balanced growth. France is an example where most regional scientists worked with the DATAR (the central planning agency) for a long time linked to the first minister, then with the minister of ecology. Well-known names in regional science, as Perroux and Guigou, were in charge of the national urban planning. Furthermore there are many examples from elsewhere including Robert E. Dickinson (UK) and Niles Hansen (USA) to name just two. We should remember also that the *Regional Science Review* was started by W. Isard, out of a concern that other regional science journals did not pay sufficient attention to planning questions or international topics.

9. Peace Science

It is appropriate that the ninth and final discussion of academic influences, past and possible, is peace science inasmuch as Walter Isard is the father of both regional science and peace science, and regional science is often the rigorous scientific foundation that many peace science questions are built upon. Isard founded the Peace Science Research Society (International) in 1963 roughly 10 years after he founded the Regional Science Association. Isard was joined in this undertaking in Malmo Sweden by distinguished social scientists Amos Rapoport and Kenneth Boulding. Isard won the Founders Medal in Peace Science in 2005. Peace Science has produced a rich and extensive literature which covers a wide range of topics including the role of defense spending in shaping national economies.

The importance of Peace Science to understanding national economies during the "cold war" was fairly obvious. Sixty years after the establishment of the Peace Science Society the exact nature of conflicts and the geographic venues of conflicts may have changed, but the need for thoughtful and scientific analysis of conflicts, arms control, and conflict resolution is as compelling as ever.

2.3 Risks and Rewards

A strong case can be built for expanding the content of regional science, but this doesn't mean that there are no risks which come with what is potentially "disciplinary overreach."

It is likely that any decision to expand the content of regional science scholarship will be made by an individual initially on a modest scale perhaps in much the same way that Walter Isard would give a public lecture on the way that sociology could, or already had contributed to the development of the discipline. There is no clearing-house to manage this issue. An individual with substantial background in public management and regional science submits a conference paper combining those two approaches, or this same paper is submitted for publication in a regional science journal. Either way we see an individual move forward into new territory. Unless such efforts are dismissed as inappropriate, it will likely continue and be recognized as a legitimate extension of regional science. Further, collaborations of this sort will lead to more conference papers and more published papers that explore public management issues through the eyes of the regional scientist.

Three possible risks are initially identified and an equal number of possible rewards.

First, if regional science tries to be all things to all people, it could obscure its distinctive focus as a quantitatively oriented theory-based spatial science. Rather than moving toward its objective of becoming a fundamental research discipline, it could find itself thought of as being a loose collection of social, humanistic, and even environmental disciplines. The fragmentation of sciences, with different forms, methods, and norms, calls for a better integration, a real transdisciplinarity. From a regional science for society to a regional science *with* society (Scholz and Steiner 2015), transdisciplinarity extends beyond interdisciplinarity to solve real-world problems and to cope with the new complex regional problems, such as identities, migration, resource use, pollution, injustice... an expansion of the context of the field.

Second, the regional science "brand" suggests strong elements of quantitative rigor and oftentimes content from the socioeconomic sciences are essential ingredients in the thing called regional science. Changes in content should preserve the sense of regional science as it has evolved since 1950.

A third possible risk is that of expanding into content areas that make regional science seems frivolous. Regional science will best be served by work that establishes its value to public and private decision-makers who deal with serious issues. Regional science should work to establish itself as essential and profound, not trivial (Haynes et al. 2008).

Possible rewards are numerous, but we shall discuss three to demonstrate that payoffs of an expanded regional sciences scope can be substantial.

First, it may be time to follow Walter Isard's lead and continue to expand regional science into areas that are the focus of other disciplines and professional fields. With this expansion will come the opportunity to welcome a new cohort of scholars to the regional science community and a new cohort of beneficiaries in both the public and private sectors.

Second, by expanding the content of regional science, there may be an opportunity to promote more broad-based participation in regional science conferences thereby encouraging a more diverse mix of participants, with scholars interested in a mutual learning process and interactions (and a more robust revenue stream for the

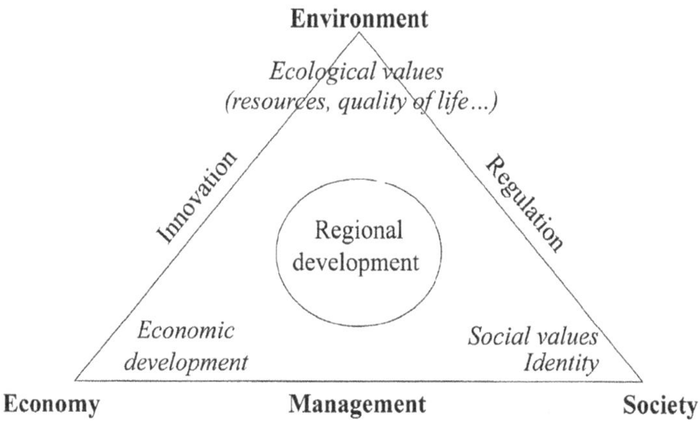

Fig. 2.2 The regional science triangle

organizers). The same might be true for publications. Enhanced quality could follow increased competition for space.

Third and finally, real-world problems typically benefit from a broader and less narrow approach than do more purely disciplinary problem-solving exercises. A broader definition of "appropriate content" could be supportive of initiatives designed to encourage applied research by regional scientists that would focus on real-world research problems (Fig. 2.2).

2.4 Concluding Thoughts

Even in the very early years of regional science, Walter Isard was at work incorporating new content from other professional fields and disciplines into the body of this evolving discipline. It would seem that current or even accelerated efforts to do this sort of thing are clearly appropriate. Some new content is intuitively more appropriate than other content, but when new content adds value, it is likely to be retained. There are a number of established and emerging disciplines and fields of scholarship that appear to have the potential to both sharpen and broaden the problem-solving power of regional science and in the process of doing so enhance their own power and usefulness.

References

Bailly A (1995) Geography teaching in the 21st century. Prospects 25(4):783–790
Bailly A, Coffey W (1994) Regional science in crisis: a plea for a more open and relevant approach. Pap Reg Sci 73(1):3–14

Berry B (1967) Geography of market centers and retail distribution. Prentice-Hall, Englewood Cliffs

Donaghy K (2014) Walter Isard's evolving sense of the scientific in regional science. Int Reg Sci Rev 37(1):78–95

Glaeser E (2011) Triumph of the city: how our best inventions makes us richer, smarter, greener, healthier and happier. Penguin Press, New York

Haynes K, Nijkamp P (2006) Infrastruture: the glue of megacities. Kenniscentrum Grote Steden, The Hague

Haynes K, Bailly A, Gibson L (2008) Applied geography for the entrepreneurial university. Economica, Paris

Isard W (1956) Location and space economy. The MIT Press, Cambridge, MA

Isard W (1960) Methods of regional analysis. The MIT Press, Cambridge, MA

Isard W (2003) History of regional science and the regional science association international. Springer, Berlin

Isard W et al (1973) Ecologic-economic analysis for regional development: some initial explorations with particular reference to recreational resource use and environmental planning. The Free Press, New York

Kahn M (2006) Green cities: urban growth and the environment. Brookings Institution Press, Washington

Rodwin L, Hollister M (eds) (1984) Cities of the mind: images and themes of the city in the social sciences. Plenum Press, New York

Scholz RW, Steiner G (2015) Transdisciplinarity at the crossroads. Sustain Sci 10(4):521–526. https://doi.org/10.1007/s11625-015-0338-0

Tobler W (1970) A computer movie simulating urban growth in the Detroit region. Econ Geogr 46 (sup1):234–240

Chapter 3
Is Regional Science Just Economics with a "d_{ij}" Added to All Equations? Some Thoughts of an Economist

Kenneth Button

Abstract This chapter looks at the extent to which "regional science" is distinctive enough to be called a unique sub-discipline. It considers the background against which the idea of a regional science was initiated and at the publications, institutions, and work that has been associated with the idea. In particular, it reviews the ways the American Economic Association has sought over the years to embrace geographical spatial analysis with the larger body of economic thinking. But this still leaves open the question of whether location and distance are really that different to the numerous elements included in modern economic analysis. The chapter looks at whether, even if there were a justification for a regional science in the 1950s, this has evaporated as economic thinking and analysis has morphed into something more integrated with other areas of social analysis. The conclusions reached are that even at the outset the notion of a specific regional science was vague and added little to what regional and urban economists were discussing. And even if differences could have been detected 75 years ago, these have now evaporated.

Keywords Regional science · Regional economics · Spatial analysis · Replication · Meta-analysis

3.1 Introduction

> Having duly recognized the significant inputs of non-economists to regional science, I am nonetheless convinced that the scientific respectability of regional science depends largely on its degree of respectability within mainstream academic economics. (Hanson 1995)

K. Button (✉)
Schar School of Policy and Government, George Mason University, Fairfax, VA, USA
e-mail: kbutton@gmu.edu

Z. Chen et al. (eds.), *Development Studies in Regional Science*,
New Frontiers in Regional Science: Asian Perspectives 42,
https://doi.org/10.1007/978-981-15-1435-7_3

> Regional economics as a sub-discipline of economics really does not exist any longer.. . .The vitality of regional science, too, is threatened by the absence of intellectual challenges from economists and by the diminished role that economists seem to play in shaping the core ideas of regional science. Both regional science and economics are the poorer from this development. (Giarratani 1995)

Some years ago, in my middle age, I found myself on a list of the "Intellectual leaders of regional science." Actually, I was number 80 out of the 94 listed individuals with 14 citations or more between 1990 and 2001 in designated regional science journals (Isserman 2004). But then again, this was in an era prior to the death by drowning in publications that now dominates academia, and the baseline of 14 was I thought quite an achievement. But what really puzzled me is that I found this an odd position to find myself. Until then I had never considered myself a regional scientist. I had a pretty good idea what some people thought regional science was, after all I had been in Kingsley Haynes' Institute of Institute of Public Policy at George Mason University for quite a few years and that had a serious interest in spatial activities. But I did ponder over exactly what regional science was, and I asked myself why a transportation, and part-time regional, economist was suddenly being reclassified.

I proceeded to do some digging into the history of regional science, and what exactly it is, or at least what it thinks it is. I was particularly stimulated by the quote of Niles Hansen at the head of this paper. Hansen was at the time an Emeritus Professor of Economics at a major university, the University of Texas, and a significant figure in regional economics. In the original article from which the quote is extracted, Hansen was reflecting on the possible future of regional science within the longer-term historical development of the subject. In particular, if regional science was at all important why did it need approbation from economists? John Meyer's (1963) seminal survey also raises definitional and credibility issues, but from the opposite perspective, "Almost from the beginning, the convention, at least in formal discourse, has been to speak of 'regional analysis' and 'regional science' rather than 'regional economics'."

This chapter looks at the extent to which this segmentation of courses, journals, and academic departments has added much to the study of, in this case, what has become known as "regional science." In other words, does the concept of regional science really add that much to conventional economic analysis? And perhaps, as flowing from Frank Giarratani quote at the beginning, "are there sorts of synergies or marketing advantages in somehow bringing the two titles together?"

There is certainly a literature that calls itself "regional science," and much of it appears in journals bearing the name, e.g., *Annals of Regional Science*, *Papers of the Regional Science Association*, *Regional Science and Urban Economics*, and *Regional Science Policy and Practice* (Boyce 2004). There are also numerous very active associations around the globe that carry the title of "regional science" and conferences and workshops associated with them. But, the issue raised is "Does this really extend our analysis of spatial activities very much beyond what economists now cover or, indeed, have historically covered?"

I successively, after briefly exploring the general patterns of specializations in economics and the factors that have been driving them, move to look at the trends regarding the ways that distance and location are treated. I ask whether there is any substantial intellectual difference with the ways that variables other than space and spatial institutions are considered in economics and, indeed, whether there should be any difference. It takes some of the ideas that have appeared under the general heading of regional science and considers whether the underlying theories, methodologies, and estimation procedures differ significantly, or at all, from those associated with what one may call mainstream economics. Put bluntly, "Is regional science just a marketing tool for selling a particular topic of analysis, not to say conferences, associations, journals and courses, rather than a genuine separate science?" Finally, it looks at whether some of the recently debated problems in applied economics, including regional economics, are also applicable to the work in regional science.

A specific factor affecting my choice of subject matter is two sets of papers, one published in 1995 in the July issue of *International Regional Science Review* and the other in the January 2005 issue of *Papers in Regional Science*. Both of these offer a range of views about the then state of regional science.[1] Both were also timely, not just because of the subject matters covered – they focused on the first 40 and first 50 years of regional science, respectively – but because they included reflections from some of the more "senior academics" in the field who had been active during what some saw at the time as the heyday of the subject. The mid-1950s was the period regional science was said to have broken away from economics into what was seen as a multidisciplinary area of study. Many things emerged from these edifying collections, not least of which was the ebb and flow of interest in regional matters, and how this had impacted on the education and research that was being conducted. I update this work to some extent.

3.2 Why Separate Out Areas of Study?

Academics have always loved to classify things, and classifying academic fields of study has been at the forefront of their endeavors. Over the years there has been a gradual fine-tuning in the way that we define what may loosely be called "academic disciplines." Disciplines have always been a somewhat difficult thing to specify with any degree of precision. The challenge has increased as the extent of global knowledge has grown, and the human brain has fallen behind in its capacity to handle it all. It became more pronounced after it reached the point when it was impossible for any individual to have universal knowledge.

[1]Other notable retrospective collections are the July 2007 issue of *Regional Science and Urban Economics* that reflects on 35 years of the journal and the April 2012 special issues of the *Journal of Regional Science* that assess the then state of spatial econometrics.

The possibility of "Renaissance man" quite literally ended after the Renaissance. This is when "knowledge" began to be divided up. Instead of Leonardo da Vinci splashing a little paint on a panel of wood prior to breakfast to produce the Mona Lisa, drawing a few lines after eating to plan out Milan's canal system, and, following lunch, proceeding to invent the helicopter and to think over the mechanics of an adding machine and, just before going to bed, dissecting a human cadaver at the Hospital of Santa Maria Nuova, modern academics tend to mull for days or weeks over the appropriate number of places of decimal for parameters in a constrained gravity model. Such a degree of specialization requires an appropriate descriptive discipline for respectability.

This pattern has manifested itself in most areas of study. As can be seen from the ever-expanding listings of economic subdivisions in the *Journal of Economic Literature* (*JEL*), economics has been gradually fragmenting over time after it ceased to exist as one area of moral philosophy.[2] In some cases, this has involved a simply dividing up of a *JEL* classification, but in others there has been a clear narrowing down as some areas of study have been seen to have shifted away from economics. So how does economics in general treat regional analysis in this world of increasing specialization? Are the complaints justified that it was being given short-shift by economists, and thus a new regional science was needed? One way of looking at this is to consider how one of the major economics bodies has treated regional analysis.

The first number of the *American Economic Review* (*AER*) published in March 1911 listed ten categories or sub-interests of economics, of which "History and Geography" was the second item (Cherrier 2017). The list was subsequently modified over the years in a largely ad hoc way until the demands of both the Social Science Research Council and the American Council of Learned Societies found it necessary to have a more complete categorization for World War II planning purposes. Registers of individual economists' expertise were compiled and then maintained after the war. Efforts to have a National Science Foundation social science division failed mainly because of issues over the political neutrality of the research involved, and, in any case, there were questions over its usefulness. Largely for practical purposes of helping editors select referees for the *AER*, the American Economic Association (AEA) was in parallel seeking an updated classification system. A genus-species 17 categorization draft list drawn up in 1940 by AEA Secretary James Bell had no mention of regional economics (although economic geography was seen as a subcategory of industrial history). Paul Homan, subsequently editor of the *AER* from 1941 to 1951, came up with a problem-oriented list of 23 categories also in 1940 that included "**4.** Economic Geography and Regional Economics."

[2] I focus mainly here on the situation in the USA. There were similar debates taking place elsewhere and especially in the UK from the mid-1980s when the Government's Research Assessment Exercise was introduced across all disciplines to assist in the award of university grants. A defined subject specialism of an academic department, as well as the quality of the faculty, affected allocations of resources.

The AEA's 17 classification subsequently adopted in 1949 was largely based on criteria to help categorize personnel in the context of job markets and articles for refereeing. Although not mentioning regional economics, the list did explicitly have "**15.** Land Economics; Agricultural Economics; Economic Geography." An updating in 1956 saw "Housing" added to the category.

Perhaps more germane, "(c) Area Studies (regional and national economics)" was explicitly added to "**3.** Economic History; Economic Development; National Economic".[3] This remained the situation for a decade when further changes to the AEA classification saw a stronger recognition of spatial economics with the introduction of "**900.** Welfare Programs; Consumer Economics; Urban and Regional Economics." Urban economics, a major growth area of interest in the late 1950s and 1960s, despite considerable pressure, was not given a separate categorization, and regional economics was assumed to embrace economic geography (Cherrier 2017).

The increasing output of economics papers, including those covering regional and urban topics, combined with the needs for the US National Science Foundation for clear classification of subject matter as more social science awards were made, led to considerable adjustments to the AEA classifications for the late 1960s. Most notable was the introduction of intermediate categories within a maximum of ten classifications. The listing was also transferred to the *JEL* in 1970, with an ongoing series of minor revisions into the mid-1980s. More detail was added to classifications. That really did little, however, to change the degree of emphasis given to regional economics. In 1991 the number of classifications rose to 19 (**R** being Urban, Rural, and Regional Economics)[4].

Perhaps even more pertinent to my discussion is the current *JEL* classification "**R** – Urban, Rural, Regional, Real Estate, and Transportation Economics." And within this are subdivisions for "**R1** – General Regional Economics" embracing such as the following:

Regional economic activity (growth; development, environmental issues, and changes; size and spatial distributions of regional economic activity; general equilibrium and welfare economic analysis of regional economies; land use patterns; and econometric and input-output models)

Household analysis (housing demand; regional migration, regional labor markets, population, and neighborhood characteristics; and government policy)

Real estate markets, spatial production analysis, and firm location (housing supply and markets, other spatial production and pricing analysis, nonagricultural and nonresidential real estate markets, and government policy)

Regional government analysis (finance in urban and rural economies; land use and other regulations; public facility location analysis, public investment, and capital stock; and regional development planning and policy)

---

[3]There was a considerable argument over the positioning of economic geography. Fritz Machlup, the international economist, along with some others, felt it should be split between "Area Studies" and "International Economics" on the basis that it entailed comparative analysis.

[4]Edwin Mills, an innovator in the new urban economics, provided blueprints for the organization of "Urban, Rural, and Regional Economics" classification, and Richard Muth, another with an interest in NUE, was consulted on urban economics.

And this does not include the listings under Transportation, a subject which many see as important in analysis of spatial behavior following the development of the new regional economics associated with the likes of Paul Krugman and Anthony Venables.

The history tells us several things. First, John Meyer is a little offtrack in saying that the subject under discussion here has almost always been known as "regional science." While terminology, for a diverse set of reasons, often adjusts and is modified, the term regional economics has a pretty well-established pedigree, at least within the academic economic field. Second, very eminent people have been concerned to have regional economics and related matter included in categorizations of economics as defined by the main US academic body. Some, such as Walter Isard as we see below, may have argued for more, and others less, but given the wide coverage of economics, it is difficult to say regional economics (and, by default in Meyer's argument, regional science) has somehow been neglected.

Given this, where is the gap regional science now seeks to fit into?

3.3 Historical Context

Delving further into definitions, at the outset it is clear that it was difficult to precisely define economics let alone elements within it. Indeed, Jacob Viner's supposed definition that "Economics is what economists do" (Spiegel 1987) and Kenneth Galbraith's view that "Economics is extremely useful as a form of employment for economists" probably sum up the situation as many still see it, but it can be defined with more precision.

Economics as we know it today has a much shorter history than many people think although the term economics goes back to the classical Greek word "Okonma" meaning "household management." This was the way, for example, the philosopher Aristotle used it. As time changed, the concept was broadened out considerably. By the eighteenth century, many elements of what we now think of as economics came within "moral philosophy." This is a branch of philosophy that contemplates what is right and wrong and examines how people should live their lives in relation to others. Adam Smith (1776), although fundamentally a moral philosopher as seen in his "other book," *The Theory of Moral Sentiments*, changed this. He argued that economics is a science that enquires into the nature and causes of the wealth of nations.

Alfred Marshall, who formalized the prevailing knowledge of the day, argued from the late 1890s that "Economics is the study of humans, in relation to the ordinary business of life. It studies that portion of the personal and social activities, which are closely related to the attainment of material resources, related to welfare and its utilization."[5] With this, Marshall offers perhaps the most cited definition of

---

[5]In his *Principles of Economics*, Marshall (1890) does include a specific chapter on "The concentration of specialized industries in particular localities" as well as introducing space and geography into a variety of economic discussions.

the discipline, but why does a subdivision such as regional economics (or regional science) need a particular delineation? In fact, most would argue that it is more of a topic than a social science sub-discipline. While it is difficult to be precise about what regional economics covers, this seems true of most sub-areas of economics and indeed of other disciplines. Most are defined by lists of interests or topics. Additionally, the pedigree of regional economics, as with economics in general, is clearly one of an applied study area rather than one that has grown from abstract theory. The distinction between regional economics and regional science, as seen below, is, therefore, difficult to make unless the topics covered vary significantly.

It was a practical matter that led to the move to establish institutional structures fostering the study of regional science. This came from a feeling that economics in the 1950s was missing an important spatial dimension and thus was not a complete social science.[6] As David Boyce (2004) explains, the catalyst for action by Isard and others was the perceived lack of attention the AEA was paying to locational analysis and regional problems despite the discussions of classifications outlined above.[7] In that sense, regional science may be seen as coming about largely by default as opposed to any major positive shift in academic thinking. Much of this perceived preoccupation of economists of the day was seen by Isard and others as refining Keynesian macroeconomics theory and in testing it by applying increasing computer power to the new national income accounting.[8] The more established microeconomists were seen as engrossed in considering the implications of the inter-war work of the likes of Edward Chamberlin, Joan Robinson, Harold Hotelling, Hall and Hitch, and others on understanding the complexities of industrial organization.[9] But countering this, as we have seen, it was also about this time that "Area Studies" was introduced into the AEA classification system, suggesting spatial economics was not being quite as strongly pushed to one side as was perhaps being claimed.

But even after the Regional Science Association (RSA) was formed in 1954 in response to a supposed neglect of spatial aspects of economics, its objectives were unclear. This was not perhaps surprising for a such a diverse group comprised largely of academics drawn from economics, geography, city planning, political science, and rural sociology. In the first issue of its *Papers and Proceedings*, the Association

[6]It was also about this time, in 1946, when, for similar reasons, the Transportation and Public Utilities Group was formed as the first associated organization to the AEA by economists such as James Nelson, Charles Dearing, and Ralph Dewey who were interested in those subjects.

[7]Isard (2003) provides a more detailed account, while Barnes (2003) offers a critical assessment. It should perhaps be noted that Isard himself seemed to publish in economics journal in the early 1950s, e.g., Isard (1951).

[8]One might also argue that the early 1950s was also the time that the embryonic ideas of regional multipliers, regional input-output analysis, regional trade-theory, etc. were laid down, albeit initially in the context of "national regions" rather than "economic regions."

[9]In fact, the inter-war theoretical literature had already said quite a bit on the effect of space on industrial organization – e.g., Hotelling (1929) on oligopolies and Chamberlain (1933) on monopolistic competition.

stated its objectives as being "...to foster exchange of ideas, and to promote studies focusing on the region and utilizing tools, methods, and theoretical frameworks specifically designed for regional analysis as well as concepts, procedures, and analytical techniques of the various social and other sciences." Isserman (1995) suggests this may be taken as meaning applying economic approaches and methodology to geographical problems. Later, Harvey Perloff (1957) did little to clarify this very broad definition when he stated "Regional studies (*sic*) tend to deal with many features and often involve the use of several academic disciplines. Thus, no general system of classification can be expected to provide self-contained categories; there is inevitable spill-over." He goes on to essentially list topics he considers covered by regional studies. Walter Isard (1960) similarly resorts to a compendium of what amount to economic problems. As Meyer (1963) puts it, "A distinctive aspect of Isard's definition is its exclusive emphasis on what economists would normally construe or recognize as economic problems."[10]

Further, Meyer, trying to setting this in the context of regional economics, finds Isard's list to be too long and suggests cutting it to "...(1) problems of regional analysis with unique conceptual characteristics, and (2) specific areas of particularly heavy interchange between conventional economic theory and regional economics." But even in doing this, Meyer also finds little to distinguish regional analysis from economics more generally, viz., "While regional definition problems do possess several reasonably unique elements not encountered in conventional economic analyses, they hardly would appear substantial enough to give regional economics a thoroughly distinct identity."

In a slightly later contribution from the other side of the Atlantic, Arthur Brown (1969) in a major survey paper also had problems in defining regional economics, let alone regional science. He looked at the situation from a more applied, policy-oriented perspective. He ends up with:

> Regional economics is a field of study which has meant different things to different people. To some it has meant primarily the study of the economy and the economic problems of a particular region – generally one that is part of a wider area within which free trade prevails, and within which movement of labour and capital are not subject to control. To others it has meant the wider study of the relative economic performances and economic interactions of a number of such regions.

Added to this is the idea, beginning in the early 1960s, that regional and urban studies could also be set on a more political science-based foundation. This movement includes the establishment of the Regional Studies Association that, through its journal *Regional Studies*, seeks to facilitate discussions involving economic development and growth and conceptions of territory and its governance and of equity and injustice. Interestingly, the Regional Studies Association did not link with the RSA

[10]Meyer also footnotes that Isard's book "constitutes a good single-volume introduction to regional economics...."

because it felt the latter was too US oriented and could not embrace the peculiarities of the British and wider European situations.[11] The Southern Regional Science Association also had morphed somewhat in this direction with its publication of *The Review of Regional Studies*. There has also been some spatial, rather than geographical, specialization with the emergence in 1964 of *Urban Studies* with a similar multidisciplinary ethos.

By the mid-1970s, there had been a slight shift in thinking, at least as portrayed by Harry Richardson (1978b) in his survey of the "State of Regional Economics." He takes a rather pragmatic position. He felt that there was a plethora of new regional problems that had just emerged offering more work for regional economists as theorists, technicians, and policy analysts. These trends, which are reflected in the current AEA classification of regional economics outlined earlier, included the role of environmental quality in regional development, the regional impacts of rising energy costs, the increasing importance of amenities as locational attractors, the decline of large cities and the growth of exurban hinterlands, and the influence of emerging communication technologies. While some of the resultant issues could be handled within the boundaries of traditional disciplines, he argues others would probably require an understanding of the process of managerial decision-making and of psychology. In the latter cases, "only the new disciple of regional science offers...freedom from the stifling influence of the great but limited neoclassical tradition."

3.4 Defining Regions

But all of this activity really begs the questions, "What is a region?" Meyer (1963) offers three possibilities, basically self-contained or nodal regions, homogeneous regions, and administrative regions.

An economist may well argue that the last of these, administrative regions, have characteristics very similar to nation-states and indeed some national states are much smaller than so-called regions within a large country – Singapore, for example, is smaller than the mid-west region of the USA by many orders of magnitude.[12] It is difficult to see in this case where the standard tools of international economics and macroeconomics are deficient for analyzing the associated regional questions. Administrative regions are, after all, largely institutional rather than

[11]This complaint is more difficult to make now since the founding of numerous national and sub-national Regional Science Associations and of the Regional Science Association International.

[12]Kristian Behrens and Jacques Thisse (2007) make the salient point "... regardless of what is meant by a region, the concept is useful if and only if a region is part of a broader network through which various types of interactions occur. Without taking this aspect into account, one may wonder what the difference between regional economics and the macroeconomics of a closed economy would be."

nature's constructions, and economists have a long tradition of analyzing matters of economic interest both within and between countries. Indeed, given the growth of common markets of various forms, there are mega-global regional structures that act very much like a single country, with countries within them being conceptually the same as metropolitan areas and the like within a nation-state. Economists contribute extensively to the analysis of these.

The tools used for looking at international trade and production flows between countries and those used to look at trade and flows between politically designated regions within a country are, in fact, technically identical. The point Machlup made nearly 50 years ago in the AEA classification debate. The gravity model used by John Stewart and William Warntz (1958) on regional migration differs little from the almost contemporaneous study of global trade flows conducted by Jan Tinbergen (1962). Equally, when considering economic activities within regions, the use of fiscal multipliers, input-output analysis (Richardson 1978a, b), and computable general equilibrium models (Giesecke and Madden 2013) is essentially no different to their macroeconomic counterparts. For estimation purposes econometrics, which had in the immediate World War II period focused mainly on time series estimation of macroeconomies, began to consider cross-sectional challenges such as handling issues of spatial autocorrelation. This was partly stimulated by macroeconomic considerations of structural industrial change and demographics, as well as the fact that relative spatial location and agglomeration economies are important in this.[13]

Where differences may be seen to exist is in the practical challenges associated with availability of data.[14] The notions of homogeneous regions and nodal regions have many attractions from a theoretical and economic modeling perspective. Homogeneous regions provide a basis for interregional trade analysis and discussions of comparative advantage and agglomeration effects, while the concept of nodal regions offers the basis for thinking about balanced growth and local externalities. The testing of hypotheses, however, has long been a a challenge in both cases because of the lack of adequate and reliable data at any sub-national level of analysis. Regional accounts, where they have existed, have normally been at the administrative region level (Brown and Woodward, 1969). Given the growth in urbanization, continually shifting administrative boundaries, and changing demographic and industrial trends, such data are often far from reliable, especially if the interest is in the dynamics of regional development. But all this applies to international economics.[15] One can use Paul Samuelson's (1954) analytical iceberg model of trade, for example, at any level of aggregation with minimal tweaking, but operationalizing it is not so easy. The problem is not unique to regional analysis.

[13]Jean Paelinck seems to have originated the term "spatial econometrics" in 1974. Moran's (1948) work is generally considered the origin of spatial autocorrelation analysis.

[14]If Isard did have a case for highlighting regional economic issues in the 1950s, it was on the grounds of inadequate official data collection rather than any intellectual neglect by the AEA. Richard Stone (1961) offers observations on the UK data situation in the 1950s.

[15]This is one reason why local case studies have been a pronounced feature of regional studies where, unlike regional science, overriding laws are not sought.

3.5 A "Science" or What?

This leads to another issue: Is regional science a "science," or, specifically in this case, a "social science," or a set of ad hoc observations and topics? Adam Smith maintained that "Science is the great antidote to the poison of enthusiasm and superstition." But it is not easy to conduct scientific experiments of the type Smith seemed to envisage with the data available. As a consequence, the argument over whether or not economics is a science or not is ongoing. But clearly with the formation of the RSA, there were those who did think that regions could be studied scientifically and systematically or else they would have adopted another title (Isard 1956).[16]

Many these days feel this view was a little optimistic. Trevor Barnes (2003), for example, argues that "...regional science would have fared better if rather than emphasizing science, it emphasized the region." Isserman (1995) also probably sums up many people's view these days that "Regional science never became a science or a discipline, and it has had a peculiar relationship to regions. Yet, the concept has had spectacular success as a basis of many international, interdisciplinary scholarly forums, and it has produced noteworthy contributions to several disciplines." The technical reasons why regional science falls short of being a "science" are returned to later. Here I offer some comments on what regional science has achieved and some observations on why trying too hard to be some sort of hard science has often been counterproductive.

As already discussed, even the definition of a region is problematic and certainly falls far short of anything like the natural elements isolated in physicals. Instead it is largely about problems and topics; location, migration, spatial concentration, etc. And this is really the point Isserman is making. These are only affected in a relatively small way by common scientific laws. They are also influenced by public policies and human reactions, including reactions to the findings of regional "scientists" and indeed regional economists. Atoms do not react to the analysis of physicists, but regions can react to policy shifts stimulated by work of regional analysts. In that sense, much of what appears as positive regional science is effectively a normative activity designed to influence human welfare as well as describing it.[17] It is akin to the old idea of moral philosophy. The uptake of the findings of regional analysis is in effect endogenous to the way that people behave over space; the information from analysis affects the outcome.

There is also another issue worthy of attention. Science usually involves measurement and with this comes the need for some form of metric. Some metrics are common across subject areas, others more specific. Economists, while talking about utility, generally use a money metrics as a proxy to value. With all its domestic challenges of needing adjustments for inflation in time series applications, and for

[16]In fact, Isard had wanted to call it "spatial science" but felt this would confuse it with physics and astronomy.

[17]Here we talk about social science in the way Lionel Robins (1932) does.

international exchange rate movements in some cross-sectional work, it is a fairly standard gauge.[18] In terms of regional analysis, distance (d_{ij}) becomes the obvious measure of impedance, and benefits can be gained by reducing journey lengths. The problem is that given diversity of terrain and climate, d_{ij} is not a good metric and indeed may in a sense well be endogenous when it comes to location and similar decisions. The result is that much of regional science resorts to the use of money as a key input into its forecasting and evaluation exercises just as economists do. It allows comparisons cross a diverse range of inputs and outputs and across both consumers and producers.[19] But its imperfections also partly explain why any area of economics, just as so-called regional science, is not a natural science and thus objective quantification is a particular issue. Both, by definition, inevitably make use of multidisciplinary approaches or at least approaches that are increasingly less rigid in their underlying assumptions.[20]

3.6 The "New Regional Economics" and "New Urban Economics"

The world does not stand still, and over the past 40 to 50 years, there have been changes in the way that regions have been analyzed and indeed why. The elder of the two papers that stimulated this chapter appeared a quarter of a century ago, and there have been subsequent changes in the tools available for looking at regions, partly due to advances in theory, partly through better analytical tools, and partly because of improved data. The prefix "new" has been attached to both regional and urban economics and to human geography to draw boundaries in thinking (Hansen 1995). The question thus concerns the extent to which regional science as seen, albeit rather opaquely, has moved on since the mid-1950s.

The new urban economics (NUE), initiated by the works of Mills, Muth, and Martin Beckmann and their likes, moved the study of cities from what was largely a set of descriptive exercises focusing on urban sectorial problems – congestion, housing, deprivations, etc. – that were largely aimed at helping urban planners to

[18]Some transportation economists have in the past discussed the idea of using time (hours or minutes) as a measure of value on the basis that it is more equitable. It never gained acceptance.

[19]There are programming techniques, such as data envelopment analysis, that are not limited to a single unit of measurement and that have a fairly long pedigree in economics, although admittedly not often used in spatial analysis. John Hicks (1960) provides an early general survey of some of these.

[20]John Maynard Keynes gives a more complete reason, "I also want to emphasise strongly the point about economics being a moral science. I mentioned before that it deals with introspection and with values. I might have added that it deals with motives, expectations, psychological uncertainties. One has to be constantly on guard against treating the material as constant and homogeneous in the same way that the material of the other sciences, in spite of its complexity, is constant and homogeneous" (Letter to Roy Harrod, 10th July 1938).

studies that are based on abstract modeling and empirical testing. The underlying NUE idea had been around since the mid-1970s – Richardson (1977) and Mills and MacKinnon (1973) provide overviews of the early works – and the result was the focus very much shifting to the dynamics of cities. This is perhaps not surprising considering the rapidly changing nature of urban form, industrial structures, and lifestyles that were taking place at the time. Intellectually, the subfield began to integrate welfare economics and urban economics within a general equilibrium framework.

What the approach has lacked, however, has been an inability to satisfactorily tie in urban change with other societal and economic shifts in the likes of information technology, migration, and the service economy. Much effort has gone into seeking to optimize city sizes or distributions without allowing for interactions between spatial attributes and other determining factors such as shifting production functions and consumer preferences (Button 2000).

The arrival of the new regional economics and geography stemmed from the adoption of Krugman's (1991) and Masahisa Fujita and Krugman's (2003) argument that perfectly competitive, partial equilibrium models of spatial interaction are not useful. The new regional economics focuses primarily on the forces that lead to agglomeration of activities at a variety of spatial levels, including the international. It relies on high-technology numerical examples that the availability of enhanced computing power and big datasets allows (Fujita et al. 1991). In a way this approached has forced analysis much more toward an empiricism that Isard (1956) had advocated 35 years previously for regional science.

Articles making use of these two "new" approaches are to be found in both the regional science and regional economics literature. One problem with these approaches, however, is that while greater quantification is welcome, there are many qualitative factors that affect, for example, decisions to relocate production, to migrate, to invest in public infrastructure, etc. As Albert Einstein put, "Not everything that counts can be counted, and not everything that can be counted counts."[21] Even with the greater appreciation of this across many areas of economics, especially with the growth of interest in the role of institutions and in behavioral economics, there has been something of a lag in the sophistication of their incorporation in regional economics. If they are included, they often come in the form of descriptive, fixed effects rather than as strict causal variables.[22]

A further criticism, and one that is increasingly less valid, is implicit in the previous doubt caste over the way spatial econometrics is deployed to examine various hypotheses, essentially the challenge one of moving from theory to quantification. Stephen Gibbons and Henry Overman (2012), however, argue, with

[21]This is very much in line with Mario Polèse's (1995) argument that the fact regions are very distinctive makes generalization along traditional scientific lines extraordinarily difficult. In a nutshell, one should focus on individual regions.

[22]In particular, the new institutional economics associated with the likes of Oliver Williamson (2000) have provided positive theories allowing a richer range of economic hypothesis to be explored.

considerable justification, that such concerns are often "...based on imprecise and ill-informed perceptions of the sophistication and diversity of the work of the spatial econometrics and wider academic community." They go on to provide illustrations of cases where, unlike the traditional strawmen analysis that is it mechanical and its results accepted purely based on the statistical significance of variables, involve careful econometric analyses. The cases reflect situations where the work considers a priori rationalizations and in which economic theory is at the core of their specifications. But there still remains in regional economics, and in economics more generally, a focus on computer output results.

But this is not to say there are no problems even when there is a wider focus, "While the theory underlying these models is often exceptionally well established and well received, nevertheless it is also true that there are cases in which spatial econometric work has been too casual in its attempt to base model specifications on economic theory." In particular, Gibbons and Overman highlight the inadequate handling of hierarchies in regional science and spatial economics. Similarly, when reviewing the theoretical and empirical rationale for network dependence and spatial externalities embodied in spatially lagged variables, Luisa Corrado and Bernard Fingleton (2012) find that a failure to acknowledge their presence at least biases inference and can cause inconsistent estimation leading to incorrect assessment of causal processes.

3.7 Replication and Meta-Analysis

A simple glance over the publications in the regional science journals indicates an expanding number of empirical studies. The gradually increasing availability of data, the development of more sophisticated estimation procedures and software, and the wide variety of theoretical hypothesis that have been generated and in need of quantitative evaluation easily explain this. But there were also intellectual forces pressing for this. The work often, for example, pays particular attention to the role of transaction costs, largely in terms of transportation, and to market imperfections – an outcome of the work of Krugman and the like.

Both Meyer (1963) and Douglas Brown (1979), following earlier pleas from Isard, argued in the late 1960s and early 1970s that it was time regional science moved away from broad conceptualizing and toward the testing of hypothesis. Brown wrote "...instead of continuously re-specifying the theory, I strongly recommend that we set our sights on empirical testing." Moves in this direction were already under way in economics in general, and regionally oriented research was part of this. Isserman (1995), however, raised the question about whether this was really being done scientifically. In particular, an important issue across many areas of social science involves the ability to replicate empirical results (Kane 1984). Application of applied scientific methods should produce results that can be reproduced to be valid.

There are a number of factors mitigating against conducting replication in the social sciences. Independent, direct replications of others' findings can be time-consuming for the replicating individual or team and can take energy and resources away from other projects that reflect one's own original thinking. Replications are also harder to publish, often because editors feel it is not original work and, even when accepted for publication, are seen as "bricklaying" exercises, rather than as major contributions to the field.

Despite this, the concern about non-replication has grown. It was a major theme at both the AEA and the Royal Economic Society (RES) annual meetings in 2017. For example, when discussing the role of empirical analysis in economics, James Berry et al. (2017) maintained at the AEA that "Replications are a key component in the scientific process, helping the profession sift robust empirical findings from mistakes." Similarly, Maniadis et al. (2017) at the RES highlighted "...a widespread concern that there is a reproducibility problem due to a sizable fraction of published findings being typed-I errors, or false positives (i.e. scientific discoveries of statistical relations that are in fact not true)."[23]

A challenge in replication is that of definition. Maren Duvendack et al. (2017) helped a little by consolidating two oft-used definitions. Michael Clemens (2017) separates replication from robustness tests, classifying "verification" (replication) as those using the same sample, population, and empirical specification; "reproduction" (replication) as those using different samples from the same population but using the same specification; "reanalysis" (robustness) using the same sample and population but different specifications; and "extension" (robustness) using different samples and populations but the same specification. Daniel Hamermesh (2007) separates "pure replications" (same methods, same sample and population) from "statistical replications" (different sample, same methods and population) and "scientific" replications (different sample and population, similar but not identical methods). Both agree on what is "pure replication" or "verification"; the "statistical replication" of Hamermesh corresponds to the "reproduction" of Clemens, while the "scientific replication" of the former incorporates the "robustness" categories defined by Clemens, although broader.

Then there is the matter of what leads to analysis that cannot be replicated. A number of possible factors have emerged. Duvendack et al. (2017) summarize them:

> First is "HARKing," or hypothesizing after the results are known. This practice turns hypothesis testing on its head, with theories being developed only after empirical results have been obtained, and then the same empirical results are used to "test" the theories.

[23]Other papers include Chang and Li (2017) who replicated 22 of 67 economics papers that used the authors' data and code files and additional 7 papers with assistance from the authors. Of articles using public data and making use of code written for software owned by the authors, 29 of 59 could be replicated. Replication has also involved several economic fields; Camerer et al. (2016) sought to replicate papers in experimental economics, Hamermesh (2017) labor economics, and Sandip Sukhtankar (2017) development economics.

> Second is data mining and estimation manipulation, commonly known as "p-hacking," by which researchers torture the data until they are able to produce the elusive p<0.05. . .Third is data error and outright fraud. . . . The last reason is publication bias, by which false positives are disproportionately reported in the literature.[24]

But there are important changes taking place to encourage work that can be replicated. Economics journals with reproducibility policies are cited more often than others. Additionally, what are normally considered the top five economics journals now have a data access policy with authors required to make data and code available to all researchers to test for replication. For the minority of journals with a mandatory and enforced policy, this is significant when controlling for time and journal effects (Höffler 2017). But there are many journals that have no such requirement, or it is voluntary. There is far less discussion, however, of the lack of replication, and how to handle it, in the regional science literature.

Meta-data analysis, the synthesis of the results of prior studies adjusting for their context, is often seen as a method of replication and is perhaps more widely used in regional science than regional or other specialisms of economics. But there are important differences. Care is necessary when applying meta-analysis in regional science or economics because, unlike psychology or the health sciences, many empirical studies in economics are non-stochastic and analyze publicly available data, although dataset selection may differ between studies (Anderson and Kichkha 2017). Meta-analysis is also not "a scientific technique" – decisions are required regarding which studies to include, what weights to attach to the studies, and how to interpret the results.

Further, few meta-analyses of regional matters have delved back into the raw data when selecting prior works for inclusion. The problem is that there is no systematic way of objectively assessing the quality of studies. In particular, gray literature (e.g., reports and working papers) and those not written in English tend to be omitted. Added to this, the material selected from peer-reviewed journals generally suffers from bias. There is a tendency for editors to favor results that support existing theories or contain findings broadly conforming to "expected" magnitudes and to reject as outliers where finding radically different results from the norm.

A more pragmatic issue is the usefulness of findings for forecasting. Milton Friedman (1953) provided a practical, ex post criteria for assessing the quality of any analysis, namely, that it should predict well or at least meet the needs of those who seek to use it for predictive or forecasting purposes. What we do know is that most analysis published in all fields concerned with regional matters is essentially cliometrics or historical econometrics in nature. It is based on past, revealed

[24]Edward Leamer (1983) highlights "p-hacking." "The econometric art as it is practiced at the computer terminal involves fitting many, perhaps thousands, of statistical models. One or several that the researcher finds pleasing are selected for reporting purposes. This research for a model is often well intended, but there can be no doubt that such a specification search invalidates the traditional theories of inference." The situation was put bluntly by the Nobel Prize winner, Ronald Coase (cited in Gordon Tullock 2001), when he joked, "If you torture the data long enough, Nature will confess."

preference data with all the challenges that this introduces for using the findings for predict purposes. Further, there are few studies that have conducted ex post analysis of the accuracy of predictions – perhaps this is because they will not be published, or it may be because checking results can prove embarrassing. Certainly, from what we know in some sub-fields within regional analysis, such as transportation (Flyvbjerg et al. 2005), forecasts can prove to be highly inaccurate. The picture is not, though, altogether bleak. Although still in the minority, there is perhaps a greater proclivity to favor stated-preference data and methodologies in regional science journals than in regional economics, although this is more of an educated guess that a scientifically supported fact. The former approach, by definition, at least seeks to introduce some forward-oriented indicators of expectations into the analysis. But the forecasting reliability of stated-preference models has also not been explored in any depth by those involved in regional analysis.

3.8 Conclusions

So, what do we concluded from these various peeps at the differences in regional economics and regional science? First, economics has from the beginning played a major, indeed dominant role in regional science, and, if anything, this has increased over time. Back in the mid-1990s, Isserman (1995) found that economists accounted for 70% of the authors to the *Journal of Regional Science*, 79% (perhaps not surprisingly) of those in *Regional Science and Urban Economics*, but under 30% of those in *Papers of the Regional Science Association*. By 2018, I find the proportions have changed a little for the *Journal of Regional Science* and *Regional Science and Urban Economics* with economists now account for 63% of the authors publishing in the *Papers in Regional Science*, the successor to *Papers of the Regional Science Association.*[25]

Secondly, it can now hardly be claimed, as did the founders of regional science, that economists pay too little attention to spatial differences in economic behavior. I simply cite the reason Paul Krugman was awarded the Sveriges Riksbank Prize in Economic Sciences in Memory of Alfred Nobel in 2008. It was "...for his analysis of trade patterns and location of economic activity."[26] Although, while perhaps a complaint could be that Isard was neglected for the award, one should also recognize that the Nobel Prize has been awarded to Daniel McFadden (recipient in 2002) for his work refining discrete analysis, an approach widely used in spatial economics; Tinbergen (recipient in 1969) who published on a variety of regional topics,

[25]The proportion may be even larger. Those not recording a specific department are classified as noneconomists.

[26]Isard (1956) argues that economics, "...rarely obtains depth of analysis in that area which touches upon the broad influence of space and physical environment upon man's behaviour and land utilization patterns."

including in *Papers of the Regional Science Association*; and Wassily Leontief (recipient in 1973) who deployed his input-output analysis extensively at the regional as well as at the national level – e.g., Leontief (1953). And more recently, Paul Romer's (recipient in 2018) work on endogenous growth theory has a strong spatial element to it, most notably in terms of the role of charter cities.

Giarratani view that there are now proportionally fewer courses focusing on regional economics or regional science than there were in the period of the 1950s through to the 1970s is perhaps true. But in absolute terms, the sheer global increase in university education makes it unlikely that the study of spatial matters has declined. Also, there has been an increased internationalization in the subject matter both as global economic growth has taken place and as larger economic units, such as the European Union, that has led to new definitions and forms of political regions requiring different forms of study. The shifts towards market economies in Eastern and Central Europe, together with the economic changes in China and other emerging economies, have raised interesting questions centered around paths of transition which extend beyond the traditional boundaries of regional science. Added to this, there are now more interdisciplinary departments and courses at universities, and many contain elements of what would in the past have gone under the guise of regional science or regional economics.

But having said this, and coming back to the original question in the chapter's title, economics still dominates regional matters. One of economics' emergent advantages has been its more catholic approach to the subject matter of interest and a shift away from the rigidities of focusing on *homo economicus* and from "the stifling influence of the great but limited neoclassical tradition." This has embraced the growth of behavioral and institutional economics, as well as developing new techniques of analysis such as experimental economics.[27] While analyses of regions have not always been at the forefront of this work, the evolving methodologies do reflect a continual changing and flexible attitude in the economics discipline. Regional science, however, seems to have been less flexible in terms of the assumptions being made when modeling and in the range of issues it is willing to address. It still in many ways lingers in the 1950s and the 1960s.

References

Anderson RG, Kichkha A (2017) Replication, meta-analysis, and research synthesis in economics. Am Econ Rev 107:56–59

Barnes TJL (2003) What's wrong with American regional science? A view from science studies. Can J Reg Sci 26:2–26

Behrens K, Thisse J-F (2007) Regional economics: a new economic geography perspective. Reg Sci Urban Econ 37:457–465

[27]The Nobel speeches of Richard Thaler (2018) and Vernon Smith (2003), respectively, highlight the nature of these approaches.

Berry J, Coffman LC, Hanley D, Gihleb R, Wilson AJ (2017) Assessing the rate of replication in economics. Am Econ Rev 107:27–31
Boyce D (2004) A short history of the field of regional science. Pap Reg Sci 83:31–57
Brown AJ (1969) Survey in applied economics: regional economics. Econ J 68:761–796
Brown AJ, Woodward VH (1969) Regional social accounts for the United Kingdom. Rev Income Wealth 15:335–347
Brown DM (1979) The location decision of the firm: an overview of theory and evidence. Papers of the Regional Science Association 43:23–39
Button KJ (2000) Where did the "new urban economics" go after 25 years? In: Regiani A (ed) Spatial economic science: new Frontiers in theory and methodology. Springer, Berlin, pp 30–50
Camerer CF, Dreber A, Forsell E, Ho T-H, Huber J, Johannesson M, Kirchler M, Almenberg J, Altmejd A, Chan T, Heikensten E, Holzmeister F, Imai T, Isaksson S, Nave G, Pfeiffer T, Razen M, Wu H (2016) Evaluating replicability of laboratory experiments in economics. Science 351:1433–1436
Chamberlain E (1933) The theory of monopolistic competition: a re-orientation of the theory of value. Harvard University Press, Cambridge, MA
Chang AC, Li P (2017) A preanalysis plan to replicate sixty economics research papers that worked half of the time. Am Econ Rev 107:60–64
Cherrier B (2017) Classifying economics: a history of the JEL codes. J Econ Lit 55:545–579
Clemens MA (2017) The meaning of failed replications: a review and proposal. J Econ Surv 31:326–342
Corrado L, Fingleton B (2012) Where is the economics in spatial econometrics? J Reg Sci 52:210–239
Duvendack M, Palmer-Jones R, Reed ER (2017) What is meant by 'replication' and why does it encounter resistance in economics? Am Econ Rev 107:46–51
Flyvbjerg B, Holm, MKS, Buhl SL (2005) How (in)accurate are demand forecasts in public works projects? The case of transportation. J Am Plan Ass 71:131–146
Friedman M (1953) The methodology of positive economics. In: Friedman M (ed) Essays in positive economics. University of Chicago Press, Chicago, pp 3–43
Fujita M, Krugman P (2003) The new economic geography: past, present and the future. Pap Reg Sci 83(1):139–164
Fujita M, Krugman P, Venables A (1991) The spatial economy: cities, regions and international trade. MIT Press, Cambridge, MA
Giarratani F (1995) Nurture the symbiosis between economics and regional science (It's worth the trouble). Int Reg Sci Rev 17:343–346
Gibbons S, Overman HG (2012) Mostly pointless spatial econometrics? J Reg Sci 52:172–191
Giesecke JA, Madden JR (2013) Regional computable general equilibrium modeling. In: Dixon PB, Jorgenson DW (eds) Handbook of computable general equilibrium modeling, vol 1. Elsevier, Oxford, pp 379–475
Hamermesh DS (2007) Viewpoint: replication in economics. Can J Econ 40:715–733
Hamermesh DS (2017) Replication in labor economics: evidence from data, and what it suggests. Am Econ Rev 107:37–40
Hansen N (1995) Regional science, regional policy, and the "new" regional economics: future possibilities in historical perspective. Int Reg Sci Rev 17:337–342
Hicks JR (1960) Linear theory. Econ J 70:671–709
Hotelling H (1929) Stability in competition. Econ J 39:41–57
Höffler JH (2017) Replication and economics journal policies. Am Econ Rev 107:52–55
Isard W (1951) International and interregional input-output analysis; A model of a space-economy. Rev Econ Stat 33:318–328
Isard W (1956) Regional science, the concept of a region, and regional structure. Papers and Proceedings of the Regional Science Association 2:13–26

Isard W (1960) Methods and regional analysis: an introduction to regional science. Wiley, New York
Isard W (2003) History of regional science and the regional science association international: the beginnings and early history. Springer, Berlin
Isserman AM (1995) The history, status, and future of regional science: an American perspective. Int Reg Sci Rev 17:249–296
Isserman AM (2004) Intellectual leaders of regional science: a half-century citation study. Pap Reg Sci 83:91–126
Kane EJ (1984) Why journal editors should encourage the replication of applied econometrics research. Q J Bus Econ 23:3–8
Krugman PR (1991) Increasing returns and economic geography. J Polit Econ 99:483–499
Leamer EE (1983) Let's take the con out of econometrics. Am Econ Rev 73:31–43
Leontief WW (1953) Interregional theory. In: Leontief WW et al (eds) Studies in the structure of the American economy theoretical and empirical explorations in input-output analysis. Oxford University Press, Oxford, pp 93–115
Maniadis Z, Tufano F, List JA (2017) To replicate or not to replicate? Exploring reproducibility in economics through the lens of a model and pilot research. Econ J 127:F209–F235
Marshall A (1890) Principles of economics, 1st edn. Macmillan, London
Meyer JR (1963) Regional economics: a survey. Am Econ Rev 53:19–54
Mills E, MacKinnon J (1973) Notes on the new urban economics. Bell J Econ Manag Sci 4:593–601
Moran PAP (1948) The interpretation of statistical maps. J R Stat Soc Ser B 10:243–251
Perloff HS (1957) Regional studies at U.S. Universities: a survey of regionally oriented research and graduate education. Resources for the Future, Washington, DC
Polèse M (1995) On the cultural origins and future direction of regional science: a voice from the periphery. Can J Reg Sci 17:311–318
Richardson HW (1977) The new urban economics and alternatives. Pion, London
Richardson HW (1978a) Input-output and economic base multipliers. Looking backward and forward. J Reg Sci 25:607–662
Richardson HW (1978b) The state of regional economics: a survey article. Int Reg Sci Rev 3:1–48
Robbins LC (1932) An essay on the nature and significance of economic science. Macmillan, London
Samuelson PA (1954) The transfer problem and transport costs, II: analysis of effects of trade impediments. Econ J 64:264–289
Smith A (1776) An inquiry into the nature and causes of the wealth of nations, 1997th edn. Oxford University Press, Oxford
Smith VL (2003) Constructivist and ecological rationality in economics. Am Econ Rev 93:465–508
Spiegel HW (1987) Jacob Viner (1892–1970). In: Eatwell J, Milgate M, Newman P (eds) The new Palgrave: a dictionary of economics, vol IV. Macmillan, London, pp 812–814
Stewart JQ, Warntz W (1958) Physics of population distribution. J Reg Sci 1:99–121
Stone JR (1961) Social accounts at the regional level: A survey. In: Issard W, Cumberland JH (eds) Regional economic planning. OECD, Paris, pp 263–296
Sukhtankar S (2017) Replications in development economics. Am Econ Rev 107:32–36
Thaler RH (2018) From cashews to nudges: the evolution of behavioral economics. Am Econ Rev 108:1265–1287
Tinbergen J (1962) Shaping the world economy an analysis of world trade flows. Twentieth Century Fund 5:27–30
Tullock G (2001) A comment on Daniel Klein's 'a plea to economists who favor liberty'. East Econ J 27:203–207
Williamson OE (2000) The new institutional economics: taking stock, looking ahead. J Econ Lit 38:595–613

Chapter 4
Sustainability and Resilience Through Micro-scale Decisions for Change

Alan T. Murray

Abstract The impacts of human-induced change are significant, affecting our environment, climate, fauna, and people in various ways. Recognition of needed change is widespread. Sustainability and resilience efforts reflect such awareness and often focus on pathways for moving forward that address current and future issues through decisions based on analysis, planning, management, and policy. The chapter highlights essential micro-scale thinking to bring about change in order to mitigate the negative impacts of human-induced growth and development. The use of spatial analytical approaches, including geographic information systems, spatial optimization, and spatial statistics, is a central theme. Application studies are reviewed to highlight the significance of micro-scale decisions for change as a component to achieving long-term sustainability and resilience.

Keywords Spatial analytics · Spatial optimization · Transit · Street lighting · Urban heat island

4.1 Introduction

Urban growth and development presents new and unique problems for society (see Cohen et al. 1996). There is recognition that past and current practices of daily life have negatively impacted the environment, changing local and regional climates and depleting what was once thought to be bountiful natural resources. Sustainability and resilience are now the ultimate goals. Interest in sustainability and its implications for better population growth and development management continues to increase. Despite this attention, defining the concept of sustainability in operational terms has proven to be a difficult and subjective task (Barbier 1987; Toman 1994; Yao et al. 2018). There are major differences between ecological, social, and economic

A. T. Murray (✉)
Department of Geography, University of California at Santa Barbara, Santa Barbara, CA, USA
e-mail: amurray@ucsb.edu

Z. Chen et al. (eds.), *Development Studies in Regional Science*,
New Frontiers in Regional Science: Asian Perspectives 42,
https://doi.org/10.1007/978-981-15-1435-7_4

interpretations of sustainability (see Batty 1995; Commons 1995; Talen 2014). Costanza (1994) suggests that sustainable development entails maintaining a fair distribution of resources and opportunities among species (current and future), a manageable scale of the economy relative to its ecological life support system, and an efficient temporal allocation of resources that considers natural capital. Considerable work has focused on operationalizing the concept of sustainable development (Hunter and Haughton 2004; Yao et al. 2018). Nijkamp et al. (1996) define sustainability as "... an ecologically compatible spatial and socio-economic development in a spatial system, taking into account mutually conflicting but also mutually supporting developments in all areas of that system." Resilience too is challenging to define and operationalize. Haynes and Georgianna (1989) discuss that resiliency reflects the ability of a natural system to restore itself. Achieving sustainable and resilient urban and regional systems requires dedication and commitment on the part of all and will be accomplished only through strategic planning, management, decision-making, and policy that is based on sound science reflecting a broad understanding of human and natural systems. This suggests an important role for spatial analytics.

At the forefront of spatial analysis and modeling has been Professor Kingsley Haynes, a legend in regional science and geography, who has sought to address contemporary public policy issues associated with sustainability and resilience, and in particular critical infrastructure investment (Haynes 1997; Yilmaz et al. 2002; Haynes et al. 2005; Chen et al. 2016), spatial equity (Bowen et al. 1995; Chen and Haynes 2017), manufacturing and employment (Haynes and Machunda 1987; Zhu et al. 2015), and regional efficiency (Dinc and Haynes 1999), among others. While the substantive and policy aspects of his work are a common theme, what is perhaps most striking is the wealth and breadth of spatial analytics that are brought to bear in his research to support sustainability and resilience efforts. This has meant that spatial analytics have had to be developed, refined, and extended in various ways to address an understanding of systems, as reflected in his research on gravity and spatial interaction (Haynes and Fotheringham 1984), optimization (Charnes et al. 1975), computable general equilibrium (Chen et al. 2016), data envelop analysis (Zhu et al. 2015), input-output (Dinc and Haynes 1999), shift-share (Haynes and Dinc 1997), and spatial statistics (Chen and Haynes 2017). With an appreciation of local, regional, national, and international issues along with a policy/planning perspective, his quantitative skills have been used to support positive change.

Inspired by his research, perspective, and general approach, this chapter suggests that achieving sustainability and resilience goals can only be accomplished through integrated decision-making that accounts for regional and micro-scale considerations. While rapidly developing countries in Asia are often the central focus of research efforts, growth and development abounds. Interest in sustainability and resilience is pervasive, with research on the smart city reflecting ongoing efforts. This means we indeed must be concerned with the bigger picture of establishing sustainability goals and targets as well as seek out resilient responses, but attention must focus on reaching them through micro-scale decisions for change. The remainder of this chapter is as follows. The next section reviews context for considering sustainability and resilience. Then spatial analytics are detailed that support decision-making. Case studies are then summarized which exemplify micro-scale decisions for change. The chapter ends with discussion and concluding comments.

4.2 Context

A theme of this Festschrift is an Asian perspective. Why Asia? No doubt this is because more than half of the world's population resides in Asia. With continued and sustained shifts to urban areas, the strains on the environment are significant. Ultimately what happens in this region clearly has impacts and implications for the rest of the world. Characteristic traits of many areas in Asia are urban growth and rapid development. Transportation has major implications for sustainability in this context. One aspect of the work that follows is a focus on transportation and, in particular, public transit access and accessibility. Another major sustainability factor is energy consumption. In particular, nighttime lighting requires a significant portion of global electricity production. Because of this, another aspect of the work that follows is focused on lighting costs and impacts. An important facet of climate change is urban heat island, where temperatures in the built environment are significantly hotter than surrounding areas. Accordingly, a final aspect of the work that follows is devoted to urban heat island. Each of these issues figure prominently for Asian cities and regions.

The implications for sustainability and resilience in transportation, energy consumption, and rising temperatures are broad and encompassing. The discussion in Borsekova and Nijkamp (2018) is suggestive that the smart city has and will continue to take advantage of information and communication technologies and use them strategically to ensure efficiency. However, this will not happen by itself but rather will be the by-product of decision-making informed and guided by analytics. This is precisely what is suggested by the notion of micro-scale decisions for change discussed in this chapter. Three particular contexts, as noted above, are utilized to highlight the need for such decision-making along these lines.

Transportation is a key aspect of sustainability and resilience efforts, with public transit playing a critical role (Currie and De Gruyter 2018). Micro-scale decisions for change focused on transit planning were addressed in Murray et al. (1998) and Murray (2001). Of particular interest were regional planning goals designed to increase public transit ridership, thereby reducing congestion, eliminating the need for more infrastructure, and decreasing environmental impacts. Murray et al. (1998) and Murray (2001) highlight that an often used approach is to ensure that a large portion of a region has suitable access to transit, so increasing access is recognized as offering potential for transit ridership increases and modal shifts in travel behavior. Such a goal is typically part of an integrated regional transport plan. This is expressed in explicit terms, such as a regional public transport goal of at least 90% of the total population served within 400 meters of a transit stop, as an example. This may be extended to address other aspects of access, such as temporal, affordability, safety, travel time, etc. The assumption is that suitable access influences public transportation utilization and travel behavior (see also Delmelle et al. 2012). Beyond this, there are important questions of efficiency in achieving sustainability and resiliency goals.

The production of energy too has an important role in sustainability and resilience, with nighttime lighting consuming a significant portion of production capacity. A second micro-scale decision for change context, therefore, is street lighting. Murray and Feng (2016) and Feng and Murray (2018) note that standards and guidelines, often through federal, state, and/or local laws and ordinances, establish explicit and detailed specifications regarding the provision of artificial nighttime lighting, typically with respect to pedestrian and transportation safety. For example, there must be street lighting at intersections, and street lighting intervals should not exceed 91.44 m. The assumption is that lighting provides visibility and ensures safety. Interestingly, efficiency with respect to economic and environmental costs is often not explicitly considered.

While growth and development are generally considered good, associated urban heat island temperature increases are problematic in many ways. Therefore, a third micro-scale decision for change context involves mitigating urban heat island. Zhang et al. (2017a) note that cities like Phoenix, Arizona, have seen significant daytime and nighttime average temperature increases, over 3.1 and 5 °C, respectively, in the past 50 years. Zhang et al. (2017b) highlight concerns for increasing temperatures in cities like Beijing due to rapid expansion and development, particularly during summer months. The public health implications and environmental impacts have prompted goals for decreasing urban heat island through the increase of green space. For example, Phoenix is making a substantial investment to boost urban vegetation significantly over the next decade. However, an increase in vegetation alone will not decrease temperature as spatial configuration of green space matters (Li et al. 2012; Turner et al. 2013). Significant decreases in average temperature are possible if green space is increased in a strategic manner.

This chapter is premised on the notion that micro-scale function and operation are fundamentally important for the sustainability and resilience of cities and regions. We must care about and focus on little details regarding how subsystems work and what are their roles as well as the essential contribution(s) that they are making. But given that a particular service is necessary, efficiency is critical. After all, how can sustainability and/or resilience be achieved without efficiency across all facets of operations, services, and functions? Long-term viability is about both need and efficiency, asking tough questions and making difficult investment decisions.

4.3 Spatial Analytics

As noted previously, the work of Professor Haynes has spanned the range of approaches. An overview perspective of quantitative methods is offered in Murray (2010). Murray (2017) characterizes such approaches and others as analytics. For addressing geographic problems and issues, it is appropriate to view these

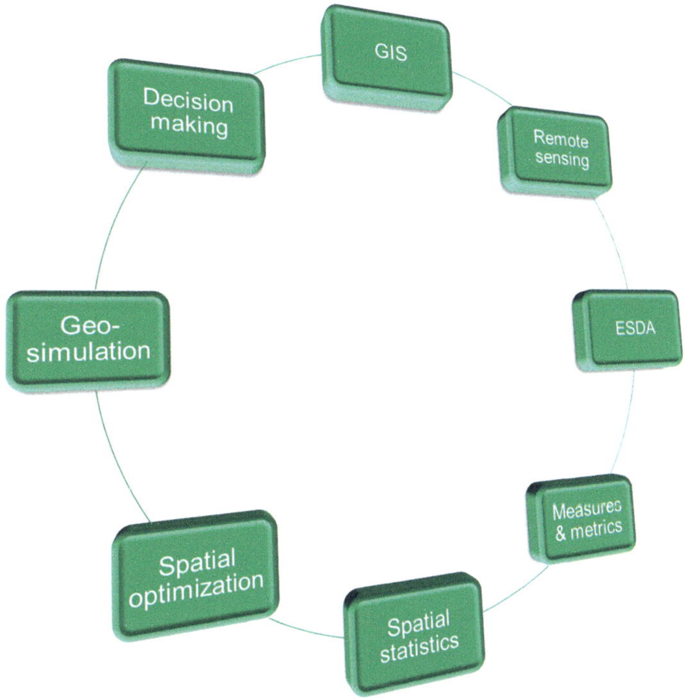

Fig. 4.1 Potential spatial analytics for addressing sustainability issues

approaches as spatial analytics, which would include all quantitative methods that support analysis, policy, and planning involving geographic space. Some of the more prominent spatial analytics are summarized in Fig. 4.1 and are often used in combination when applied to address urban and regional problems/issues. While each category noted in Fig. 4.1 is not reviewed here due to space constraints, further detail regarding ESDA (exploratory spatial data analysis) and spatial statistics can be found in Anselin et al. (2013) and Chen and Haynes (2017); examples of measures and metrics (e.g., spatial interaction, shift-share, input-output, computable general equilibrium, etc.) are included in Haynes and Fotheringham (1984) and Haynes and Dinc (1997); and discussion of spatial optimization is given in Charnes et al. (1975) and Murray (2010, 2017), highlighting the different ways that geographic details may be explicitly and implicitly incorporated in analytics.

Spatial analytics play a central role in the micro-scale efforts that follow. These include GIS (geographic information system), remote sensing, spatial statistics, and spatial optimization, all within the context of decision-making processes. In particular, GIS is utilized for geographic data creation, management, manipulation, analysis, and display. Remote sensing too provides data input through aerial imagery, observation, and associated processing. Spatial statistics are used to identify patterns and relationships, based upon which estimation of parameters and other attribute characteristics is possible. Building on these methods, spatial optimization has proven to be an essential integrating spatial analytic technique behind microlevel decisions for change. The remainder of this section is devoted to discussion of problem context and the technical details of associated methods.

Transit planning was addressed in Murray et al. (1998) and Murray (2001). Of particular interest were regional planning goals designed to increase public transit ridership. An often used approach is to ensure that a large portion of a region has suitable access to transit, so increasing access is recognized as offering potential for transit ridership increases. Murray et al. (1998) demonstrated that GIS and associated analysis functionality like overlay could be used in such an assessment. Murray (2001) took this a step further, suggesting an approach to examine system performance efficiency based on access goals. This was done through the use of the location set covering problem (LSCP). The LSCP enables transit stop placement efficiency evaluation with respect to suitable access, considered to be the area within 400 meters of a transit stop. Such an access standard is commonly viewed as a reasonable walk under normal conditions. The model then provides a mechanism for determining whether any stop(s) are unnecessary with respect to the access standard and regional transportation goals. This is significant because superfluous stops degrade transit system performance by slowing average travel times.

Consider the following notation:

i= index of demand objects

j= index of potential facility siting locations

N_i= set of potential facilities capable of suitably serving demand object i

$$X_j = \begin{cases} 1 \text{ if potential facility location } j \text{ is selected} \\ 0 \text{ otherwise} \end{cases}$$

The demand object in this case could be a land parcel, neighborhood, or census reporting unit, and the facility is a transit stop. Given a set of potential facility locations (existing transit stops in this case), it is possible to carry out evaluation to determine precisely which facility sites are capable of serving an individual service demand i. The set N_i therefore reflects this evaluation, denoting which potential facility sites can suitably serve demand i. Often such evaluation is based on travel distance or time between any pair of geographic locations, with a desired or mandatory response standard established. In the case of transit access, the 400 m standard is generally assumed for bus-based systems. With this notation a particular spatial optimization model can be structured, the LSCP is as follows:

$$\text{Minimize } \sum_j X_j \tag{4.1}$$

$$\text{Subject to } \sum_{j \in N_i} X_j \geq 1 \quad \forall i \tag{4.2}$$

$$X_j = \{0, 1\} \quad \forall j \tag{4.3}$$

The objective, (4.1), seeks a minimum number of facilities, equivalent to a minimum cost configuration if each potential facility site has the same fixed costs. Constraints (4.2) stipulate that each demand must be serviced by one or more sited facilities within the desired service standard. Binary integer restrictions are imposed on decision variables in Constraints (4.3).

The next micro-scale decision for change context to be discussed is street lighting. With standards and guidelines largely dictating the nature of nighttime lighting for safety and security, the provision of lighting has often been accomplished in rather ad hoc ways. Efficiency with respect to economic and environmental costs is often not explicitly considered, though it has generally been assumed as part of the overall engineering design process. In practice, this does not appear to be the case outside of more recent spatial analytic efforts. A model based on the LSCP was detailed in Murray and Feng (2016) for evaluation and assessment of street lighting system configuration. An extension to account for a limited budget in facility investment was structured in Feng and Murray (2018). The idea is to identify a configuration of street lights that illuminates the greatest amount of demand for service possible given a fixed budget on street light investment and operation. In this case, illumination is determined to be suitable out to 45.72 m. Consider the following additional notation:
α_i= expected service demand associated with object i
p= number of facilities to site

$$Y_i = \begin{cases} 1 \text{ if demand } i \text{ is suitably served by one or more sited facilities} \\ 0 \text{ otherwise} \end{cases}$$

The demand object in this case could be a land parcel, street segment, and/or intersection, and the facility is a street light. The number of facilities to site, p, represents a budget or limit on service to be provided. Using this notation, the spatial optimization model that follows is known as the maximal covering location problem (MCLP):

$$\text{Maximize } \sum_i \alpha_i Y_i \tag{4.4}$$

$$\text{Subject to } \sum_{j \in N_i} X_j \geq Y_i \quad \forall i \tag{4.5}$$

$$\sum_j X_j = p \tag{4.6}$$

$$X_j = \{0, 1\} \quad \forall j \tag{4.7}$$

$$Y_i = \{0, 1\} \quad \forall i \tag{4.8}$$

Objective (4.4) seeks the greatest total service demand covered. Constraints (4.5) track coverage of an area by facilities sited that are able to serve it within the stipulated standard. Constraints (4.6) set the number of facilities to be sited at p. This is effectively a budget limit when the cost of each potential facility location is essentially the same. Binary integer restrictions are imposed on decision variables in Constraints (4.7) and (4.8).

The final micro-scale decisions for change modeling approach detailed here involve urban heat island. As noted above, significant public health and environmental impact issues are associated with temperature increases attributable to non-impervious surfaces and materials in the built environment. These materials absorb and magnify solar radiation. To mitigate such impacts, cities and urban regions have recognized that increased green space can help cool urban areas. But challenges remain because spatial configuration of green space matters. It is not enough to merely add green space but to do so in a manner that lowers average temperatures the most. Zhang et al. (2017a) structured and applied a spatial optimization model to support green space decision-making. The idea is to identify a spatial configuration of green space that mitigates the impacts of urban heat island to the greatest extent possible. This is accomplished by tracking direct and indirect cooling benefits. Specifically, the conversion of a parcel or land area to green space results in direct cooling of the area. Alternatively, an area in close proximity to converted green space experiences cooling, but this is deemed an indirect effect. Collectively, direct and indirect cooling offer local relief of urban heat island effects but also work to bring down average temperatures across a region.

Consider the following additional notation:

β_j= direct benefit associated with selecting facility j

δ_{ik}= local (indirect) benefit to demand object i if facility k selected.

$$Z_{ik} = \begin{cases} 1 \text{ if demand } i \text{ is suitably served by } k \text{ sited facilities} \\ 0 \text{ otherwise} \end{cases}$$

The demand object in this case is a land parcel and the facility is green space. Selection of a land parcel, e.g., $X_j = 1$, means that it should or will be converted to green space. Using this notation, a spatial optimization model to support parcel selection is as follows:

$$\text{Maximize} \sum_j \beta_j X_j \tag{4.9}$$

$$\text{Maximize} \sum_i \sum_k \delta_{ik} Z_{ii} \tag{4.10}$$

$$\text{Subject to} \sum_{j \in N_i} X_j \geq k\, Z_{ik} \quad \forall i, k \tag{4.11}$$

$$\sum_{k} Z_{ik} + X_i \leq 1 \quad \forall i \tag{4.12}$$

$$\sum_{j} X_j = p \tag{4.13}$$

$$X_j = \{0, 1\} \quad \forall j \tag{4.14}$$

$$Z_{ik} = \{0, 1\} \quad \forall i, k \tag{4.15}$$

Objectives (4.9) and (4.10) seek the greatest total cooling benefit of demand, directly and indirectly. Constraints (4.11) relate the level of cooling benefit to proximally sited green spaces. Constraints (4.12) limit cooling benefit to be either direct (area selected for green space conversion) or indirect (green space sited nearby). Constraints (4.13) set the number of sites to be selected for green space at p. Binary integer restrictions are imposed on decision variables in Constraints (4.14) and (4.15).

The spatial analytics outlined in Fig. 4.1 along with the spatial models specified in this section help us to formalize sustainability and resilience goals. This facilitates and enables real progress to be made in order to move forward at a micro-scale. Spatial analytics have an important role in decision-making but must be structured and applied in meaningful ways. Linkage of regional goals to detailed operational changes and behavior is essential.

4.4 Micro-scale Decisions for Change

Boulding (1975) observed that the world changes as a result of decisions not plans. Addressing sustainability and resilience issues, accordingly, must be directed at decisions, hopefully those decisions that will bring about a positive change. Decisions then reflect operational mechanisms of systems that provide goods and services; enable travel, movement, and interaction; protect natural resources; rehabilitate contaminated lands; bolster ailing processes; etc. I characterize a focus on operational mechanisms as micro-scale decisions for change, where essential questions of need and efficiency are at the heart of achieving sustainability and resilience. Service-based systems generally evolve over time, and with growth and change, such systems become inefficient, though in some cases they may not have been needed and/or were not efficient to begin with. The service systems reviewed below are meant to highlight ways in which spatial analytics can be brought to bear in moving toward a more sustainable and resilient future, though clearly many more subsystems must ultimately be considered, examined, and enhanced.

The situation detailed in Murray et al. (1998) and Murray (2001) involved transit service provision in the South East Queensland (Australia) region. With less than 7%

of all trips in the region using transit, a public transport goal in their integrated plan was to ensure that at least 90% of people are within 400 meters of a transit stop. Again, the assumption is that increased access will result in greater transit ridership. Through the use of GIS and associated spatial information, including census-based data and transit stop locations, applied spatial analytics indicated that some 55% of the total population had suitable access to transit. Thus, relative to the stipulated goal of 90%, there is room for improvement. Murray (2001) went beyond this goal, essentially questioning the ability to increase ridership through a focus solely on the provision of access. In particular, it was suggested that there were significant inefficiencies in the existing system. Such inefficiencies were the by-product of an excessive number of transit stops along a given route of the bus-based system. That is, too many stops along a route mean that a bus must slow down, stop, alight passengers, board passengers, and then accelerate and reenter traffic. The result is slower average travel speeds on transit between an origin and destination.

To highlight this point, Murray (2001) examined the 7589 bus stops along with sources of travel demand (1538 collection districts). Applying the LSCP to find the most efficient configuration of transit stops that would continue to serve the 1538 collection districts within the 400 meters standard, Murray (2001) reports that only 1176 of the existing 7589 stops are actually needed. Relative to the 400 meters access standard, less than 16% of the existing transit stops would be necessary to maintain the current level of bus based service. Figure 4.2 shows the transit line

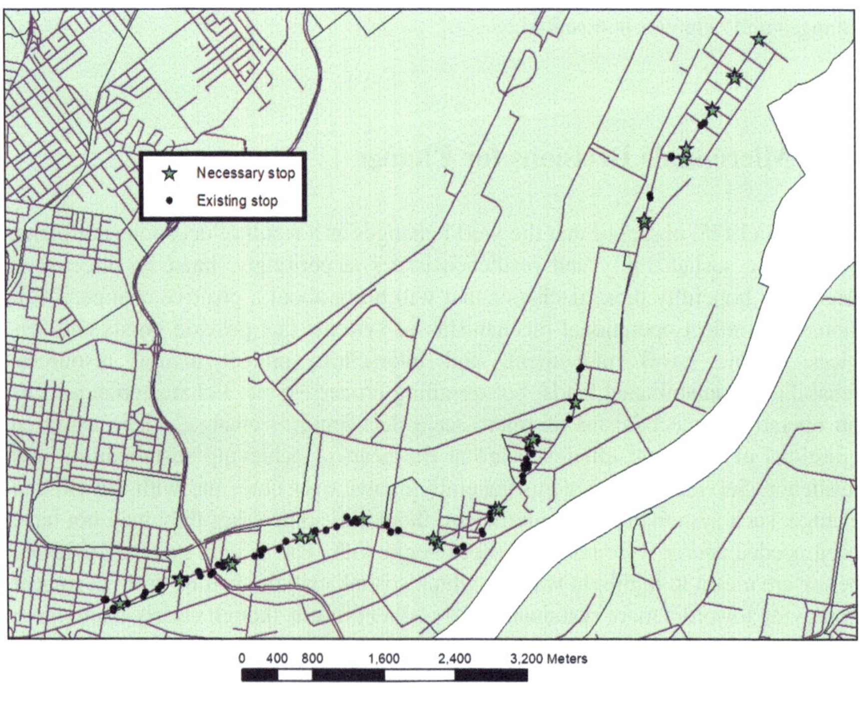

Fig. 4.2 Transit planning for ensuring the best performance possible

along Kingsford Smith Dr./Eagle Farm Rd./Main Beach Rd. near Brisbane Airport. In total there are 89 bus stops along this route. Many represent stop pairs, with one stop for one direction of travel and the other stop serving the other direction (on the other side of the road). In this case only 25 stops are actually necessary along this route in order to ensure that all potential demand is within 400 meters of a stop. Similar results are reported as well in Delmelle et al. (2012) for transit in Charlotte, North Carolina. Both studies illustrate the nature of stop spacing impacting travel times, with too many stops along a route during peak periods of travel. This creates systematic inefficiencies but also impacts behavioral decision-making of potential ridership. Increasing transit ridership and bringing about change in regional travel mode behavior means that the system must be as efficient as possible.

Murray and Feng (2016) and Feng and Murray (2018) examined nighttime street lighting. The premise of their work is that there are inherent inefficiencies in systems and they have considerable implications for sustainability efforts. Cities, large and small, spend a significant portion of their annual budgets on nighttime lighting. San Diego, California, with over 1.3 million people, operates approximately 40,000 street lights, spending some $4,700,000 annually on lighting. Goleta, California, with nearly 31,000 people, operates approximately 1650 street lights, spending $273,072 per year on lighting. Los Angeles, California, with over 3.8 million people, operates approximately 220,000 street lights. There are no publicly available figures on annual operations costs but are likely in the $25 to $36 million range for Los Angeles to provide street lighting. Continuing unnecessary or nonessential nighttime lighting burdens resource demands but also necessitates further electricity generation. Indeed, nighttime lighting is estimated to require some 20% of overall energy production. Beyond this, Gaston (2018) highlights other negative issues associated with lighting. Examined in Feng and Murray (2018) was a neighborhood in San Diego. The existing lighting system had 104 lights serving some 68% of service demand. From an efficiency perspective, the MCLP was applied to the area, finding that it is possible to site only 89 lights and still serve 68% of service demand. This spatial configuration and associated service is depicted in Fig. 4.3, where lighting has an effective illumination range of 45.72 m. Thus, it is possible to use fewer resources to provide an equivalent level of lighting coverage. In this case, a reduction of 14% of annual costs is possible through system reconfiguration and would provide the same degree of service. Of course, further reduction too is possible, if it is acceptable to illuminate less than 68% of area demand.

Zhang et al. (2017a) report an assessment of urban heat island in Phoenix, Arizona, and consider goals to mitigate systemic temperature increases through the addition of green space. Noted are real and significant public health concerns, including heat-related illnesses and increased death rates for vulnerable groups like the elderly, but also sustainability implications, including high electricity loads during extreme heat periods as well as high water usage. Evaluation has shown that green space offers direct cooling of up to 6.7 °C during the day and 2.6 °C during the night and indirect cooling of 2.7 °C during the day and 1 °C during the night in the Phoenix region, consistent with other studies such as those focusing on Beijing (see Li et al. 2012, Zhang et al. 2017b). Using this information, the above-noted spatial optimization model was applied to determine that overall regional

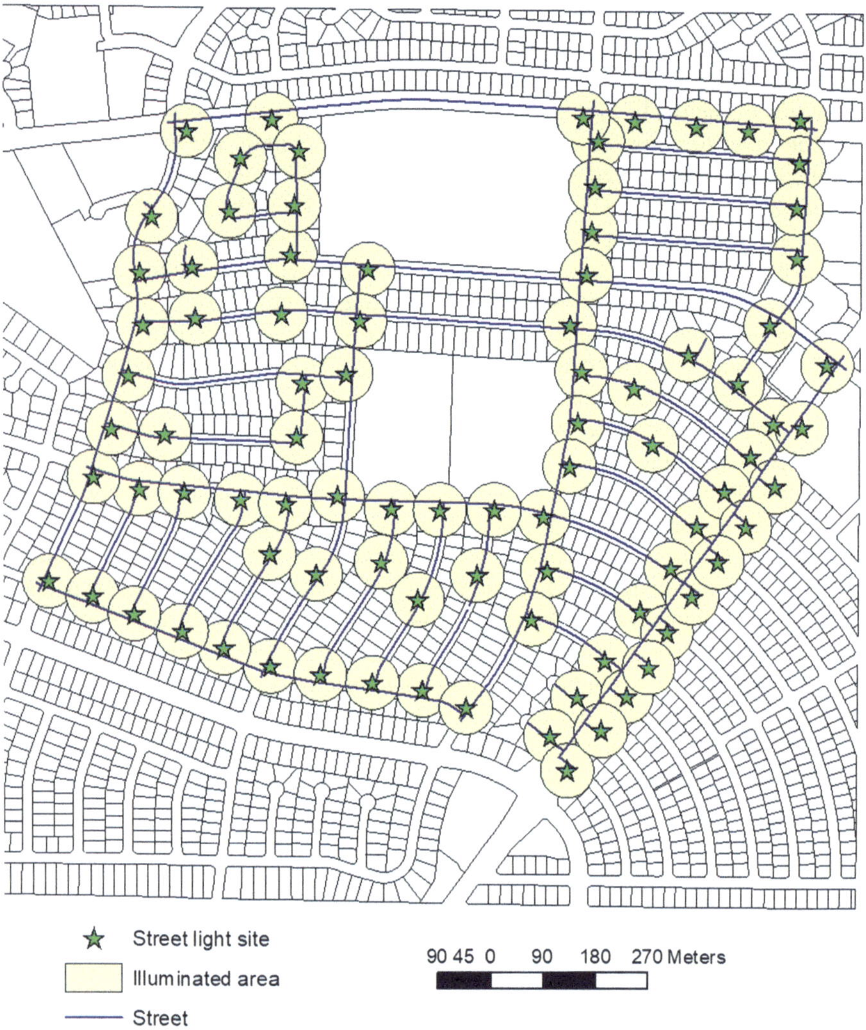

Fig. 4.3 Street lighting design for serving the greatest demand possible

cooling of approximately 0.5 °C was possible through green space conversion involving as little as 1% of the land area, with local cooling of up to 2 °C. This is illustrated in Fig. 4.4 where the direct benefits are shown as well as the indirect benefits. The point then is that decisions focused on the parcel or sub-parcel level can indeed have a cumulative effect, decreasing the impact of urban heat island in this case. Spatial configuration matters, and this can be reflected in spatial analytics used to support decisions seeking to make regions more sustainable and resilient.

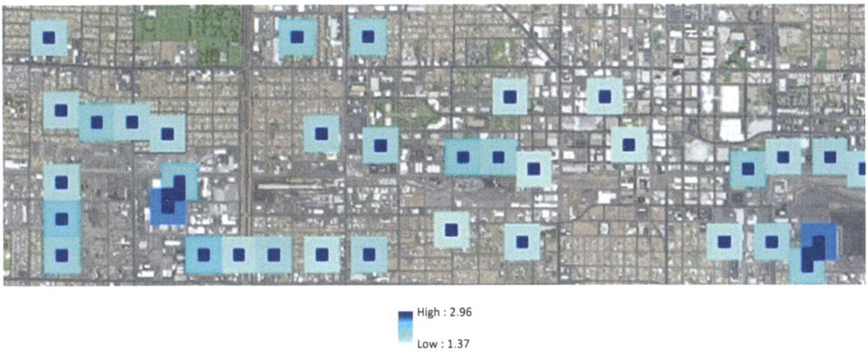

Fig. 4.4 Green space planning to mitigate urban heat island

4.5 Discussion and Conclusions

The micro-scale decisions for change examples have highlighted that any and all operational components of urban and regional systems must be subjected to considerable scrutiny if sustainability and resiliency are to ever be attained. Of course, change is incremental, resulting from growth, development, migration, movement, behavior, technology, etc. As a result, systems become inefficient as they evolve for different reasons. Urbanization is clearly a factor, but there are many other causes as well.

Through the use of spatial analytics, it is possible to identify inefficiencies and establish micro-scale decisions for bringing about change to make systems more efficient. Consider public street lighting in San Diego where 14% savings is possible for equivalent levels of illumination. Such a situation suggests that large publicly supported systems, like that of Los Angeles with 220,000 street lights, would likely save millions of dollars annually. Beyond this, spatial analytics enable exploration of alternative futures, where systems can be reconfigured, contracted, or eliminated in order to assess the impact of such changes. Of course when inefficiencies are identified, it becomes possible to expand service in various ways or perhaps redirect savings to other services.

Urban areas are very reflective of a system comprised of many subsystems that evolve in various ways over time. Negative by-products of such evolution may include poor utilization of public transit because of excessive travel times, exorbitant expenditures on public lighting, and dangerous conditions posed by urban heat island, all highlighted in this chapter. Through the use of spatial analytics and a focus on micro-scale decisions, it is possible to make changes to spatial structure and composition, which offer strategies to decrease transportation impacts, reduce the costs of public services, and mitigate local heating effects, as examples touched upon in this chapter. Strategic thinking and systematic decision-making offer a path forward but are reliant upon integrated spatial analytics. Such approaches reflect micro-scale spatial detail but account for important local interactions.

References

Anselin L, Murray AT, Rey SJ (2013) Spatial analysis. In: Little TD (ed) The Oxford handbook of quantitative methods, vol 1. Oxford University Press, Oxford, pp 154–174
Barbier E (1987) The concept of sustainable economic development. Environ Conserv 14:101–110
Batty M (1995) Cities and complexity: implications for modelling sustainability. In: Brotchie J, Batty M, Blakely E, Hall P, Newton P (eds) Cities in competition. Longman, Melbourne, pp 467–486
Borsekova K, Nijkamp P (2018) Smart cities: a challenge to research and policy analysis. Cities 78:1–3
Boulding KE (1975) Reflections on planning: the value of uncertainty. Plan Rev 3(2):11–12
Bowen WM, Salling MJ, Haynes KE, Cyran EJ (1995) Toward environmental justice: spatial equity in Ohio and Cleveland. Ann Assoc Am Geogr 85(4):641–663
Charnes A, Haynes KE, Hazleton JE, Ryan MJ (1975) A hierarchical goal-programming approach to environmental land use management. Geogr Anal 7(2):121–130
Chen Z, Haynes KE (2017) Impact of high-speed rail on regional economic disparity in China. J Transp Geogr 65:80–91
Chen Z, Xue J, Rose AZ, Haynes KE (2016) The impact of high-speed rail investment on economic and environmental change in China: a dynamic CGE analysis. Transp Res A Policy Pract 92:232–245
Cohen M, Ruble B, Tulchin J, Garland A (1996) Preparing for the urban future. Woodrow Wilson Center Press, Washington
Commons M (1995) Sustainability and policy: limits to economics. Cambridge University Press, Cambridge
Costanza R (1994) Ecological economics and sustainable development. International Experts Meeting for the Operationalization of the Economics of Sustainability. Manila, 28–30 July
Currie G, De Gruyter C (2018) Exploring links between the sustainability performance of urban public transport and land use in international cities. J Transp Land Use 11(1):325–342
Delmelle EM, Li S, Murray AT (2012) Identifying bus stop redundancy: a GIS-based spatial optimization approach. Comput Environ Urban Syst 36(5):445–455
Dinc M, Haynes KE (1999) Sources of regional inefficiency an integrated shift-share, data envelopment analysis and input-output approach. Ann Reg Sci 33(4):469–489
Feng X, Murray AT (2018) Spatial analytics for enhancing street light coverage of public spaces. LEUKOS 14(1):13–23
Gaston KJ (2018) Lighting up the nighttime. Science 362(6416):744–746
Haynes KE (1997) Labor markets and regional transportation improvements: the case of high-speed trains an introduction and review. Ann Reg Sci 31(1):57–76
Haynes KE, Dinc M (1997) Productivity change in manufacturing regions: a multifactor/shift-share approach. Growth Chang 28(2):201–221
Haynes KE, Fotheringham AS (1984) Gravity and spatial interaction models. Sage, Beverly Hills
Haynes KE, Georgianna TD (1989) Risk assessment of water allocation and pollution treatment policies in a regional economy: reliability, vulnerability and resiliency in the Yellowstone Basin of Montana. Comput Environ Urban Syst 13(2):75–94
Haynes KE, Machunda ZB (1987) Spatial restructuring of manufacturing and employment growth in the rural Midwest: an analysis for Indiana. Econ Geogr 63(4):319–333
Haynes KE, Gifford JL, Pelletiere D (2005) Sustainable transportation institutions and regional evolution: global and local perspectives. J Transp Geogr 13(3):207–221
Hunter C, Haughton G (2004) Sustainable cities. Routledge, London
Li X, Zhou W, Ouyang Z, Xu W, Zheng H (2012) Spatial pattern of greenspace affects land surface temperature: evidence from the heavily urbanized Beijing metropolitan area, China. Landsc Ecol 27(6):887–898
Murray AT (2001) Strategic analysis of public transport coverage. Socio Econ Plan Sci 35 (3):175–188

Murray AT (2010) Quantitative geography. J Reg Sci 50(1):143–163
Murray AT (2017) Regional analytics. Ann Reg Sci 59(1):1–13
Murray AT, Feng X (2016) Public street lighting service standard assessment and achievement. Socio Econ Plan Sci 53:14–22
Murray AT, Davis R, Stimson RJ, Ferreira L (1998) Public transportation access. Transp Res Part D: Transp Environ 3(5):319–328
Nijkamp P, Baggen J, van der Knaap B (1996) Spatial sustainability and the tyranny of transport: a causal path scenario analysis. Pap Reg Sci 75(4):501–524
Talen E (2014) Urban and regional sustainability. In: Fischer MM, Nijkamp P (eds) Handbook of regional science. Springer, Berlin, pp 1071–1083
Toman M (1994) Economics and 'sustainability': balancing trade-offs and imperatives. Land Econ 70:399–413
Turner BL, Janetos AC, Verbug PH, Murray AT (2013) Land system architecture: using land systems to adapt and mitigate global environmental change. Glob Environ Chang 23:395–397
Yao J, Zhang X, Murray AT (2018) Spatial optimization for land-use allocation: accounting for sustainability concerns. Int Reg Sci Rev 41(6):579–600
Yilmaz S, Haynes KE, Dinc M (2002) Geographic and network neighbors: spillover effects of telecommunications infrastructure. J Reg Sci 42(2):339–360
Zhang Y, Murray AT, Turner BL (2017a) Optimizing green space locations to reduce daytime and nighttime urban heat island effects in Phoenix, Arizona. Landsc Urban Plan 165:162–171
Zhang Y, Zhan Y, Yu T, Ren X (2017b) Urban green effects on land surface temperature caused by surface characteristics: a case study of summer Beijing metropolitan region. Infrared Phys Technol 86:35–43
Zhu Y, Xue JB, Zhu Y, Haynes K (2015) Innovation efficiency of manufacturing industry: a case study of Shandong province in China. In: 2015 12th International conference on service systems and service management (ICSSSM), pp 17–4. IEEE

Chapter 5
Residency, Race, and the Right to Public Employment

Richard Wright

Abstract Residency requirements impose restrictions on the domicile of individuals. Contemporary debates over residency and rights increasingly foreground immigration, citizenship, and belonging. This essay, however, shifts scale and addresses the exclusionary power of residency requirements associated with municipal employment. And just as race continues to play a central role in national debates over belonging, I illustrate that race continues to matter in local public employment. The analysis centers on a cluster of towns in northern New Jersey that required firefighters to live in member municipalities. The towns used the exclusionary power of residency requirements to privilege the employment of local residents, thereby reducing the employment chances of Blacks who lived near, but not in, the towns. The NAACP joined several individual plaintiffs in successfully challenging this tactic. This case study relates then to recent court decisions on race and public employment but also offers a critique of the role of municipal residency requirements as a tool for reform. The analysis points to the irony that residency requirements designed to be inclusive can operate to be exclusive at the same time.

Keywords Municipal residency requirements · Public policy · Firefighters · Labor markets · Race

> "Do you like my city?" she asked . . .
> "Yes. Very much."
> "What do you like about it? . . . "
> "It's a real city, with people living where they work." John Grisham (*The Broker* 2005)

R. Wright (✉)
Dartmouth College, Hanover, NH, USA
e-mail: richard.a.wright@dartmouth.edu

Z. Chen et al. (eds.), *Development Studies in Regional Science*,
New Frontiers in Regional Science: Asian Perspectives 42,
https://doi.org/10.1007/978-981-15-1435-7_5

5.1 Introduction

In the United States, rights associated with residency play out at various scales from the local to the national. Discussions about residency rights today tend to focus on the foreign born and their rights of domicile, citizenship, voting, driver's licenses, and so on. In the age of increasing nationalism and bordering, the issue of territorially conferred rights has risen to the top of the social science research agenda. In such public policy debates about membership and belonging, residency becomes associated with the *consumption* of public services: for example, should the foreign born qualify for social support and social security, or have access to higher education, K through 12 education, or educational loans?

When we consider the *provision* of public services and residency, however, attention often shifts geographic scale, away from nativity and nationhood toward questions of where people live and where they work. Laws concerning place of work and place of residency shape the operation of local labor markets for certain municipal employees. Towns and cities that enact residency requirements compel some or all municipal workers to live in or near the city as a condition of employment. Accordingly, previous research on residency requirements assesses, for example, the effects on local housing and labor markets, such as the discriminatory effects of these rules on wages and employment between those with the eligible domicile and those with not. Residency rules were often implemented to slow white flight from central cities to suburbs in the 1950s and 1960s, but the potential for residency requirements to discriminate along the lines of race has garnered little attention from scholars (cf. Ungar-Sargon and Flowers 2014).

This essay helps redress this imbalance. Residency requirements can be seen as, in the words of Omi and Winant (2014), "racial projects." Racial projects often come in the form of public policy designed to redistribute resources along racial lines. As such they can be either regressive (e.g., Jim Crow) or progressive (e.g., affirmative action). This essay explores the paradox that residency requirements in municipal employment can be both. In some contexts, they have been set up to be inclusive: many cities, for example, used these requirements to help attenuate a white exodus and thus maintain not only the tax base but also a racially diverse residential population. Some other municipalities have used residency requirements as exclusionary instruments to sustain a predominantly white municipal workforce. Such an application likely violates Title VII of the Civil Rights Act of 1964. This essay analyzes residency requirements, racial discrimination, and public employment in the context of a recent court case in northern New Jersey that committed such a violation.

Peake and Kobayashi (2002, 52) used a geological metaphor to call for geographers to clarify relations between racism and the law. The geographical effects of the law in terms of racialization requires, they said, "more than a surface analysis...we need to understand the law as a fundamental form of racialized social relationships that affects how people inhabit their homes, streets, and workplaces." It is precisely these spaces and relationships I seek to explore in this analysis. The northern New

Jersey case hinged in large part on a set of comparisons involving the racial composition of the towns themselves, the towns' workforce, the neighboring jurisdictions, and the list of qualified applicants and their residential location. Accordingly, the essay situates the contemporary use of residency requirements and race in historical context and then, via this case study, positions them spatially to reveal their discriminatory effects in this particular setting.

5.2 Background

Public policy debates about residency and the provision of public services have a long history, predating the founding of the United States and even European settlement of North America. Colonial era statutes that decided the responsibility for the poor and indigent trace back to English feudal society and Elizabethan Poor Laws. In colonial Massachusetts, for instance, towns bore financial responsibility for the poor. Poor relief, in other words, had a residency requirement. Poor people seeking support from a community in which they had not established residence were forced to return to their place of "settlement" – their place of legal residence or even their place of birth (Simon 1991–1992). If they could not return (for whatever reason), the town providing relief billed the town where settlement was established.

This example highlights one dimension of residency – that of establishing domicile in a place. More formally, residency requirements can take the form of durational or continuous obligations. Durational requirements compel someone to live in a place in a prescribed time before being entitled to locally furnished benefits (or run for public office, Mazo 2015). For instance, immigrants seeking to acquire US citizenship must pass through legal permanent resident status for either 3 years (if married to a US citizen) or 5 years (if not). Similarly, temporary protected status beneficiaries lose their rights if they depart the United States. Continuous residency requirements, the subject of this essay, pertain to municipal administration and public employment and require residency within specified space (city, state) or within a certain distance and a grace period for living outside the municipality as a condition of that employment.

Public employment refers to a variety of jobs. Residency requirements can be comprehensive and cover every municipal employee or, more likely, involve specific occupations such as teachers, senior officials, or firefighters. For example, Roanoke VA requires only heads of departments to live within the city limits. Police and firefighters, however, represent a special category public service employment; these lines of work stand apart from other types "because of the compelling interest in providing the community with day and night fire and police protection" (Myers 1986, 25). Accordingly, many residency requirements are specifically tailored to restrict where first responders live.

The practice of requiring residency for public employees goes back over 100 years. They burgeoned in the late nineteenth century as politicians used them within a spoils system, whereby the winning party apportioned jobs to supporters and support was tied to patronage; all this was part and parcel of the urban Gilded Age political corruption (Eisinger 1983). Residency requirements became one of the tools to manage the system, restricting the pool of potential employees to the residents of the ward or municipality. Opposition to these targeted residency requirements emerged almost simultaneously because such practices were prone to corruption and they artificially limit the spatial extent of the labor market, opening up the chance that highly qualified candidates living nearby would have no chance of employment.

The arguments opposing the restrictions on residency, which carry through to the present day, began to prevail in the Progressive Era but especially after World War 1 (Eisinger 1983). Between 1920 and 1960, many municipalities either abolished the practices or simply did not enforce the laws (Eisinger 1983). By 1960, only Buffalo, Milwaukee, Philadelphia, and a few other major cities had residency requirements for public employment (Fogelson 1977). It is no coincidence that these large cities in the Midwest and Northeast maintained these requirements. Unlike other areas of the country, many states in the Manufacturing Belt in the nineteenth century had granted town and city officials substantial independent authority. Such autonomous suburbs came to surround central cities, a political geography that produced a racial geography when the Great Migration of Blacks occurred. These independent municipalities kept Blacks at a remove (Logan et al. 2004).

Residential segregation has deleterious consequences for Blacks. Despite the fact that overt racial discrimination has been outlawed in the United States, current public policies continue to disadvantage Black people and their communities (Massey and Denton 1993; Hardy et al. 2018). The most obvious is the criminal justice system wherein Blacks face higher bail and other monetary sanctions and where Black communities are differentially policed. Blacks are also disadvantaged in public education, which has often been underfunded in African-American majority schools, limiting skill acquisition and upward mobility for Blacks. Blacks also suffer disproportionately from employment discrimination, hamstringing efforts for Blacks to move out of poor neighborhoods and build wealth. Such labor market discrimination carries with it further deleterious effects as victims of discrimination (real or perceived) are more likely to suffer negative health outcomes such as depression or anxiety (Pager and Shepherd 2008).

The decline in the number of municipalities with residency requirements bottomed out the 1960s. The reasons for the (re-) implementation of residency requirements at this time vary, with race again playing a role (e.g., Eisinger 1983; Lowry 2006). Some cities used them to prevent white flight and to develop a racially diverse employment base. Other towns cited the loss of qualified workers to the suburbs. "Public coffer" arguments gained traction in other ways: inflation and especially the oil price hikes of the 1970s led to increased unemployment. Residency requirements evolved to become one of the tools to keep well-paying jobs and spending deriving from that income, in the city, and to maintain the tax base. Public safety debates also came into play. Violent crime rates fluctuate over time, but in many large US cities, these peaked in the 1960s and 1970s. Residency in the municipality of employment came to be associated with the argument that first responders were better able to do their jobs if they lived nearby and if they knew, had a stake in, the community. Proximity mattered in another way; people who live close to their place of employment were less likely to be late for work or absent entirely (Lowry 2006). With that in mind, some jurisdictions adopted a distance criterion rather than a jurisdictional one, that is, they required employees to live within a certain physical distance from the town. Whitehall PA, for example, requires police officers to "... be able to meet the Township residency requirement of 10 miles within 6 months of hire" (http://www.whitehalltownship.org/police_employ.html).

Courts became more involved. Court approval of residency rules require the demonstration of compelling governmental interest that justifies the discrimination against nonresidents and the deprivation of the right to travel freely. In 1971, the Michigan Supreme Court held that Detroit's requirement for police officers was neither irrational nor violated the Due Process Clause or the Equal Protection Clause of the Fourteenth Amendment (*Detroit Police Officers Assn. v. City of Detroit,* 385 Mich. 519, 190 N.W.2d 97 (1971)). Similarly, the US Supreme Court in the 1976 *McCarthy v. Philadelphia* decision opined that the firefighter in Philadelphia who lost his job after 16 years of service because he moved residence from the City to New Jersey had not had his constitutional rights (i.e., the freedom travel across state lines) infringed upon. More generally, courts have held that residency requirements are constitutional "if it is rationally related to a legitimate government purpose" (Kennedy et al. 2017, 67). Those challenging the law bear the burden of proving otherwise.

The reassertion of residency requirements in the 1960s and 1970s, however, was by no means universal. For example, California banned them in 1974, as did Seattle in 1977. Nevertheless, by 1980 roughly half of all large US cities had some sort of residency requirement in place (Ungar-Sargon and Flowers 2014). Another estimate (of all US jurisdictions) found that over 40% in 2001 had some sort of residency provision for employment (Lowry 2006). Recent years have seen another period of decline in their application. Kennedy et al. (2017), for example, reported that 54% of cities in their sample had a residency requirement for police officers in 1993; that share had shrunk to just 20% in 2013.

Courts now are hearing cases and deciding on the constitutionality not of the *implementation* of residency requirements but rather of their *removal*. Kennedy et al. (2017) report the story of Denver's gradual relaxation of its strict residency requirements for city employees (from the city to a six-county area) and their subsequent elimination. The arguments that won the day involved the larger labor market argument along with the rising housing costs in the city and environs. Thus, the "public coffer" arguments that held sway several decades ago have lost some of their weight. Relatively wealthy white people are helping drive increasing housing costs in and near the downtowns of many US cities (Badger et al. 2019), which undermines another pro-residency requirement argument: white flight. Whites are no longer fleeing the central cities of US metropolitan areas – wealthy white homeowners are increasingly seeking housing in those very same places. The key issue that courts now rule on is is the public interest served by removing or implementing residency requirements? (Kennedy et al. 2017).

Residency laws produce geographically circumscribed local labor markets. As towns and cities that enact them require municipal workers to live in the city as a condition of employment, much of the previous research on residency requirements assesses the effects of these rules on wages, school choice, employment probabilities, or the housing market (e.g., Duncan 2005; Dehring and Fisher 2013; Gonzalez et al. 1991; O'Brien 1997; Rindosh 2012). Given that race played an important role in the revival of their implementation and now race is playing another role in the removal, it is surprising that scholars have tended to sidestep the racial dimensions of residency requirements in their analyses of such statutes. Two recent studies (Ungar-Sargon and Flowers 2014; Kennedy et al. 2017) buck that trend.

Kennedy et al. (2017) tested the hypothesis that residency requirements would increase the demographic share of nonwhites in the workforce of police officers. In an analysis of over 200 police departments, they found that the addition of a residency requirement indeed resulted in a decline in the share of whites on the force as well as an increase in Asians and Latinos. The share of Black officers, however, was unaffected. In a related study, Ungar-Sargon and Flowers (2014) sought to understand the following: did municipalities with the requirement have police forces that were more racially similar to the population of city as a whole compared with those that did not have such a requirement? They looked at the largest 75 cities in the United States using US Equal Employment Opportunity Commission (EEOC) data on police officers and the Census Bureau's American Community Survey (ACS) data for the city's population using four racial groups: Whites, Blacks, Asians, and Latinos. Paradoxically, they found that many police departments with a residency requirement tended to have forces that were *less* demographically similar to their cities compared with those cities that had no such requirement.

How can this be? In a previous study, Murphy and Worrall (1999) found that residency requirements *negatively* affected citizens' perceptions of the police. They explained their counterintuitive results by speculating that residency requirements interfered with and compromised recruiting the best-qualified officers for the force. While they did not test this theory, the remainder of this essay provides such an examination. The case study I will share demonstrates that a tool designed to maintain a racially diverse workforce can operate in precisely the opposite kinds of ways: effectively keeping some people out and cultivating a workforce from a narrow racial base.

5.3 Analysis

On September 21, 2010, New Jersey Senior District Judge Dickinson Debevoise ruled in favor of the National Association for the Advancement of Colored People (NAACP) and Allen Wallace, Lamara Wapples, and Altarik White in the case they brought against North Hudson Regional Fire & Rescue (NHRFR). NHRFR, or, in short, North Hudson, is the collective name of the municipalities of Guttenberg, North Bergen, Union City, Weehawken, and West New York in Hudson County,

New Jersey. Each municipality has an independent local government and school district. The towns collaborated on certain public services such as emergency medical services and firefighting. Until this ruling, applicants had to have lived in the member municipalities to be eligible to join NHRFR. The plaintiffs claimed that this residency requirement racially discriminated against African-Americans who resided in nearby municipalities – the southern part of Hudson County and neighboring Essex and Union counties. The judge had to weigh court precedent and evidence. Court precedent involved previous rulings in favor of the rights municipalities to require residency of some employees in the context of Title VII of the Civil Rights Act of 1964 wherein it is unlawful for an employer "to limit, segregate or classify his employees or applicants for employment in any way which would deprive or tend to deprive any individual of employment opportunities . . . because of such individual's race, color, religion, sex, or national origin" 42 U.S.C. § 2002e-2 (a)(2). For evidence, I was the NAACP's expert witness in this case, so I will explain my analysis before proceeding to a consideration of the ruling.

The data I used came from various sources. To become a firefighter in New Jersey, candidates must pass a physical exam as well as a written test. The New Jersey Department of Personnel (NJDOP) administers these exams. Applicants are then ranked on a list based on their test scores on the written and, sometimes, physical examinations. Based on these scores, the NJDOP creates eligibility lists from which organizations, such as the NHRFR, may hire candidates in rank order. If applicants did not live in the member municipalities at the time of the exam, their names would not be placed on the NHRFR's list, and, thus, the candidate will not be eligible to be hired by the NHRFR, no matter how high their test score.

I also used US Census Data for demographic analysis and US Equal Employment Opportunity Commission (EEOC) data for labor market analyses. The 2000 US Census reported that the 5 towns comprising North Hudson together had a population of about 195,000 and made up of 69.6% Latinos, 22.9% Whites, and 3.4% Blacks. Based on EEOC data from its 2005 EEOC-4 report, in July 2008, NHRFR had 323 full-time employees: 2 Blacks, 64 Latinos, 255 Whites, and 2 who claimed some other race. Of the 323 full-time employees, 308 were firefighters. Of these, 2 were Black, 58 were Latino, and the rest were white. Was this count of two Black firefighters lower than what we would expect if NHRFR had no residency requirements?

The analysis thus hinged on two main issues: the chances that Blacks work for city and state governments in general and as first responders and firefighters in particular and defining the "local labor market" for such workers. Accordingly, I started broadly and simply determined whether Blacks were more or less likely to work in state and local government. 2008 EEOC data showed that for the United States as a whole, employment of Blacks in state and local government comprised 18.9% of total state and local municipal government in the United States. Employment of Blacks in private establishments in the United States made up 14.1% of total employment in 2005. Blacks were thus 1.34 times more likely to work in state and local government employment than in private sector employment in the United States as a whole. The same data source revealed that in New Jersey, the employment of Blacks in state and local government made up 23.8% of total municipal and state full-time employment in 2008. Employment of Blacks in private establishments in New Jersey was 15.3% of the total. Thus, Blacks were thus 1.56 times more likely to work in public sector jobs as a whole than in private industry in New Jersey.

Second, I asked: were Blacks more or less likely to work as firefighters, and is the share of firefighters significantly low in NHRFR compared to municipal employment in the state and the local county? In 2008, NHRFR had a total of 308 firefighters, just 2 self-identified as Black. Using the proportion of Blacks in Hudson County in full-time state and local government employment for comparison (12% of total state and local government employment), the expected number of Blacks would be 37 (308×0.12). Using the proportion of Blacks in New Jersey in full-time state and local government employment for comparison (23.8% of total state and local government employment in 2005), the expected number of Blacks would be 73 (308×0.238). I took these (and other) expectations of the Black share of the labor force and used them as referents to test whether the actual count of Black firefighters could have been a chance occurrence.

A binomial probability analysis shows that the likelihood that a Black employment of 2 out of a total of 308 was unlikely due to chance. Using 12% (proportion of Blacks in Hudson County in full-time state and local government) as the expected number, I calculated a difference of over six standard deviations between the expected number of Black employees and the actual number employed. Thus, the probability of a chance occurrence of this happening is almost zero. Using 23.8% (the proportion of Blacks in full-time state and local government employment in New Jersey) as the expected proportion of Blacks in NHRFR and the same hypothesis test, I calculated a difference of over nine standard deviations – a probability of occurrence by chance again indistinguishable from zero.

To dig deeper, I next focused on state and municipal protective service work specifically. Blacks were underrepresented in state and municipal protective service work before the Civil Rights Act of 1972. EEOC data provide that in state and municipal protective service jobs (mainly police officers and firefighters) nationwide, they represented 17.6% of these jobs in 2008 – a figure greater than 14.1% Black representation in private industry. In New Jersey, Black representation in the protective service category reached 20% in 2008. This is considerably greater than the proportion of Blacks in jobs in the private sector in New Jersey (15.3%) and slightly less than the Black representation in all state and local government full-time work in New Jersey (23.6%).

In analyzing Black representation in firefighter employment in North Hudson, the question also hinges on the appropriate area from which municipalities may hire their firefighters. I considered several different labor markets. One appropriate labor market from which North Hudson may be expected to draw its protective service personnel could be the entire state. Many occupations, such as barbers and psychiatrists, are constrained by states' requirements, such as licenses to practice. This proscribes their job search and, for example, may account for reduced interstate migration of certain occupations. Firefighters in New Jersey must have passed various firefighter exams, which are statewide tests. It follows that their job search field may be considered statewide. In 1999, the pass rate of Blacks was 52%. The same binomial probability test using these data revealed a miniscule probability of two Blacks in protective service employment in North Hudson being a chance occurrence. Similarly, 20% workers statewide in full-time protective service work are Black. The employment disparity is about 8.6 standard deviations from the state mean: the expected value of 61. There was virtually no probability of this outcome occurring by chance.

Shifting scales, N. Hudson Regional Fire and Rescue is located in Hudson County. The neighboring counties are Essex and Union. Thus, statistics on employment of Blacks in protective service employment in the three surrounding counties offer another relevant perspective on determining the availability of Blacks for employment in N. Hudson Regional Fire and Rescue's protective service work. Based on the 29.9% Black employment representation in protective service work in the three-county area, I calculated the disparity between two Black employees and an expected proportion of 29.9% to be more than 10 standard deviations. The probability of a chance occurrence of this difference is virtually zero.

If we narrow the focus to the proportion of Blacks in North Bergen, Guttenberg, West New York, Weehawken, and Union City, where Blacks make up 3.4% of the population, we would expect to see 11 Black employees as opposed to the actual number of 2. I calculated a difference of 2.76 standard deviations between the expected number and the actual. If a disparity is 2.76 standard deviations, the probability of a chance occurrence of this happening is extremely small, about 3 in 1000 times.

Commute times also provide an indication of local labor market extent and are commonly used in other contexts to delimit residency when a town circumscribes the area in which first responders may live. Analyses of commuting data in the United States as a whole and New Jersey indicate that local labor markets in general are broader than most municipal boundaries. According to the US Census Bureau, the average daily commute to work in 2003 was about 24 min. The 2000 US Census revealed that residents of Hudson County as a whole have a mean travel time to work of 29 min. If local authorities draw on an employment base from outside the municipality, then we can consider different commute times to determine labor market extent. I derived the centroid coordinates and the population data from that same data source. With the centroid as the focus point, I found that Blacks comprised 5.8% of the surrounding total population at a 5-mile radius and 15.8% of the surrounding total population at a 10-mile radius. I reckoned that much of even this larger area to be within 29 min average commute time for Hudson County.

To determine the probability that a Black employment of 2 out of a total of 308 could have been due to chance in light of these census data, I again subjected the data to same binomial probability analysis.

1. Using 3.4% (proportion of Blacks in North Bergen, Guttenberg, West New York, Weehawken, and Union City) as the expected number, I calculated a difference of 2.89 standard deviations between the expected number of Black employees

(10) and the actual number employed (2). If a disparity is 2.89 standard deviations, the probability of a chance occurrence of this happening was extremely small, 2 in 1000 times.

2. Using 5.8% (the proportion of Blacks residing within 5 miles in 2000) as the expected proportion of Blacks in N. Hudson Regional Fire and Rescue, I calculated a difference of over four standard deviations – a probability of occurrence by chance indistinguishable from zero.
3. Using 15.8% (the proportion of Blacks residing within 5 miles in 2000) as the expected proportion of Blacks in N. Hudson Regional Fire and Rescue, I calculated a difference of over seven standard deviations – a probability of occurrence by chance also indistinguishable from zero.

All these referents, when tested using a binomial probability analysis, demonstrated effectively that Blacks are significantly underrepresented in N. Hudson Regional Fire and Rescue's workforce, results that stem from discriminatory hiring practices shaped by the municipal residency requirements for firefighters. But in matters of race and the courts, the path forward is never easy or straightforward. In the midst of the deliberations, depositions, and arguments, six Latino residents of the member municipalities filed a third-party motion to intervene. They asserted that if the residency requirements were to be lifted, adding Black firefighters would come at the expense of Latino applicants. And North Hudson hired their own expert.

The six Latinos who tried to intervene had sat the NJDOP firefighter examination and earned good scores. Of the subgroup of test takers who met NHRFR's residency requirements, they were ranked at 21, 25, 26, 45, 49, and 70. At the time, NHRFR needed to hire at least 30 new firefighters but were unable to do so because of the court case. The intervenors argued that it was likely they would have been hired had a court injunction not barred the NHRFR from hiring using the residency criterion.

Should the court have required NHRFR to hire from list derived, say, from the three counties of Hudson, Essex, and Union, the intervenors would have shrunk their chances to be hired, since their rankings would be significantly altered. For example, the candidate ranked in 21st place on NHRFR's list would be ranked at far lower on any larger list. The intervenors correctly assumed that changing or eliminating North Hudson's firefighter residency requirements would have eroded their prospects for employment with the NHRFR.

The Latino intervenors found support from NHRFR's expert whose argument centered on interest in, and qualifications for, being a firefighter. Their expert asserted that Blacks make up 0.62% of the employees in the NHRFR while constituting 3.6% of the population of the member municipalities. This ratio (0.62/3.6 = 17.22%) became the link between the racial/ethnic mix of the population and the racial/ethnic mix among those interested in, and qualified for, the position (never mind that the Black share of the NHFRF workforce was being challenged because it was constricted by the extant residency requirements.) This logic produced the following analysis. First, the expert witness assumed this same relationship existed in the other areas. He then estimated the expected number of Blacks in the North Hudson workforce if it were expanded to Hudson County to be eight. If it were expanded to the three-state area, 15; if it were expanded to all of New Jersey, 8. For 5- and 10-mile radii, then the expected numbers of Blacks would be three and nine, respectively. Accepting this odd reasoning for the sake of argument, I subjected these estimates to same analysis I performed on the EEOC data (above). For all but the 5-mile radius estimate, the probability that these occurred by chance was, again, indistinguishable from zero.

Judgment hinged, to a significant extent, on geography. The court cited[1] New Jersey precedent wherein to demonstrate causation in statistical analysis, the "proper comparison [is] between the racial composition of [the at-issue jobs] and the racial composition of the qualified ... population in the relevant labor market." City of Bayonne, 134 F.3d at 121 (quoting Wards Cove, 490 U.S. at 650). The "at issue" jobs were known: NHRFR employed two Blacks as firefighters. The court then considered the appropriate labor market, finding it to be, following my argument, either the tri-county area or the entire state of New Jersey. These options were "sound in reasoning," and NHRFR did not dispute this particular conclusion.

The court also thought through what was the "qualified population." The court found compelling that Blacks in full-time protective service work in the tri-county area make up 37% of workers and that Blacks in full-time protective service work in New Jersey area make up 22% of the workforce. Furthermore, the court found that expanding the residency requirement to the tri-county area added between 8 and 12 Blacks to the top 35 candidates on the list of those who passed the qualifying exam (depending on year). This addition was "sufficiently substantial." Put differently, NHRFR's residency requirements for firefighters discriminated against well-qualified Black applicants who lived nearby, but not in, the fire district.

Last but not least, the court brought to light an aspect of the residency requirements that had escaped my attention as I did not have any idea that these, actual residence, data existed. That is, North Hudson's residency requirement was based exclusively on an applicant's residence *at the time of the exam*. In other words, once hired, NHRFR employees were free to live anywhere they chose. Only about a third of all firefighters employed by North Hudson lived in the member municipalities at the time of the lawsuit.

5.4 Conclusions

The argument that public employees should live in the municipality that employs them is centuries old. The counterargument deploys the powerful rhetoric of freedom – freedom to live where you want and the right to move about without encumbrance. In the United States, municipal residency requirements perhaps evoke a time when civic life clustered in small, tightly knit communities where the geographic range of

[1] https://www.gpo.gov/fdsys/pkg/USCOURTS-njd-2_07-cv-01683/pdf/USCOURTS-njd-2_07-cv-01683-2.pdf

daily life was relatively limited. NHRFR's history, however, does not trace back not to colonial times; it was formed in the late 1990s and lies near the middle of the New York metropolitan area where long commutes to work are not uncommon.

This analysis of residency requirements, racial discrimination, and public employment in the context of the fragmented municipal landscape of northern New Jersey involves several considerations. The court found in favor of the plaintiffs based on a consideration of precedents and a determination of the geography of the labor pool of qualified applicants. It ended a practice in this district that racially discriminated against a population of qualified Black candidates who were effectively barred from employment consideration because of where they lived at the time they qualified for being a firefighter. The case did not put an end to residency requirements in New Jersey or anywhere else. As already mentioned, courts have upheld or modified these requirements in many instances. If NHRFR had had requirements wherein firefighters lived within the tri-county area, they would have endured no court challenge. It was the specific architecture of NHRFR's requirements that were found in violation of the law.

Thus, while the residency requirements in NHRFR were struck down, residency requirements have been around for decades and will likely be with us for some time to come. Public employees, first responders as well as others, may face some restrictions, such as living within their locality's county or in a set of adjacent counties, so long as the law serves the public interest and does not violate equal protection clauses US Constitution. In addition, high-level public servants such as mayors and school-district superintendents may continue to face residency restrictions under "emergency and disaster" exceptions under local or state law. The clear trend, however, is away from tightly circumscribed labor markets for public employees toward a broader conceptualization of a "local" labor market. It follows that when it comes to the *provision* of public services, borders are not being hardened. Quite the opposite. When Cincinnati attempted to restrict the residences of local government employees in 2013 to the state of Ohio, the courts disagreed. Employees were free to live wherever they wanted. These less-geographically constrained labor markets, as in the NHFRF case, can open up employment opportunities to groups that were previously excluded.

The case study and analysis of an important municipal policy brings together several scholarly enterprises. The essay's epigraph signals that the concern of this research is the mediation of housing markets and labor markets. There is a large literature on place of residence, place of work, and space. Hanson and Pratt (2003), for example, studied types of work, the place of residence, and the segregation of men and women into different occupations. Ellis et al. (2004), in a related analysis, compared racial segregation by place of residence and place of employment finding that segregation was lower when measured by the census tract of work compared with the census tract of residence. The NHRFR case study fits easily in these research areas.

The sorts of analyses wherein geographers take on the role of expert witness are examples of "applied geography" (see, e.g., Clark 1981, 1991; Green 1986; Mitchell 1978) and legal geographies (Blomley 1994; Platt 1996) *par excellence*. This case study shows how the application of some simple statistics can be used to open up employment opportunities to a protected class. Protected classes, of course, include groups other than those defined through racialization (e.g., gender, sexual orientation, age, disability), but this case study concerns race. The analysis serves to remind us that race remains a fundamental organizing principle of social and economic life (Omi and Winant 2014). Geographers have tended to lag other disciplines in foregrounding race in their research. This incident revealed how a requirement for employment, rather than slowing white flight, produced racial exclusion in a local labor market.

Acknowledgments Carla Castillo and Jonathan Chipman provided valuable research assistance. Sheila Culbert and Serin Houston offered guidance and lively debate during the framing of this essay. They, of course, bear no responsibility for the ideas herein. And last, but not least, thanks Kingsley. Your support in grad school helped build the foundations of a career I could not have imagined in the early 1980s. This essay on applied geography, municipal employment, race, and public policy is for you.

References

Badger E, Bui Q, Gebeloff R (2019) The neighborhood is mostly black. The home buyers are mostly white. New York Times, April 27

Blomley NK (1994) Law, space, and the geographies of power. The Guilford Press, New York

Clark WAV (1981) The social scientist as expert witness. Environ Plan A 13:1468–1470

Clark WAV (1991) Geography in court: expertise in adversarial settings. Trans Inst Br Geogr 16 (1):5–20

Dehring CA, Fisher EN (2013) Residency requirements and house prices: a natural experiment from Ohio. https://athenaeum.libs.uga.edu/handle/10724/36416

Duncan B (2005) Using municipal residency requirements to disguise public policy. Public Financ Rev 33(1):84–116

Eisinger PK (1983) Municipal residency requirements and the local economy. Soc Sci Q 64 (1):85–96

Ellis M, Wright R, Parks V (2004) Work together, live apart? Geographies of racial and ethnic segregation at home and at work. Ann Assoc Am Geogr 94(3):620–637

Fogelson R (1977) Big city police. Harvard University Press, Cambridge, MA

Gonzalez RA, Mehay SL, Duffy-Deno K (1991) Municipal residency laws: effects on police employment, compensation, and productivity. J Lab Res 12(4):439–452

Green HP (1986) Commentary: the academic as expert witness. Sci Technol Hum Values 11 (2):74–75

Hanson S, Pratt G (2003) Gender, work and space. Routledge, New York

Hardy B, Logan TD, Parman J (2018).The historical role of race and policy for regional inequality. Place-Based Policies for Shared Economic Growth, pp 43–69

Kennedy BA, Butz AM, Lajevardi N, Nanes MJ (2017) Causes of passive representation in American policing: politics and officer selection. In: Race and representative bureaucracy in American policing. Palgrave Macmillan, Cham, pp 61–82

Logan JR, Stults BJ, Farley R (2004) Segregation of minorities in the metropolis: two decades of change. Demography 41(1):1–22

Lowry R (2006) Personnel practices: residency requirements. International Public Management Association for Human Resources. http://www.yorkcity.org/user-files/file/City%20Council/Miscelaneous/IPMA%20Residency%20Guides.pdf

Massey DS, Denton NA (1993) American apartheid: segregation and the making of the underclass. Harvard University Press, Cambridge, MA

Mazo ED (2015) Residency and democracy: durational residency requirements from the framers to the present. Florida State Law Rev 43:611–677

Mitchell JK (1978) The expert witness: a geographer's perspective on environmental litigation. Geogr Rev 68:209–214

Murphy DW, Worrall JL (1999) Residency requirements and public perceptions of the police in large municipalities. Policing Int J Police Strateg Manag 22(3):327–342. https://doi.org/10.1108/13639519910285080

Myers RS (1986) The constitutionality of continuing residency requirements for local government employees: a second look. Calif West Law Rev 23:24–41

O'Brien KM (1997) Do municipal residency laws affect labour market outcomes? Urban Stud 34 (11):1759–1769

Omi M, Winant H (2014) Racial formation in the United States, 2nd edn. Routledge, New York

Pager D, Shepherd H (2008) The sociology of discrimination: racial discrimination in employment, housing, credit, and consumer markets. Annu Rev Sociol 34:181–209

Peake L, Kobayashi A (2002) Policies and practices for anti-racist geography at the millennium. Prof Geogr 54(1):50–61

Platt RH (1996) Land use and society: Geography, law, and public policy. The Island Press, Washington, DC

Rindosh J (2012) Continuing residency requirements: questioning burdens on public employment in New Jersey. Seton Hall L Rev 42:1635

Simon H (1991–1992) Towns without pity: constitutional and historical analysis of official efforts to drive homeless persons from American cities. Tulane Law Rev 66(4):631–676

Ungar-Sargon B, Flowers A (2014) Reexamining residency requirements for police officers. https://fivethirtyeight.com/features/reexamining-residency-requirements-for-police-officers/

Chapter 6
Humanitarian Local and Regional Economic Development: A Potential Answer to Sustainability and Conflict Prevention in the Information Age

Mustafa Dinc

Abstract We live in a new world made and remade by many factors ranging from disruptive technological revolutions, globalization, conflict and migration, depletion of national resources and environmental degradation, and deterioration of traditional protective institutions. Their impact on the local and regional economic development process appears to become more pressing, and the magnitude of the challenges is immense. There is a circular and cumulative relationship between these issues and local and regional economies, in some cases resulting in a vicious cycle that requires a clear understanding of the entire set of factors to interrupt this cycle. This paper tries to understand the relationship between these factors within the local and regional development framework.

Keywords Development · Local and regional development · Conflict · Sustainability · Artificial intelligence · Machine learning · Additive manufacturing

---

I would like to thank Tanju Yurukoglu, Serdar Yilmaz, and Murat Tarimcilar for their valuable comments and suggestions to an earlier version of the paper.

Disclaimer: The findings, interpretations, and conclusions expressed in this work are entirely those of the authors and should not be attributed in any manner to the World Bank, its Board of Executive Directors, or the governments they represent.

M. Dinc (✉)
The World Bank, Washington, DC, USA
e-mail: mdinc@worldbank.org

Z. Chen et al. (eds.), *Development Studies in Regional Science*,
New Frontiers in Regional Science: Asian Perspectives 42,
https://doi.org/10.1007/978-981-15-1435-7_6

6.1 Introduction

Over the past few decades, Schumpeterian "creative destruction" is in full swing around the world in different forms and scales ranging from economic, social, political, and environmental, to technological disruptions. These disruptions have, in turn, had a significant impact on the regional and local economies and communities. They created both opportunities and challenges. To benefit from opportunities and manage challenges, it is essential to understand the root causes and implications of the paradigm shifts taking place in economic, social, and ecological space. This paper aims to discuss some of these issues in general but also initiate a debate that focuses on the effects of these disruptions in the regional and local development discussions.

The world output of goods and services increased from $19.1 trillion in 1970 to $80 trillion in 2017 in constant 2010 US$.[1] Although most countries enjoyed similar growth in their GDP, not everyone within each country benefited from these developments equally. In many countries, economic inequality increased dramatically as the benefits of growth flowed primarily to the wealthy, well-educated, and the privileged (Fukuyama 2018).

Due to globalization and liberalized international trade, distances and national boundaries have substantially diminished. Most of the obstacles in accessing to the external markets have been removed. New technologies are now readily available to facilitate coordination and monitoring of economic activities and transactions across continents. As the framework for the global economic activity is getting larger and naturally more complicated, its impact on regional and local economies may be considered less important or not get the attention it deserves. It would be a fundamental mistake to detach globalization from national, regional, and local economic development and to see it as simply spreading of economic activity or the transformation of the economic order across the world.

It is well documented that the effects of globalization have been uneven among nations and even among regions of a nation, and benefits and costs associated with the process have differed noticeably. Increased integration and a higher share of international goods and services in national and regional economies impose certain adjustments in production processes and resource allocation. Such adjustments often associated with social costs and tension. In most cases, inefficient domestic production processes could not compete with externally produced relatively cheap and higher quality goods and services. This could cause job losses in host countries (Dinc 2015).

Meanwhile, wars and conflicts have become daily occurrences in many parts of the world. The Institute for Economics and Peace (IEP 2016) reports that of the 163 countries covered in the report, just 11 could be seen as peaceful without any

[1] https://data.worldbank.org/indicator/NY.GDP.MKTP.KD

conflict.[2] The prospect of a peaceful and harmonious world seems elusive. The UNCHR reported that by the end of 2017, an estimated 68.5[3] million people were forcibly displaced due to wars and violent conflicts. This means that 1 in every 113 people was either internally displaced, a refugee, or an asylum seeker. The impact of violent conflict is not limited to humanitarian and social tragedies. It also has an enormous economic cost to all involved parties around the world. IEP (2016) estimated the economic impact of violence to the global economy as $13.6 trillion in 2015, in purchasing power parity (PPP) terms[4] or 13.3% of the world GDP. The global economic impact of armed conflict was $742 billion in PPP terms in 2015.

The environment is another global event with immense local roots and implications. It has come to the focus of local, regional, national, and international institutions over the past 45 years or so (Williams 1998) due to the increasing level of pollution and deforestation. These initial concerns about pollution and depletion of natural resources have subsequently been adopted as a broad slogan under the concept of sustainability. The World Commission on Environment and Development (WCED) released a report in 1987, Our Common Future, which brought the term sustainable development to the center stage of the development discourse (Lele 1991). The report defined sustainable development as development that meets the needs of the present without compromising the ability of future generations to meet their own needs (WCED 1987). Suddenly, sustainable development has become a catchphrase for everyone including international development agencies, development planners, and developmental and environmental activists.

We have been witnessing revolutionary developments in information and communications technologies that had a substantial impact on practically all aspects of our society, life, firms, and employment. We are now living in a time of astonishing progress with digital technologies and heading into an era that will no longer be the same. The digital revolution has some outstanding features such as exponential improvement in most aspects of computing, extraordinarily large amounts of digitized information, and recombinant innovation that brought artificial intelligence, machine learning, and additive manufacturing (3D printing) in our living rooms. These developments have brought and will continue to bring great benefits for all. However, they will also bring some challenges and will have unpleasant consequences that must be managed. For example, there will be some economic and social disruptions as the increased use of powerful computers and smart machines for certain types of work as a substitute for human labor. It is more likely that this

[2]The Global Peace Index (GPI) is composed of 23 qualitative and quantitative indicators, which ranks 163 independent states and territories according to their level of peacefulness, covering 99.7% of the world's population.

[3]https://www.unhcr.org/en-us/statistics/unhcrstats/5b27be547/unhcr-global-trends-2017.html

[4]Includes security services and prevention-oriented costs, armed conflict-related costs, and cost resulting from interpersonal violence based on direct and indirect costs and a multiplier effect. The multiplier effect calculates the additional economic activity that would have accrued if the direct costs of violence had been avoided and allocated to more productive areas of the economy.

progress will leave some people behind while making a few extremely rich (Brynjolfsson and McAfee 2016).

These disruptions or problems are socially, economically, and environmentally damaging, and it is more likely that in the coming years, such damages will increase if not managed right. Over the past 60 years, there have been continuing attempts to prevent or reduce these damages around the world. In different periods and different places, there have been philosophers, scholars, and policymakers who have believed that a better world is possible. They proposed and advocated different approaches to attain such a world. They also believed that while it is possible to change the world, it is necessary to change ourselves in the process. The world we would like to live in is very much linked to the type of people we want to be, the social relations we are interested in, our interaction with nature, and our value system that is important for us (Harvey 2014).

However, we frequently fail to recognize and integrate different concepts, value systems, and nature of human interests in our analysis, understanding, and interpretation of world events. They are, in fact, closely interlinked. In a sense, we generally overlook what Max Weber described as “the fundamental analytical problem of integrating the different value spheres or fields of human life” (Lejano and Stokols 2013, p. 1). When specific logical methods or approaches are developed, we tend to make decisions focusing on one approach and excluding the others. Such an approach artificially separates economic or social analysis into different systems and allows each system to operate separately (Lejano and Stokols 2013). This has been a problem for the past 60 years and still is a problem we face today in reconciling various essential components and elements of the local and regional development process. Therefore, an integrated approach is needed that will allow making simultaneous progress on different fronts including different actors and institutions that influence and reinforce each other.

Such an approach should have certain tenets that remain the same over time. Humanist tradition (secular, religious, revolutionary, socialist, or Marxist humanism) could offer some principles: dignity, integrity, tolerance, compassion, love, and respect for others. These principles are and should be the pillars of the development process to achieve the liberation of human potentialities, capacities, and powers. Humanist tradition subscribes to the true flourishing of individuals and the construction of the good life. Humanists believe that it is possible to change ourselves and the world we live in for the better through mindful ideas and action (Harvey 2014). For some such an approach is seen as a bundle of utopic ideas that are disconnected from the realities of life and, for others, even if they may sound utopic, should be the foundation of any development process. The humanist approach could be a good starting point in addressing the problems mentioned above at the local, regional, and national levels.

This paper will review these issues from a local and regional development perspective and try to link them to the regional and local development discourse. The next section will discuss the local and regional development concept. The third section will focus on conflict and related issues. The fourth section looks into sustainability with a critical view to understand its local and regional implications.

The fifth section is about the developments in information and communications technologies and their implications on local and regional economies. The final section will try to put all these together from a regional development perspective and offer some suggestions for future research.

6.2 Local and Regional Development

It is now a well-established fact that economic development varies spatially at varying scales. While some countries, regions, and cities prosper, others decline economically and socially, and often the success of some is connected to the failure of others. This indicates that local and regional economic development is combined and uneven. It means that development in one place not only depends on its own institutional arrangements and human and natural resources but also on its connections to other places. Combined and uneven economic development is a product of different causal mechanisms that are specific to particular forms of social and economic and political organization. Additionally, it is important to note that different modes of production with different causal mechanisms will influence the patterns of combined and uneven development (Hudson 2007). The uneven development is also explained as the outcome of geographical expansionary tendencies of capitalism to find a new "spatial fix" (dispersing or exporting capital and labor surpluses into new and more profitable spaces) for its problems. Without such expansions and perpetually seeking out spatial fixes, capitalism cannot survive (Harvey 2001).

Defining space is seemingly a simple and straightforward task, but it is quite the opposite. The definition of space, territory, or region is quite complicated and often prompts some modification or qualification (Harvey 2006) such as material space, social space, personal space, absolute space, relative space, relational space, city region, mega-region, learning region, creative region, competitive region, resilient region, or bioregion. All these modifications and qualifications have attached new meanings to the idea of space and region. Even if we include all possible modification, it is still quite difficult to come up with a generic definition. For example, critical scholars of regional studies raised two points that were missing from the debate: power dynamics in the region and the subjective nature of human behavior and experience. Regions, in this view, are social constructs that were produced and reproduced by social actors through social practices (Paasi and Metzger 2017).

Similarly, the definition of regional and local economic development is quite a challenging starting point, although it is vitally important. Such a definition should address the basic meaning of what it is, what it is for, and what it should be about, which will help to understand the form and nature of local and regional development. An important aspect of the definition is that it is context-dependent, and in different historical and geographic contexts, local and regional development could adopt different forms and meanings. Therefore, the focus of local and regional development analyses should follow the changing context and shift accordingly. Failing to do so may result in overlooking other critically important external factors that influence local and regional development (Pike et al. 2017) such as the restructuring of international and interregional divisions of labor resulting from economic crises, conflict, technological progress, or sustainability-related policy changes. Local and regional economic development is a multidimensional process and has geographic, economic, social, and political aspects that should be taken into account.

Due to all these complexities, there is no agreed definition and understanding of local and regional economic development. Regardless of the definition, local and regional development is a geographical phenomenon (Pike et al. 2007), and certainly, all economic and social activities must take place in a place (Hudson 2016) either absolute/material, relative, or relational. Space is an integral part of economic, social, ecological, political, and cultural relations and processes (Harvey 1982; Markusen 1987), and there is a dialectical relationship between space and such processes that influence and shape each other.

The local and regional economic development is, by definition, an economic phenomenon involving concepts such as investment, job creation, income, production, trade and financial transactions, research and development, innovation, and the like. These are fundamental components of the local and regional economic development process that takes place in either abstract space (Perroux 1950), absolute space (Harvey 2006), or relational space (Harvey 2006; Massey 1979, 2004).

In the old mainstream approaches and definitions, the focus was mainly on economic growth and productivity gain. There are, however, several social issues such as living conditions and lifestyles, social and environmental justice and equity, education, health, and well-being that local and regional economic development agenda should pay attention. In that sense, it is largely a social process through the actions of various agents in the region to achieve socially acceptable goals. Following the concept of human flourishing (Sen 1999), some scholars have broadened the definition of economic development in recent years to address social, ecological, political, and cultural concerns (Hudson 2007, 2016; Pike et al. 2007, 2016, 2017; Perrons and Dunford 2013; Dunford et al. 2016). Therefore, local and regional development should include and emphasize social justice, citizen participation and inclusive governance, recognition, and respect for cultural, ethnic, religious, and gender diversification (Pike et al. 2017).

Local end regional economic development also has a political aspect that requires a clear understanding of power relationship, the nature of politics, and political process in the region and nation. Sometimes, political or politically motivated economic decisions at the national level could have a profound impact on local and regional economies. Import-export regulations and national tax regime are some examples that could affect local and regional economies positively or negatively. Decentralization movement is another example that could shift the responsibility of formulating their own socioeconomic development strategies, sometimes together with the necessary power and resources, to local governments (Hudson 2007). In some cases, decentralization could work; in others, it may not. Therefore, local and regional economic development process should recognize the importance of political practices and their impacts on local and regional economic development.

Today, the world is going through a period of political and economic turmoil. Populist politics with incredibly false promises are in rise everywhere, and citizens have lost their trusts in political leaders, public institutions, and traditional modes of exercising power. In such a time and environment, local and regional development becomes an urgent priority as a stepping stone addressing these problems. It becomes imperative to develop concepts, theory, policy, and practice in local and regional development that encourage widespread participation of all relevant actors and establish mechanisms and networks to facilitate and promote dialogue, debate, and deliberation about the common concerns and problems we are facing and will continue to face in coming years (Pike et al. 2017). While recognizing the positive developmental potential of the local and regional economic development process, it is equally important to recognize its limitations. The national governments still have responsibilities for the social and economic well-being of its citizens, wherever they live (Hudson 2007).

6.3 Conflict in Local and Regional Development: Causes and Implications

With a few exceptions (see Dinc 2015) the concept of conflict has not been a part of regional science literature. In fact, the local and regional economic development is a multidimensional and complex process and involves many actors often with conflicting interests. Therefore, by its very nature, the entire local and regional economic development process is or should be about conflict prevention and management. The current state of the world suggests that the local and regional economic development process could not have addressed the conflict issue in the past, at least in certain parts of the world.

Conflict is an expression of differences in interests, values, and beliefs that sometimes manifests itself in a violent confrontation. In fact, conflict is quite an ordinary phenomenon and an integral part of daily life, and when managed properly, it could help create a productive force to promote social change and address social injustices. Hence, some conflicts may be instrumental in big economic and social changes.

In recent years, there have been growing community concerns around the world about the impact of the abovementioned disruptions on sustainability, social justice, and quality of life. Today, environmental issues, inequality, and social justice are everyone's concern around the world. This new paradigm has brought additional challenges to the regional economic development process and deepened the existing conflicts in producing economically, socially, and environmentally sustainable results in an environment of rapid change and uncertainty.

To a large extent, development process, local, regional, or national, is inherently a conflict-prone process. Apparent conflicts between environmental issues, economic growth and development, and social justice are not abstract and simple notions arising from personal preferences nor temporary problems triggered by a trendy wave of awareness of these issues. These are quite real and part of everyday life. Historically, the general tendency has been to promote the economic growth and development of cities and regions at the cost of nature and the environment where forests were cleared, rivers and air were polluted, and mountains were leveled (Dinc 2015). In the process, social justice has been mostly ignored. What is important here is that all three areas are linked to nature and have an interactive relationship with it.

There are different interest groups or stakeholders with different views, needs, and objectives in society. This implies that there will be conflicts among these different interest groups or stakeholders. Each stakeholder group consists of individual actors with different needs and different views on how to satisfy them. Conflicts may emerge in many different areas of economic, social, and ecological life in a region or nation and in some cases may result in no-win situations. For example, miners, lumberjacks, and mill workers worry about poverty before worrying about environmental protection. In almost everywhere, for poor urban communities, economic survival comes before environmental quality, which suggests that economic isolation will lead to environmental inequity (Dinc 2015). Given that the price mechanisms of the markets have not been able to resolve these problems, it is necessary to look at them from different perspectives.

Is it possible that the abovementioned conflicts could be the causes of displacement of 68.5 million people due to wars and violent conflicts? The answer to this question is a resounding no. To some degree, these conflicts could be seen as the starting point for deeper and in some cases violent conflicts. One may argue that if local and regional economic development policies were collaborative, transformative, and inclusive that could identify priorities among issues and needs of actors and align the objectives and goals accordingly, it would be possible to prevent acceleration of such conflicts into violent ones. This may sound quite reasonable, but it can only partially explain violent conflict and its devastating consequences. There are some other factors that could trigger or intensify conflicts, and these may be beyond the control of local and regional economic development process.

There is, for example, the class conflict that is an inherent part of the capitalist economic system and time to time may become violent as in recent cases of Venezuela, Brazil, Greece, and France. Identity-based conflict is another example that is becoming more and more prevalent. As Fukuyama (2018) argued, in recent years, groups have come to believe that their identities, whether national, religious, ethnic, sexual, and gender, are not receiving adequate recognition. Hence, identity politics has become a major concept that was both abused by different interest groups and politicians and used for explaining much of what is going on around the world.

The impact of globalization in certain parts of the world is considered another source of conflict. Generally seen as a process of economic rationality, the contemporary form of globalization has also been criticized as a tool for promoting western culture and interests of corporations. Critics argue that globalization helps exploit cheap labor in the poorer countries by multinational corporations and in the process increases threats to the environment. It could also undermine the foundations of social stability by subjecting national institutions to forces of economic change. In the literature, there is a distinction between conflicts resulting from social, cultural, and identity differences and conflicts resulting primarily from economic reasons. It should be noted that in real life these two areas are closely related. If the basic human needs and universally accepted human rights are not satisfactorily addressed, we should expect that the incidence and intensity of social conflict resulting from globalization are likely to increase in coming years (Lerche III 1998).

Another factor that could trigger conflict is the rapid pace of technological developments, particularly in information and computing technologies. Today, information technologies reached to a level that favor more-skilled over less-skilled workers and created winner-take-all markets. At the same time, the return to capital increased significantly, while the share of labor income declined. These trends increased the gap between those that have a job and those that do not, between highly skilled and educated workers and less advanced ones. It is reasonable to expect future advancements in these technologies will more likely to widen the gap. Resulting economic inequality will tend to create greater political inequality, and those who are further empowered politically will use this to gain greater economic advantages, which create a vicious cycle (Brynjolfsson and McAfee 2016). Similarly, Autor (2015) argued that changes in technology indeed altered the types of jobs available and caused the polarization of the labor market. These developments will have a more profound impact on poorer regions and nations and could trigger and/or intensify social conflicts.

Once a famous Turkish poet fittingly wrote in 1939, "those who create and destroy, there will be only their accounts in our stories.[5]" Since the people are or should be in the center of all these discussions as the object of the local and regional development process, a good starting point would be to understand the nature of human experience and psychology. As Fromm (1941) argued, there is a dynamic relationship between man and society. On the one hand, there are certain physiologically conditioned needs which are an indispensable part of human nature that require satisfaction in any condition. The lack of satisfaction of such needs is unbearable. These physiologically conditioned needs are labeled as the need for self-preservation that is part of human nature and forms the primary motive of human behavior. In other words, man must eat, drink, sleep, and protect himself, and in order to satisfy these needs, he must work and produce. The type of work the individual performs is heavily dependent on the type of economic system he lives in. This is very important because the mode of life of the individual is mainly determined by the peculiarity of the economic system he was born into. This, in turn, shapes the character structure of the individual because the need for self-preservation forces him to accept the conditions under which he must survive (Fromm 1941). The need theory was further elaborated by Maslow (1943) and was applied to social and political conflicts by Burton (1979, 1990, 1998).

[5]Nazim Hikmet Ran, 1968, Kuvayi Milliye Destani, Bilgi Yayinevi, Istanbul (in Turkish).

On the other hand, there is a social dimension of human psychology that deals with the relationship between the individual and society. At this point, social psychology helps us understand how passions, desires, and anxieties of man change and develop as part of the social process. It also shows how man's energies are shaped into specific forms and became productive forces. In connection with the need for self-preservation, certain external circumstances could provoke new drives and anxieties. Man could develop different strivings and fears as a reaction to certain living conditions, which are not necessarily flexible (Fromm 1941). In an environment where rapidly changing economic and social conditions, man's not so flexible strivings and fears could likely cause major social conflicts.

The impact of violent conflict is not limited to humanitarian and social tragedies. It also has an enormous economic cost to all involved parties around the world. Given that the most affected countries are relatively poor developing countries and conflict and violence are not limited to involved regions and countries, this brings additional burden to their neighbors and the rest of the world. In such an environment, poor localities and regions face insurmountable challenges for development.

Opinions vary about the direction of causality between conflict and development and need further investigation. Apart from the long-lasting identity-based conflicts (ethnic, religious, racial), the anecdotal evidence shows that the underlying cause of conflict is mostly economic. In almost every society, there is a strong link between income and status of individuals that are open to manipulation and exploitation. The existence of persistent inequality in income and wealth, poverty, and marginalized groups in a nation or region creates an environment where resentment and social conflict thrive. In a sense, such conflicts start with real economic distress (Fukuyama 2018), and one way of addressing these problems is to create a just society where basic human needs are met. This is a challenging task for all, local communities, policymakers, and academics, to develop and promote programs that could transform local, regional, and national economies.

6.4 Sustainability and Regional Development

In addition to these conflict-related problems, environmental degradation, depletion of natural resources, pollution, and climate change are other pressing issues that create major challenges to particularly developing countries and poorer regions. These topics are generally discussed under sustainability. Therefore, it would be useful to take a quick look at the evolution of the concept of sustainability and its connection to development.

A series of international conferences and summits on environment and development under the auspices of the United Nations have been held since 1972 (Stockholm in 1972, Rio de Janeiro, 1992, Johannesburg, 2002) to discuss and respond to the growing problems of environmental deterioration and the relationship between environment and development. Each summit produced a declaration stating that all participants (representatives of the UN member countries) assume a collective responsibility to address these problems. Finally, at the seventieth anniversary of the United Nations, the Heads of State and Government and High Representatives met in New York in September 2015 and decided on new global Sustainable Development Goals (SDGs), 17 goals with 169 associated targets. The Resolution that was adopted by the General Assembly made a bold statement that all members "commit themselves to work tirelessly for the full implementation of this Agenda by 2030."

Setting up measurable and monitorable goals and targets may look and sound very useful and respectable. However, categorizing these Sustainable Development Goals and targets shifts the focus to metrics and measurements, which is heavily based on indicators and data. This means that overattention to metrics and measurements could obscure the complex causal relations between potential problems, and certain aspects of human life could be potentially sidelined. It looks like the normative and rights-based approaches have been marginalized in the SDGs because of a simple logic; without measurement, there cannot be a metric; without a metric, there cannot be a target; and without a target, there cannot be a program of intervention (Caprottia et al. 2017).

The concept of sustainable development has been quite successful in raising awareness and serving as a common ground for everyone regardless of their primary interest. It has been widely embraced and is now used for almost everything. Despite such widespread acceptance and support, the joint efforts of world leaders and international development organizations over the past 45 years have not been so successful on the ground. Billions of people are still in poverty and denied a dignified life. The inequality among people is rising. Global health threats, spiraling conflict, violent extremism, and forced displacement of people have become major problems. Natural resource depletion and environmental degradation, freshwater scarcity, and loss of biodiversity are other serious problems that humanity faces. The survival of many societies and of the biological support systems of the planet is at risk (UN 2015; p. 5). It appears that the advocates of sustainable development have primarily focused on gaining widespread support instead of action.

This disappointing progress in attaining intragenerational needs and equities (equitable access to resources within existing generations) prompts the question whether it is possible to secure the satisfaction of inter-generational needs and equities (leaving the next-generation resources no less than what is available now). Obviously, it would be quite difficult to encourage conservation of resources for the satisfaction of future generations if the current generation is starving (Vojnovic and Darden 2013).

There are also conceptual flaws in sustainable development; hence it has been criticized from different perspectives since its early days. One major criticism is about its emphasis on economic growth. While the definition of sustainable development focuses on meeting needs, the operational part focuses on economic growth, suggesting that growth, even in the developed countries, is essential for meeting these needs (Lele 2013). This growth-centric approach has been the basis of a growing literature that questions the feasibility of continued economic growth particularly in the overdeveloped part of the world. Degrowth movement, heavily influenced by the work of Nicholas Georgescu-Roegen and Herman Daly, emerged as a response to growth economics.

Supporters of this movement advocate the abolition of economic growth as a social objective and seeks a new direction for society, one in which societies will use fewer natural resources and will organize and live differently from today. Daly (1974) developed the concept of the steady-state economy and defined it as an economy with constant stocks of people and artifacts, maintained at some desired, sufficient levels by low rates of maintenance throughput (raw material, energy, and waste). The steady-state economy became the foundation of the vast literature on degrowth movement and critique of sustainable development. Within this framework, the concept of sustainable development is questioned from different perspectives. Daly and Townsend (1993) argued that in a finite, nongrowing and materially closed ecosystem, sustainable growth is impossible; the sustainable development is only possible without growth. There are absolute physical limits to growth and resource extraction as defined by the laws of thermodynamics (Hornborg 2014). The logic behind this argument is that economic growth means more consumption and hence more production that, in turn, requires more raw material, energy, and built environment, all of which contribute to the depletion of natural resources.[6] Despite all these growing literature, the growth paradigm still enjoys a favorable status both within academia and in society (Buch-Hansen 2014).

The downside of the steady-state economy is the assumption that capitalism could be reconstructed in a way that it could stop growing quantitatively at least in developed countries but continue to develop internally. In other words, Daly and his followers assume that capitalist production system is sufficiently malleable that corporations can focus more on saving the earth than making a profit (Smith 2010). The important point they overlook is that capital accumulation and economic growth are vital for the functioning of capitalism (Harvey 2014, 2016, 2018; Buch-Hansen 2014); the growth requirement is virtually a law of nature built into in any conceivable capitalism. Corporations have no choice but to seek to grow (Smith 2010). Further, the consumption choices of people are mainly driven by the very structure of the economy. Citizens are taught and even overwhelmed by corporations through commercials to consume more, to never be satisfied, because the capitalist system of production depends on ever-increasing profits and ever-increasing economic growth (Lele 2013); otherwise, the system collapses into crisis.

Therefore, it is argued that sustainable economic development cannot be realized under capitalism. What is needed is a completely different kind of economic system that is based on human needs, environmental needs and a completely different value system. It should be a practical, workable post-capitalist ecological economy by the people, for the people, that is geared to production for need, not for profit (Smith 2010). All these suggest that without making major shifts in production and consumption patterns, sustainable development would be no more than another bright idea in a long list of approaches to economic development.

[6]For further discussion about growth criticisms, see Assadourian (2012), Daly (2013), D'Alisa et al. (2015), and Mastini (2017, 2018).

In addition to above-discussed issues, local and regional communities face grave environmental and sustainability problems resulting from unrestrained exploitation of their natural resources (Dunford et al. 2016) to catch up with the rest of the world. Poorer nations and regions with weaker environmental regulations offer attractive locations for corporations to relocate routine production of both material commodities and services (Hudson 2016) with an expectation of more jobs and faster development that adversely affect the environment. In poorer regions, limited resources for environmental protection exacerbate the impact of total emissions and climate change on local and regional ecosystems, particularly in developing countries. Food security, water scarcity, and the growing phenomenon of land grab in impoverished countries by multinational corporations are other pressing issues that are vital for the local and regional communities (Dunford et al. 2016). Sustainable development essentially requires the involvement of diverse groups (from local, regional, national to global) to create a positive vision of a world in which basic human needs are met without destroying or irreversibly degrading the natural systems on which we all depend (Kates et al. 2005).

6.5 Information and Computing Technology and Regional Development

The digital revolution has a significant impact on localities and regions particularly on urban areas on two fronts. First, it created and reshaped the space, abstracts, and real. Second, it caused rearranging employment and production processes that could change the socioeconomic structure of regions. Information and communications technologies have been an integral part of everyday urban life for a long time. In a sense, widely available information produces space and the urban environment, and at the same time, it becomes a commodity which can be accumulated, bought, and sold. Citizens, corporations, and governments have become increasingly dependent upon it. The digital information and communications technologies produce and reshape abstract space and become central to the reproduction of physical urban space (Shaw and Graham 2017). The notion of "smart city" is now part of everyday discussions of those who are involved or interested in urban development.

We are now living in a world where computing power is growing exponentially; artificial intelligence (AI) is now part of the daily life and getting better every day; robots are replacing labor on a scale not previously observed; and, finally, new manufacturing techniques such as 3D printing or additive manufacturing are disrupting production methods.

Brynjolfsson and McAfee (2016) argued that recent improvements in computing technology have made digitization of just about everything possible, which, in turn, has become the most important phenomenon of recent years. There have been two great outcomes of this process. It made obtaining knowledge and information much easier. We can reach a wealth of information from our living rooms by using our computers or mobile devices. It also significantly increased the rate of innovation, which helped create a circular and cumulative process for further development. Digitization, in a sense, provides the input for machine learning and/or AI to design, improve, and utilize programs and tools for the benefit of individuals, corporations, and governments.

Over the past few decades, machine learning has become one of the key pillars of information technology. With the increasing amounts of digitized data, machine learning will become an even more important ingredient for future technological progress (Smola and Vishwanathan 2008). Although sometimes confused, machine learning is a subfield of artificial intelligence that focuses on understanding the structure of data. By supplying data into computer models, machine learning can make it understandable and useful for the people. Machine learning utilizes the digitized data and desired result as input and produces an algorithm that turns this input into another algorithm, which is called learning algorithms. In a sense, with machine learning, computers can write their own programs (Domingos 2015). In this way, machine learning enables computers to build models from sample data that could, in turn, automate decision-making processes (Tagliaferri 2017). AI, then, utilizes these machine learning algorithms and teaches computers to perform certain tasks that are currently performed by humans.

Today, algorithms are everywhere: not just in cell phones or computers but in cars, houses, appliances, and toys. Algorithms now schedule flights and even fly airplanes, help run factories, manage trading goods and services, and manage financial transactions and keep the records. Imagine a world where every algorithm suddenly stopped working, it would be chaos everywhere; there will be no transportation and no financial transaction, and government agencies, hospitals, and education institutions will not be able to perform their routine duties. It will be the end of the world as we know it. The machine learning revolution will certainly cause extensive economic and social changes in the coming years (Domingos 2015).

These current technological revolutions, by definition, bring major changes in all aspects of life; some are quite beneficial for all, while others are a little problematic. The first Industrial Revolution introduced the large industrial firm that heavily utilized the machine power to substitute and/or supplement the manual work and significantly increased productivity, hence offered affordable products to consumers and improved living standards (Makridakis 2017; Autor 2015). Current technological progress also created unprecedented bounty and more wealth with less work (Brynjolfsson and McAfee 2016), but such progress inevitably caused inequality in employment opportunities and in the distribution of income and wealth.

Increasing computing power, digitization, and machine learning has accelerated enhancements in manufacturing technologies and created changes in the production process. One such major development is additive manufacturing (AM), commonly known as 3D printing. It is a manufacturing technology that enables companies to manufacture products in a more cost and resource-efficient way than traditional manufacturing (Ford and Despeisse 2016). AM is a suite of computer-automated processes that produce physical objects usually layer by layer from computer-aided design models using metallic, plastic, ceramic, composite, or biological materials (Huang et al. 2015).

The AM technology is not new, but it has made significant progress over the past 30 years. There is now a growing interest in its capabilities and potential uses. The pace of research and development both in academia and in corporations for further improvements is increasing (Roca et al. 2017; Bingheng et al. 2015). It is anticipated that AM will revolutionize production modes in customized fabrication. It allows the use of almost any material to fabricate any part, in any quantity and any location, for any industrial field (Bingheng et al. 2015). Its impact is not limited to the production process. It will also affect the backward and forward linkages in the production and distribution process. It signals that value chains will become shorter, smaller, more localized, and more collaborative and offer significant sustainability benefits. AM is identified as potentially less wasteful during manufacturing and capable of creating lightweight components that reduce material consumption in manufacturing and energy consumption in use. It also helps reduce transportation costs in the supply chain due to the light weight of the final product. AM makes it possible to create spare parts on demand and hence reduce inventory waste (Huang et al. 2015; Ford and Despeisse 2016).

AM also has the potential for rearranging the location of manufacturing activities. Since the beginning of Industrial Revolution, manufacturing has been mainly a centralized activity. AM is now creating opportunities for manufacturing to become decentralized as more localized manufacturing becomes economically attainable. In such a world, more localized manufacturing could radically transform supply and distribution networks (Ford and Despeisse 2016).

Regardless of the great progress AM systems have made in recent years, there are several challenges that need to be addressed. Some of them are limited material availability, relatively poor part accuracy and insufficient consistency in the produced parts, and lack of certification for AM processes (Huang et al. 2015). The AM technology is still under development, and resolving its problems may take decades. In its current level, AM is more suitable for small batch production in niche applications (Roca et al. 2017). Perhaps, a fusion of AM technology with equivalent and subtractive manufacturing could open new avenues and create additional benefits for advanced manufacturing (Bingheng et al. 2015).

Since the invention of the steam engine, Industrial Revolutions have substantially increased the standards of living, but at the same time have reduced the role and share of labor power in the production process. Over the last two centuries, there have been anxiety and periodic warnings that such developments will wipe out a large number of jobs. However, the past automation and technological progress have not made human labor obsolete; in fact, the employment-to-population ratio rose during the twentieth century (Autor 2015). It is more likely that expansion of the economy across the world has helped to keep the employment reduction at bay during this period. It should be noted that there are significant qualitative differences between past developments and recent information computing technologies. One may ask then whether observations about the past interactions between automation and employment change can provide reasonable guidance for future interactions.

Over the years with each new development, skill requirements of labor changed and shifted toward more-skilled and better-educated ones. Computers and robots have been replacing human labor in performing codifiable tasks. These tasks have precise, well-understood procedures that could be easily automated. This skill-biased technical change has increased the demand for workers with the relevant education and skill set while reducing demand for less-educated workers whose jobs are easily automated. This created the so-called labor market polarization (Brynjolfsson and McAfee 2016; Autor 2015). There are certain tasks that are quite difficult to computerize or automate that involve problem-solving capabilities, intuition, creativity, situational adaptability, and in-person interactions. These tasks require flexibility, judgment, and common sense that people generally understand only tacitly (Autor 2015). In a sense, intangible assets are now more important in the production process than physical equipment and structures.

One may argue that improved productivity through automation will create employment opportunities in other sectors, particularly in services sectors. This means that the service sector needs to be broadened to absorb additional employment for those who lost their jobs in other sectors. However, it is still unclear whether future jobs are also potentially automatable (Makridakis 2017).

Another downside of capital-biased technological changes resulting from the substitution of robots and computers for labor is the unequal distribution of gains from such developments. While profits earned by capital owners have been increasing, the share of labor income diminished (Harvey 2014; Brynjolfsson and McAfee 2016). Digitization and AI coupled with the exponential growth of the Internet also created the winner-take-all markets that contributed to increasing inequality. Due to the almost negligible marginal cost of additional production, capacity constraints for digital goods are no longer relevant. Technological improvements in communications and transportation diminished distance and expanded the market for individuals and companies. Now, top performers in a given sector can reach wider markets and win even more customers. Once these markets merge into one global market, local providers and even the second-best performer face tougher competition from all directions (Makridakis 2017; Brynjolfsson and McAfee 2016). The result of this intense competition would be monopoly or oligopoly as the strong drives out the weak in a Darwinian struggle for survival (Harvey 2001).

Most people are laborers not owners of capital, and they must sell their labor to buy things they need. As the replacement of human labor by robots and digital labor becomes more pervasive, they will become and remain unemployed. This, in turn, will reduce the demand for goods and services now produced by robots in large quantities and cheap, which will eventually slow down the overall economic growth. This will create one of the chronic crises of the capitalist system.

The major concern is whether the current social structure could survive such massive reductions in jobs coupled with the unequal distribution of wealth and income. Even if extensive retraining programs are organized, this may not be enough to avoid social disruptions and conflicts because required skills for new jobs may not be easily attainable (Makridakis 2017). In fact, there is a growing fear among the superrich that social unrest is looming as evidenced by the increased spending on doomsday preparation (Osnos 2017). It is not too late to start discussing how to transform the society around a labor-light economy to avoid such social disruptions.

To remedy the financial distress resulting from job loss, some suggested that an unconditional universal basic income, a regular income paid in cash to every individual member of the society, should be provided (Van Parijs and Vanderborght 2017). Another suggestion is the provision of a negative income tax that combines a guaranteed minimum income with an incentive to work (Brynjolfsson and McAfee 2016). The concept of basic income and negative income tax is not part of the policy discussion today, and the questions about the size and source of the necessary funds remain to be addressed, as well as its feasibility within the current capitalist economic system.

It should be emphasized that the impact of the digital and AI revolution will be more prominent in poorer regions and nations than in advanced ones for two reasons. First, as computers and robots replace human labor for codifiable tasks, it will be difficult for these poor regions to attract new investments, if not lose the existing ones to the increasing reshoring back to advanced countries or regions. Second, these regions and nations will have significant disadvantages to invest in expensive AI technologies due to lack of necessary financial and human resources (Makridakis 2017).

These developments will have significant implications on local and regional economies particularly on employment opportunities and warrant careful investigation and good understanding.

6.6 Concluding Remarks and Future Directions for Research

It is obvious that the issues discussed in this paper are not exhaustive, but even with this subset of factors, the magnitude of the challenges is immense. Their impact on the local and regional economic development process appears to become more pressing. There is a dialectical or circular and cumulative relationship between the above-discussed issues and local and regional economies, in some cases resulting in a vicious cycle that requires a clear understanding of the entire set of factors to interrupt this cycle.

We live in a new world made and remade by many factors ranging from disruptive technological revolutions, globalization, conflict and migration, depletion of national resources and environmental degradation, to deterioration of traditional protective institutions. We are faced with unprecedented threats to our future along with many opportunities to make significant positive changes. We need to have a normative standard focusing on not only what it is but also what it should be in order to evaluate these threats and opportunities and take action. It is essential to restore hope and confidence for a harmonious, peaceful, and just society where the true flourishing of individuals and the construction of the good life are possible. We need to challenge the perceived wisdom, abandon our prejudices, and, more importantly, be open to welcome new, sometimes radical, ideas.

Today, every community is facing certain social, political, and economic instability that is damaging the social construct of the society due to abovementioned factors. In such a time and environment, local and regional economic development could be a good starting point to address these problems through rational, integrated, and scientific approaches and sound policies. There is no denying that all politics are local. It becomes imperative to develop concepts, theory, policy, and practice in local and regional development that encourage widespread participation of relevant actors from all corners and establish mechanisms and networks to facilitate and promote dialogue and deliberation about the common concerns and problems we are facing and will continue to face in the coming years. These policies and theories should emphasize that the focus of development is the people and their undeniable needs. They should also realize that the world we would like to live in is very much linked to the type of people we want to be, the social relations we are interested in, our interaction with nature, and our value system that is important for us. This requires a holistic and progressive approach that can address the relations and integration between the economic, social, political, ecological, and cultural dimensions of local and regional development as well as the potential trade-offs and conflicts.

The future research should focus on a critical review of existing theories of regional science in light of the above discussions, developing new ones and testing them.

References

Assadourian E (2012) The path to degrowth in overdeveloped countries, in state of the world 2012: moving toward sustainable prosperity. Worldwatch Institute, Washington, DC. ISBN:978-1-61091-037-8

Autor DH (2015) Why are there still so many jobs? The history and future of workplace automation. J Econ Perspect 29(3):3–30

Bingheng L, Li D, Tian X (2015) Development trends in additive manufacturing and 3D printing. Engineering 1(1):85–89

Brynjolfsson E, McAfee A (2016) The second machine age. W.W. Norton and Company, New York

Buch-Hansen H (2014) Capitalist diversity and de-growth trajectories to steady-state economies. Ecol Econ 106:167–173

Burton JW (1979) Deviance, terrorism, and war: the process of solving unsolved social and political problems. Martin Robertson, Oxford

Burton JW (1990) Conflict: basic human needs. St. Martins Press, New York

Burton JW (1998) Conflict resolution: the human dimension. Int J Peace Stud 3(1)

Caprottia F, Cowleyb R, Dattab A, Brotoc VC, Gaod E, Georgesone L, Herrickf C, Odendaalg N, Jossh S (2017) The new urban agenda: key opportunities and challenges for policy and practice. Urban Res Pract 10(3):367–378

D'Alisa G, Demaria F, Kallis G (eds) (2015) Degrowth: a vocabulary for a new era. Routledge, London. ISBN:9781138000766

Daly HE (1974) The economics of the steady state. Am Econ Rev 64(2). In: Papers and proceedings of the eighty-sixth annual meeting of the American Economic Association, pp 15–21

Daly HE (2013) A further critique of growth economics. Ecol Econ 88:20–24
Daly HE, Townsend KN (1993) Valuing the earth: economics, ecology, ethics, 2nd edn. MIT Press, Cambridge, MA
Dinc M (2015) Introduction to regional economic development. Edward Elgar Publishing, Cheltenham/Northampton
Domingos P (2015) The master algorithm. Basic Books, New York
Dunford M, Aoyama Y, Campolina Diniz C, Kundu A, Limonov L, Lin G, Liu W, Park SO, Turok I (2016) Area development and policy: an agenda for the 21st century. Area Dev Policy 1(1):1–14
Ford S, Despeisse M (2016) Additive manufacturing and sustainability: an exploratory study of the advantages and challenges. J Clean Prod 137:1573–1587
Fromm E (1941) 1994, escape from freedom. Henry Holt and Company, New York
Fukuyama F (2018) Identity: the demand for dignity and the politics of resentment. Farrar, Straus and Giroux, New York
Harvey D (1982) The limits to capital. Blackwell, Oxford
Harvey D (2001) Globalization and the "Spatial Fix", in Geographische Revue, Zeitschrift für Literatur und Diskussion, Jahrgang 3, Heft 2
Harvey D (2006) Spaces of global capitalism. Verso, London
Harvey D (2014) Seventeen contradictions and the end of capitalism. Oxford University Press, New York
Harvey D (2016) The ways of the world. Oxford University Press, New York
Harvey D (2018) Marx, capital, and the madness of economic reason. Oxford University Press, New York
Hornborg A (2014) Ecological economics, Marxism, and technological progress: some explorations of the conceptual foundations of theories of ecologically unequal exchange. Ecol Econ 105:11–18
Huang Y, Leu MC, Mazumder J, Donmez A (2015) Additive manufacturing: current state, future potential, gaps and needs, and recommendations. J Manuf Sci Eng 137:014001
Hudson R (2007) Regions, and regional uneven development forever? Some reflective comments upon theory and practice. Reg Stud 41(9):1149–1160
Hudson R (2016) Rising powers and the drivers of uneven global development. Area Dev Policy. https://doi.org/10.1080/23792949.2016.1227271
Institute for Economics and Peace (IEP) (2016) Global PEace Index, ten years of measuring peace. New York, NY
Kates RW, Parris TM, Leiserowitz AA (2005) What is sustainable development? Goals, indicators, values, and practice. Environ Sci Policy Sustain Dev 47(3):8–21
Lejano RP, Stokols D (2013) Social ecology, sustainability, and economics. Ecol Econ 89:1–6
Lele SM (1991) Sustainable development: a critical review. World Dev 19(6):607–621
Lele SM (2013) Rethinking sustainable development. Curr Hist 112:311–316
Lerche III CO (1998) The conflicts of globalization. Int J Peace Stud 3(1)
Makridakis S (2017) The forthcoming Artificial Intelligence (AI) revolution: its impact on society and firms. Futures 90:46–60
Markusen A (1987) Regions: the economics and politics of territory. Rowman, and Allenheld, Totowa
Maslow AH (1943) A theory of human motivation. Psychol Rev 50:370–396
Massey D (1979) In what sense a regional problem? Reg Stud 13(2):233–243
Massey D (2004) Geographies of responsibility. Geografiska Annaler B 86:5–18
Mastini R (2017) Degrowth: the case for a new economic paradigm. Originally published by openDemocracy. http://www.resilience.org/stories/2017-06-12/degrowth-case-new-economic-paradigm/
Mastini R (2018) Degrowth as a Concrete Utopia. Originally published by openDemocracy. https://www.resilience.org/stories/2018-11-19/degrowth-as-a-concrete-utopia/
Osnos E (2017) Survival of the richest. The New Yorker, January 30 issue
Paasi A, Metzger J (2017) Foregrounding the region. Reg Stud 51(1):19–30

Perrons D, Dunford R (2013) Regional development, equality, and gender: moving towards more inclusive and socially sustainable measures. Econ Ind Democr 34:483–499. https://doi.org/10.1177/0143831X13489044

Perroux F (1950) Economic space: theory and applications. Q J Econ 64(1):89–104

Pike A, Rodríguez-Pose A, Tomaney J (2007) What kind of local and regional development and for whom? Reg Stud 41(9):1253–1269

Pike A, MacKinnon D, Cumbers A, Dawley S, McMaster R (2016) Doing evolution in economic geography. Econ Geogr 92(2):123–144

Pike A, Rodríguez-Pose A, Tomaney J (2017) Shifting horizons in local and regional development. Reg Stud 51(1):46–57

Ran NH (1968) Kuvayi Milliye Destani. Bilgi Yayinevi, Istanbul. (in Turkish)

Roca JB, Vaishnav P, Mendonça J, Granger Morgan M (2017) Getting past the hype about 3-D printing. MIT Sloan Manag Rev 58(3):56–62

Sen A (1999) Development as freedom. Knopf/Oxford University Press, New York

Shaw J, Graham M (2017) An informational right to the city? Code, content, control, and the urbanization of information, antipode. ISSN:0066-4812, pp 1–21

Smith R (2010) Beyond growth or beyond capitalism? Real-world economics review, issue no. 53, pp 28–42. http://www.paecon.net/PAEReview/issue53/Smith53.pdf

Smola A, Vishwanathan SVN (2008) Introduction to machine learning. Cambridge University Press, Cambridge

Tagliaferri L (2017) An introduction to machine learning. https://www.digitalocean.com/community/tutorials/an-introduction-to-machine-learning

United Nations (1972) Report of the United Nations Conference on the Human Environment, Stockholm, 5–16 June 1972 (United Nations publication, Sales No. E.73.II.A.14, and corrigendum)

United Nations (1992) United Nations Conference on Environment & Development Rio de Janeiro, Brazil. https://sustainabledevelopment.un.org/content/documents/Agenda21.pdf

United Nations (2002) Report of the World Summit on Sustainable Development, Johannesburg, South Africa, United Nations publication, Sales No. E.03.II.A.1. ISBN:92-1-104521-5

United Nations (2015) Transforming our world: the 2030 Agenda for Sustainable Development A/RES/70/1, Resolution adopted by the General Assembly

Van Parijs P, Yannick V (2017) Basic income, a radical proposal for a free society and a sane economy. Harvard University Press, Cambridge, MA

Vojnovic I, Darden JT (2013) Class/racial conflict, intolerance, and distortions in urban form: lessons for sustainability from the Detroit region. Ecol Econ 96:88–98

Williams M (1998) Aid, sustainable development and the environmental crisis. Int J Peace Stud 3 (2):19–33

World Commission on Environment and Development (WCED) (1987) Our common future. Oxford University Press, Oxford/New York

Chapter 7
Regional Policy Analysis in the Era of Spatial Big Data

Laurie A. Schintler

Abstract New and expanding sources of spatial big data hold tremendous potential for regional policy analysis. Such data enable us to analyze regional policies in ways not possible with traditional sources of data, such as administrative records. At the same time, the use of spatial big data is fraught with issues and challenges that must be addressed. In this paper, we discuss both the opportunities and challenges of using spatial big data for regional policy analysis. We also explore analytical issues tied to the use of regional policy analysis methods in the era of big data, as well as the state of art in applying such methods to spatial big data. Our discussion focusses on three types of methods: (1) statistical and regression modeling, (2) traditional nonparametric modeling, and (3) deep neural learning.

Keywords Big data · Emerging technology · Regional methods · Policy analysis

7.1 Introduction

Recent socio-technological trends and developments, including the increasing use and diffusion of mobile devices and sensors, are contributing to the production of vast amounts of fast-streaming, rich, and detailed spatial data, generally referred to as spatial big data. These new and abundant sources of spatial data are giving us a vivid and real-time picture of the interests, preferences, needs, and activities of individuals in nearly every corner of the globe and of the places in which individuals live and interact (Schintler and Fischer 2018). Accordingly, we are now able to understand and analyze urban and regional phenomena in ways not possible with traditional sources of data (Mennis and Guo 2009), but we also now have new avenues and approaches for regional policy analysis, which can further improve our

L. A. Schintler (✉)
Schar School of Policy and Government, George Mason University, Arlington, VA, USA
e-mail: lschintl@gmu.edu

Z. Chen et al. (eds.), *Development Studies in Regional Science*,
New Frontiers in Regional Science: Asian Perspectives 42,
https://doi.org/10.1007/978-981-15-1435-7_7

understanding of urban and regional systems and our ability to design more efficient and targeted policies (Guldmann 2013).

Given the potential of spatial big data for regional policy analysis, there are increasing calls to address the opportunities and challenges created by the use of the data for this purpose (Stimson 2016). To fully harness the benefits of spatial big data for the analysis of regional policies, there are several analytical, computational, organizational, and institutional difficulties and issues that must be addressed (Schintler and Kulkarni 2014). Moreover, we do not yet fully understand the policy relevance of big data for regional science in the first place (Aroca et al. 2015) or how big data fits into existing spatial analytical frameworks (Stimson 2016). There also is a need to understand better how nonparametric, data-driven methods may play a role in supporting regional policy analysis (Nijkamp and Ratajczak 2015).

In this paper, we attempt to address some of these issues and concerns. What opportunities do spatial big data provide for regional policy analysis? What are the special challenges posed in the application of regional policy analysis methods, such as data envelope analysis (DEA), shift-share analysis, and spatial econometrics and statistical models, to spatial big data? Are other techniques more suitable in handling the nuances and complexities of spatial big data? What does the future hold in terms of the perils and prospects of big data for regional policy analysis?

7.2 Changing Spatial Data Landscape

Regional policy analysis has traditionally relied on data from censuses, surveys, and fixed sensors – e.g., road loop detectors and weather monitoring stations. While these sources of data will continue to be necessary for policy analyses, there is an increasing interest in alternative data sets as a means of addressing limitations of traditional sources of data (Thakuriah et al. 2017). Spatial big data is a new and emerging source of data, which helps to overcome the shortcomings of information collected via surveys, censuses, conventional sensors, and other customary data sourcing mechanisms.

Spatial big data is defined as data that is too large or complex to be processed in an existing geospatial database and analytical systems, such as in a Geographic Information System (GIS) (Lee and Kang 2015). That is, it tends to exceed the capacity of spatial computing and database technologies – including hardware and software – in terms of learning, managing, and processing the data with reasonable ease and effort (Shekhar et al. 2009).

Similar to a-spatial big data, spatial big data is typically described in terms of four dimensions – volume, velocity, variety, and veracity. However, spatial big data also comprise features tied to some geographic referencing system or set of locations (Li et al. 2015). First, big data tends to comprise massive amounts of observations or variables. The size and dimensionality of spatial big data are much more significant than that of a-spatial big data, given that space is an additional feature or attribute in the data. Further, spatial big data often have a high level of spatial and temporal resolution, with information down to latitude and longitude coordinates and seconds of the day, and geospatial coverage spanning the globe, which adds to the scope and volume of the data. Second, spatial big data tends to stream in at a rapid clip and often from multiple locations simultaneously rather than from a single point in space. Georeferenced social media posts and transactions, along with sensor data tied to the Internet of Things (IoT), are prime examples. Third, spatial big data is very heterogeneous. Similar to a-spatial big data, it can be represented and summarized in various ways, including in both structured and unstructured formats. Structured data include tabular and ordered formats, whereas unstructured data are not organized in a pre-defined manner. Video, imagery, text, and audio are examples of unstructured data. Spatial big data also are varied in terms of the granularity of the spatial and temporal aspects of the data. For example, spatial data comprises differing spatial and temporal scales, levels of resolution, extents of coverage, and spatial referencing systems (Fischer et al. 1996). Lastly, veracity relates to the quality and trustworthiness of the data. Big data, in general, tend to be fraught with noise, incompleteness, redundancy, uncertainty, and other undesirable artifacts (Schintler and Fischer 2018).

Several trends are contributing to the production of massive amounts of spatial big data. These developments include the (1) advent and continuing evolution of the Internet of Things (IoT); (2) increasing use and sophistication of mobile devices; (3) rise of crowdsourcing and citizen sensing platforms; (4) proliferation of e-commerce, social media websites, and other services which allow people and organizations to conduct digital transactions; and (5) rise of the open data movement. In this context, spatial data is categorized as follows: (1) data from human and social actions and interactions, (2) process-mediated data, (3) machine-generated data, and (4) synthetic data. Such data also can be delineated in terms of user communities, methods of generation, and modes of ownership and access (Thakuriah et al. 2017).

Human-sourced data is just what it implies; it is data that is produced from human activity, behavior, and interaction. Participatory sensing systems, citizen science projects, social media, Internet activity (e.g., web searches), and photo-sharing platforms are a few examples of human-generated data. Indeed, with the advent of information communications technology (ICT), anyone who has access to a digital communications device, e.g., a computer or the Internet, can act as a sensor. Further, given that many devices today are equipped with location tracking mechanisms and systems, e.g., GPS, much of the data that is sourced by humans contains spatial features and attributes.

Human-generated data – or human and social sensing data – is either actively or passively collected via digital crowdsourcing. Actively collected data, which is generally referred to as user-generated content (UGC), is information that is willingly contributed by individuals or communities of people. Volunteered geographic information (VGI) is a particular type of UGC, which contains information about locations and places contributed by users and shared with others. An example of VGI is data produced from location-sharing services, which enable individuals to digitally share their current locations and activities at those locations with their friends and acquaintances. Crowdsourced mapmaking systems, such as OpenStreetMap, are another instance of VGI. VGI has evolved as part of the "neography" movement, which unlike older geographic epistemologies and paradigms encompasses or enforces no restrictions on the roles, ownership, and interactions of the audience, the information, the presenter, and the subject (Goodchild 2008). Spatial big data also is collected passively from the movements of individuals and the activities and behavior of people and groups at different locations. Mobile phone traces are a prime example of passively collected human-generated data. Internet search activity is a particular type of passively collected big data. For example, Google Insights is a database of search queries in Google, which can be compared for keywords across countries, regions, and cities by time.

Process-mediated data include data that are generated by the transactions of government agencies and companies (Lansley et al. 2019). Indeed, new technologies are enabling organizations to gather massive amounts of data about their constituents and customers at a much higher scope and velocity. Government agencies and administrative organizations routinely collect data on citizens, including registrations, transactions, and records tied to the demand for and delivery of municipal services. For example, fiscal agencies report data on taxes and other financial undertakings, along with revenue generated by such activities (Thakuriah et al. 2017). Businesses, including retailers, utility providers, transport providers, and banking and financial services, also regularly assemble massive amounts of data, such as consumption patterns and demographics of customers at different venues and locations, as well as information on business climate, future supply and demand of goods and services, and competitive forces and dynamics. (Lansley et al. 2019).

Increasingly, vast amounts of data on our natural and human-made environment are being sensed by machines. Building structures, nightlights, land use cover, meteorological conditions, energy consumption, and air and water quality are just a few examples of the kinds of information collected by machines (Schintler and Fischer 2018). The amount of data being produced by machine sensors is far from trivial. In fact, it could soon comprise half of all the data in the world (Gantz and Reinsel 2012). There are a couple of factors behind the germination of machine-generated data. First, technology has reduced (and, in some cases, removed) the need for a human in the creation, curation, and computational processing of data (Lansley et al. 2019). For example, it is now possible to automate the production and spatial referencing of data from the use of mobile devices. Second, the Internet of Things (IoT), which comprises a large and rapidly amassing assemblage of devices connected to the Internet, is producing massive amounts of real-time information on various aspects of our behavior, homes, infrastructure, and environment.

Machine sensors are fixed, mobile, or a-spatial (Lansley et al. 2019). Fixed sensors collect data at a particular location, e.g., energy meters, whereas mobile sensors harvest information on spatial trajectories – e.g., mobility patterns derived by mobile phones. Autonomous vehicles also are a type of mobile sensor, which continuously monitors the surrounding environment as well as the performance characteristics of the vehicles themselves. Other kinds of machine sensors are unfettered by location altogether – e.g., satellites which monitor the earth.

Synthetic data – or processed data – is that that is not obtained by direct measurement; instead, it is generated by simulation or machine learning of source data.

Generally, the purpose of synthetic data is to mask personally identifiable or proprietary information or to meet specific needs or certain conditions that are not available in the raw data. Synthetic data on micropopulations, for example, are used to predict possible individual-level outcomes of policy interventions (Smith et al. 2009).

7.3 Overview of Opportunities and Challenges

New and emerging sources of spatial data produced from the digital transactions of humans and organizations, systems of sophisticated machine sensors, and synthetic processing methods can be used to support the regional policy process in various ways. In general, the policy process comprises the following steps: (1) problem definition, (2) formulation of alternative solutions, (3) projection of outcomes, (4) ex ante evaluation of alternatives, (5) selection of the solution, (6) implementation, and (7) ex post evaluation. Thus, the analysis and evaluation factor in all stages of the policy process and big data can play new and innovative roles in supporting in these efforts.

First, intelligence gathering is needed to identify a problem to be solved clearly. Crowdsourcing and citizen sensing systems – i.e., human and social-generated data – provide a low-cost, real-time, and automated mechanism for gathering information on the behavior, activities, needs, and preferences of people in a region, unlike surveys and censuses which are generally very costly and time-consuming to carry out and administer. The Internet of Things (IoT) will play an increasing part in detecting and anticipating problems in real-time mode but also in seamlessly tracking the impacts of policies after they have been implemented. Spatial big data also support the use of "nowcasting" – i.e., on-the-fly, near real-time forecasting of economic and other kinds of activity (Glaeser et al. 2017). Second, as spatial big data tends to have extensive spatial and temporal coverage – e.g., second-to-second coverage of many places in the world – it can be used to track and measure phenomena where erroneous, incomplete, or inaccessible data hinders the development of useful and comprehensive performance indicators. It also can be used as a supplement to administrative data and to create proxies for different aspects of regional systems at levels of spatial resolution that may not be possible with administrative data (Kulkarni et al. 2011). Third, given spatial big data tend to have a high degree of spatial and temporal resolution, it helps to address the challenge in regional policy analysis of finding data that is consistent in spatial and temporal terms. The high degree of granularity in spatial big data means that the summarization of urban and regional phenomena need not be confined to particular time intervals and/or boundaries – i.e., administrative units. Thus, the data can be used to conduct cross-regional and cross-city comparative policy analyses, which has long been a challenge with traditional sources of data (Haynes 1971). Lastly, spatial big data can be used to delineate the boundaries of regions in new ways altogether new regional boundaries, based on the detailed accounts of individuals, firms, and organizations in a region (see, e.g., Schintler et al. 2014).

At the same time, there are several issues and challenges in the use and application of spatial big data for regional policy analysis. Not only does the sheer size of the data complicate matters but also does the depth and dimensionality of the data. The dimensions of space and time in spatial big data create challenges which are distinct from those faced with the use of a-spatial big data. We discuss four issues: data formatting, data cleaning, data integration or fusion, and data aggregation.

As a preliminary step, it is often necessary to convert spatial big data into a form appropriate for the intended policy analysis. Thus, the data must be reformatted. For example, it may be essential to convert unstructured data to structured data to be able to apply quantitative modeling and analytical methods. Spatial big data, in particular, must be geocoded before it can effectively be used to support regional policy analysis in a Geographic Information System. Further, whereas specific sources of big data contain explicit geographic references – e.g., place names or latitude and longitude coordinates – many others do not, and location-based information may be hidden in the data, as is the case with social media feeds and website content. Thus, part of the process in formatting spatial big data involves the extraction and assignment of spatial information to the data.

Big data, in general, tend to be fraught with imperfections and other undesirable qualities. Often, the data contains redundant information or records, a source of the noise. For example, real-time imagery collected by satellites tends to have repetitive coverage, as multiple snapshots must be produced at any given time to achieve adequate spatial coverage. In other cases, the data are merely incomplete. For instance, given that location positioning technologies are not capable of producing proper signals in certain kinds of environments – e.g., dense foliage and valleys – spatial trajectories collected from mobile phone use often contain gaps. Human- and social-generated data are notoriously skewed toward the demographic characteristics, preferences, interests, motivations, and activity patterns of their users. They also are susceptible to bias when users have the option to "opt-in" to location sharing in the first place. Lastly, there may be variations in the extent and quality of government data from one region to another, or at different spatial administrative scales within a region (Lansley et al. 2019).

Considering that many sources of big data are far from perfect, it is usually necessary to clean or scrub the data before it can be used for policy analysis. Otherwise, the analysis can produce spurious correlations, faulty conclusions, and misleading predictions about the state of a region or the impacts of regional policies. Unfortunately, while there are international standards and procedures for assessing the quality of and cleaning small spatial data, appropriate practices and guidelines for spatial big data are generally lacking (Goodchild 2013). Detecting and correcting for noise and bias in spatial big data is especially challenging, given that the type and extent of these problems vary from place to place. Good data provenance, e.g., making sure that metadata is produced and updated as big data changes hands, can help to alleviate this problem (Getis 1999). One can also exploit redundancy in big data for detecting errors and inconsistencies (Goodchild 2013). Lastly, anomaly detection methods, which look for events and patterns in data different than what one expects, also can be used to identify imperfections in spatial big data. However, anomaly detection is difficult as it requires knowledge of what is considered abnormal in the first place (Li et al. 2015).

To gain a robust and comprehensive picture of a region, and to be able to evaluate policies along multiple and diverse dimensions, it is often necessary to merge and aggregate big data or to combine it with traditional sources – e.g., administrative records. Spatial big data fusion is rapidly growing area of research in the field of geocomputation, and its primary aim is the "creation of new datasets and making existing ones more readily available to a broader array of users" (Haynes et al. 2018). Through the process of data fusion, new data sets are created to make them compatible with existing data and analytical processes. Thus, in the case of regional policy analysis, new data sets created through data integration should ideally be congruous with the methods that are used to assess policies in the first place. However, data integration or fusion is especially challenging in the case of spatial big data, considering that the data comprises varying levels of resolution, scale, and coverage and the different formats of the data – i.e., raster, vector, and graph – pose additional hurdles. Linking data that has been collected by multiple organizations, including government agencies, is particularly challenging. Multivariate linkage approaches may help out in this regard (Lansley et al. 2019). Integrating spatial big data with conventional sources of big data is an ongoing challenge, which will no doubt need to be addressed, especially in the context of smart cities (Batty et al. 2012).

Impact assessment of regional policies tends to be sensitive to the time period, scale, and location of the analysis at hand (Chen and Haynes 2015). Issues of spatial and temporal scale-variant outcomes relate closely to the modifiable areal unit problem (MAUP) and modifiable temporal unit problem (MTUP), which are sources of statistical bias and error potentially contributing to faulty decisions regarding regional policies. Both problems are compounded in spatial big data given that there are countless ways to aggregate and disaggregate the data spatially and temporally. At the same time, spatial big data give us an opportunity to more robustly understand to what extent and under what circumstances MAUP and MAUT create bias (Schintler and Fischer 2018). Similar explorations can be done with synthetically created data (Arbia and Petrarca 2016).

7.4 Regional Policy Analysis Methods and Spatial Big Data

With the opportunities and challenges just discussed in mind, we now look more closely at the analytical issues tied to the use of regional policy analysis methods in the era of big data, as well as the state of art in applying such methods to spatial big data. We first examine statistical and econometric modeling and then turn our attention to nonparametric data-driven methods, such as data envelope analysis (DEA), shift-share analysis, and newer methods based on deep neural learning.

7.4.1 Spatial Econometrics and Statistical Modeling

Econometric models and techniques, including spatial and panel regression, Granger causality, and discrete choice modeling, are ordinarily used for regional policy analysis (see, e.g., Ding et al. 2008; Chen and Haynes 2012, 2015, 2017; Ding and Haynes 2006). Spatial econometrics, in particular, is gaining increasing interest and use across a wide array of policy applications, including transportation, housing, and urban development (Arbia 2016). Some of the benefits of spatial econometric modeling include its ability to account for spatial autocorrelation and its ability to analyze local effects and spillover effects of regional policy investments, such as in transportation infrastructure (Chen and Haynes 2015).

Big data offer numerous opportunities such kinds of modeling, and accordingly, there are increasing efforts to apply econometric and statistical modeling to spatial big data. To this point, Google econometrics is an emerging paradigm, which utilizes information on Internet searches as independent variables in regression and statistical models for predicting different urban and regional phenomena. For example, Kulkarni et al. (2009) used a Google search index to forecast housing prices at the city level using Granger causality modeling.

However, traditional statistical and econometric methods were not designed for spatial big data. Conventional methods cannot easily or effectively handle new kinds of spatial data forms and formats, such as trajectories of moving objects, geographic information embedded in web pages, and surveillance videos (Mennis and Guo 2009). Nor can they manage the size and dimensionality of spatial big data. Moreover, spatial big data tends to violate the assumptions that must hold when using statistical parametric methods. More to the point, such data is fraught with spatial and temporal dependence, autocorrelation, heterogeneity, and non-normality (Schintler and Fischer 2018).

Spatial econometric modeling in the era of big data faces particular challenges. For example, spatial (and temporal) dependence must be fully understood and controlled for in the specification of spatial regression models, a problem which is complicated in the case of spatial big data in that the nature of spatial and temporal association can change depending on how the data is parsed or aggregated. Additionally, data problems associated with geographic attributes, areal framework, and area/attribute interaction, which can affect the performance of spatial econometric modeling, are magnified with larger spatial data sets (Getis 1999).

Other concerns raised about spatial econometric modeling relate to the size and dimensionality of spatial big data and added computational complexity from the spatial weights matrix. Accordingly, there are active efforts to develop techniques, methods, and model specifications for overcoming the computational problems in terms of statistical estimation and hypothesis testing of regression models based on large, complex data sets (Arbia 2016; Burden et al. 2015; LeSage and Pace 2008). Another problem relates to the spatial weight matrix used in spatial econometric models to describe the arrangement of observational units in space. Given that computational complexity increases exponentially as the number of locations increases linearly, such models tend to suffer from the curse of dimensionality (Li et al. 2015). This problem compromises the computational efficiency of maximum likelihood estimation (a problem not arising in the case of Bayesian model estimation) in spatial autoregressive modeling (Smirnov and Anselin 2001). For spatial network data – e.g., georeferenced social media data, where a spatial weight matrix represents relationships between origin-destination locations – this problem is even more extreme (Zhou et al. 2017). While we can apply sampling strategies to reduce the size and dimensionality of the spatial weight matrix, this approach can lead to underestimation of spatial autocorrelation (Zhou et al. 2017). "Divide-and-conquer" methods, which iteratively reduce complex problems into subtasks, until the solution of subproblems is scalable, may be better suited for dealing with dimensionality in spatial regression modeling (Smirnov and Anselin 2001). Further, big data tools can be used to create spatial weights from huge spatial data sets to manage computing resources efficiently (Li et al. 2014). Additional research is aimed at addressing issues related to the quality or veracity of big data and uncertainties such as those that are present in location data which has been processed such that the identities of individuals are masked (Arbia et al. 2016). Uncertainties and flaws in the data can introduce error in models and potentially inefficient estimators of the parameters, thus potentially leading to inadequate or inappropriate policy recommendations based on the model results. Use of alternative analytical methods, such as the Bayesian model averaging approach, can be an effective means for addressing model uncertainty in the context of spatial econometric models (LeSage and Fischer 2008). In addition to computational and analytical solutions, another way to address the issue of gaps and other sources of uncertainty in big data is to exploit the models of the very phenomena that the underlying raw data corresponds to (Batty et al. 2012).

One final problem associated with the application of spatial econometric models to big data is that there are many viable model approaches, methods, and techniques that can be adopted. Thus, systematic, comprehensive, and efficient procedures for selecting and formulating robust models are needed (Doornik and Hendry 2015).

Spatial interaction modeling is an application of econometrics that merits separate attention. Opportunities for such modeling in the era of spatial big data are enormous, especially considering that many sources of big data contain rich and timely information on the location activities, choices, and preferences and on movement patterns of individuals in space and time. Such models have been widely applied to anticipate how the choices of individuals, firms, and organizations may be affected by the implementation of different policies, such as those that relate to transportation. Considering that many sources of spatial big data contain detailed and timely information on the activities, preferences, and needs of people, and their movement and mobility patterns and trajectories in space and time, there are currently active efforts to apply location choice and spatial interaction models using location-based big data. Moreover, there are attempts to develop models of socio-spatial interaction which account for both the physical and virtual activities and patterns of interaction of individuals in regions (see, e.g., Schintler et al. 2014).

The use of spatial big data for econometric spatial interaction modeling poses unique challenges and issues. For example, the assumption of independence from irrelevant alternatives (IIA) in discrete choice modeling is easily violated in a spatial context, especially if large numbers of locations are being modeled. While there are formal tests and alternatives (e.g., probit model) for managing this problem, such solutions often lead to necessarily more complex models, which can generate additional difficulties (Haynes et al. 1988). Further, the aggregation of elemental alternatives as a strategy for ensuring that IIA is satisfied is particularly challenging with large spatial data sets. Specifically, there are complicating issues in terms of ensuring that the equal substitutability constraint holds discrete choice modeling (Haynes et al. 1988).

7.4.2 Conventional Nonparametric Modeling

Nonparametric methods, such as data envelope analysis (DEA) and shift-share analysis, are standard tools for regional policy analysis. As such methods are data-driven, they are particularly well-suited for spatial big data. They also avoid some of the problems that are associated with the application of parametric econometric modeling to big data; at the same time, they are not without their concerns and issues, especially in the era of big data.

Data envelope analysis (DEA) is a linear programming method for measuring the relative efficiency of so-called decision-making units (DMUs) based on some set of inputs and performance outputs. Specifically, DMUs are compared to each other by selecting the most efficient units relative to other units, unlike the averaging methods used in econometric regression modeling. Thus, DEA creates an efficiency frontier comprised of the most efficient decision-making units, which can then be used to infer information on the relative efficiency of all the units concerning factors that affect the efficiency of production (Haynes and Dinc 2005).

DEA has been applied extensively in an urban and regional context, including for environmental policy analysis and transportation performance assessment. One of the benefits of DEA is that it allows for the decomposition of different sources of efficiency, which can help in prescribing policies aimed at increasing the efficiency of underperforming DMUs (Haynes and Dinc 2005). Further, as a nonparametric method for estimating regional production functions (Stolp 1990), DEA enables us to evaluate the relative productivity of cities and regions vis-à-vis factors that drive productivity and growth, such as labor and capital investments.

For many years, the application of DEA to data sets comprising either large numbers of DMUs or input factors was hindered by the lack of appropriate computational infrastructure and resources. Some 25 years ago, Haynes et al. (1990) rightly argued, however, that such concerns would lessen as computing power advances and parallel computing becomes standard in the computation of massive data sets. Indeed, the size and complexity of data used for DEA have expanded over time vis-à-vis advancements in computational efficiency, but also with the growing availability of spatial big data (see, e.g., An et al. 2017; Chen and Jia 2017; Li et al. 2017; Zhu et al. 2017; Song et al. 2018). Nevertheless, computational time still can be quite significant (Song et al. 2018), especially when applying dynamic DEA to big data (Chen and Jia 2017; Zhu et al. 2017). In these instances, stylized parallel processing algorithms can help in managing the size and dimensionality of the data (Song et al. 2018), as can filtering and compression methods such as principal component analysis (Mariz et al. 2018).

As with other nonparametric data-driven methods, DEA is criticized for being a "black box" with little or no theoretical grounding. To this point, DEA does not give us any information on the underlying production function, including parameter estimates, and thus drawing theoretical inferences based on the results is problematic. On the other hand, such concerns may not be as grave as they seem, especially given that "model parameters are little more than data summary devices, 'placeholders' for theoretical concepts that may have little life outside of the theory that informs them" (Stolp 1990). Moreover, the idea that one does not need to specify a priori a particular functional form and related parameterization is appealing. Lastly, network DEA modeling could provide fruitful avenues for getting inside the "black box," as such models are designed explicitly for capturing internal interactions and dynamics within and across DMUS. In this context, spatial big data such as real-time information on the movement of vehicles and goods generated by RFID tags in logistics supply chains provide tremendous opportunities for the use of network DEA for policy analysis of systems defined by complex linkages in space and time (Badiezadeh et al. 2018).

Shift-share models are another commonly used nonparametric method for regional policy analysis. The traditional shift-share approach analyzes the evolution of regional economic performance between time periods by identifying three components: a national effect, a sectoral effect, and a competitive effect (Wang and Chen 2019). A region with below-average output or employment growth has either an unfavorable industrial mix or it is at a competitive disadvantage relative to other regions (Haynes and Dinc 1997). Accordingly, a shift-share analysis is especially useful in identifying regions where policy interventions may be needed to boost economic growth and productivity and to evaluate the impact of regional economic policies after they have been instituted.

Spatial big data create new opportunities for the use of shift-share analysis for regional policy assessment. Big data containing information on the economic exchanges between firms as well as those between producers and consumers give us novel ways to characterize regional economic activity, including the nature and composition of labor markets. Along these lines, data from online job postings can help in sensing the industrial structure of a region in real time. Moreover, big data enable us to apply shift-share analysis to spatial and temporal scales much more refined than those afforded by traditional administrative data. However, on the other side of the coin, MAUP and MTUP then become complicating factors.

7.4.3 Machine Learning and Neural Networks

Neural networks and machine learning methods have the potential to help in addressing the issues and challenges associated with the use of spatial big data for regional policy analysis. While indeed such techniques have been applied widely to understand and model regional systems (see, e.g., Kulkarni et al. 2000; Fischer and Gopal 1994), there remain many untapped opportunities in the use of neural learning for regional policy analysis. Many types of neural networks can capture nonlinearity, heterogeneity, noise, and other complexities in spatial and temporal data, and some do not require specification of a particular functional form making them well-suited for nonparametric statistical inference as they do require specification of any particular functional form (Fischer 2015). Unsupervised machine learning – e.g., clustering methods – can aid in reducing the dimensionality of spatial big data, while supervised machine learning methods can support the use of predictive analytics for different regional policy scenarios.

At the same time, neural learning is not without challenges and issues, especially in the era of big data. First, given that there is a network topology embedded in the architecture of neural models, they cannot yet scale to massive, high-dimensional data sets (Schintler and Fischer 2018). Further, machine learning models cannot be generalized to different situations and circumstances. To this point, they need to be retrained and retested when moving from one region, time period, or policy context to another (Li et al. 2015). While deep learning, an emerging computational paradigm, has tremendous potential for regional policy analysis in the big data era, the method is still very much a black box with multiple layers of hidden and uninterpretable parameters (Schintler and Fischer 2018). Accordingly, analogous to other methods such as DEA and shift-share analysis, deep learning lacks a theoretical grounding. To better understand the inner workings of deep learning to make it a more meaningful approach for regional policy analysis, it may be worthwhile to explore recent theories about the method (see, e.g., Wolchover 2017).

There are many other avenues for future research in terms of the use of neural learning methods for regional policy analysis. For example, how can we use deep learning (and machine learning, in general) for causal inference, such as in analyzing the potential effects of different policies? Moreover, how can machine learning techniques be used in combination with econometric/statistical methods, specifically to adequately address the array of challenges related to modeling of big data (Varian 2014)? Indeed, there are active efforts to integrate regional policy analysis modeling frameworks – e.g., CGE modeling and spatial econometrics (see, e.g., Chen and Haynes 2015). However, integration of traditional methods with machine learning techniques has yet to be explored in any robust manner. More research also is needed on how to validate neural models for regional policy analysis. To this point, we must be able to assess the performance of different machine learning algorithms from a standard base (Li et al. 2015) and to match big data with "ground truth" (Chen and Schintler 2015).

7.5 Role of Visualization

Visualization can play a pivotal role in the use and application of spatial big data for regional policy analysis. The purpose of visualization in this context is multifold. First, it helps in exploring the properties of the data, including outliers, patterns of association, and spatial and temporal dependence. In this manner, it can contribute to the identification of problems in a region and the formulation of hypotheses about the possible implications of different policies. Visualization also can help in developing efficient ways to partition the data for further computational analysis and to the appropriate selection of methods. Indeed, visualization is needed to represent data in computational structures, so that spatial big data and their interrelations can be effectively and efficiently modeled (Robinson et al. 2017). Exploratory spatial data analysis (ESDA) comprises a set of tools for visualizing and analyzing geospatial data for exploratory purposes. Second, it helps to communicate patterns, relationships, and other findings that stem from big data analysis (Li et al. 2015). Dashboards, which encapsulate benchmarks, indicators, and visualization, provide a compelling way of presenting the results of regional policy analysis using big data to citizens and policymakers.

There are several challenges associated with the visualization of spatial big data for regional policy analysis. In particular, the four dimensions of big data, volume, variety, velocity, and veracity, add a set of complicating factors (Robinson et al. 2017). The key issues include how to:

1. Develop visual policy analytical reasoning systems that help policy analysts and policymakers glean meaning from and organize spatial big data
2. Design useful interfaces to support continued engagement with spatial big data – i.e., between those who are analyzing the data, those who are affected by the analysis, and those who are making policies based on the analysis
3. Develop new visualization approaches and platforms for supporting collaborative decision-making
4. Develop techniques that allow users to express spatial patterns with a graphical interface
5. Understand when, how, and if visualization (e.g., maps) are appropriate in understanding spatial big data

7.6 Ethics and Privacy

Spatial big data often reveal very sensitive information about the activities, behavior, and sentiment of individuals at different locations and points in time. Information across multiple sources of data can be easily combined to create a comprehensive picture of someone's activity in space and time. In other cases, personally identifiable information can be inferred from the data. As big data becomes more and more open – e.g., available online – issues related to privacy will become increasingly pronounced (Batty et al. 2012). Indeed, many online services today require us to share private information, but beyond record-level access control, we do not understand what it means to share data and how the shared data can be linked. Considering the concerns above, some claim that research ethics are obsolete in the era of big data (Leetaru 2016). Thus, in using spatial big data for regional policy analysis, it is imperative to take steps to ensure the privacy and confidentially of the subjects under study are protected. However, doing this with big data is extraordinarily complex and challenging.

While many professional associations, government agencies, and universities have specific codes, rules, and policies relating to the ethical conduct of research, such formalized standards do not exist for big data. Thus, the researcher is ultimately responsible for ensuring the fair and ethical use of big data. To this end, data ideally should be de-anonymized or stripped of sensitive and personally identifiable information. In particular, references to precise locations – e.g., street addresses or names of individuals and organizations – should be eliminated or masked. Synthetic data, which is necessarily a fuzzified version of the raw data, is one approach for desensitizing big data.

7.7 Conclusion

Spatial big data can be expected to continue to grow at an accelerated rate, and we will likely see new sources and types of spatial big data in the coming years. While new and emerging sources of data have the potential to support meaningful and productive regional policy analysis, the issues and challenges associated with their use in this context must be appropriately and effectively addressed. We also need to explore how machine learning models, traditional nonparametric regional analysis methods, and econometrics models can be integrated to address difficulties associated with the use of spatial big data for regional policy analysis. Such modeling frameworks could help to augment all stages of the policy analysis process and to contribute to the formulation and implementation of policies that support livable and sustainable regions. For spatial big data to achieve its full potential in this context, multidisciplinary approaches, strategies and solutions are ultimately needed.

References

An Q, Wen Y, Xiong B, Yang M, Chen X (2017) Allocation of carbon dioxide emission permits with the minimum cost for Chinese provinces in big data environment. J Clean Prod 142:886–893

Arbia G (2016) Spatial econometrics: a rapidly evolving discipline

Arbia G, Petrarca F (2016) Effects of scale in spatial interaction models. In: Spatial econometric interaction modelling. Springer, Cham, pp 85–101

Arbia G, Espa G, Giuliani D (2016) Dirty spatial econometrics. Ann Reg Sci 56(1):177–189

Aroca P, Haynes K, Stimson R (2015) Research challenges in regional science. Presentation to plenary session. In Annual meeting of the Argentina Section of the Regional Science Association International

Badiezadeh T, Saen RF, Samavati T (2018) Assessing sustainability of supply chains by double frontier network DEA: a big data approach. Comput Oper Res 98:284–290

Batty M, Axhausen KW, Giannotti F, Pozdnoukhov A, Bazzani A, Wachowicz M et al (2012) Smart cities of the future. Eur Phys J Spec Top 214(1):481–518

Burden S, Cressie N, Steel D (2015) The SAR model for very large datasets: a reduced rank approach. Dent Econ 3(2):317–338

Chen Z, Haynes KE (2012) Re-examining linkages between surface transportation infrastructure and economic performance: a panel granger causality test on the northeast corridor. GMU School of Public Policy Research Paper (2013–02)

Chen Z, Haynes KE (2015) Multilevel assessment of public transportation infrastructure: a spatial econometric computable general equilibrium approach. Ann Reg Sci 54(3):663–685

Chen Z, Haynes K (2017) Impact of high-speed rail on regional economic disparity in China. J Transp Geogr 65:80–91

Chen L, Jia G (2017) Environmental efficiency analysis of China's regional industry: a data envelopment analysis (DEA) based approach. J Clean Prod 142:846–853

Chen Z, Schintler LA (2015) Sensitivity of location-sharing services data: evidence from American travel pattern. Transportation 42(4):669–682

Ding L, Haynes K (2006) The role of telecommunications infrastructure in regional economic growth in China. Aust J Reg Stu 12(3):281

Ding L, Haynes KE, Liu Y (2008) Telecommunications infrastructure and regional income convergence in China: panel data approaches. Ann Reg Sci 42(4):843–861

Doornik JA, Hendry DF (2015) Statistical model selection with "Big Data". Cogent Econ Financ 3(1):1045216

Fischer MM (2015) Neural networks. A class of flexible non-linear models for regression and classification. In: Karlsson C, Andersson M, Norman T (eds) Handbook of research methods and applications in economic geography. Edward Elgar, Cheltenham, pp 172–192

Fischer MM, Gopal S (1994) Artificial neural networks: a new approach to modeling interregional telecommunication flows. J Reg Sci 34(4):503–527

Fischer MM, Scholten H, Unwin D (eds) (1996) Spatial analytical perspectives on GIS. Taylor & Francis, Basingstoke

Gantz J, Reinsel D (2012) The digital universe in 2020: big data, bigger digital shadows, and biggest growth in the far east. IDC iView IDC Analyze Future 2007(2012):1–16

Getis A (1999) Some thoughts on the impact of large data sets on regional science. Ann Reg Sci 33(2):145–150

Glaeser EL, Kim H, Luca M (2017) Nowcasting the local economy: using Yelp data to measure economic activity (No. w24010). National Bureau of Economic Research

Goodchild MF (2008) Commentary: whither VGI? GeoJournal 72(3–4):239–244

Goodchild MF (2013) The quality of big (geo) data. Dialogues Hum Geogr 3(3):280–284

Guldmann JM (2013) Analytical strategies for estimating suppressed and missing data in large regional and local employment, population, and transportation databases. Wiley Interdiscip Rev Data Min Knowl Discov 3(4):280–289

Haynes KE (1971) Spatial change in urban structure: alternative approaches to ecological dynamics. Econ Geogr 47(sup1):324–335

Haynes KE, Dinc M (1997) Productivity change in manufacturing regions: a multifactor/shift-share approach. Growth Chang 28(2):201–221

Haynes KE, Dinc M (2005) Data envelopment analysis (DEA)

Haynes KE, Good DH, Dignan T (1988) Discrete spatial choice and the axiom of independence from irrelevant alternatives. Socio Econ Plan Sci 22(6):241–251

Haynes KE, Stough RR, Shroff HF (1990) New methodology in context: data envelopment analysis

Haynes D, Jokela A, Manson S (2018) IPUMS-Terra: integrated big heterogeneous spatiotemporal data analysis system. J Geogr Syst 20(4):343–361

Kulkarni RG, Stough RR, Haynes KE (2000) Towards modeling of communities of practice (CoPs): a Hebbian learning approach to organizational learning. Technol Forecast Soc Chang 64(1):71–83
Kulkarni R, Haynes KE, Stough RR, Paelinck JH (2009) Forecasting housing prices with Google econometrics
Kulkarni R, Haynes K, Stough R, Riggle J (2011) Light based growth indicator (LBGI): exploratory analysis of developing a proxy for local economic growth based on night lights. Reg Sci Policy Pract 3(2):101–113
Lansley G, de Smith M, Goodchild M, Longley P (2019) Big data and geospatial analysis. arXiv preprint arXiv:1902.06672
Lee JG, Kang M (2015) Geospatial big data: challenges and opportunities. Big Data Res 2(2):74–81
Leetaru K (2016) Are research ethics obsolete in the era of Big Data. Forbes. Retrieved from http://www.forbes.com/sites/kalevleetaru/2016/06/17/are-research-ethics-obsolete-in-the-era-of-big-data
LeSage JP, Fischer MM (2008) Spatial growth regressions: model specification, estimation and interpretation. Spat Econ Anal 3(3):275–304
LeSage JP, Pace RK (2008) Spatial econometric modeling of origin-destination flows. J Reg Sci 48(5):941–967
Li X, Li W, Anselin L, Rey S, Koschinsky J (2014) A MapReduce algorithm to create contiguity weights for spatial analysis of big data. In: Proceedings of 3rd ACM SIGSPATIAL International Workshop on Analysis for Big Geospatial Data, November 4, 50–53 ACM
Li D, Wang S, Li D (2015) Spatial data mining. Springer, Berlin/Heidelberg
Li L, Hao T, Chi T (2017) Evaluation on China's forestry resources efficiency based on big data. J Clean Prod 142:513–523
Mariz FB, Almeida MR, Aloise D (2018) A review of dynamic data envelopment analysis: state of the art and applications. Int Trans Oper Res 25(2):469–505
Mennis J, Guo D (2009) Spatial data mining and geographic knowledge discovery – an introduction. Comput Environ Urban Syst 33(6):403–408
Nijkamp P, Ratajczak W (2015) The spatial economy: a holistic perspective. In: Regional science matters. Springer, Cham, pp 15–26
Robinson AC, Demšar U, Moore AB, Buckley A, Jiang B, Field K et al (2017) Geospatial big data and cartography: research challenges and opportunities for making maps that matter. Int J Cartogr 3(sup1):32–60
Schintler LA, Fischer MM (2018) Big data and regional science: opportunities, challenges, and directions for future research
Schintler LA, Kulkarni R (2014) Big data for policy analysis: the good, the bad, and the ugly. Rev Policy Res 31(4):343–348
Schintler LA, Kulkarni R, Haynes K, Stough R (2014) 5. Sensing 'socio-spatio' interaction and accessibility from location-sharing services data. Part I: Advances in modelling accessibility and spatial interaction, 92
Shekhar S, Kang J, Gandhi V (2009) Spatial data mining. In: Encyclopedia of database systems, pp 2695–2698
Smirnov O, Anselin L (2001) Fast maximum likelihood estimation of very large spatial autoregressive models: a characteristic polynomial approach. Comput Stat Data Anal 35(3):301–319
Smith DM, Clarke GP, Harland K (2009) Improving the synthetic data generation process in spatial microsimulation models. Environ Plan A 41(5):1251–1268
Song ML, Fisher R, Wang JL, Cui LB (2018) Environmental performance evaluation with big data: theories and methods. Ann Oper Res 270(1–2):459–472
Stimson RJ (2016) Some challenges for regional science research
Stolp C (1990) Strengths and weaknesses of data envelopment analysis: An urban and regional perspective. Comput Environ Urban Syst 14(2):103–116
Thakuriah PV, Tilahun NY, Zellner M (2017) Big data and urban informatics: innovations and challenges to urban planning and knowledge discovery. In: Seeing cities through big data. Springer, Cham, pp 11–45

Varian HR (2014) Big data: new tricks for econometrics. J Econ Perspect 28(2):3–28
Wang K, Chen Z (2019) Infrastructure and regional economic growth in the One Belt and One Road regions: a dynamic shift-share approach. In: Development studies in regional science: essays in honor of Kingsley E. Haynes. Springer
Wolchover N (2017) New theory cracks open the black box of deep learning. Quanta Magazine, 3
Zhou J, Tu Y, Chen Y, Wang H (2017) Estimating spatial autocorrelation with sampled network data. J Bus Econ Stat 35(1):130–138
Zhu Q, Wu J, Li X, Xiong B (2017) China's regional natural resource allocation and utilization: a DEA-based approach in a big data environment. J Clean Prod 142:809–818

Chapter 8
A Spatial Interaction Model Based on Statistical Mechanics

Zheng Wang

Abstract In this chapter, a new model of spatial interaction is proposed with a view of statistical mechanics. It argues that spatial interaction is microscopically independent of macroscopic phenomenon and that patterns of interaction based upon individual agents emerge in space through Brownian motion. Using principles of statistical mechanics, we solve this complex process problem. This contrasts with Wilson's model in which spatial interaction exponentially decays in geographical space and the maximum entropy method is used to obtain the form of distance decay. In this paper, the empirical method is used to test the model. The model shows that the coefficient of the spatial interaction cannot be simply treated as a Lagrange parameter, which is related to both the average spatial scale of an agent particle migration and the likelihood of agent impulses. Finally, this model suggests that the free flow of population (or capital) enhances spatial interactions.

Keywords Spatial interaction · Micro-mechanisms model · Statistical mechanics

8.1 Introduction

A spatial interaction model is a classic issue in regional science (Isard 1975; Roy and Thill 2004; Karlsson et al. 2015). The most widely used and conventional model is the gravity model of Newtonian mechanics, where the interaction force is formed by decaying spatial interaction. The effect of intensity attenuates in the form of a negative square of the distance. In economics research, the spatial interaction model is called the "gravity model in theory" (Anderson 1979). However, regional scientists pay more attention to its application (Haynes and Fotheringham 1984).

Z. Wang (✉)
School of Geography, East China Normal University, Shanghai, China

Institute of Science and Development, Chinese Academy of Sciences, Beijing, China
e-mail: wangzheng@casisd.cn

Z. Chen et al. (eds.), *Development Studies in Regional Science*,
New Frontiers in Regional Science: Asian Perspectives 42,
https://doi.org/10.1007/978-981-15-1435-7_8

Haynes and Fotheringham (1984) strongly promote the popularization and application of the spatial interaction theory.

One problem with the conventional spatial interaction model is that, when two regions are sufficiently close to each other, their interaction intensity tends toward infinity—this is obviously unreasonable. In addition, the power of distance parameters in the model is still unclear; therefore, a crucial element of the model has not yet been resolved. Although Smith (1987) and Sen and Smith (1995) attempted to provide an axiomatic system to answer basic scientific questions about spatial interaction (SI), their conception of SI is physically oriented and should, therefore, be understood strictly on a physical level.

At present, many authors use Wilson's model (e.g., Drezner and Drezner 2001 and Niamsiri et al. 2009). In fact, Wilson's (1970) model assumes that regional logistics systems are closed; hence, the model indicates that interaction decays exponentially with variables that reflect distance, such as cost. However, regional systems in reality are certainly not closed; therefore, the assumption of maximum entropy in regional logistics is a flaw in Wilson's proof.

This paper discusses the modeling of spatial interactions and the development of solutions to difficulties in maximum entropy. In order to develop a new model of spatial interaction unrelated to (maximum) entropy, we assumed that N regions are composed of closed systems. When beginning to explore them, we have no reason to suppose their interaction is exponential. In principle, the form of spatial interactions should not be related to the number of regional systems. Moreover, since the current SI model of the attenuation factor has been introduced as a Lagrangian parameter, its geographical significance is unclear. Furthermore, although Wilson found that SI exponentially decays and resolved the problem of close proximity expansion, his model assumes that the regions of space constitute a closed system. Only when this assumption holds can the entropy of the space system reach its maximum. Otherwise, it is difficult to understand the space system. Therefore, a mechanistic model is indispensable. Because this issue is important, it is necessary to address in order to continue the study.

In this chapter, in order to resolve the theoretical problem of SI, we attempt to focus on the microcosmic basis of SI through a *statistical mechanics* analysis of physics, which is based on the economic and geographic principles of spatial interaction mechanism model.

8.2 Physical Features of Spatial Interaction

8.2.1 Population, Agent, and Diffusion

To recognize the nature of spatial interactions, we first need to discuss physical features. Why are there interactions between two spatial regions or cities? When a population particle moves from one region to another, information exchanges will occur between them; these exchanges generate spatial interactions. Information exchange constitutes the microscopic basis of interactions.

In the theory of geographical diffusion, Hägerstrand and his followers have applied the conception of a mean information field (MIF). An MIF is a basic pixel in diffusion; however, it is not regarded as diffusion as it only moves the inner pixels of an MIF. The concept of MIFs has been extended. An MIF can additionally be defined as the least spatial element, of which a certain geographical process has meaning. While a geographical process occurs in a certain geographical spatial field, one can divide the field into many small fields in a microscope in order to show processes acting in a small area with the same intensity and direction. It is known that such division cannot be infinite because a geographical observation needs a spatial size; this spatial size is just an MIF. The MIF provides such a scale as a small amount h and area in the amount h; in other words, an MIF is a significant minimum pixel in a certain geographical process.

The concept of an MIF has often been used in geography. Let us consider population diffusion. For example, if we consider a scale only for a residential area or a street, it is usually meaningless for population diffusion. Another example is the division of a region in physical geography; while the width of "region" attains to that of a plant sample district or of a minimum area where an organism lives, the region has been defined by observation. A pixel in a remote sensing image is a functional pixel (FP); the characteristics of pixels enable feature recognition (Wang et al. 1991). The functional pixel can only be used to estimate the percent of geographical objects in it, rather than demarcate the boundary of those geographical objects. When a space's scale is less than an FP or its length is shorter than h, it cannot be measured in a geographical aspect. In other words, FP is the minimum functional pixel observed under geographical meaning.

Once the concept of dimension is also considered, we can introduce the concept of a homogeneous field, which is the natural extension from the concept of homogeneous planes in location theory. In many early agent studies, geographers have applied the concept of homogeneous planes to analyze a geographical aspect of a non-plane. The effects or disturbances of geographical factors on a geographical process show the same statistical properties as an MIF. In other words, one might refer to a field as homogeneous in relation to a certain kind of regional process; the regional process of the field either has equal intensity and direction or holds invariable random processes, both of which have the same probability distribution.

8.2.2 Characteristics of Population Diffusion

A model of the geographical diffusion of a population is generally understood with reference to physical particle diffusion. However, a real geographical particle has different characteristics than a physical particle. A monomer of a geographical population has only finite longevity, which is not the same as a physical particle.

Each person only has a finite life, whereas sediment particles in a river persist indefinitely. We refer to these geographical particles as agents when they have the following features:

(1) A monomer of an agent has only limited life; its longevity is satisfied by various kinds of probability distributions.
(2) An agent is a random particle. Though monomeric agents have separately migrating objects and life meanings, they are the same nature under certain geographical processes; in other words, they are identical particles about a certain geographical observation. It is significant for us to study a geographical process only when it is regarded as a single group. For example, a tourist may be considered a particle, whose tourism life starts at the beginning of the tour and ends when they arrive back home. However, when we research tourists' behaviors, we do not study their personal behaviors but rather the behaviors of tourists as a whole; we do not distinguish them from others. This characteristic results in an agent being considered the same as a physical particle.
(3) The movement of an agent is a spatial process; this action process is called geographical diffusion, in which a great amount of agent movement occurs at the same time, with agents playing the same role as particles in a diffusion process in statistical mechanics.

8.3 Model of Agent Diffusion on a Homogeneous Field

With the physical feature, one might establish a model agent in a homogeneous field. Suppose that these conditions are sufficient; in many resident places on a homogeneous field, starting from any resident place, the agent can reach any of them within a finite distance during a finite time, including a return to the resident's own place. Let an agent set of all of the agents who were born in a given resident place at a given time be referred to as an A. Because the field is homogeneous, the probability characteristic of any agent group migrating to any other residential place is the same; that is, the action of the agent particle is a form of two-dimensional Brownian movement. Although human mobility patterns are more complicated than particle migration, they are quite similar in their macro-emergent meaning. Because of multifactor complexity, human mobility is shown as a stochastic process. The two-dimensional Brownian movement has been sufficiently studied in statistical physics. For a particle that starts in Brownian movement at any given time, its probability density function in space is denoted as

$$f(r,t) = \frac{1}{2\pi D(t-\tau)} \exp\left(-\frac{r^2}{2D(t-\tau)}\right) \tag{8.1}$$

where r is the distance to place a and t is the age of agent group A_t D is the diffusion coefficient and is defined as

$$D = \frac{h^2}{2T} \tag{8.2}$$

where h is a diameter of FP and T is the time in which an agent particle from an FP spreads to another FP or is the time of agent particle delay in an FP if we ignore the journey time; we refer T to as mean migration time. For the agent, the diffusion movement begins at life starting at 0, and we get

$$f(r,t) = \frac{1}{2\pi Dt} \exp\left(-\frac{r^2}{2Dt}\right) \tag{8.3}$$

The Brownian movement of an agent in a homogeneous field is an ergodic process. Hence, Formula (8.3) may be regarded as the spatial distribution of the probability of members of an agent at time *t*, appearing far from the center with a distance of *r*.

Suppose that the migration rate of agent group *A* is *g(t)*. We then have the spatial aspect of the migratory agent:

$$W(r,t) = kg(t)f(r,t) \tag{8.4}$$

k in the above formula is the unitary constant. If *g(t)* is constant, the agent life will be infinite and will result in *W(r, t)* = *f(r, t)*. However, the agent has a life and migration custom, *g(t)*≠constant; thus, it is necessary for us to estimate *g(t)*.

Let *K(t)* be the agent out-migratory rate of the agent of place *a*, i.e., the age distribution of agent group *A* around place *a*. Then there is

$$K(t) = \int_0^\infty \int_0^{2\pi} W(r,t) r d\theta dr \tag{8.5}$$

By substituting Formulas (8.3) and (8.4) into (8.5), and paying attention to the probability density function *f(r, t)*, we obtained

$$K(t) = kg(t) \tag{8.6}$$

However, we know that the out-migratory rate of an agent has certain features, such as that it is impossible for a baby or child to migrate by itself, or that it is impossible for a deceased person to take part in migration. As *K(t)* is a function that has a summit, we suggest *K(t)* or *g(t)* has the following:

$$g(t)t^{\tilde{\frac{1}{2}}} \exp(-a \cdot t) \tag{8.7}$$

where *a* is a parameter depending on the geographical condition, such as migratory policy and the economy, during the agent process. In fact, Ding's (1994) analysis of population migration laws in the Panyu District, Shandong Province, China, is similar to the pattern. Thus, we can also derive the maximum out-migratory rate age from Formula (8.7)

$$t_{\max} = \frac{1}{2a} \tag{8.8}$$

The existence of the maximum out-migratory rate has been proven by many researchers (see, e.g., Ding 1994). It has been found that the maximum out-migratory rate is approximately equal to a number ranging from 19 to 21 years in China, which depends on gender, agent policy, and geographical condition, but is not directly affected by the quantity of agents in a residential area.

8.4 The Kernel Spatial Interaction in a Geographical Space

Now let us directly consider spatial interaction. As mentioned above, spatial interaction results from the diffusion of agent particles, and the agent's exchange amount is similar to the photon in an electromagnetic interaction. The diffusion of variously aged agents results in a potential *G(r)*, where *r* is the distance from place *a*. The potential of a field results from interaction, and the interaction force is the negative value of the derivative of potential of the spatial coordinate. We first solved the potential function G(r):

$$G(r) = \int_0^\infty W(r,t)dt \tag{8.9}$$

In accordance with the definition of *W(r, t), G (r)* is actually a boundary probability distribution density function of an agent; one can obtain it after *g(t)* is made integral. Substituting Formula (8.7) into Formulas (8.3) and (8.9), we have

$$G(r) = \int_0^\infty \frac{k}{2\pi D\sqrt{t}} \exp\left[-\left(at + \frac{r^2}{2Dt}\right)\right] dt \tag{8.10}$$

By including integral (8.10) in the appendix, we have proven

$$G(r) = \frac{k}{2\sqrt{\pi D^2}} \exp\left(-\sqrt{\frac{2a}{D}}r\right) \tag{8.11}$$

This may be abbreviated as

$$G(r) = K\exp(-\beta \cdot r) \tag{8.12}$$

Formula (8.12) is the kernel of geographical spatial interaction. It is conventionally called a Wilsonian kernel in honor of A. E. Wilson, who first discovered that geographical spatial interaction is an exponential function in 1970.

Wang et al. (2004), based on data analysis, analyzed a type of spatial interaction and found that spatial knowledge spillover can be expressed as

$$s_{ij} = \alpha_i e^{-\left(\frac{1}{\delta_i^{(k)}}G_{ij}^{(k)} - \mu_i\right)^2 + \sum_{m=0}^{M-1}\frac{1}{\delta_i^{(m)}}G_{ij}^{(m)} - \beta r_{ij}} \tag{8.13}$$

where s_{ij} is knowledge spillover strength from region j to region i, δ_i is learning capacity, r_{ij} is the spatial distance between regional i and region j, and $G_{ij}^{(m)}$ are knowledge gaps between region i and j, M may be zero, and β is a regional parameter. This model shows that the spatial interaction satisfies Eq. (8.12).

8.5 Empirical Test

Wang et al. (2004), based on data analysis, considered knowledge spillovers, which is a spatial interaction with the spatial decay exponential and/or newton form. By observing spatial variation in the strength of spatial knowledge of the data, one can see this feature. Therefore, it can be considered that knowledge spillovers are a form of spatial interaction, which is similar to the Newtonian gravity potential in the spatial attenuation. Verspagen (1992) and Canie and Verspagen (2001) found that knowledge spillover declines with distance, with an inverse proportion. Wang et al. (2004), using Wilson's (1967) model, stipulated that the decline correlating with distance is in a negative exponent. So Wang et al. (2004) considered the spatial propagation of the concept of sustainable development and the concept of the knowledge economy. For example, they studied the spatial variation of knowledge spillovers under spatial interaction; they made use of two forms to fit with the knowledge of the overflow intensity in space, with the attenuation of distance:

$$s_{ij} = \delta_i \exp\left(-\frac{1}{\delta_i^{(k)}}\left(G_{ij}^{(k)} - \mu_i\right)^2 + \frac{G_{ij}^{(d)}}{\delta_i^{(1)}} - \beta r_{ij}\right) \tag{8.14a}$$

$$s_{ij} = \frac{\delta_i}{r_{ij}^{\beta}} \exp\left(-\frac{1}{\delta_i^{(k)}}\left(G_{ij}^{(k)} - \mu_i\right)^2 + \frac{G_{ij}^{(d)}}{\delta_i^{(1)}}\right) \tag{8.14b}$$

where s_{ij} is the intensity of knowledge spillover from place i to place j, δ_i is the learning capacity, $G_{ij}^{(k)}$ is the knowledge gap, and $G_{ij}^{(d)}$ is the demand gap and ecological gap, measured by the ratio of regional ecological levels in the issue of sustainable development. β is the spatial resistance. For example, Wang et al. (2004) found that knowledge spillover change better satisfied (8.13) rather than (8.14a, 8.14b), because the correlation coefficient on $e^{-\beta r}$ in (8.13) was greater than the correlation coefficient on $1/_r$ in (8.14a, 8.14b) (which are 0.890 and 0.876, respectively). The corresponding F tests are 22.0 and 18.9, respectively. In other words, the empirical analysis of the data confirmed that spatial interaction intensity is attenuated with the distance exponent. In another work, Liu (2004) studied the spatial diffusion of the ISO9000 standard and found that the spatial decay of diffusion is in the form of $e^{-\beta r}$, which is more in line with the actual data than $1/_r$.

In (8.11), Wang et al. calculated the formula of the spatial damping coefficient. The damping coefficients of spatial interaction in the model in this chapter can be calculated through the geographic feature

$$\beta = \sqrt{\frac{2T}{t_{\max} D}} \tag{8.15}$$

In Formula (8.15), T is the diffusion element that is the transfer of sub-average migration-residence time scale in a diffusion spatial element, and D is the diffusion field element area TF. It shows that there are two factors that affect the β value. Regarding tourism in China, Li (2007) estimated the corresponding coefficient based on China's tourist population. Li determined the spatial damping parameter as 0.00527 in cross-county tourism, which takes 3000 square kilometers for the estimation of a county scale. After he took the estimated value of 200,000 square kilometers for the provincial domain scale, the corresponding spatial damping parameter was calculated to be 0.00065.[1] We see that the spatial damping parameter values correspondingly reduce as the field size increases. From the decay of interaction in tourism space, the smaller the damping value, the slower the decay, showing the "strange effect" of tourist destinations: the farther away from the source, the more attractive, that is, interprovincial tourism forces are greater than cross-county tourism, which is consistent with actual life experience.

[1]Li (2007). According to the average tourist rate of Chinese citizens survey, the average time distance of Chinese citizens travel is T = 0.6 years old. Chinese people are most likely to travel at the age of 40 years.

8.6 Discussion

In Formula (8.12), parameter β is important. In previous literature, β was treated as a Lagrangian parameter, so its geographical meaning is not clear. With the statistical mechanism model developed in this chapter, one can easily find:

$$\beta = \sqrt{\frac{2T}{t_{\max} h^2}} \tag{8.16}$$

Formula (8.14a, 8.14b) shows that the force of a spatial interaction depends on the area of FP h and mean migration time T. In turn, the size of an FP depends on geographical observation. Migration arises from both cities and a city is an FP, since a city as a monolith acts on another city. Migration arises from both villages and a village is an FP, since a village as a monolith acts on another village. Therefore, when we use the state as the observation scale h, the damping factor will be small. This shows that international migration is greater than inter-village migration. The spatial interaction of the parameters for different viewing scales is inconsistent. Formula (8.16) tells us:

1. While discussing spatial interactions, we need to pay more attention to the consistency of places. For example, migration in a community is quite different from the migration between cities. All of the migration factors, especially "h," are divergent.
2. The term "Ť" is a secondary important factor related to spatial interaction. Migration policies and communication conditions determine migration time. Therefore, free migration policies strengthen regional and urban regional advantages.

Acknowledgment The author would like to thank the anonymous reviewers for their suggestions and comments. The author would also like to thank Zhao Zuoquan, Guo Rongxing, and Xue Junbo for their help in revising this paper.

Appendix

For integration

$$G(r) = \int_0^{\infty} \frac{k}{2\pi D\sqrt{t}} \exp\left[-\left(at + \frac{r^2}{2Dt}\right)\right] dt \tag{8.17}$$

$$x = \sqrt{at} \tag{8.18}$$

Let

$$dx = \frac{\sqrt{a}}{2\sqrt{t}} dt \tag{8.19}$$

$$G(r) = \int_{0}^{\infty} \frac{k}{\pi D\sqrt{a}} \exp\left[-\left(x^2 + \frac{r^2 a}{2Dx^2}\right)\right] dx \tag{8.20}$$

$$\int_{0}^{\infty} \exp\left[-\left(x^2 + \frac{b}{x^2}\right) dx\right] = \frac{\exp(-2b)}{2}\sqrt{\pi} \tag{8.21}$$

We have

The second integration is a general integration. Comparing (8.20) with (8.21), we could obtain

$$b = r\sqrt{\frac{a}{2D}} \equiv \beta r \tag{8.22}$$

$$G(r) = \frac{k}{2\sqrt{\pi D^2}} \exp\left(-\sqrt{\frac{2a}{D}}r\right) \tag{8.23}$$

$$or \qquad K = \frac{k}{\delta\sqrt{\pi D^2}} \tag{8.24}$$

So, we obtain Formulas (8.11) and (8.12).

References

Anderson JE (1979) A theoretical foundation for the gravity equation. Am Econ Rev 69:106–116

Caniëls MC, Verspagen B (2001) Barriers to knowledge spillovers, and regional convergence in an evolutionary model. Evol Econ 11:307–329

Ding J (1994) On the level and mechanism of urbanization of population in China. In: Wang Z (ed) Progress in Earth surface system sciences. The Publishing House of Surveying & Mapping, Beijing, pp 94–105. (in Chinese)

Drezner T, Drezner Z (2001) A note on applying the gravity rule to the airline hub problem. J Reg Sci 41(1):67–73

Haynes KE, Fotheringham AS (1984) Gravity and spatial interaction models. SAGE Publication, Beverly Hills
Isard W (1975) Introduction to regional science. Prentice-Hall, Englewood Cliffs
Karlsson C, Andersson M et al (2015) Handbook of research methods and a pplications in economic geography. Edward Elgar, Cheltenham, pp 491–493
Li S (2007) Research on basic theories and geographical computing of tourism destination circles. East China Normal University. Doctoral Dissertation
Liu L (2004) Research on the spatial diffusion of ISO9000 product quality standards in China. China Agricultural University, PhD Dissertation, Beijing
Niamsiri N, Bergkvist M et al (2009) Spatial interaction modelling of cross-region R&D collaborations: empirical evidence from the 5th EU framework program. Pap Reg Sci 88(3):531–546
Roy R, Thill CL (2004) Spatial interaction modelling. Pap Reg Sci 83:339–361
Sen A, Smith TE (1995) Gravity model of spatial interaction behavior. Springer, Berlin/Heidelberg/New York
Smith TE (1987) Poisson gravity model of spatial flows. J Reg Sci 27:315–340
Verspagen B (1992) Endogenous innovation in neoclassical growth models: a survey. J Macroecon 14(4):631–662
Wang Z, Deng F, Yang YY (1991) A Connaction with spatial interaction and diffusion. Geogr Res 1(10):48–55
Wang Z, Ma C, Weng G, Wang Y (2004) A study on temporal and regional process of knowledge spillover. Ann Reg Sci 38:595–606
Wang Z, Ma C, Weng G, Wang Y (2004) A study on temporal and regional process of knowledge spillover. The Annals of Regional Science 38:595–606
Wilson AG (1967) A statistical theory of spatial distribution models. Transp Res 1(3):253–269
Wilson AG (1970) Inter-regional commodity flows: entropy-maximizing approaches. Geogr Anal 2:255–282

Chapter 9
Regional Modeling of Major Projects: What Factors Determine Net Social Benefits?

James A. Giesecke and John R. Madden

Abstract Regional governments frequently seek to attract major projects to promote their region's economic development, often by means of subsidies, publicly provided infrastructure, and environmental clearance. Justification for such measures is routinely provided in economic impact statements indicating the new project will increase regional and national output and employment, which are taken as proxies for economic welfare. Increasingly in Asian and Pacific countries, these impact assessments are made with the aid of computable general equilibrium (CGE) models. With their key characteristics of resource constraints and price responsiveness, CGE models are well equipped for analyzing major projects' economic impacts. Frequently, however, CGE assessments do not report results in economic welfare terms, and simulation design is often ill suited to correctly estimating net social benefits. In this paper, we simulate, under a variety of stylized scenarios, a hypothetical example of a major mining project in the Western Australian region to test whether output measures like GDP and gross regional product are good indicators of economic welfare. We show that key factors in determining gross national disposable income (GNDI), an economic welfare measure, are terms of trade effects, profitability, public concessions and infrastructure, cost of foreign financing, and taxation of foreign-owned returns. However, while GNDI is sensitive to these determinants, GDP is not and thus forms a poor indicator of economic welfare.

Keywords Computable general equilibrium (CGE) · Regional policy · Major projects · Multiregional modeling · Gross national disposable income

JEL D58 · D61 · Q33 · Q38

J. A. Giesecke · J. R. Madden (✉)
Centre of Policy Studies, Victoria University, Melbourne, VIC, Australia
e-mail: james.giesecke@vu.edu.au; john.madden@vu.edu.au

Z. Chen et al. (eds.), *Development Studies in Regional Science*,
New Frontiers in Regional Science: Asian Perspectives 42,
https://doi.org/10.1007/978-981-15-1435-7_9

9.1 Introduction

For many years now, major new projects and events have been frequently accompanied by an economic impact study. The proponents of private projects, particularly in the areas of mining and manufacturing, may be motivated by the need to get environmental or other regulatory clearance, or a desire to support their case for publicly funded infrastructure to accompany the project, or perhaps to bolster their request for some form of assistance. Similarly governments seek favorable research findings that might assist in justifying large public expenditure on infrastructure and other major investments.

Over the past two decades in Australia, economic impact studies have been conducted largely with computable general equilibrium (CGE) models.[1] Frequently, these studies report results mainly in terms of the impacts on real GDP and employment.[2] While, typically, these economic impacts are lower than those produced by unconstrained input-output (IO) models – since CGE results are conditioned by aggregate resource constraints on the economy – it is not unusual for CGE studies to report very large economic impacts.

In the normal course of events, it is to be expected that a profitable project gives rise to an increase in GDP through returns to the newly installed capital. Many CGE studies also allow for a short-term impact on employment that also temporarily adds to GDP. This assumption, however, has been less popular during the last 15 years, a period in which Australian labor markets generally have been tight and in which economists have sought to keep project analysis separate from countercyclical policies.

While a project that will increase a nation's effective capital stock will add to the present value of GDP, it need not have a similar effect on the present value of real consumption. In order to create the new capital, it is necessary that some (public or private) consumption be forgone while the investment occurs (i.e., funding through domestic savings) or that there be an increase in external obligations (i.e., funding out of foreign savings). Recognizing this helps identify the sources of welfare gain from a project. Key factors are the productivity of a project (i.e., private profitability and the degree to which it relies on government inputs such as infrastructure, tax concessions, and the like), the cost of foreign financing, the degree of taxation of foreign-owned profits, and effects on the terms of trade.

In this paper, we concentrate on those factors which relate to the distribution of project returns between domestic and foreign economic agents. We conduct simulations with a dynamic CGE model for a typical (hypothetical) project spanning a

[1]While the use of CGE modeling for economic impact analysis is probably more common in Australia than most other countries, it is in widespread use globally. Some examples of CGE economic impact modeling in other countries in the Asia-Pacific region are Ahmed et al. (2013), Corong et al. (2013), Dixon et al. (2010), Fan (2010), Khan and Gottschalk (2017), and Liu (2006).

[2]There are many examples of CGE economic impact studies which emphasize impacts on GDP and employment. See ACE Group (2011) for one example.

15-year period under 20 different scenarios relating to the degree of foreign ownership, the rate of tax on capital returns, and the rate of a natural resource rent tax.

9.2 The Victoria University Regional Model (VURM)

9.2.1 VURM Overview

VURM is a dynamic multiregional CGE model.[3] When implemented in its full regional detail, it explicitly models the behavior of economic agents within each of Australia's eight states and territories. For this paper, we use a two-region implementation of the model, with the two regions being Western Australia (WA) and the rest of Australia (RoA).[4] The model features detailed sectoral disaggregation, identifying 65 industries and commodities. Neoclassical assumptions govern the behavior of the model's economic agents. Each of the 65 representative industries operating within each of the 2 regions is assumed to minimize costs subject to constant-returns-to-scale production technologies and given input prices. A representative utility-maximizing household resides in each of the model's two regions. Investors allocate new capital to industries on the basis of expected rates of return. Units of new capital are assumed to be a cost-minimizing combination of inputs sourced from each of the model's three sources of supply (the two domestic regions plus imports). Imperfect substitutability between the imported and two domestic sources of supply for each commodity is modeled using the CES assumption of Armington. In general, markets are assumed to clear and to be competitive. Purchasers' prices differ from basic prices by the value of indirect taxes and margin services. Taxes and margins can differ across commodity, user, region of source, and region of destination. Foreign demands for each of the 65 commodities from each of the 2 regions are modeled as inversely related to their foreign currency prices. The model includes details of the taxing, spending, and transfer activities of two levels of government: a regional government operating within each region and a federal government operating Australia-wide. Intergovernmental transfer payments and personal transfer payments to households are also modeled. Dynamic equations describe stock-flow relationships, such as those between regional industry capital stocks and regional industry investment levels. Dynamic adjustment equations allow for the gradual movement of a number of variables toward their long-run values. For example, the national real wage is assumed to be sticky in the short run, adjusting over a period of about 5 years to return the level of national employment to its base

[3]VURM was formerly known as MMRF (see Naqvi and Peter 1996).

[4]Our paper reports results for dozens of simulations undertaken over a lengthy forecasting run. The full eight-state implementation of the model takes a substantial time to run. With no loss of generality to our research findings, significant computational time is saved by implementing a two-region (a region of focus – Western Australia and the rest of Australia) implementation of the model.

case level following an economic shock.[5] Equality of deviations in regional real consumer wages across regions is maintained through labor movements between regions.[6] Regional economic linkages arise from interregional trade, factor mobility, the taxing and spending activities of the federal government, and long-run economy-wide employment and balance of trade constraints. The model also evaluates a full set of national and regional income accounts and associated deflators. The reader is referred to Adams et al. (2015) for a detailed technical description of the model.[7] VURM is solved with the GEMPACK economic modeling software (Harrison and Pearson 1996).

[5]This is equivalent to gradually returning the national unemployment rate to base case (a standard assumption in macro models) with national labor supply remaining on base case throughout the policy simulation. Hence, we implicitly assume that the working age population, the participation rate, and hours worked per worker are all unaffected by the shock. There are some empirical grounds for these assumptions, but they are made chiefly to quarantine our core results from second-order labor market adjustments, some of which would require additional strong policy response assumptions. Regarding the labor supply elasticity (which governs participation and hours per worker), at the level of the aggregate labor market, these are likely to be quite low. For example, Nassios et al. (2019), in their review of labor supply elasticities in CGE models, find support for an estimate around 0.15 at the economy-wide level but note that the value is likely to be lower (or even negative) for male workers and higher for female workers. The version of VURM used in this paper does not distinguish labor market categories at this level, nor do we consider the gender or occupational composition of the workforce of the major project examined herein. A deviation in the working age population would require a national immigration policy response to the major project. In this paper, we wish to isolate the effect of the major project from changes in immigration policy. We do not think a relaxation of these assumptions would change the direction of results reported herein. A positive labor supply elasticity would generate an employment response positively related to both the GDP and real consumption deviations reported herein. The net welfare consequences of the labor supply response would need to account for the value of foregone activities outside the formal labor market. A positive immigration response could further lift real GDP (via additional factor supply) while depressing real consumption per capita (via congestion of fixed factors and damping of the terms of trade (Giesecke 2006).

[6]This is a somewhat strong assumption in the short run, but not one that materially affects our conclusions. For example, Giesecke and Madden (2013) allow for gradual adjustment of regional populations in response to changes in regional per capita living standard relativities and the possibility that these relativities do not fully close in the long run because of differences in regional location preferences. Regional migration dynamics like these, if applied to the case investigated herein, would damp the short-run WA activity responses reported in Charts 9.4 and 9.6 and augment the short-run WA price response reported in Chart 9.5 while having little impact on the long-run deviations reported in these charts. At the level of the national economy, the regional migration assumptions are unlikely to exert a material influence on key macro variables and are thus unlikely to affect any conclusions reached on the basis of the results reported in Charts 9.7, 9.8, 9.9, 9.10, 9.11, and 9.12.

[7]Also, see Giesecke and Madden (2013).

9.2.2 Enhancements to VURM for This Study

We make a number of changes to the standard VURM model to facilitate the simulations reported in this chapter. In particular, we build into the model's theory and database two new nascent or embryonic industries: one representing the *construction activity* associated with the development of the hypothetical resource project and one representing the *operating activity* of the hypothetical resource project.[8] We locate both nascent industries in Western Australia (WA), Australia's most resource-intensive region. The two new industries are characterized by the cost and sales structures of the construction and operating phases of the project. These cost and sales structures are based on the project's financial aggregates as discussed in Sect. 9.2.4, expanded to the model's full commodity and sourcing detail using input cost shares of the WA mining industry, as described in the standard VURM database. As discussed in Sect. 9.2.4, we describe the project via time paths for:

1. Capital expenditure
2. Sales
3. Payments for intermediate inputs and labor
4. Capital returns
5. Natural resource rent tax payments
6. Repatriated foreign capital and interest income

To implement in the model the operations of the project, we require further information on the composition of its inputs and the sales destination of its outputs. On the output side, we assume all sales are destined for the export market, typical of Australian resource development projects. On the operational input side, our thumbnail financial assumptions described in Sect. 9.2.4 allow us to tie down important aggregates such as:

1. The total value of payments for intermediate inputs and labor
2. Total capital payments
3. Natural resource rent tax payments

However, to model the project explicitly in VURM, we must divide the total value of intermediate inputs and labor into:

1. The basic value of intermediate inputs, distinguished by commodity and source
2. The value of margin payments associated with individual source- and commodity-specific intermediate inputs
3. The value of indirect taxes paid on purchases of individual source- and commodity-specific intermediate inputs
4. Payments to labor

To provide this compositional information for the present exercise, we simply use the relevant input shares of the existing VURM WA Iron Ore industry. We divided

[8]See Dixon et al. (1992) for an early application of this method.

capital expenditure into its commodity, source, basic value, margin value, and indirect tax components in the same way, using the input composition of the VURM WA Iron Ore construction activity as a template. With the input-output composition of the project's operations and construction activities thus specified, we introduce these activities to the model's database as very tiny industries. In our simulations, variables determining the levels of the operations and construction activities of these new industries are shocked by amounts sufficient to ensure they follow the time paths specified in Sect. 9.2.4. Shocks reflecting these time paths are implemented in both the base case (no project) simulation and the counterfactual (project) simulation. In the base case (no project) simulation, the embryonic industries are maintained at their initial tiny size. The counterfactual (project) simulation is identical to the base case simulation in all respects; other than that, the hypothetical project is expanded up to its full size via exogenous determination of the project's investment spending and demands for its output by foreigners.

9.2.3 Simulation Design

We model the economy over two time paths over a 19-year period[9]:

1. *Base case scenario.* We run one base case scenario, describing a projection for the national and state economies, compiled on the assumption that the hypothetical resource project does not occur.
2. *Counterfactual scenarios.* We run many project scenarios. These scenarios show the effects of the construction and operating phases of the resource project, under different assumptions relating to:
   (i) The extent of foreign ownership of the project
   (ii) The rate of capital income tax applying to the project
   (iii) The rate of resource rent taxation

We report impacts on a number of national and regional economic variables typical of the type reported in regional economic impact studies. We contrast these with outcomes for aggregate real consumption, the relevant measure of the project's impact on national welfare. All impacts are reported as differences between the values of the variables in the project scenario and their values in the base case scenario.

[9]That is, for the 15 years of the project, plus a 4-year post-project adjustment period.

9.2.4 Other Assumptions

9.2.4.1 Specification of the Hypothetical Project

We describe the hypothetical project by specifying:

$SALES_n$	The value of project sales in year n. We assume all project output is exported.
$INTRM_n$	The value of intermediate commodities used as an input to project operations in year n.
$LABOR_n$	The value of the project's total wage bill in year n.
INV_n	Project investment in year n.
$CAPTAX$	The effective corporate tax rate applying to the project.
$NRRTAX$	The effective natural resource rent tax rate applying to the project.
$FINSHR_{Debt}$	The share of debt in the project's total financing cost.
r_{Debt}	Cost of foreign debt finance to the project.
$OWNSHR_{Foreign}$	The share of the enterprise that is beneficially foreign-owned.
$FINSHR_{Equity}$	The share of equity in the project's total financing cost (1 – $FINSHR_{Debt}$).
$OWNSHR_{Domestic}$	Share of the enterprise that is beneficially domestically owned (1 – $OWNSHR_{Foreign}$).

Given our assumptions for the values of the above, we can determine the hypothetical project's gross operating surplus (GOS_n) and pretax accounting profit ($PROFIT_n$) as follows:

$$GOS_n = SALES_n(1 - NRRTAX) - INTRM_n - LABOR_n \tag{9.1}$$

$$PROFIT_n = GOS_n - \left[\sum_{t=1\ldots n} INV_t\right] \times FINSHR_{Debt} \times r_{Debt} \tag{9.2}$$

For our simulations, we must specify values for INV_n, $SALES_n$, $INTRM_n$, $LABOR_n$, $FINSHR_{Debt}$, r_{Debt}, $CAPTAX$, $NRRTAX$, and $OWNSHR_{Foreign}$. Our assumptions for these values are outlined below.

(A) The project is constructed over 3 years. Annual investment is \$1605 m. That is, $INV_t = 1605$ for $t =$ years 1–3 inclusive.
(B) The project commences operations in year 4 and ceases operations after 12 years (year 15). Annual sales, all of which are exported, are \$3000 m. That is, $SALES_n = 3000$ for t = years 4–15 inclusive.
(C) The annual value of intermediate inputs is \$1125 m. That is, $INTRM_n = 1125$ for $t =$ years 4–15 inclusive.
(D) The annual wage bill is \$225 m. That is, $LABOR_n = 225$ for $t =$ years 4–15 inclusive.

(E) The debt/equity ratio is 1. That is, $FINSHR_{Debt} = FINSHR_{Equity} = 0.50$.

(F) The cost of debt finance for the project is 8%. That is, $r_{Debt} = 0.08$.

In all simulations, assumptions (A) to (F) are unchanged. With assumptions (A) to (D) in place, the project generates a pretax internal rate of return (IRR) of 25 percent, a typical hurdle rate for Australian natural resource extraction projects.

Our paper investigates the effects of varying assumptions (G) to (I):

(G) We vary the project-specific effective capital tax rate, *CAPTAX*, between 0.30 and 0. For values of *CAPTAX* below 0.30 (the full corporate income tax rate for Australia), we are investigating the effects of project-specific corporate tax concessions or effective corporate tax minimization activities by the project owners.

(H) We vary the project-specific effective natural resource rent tax, *NRRTAX*, between 0.05 and −0.05. For values of NRRTAX below 0, we are investigating the effects of subsidizing the project.

(I) We vary the share of the project's equity that is foreign-owned, $OWNSHR_{Foreign}$, between 1 and 0.

9.2.4.2 Private and Public Consumption

In both the base case and project scenarios, we assume that national consumption (private plus public) is a fixed proportion of gross national disposable income (GNDI). Hence, at the national level, the percentage deviation in real consumption (private plus public) is equal to the percentage deviation in real (consumption price deflated) GNDI. In calculating GNDI, we are careful to explicitly account for project-related financing costs. In particular, we must calculate the amount of project income that is repatriated in each year of the base case and project scenarios. To do this, we must understand how the nation (not simply the project owner) finances project-related construction spending. Equation (9.3) summarizes our project financing assumptions.

$$\begin{aligned} REPAT_n = & \left[\sum_{t=1\ldots n} INV_t\right] \times FINSHR_{Debt} \times r_{Debt} + \\ & PROFIT_n \times (1 - CAPTAX) \times OWNSHR_{Foreign} + \\ & \left[\sum_{t=1\ldots n} INV_t\right] \times \left(FINSHR_{Equity}\right) \times OWNSHR_{Domestic} \times r_{For} \end{aligned} \tag{9.3}$$

where:

$REPAT_n$ is project-related net primary factor payments to non-residents in year n.

r_{For} is the foregone rate of return/cost of foreign capital faced by domestic owners of the project.

In specifying r_{For}, we assume $r_{Debt} = r_{For} = 8\%$.[10]

Equation (9.3) recognizes that project-related repatriation of primary factor income is comprised of three parts. The first term on the right-hand side of Eq. (9.3) relates to the cost of debt financing. So that we need not adjust the base case or project consumption paths to reflect changes in the holding of project debt by domestic agents, we assume that all of the debt financing is ultimately raised offshore. Hence, interest payments on the debt component of the project's financing costs are repatriated. The second and third terms capture the cost of equity finance. The second term captures repatriation of the foreign-owned share of project-related posttax profits. The third term measures the opportunity cost to domestic shareholders of project-related financing from retained profits. We assume that domestic shareholders forego a foreign rate of return of 8% on the earnings that are retained by the project for investment financing. Alternatively, the third term can be interpreted as the foreign cost of capital to domestic shareholders, under a scenario in which the project finances the equity component of its project-related capital costs via expansion of issued shares, with such shares acquired by domestic and foreign agents in proportion to the initial domestic/foreign ownership ratio.

With aggregate national consumption spending a fixed proportion of GNDI, our final task is to determine the split between private and public consumption. In *each region*, we assume that the ratio of real regional public consumption spending to real regional private consumption spending, in each year of the project scenario, follows its base case path. At the *national level*, we assume that the ratio of real federal public consumption spending to real national private consumption spending, in each year of the project scenario, follows its base case path. With private and public consumption spending thus moving in fixed proportions, the welfare consequences of the project are calculated as the sum of the deviations in private and public consumption spending.

9.2.4.3 Labor Markets

At the national level, we hold economy-wide employment fixed at its base case level in each year of the project scenario. This labor market closure can be interpreted in one of two ways. First, it can be interpreted as reflecting a situation of full employment.[11] Second, it can be interpreted as a situation in which government has engaged

[10]In distinguishing r_{debt} and r_{for}, we anticipate scenarios in which rates of return on investment opportunities available to domestic shareholders and the cost of foreign debt to the firm may differ.

[11]During the decade to 2015, which contained the peak of the most recent Australian mining boom, Australia's unemployment rate averaged 5.2% and was as low as 4.5% for a substantial period (3 years, 2006–2008). In 2018, the national unemployment rate remains low, falling to 5.1% in October. With unemployment at such low levels, peak industry lobby groups made frequent claims of "skill shortages" and gave strong support to the expansion of Australia's skilled migrant intake. In VURM, this situation of full or near-full employment is modeled by the closure assumption described in Sect. 9.2.4.3.

employment-promoting policy levers, independent of the particular investment project under evaluation, to target full employment.

At the regional level, we assume labor is free to move between state economies. Labor moves between regions so as to maintain initial interstate wage differentials.

9.2.4.4 Rates of Return on Capital

In deviation simulations, VURM allows for short-run divergences in rates of return on industry capital stocks from their levels in the base case forecasts. Such movements in rates of return cause divergences, from base case values, in investment and capital stocks. The divergences in capital stocks gradually erode the divergences in rates of return.

9.2.4.5 Production Technologies

VURM contains many types of technical change variables. In the project scenario, we assume that all technology variables follow their base case scenario values.

9.3 Results

9.3.1 National and Regional Impacts: Central Case Scenario

We begin by reporting results for a Central Case in which:

(i) The capital tax rate is 30% ($CAPTAX = 0.30$).
(ii) The natural resource rent tax is 5% ($NRRTAX = 0.05$).
(iii) The project's capital is owned equally by foreign and domestic agents ($OWNSHR_{Foreign} = OWNSHR_{Domestic} = 0.50$).

Key regional and national macroeconomic results are reported in Charts 9.1, 9.2, 9.3, 9.4, 9.5, and 9.6. We begin by considering the project construction (or investment) phase – years 1–3 inclusive. For these initial years of the simulation period, the national real investment deviation is positive (Chart 9.2), reflecting project-specific investment spending. Real GDP is largely unaffected by the construction phase (Chart 9.1). As discussed in Sect. 9.2.4.3, in every year of the project simulation, we hold employment at its base case level. With employment unchanged, and capital stocks adjusting slowly, there is little scope for the project investment phase to positively affect real GDP. Indeed, in Chart 9.1, we see that the investment phase causes a slight negative deviation in real GDP. This is due to crowding out of capital-intensive industries. In particular, with real GDP largely unchanged from base case during the project construction phase, project-related investment spending must move the real balance of trade toward deficit. In Chart 9.2,

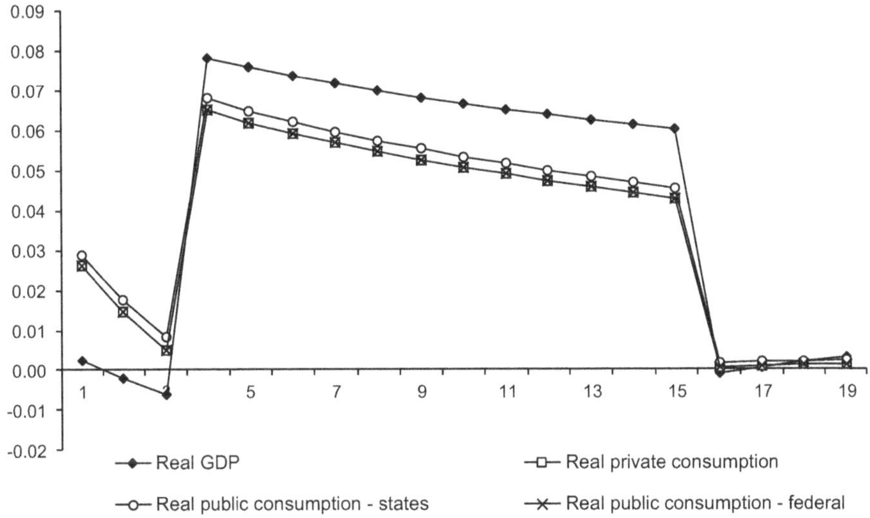

Chart 9.1 Real GDP and real consumption (% deviation from base case scenario)

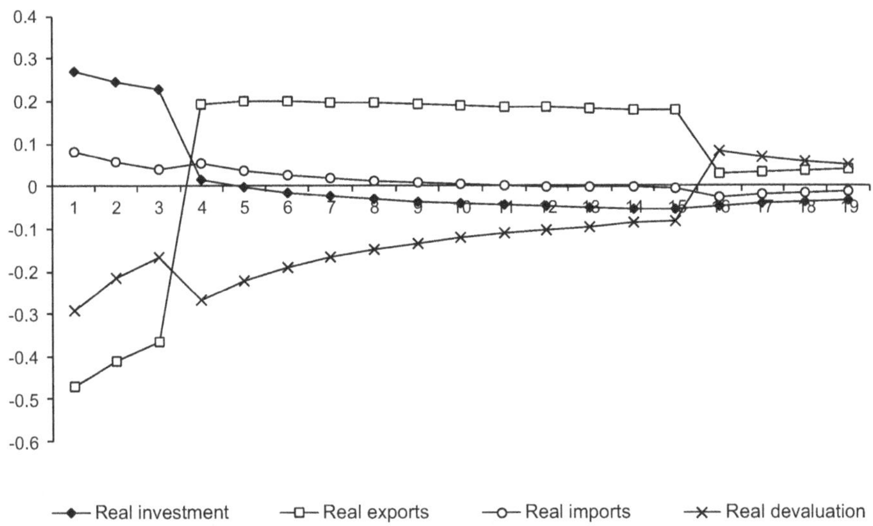

Chart 9.2 Real investment, balance of trade, and the exchange rate (% deviation from base case scenario)

this is manifested as a negative export deviation and positive import deviation over the first 3 years of the simulation. This movement toward trade deficit requires the real exchange rate to appreciate (Chart 9.2). The resulting crowding out of capital-intensive trade-exposed industries accounts for the small negative real GDP deviation in the second and third years of the project construction phase (Chart 9.1).

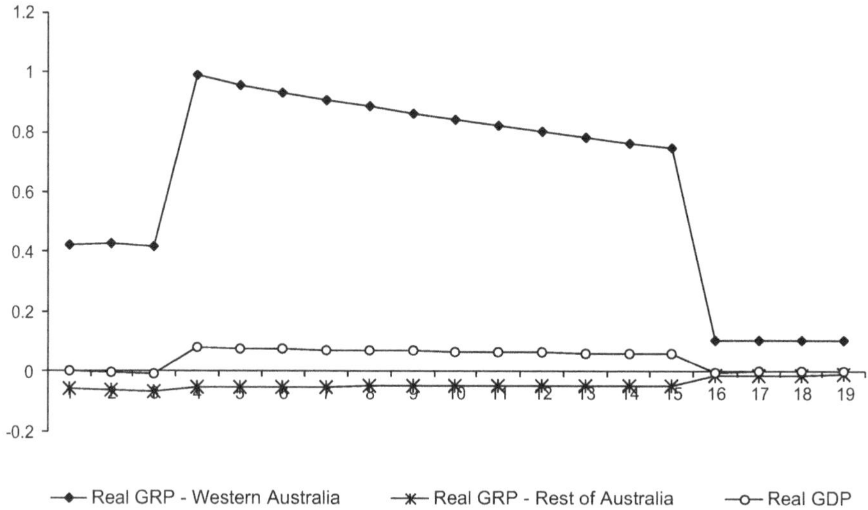

Chart 9.3 Real GDP: Australia, Western Australia, and the rest of Australia (% deviation from base case scenario)

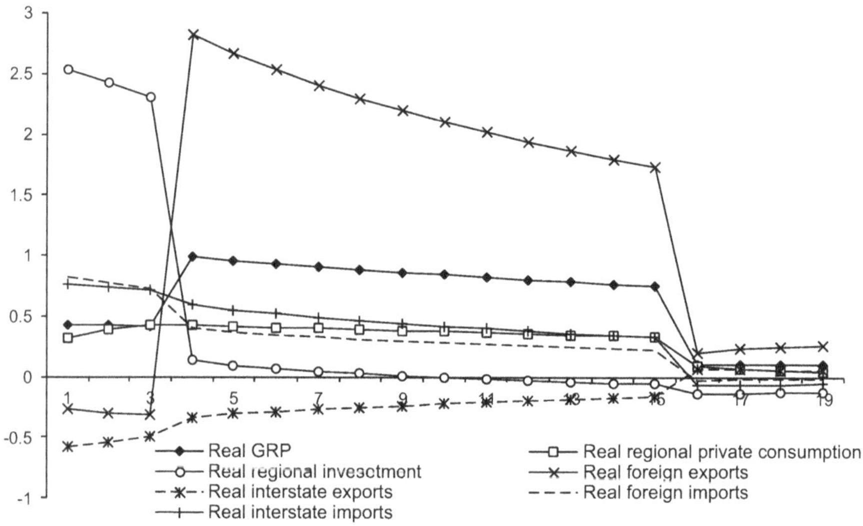

Chart 9.4 Western Australian macroeconomic outcomes (% deviation from base case scenario)

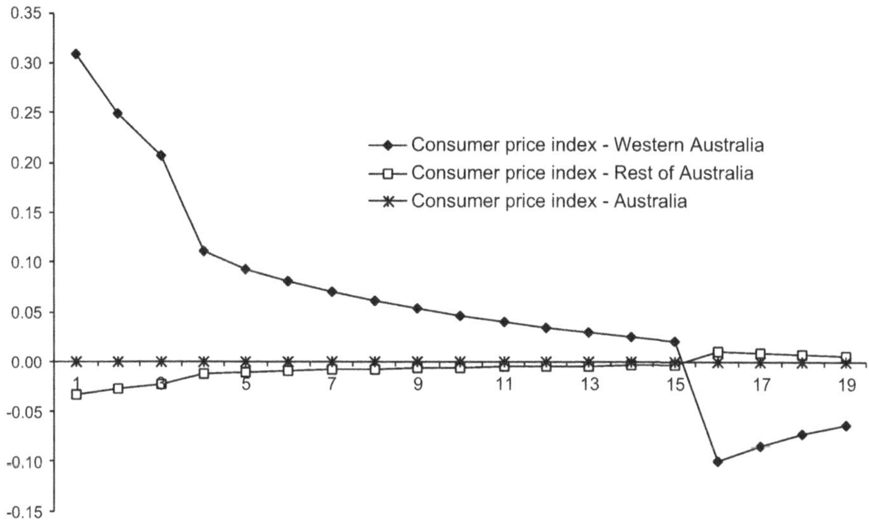

Chart 9.5 Relative consumer prices: Western Australia, the rest of Australia, and Australia (% deviation from base case scenario)

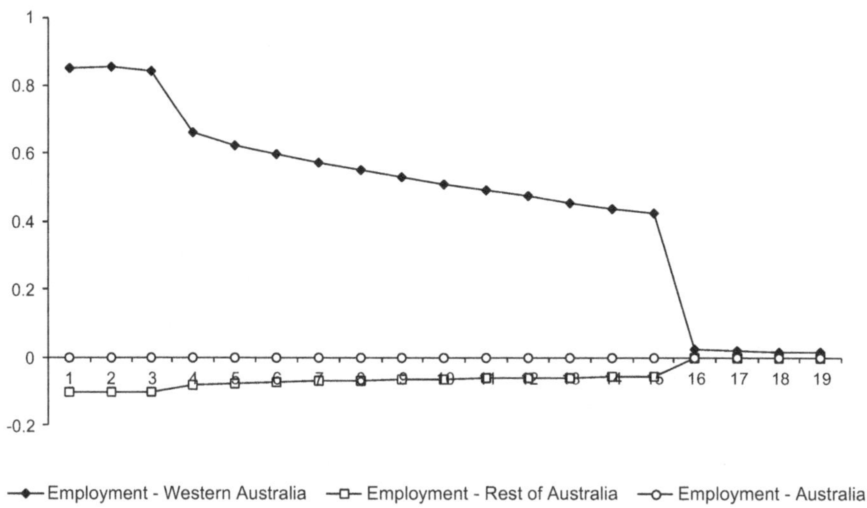

Chart 9.6 Employment: Western Australia, the rest of Australia, and Australia (% deviation from base case scenario)

The negative export deviation during the project's construction phase causes the terms of trade to improve.[12] The positive terms of trade deviation allows the deviation in real (consumption price deflated) gross national disposable income (GNDI) to exceed the deviation in real GDP. Since we assume that consumption (private and public) is a fixed share of GNDI, the consumption deviation exceeds the GDP deviation over years 1–3 (Chart 9.1).

As we have seen, the project investment phase has little impact on national real GDP. However, it does alter the national distribution of final demand and primary factors across regions. As such, project investment can have a substantial impact on indicators of economic activity in the host region. In Chart 9.4, we see project-specific investment causes a sharp positive deviation in WA real investment over years 1–3. This accounts for the positive deviation in WA employment over this period (Chart 9.6). Since national employment follows its base case path throughout the project simulation (see Sect. 9.2.4.3 above), WA's employment gain must be RoA's employment loss (Chart 9.6). This accounts for the decline in real GDP in RoA (Chart 9.3). The positive deviation in WA investment places positive demand pressure on fixed factors (land) and sticky factors (capital) in the region. By driving up the short-run rental prices of these factors, this demand pressure causes prices in WA to rise relative to those in the RoA (Chart 9.5). The positive deviation in relative WA prices accounts for the negative deviations in WA interstate and foreign exports (Chart 9.4). Together with the increase in investment activity in WA, the rise in relative WA prices also explains part of the positive deviation in interstate and foreign imports into WA (Chart 9.4). The short-run increase in the rental price of WA capital is gradually attenuated by a rise in WA capital supply. This accounts for the deviation in their regional CPI commencing to decline steadily after the first year of the simulation period (Chart 9.5).

Project operations commence in year 4 and continue to year 15. The project's gross operating surplus and natural resource rent tax fully account for the positive real GDP deviation (Chart 9.1). As discussed in Sect. 9.2.4.2, we allow consumption spending to be a fixed proportion of GNDI. Our GNDI calculation takes explicit account of repatriation of foreign profits and interest payments. In the Central Case, just under half ($747 m.) of the project's capital returns (GOS plus NRRT = 1650) are repatriated to foreign suppliers of capital. The remainder is available for domestic consumption. Since only part of the real GDP gain is available for domestic consumption, the real consumption deviation during the project operating phase must lie below the real GDP deviation (Chart 9.1). This causes the real balance of trade to move toward surplus (Chart 9.2). Despite the movement toward surplus in the balance of trade, the deviation in the real devaluation index remains negative, reflecting real appreciation (Chart 9.2). We assume that all of the project's output is

[12]As discussed in Sect. 9.2.1, foreign demands for each region-specific commodity are modeled as inversely related to their foreign currency price via constant elasticity export demand functions. Hence, contraction in export volumes must be associated with a rise in foreign currency export prices, that is, a terms of trade gain in the absence of countervailing import price movements.

exported. The project's exports alone are more than sufficient to generate the movement toward surplus implied by the gap between consumption and GDP in Chart 9.1. Hence, real appreciation is required to crowd-out activity in other traded goods industries. Since these industries tend to be capital-intensive, the negative deviations in activity in these industries account for the negative deviation in national investment during the project operating phase (Chart 9.2).

The sizeable deviation in WA's real gross regional product (GRP) (Chart 9.3) simply reflects the physical location of the project in this region. The expansion in WA's real GRP requires labor to move from the rest of Australia (Chart 9.6). This accounts for the contraction in real GRP in the rest of Australia (Chart 9.3). The expansion in WA's economic activity places demand pressure on fixed and sticky factors (land and capital, respectively). For land, this results in an increase in rental prices that lasts the duration of the project's operating phase. For capital, it causes a short-run increase in capital rental prices, but a long-run increase in capital supply. This accounts for the positive but declining deviation in WA prices during the project's operating phase (Chart 9.5). The rise in relative WA prices places pressure on trade-exposed sectors in WA. This accounts for the negative deviation in WA interstate exports (Chart 9.4). Together with the expansion in WA economic activity, it also accounts for the positive deviations in WA interstate and foreign imports (Chart 9.4). The negative deviation in WA prices following the cessation of project operations reflects excess capacity (Chart 9.5). The positive deviation in WA real GRP over year 4 to year 15 induces capital supply into WA sectors only indirectly related to the project. For example, capacity slowly expands in sectors supplying consumption goods to the additional workers in WA. With the cessation of project operations in year 16, capital is in excess supply in WA, requiring WA capital rental prices to fall. This causes the WA price level to fall (Chart 9.5). It also accounts for the negative deviation in real WA investment in the last years of the simulation period (Chart 9.4). The magnitude of the negative WA price deviation declines over time as investors gradually adjust the WA capital stock to the new lower level required following cessation of project operations.

9.3.2 Economic Impact Versus Welfare Under Alternative Ownership and Tax Assumptions

We undertake 20 variations on the Central Case discussed in Sect. 9.3.1. Our aim is to show that variations in tax and ownership assumptions have little effect on the "economic impact" of the project, as traditionally measured by real GDP and real GRP deviations, but do have a substantial effect on our welfare measure, real national consumption. We argue that policy-makers focused on economic impact as a measure of project benefit may risk overproviding public support to certain projects. This risk is magnified when project proponents use activity-based economic impact measures (such as GDP and GRP) to argue for concessional tax rates and subsidized infrastructure provision.

Recall that under the Central Case, discussed in detail in Sect. 9.3.1, we assumed $CAPTAX = 0.30$, $OWNSHR_{Foreign} = 0.50$, and $NRRTAX = 0.05$. In this section, we discuss real GDP and real consumption results under 20 combinations of values for *CAPTAX*, $OWNSHR_{Foreign}$, and *NRRTAX*. We group these into four sets of five simulations each:

Set I: 5 simulations in which we set $OWNSHR_{Foreign}$ alternatively at 0, 0.25, 0.50, 0.75, and 1.00, with $CAPTAX = 0.30$ and $NRRTAX = 0.05$

Set II: 5 simulations in which we set $OWNSHR_{Foreign}$ alternatively at 0, 0.25, 0.50, 0.75, and 1.00, with $CAPTAX = 0.15$ and $NRRTAX = 0.05$

Set III: 5 simulations in which we set $OWNSHR_{Foreign}$ alternatively at 0, 0.25, 0.50, 0.75, and 1.00, with $CAPTAX = 0.00$ and $NRRTAX = 0.05$

Set IV: 5 simulations in which we set *NRRTAX* alternatively at 0.05, 0.025, 0.00, −0.025, and −0.050, with $CAPTAX = 0.00$ and $OWNSHR_{Foreign} = 1.00$

Chart 9.7 reports the percentage deviations in real GDP under these 20 combinations of $OWNSHR_{Foreign}$, *CAPTAX*, and *NRRTAX* outlined above. It is clear from Chart 9.7 that the real GDP deviation is insensitive to changes in these parameters. However, the national real consumption deviation is very sensitive to changes in $OWNSHR_{Foreign}$, *CAPTAX*, and *NRRTAX*, because these parameters determine the distribution of project capital returns between domestic and foreign agents. We explore real consumption effects below.

Chart 9.8 reports deviations in national real aggregate consumption ($m.) under the Central Case assumptions relating to *CAPTAX* and *NRRTAX*, but with $OWNSHR_{Foreign}$ ranging over five values from 0 to 1. Higher values for

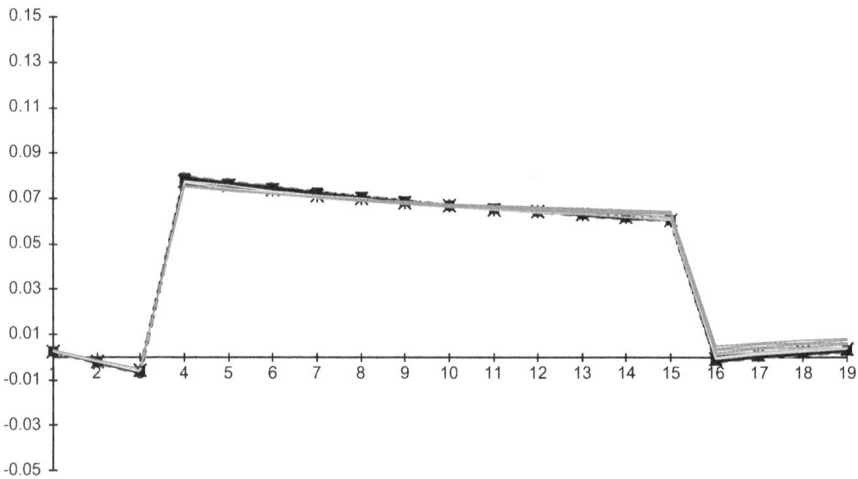

Chart 9.7 Real GDP under 20 variations in ownership share, capital tax, and resource rent tax (% deviation from base case)

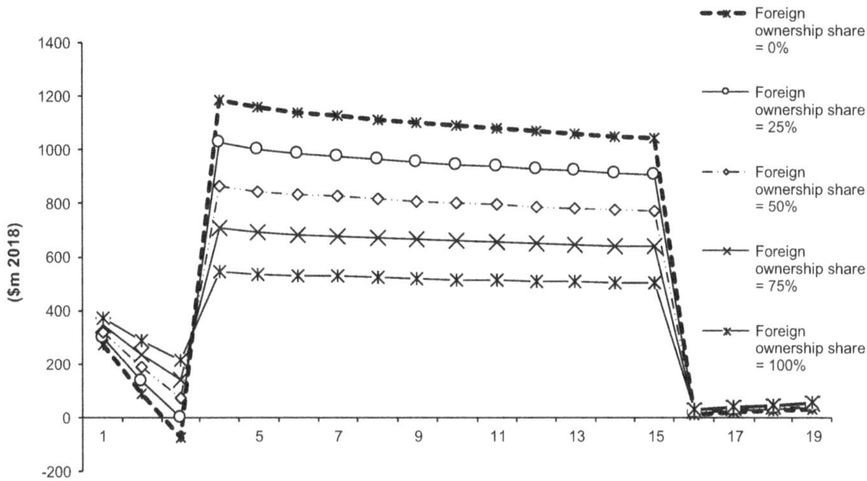

Chart 9.8 Real consumption deviations ($m.) under alternative ownership shares (CAPTAX = 0.3, NRRT = 0.05)

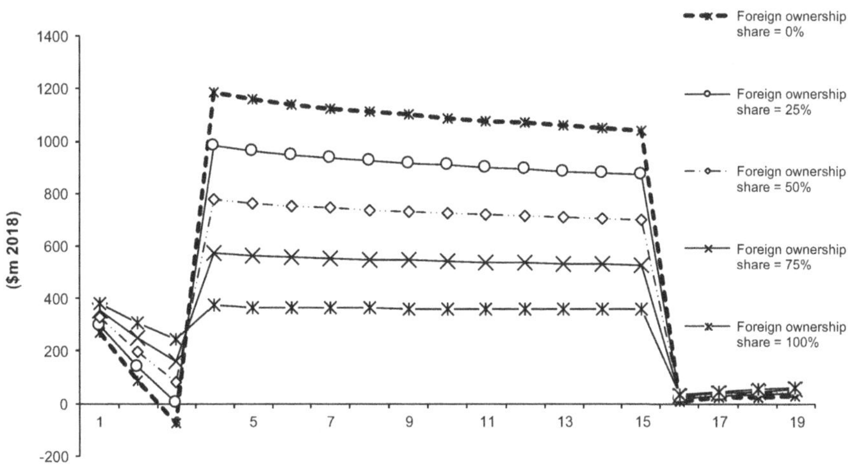

Chart 9.9 Real consumption deviations ($m.) under alternative ownership shares (CAPTAX = 0.15, NRRT = 0.05)

$OWNSHR_{Foreign}$ are associated with lower real consumption deviations. The cause is clear from Eq. (9.3): with $OWNSHR_{Foreign}$ higher, so too is $REPAT_n$. As discussed in Sect. 9.2.4.2, we assume that consumption is a fixed share of GNDI. By definition, GNDI is calculated net of $REPAT_n$.

However, foreign owners of the project can repatriate only posttax profits. From Eq. (9.3), it is clear that, ceteris paribus, lower values for *CAPTAX* will be associated

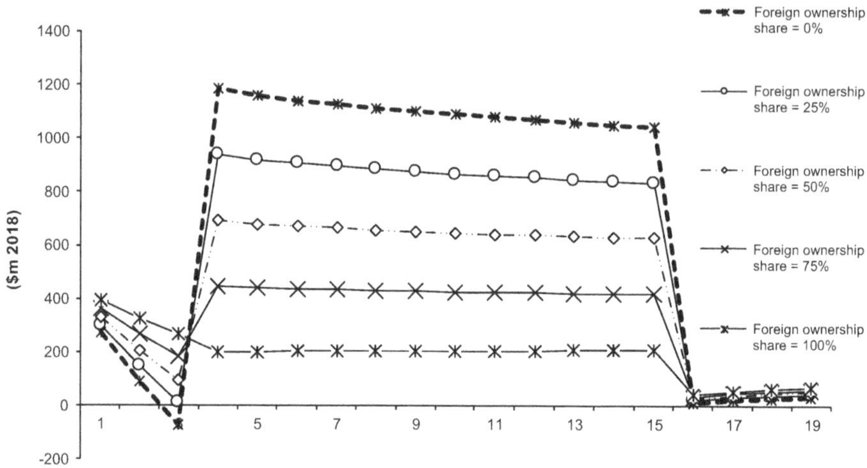

Chart 9.10 Real consumption deviations ($m.) under alternative ownership shares (CAPTAX = 0.00, NRRT = 0.05)

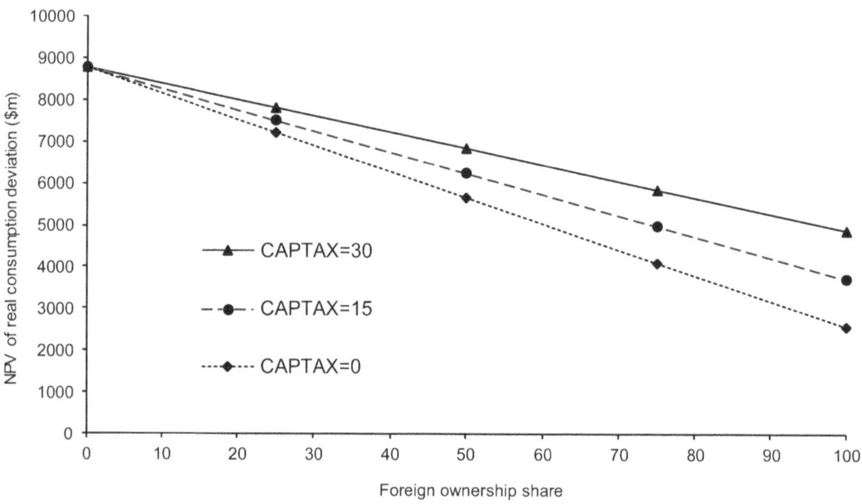

Chart 9.11 NPV of real consumption deviations ($m) under alternative CAPTAX and OWNSHR values

with higher values for $REPAT_n$. Hence, given that domestic consumption is out of GNDI, lower values for *CAPTAX* will be associated with lower real consumption deviations. Charts 9.9 and 9.10 report real consumption deviations for the simulations defined by Sets II and III above – that is – project-specific *CAPTAX* at 15% and 0%, respectively, under alternative values for $OWNSHR_{Foreign}$.

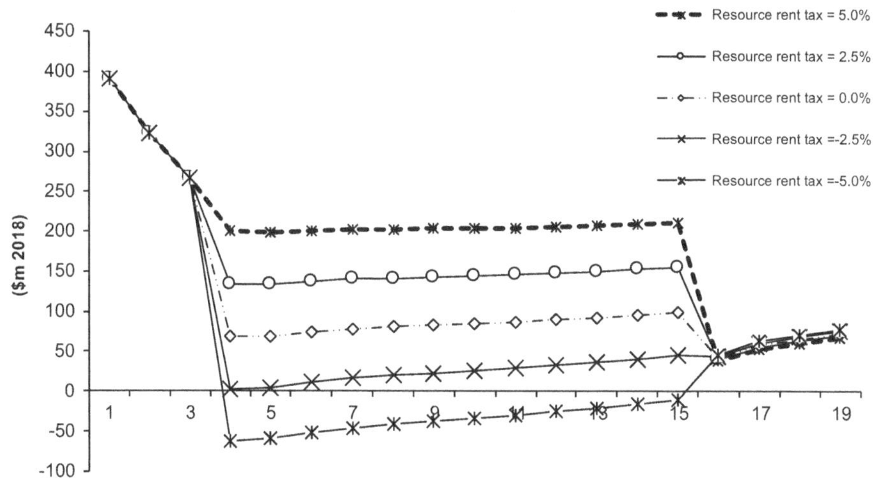

Chart 9.12 Real consumption deviations ($m.) under alternative resource rent taxes (CAPTAX = 0.00, $\text{OWNSHR}_{\text{Foreign}} = 1$)

The relationship between domestic real consumption and alternative values for $OWNSHR_{Foreign}$ and $CAPTAX$ is made clearer by Chart 9.11. Together, Charts 9.8, 9.9, and 9.10 report real consumption deviations for 15 combinations of $OWNSHR_{Foreign}$ and $CAPTAX$ with $NRRTAX$ held fixed at 0.05. Chart 9.11 plots the net present value[13] of these 15 real consumption deviations, linking observations of given values for *CAPTAX*. Chart 11 makes clear that the capital tax rate is irrelevant to the national welfare calculation where the project is entirely domestically owned. Under complete domestic ownership, *CAPTAX* merely determines the allocation of the project's surplus between domestic household and government sectors, leaving GNDI unaffected.

Our fourth set of simulations investigates scenarios in which substantial tax concessions are offered to the new project. In simulation Set IV, we assume that $OWNSHR_{Foreign} = 1$ and $CAPTAX = 0$ and investigate the effects of progressively lowering the natural resource rent tax, from its typical value of 5% down to a production subsidy of 5%. Chart 9.12 reports real consumption deviations under alternative values for *NRRTAX*. Even with the resource rent tax at 0, and no company tax collected from the project, a small welfare gain remains under 100% foreign ownership. This reflects real consumption gains from the positive deviation in the terms of trade. The real consumption deviation is negative under a 5% production subsidy and no capital taxation. In reality, provision of a direct production subsidy is unlikely. However, public provision of what is essentially private infrastructure is common. In particular, major projects often come with private demands for

[13]The 15 sets of flows are in constant dollars. In calculating the NPV values plotted in Chart 9.11, we discount these flows at a real rate of 5%.

substantial tax-funded investment in infrastructure that would not be required if the project did not proceed. In terms of the project's private (post*NRRTAX*) IRR, our 5% production subsidy is equivalent to public financing of 17% of the project's initial physical capital requirements.

9.4 Conclusions

It is customary for economic modeling studies of major projects to report their results in terms of economic impacts on output and employment. GDP results are often headlined as though this variable is a good indicator of the economic benefits of a project. In this paper, we demonstrate that the GDP impact serves as a poor proxy for the effect on economic welfare. We undertake a wide range of scenarios which demonstrate that while the real GDP deviation hardly varies for changes in tax and ownership assumptions, these assumptions have a substantial effect on the economic welfare results.

We thus conclude that CGE modelers should pay less attention in reporting their results on the economic impacts of a project and focus their attention more on the consequences of the particular project for economic welfare. Only then will their results form a proper basis for assessing the benefits that individual projects might bring.

References

Adams, PD, Dixon JM, Horridge JM (2015) The Victoria regional model (VURM): technical documentation, version 1.0, CoPS working paper number G-254. Centre of Policy Studies, Victoria University, Melbourne

AEC Group (2011) Economic impact assessment: Surat gas project, final report. Report prepared for Arrow Energy Pty Ltd and Coffey Environments Australia Pty Ltd, August. (Downloaded from: https://www.arrowenergy.com.au/data/assets/pdf_file/0006/28734/Appendix20020-20Economic20Assessment.pdf on 16 December 2018)

Ahmed V, Abbas A, Ahmed S (2013) Public infrastructure and economic growth in Pakistan: a dynamic CGE-microsimulation analysis. In: Cockburn J, Dissou Y, Duclos JY, Tiberti L (eds) Infrastructure and economic growth in Asia. Springer, Dordrecht

Corong E, Dacuycuy L, Reyes R, Taningco A (2013) The growth and distributive impacts of public infrastructure investments in the Philippines. In: Cockburn J, Dissou Y, Duclos JY, Tiberti L (eds) Infrastructure and economic growth in Asia. Springer, Dordrecht

Dixon PB, Horrdge M, Johnson DT (1992) A general equilibrium analysis of a major project: the multifunction polis. Aust Econ Pap 31(59):272–290

Dixon PB, Kauzi G, Rimmer MT (2010) Effects on the PNG economy of a major LNG project. Econ Rec 29:143–155

Fan Z (2010) The benefits of regional infrastructure investment in Asia: a quantitative exploration. ADBI working paper no. 223. Asian Development Bank Institute (ADBI), Tokyo

Giesecke JA (2006) The economic impact of a general increase in skilled immigration. People Place 14(3):48–63

Giesecke JA, Madden JR (2013) Regional computable general equilibrium modeling. In: Dixon PB, Jorgenson DW (eds) Handbook of computable general equilibrium modeling. Elsevier, Amsterdam, pp 379–475

Harrison WJ, Pearson KR (1996) Computing solutions for large general equilibrium models using GEMPACK. Comput Econ 9:83–127

Khan S, Gottschalk T (2017) Investigating the transmission channels behind Dutch disease effects: lessons from Mongolia using a CGE model. The World Bank, policy research working series: 8183

Liu CC (2006) A computable general equilibrium model of the southern region of Taiwan: the impact of the Tainan science-based industrial park. Appl Econ 38:1655–1661

Naqvi F, Peter MW (1996) A multi-regional multi-sectoral model of the Australian economy with an illustrative application. Aust Econ Pap 35(66):94–113

Nassios J, Madden J, Giesecke J, Dixon J, Tran N, Dixon P, Rimmer M, Adams P, Freebairn J (2019) The economic impact and efficiency of state and federal taxes in Australia. Centre of policy studies working paper no. G-289. Victoria University, Melbourne, April 2019

Part II
Asian Perspective

Chapter 10
Environmental Equity and Nuclear Waste Repository Siting in East Asia

Barry D. Solomon and Fei Li

Abstract Research by Kingsley Haynes and colleagues has emphasized the importance of spatial scale in the analysis of environmental (in)equity in the patterns of toxic chemical releases vs. residential location, especially at county and census tract levels. Earlier work has explored the use of multiple-criteria decision tools in siting electric power plants and waste disposal repositories, where technical, geologic, political, and socioeconomic criteria and standards operate at county and higher spatial scales. For these problems, appropriate consideration of environmental equity will be different than when operating at solely the county and census tract scale. The nuclear waste problem in particular takes on regional dimensions and raises vexing questions of intergenerational as well as intragenerational environmental equity when a decision process for repository siting is developed. In this chapter, these issues will be explored in the context of nuclear waste repository siting, for both high-level and low-level wastes, and potential population exposure to long-lived radioactive wastes. Four case studies in East Asia will be presented: Japan, South Korea, China, and Taiwan. Three equity principles are applied to the case studies: voluntary assumption of a harm or burden, risk avoidance and risk reduction, and benefit-burden concordance. None of the cases meet all of the principles, while only Japan meets two of them. Thus, governments in all of the cases have more work to do to establish equitable programs for nuclear waste repository siting.

Keywords Environmental equity · High-level radioactive waste · Low-level radioactive waste · Repository siting · Wicked problem

B. D. Solomon (✉)
Department of Social Sciences, Michigan Technological University, Houghton, MI, USA
e-mail: bdsolomo@mtu.edu

F. Li
CDP China, Beijing, China

Z. Chen et al. (eds.), *Development Studies in Regional Science*,
New Frontiers in Regional Science: Asian Perspectives 42,
https://doi.org/10.1007/978-981-15-1435-7_10

10.1 Introduction

Since the mid-1990s, research by Kingsley Haynes and his colleagues has emphasized the importance of spatial scale in the analysis of environmental equity in the patterns of toxic chemical releases vs. residential location, especially at the county and census tract level. Indirectly related, earlier work of his has explored the use of multiple-criteria decision tools in siting electric power plants and waste disposal repositories, where technical, geologic, political, and socioeconomic criteria and standards are considered. However, the appropriate consideration of environmental equity may be different at different spatial scales. The nuclear waste problem in particular takes on dimensions of intergenerational equity as well as intragenerational and interregional equity and raises vexing questions when a decision process for repository siting is developed. In this chapter, these issues will be explored in the context of nuclear waste repository siting and potential population exposure to long-lived radioactive wastes (hereafter, we will use the terms nuclear waste and radioactive waste interchangeably) in four case studies in East Asia: Japan, South Korea, China, and Taiwan. These four states account for over 90% of the nuclear power capacity in Asia. While not developing a new model, the chapter will review traditional approaches to nuclear waste repository siting and apply the conceptual framework to environmental equity in the context of the case studies.

There is a large literature on environmental equity and environmental justice, and the contribution of Haynes and his colleagues has been influential in addressing spatial issues. The intent of most of these studies is to determine whether the siting or location of toxic waste sources, landfills, electric power plants, and other noxious facilities is "just," "right," or "fair" with respect to the residential location of racial or ethnic minorities or low-income people (Bullard 1983, 1990; Cutter 1995). These definitions and analyses vary depending on the region, nation, or environmental hazard or technology under consideration. The traditional rationale for such studies has been that minorities or low-income people (or both) may be disproportionately exposed to environmental harms or have inadequate access to environmental benefits. At the extreme some have argued that environmental racism exists, which in environmental law and policy refers to racial discrimination against people or the targeting of communities by race or color, in the siting of noxious facilities (Bullard 1993; Pulido 2000; Cole and Foster 2001). Bowen et al. (1995) used US Toxic Release Inventory (TRI) data to analyze environmental equity with respect to industrial emissions in Ohio and Cuyahoga County (including at the census tract level). The authors examined the spatial coincidence between residential locations and the relevant industrial facilities. While they found strong correlations at the state level between minority populations and toxic releases, these associations did not hold at the coarse, county level of analysis. However, they found some evidence of income discrimination at the metropolitan-area census tract level, though not based on minority group. Follow-up work on the Cuyahoga County case by Haynes et al. (2001) examined methodological issues raised by such studies, using geographic information systems (GIS) and spatial analyses to correct for biases and inconsistencies among spatially dependent results.

More than a decade before Haynes began working on environmental equity, one of us collaborated with him on power plant siting research (e.g., Solomon et al. 1980; Solomon and Haynes 1984). This research focused on multiobjective programming and the siting of large-scale nuclear and coal-fired power plants, which emit substantial water and or air pollution among other environmental externalities. At the time, two research methods were popular for addressing the energy facility siting problem: a siting criteria matrix, based on a site suitability score for potential county locations based on their compatibility indexes and importance weights for a series of variables (e.g., Dobson 1979), and multiobjective location analyses (e.g., Cohon et al. 1980). Typical siting attributes or variables and constraints included population density, water availability, air pollution and other ecological impacts (e.g., seismicity, flood hazard, presence of endangered species), socioeconomic impacts, transmission distance, energy resource supply and demand, and construction and operating costs. Solomon et al. (1980) added a hierarchical screening step to the classic multiobjective programming model. While population density and proximity to a technological hazard is one dimension of environmental equity, it is largely a safety concern. Moreover, as we will argue below, these classic models and procedures omit other important aspects of environmental equity.

After being a highly touted energy option for developed countries in the 1960s and 1970s, nuclear power has been slowed ever since by a series of high-profile accidents and disasters (i.e., Three Mile Island, United States in 1979; Chernobyl, Ukraine, in 1986; and Fukushima Daiichi, Japan, in 2011), high cost, and the lack of disposal sites for long-lived radioactive wastes. Indeed, the share of global electric power generated by nuclear peaked in 1996 at 17.6%. In the last two decades, new nuclear development has been concentrated in Asia. Most of Asia's operating nuclear plants are in Japan, China, South Korea, and India. Asia also accounts for two thirds of the nuclear reactors currently being built worldwide (WNA 2018). As a result, these countries will need to catch up with the West (especially Scandinavia) to address the radioactive waste disposal problem and concomitant equity issues.

Nuclear power plants generate multiple categories of radioactive wastes (Solomon and Shelley 1988). Internationally, these are divided into high-level (spent fuel rods and some reprocessing wastes), intermediate-level (mostly from nuclear reprocessing plants), low-level, and extremely low-level (below-regulatory concern). While most regulatory and research focus has been on high-level nuclear wastes, all except for extremely low-level wastes will be hazardous to human health and the environment for thousands to hundreds of thousands of years. Consequently, Asian countries need to manage multiple categories of nuclear wastes as well.

This chapter will provide four Asian case studies of the role of environmental equity in nuclear waste repository siting. Since these areas are at different stages of nuclear development and consideration of nuclear waste management, we will unite them by a conceptual framework for how nuclear waste facilities are normally considered as a regional or spatial siting decision problem. This will be addressed in the next section. Following this, we will address environmental equity in the context of nuclear waste: this will include procedural vs. distributional equity, as well as interregional vs. intergenerational dimensions. The next section will present the four case studies. Finally, some conclusions will close the chapter.

10.2 Nuclear Waste Disposal as a Regional or Spatial Decision Problem

10.2.1 Background

One of the essential requirements of nuclear power development is the management and disposal of nuclear waste – both high-level wastes (HLW), low-level wastes (LLW), and in some countries intermediate-level wastes (ILW). There are only a few technical options that can be considered by nuclear electric utilities and government policy-makers, namely, some type of waste storage (whether short term or long term) or disposal (e.g., in shallow trenches or deep geological repositories). Unfortunately, in many cases in many countries, these decisions have been postponed because of their political and cost implications. When this has happened, nuclear-powered utilities have been forced to keep spent fuel rods on racks in their water storage pools at reactors longer than is considered safe, which is usually 5–10 years (Sloan 2017). This has led many utilities to further optimize wet storage capacity by re-racking the spent fuel rods in the pools at higher densities or to turn to at-reactor dry cask storage or away from reactor storage facilities. Dry cask storage (using passive cooling) can be done safely above ground for a much longer period, around 100–120 years and is popular in many advanced economies.

Since nuclear waste storage, even in dry casks, is not a long-term solution, disposal sites will still be needed. Thus, notwithstanding technical issues and challenges, radioactive waste disposal becomes an inherently regional or spatial decision problem ripe with political conflict (Easterling and Kunreuther 1995). Nuclear waste sites need to be developed *somewhere*, and the vast majority of communities do not want these facilities in their backyard (Blowers et al. 1991; Solomon et al. 2010). Nonetheless there are exceptions, and all nuclear-powered nations must undertake the siting of such facilities sooner or later.

The next section will discuss siting methods for nuclear waste repositories. Technology and safety are given priority in the processes, and these methods have become more sophisticated over time. However, given the failure of the United States to develop its HLW site at Yucca Mountain, Nevada, it has become imperative to look beyond conventional siting methods (Ewing and von Hippel 2009; Adams 2009–2010; Macfarlane and Ewing 2017).

10.2.2 Siting Methods

As discussed by Merkhofer and Keeney (1987), Keeney (1987), and Bowen and Haynes (1992) in the US case, the most common siting methods in the 1980s for nuclear waste repositories were some form of multicriteria analysis (MCA) or multiattribute utility analysis (MUA). For a European case, Briggs et al. (1990) applied the multicriteria PROMETHEE methods for repository siting and also considered different timeframes and financing methods for $3 \times 3 \times 3 = 27$ possible actions. In the US case, a series of geological variables was incorporated into site selection, including subsurface hydrology, stratigraphy, and geochemical factors. Since the siting was sequentially narrowed down from large geological provinces to multistate regions, then to areas, locations, and site alternatives, this was a form of hierarchical screening (c.f. Solomon et al. 1980 for an example of this in the case of power plant siting). The final site selection process for the United States for the Department of Energy (DOE), which focused on five nominated locations, was mandated to be based upon multiple attributes: (1) health and safety; (2) biological impacts; (3) archeological, historical, and cultural impacts; (4) aesthetic impacts; (5) socioeconomic impacts; and (6) economic costs (Bowen and Haynes 1992). After the siting process was terminated in the mid-1980s and thereafter focused exclusively on Yucca Mountain, Nevada (the favored site based on the DOE's MUA), the siting became a notorious failure, at least on political grounds and possibly on technical grounds as well (Blowers et al. 1991: 207–217; Macfarlane and Ewing 2006; Ewing and von Hippel 2009). This siting failure will be discussed in the next section.

MUA was used in the United States to evaluate the pre-closure impacts of the site alternatives for HLW disposal (Keeney 1987: 199). To do so, the impact estimates for each performance measure were evaluated and combined based on value judgments, which elicited information about value trade-offs and risk attitudes. The model was scaled from 0 to 100 in the additive form and was normalized into the following form:

$$u(x_1, \ldots, x_{14}) = 121 - 1/200\ [\Sigma_{i=1}^{14} K_i C_i x_i] \tag{10.1}$$

where C_i (i = 1,. . .,14) are component disutility functions that represent units of the x performance measures (14 in this case) with natural scales and percentages of the range of impacts for the measures that had constructed scales. K_i (i = 1,. . .,14) are positive scaling factors that represent the value trade-offs between units of the corresponding performance measure and repository costs measured in US dollars.

In a critique of MUA in the US case, Bowen and Haynes (1992) highlighted the limiting assumptions of value judgment agreement among the DOE siting team managers with respect to which siting attributes to include in the analysis and which alternative sites to include and the structure of the relations between attributes. As an alternative, a probabilistic multidimensional scaling algorithm (PROSCAL) was used and tested with a group of environmentally aware students. While approaching the siting problem differently and with 13 possible sites instead of 5, the students also selected Yucca Mountain as their first choice for the repository.

As geographic information systems (GIS) became increasingly commercialized and used on personal computers in the mid- to late-1980s, their value in addressing siting problems became apparent. For example, Openshaw et al. (1989) used Arc/Info overlay routines to search for areas suitable for nuclear waste disposal in the United Kingdom. Their analysis considered four siting attributes: suitable geology, population density, accessibility to transportation, and conservation areas. Creating GIS map overlays alone only amounts to a deterministic screening procedure for feasible areas based on all siting criteria, however, and does not select an optimal disposal site. Thus, in a follow-up work, Carver (1991) combined GIS with MCA for waste repository siting.

Carver (1991) discussed several MCA techniques and applied a modified concordance-discordance analysis for a pair-wise comparison of the choice alternatives for nuclear waste repository siting in the United Kingdom. His example included a seven-point weighting scale for the siting factors. After using GIS to survey a large range of potential sites for the facility location, MCA techniques were embedded in the GIS framework with additional site-specific information with the siting factors weighted in a second stage of the analysis for preliminary site identification. The evaluation matrix containing site information was built using the data-handling facilities provided by the GIS. In his study, Carver (1991) compared the results and technique bias based on criterion weights for the nuclear industry vs. the general public vs. environmentalists and also demonstrated the robustness of the analysis. While this siting method is demonstrably useful, the United Kingdom also has failed to site an HLW repository (Blowers 2017). Additional work has demonstrated the value of GIS in the selection of nuclear waste transport routes (Chen et al. 2008).

10.3 Nuclear Waste Management and Environmental Equity

We have briefly noted the general failure of nuclear waste repository siting worldwide, though Sweden and Finland are notable exceptions for HLW (Solomon et al. 2010). In the case of the United States (among other nations), the siting process has often changed over time, false promises were made, and there have been technical surprises along with restricted public and stakeholder participation. As a result, some have referred to nuclear waste disposal as a "wicked problem," i.e., a problem that is resistant to resolution because of contradictory, incomplete, and changing requirements that are often difficult to recognize (Di Nucci and Brunnengräber 2017). The lack of public trust is a serious obstacle to radioactive waste disposal (Suzuki 2015; Carter 2017). Moreover, as argued by Shrader-Frechette (1993), Cameron and Solomon (1990), Macfarlane and Ewing (2006) among others, the huge time horizon for nuclear waste management increases the uncertainty of facility risks and impacts to unmanageable (and perhaps unimaginable) proportions. Thus, the siting models discussed in the last section may have little applicability to nuclear waste decision-making. The factors behind the success stories of Sweden and Finland in HLW repository siting have included the presence of preexisting nuclear facilities, public trust, strong local stakeholder participation and support, voluntarism, management flexibility, and compensation, i.e., a sense of environmental equity among host communities (Di Nucci and Brunnengräber 2017). Thus, environmental equity is worth exploring for the nuclear waste siting problem.

10.3.1 Procedural vs. Distributional Equity

We prefer to use the phrase environmental equity here instead of environmental justice, though both of these related terms are found in the nuclear waste literature. The phrase environmental justice is used more when there is concern that communities of color or other minorities may be discriminated against, and this is not normally the case with nuclear waste (for an exception see the Taiwan case in Sect. 10.4.4).

Procedural equity refers to a fair siting process and stakeholder engagement. We hasten to add that reasonable people may have different judgments on whether or not a fair siting process is being followed. An important principle of procedural equity is the voluntary assumption of any harm or burden from nuclear waste by a local population and ideally local veto power over that decision. This requires strong consultation and concurrence for siting and full disclosure of the potential harm or burden upon the host community, which was critical in the Swedish and Finnish cases. This suggests that the voluntary principle may be important internationally (Kasperson and Rubin 1983; Di Nucci et al. 2017; Kelleher 2017). Moreover, the voluntary assumption of any harm or burden is predicated upon a comprehensive scientific assessment and disclosure of the risks of nuclear wastes.

While nations have varying political systems and levels of local public, government, and other stakeholder input, some process for local engagement in siting (if not fully participatory democracy) will usually be welcomed and should be encouraged. To test the importance of procedural justice, Krütli et al. (2012) conducted three quasi-experimental analyses using conjoint analysis to analyze people's concerns regarding justice in the siting of nuclear waste facilities in Switzerland. The authors reported consistent findings that a fair process was more highly ranked than distributional justice and outcome valence. The lack of a fair process helps to explain the rejection of an HLW repository in the United States, which the State of Nevada strongly opposed at every stage of the process (Adams 2009–2010).

Distributional equity, in turn, has two additional important principles. These are risk avoidance and risk reduction and benefit-burden concordance, the latter with compensation for those who receive unfair burdens (Kasperson and Rubin 1983). These two principles along with voluntariness will be discussed and evaluated in our case studies. The three equity principles have interregional (locus or spatial) and intergenerational (legacy) aspects, which will be discussed in the next section.

10.3.2 Interregional vs. Intergenerational Equity

The risk avoidance and risk reduction principle requires that in the interest of public safety, nuclear waste be disposed as far away from human population centers as possible, the risk of transport accidents aside (which is usually assumed to be small). The timing, placement, and number of waste repositories should be determined on the basis of minimizing the overall systemwide risk (Solomon and Cameron 1985:

572). This risk is the product of the accidental release of radiation from nuclear waste disposal and transport times the health and environmental effects of the radiation. But would the use of remote sites minimize systemwide risk and be fair? Not necessarily. A counterargument is that beneficiaries of nuclear power generation have received jobs and business revenue from the construction and operation of nuclear plants, and thus the same region with the power plants should receive the burden of a waste repository. However, the communities that host nuclear power plants have arguably experienced increased health and environmental risks for the benefit of society as a whole, so perhaps now it is the turn of other regions to assume their responsibility and host waste repositories (Di Nucci et al. 2018: 11). In either case, compensation payments to host communities might be justified in the interest of fairness (see below), although some have argued that this constitutes a form of bribery (e.g., Frey et al. 1996).

The benefit-burden concordance principle requires that for any risks that cannot be avoided, some compensating benefit should be provided to those who assume the risks of a waste repository (Gerrard 1996). In addition to compensation payments, this principle also requires that those who have benefited from nuclear power generation in their region should receive their fair share of the waste burden. Other requirements that flow from this principle include liberal insurance coverage for waste transport risks and the highest safety standards to protect future generations that do not share the benefits (Solomon and Cameron 1985: 572).

What more might intergenerational equity require based on these two principles? If the current generation does not consent to the risks of a waste repository, it cannot be assumed that future generations would give their proxy consent for the same decision (Shrader-Frechette 2000). However, delaying decisions on wastes can leave future generations with problems they did not create (Di Nucci et al. 2018: 11). Of course, it is much more difficult (if not impossible) to secure the informed consent of future generations for a waste repository site. This problem underscores the need to resolve or dramatically reduce the radioactive waste problem in the near term. In addition, the creation and funding of a public defender for the future and a public legacy trust fund to cover the costs of future monitoring, storage, and liability associated with a repository have been proposed to address these problems (Kasperson et al. 1983; Shrader-Frechette 1993: 217–231). In contrast, Ahearne (2000) has argued that in setting radiological health standards for protecting the lives of generations far into the future, future generations have been given too much weight vs. current generations, and instead discounting should be used.

10.4 Four Case Studies

10.4.1 Japan

While Japan once had the third highest nuclear power-generating capacity in the world after the United States and France, with 54 reactors totaling 48.8 GWe, it closed all of its nuclear plants 1 year after the disastrous accident at Fukushima

Daiichi of March 2011 (Suzuki 2015). These plants had accounted for 25% of Japan's electricity. As of June 2018, 12 of the reactors were permanently closed and just 9 reactors in 5 nuclear plants had passed the stronger post-Fukushima safety assessments and were operating (Okamura 2018: 96). Fukushima has thus had a significant impact on Japan's nuclear power policy, including nuclear waste management, which has been under review and revision ever since. Indeed, Fukushima Reactor Units 1, 3, and 4 experienced hydrogen explosions that damaged the spent fuel pool handling facilities and equipment and provided enhanced pathways for the release of radiation into the environment (NASEM 2016).

Nuclear waste management in Japan has historically been discussed separately from nuclear power policy (Okamura 2018: 95). Overall, with a high buildup of nuclear wastes, one might expect that waste management policy would be a high priority, but this has not happened. In fact, nuclear waste policy in the 1970s and 1980s focused on avoidance of waste disposal in Japan with serious consideration given to ocean dumping, sub-seabed burial, and waste storage on one or more uninhabited Pacific Islands outside of its territory (Solomon 1987).

Over 80% of Japan's nuclear spent fuel is stored at reactor sites, with the rest at the Rokkasho Reprocessing Plant (after long delays, now set to open in 2021). Japan used to have its spent fuel reprocessed in France and England, with vitrified HLW returned. The reprocessing facility is in Rokkasho-mura, an isolated rural village in the northeast peninsula on Honshu Island in Aomori prefecture. The municipal government signed an agreement in 1994 with Japan Nuclear Fuels Ltd. to store vitrified waste there for 30–50 years. An away-from reactor spent fuel storage facility has been built in Mutsu City (Suzuki 2015: 597), but as of mid-2018, storage had been blocked by local political opposition and the opening delayed for safety reasons (Hayashi 2018). Additional high-level liquid reprocessing waste that has been vitrified and sealed is stored at the older Tokai reprocessing plant (which will be decommissioned) in the Central Ibaraki prefecture. The damaged reactors from the Fukushima Daiichi accident will also need decommissioning and disposal, along with contaminated water, soil, and other debris in the area. Only the Fukushima Daiichi plant and one other in Japan use dry cask storage for spent fuel. For now, interim storage for several decades in the prefecture is envisioned (Okamura 2018). Finally, LLW are stored at Rokkasho-mura, where the local residents are pronuclear (Park and Sovacool 2018).

Japan's Diet passed the Specified Radioactive Waste Final Disposal Act in 2000, which was amended in 2007. This law requires deep geological disposal in Japan of HLW and transuranic nuclear wastes. The law is implemented by the Nuclear Waste Management Organization of Japan, including site selection and construction. A multistep process was authorized: selection of preliminary investigation areas along with a survey of geological literature, selection of detailed investigation areas, and then final site selection and construction. Agreement of the local population, municipal mayor, and prefectural governors is required, and thus public participation is very important. Grants of 1 and 2 million yen were authorized for host areas for the literature survey and preliminary investigation stages (Okamura 2018). This process is challenging since Japan is located in the seismically active Pacific Ring of Fire, though its geological modeling and site screening siting criteria were given international peer review (NEA 2016).

Only one municipality applied for a literature survey – Toyo-machi in Kochi Prefecture in January 2007 – though two regional prefectural governors objected, and the application for this literature survey was withdrawn a few months later. Because of this challenge and growing antinuclear sentiment post Fukushima, the Prime Minister's Cabinet revised the Final Disposal Act in May 2015 to switch from a voluntary system of repository site selection to one in which the central government preselects geologically suitable sites and then discusses the possibility with municipalities. While two thirds of Japan's land area have been deemed potentially suitable, the process of narrowing down the sites is expected to take 20 years (Okamura 2018: 110–111).

Japan's nuclear waste repository siting program can be evaluated based on our environmental equity criteria. It meets the voluntary assumption of a harm or burden principle, even with the HLW policy revision of 2015. While the new siting policy is being slowly implemented, thus far it does not appear that the central government will impose a repository on a community that does not want it. In addition, the 1994 decision to establish nuclear waste facilities at Rokkasho-mura appeared to be voluntary, despite initial opposition (Johnstone 1985; Park and Sovacool 2018: 701). As for risk avoidance and risk reduction, this principle has not been followed. The potential health effects of the Fukushima Daiichi accident alone are devastating enough, but it will be very difficult if not impossible to find a remote and geologically suitable area in Japan to host an HLW repository. Early policy in Japan attempted to ship its nuclear wastes overseas, though that could have been ecologically unsound or inequitable for other people, if not both. Finally, the benefit-burden concordance principle is being met. Not only are grants being offered to potential host communities as well as significant tax revenues for Rokkasho, but government policy requires deep geological disposal in Japan (where residents have benefited from nuclear power), as challenging as that will be to achieve.

10.4.2 South Korea

With the decline of nuclear power in Japan since the Fukushima accident, South Korea is now the fifth largest producer of nuclear energy worldwide. South Korea has 24 reactors at six nuclear plants (a 25th reactor, Kori 1, closed in 2017). All nuclear power stations are in coastal areas, with 22.5 GWe of installed generating capacity. Nuclear power accounts for 33% of South Korea's electricity production. However, while significant new capacity had been planned or under construction, additional nuclear reactors that were in the planning stages as well as life extensions on existing ones were cancelled by President Moon Jae-in in 2017 (Leem and Schreurs 2018: 75). Moreover, the Moon government favors an eventual phaseout of nuclear power in favor of natural gas and renewable energy, though that may take many decades.

Low- and intermediate-level nuclear wastes (LILW) in South Korea are stored at the six-plant sites (78%), with an additional 17% of these wastes generated by Korea Nuclear Fuel, industries, hospitals, universities, and research institutes temporarily stored in Daejeon. Another 5% is stored in an underground repository in the City of Gyeongju on South Korea's east coast, with plans to eventually store all LILW there (Leem and Schreurs 2018).

South Korea has separate policies and procedures for LILW vs. spent fuel and high-level waste management and disposal. For LILW, policy has been in effect since the mid-1980s. Under the Atomic Energy Act of 1986, the Korea Atomic Energy Research Institute (KAERI) was granted authority for waste management, though this power shifted to the Nuclear Environment Technology Institute (NETC) under Korea Electric Power Corporation in 1996. NETC was then transferred to the new Korea Hydro and Nuclear Power Company (KHNP) in 2001 (Song 2002). Attempts to site a LILW facility failed nine times. After its first failure in the late 1980s, NETC switched to a policy of open consultation with potential host communities, voluntary siting, and significant financial incentives. Siting efforts had met with consistent public mistrust and opposition (Kelleher 2017: 299–303). Finally, NETC recognized local referendums on a potential disposal site and in 2005 accepted Gyeongju for the repository, since it had the highest rate of acceptance, at 89.5% (Kang 2011). The LILW repository site is very close to the Wolsong Nuclear Power Plant, undoubtedly a factor in the high acceptance rate. The repository was partially opened in July 2015. The central government offered 300 billion won (about $270 million) to Gyeongju upfront plus an additional 637,500 won for each waste drum accepted until the facility reaches its design capacity of 800,000 drums (Kang 2011). KHNP also moved its headquarters to Gyeongju. However, there is concern over environmental safety, as a strong earthquake occurred nearby in September 2016 (Park and Sovacool 2018: 699).

With the repeated failures of siting the LILW facility in South Korea, efforts to site an HLW repository or away from reactor spent fuel storage facility have also been very difficult. Since South Korea does not reprocess spent fuel (though it would like to in order to keep up with North Korea and Japan, KAERI is researching pyrochemical processing in Daejeon), the rods are stored at nuclear power plants, and space is filling up rapidly. In 2013, the Ministry of Trade, Industry and Energy (MOTIE) created a Public Engagement Commission on Spent Fuel Management (PECOS) though it has been unable to change public perceptions about nuclear safety risks. To supplement the efforts of PECOS, Kang et al. (2015) conducted 2000 telephone surveys and 66 follow-up focus group meetings with residents near nuclear power plants. They found that if residents received additional balanced, unbiased information about nuclear power, wastes, and safety risks, their support for additional nuclear waste storage, especially in dry casks, significantly increased. KHNP uses dry cask storage at two nuclear power plants. At the other four plants, wet storage capacity has been expanded and extended with high-density racks.

MOTIE will select a final repository site for deep disposal of HLW by 2028, which would open in 2053. Local referendums will again be used to help select the site (Leem and Schreurs 2018: 84). However, the central government would also consider participating in a permanent spent fuel storage facility overseas. The Radioactive Waste Control Act went into effect in 2009 and established the Korea Radioactive Waste Agency (KORAD). KORAD is a quasi-governmental organization affiliated with MOTIE and is in charge of repository site selection, construction, operation, and management. Unfortunately, due to the perceived pronuclear bias of PECOS, the antinuclear groups in South Korea have refused to participate in its proceedings, making the HLW repository siting task of KORAD more difficult (Leem and Schreurs 2018: 88–89).

South Korea's nuclear waste repository siting program can be evaluated based on our environmental equity criteria. The LILW repository at Gyeongju has a very high rate of acceptance among the local population, and MOTIE will use local referendum to help select an HLW site. Thus, the nuclear waste program meets the voluntary assumption of a harm or burden principle. Regarding risk avoidance and risk reduction, it is too early to determine if this principle is being followed. The HLW repository location will not be chosen until 2028. South Korea is less seismically active than Japan, but it does have earthquakes, and the timeframe of long-lived radionuclides complicates site selection. Lastly, the benefit-burden concordance principle is only partially being met. The financial compensation that was paid to Gyeongju has been generous and similar if not higher support can be expected for a South Korea community that accepts the HLW site. But if its spent fuel is shipped overseas, South Korea will be avoiding responsibility for accepting its HLW disposal burden.

10.4.3 China

While the electricity generated by nuclear power represents only 3% of China's total (IAEA 2018), its nuclear development has been rapid in recent decades. China is the third largest producer of nuclear energy worldwide after the United States and France and has 45 operating reactors with 44.8 GW of capacity (IAEA 2018). During the 12th 5-year plan period (2010–2015), 15 nuclear reactors were put into commercial operation with 13 more being built (Chen and Zheng 2016). According to the 13th 5-year Plan for Energy Development, the installed nuclear capacity is expected to reach 58 GW by 2020 (NDRC 2016). Increasing the proportion of nuclear energy in the national energy system will help the government realize its climate change commitment to the international community under the Paris Agreement and achieve its goal of 20% non-fossil primary energy consumption set in the National Climate Change Plan (2014–2020) (NDRC 2014).

With the expansion of nuclear power, the treatment of nuclear waste becomes more challenging. By the end of 2015, the total reactor years of nuclear power in China reached 196.9. According to the experience of other nuclear-powered countries, 200 reactor years is the warning line for the post-processing of nuclear reactor fuel. It is estimated that 13 nuclear reactor units will be saturated by 2020, and all existing units will be saturated by 2025 (Su and Zhu 2016).

LLW in China is stored in stainless steel casks in concrete vaults at regional facilities. These include the Beilong aboveground repository in Guangdong Province near the Daya Bay nuclear power plant in Shenzhen; a shallow underground LILW site near Yumen (Gansu Province); and three other sites planned for the northeast, east, and central regions (Zhou 2013: 8; Sternfeld 2018: 30). Spent fuel in China is generally stored at reactor sites. The oldest nuclear plants were designed to store spent fuel for 10 years, though those built after 2005 have 20-year storage capacity and the earlier plants have had their capacity extended. According to Wang et al. (2017), by 2020 China will accumulate 10,300 tHM of spent fuel, and the annual discharge rate will be 1000 tHM. Thus, it is very urgent to find away from reactor storage sites.

China's government has established institutions and laws to regulate nuclear waste repository siting and prevent any nuclear waste pollution (Sternfeld 2018). For example, the Law on Prevention and Control of Radioactive Pollution (2003) and the Nuclear Safety Law (2017) have requirements on selecting and planning of sites for the disposal of radioactive solid wastes. The State Administration of Science, Technology and Industry for National Defense (SASTIND) is in charge of the nuclear sector and responsible for radioactive waste management. Also, it leads in preparing site selection plans for radioactive waste disposal sites (Sternfeld 2018). The State Council must give final approval prior to implementation. In addition, there are many guidelines and regulations to help implement the siting procedures (Gan and Yang 2017). These guidelines and regulations require that the potential environmental, human health, and social impacts of establishing an HLW repository should be considered.

Some guidelines and regulations also have explicit requirement for public participation and involvement during the siting process (Gan and Yang 2017). According to geological disposal of high-level radioactive waste research and development planning guidelines (2006), research on the measures and procedures for public and stakeholders participation has to be conducted, and the mechanisms for information exchange and public participation should be established and improved. Also, the public must be informed of the relevant plans, schedules, activities, and progress in an appropriate manner. Considering public opinion will ensure the smooth research and development of siting for HLW disposal.

A nationwide screening for HLW sites in China began in 1985. The process considered technical, scientific, and socioeconomic factors. Currently, an HLW repository is proposed in the northwest in Beishan, Gansu Province, with three sites under consideration (Sternfeld 2018). The facility may be opened by 2050. The siting procedure has lacked controversy because the region used to be a military base with sparse population and favorable geological and environmental conditions. However, most of China's nuclear power plants are located on the southeast coast. If all the HLW is transported to Gansu Province, it will be costly with risk of radiation leakage. Thus, other suitable sites need to be explored.

China's nuclear waste repository siting program can be evaluated based on our environmental equity criteria. While equity was considered by the government during the selection of nuclear waste sites, the decision-making process has not been very open. Stakeholder involvement and public communication have been inadequate. Typically, the public has not been fully informed in advance. In one example, due to public objections, the plan to build a nuclear spent fuel reprocessing plant in Lianyungang, Jiangsu Province, was concealed and met with protests (Hornby and Lin 2016). Thus, China does not meet the voluntary assumption of a harm or burden principle. As for risk avoidance and risk reduction, this principle has been followed. In the case of the Beishan HLW site, the location is far from populous regions. The benefit-burden concordance principle is partially met, though this is uncertain since detailed information is not available. For example, in the case of LLW, the repository sites are located mostly near the nuclear power plants. In the case of HLW, it has been reported that for the Beishan disposal site, the Gansu Province Environmental Protection Bureau has demanded compensation for the risk (Feng 2014). In the meantime, the areas with nuclear power plants are assuming the risks of accidental radiation releases until a permanent repository is ready. Regarding intergenerational equity, China takes serious the need to determine the sites for nuclear waste disposal as soon as possible to resolve the problem that large quantities of spent fuel have to be processed and stored in the near future.

10.4.4 Taiwan

Taiwan has six reactors at three nuclear power plants, accounting for 5 GWe of installed capacity. Two plants are on the north coast, and one is on the south coast (Huang et al. 2013). Nuclear power currently accounts for 15% of electricity generation in Taiwan. Construction of two additional reactors at the Lungmen nuclear power plant was suspended. Similar to the situation in South Korea, since 2016 President Tsai Ing-wen has supported phasing out nuclear power (by 2025) to be replaced with renewable energy, though as in South Korea these plans are controversial (Hsiao et al. 2018).

Taipower (Taiwan Power Company), the state-run utility, began secretly building a temporary storage facility for LLW on Orchid Island (Lan Yu) off Taiwan's southeastern coast in 1978 with approval of the Atomic Energy Council (AEC), the same year that its first nuclear plant at Jinshan began operations on the north coast. The original plan was to dump LLW into an ocean trench. The Orchid Island facility began operations in 1982 with minimal oversight from the AEC but stopped receiving waste shipments in 1996 (Baldacchino and Tsai 2014). This site has been the focus of a long-running environmental justice conflict, given the lack of consent given by the aboriginal Tao (Yami) tribe, strong antinuclear waste protests, and a high cancer death rate among islanders (Fan 2006a, b; Hsu 2015: 653–654). Around 70% of the roughly 5000 residents are Tao/Yami people. Poorly packaged LLW remains there to this day in nearly 100,000 steel barrels, though residents also receive around $2000 US a year in compensation.

Taiwan has unsuccessfully searched for a permanent LLW site to replace Orchid Island since 1996. First, North Korea in 1997 agreed to take the wastes, but following protests from South Korea, among other problems, the deal fell through. Next, Taiwan secretly pursued plans with China, the Marshall Islands, and Russia to export LLW, but these plans also failed (Eckholm 2000). More recently, Taipower and the Ministry of Economic Affairs have tried to site an LLW repository on Taiwan. For example, in 2009 sites in Da-Ren and Wang-An townships were considered following approval of the 2006 Act on Sites for Establishment of Low Level Radioactive Waste Final Disposal Facility (Huang et al. 2013). While the legislation requires local referenda, consent, and compensation before approval, Huang et al. (2013) argued that selection of either site would be environmentally unjust. Finally, Taipower is also searching for a site to store nuclear waste when it starts decommissioning the Jinshan nuclear power plant in December 2019 (Staff Writer 2018).

Taiwan has followed the model of most advanced economies with respect to HLW disposal. The plan is to store spent fuel rods in at-reactor pools in the near term, onsite dry casks in the medium term, and in deep geological repositories in the long term. Construction of the first dry cask storage site at the Jinshan power station is underway, though it has been met with protests (Fan 2018). The Nuclear Materials and Radioactive Waste Management Act of 2002 sets the requirements for Taipower, including locational factors (e.g., geological, hydrological, avoidance of highly populated areas) with an expected repository operational date in 2055 (AEC 2017).

Taiwan's nuclear waste repository siting program can be evaluated based on our environmental equity criteria. The program does not meet the voluntary assumption of a harm or burden principle. LLW remains on Orchid Island, despite significant local opposition and government commitment to move these wastes elsewhere. There is also local opposition to continued storage of nuclear waste at the Jinshan plant and little progress in HLW disposal. Similarly, the risk avoidance and risk reduction principle has not been followed. Like Japan, it will be very difficult if not impossible to find a remote and geologically suitable area to host nuclear waste repositories given Taiwan's high level of seismicity (Wu et al. 2013). Finally, the benefit-burden concordance principle is being met. Compensation has been given to residents on Orchid Island and offered to other potential sites, and government policy requires deep geological disposal in Taiwan, as challenging as that might be.

10.5 Conclusions

Kingsley Haynes, among others, has demonstrated the value of spatial analysis in determining the environmental equity or inequity with respect to the existing residential locational patterns of racial and ethnic minorities and low-income people in relation to noxious facilities. Similar analysis would seemingly be relevant for planning the successful siting of electric power plants and nuclear waste repositories,

Table 10.1 Summary of the performance of the case studies on the environmental equity principles

Case	Voluntary assumption of a harm or burden	Risk avoidance and risk reduction	Benefit-burden concordance
Japan	Yes	No	Yes
South Korea	Yes	Unclear	Partially
China	No	Yes	Partially
Taiwan	No	No	Yes

as opposed to analyses of past locational patterns. Indeed, population density and distribution are common variables in energy facility siting. However, what is notable about nuclear waste sites in particular is that very few countries are adequately managing their radioactive waste inventories, and only a few repositories have been successfully sited. Moreover, facilities such as electric power plants and nuclear waste repositories have regional effects well beyond their immediate locality, and equity issues are not restricted to racial and ethnic minorities and low-income populations (though in a major exception to this pattern, an ethnic minority group in Taiwan has been forced to live near an LLW facility without its consent). Equity, in this context, has more to do with who benefits from specific energy development projects and who bears the costs or burdens associated with these developments.

There are only a few examples of successful nuclear waste repository siting worldwide, most notably for HLW disposal in Sweden and Finland. However, the siting in these cases was not due to formal mathematical models, though research has suggested that equity issues have been an important dimension of the success in these two countries. In our study, we have chosen three equity principles as criteria to evaluate nuclear waste repository siting in East Asia: voluntary assumption of a harm or burden, risk avoidance and risk reduction, and benefit-burden concordance. The scoring of these criteria for our four case studies is shown in Table 10.1. Japan was the only case that met even two of the three criteria – voluntary assumption of a harm or burden and benefit-burden concordance – while it did not meet the risk avoidance and risk reduction principle (in part because of its high population density and high level of seismic activity). Our other three case studies only met one each of the three equity principles.

Nuclear waste repository siting is a very difficult, even wicked problem. Only a few successful examples of such siting exist worldwide. The literature has only a few studies of the use of mathematical models for this problem, no doubt due to lack of real-world utility. Our study of the role of environmental equity in four East Asian cases found that none of them met all three equity principles, which in and of itself appears to be a necessary if not sufficient condition for successful siting. Thus, governments in all of the cases have more work to do to establish equitable and successful programs for nuclear waste repository siting. Of course, it may be possible to select locations for nuclear waste repositories in these cases without meeting the equity criteria, though we would be skeptical that sites established under such a scenario could be successfully developed and sustained over the long term.

References

Adams M (2009–2010) Yucca Mountain: Nevada's perspective. Idaho L Rev 46(2):423–448

AEC (Atomic Energy Council, Republic of China) (2017) High level radioactive waste final disposal, 5 April. Available online at https://www.aec.gov.tw/english/radwaste/article07.php

Ahearne JF (2000) Intergenerational issues regarding nuclear power, nuclear waste, and nuclear weapons. Risk Anal 20(6):763–770

Baldacchino G, Tsai H-M (2014) Contested enclave metageographies: the offshore islands of Taiwan. Polit Geogr 40:13–24

Blowers A (2017) The legacy of nuclear power. Routledge, Abingdon

Blowers A, Lowry D, Solomon BD (1991) The international politics of nuclear waste. Macmillan Press, London

Bowen WM, Haynes KE (1992) Decision theory and individual differences in policy analysis: the nuclear waste repository site decision, Working paper #92:14. The Institute of Public Policy, George Mason University, Fairfax, VA

Bowen WM, Salling MJ, Haynes KE, Cyran EJ (1995) Toward environmental justice: spatial equity in Ohio and Cleveland. Ann Assoc Am Geogr 85(4):641–663

Briggs T, Kunsch PL, Mareschal B (1990) Nuclear waste management: an application of the multicriteria PROMETHEE methods. Eur J Oper Res 44(1):1–10

Bullard RD (1983) Solid waste sites and the black Houston community. Sociol Inq 53 (2–3):273–288

Bullard RD (1990) Dumping in Dixie: race, class, and environmental quality. Westview Press, Boulder

Bullard RD (1993) Confronting environmental racism: voices from the grassroots. South End Press, Boston

Cameron DM, Solomon BD (1990) Nuclear waste landscapes: how permanent? In: Cullingworth B (ed) Energy, land and public policy. Transaction Publishers, New Brunswick, pp 137–186

Carter LJ (2017) Nuclear imperatives and public trust: dealing with radioactive waste (Routledge revivals). Routledge, Abingdon/New York

Carver SJ (1991) Integrating multi-criteria evaluation with geographical information systems. Int Geogr Inf Syst 5(3):321–339

Chen R, Zheng Y (2016) The outlook for the development of China's nuclear power sector in the 13th five-year plan (in Chinese). Available online at http://china-nea.cn/site/content/15221.html

Chen Y-W, Wang C-H, Lin S-J (2008) A multi-objective geographic information system for route selection of nuclear waste transport. Omega-Int J Manag Sci 36(3):363–372

Cohon JL, Revelle CS, Current J, Eagles T, Eberhart R, Church R (1980) Application of a multiobjective facility location model to power plant siting in a six-state region of the U.S. Comput Oper Res 7(1–2):107–123

Cole LW, Foster SR (2001) From the ground up: environmental racism and the rise of the environmental justice movement. New York University Press, New York

Cutter SL (1995) Race, class and environmental justice. Prog Hum Geogr 19(1):111–122

Di Nucci MR, Brunnengräber A (2017) In whose backyard? The wicked problem of siting nuclear waste repositories. Eur Policy Anal 3(2):295–323

Di Nucci MR, Brunnengräber A, Isidoro Losada AM (2017) From the "right to know" to the "right to object" and "decide". A comparative perspective on participation in siting procedures for high level radioactive waste repositories. Prog Nucl Energy 100:316–325

Di Nucci MR, Isidoro Losada AM, Schreurs MA, Brunnengräber A, Mez L (2018) The technical, political and socio-economic challenges of governing nuclear waste. In: Brunnengräber A, Di Nucci MR, Isidoro Losada AM, Mez L, Schreurs MA (eds) Challenges of nuclear waste governance: an international comparison, vol II. Springer, Wiesbaden, pp 3–22

Dobson JE (1979) A regional screening procedure for land use suitability analysis. Geogr Rev 69 (2):224–234

Easterling D, Kunreuther H (1995) The dilemma of siting a high-level nuclear waste repository. Springer, New York

Eckholm E (2000) China and Taiwan pursue secret nuclear waste deal. New York Times, 14 March 2000. Available online at https://www.nytimes.com/2000/03/14/world/china-and-taiwan-pursue-secret-nuclear-waste-deal.html

Ewing RC, von Hippel F (2009) Nuclear waste management in the United States - starting over. Science 325(5937):151–152

Fan M-F (2006a) Environmental justice and nuclear waste conflicts in Taiwan. Environ Polit 15 (3):417–434

Fan M-F (2006b) Nuclear waste facility on tribal land: the Yami's struggle for environmental justice. Local Environ 11(6):433–444

Fan M-F (2018) Risk discourse and governance of high-level radioactive waste storage in Taiwan. J Environ Plan Manag. https://doi.org/10.1080/09640568.2017.1418303

Feng J (2014) Where to place the nuclear waste? (in Chinese). Southern Weekly, 19th June. Available online at http://www.infzm.com/content/101618

Frey BS, Oberholzer-Gee F, Eichenberger R (1996) The old lady visits your backyard: a tale of morals and markets. J Polit Econ 104(6):1297–1313

Gan L, Yang S (2017) Legal context of high level radioactive waste disposal in China and its further improvement. Energy Environ 28(4):484–489

Gerrard MB (1996) Whose backyard, whose risk: fear and fairness in toxic and nuclear waste siting. The MIT Press, Cambridge, MA

Hayashi Y (2018) Mayor rebukes utility's reported plan on storing nuclear waste. Asahi Shimbun, 8 January. Available online at http://www.asahi.com/ajw/articles/AJ201801080030.html

Haynes KE, Lall SV, Trice MP (2001) Spatial issues in environmental equity. Int J Environ Technol Manag 1(1–2):17–31

Hornby L, Lin L (2016) China protest against nuclear waste plant. Financial Times, 7 August

Hsiao C-T, Liu C-S, Chang D-S, Chen C-C (2018) Dynamic modeling of the policy effect and development of electric power systems: a case in Taiwan. Energ Policy 122:377–387

Hsu K-J (2015) To regulate or not to regulate: the conundrum of Taiwan's nuclear power. Asian Perspect 39(4):637–655

Huang GC-L, Gray T, Bell D (2013) Environmental justice of nuclear waste policy in Taiwan: Taipower, government, and local community. Environ Dev Sustain 15(6):1555–1571

IAEA (International Atomic Energy Agency) (2018) Power reactor information system (PRIS): China, People's Republic of. Available online at https://pris.iaea.org/PRIS/CountryStatistics/CountryDetails.aspx?current=CN

Johnstone B (1985) A country without a 'nuclear toilet'. New Sci 108(1476):25

Kang JM (2011) South Korea in focus: the politics of spent fuel. Bull At Sci 67(3):51–58

Kang JM, Kim S-W, Lee B-C (2015) Hot potato in South Korea: the spent fuel storage dilemma. Bull At Sci 71(3):76–83

Kasperson RE, Rubin BL (1983) Siting a radioactive waste repository: what role for equity? In: Kasperson RE (ed) Equity issues in radioactive waste management. Oelgeschlager, Gunn & Hain, Cambridge, MA, pp 118–136

Kasperson RE, Derr P, Kates RW (1983) Confronting equity in radioactive waste management: modest proposals for a socially just and equitable program. In: Kasperson RE (ed) Equity issues in radioactive waste management. Oelgeschlager, Gunn & Hain, Cambridge, MA, pp 331–368

Keeney RL (1987) An analysis of the portfolio of sites to characterize for selecting a nuclear repository. Risk Anal 7(2):195–218

Kelleher DS (2017) Public participation in the siting of nuclear waste facilities: international lessons and the Korean experience. Korea Obs 48(2):277–323

Krütli P, Stauffacher M, Pedolin D, Moser C, Scholz RW (2012) The process matters: fairness in repository siting for nuclear waste. Soc Justice Res 25(1):79–101

Leem S-J, Schruers M (2018) Transitioning away from opaque governance: nuclear waste policy in South Korea. In: Brunnengräber A et al (eds) Challenges of nuclear waste governance: an international comparison, vol 2. Springer, Weisbaden, pp 73–94

Macfarlane AM, Ewing RC (eds) (2006) Uncertainty underground: Yucca Mountain and the nation's high-level nuclear waste. MIT Press, Cambridge, MA

Macfarlane A, Ewing R (2017) Déjà vu for U.S. nuclear waste. Science 356(6345):1313

Merkhofer MW, Keeney RL (1987) A multiattribute utility analysis of alternative sites for the disposal of nuclear waste. Risk Anal 7(2):173–194

NASEM (National Academies of Sciences, Engineering and Medicine) (2016) Lessons learned from the Fukushima nuclear accident for improving safety and security of U.S. nuclear plants: phase 2. The National Academies Press, Washington, DC

NDRC (National Development and Reform Commission) (2014) National Climate Change Plan (2014–2020) (in Chinese). Available online at http://www.ndrc.gov.cn/zcfb/zcfbtz/201411/W020141104584717807138.pdf

NDRC (National Development and Reform Commission) (2016) The 13th five-year plan for energy development (in Chinese). Available online at http://www.ndrc.gov.cn/zcfb/zcfbghwb/201701/W020170117350627940556.pdf

NEA (Nuclear Energy Agency) (2016) Japan's siting process for the geological disposal of high-level radioactive waste: an international peer review. Organisation for Economic Co-operation and Development, Paris

Okamura L (2018) False premise, false promise: governance and management of nuclear waste in Japan. In: Brunnengräber A, Di Nucci MR, Isidoro Losada AM, Mez L, Schreurs MA (eds) Challenges of nuclear waste governance: an international comparison, vol 2. Springer, Weisbaden, pp 95–122

Openshaw S, Carver SJ, Fernie J (1989) Britain's nuclear waste: siting and safety. Belhaven Press, London/New York

Park J, Sovacool BK (2018) The contested politics of the Asian atom: peripheralisation and nuclear power in South Korea and Japan. Environ Polit 27(4):686–711

Pulido L (2000) Rethinking environmental racism: white privilege and urban development in Southern California. Ann Assoc Am Geogr 90(1):12–40

Shrader-Frechette K (1993) Burying uncertainty: risk and the case against geological disposal of nuclear waste. University of California Press, Berkeley/Los Angeles

Shrader-Frechette K (2000) Duties to future generations, proxy consent, intra- and intergenerational equity: the case of nuclear waste. Risk Anal 20(6):771–778

Sloan RD (2017) Multinational storage of spent nuclear fuel and other high-level nuclear waste: a roadmap for moving forward. American Academy of Arts & Sciences, Cambridge, MA

Solomon BD (1987) Nuclear waste management in Japan and the Soviet Union. In: Proceedings of the eighth international symposium on Asian studies, 1986, Vol. 5. Asian Research Service, Hong Kong, pp 1491–1502

Solomon BD, Cameron DM (1985) Nuclear waste repository siting: an alternative approach. Energ Policy 13(6):564–580

Solomon BD, Haynes KE (1984) A survey and critique of multiobjective power plant siting decision rules. Socio-Econ Plan Sci 18(2):71–79

Solomon BD, Shelley FM (1988) Siting patterns of nuclear waste repositories. J Geogr 87(2):59–71

Solomon BD, Haynes KE, Krmenec AJ (1980) A multiobjective location model with hierarchical screening: nuclear power in Northern Indiana. Rev Reg Stud 10(3):9–22

Solomon BD, Andrén M, Strandberg U (2010) Three decades of social science research on high-level nuclear waste: achievements and future challenges. Risk Hazards Crisis Pub Policy 1 (4):13–47

Song MJ (2002) Radioactive waste management in Korea. The 7th nuclear energy symposium, Daejeon, South Korea, August 26–28, 2002

Staff Writer (2018) Nuclear waste storage site to be decided by year-end. Taipei Times, 6 March 2018. Available online at http://www.taipeitimes.com/News/taiwan/archives/2018/03/06/2003688769

Sternfeld E (2018) A long way off: nuclear waste governance in China. In: Brunnengräber A et al (eds) Challenges of nuclear waste governance: an international comparison, vol 2. Springer, Wiesbaden, pp 25–50

Su C, Zhu Y (2016) The local leaders are bidding for the emerging hundreds of billions nuclear waste treatment market (Chinese report). Industrial Securities Company Ltd, Funzhou

Suzuki T (2015) Nuclear energy policy issues in Japan after the Fukushima nuclear accident. Asian Perspect 39(4):591–605

Wang J, Ling H, Chen W (2017) Study on the safety functions of repository for geological disposal of high level radioactive waste (in Chinese). China Nucl Power 10(2):270–278

WNA (World Nuclear Association) (2018) World nuclear power reactors & uranium requirements. Available online at http://www.world-nuclear.org/information-library/facts-and-figures/world-nuclear-power-reactors-and-uranium-requireme.aspx

Wu Y-H, Chen C-C, Turcotte DL, Rundle JB (2013) Quantifying the seismicity on Taiwan. Geophys J Int 194(1):465–469

Zhou Y (2013) China's nuclear waste management and disposal. Available online at ppt. http://nautilus.org/wp-content/uploads/2013/08/China_Zhou_May-28th-2013-version-2.pdf

Chapter 11
Proximate Causes of Worldwide Mega-Regional CO_2 Emission Changes, 1995–2009

Inácio Fernandes de Araújo, William M. Bowen, Randall Jackson, and Amir B. Ferreira Neto

Abstract Evidence suggests that climate change is real and accelerating. This has led to a great deal of research on improving energy efficiency and reducing per capita energy consumption, as well as on the sources of air polluting emissions such as carbon, and possible policy options for limiting permanent environmental damage. The top regions in the world in terms of these carbon emissions are China, the United States, the European Union, India, Russia, and Japan. This chapter uses the World Input-Output Database (WIOD) and structural decomposition analysis to determine for these six countries and regions whether observed improvements in energy intensity and carbon dioxide emissions are due to the adoption of new energy technology or changes in trade relationships, final demand structures, or other structural economic changes.

Keywords Global climate change · Mega-regional carbon emissions · Energy and the environment · Structural decomposition analysis

---

I. F. de Araújo
The University of Sao Paulo Regional and Urban Economics Lab (NEREUS), Department of Economics, University of Sao Paulo (USP), São Paulo, Brazil
e-mail: inacio.araujo@usp.br

W. M. Bowen (✉)
Department of Urban Studies, Levin College of Urban Affairs, Cleveland State University, Cleveland, OH, USA
e-mail: w.bowen@csuohio.edu

R. Jackson
Geology and Geography, Regional Research Institute, West Virginia University, Morgantown, WV, USA
e-mail: randall.jackson@mail.wvu.edu

A. B. Ferreira Neto
Department of Economics and Finance, Florida Gulf Coast University, Fort Myers, FL, USA
e-mail: aborgesferreiraneto@fgcu.edu

Z. Chen et al. (eds.), *Development Studies in Regional Science*, New Frontiers in Regional Science: Asian Perspectives 42,
https://doi.org/10.1007/978-981-15-1435-7_11

11.1 Introduction

Evidence suggests that climate change is real and accelerating. This evidence is based largely upon global surface temperature readings from around the world dating back to 1850 (Brohan et al. 2006). The increases in global temperature since the advent of the industrial revolution are unequivocally and directly a result of the addition of greenhouse gasses such as CO_2 to the atmosphere (Masson-Delmotte et al. 2018; Petit et al. 1999; Ramanathan 1988). The expectation of future climatic effects attributable to additional greenhouse gasses in the atmosphere has led to a great deal of research in areas centered around improving energy efficiency (Kangas et al. 2018; Brown et al. 2017; Zhang et al. 2017a), reducing per capita energy consumption (Chen et al. 2014; Ozan et al. 2011; Steinberger et al. 2009; Haynes et al. 1993), the sources of air polluting emissions such as carbon (Peters et al. 2011; Hertwich and Peters 2009; Wiedmann et al. 2007; Turner et al. 2007), and possible policy and other options for limiting permanent environmental damage (Minx et al. 2018; Moss et al. 2010; Hallegatte 2009; Haynes et al. 1997).

The top mega-regions in the world in terms of these carbon emissions are the United States, the European Union, India, Russia, Japan, and China. Figure 11.1 depicts the relative magnitudes and trends in CO_2 emissions among these regions from 1974 through 2014. The category "rest of Asia" here includes India and Russia, as well as a host of other relatively minor CO_2 contributors such as Iran, Saudi Arabia, Korea, Indonesia, Malaysia, and Vietnam. The relative CO_2 contributions of the United States and the European Union have steadily declined; Japan along with the "rest of the world" has slightly declined; and both China and the "rest of Asia" have significantly increased.

Figure 11.2 depicts CO_2 emissions among countries within Asia over the past two decades. Japanese and Russian emissions have remained more-or-less constant. Indian emissions have been slowly trending upward. Emissions from the "rest of Asia" region have increased considerably, and those from China have approximately tripled over this period. Figure 11.3 shows Chinese emissions relative to those from

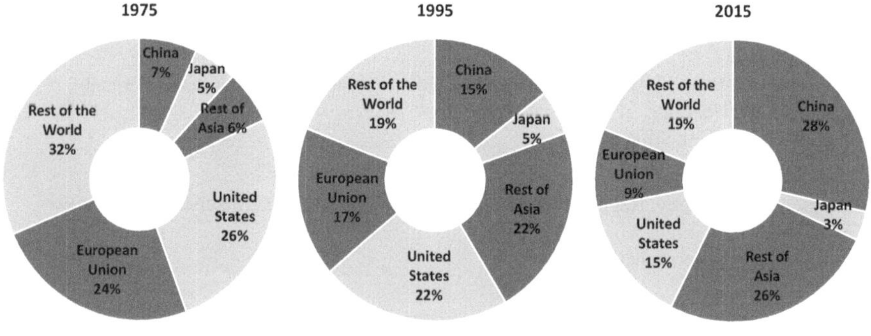

Fig. 11.1 Relative magnitudes and trends in regional CO_2 emissions

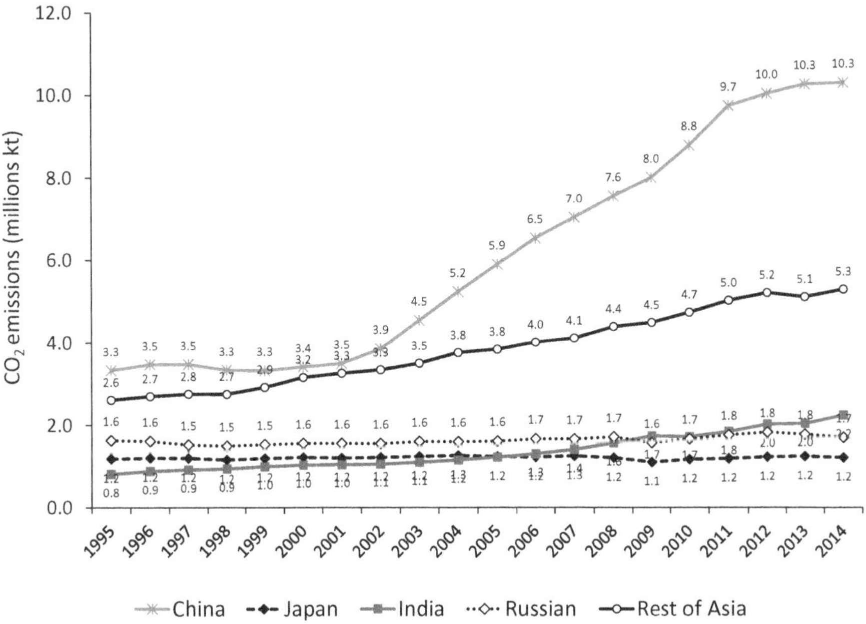

Fig. 11.2 CO_2 Emissions (millions kt) – Asia

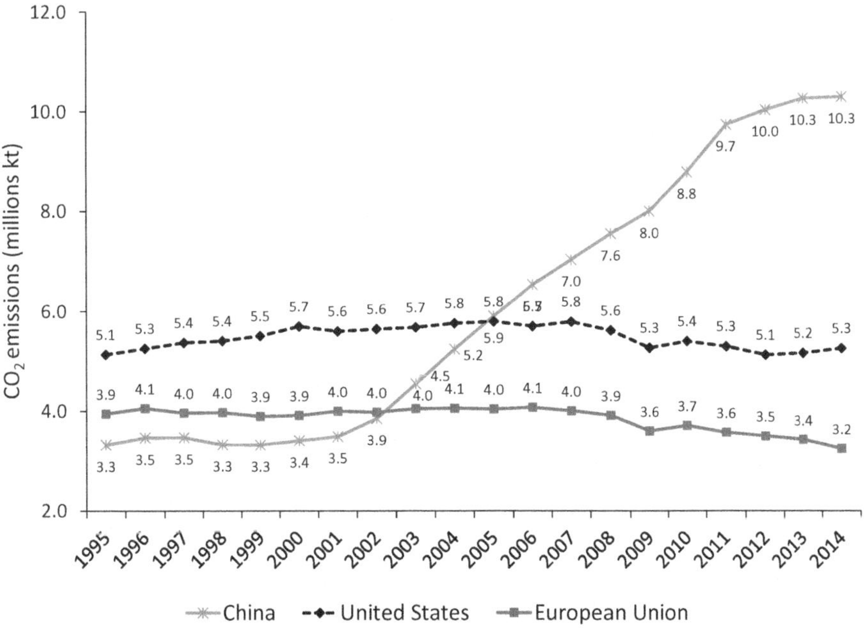

Fig. 11.3 CO_2 Emissions (millions kt) – China, United States and European Union

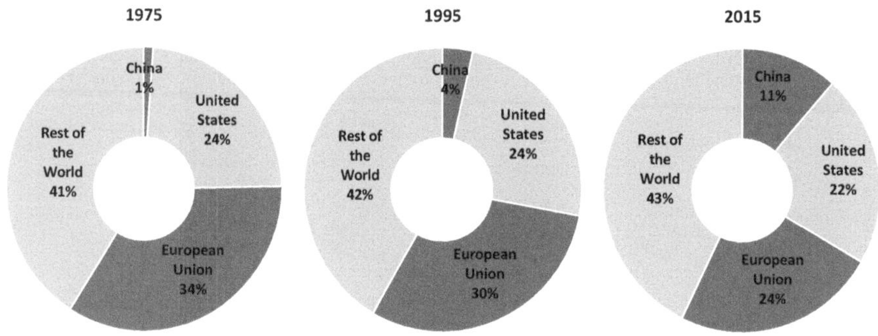

Fig. 11.4 Relative Magnitudes and Trends in Regional GDP

the United States and the European Union. Clearly, the most rapidly increasing worldwide CO_2 emissions among major emitters are Chinese.

China's rapidly expanding urban areas and booming economy have been major drivers behind its quickly increasing CO_2 emissions. Between 1980 and 2012, the percentage of China's population living in urban areas grew from 19.4% to 52.6% (Yang 2013) and on to 58% today and rising. While rapid urbanization has precipitated massive economic growth, at the same time, it has greatly increased mass production and consumption of industrial products, triggered a range of environmental problems, and brought proposals for new types of urbanization (Qu and Long 2018; Wang et al. 2015). Figure 11.4 provides insight into the economic trends: China grew from 1% of the world's GDP in 1975 to 4% in 1995 to 11% in 2014. Recent proposals for new forms of urbanization, slowing economic growth and decreases in energy intensity, all promise to help countervail against the trend toward increasing emissions (Meng et al. 2018). Figure 11.5 depicts these decreases in the rate of growth of the Chinese economy and shows them relative to growth in the United States and the European Union.

This chapter follows an established body of research in regional science and development. Its focus is on energy and the environment, a research area in which Kingsley Haynes has had a long-standing interest (Haynes 1984; Haynes et al. 1977). It uses the World Input-Output Database (WIOD) and structural decomposition analysis (SDA) to help gather insight into the proximate causes of change in various indirect environmental costs, such as those embodied in CO_2. Among other related applications, it has been used to evaluate the environmental costs of European Union membership (Araújo et al. 2018); identify factors and sectors that affect production-source CO_2 emissions in China (Chang and Lahr 2016); help understand the effects of changes in trade patterns on global CO_2 emissions growth (Hoekstra et al. 2016); examine the worldwide shifting of emission-intensive production across borders (Malik and Lan 2016); understand the drivers of change in China's energy intensity and energy consumption (Zhang and Lahr 2014); provide an overview of the origin and destination of pollution in the Dutch economy (De Hann 2001); quantify the economic factors driving greenhouse gas emissions

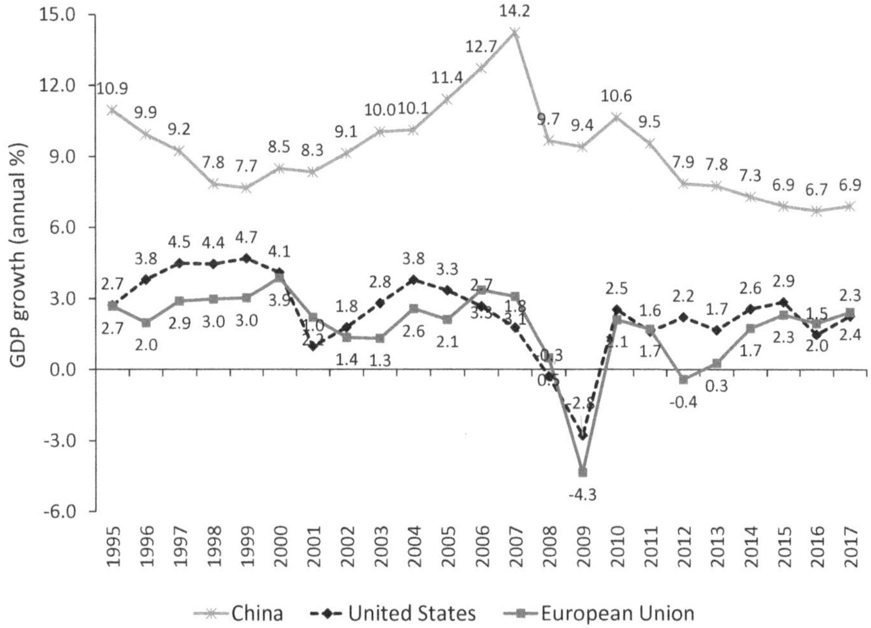

Fig. 11.5 Gross domestic product (GDP) growth (annual %)

in Norway (Yamakawa and Peters 2011); and explore the anatomy of Danish energy consumption and emissions of carbon dioxide (CO_2), sulfur dioxide (SO_2), and nitrogen oxides (NO_x) (Wier 1998). Here it is used to examine the aforementioned six regions to determine whether observed changes in CO_2 emissions are due to (a) the adoption of new energy technology or (b) changes in trade relationships, final demand structures, or other structural economic changes.

Therefore, the aim of this chapter is to decompose the change in level of CO_2 emissions in the top mega-regions in the world between 1995 and 2009 into six explanatory components. By doing so, we are able to quantify the proximate causes of these changes in CO_2 emissions and how they differ between the mega-regions which differ in terms of economic development. The remaining of the chapter is as follows: Sect. 11.2 describes the methodology and data; Sect. 11.3 presents and discusses the results; and Sect. 11.4 concludes the chapter.

11.2 Methodology and Data

The decomposition of CO_2 emissions growth starts with the basic interregional input-output model (Miller and Blair 2009). The solution of this model, with *I* sectors and *R* countries, may be summarized as:

$$\mathbf{s} = \widehat{\mathbf{e}}\mathbf{x} = \widehat{\mathbf{e}}\mathbf{L}\mathbf{f} \tag{11.1}$$

where $\mathbf{s}$ is an IR vector with total emissions directly and indirectly required to satisfy final demand per sector i, per country r, and $\widehat{\mathbf{e}}$ is the diagonal matrix vector $\mathbf{e}$ of emission intensity, i.e., the amount of CO_2 emission per unit of output i. $\mathbf{L}$ is the IR x IR interregional Leontief inverse. $\mathbf{f}$ is an IR vector with final demand for products from sector i in country r.

We follow Oosterhaven and Van Der Linden (1997) and Hoekstra et al. (2016) to distinguish trade and technology changes, both for intermediate and for final demand. Hence, instead of the basic interregional model of Eq. (11.1), we want to decompose the following extension of the basic model:

$$\mathbf{s} = \widehat{\mathbf{e}}\mathbf{L}\mathbf{G}\mathbf{y} = \widehat{\mathbf{e}}(\mathbf{I} - \mathbf{C}\circ\mathbf{A}^{*})^{-1}(\mathbf{F}\circ\mathbf{B})\mathbf{y} \tag{11.2}$$

where $\mathbf{I}$ is an $IR \times IR$ identity matrix. $\mathbf{A}$ is the matrix of technical coefficients decomposed into $\mathbf{A} = (\mathbf{C} \circ \mathbf{A}^{*})$. $\mathbf{C}$ is an $IR \times IR$ matrix of trade coefficients ($c_{ij}^{rs} = z_{ij}^{rs}/z_{ij}^{*}$), where z_{ij}^{*} is the total input requirements of industry j for input of industry i in country r, indicating which fraction of this intermediate demand for (worldwide) products i (exercised by sector j in country s) is actually satisfied by supply from country r. A^{*} is an $IR \times IR$ matrix, built up of R mutually identical $I \times IR$ matrices with technical coefficients ($a_{ij}^{\prime s}$), indicating the total need for products from (worldwide) sector i, per unit of output of sector j in country s. $\mathbf{G} = (\mathbf{F} \circ \mathbf{B})$ where $\mathbf{F}$ is an $IR \times R$ matrix with trade coefficients (f_{ij}^{rs}), which capture the trade coefficients for the final demand, and is created following the same steps presented for $\mathbf{C}$, indicating which fraction of this final demand for (worldwide) products i in country s is actually satisfied by sector i from country r. $\mathbf{B}$ is an $IR \times R$ matrix, built up of R mutually identical $I \times R$ matrices with final demand composition or preference coefficients (b_i^s) indicating the total need for products from (worldwide) sector i, per unit of final demand in country s. $\mathbf{y}$ is a R column with the final demand, i.e., consumption, level, per country s. $\circ$ is the Hadamard product, i.e., cell-by-cell multiplication.

The changes in $\mathbf{s}$ can be decomposed into different components using SDA.

11.2.1 Structural Decomposition Analysis

SDA is a major tool for distinguishing shifts in the growth in some variable over time and separating the changes in its constituent parts. The use of structural decomposition techniques allows us to quantify, analyze, and gather insight into the underlying sources of change in a wide variety of variables (Dietzenbacher and Los 1998).

In SDA, the effect of $\Delta\widehat{\mathbf{e}}$ on $\Delta\mathbf{s}$ in Eq. (11.2) represents the first component that relates to sectoral technology changes. The second sectoral technology component is derived from the change in the interregional Leontief inverse. We follow

Oosterhaven and Van Der Linden (1997) to separate the technological component from the trade component in ΔL. Therefore, the interregional input-output coefficients are decomposed into a trade part and a technical part, as follows:

$$\Delta \mathbf{L} = \mathbf{L}_1 - \mathbf{L}_0 = \mathbf{L}_1 \Delta (\mathbf{C} \circ \mathbf{A}^*) \mathbf{L}_0 \tag{11.3}$$

Pre- and post-multiplying Eq. (11.3) for $(\mathbf{I} - \mathbf{A}_1)$ and $(\mathbf{I} - \mathbf{A}_0)$:

$$\Delta \mathbf{L} = \mathbf{L}_1 (\mathbf{C}_{1/2} \circ \Delta \mathbf{A}^*) \mathbf{L}_0 + \mathbf{L}_1 \left(\Delta \mathbf{C} \circ \mathbf{A}^*_{1/2} \right) \mathbf{L}_0 \tag{11.4}$$

where $\mathbf{\Delta L} = (\mathbf{L}_1 - \mathbf{L}_0)$ and the subscript 1/2 is the average of times $t = 0$ and $t = 1$, that is, $\mathbf{C}_{1/2} = \frac{1}{2}\mathbf{C}_1 + \frac{1}{2}\mathbf{C}_0$. This is the principle of polar decomposition by Dietzenbacher and Los (1998) used for analysis of the change in $\mathbf{L}$ between two points in time.

The first part of Eq. (11.4) indicates the magnitude of the change in the technical coefficients, whereas the second part indicates the effect of the change in the trade coefficients.

Similarly, the final demand in $\mathbf{G}$ relates final demand for products from sector i in country r to macroeconomic demand $\mathbf{y}$ in Eq. (11.2). To assess the effects of changes in products' geographical source locations (sourcing patterns) ($\mathbf{F}$) from the effect of changes in the distributions of final demands ($\mathbf{B}$), the matrix $\mathbf{G}$ is decomposed as follows:

$$\Delta \mathbf{G} = \mathbf{F}_{1/2} \circ \Delta \mathbf{B} + \Delta \mathbf{F} \circ \mathbf{B}_{1/2} \tag{11.5}$$

The first part in Eq. (11.5) indicates the effect of changes in consumers' preferences, and the second part indicates the effect of the changes in the sourcing pattern for final demand.

Using Eqs. (11.4) and (11.5), it is possible to rewrite Eq. (11.2). Doing so gives the following decomposition of $\mathbf{\Delta s}$ into six separate components:

$$\Delta \mathbf{s} = (\Delta \widehat{\mathbf{e}}) \mathbf{L}_{1/2} \mathbf{G}_{1/2} \mathbf{y}_{1/2} \tag{11.6a}$$

$$+ \widehat{\mathbf{e}}_{1/2} \left[\mathbf{L}_1 (\mathbf{C}_{1/2} \circ \Delta \mathbf{A}^*) \mathbf{L}_0 \right] \mathbf{G}_{1/2} \mathbf{y}_{1/2} \tag{11.6b}$$

$$+ \widehat{\mathbf{e}}_{1/2} \left[\mathbf{L}_1 \left(\Delta \mathbf{C} \circ \mathbf{A}^*_{1/2} \right) \mathbf{L}_0 \right] \mathbf{G}_{1/2} \mathbf{y}_{1/2} \tag{11.6c}$$

$$+ \widehat{\mathbf{e}}_{1/2} \mathbf{L}_{1/2} (\mathbf{F}_{1/2} \circ \Delta \mathbf{B}) \mathbf{y}_{1/2} \tag{11.6d}$$

$$+ \widehat{\mathbf{e}}_{1/2} \mathbf{L}_{1/2} (\Delta \mathbf{F} \circ \mathbf{B}_{1/2}) \mathbf{y}_{1/2} \tag{11.6e}$$

$$+ \widehat{\mathbf{e}}_{1/2} \mathbf{L}_{1/2} \mathbf{G}_{1/2} (\Delta \mathbf{y}) \tag{11.6f}$$

Accordingly, the change in CO_2 emissions between two points in time ($\mathbf{\Delta s}$) may be decomposed in emission intensity, i.e., the emission per unit of output, ($\mathbf{\Delta} \widehat{\mathbf{e}}$) in

Eq. (11.6a); technology change, i.e., changes in the region's production structure, ($\mathbf{\Delta A}^*$) in Eq. (11.6b); intermediate trade sourcing, i.e., changes in where intermediate goods are being purchased, ($\mathbf{\Delta C}$) in Eq. (11.6c); consumer's preferences, i.e., changes in the mix of final demand goods, ($\mathbf{\Delta B}$) in Eq. (11.6d); final demand sourcing, i.e., locations from which final demand goods are being purchased, ($\mathbf{\Delta F}$) in Eq. (11.6e); and consumption level, i.e., how much is being purchased, ($\mathbf{\Delta y}$) in Eq. (11.6f).

11.2.2 Database

Our research used the World Input-Output Tables (WIOTs) and the environmental accounts for CO_2 emissions provided in the World Input-Output Database (WIOD) Release 2013 (Timmer et al. 2015). The database covers 27 EU countries and 13 other major countries in the world for the period from 1995 to 2009. The WIOD provides details for 35 industries classified according to the International Standard Industrial Classification scheme (see Table 11.3 in the Appendix). According to Genty et al. (2012), the CO_2 emissions in the WIOD accounts include emissions from energy use and process-based emissions.[1]

SDA requires the use of input-output tables expressed in constant prices (Lenzen et al. 2012). Therefore, we used the input-output tables in previous year's prices available from WIOD. These tables were constructed using exogenous value added as per the RAS approach proposed by Dietzenbacher and Hoen (1998) and the generalized RAS (GRAS) algorithm, originally proposed by Junius and Oosterhaven (2003) and modified by Lenzen et al. (2007). Los et al. (2014) discuss more details about the construction of WIOTs in terms of previous year's prices.

11.2.2.1 Characterization of Countries

This subsection presents a description of the production structure and CO_2 emissions of the selected countries based on the World Input-Output Database (WIOD). This description is made by specifying the industrial characteristics of the countries. The groups of activity sectors are classified according to the intensity of energy consumption (Table 11.3 in the Appendix).

Table 11.1 presents value added and CO_2 emissions from 1995 and 2009. The services sectors have the greatest single percentage of value added in all countries. However, the relative percentages from these sectors in China, India, and Russia are smaller than in developed countries. At the same time, with the exceptions of 1995 energy-intensive industrializing China and 1995 then-relatively-nuclear-intensive

[1]Please refer to Genty et al. (2012) for a detailed explanation of the environmental accounts in the WIOD.

Table 11.1 Value added and CO_2 emissions by group of sectors

		Value added (%)		CO_2 emissions (%)		CO_2 emissions (Mt)/value added (bi US$)	
		1995	2009	1995	2009	1995	2009
China	Non-manufacturing	24.0	14.7	7.4	5.0	1.2	0.4
	Energy-intensive	20.5	17.9	40.9	29.9	7.5	2.1
	Non-energy-intensive	14.3	14.7	5.8	2.5	1.5	0.2
	Electricity	2.2	2.7	38.6	53.5	66.0	24.3
	Services	39.0	49.9	7.3	9.0	0.7	0.2
India	Non-manufacturing	28.0	19.4	9.3	10.6	0.7	0.7
	Energy-intensive	9.5	8.7	26.0	25.7	5.6	3.5
	Non-energy-intensive	9.0	6.8	2.7	3.0	0.6	0.5
	Electricity	2.7	1.8	51.4	54.2	39.7	36.8
	Services	50.8	63.3	10.6	6.5	0.4	0.1
Russia	Non-manufacturing	15.6	13.8	10.2	8.5	2.9	0.8
	Energy-intensive	11.8	11.3	19.0	26.7	7.2	3.1
	Non-energy-intensive	5.6	3.7	0.8	0.6	0.7	0.2
	Electricity	4.5	3.2	58.1	50.6	57.4	20.8
	Services	62.4	68.0	11.9	13.6	0.9	0.3
Japan	Non-manufacturing	2.0	1.5	4.1	3.7	0.4	0.5
	Energy-intensive	12.7	10.7	34.5	29.0	0.5	0.5
	Non-energy-intensive	9.9	6.6	3.7	2.1	0.1	0.1
	Electricity	2.6	2.3	23.6	33.8	1.8	2.9
	Services	72.8	78.9	34.1	31.3	0.1	0.1
United States	Non-manufacturing	2.3	2.7	4.3	3.8	1.1	0.4
	Energy-intensive	8.7	6.7	18.4	15.7	1.2	0.7
	Non-energy-intensive	6.8	4.7	2.5	1.8	0.2	0.1
	Electricity	2.2	1.9	42.3	48.5	11.1	7.7
	Services	80.0	84.1	32.5	30.1	0.2	0.1
European Union	Non-manufacturing	3.9	2.4	5.1	4.5	1.3	0.4
	Energy-intensive	11.2	8.3	30.4	25.3	2.7	0.7
	Non-energy-intensive	8.8	6.4	3.5	2.4	0.4	0.1
	Electricity	2.7	2.4	39.8	39.7	14.6	3.5
	Services	73.3	80.4	21.2	28.1	0.3	0.1

Source: Prepared by the author from WIOD (Release 2013)
Note: Europe includes Austria, Belgium, Bulgaria, Cyprus, the Czech Republic, Germany, Denmark, Spain, Estonia, Finland, France, the United Kingdom, Greece, Hungary, Ireland, Italy, Japan, Lithuania, Luxembourg, Latvia, Malta, the Netherlands, Poland, Portugal, Romania, Slovak Republic, Slovenia, and Sweden

Japan, the electricity industry is the single largest source of CO_2 emissions. This is mainly due to the burning of fossil fuels (primarily coal) for generating electricity in the electricity industry. It is noteworthy that the value-added share of CO_2 emissions from the energy-intensive sector is larger in developing countries.

11.3 Results

Table 11.2 summarizes our decomposition of observed changes in CO_2 emissions in China, India, Russia, Japan, the United States, and Europe. Effects are aggregated into the five categories used in the structural decomposition analysis (SDA): emissions intensity, technology change, sourcing (intermediate and final demand), consumer preferences, and consumption level. All results in the table are expressed in Mt of CO_2 over 1995–2001 and 2002–2009. These periods coincide with distinct phases of growth of the Chinese economy.

Global CO_2 emissions increased 5953 Mt over 1995–2009. While China and India increased their levels of CO_2 emissions over 1995–2009, Russia, Japan, the United States, and Europe decreased their levels of CO_2 emissions. Increases in CO_2

Table 11.2 SDA results: decomposition of changes in CO_2 emissions (in Mt) between 1995 and 2009

Countries	Emissions intensity	Industrial structure	Sourcing	Consumer preferences	Consumption level	Total emissions
1995–2001						
China	−1229	−125	185	50	1247	128
India	−57	−23	31	−11	248	187
Russia	−66	−108	−78	−88	301	−39
Japan	45	−12	−53	−21	70	29
United States	−774	385	−214	−146	1147	399
Europe	−533	37	−76	−53	645	21
Rest of the world	−1227	389	518	182	951	813
Total	−3841	544	313	−87	4609	1537
Total (%)	−250	35	20	−5	300	100
2002–2009						
China	−2012	1074	1458	−15	2872	3377
India	−123	−32	42	66	641	595
Russia	−201	−164	−53	−75	530	37
Japan	−41	−54	−59	−16	71	−99
United States	288	−1174	−168	−161	662	−552
Europe	−603	−54	−56	−55	530	−237
Rest of the world	−1762	838	130	115	1975	1296
Total	−4454	434	1294	−140	7282	4416
Total (%)	−101	10	29	−3	165	100

Source: Calculated by the authors

Note: Europe includes Austria, Belgium, Bulgaria, Cyprus, the Czech Republic, Germany, Denmark, Spain, Estonia, Finland, France, the United Kingdom, Greece, Hungary, Ireland, Italy, Japan, Lithuania, Luxembourg, Latvia, Malta, the Netherlands, Poland, Portugal, Romania, Slovak Republic, Slovenia, and Sweden emissions in China, India, and the United States accounted for 42.55% of the global emissions growth over 1995–2001, while only China was responsible for the 76.45% increase in global CO_2 emissions over 2002–2009.

Increases in consumption level were the primary proximate cause of increases in global CO_2 emissions in both periods. A decrease in emissions intensity played a major role in reducing the global CO_2 emissions. Consumer preferences had relatively little impact on emissions changes. While changes in industrial structure contributed to the increase in global emissions, the relative magnitude of its effect varied without discernable pattern between countries.

The sourcing effect, which captures CO_2 emissions embodied in international trade, has led to an increase of 1607 Mt in global CO_2 emissions (27% of global emissions). Increases in levels of international trade appear to correspond with increases in CO_2 emissions, as the shift in sourcing pattern moves from lower- to higher-emission countries. This result is the same as reported in Hoekstra et al. (2016), who analyzed emission cost of international sourcing for low-wage, medium-wage, and high-wage country groups.

For the period over 2002–2009, change in sourcing led to increased emissions of 1458 Mt of CO2 in China. At the same time, other regions, with the exception of India, reduced emissions due to the sourcing effect. This is likely to be the result of greater integration into international trade by the Chinese. This integration coincides with intensification of fragmentation in global production. With such fragmentation, countries send part of their production to countries abroad with lower wage costs. Accordingly, the activities sent abroad tend to be more emission intensive. Developed countries thus outsource parts of their production process to developing countries mainly due to low production cost and moderate environmental regulations Zhang et al. (2017b). Consequently, the developed countries transfer part of the responsibility for emissions to countries with lower wage costs, such as China and India. The evidence presented in Arto and Dietzenbacher (2014), Hoekstra et al. (2016), Vale et al. (2018), and Araújo et al. (2018) reinforces this result.

Decomposition results for global emissions are illustrated on an annual basis in Fig. 11.6. Change in CO_2 emissions is shown in three groups: technology (emissions intensity and industrial structure), sourcing (intermediate trade and final demand), and consumption (consumer preferences and consumption level). The black line depicts total CO_2 emissions. In all years except 1999, 2000, and 2009, China's emissions increased due to changes in sourcing patterns – this increase has been growing since 2001. For illustration, changes in sourcing patterns might involve purchasing intermediate goods used in production from the United States and the rest of the world, instead of relying on domestic production or purchases from former Soviet countries. The sourcing effect contributes to reducing emissions in almost every year for the United States and Europe. For all countries, the technology component has tended to reduce CO_2 emissions; however, its effect was not large enough to compensate for changes in emissions due to increased consumption. Note that China and India are countries less affected by the great recession in terms of

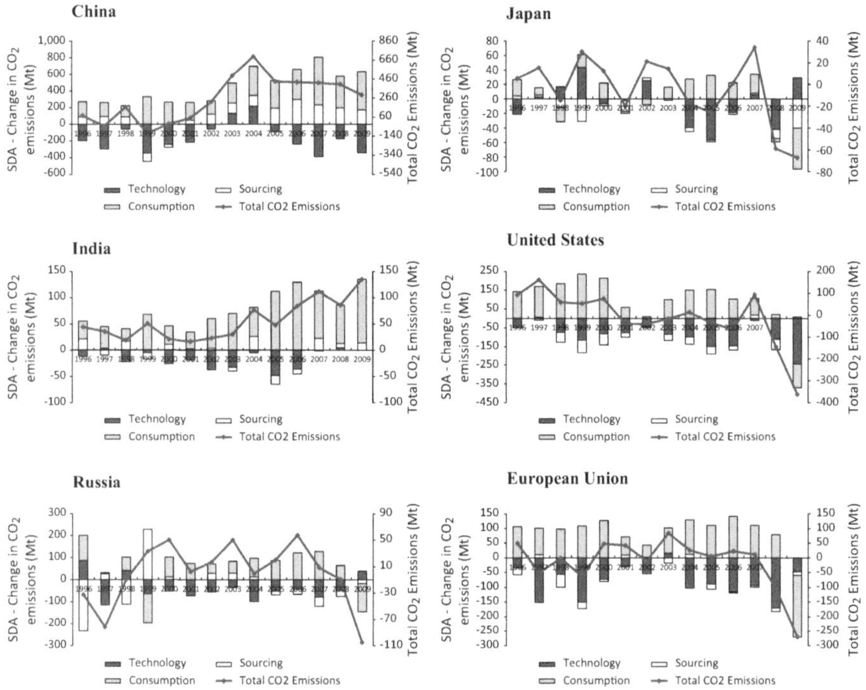

Fig. 11.6 SDA Results: The effects of change in technology, sourcing, and consumption in CO_2 emissions (in Mt), 1995–2007

Note: Europe includes Austria, Belgium, Bulgaria, Cyprus, the Czech Republic, Germany, Denmark, Spain, Estonia, Finland, France, the United Kingdom, Greece, Hungary, Ireland, Italy, Japan, Lithuania, Luxembourg, Latvia, Malta, the Netherlands, Poland, Portugal, Romania, Slovak Republic, Slovenia, and Sweden

Source: Calculated by the authors

emissions, with India actually increasing its CO_2 emission in 2009. All other countries have a significant decrease in emissions levels during these years.

Figure 11.7 shows detailed decomposition results for emissions changes in five groups of sectors (non-manufacturing, energy-intensive manufacturing, non-energy-intensive manufacturing, electricity, and services). All results in the figure are expressed in percent of the change in emissions over 1995–2009 for each country. This analysis is presented by components of the SDA. The complete results for 35 sectors are provided in Tables 11.4, 11.5, 11.6, 11.7, 11.8, and 11.9 in the Appendix.

The decomposition results reveal a very substantial decrease in global CO_2 emissions due to emission intensity (−8295 Mt). In China this reduction is concentrated mainly in the energy-intensive sectors (–38%) and electricity (–47%). Japan is

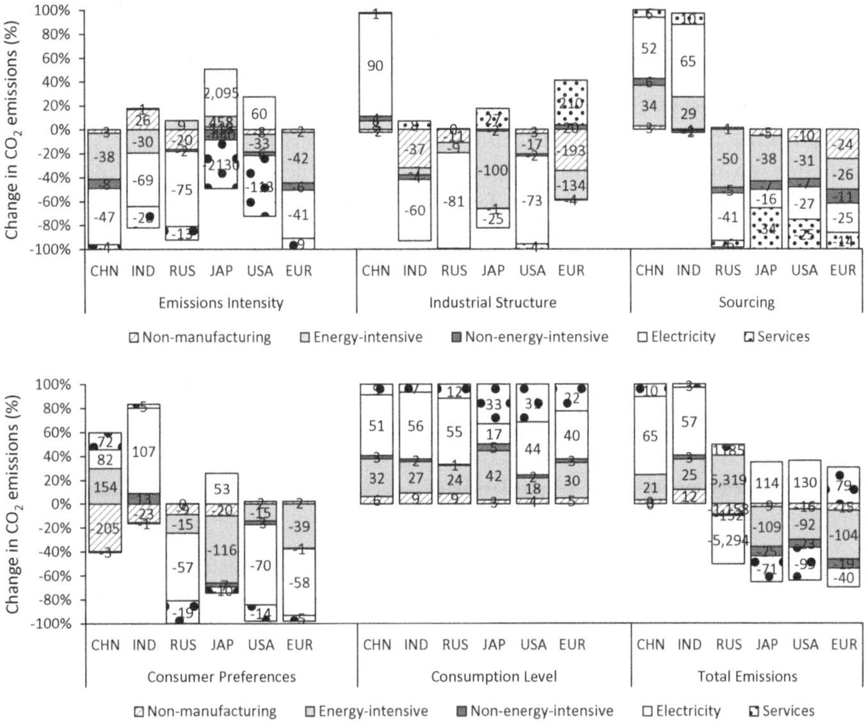

Fig. 11.7 SDA Results: Decomposition of changes in CO_2 emissions (in Mt) by group of sectors between 1995 and 2007
Note: CHN (China), IND (India), RUS (Russia), JAP (Japan), USA (United States), and EUR (Europe)
Source: Calculated by the authors

the only country the effect of emission intensity is positive (3 Mt) – this is caused by the increase in emissions of the non-manufacturing sector (12%) and electricity (2095%).[2] Emissions changes driven by the industrial structure effect are concentrated in the electricity sector – with a positive effect only in China.

The changes in the sourcing pattern caused an increase in emissions embodied in the trade only in China and India. The intensification of international outsourcing, with the production processes distributed globally, has provided economic growth in these countries. However, this has also brought production fragmentation and a corresponding negative externality caused by the increase of emissions incorporated

[2]The reason the electricity value (2095%) is so out of line with all of the other values may be that "The Liberal Democratic Party, which governed Japan almost continuously from 1955 to 2009 and returned to power in December, wasn't proactive in cleaning up the country's air and water." https://latitude.blogs.nytimes.com/2013/02/15/japans-pollution-diet/ (last accessed on 5/6/2019).

in the trade, largely through transportation. This increase is concentrated in the recipient countries to which the most energy-intensive production stages are transferred. Zhang et al. (2017b) showed that the share of emissions in developing countries induced by the global value chain-related trade is increasing gradually.

Consumer preferences reduced the global emissions by 228 Mt of CO_2. Consumption growth was mainly responsible for the increase in global emissions (11,890 Mt CO_2 over 1995–2009). This increase was concentrated in the electricity sector in China (50%), India (56%), and Russia (55%). While in the United States and Europe, the services sector accounted for an important part of the increase in emissions caused by the consumption growth. In Japan, the energy-intensive manufacturing and services sectors together accounted for 69% of the increase in emissions due to variations in consumption.

11.4 Discussion and Conclusion

In this research we used structural decomposition analysis to estimate the proximate causes of change in CO_2 emissions for six worldwide mega-regions. Our objective was to determine whether observed changes in CO_2 emissions from 1995 to 2009 were attributable to the adoption of new energy technology or to changes in trade relationships, final demand structures, or other elements of these six mega-regional economic structures. In achieving this objective, it became evident that the causal structure of change in CO_2 emissions is multifaceted and nuanced from region to region.

A substantial percentage of the increase in CO_2 emissions (27%) over this time period was attributable to increases in levels of international trade associated with changes in where intermediate goods were purchased. Sourcing patterns apparently moved from lower- to higher-emission countries as production moved from high-wage to medium-wage to low-wage countries.

In China, total emissions growth from 1995 to 2009 was slowed greatly by decreases in emissions intensity (probably attributable in large measure to the adoption of new and advanced energy technologies in its electricity industry). Over this same period, however, increased emissions attributable to all other factors, particularly change in industrial structure, sourcing, and consumption (largely of electricity), combined to make China's total emissions growth greater than the total from the rest of the world combined. Fortunately, the Chinese have subsequently made major strides toward reducing the rate of growth of their greenhouse gas emissions, largely through a combination of reduced growth in coal use, widespread deployment of renewable energy sources, decreases in energy intensity, increased use of electric vehicles, proposals for new forms of urbanization, development of carbon capture and storage capacity, and the recent creation of a national-level emission trading market (Xu et al. 2014; Mi et al. 2017).

In contrast, during this same period, both Russia and the United States improved across all factors other than emissions attributable to consumption. Europe is similar with the exception that changes in its industrial structure over the period 1995–2001 led to increases in its CO_2 emissions (though these were more than offset by improvements made between 2002 and 2009). In all three of these regions, the improvements reflect a combination of the adoption of new energy technologies as well as changes in trade relationships, final demand structures, and other economic factors. In India, the adoption of new energy technology decreased CO_2 emissions vis-à-vis improvements in emissions intensity and industrial structure: but these improvements were nevertheless considerably outweighed by increases attributable to final demand sourcing, consumer preferences, and levels of consumption. While Japan's growth in CO_2 emissions attributable to consumption was the smallest of any of the six countries or mega-regions, total emissions attributable to increased consumption grew there as well.

In terms of policy implications, the largest single contributing factor to increases in total CO_2 emissions in all of the observed regions from 1995 to 2009 was consumption levels. These increases occurred along with an increase of just under 50% in gross world product, according to World Bank estimates.[3] As levels of production increased, incomes grew, consumption increased, and more CO_2 was produced. Thus, the policy implications go to possible mechanisms for reversing trends toward greater consumption. These could include widespread reductions in working hours, restrictions on the quantity and nature of marketing messages (e.g., bans on advertising and sponsorship from all public spaces, restrictions on advertising time on television and radio, and tax laws in which the costs of advertising are not deductible business expenses), and education aimed not as much toward consumer capitalism as toward self-understanding and greater knowledge about the world in which we live.

When comparing the 1995–2001 period with the 2002–2009 period, total emissions increased in China, India, and Russia, while at the same time, they decreased in Japan, the United States, and Europe. China, India, and Russia are, of course, all members of the trilateral relationship known as Russia-India-China Triangle, and all are members of the BRICS (short for Brazil, Russia, India, China, South Africa) economic trade block. All three are large developing countries with similar development paths. Probably more importantly, however, is that Japan, the United States, and Europe are all characteristically more advanced technologically and have considerably fewer problems with functioning democratically than the other three. So their citizens and local governments are more likely to accept greater responsibility for taking the sorts of local policy and other actions necessary to minimize CO_2 emissions.

[3]http://statisticstimes.com/economy/gross-world-product.php (last accessed on 4/25/2019).

Past this, the dominant view among scholars and policy makers has been that the governance of climate change should be based on international agreements. The variegation in causal structures found in this research implies that policy makers should not attempt to take a "one-size-fits-all" approach to these agreements. Generally, when the causal structures of two or more problems in two or more regions, locations, or levels are invariant, this would imply invariant solutions to the problems that arise within them. But when the causal structures vary from one region, location or level to the next, as they do throughout these mega-regions, they warrant consideration of correspondingly different policy solutions. The only consistent contributing factor to increased CO_2 emissions found throughout this time period in these regions is consumption. Past this, the policy implications of this research for China differ from those for other countries and regions. International agreements that recognize and respect regional, national, and perhaps local institutional diversity and corresponding approaches for reducing emissions are thus critical.

Appendix

Table 11.3 Industrial composition used in the structural decomposition analysis (SDA)

Industrial sector energy consumption	Industry	Description
Non-manufacturing	Agriculture	Agriculture, hunting, forestry, and fishing
Non-manufacturing	Mining	Mining and quarrying
Energy-intensive	Food	Food, beverages, and tobacco
Non-energy-intensive	Textiles	Textiles and textile products
Non-energy-intensive	Leather	Leather and footwear
Non-energy-intensive	Wood	Wood and products of wood and cork
Energy-intensive	Paper	Pulp, paper, paper, printing, and publishing
Energy-intensive	Ref. petroleum	Coke, refined petroleum, and nuclear fuel
Energy-intensive	Chemicals	Chemicals and chemical products
Energy-intensive	Rubber	Rubber and plastics
Energy-intensive	Non-metallic	Other non-metallic mineral
Energy-intensive	Metals	Basic metals and fabricated metal
Non-energy-intensive	Machinery	Machinery, Nec
Non-energy-intensive	Electrical	Electrical and optical equipment
Non-energy-intensive	Transport	Transport equipment

(continued)

Table 11.3 (continued)

Industrial sector energy consumption	Industry	Description
Non-energy-intensive	Manufacturing	Manufacturing, Nec; recycling
Electricity	Electricity	Electricity, gas, and water supply
Services	Construction	Construction
Services	Maintenance	Sale, maintenance, and repair of motor vehicles and motorcycles; retail sale of fuel
Services	Wholesale trade	Wholesale trade and commission trade, except of motor vehicles and motorcycles
Services	Retail trade	Retail trade, except of motor vehicles and motorcycles; repair of household goods
Services	Hotels	Hotels and restaurants
Services	Inland transport	Inland transport
Services	Water transport	Water transport
Services	Air transport	Air transport
Services	Other transport	Other supporting and auxiliary transport activities; activities of travel agencies
Services	Telecommunications	Post and telecommunications
Services	Financial intermediation	Financial intermediation
Services	Real estate activities	Real estate activities
Services	Renting M & Eq	Renting of M & Eq and other business activities
Services	Public admin	Public Admin and Defense; compulsory social security
Services	Education	Education
Services	Health	Health and social work
Services	Personal services	Other community, social, and personal services
Services	Private HH	Private households with employed persons

Source: Industrial composition of the World Input-Output Tables of the WIOD, 2013 Release. Industrial sector energy consumption from the US Energy Information Administration, International Energy Outlook

Table 11.4 Decomposition of change in CO_2 emissions (in Mt) between 1995 and 2009 by industry: China

Sector	Emissions intensity	Industrial structure	Industrial sourcing	Consumer preferences	Final demand sourcing	Consumption level	Total emissions
Agriculture	−54	−13	5	−68	11	133	13
Mining	−38	−10	8	−2	21	120	99
Food	−95	20	4	−10	6	68	−8
Textiles	−76	12	14	−11	22	32	−8
Leather	−5	0	1	−1	1	3	−1
Wood	−13	4	3	0	2	9	3
Paper	−48	9	11	−2	5	37	12
Ref. petroleum	−46	−7	21	0	12	72	51
Chemicals	−298	40	71	−16	40	203	39
Rubber	−44	7	8	0	6	18	−5
Non-metallic	−279	−71	67	41	46	527	332
Metals	−437	74	161	40	101	385	324
Machinery	−65	7	7	1	14	32	−3
Electrical	−35	8	7	4	7	11	3
Transport	−33	7	5	5	4	19	8
Manufacturing	−18	0	1	0	5	5	−7
Electricity	−1532	855	473	28	373	2089	2286
Construction	−9	0	0	13	0	51	55

Maintenance	0	0	0	0	0	0	0
Wholesale trade	−20	−5	4	0	2	12	−8
Retail trade	−5	−2	1	0	2	7	2
Hotels	2	1	1	−1	1	11	15
Inland transport	−30	−14	11	−2	11	79	55
Water transport	−27	13	22	3	12	59	83
Air transport	20	−4	12	1	8	26	63
Other transport	−1	9	1	1	1	17	27
Telecommunications	−3	1	0	2	0	4	5
Financial intermediation	−3	−1	0	0	0	3	0
Real estate activities	−10	−1	0	0	0	6	−5
Renting M & Eq	−5	3	4	0	2	14	18
Public admin	−3	0	0	0	0	17	15
Education	−20	1	0	3	0	18	1
Health	4	1	0	2	0	10	17
Personal services	−17	6	2	3	1	26	22
Private HH	0	0	0	0	0	0	0
Total	−3241	949	926	34	717	4120	3505

Source: Calculated by the authors

Table 11.5 Decomposition of change in CO_2 emissions (in Mt) between 1995 and 2009 by industry: India

Sector	Emissions intensity	Industrial structure	Industrial sourcing	Consumer preferences	Final demand sourcing	Consumption level	Total emissions
Agriculture	4	−7	0	−16	0	36	16
Mining	43	−14	−5	4	4	43	76
Food	27	2	−2	−11	0	38	54
Textiles	−11	−1	0	0	3	8	−1
Leather	−1	0	0	0	0	0	0
Wood	9	−1	0	7	−7	3	11
Paper	−3	−1	0	−2	0	6	2
Ref. petroleum	−8	3	7	0	3	28	33
Chemicals	−36	2	4	1	3	34	8
Rubber	0	0	0	0	0	1	2
Non-metallic	−31	−2	−6	6	0	66	33
Metals	−4	−8	2	6	8	63	68
Machinery	1	0	0	0	0	2	4
Electrical	0	0	0	1	1	2	3
Transport	4	0	0	0	1	3	9
Manufacturing	−1	0	0	0	0	1	0
Electricity	−125	−33	12	59	35	495	443
Construction	−5	1	0	2	0	9	6

Maintenance	0	0	0	0	0	0	0
Wholesale trade	0	0	0	0	0	1	0
Retail trade	−2	0	0	0	0	3	1
Hotels	−10	1	1	1	1	9	2
Inland transport	−21	3	1	2	1	21	7
Water transport	1	0	0	−1	0	3	4
Air transport	−6	−1	0	−1	0	4	−3
Other transport	−1	0	0	−1	0	2	1
Telecommunications	−4	2	0	1	0	1	1
Financial intermediation	0	0	0	0	0	0	0
Real estate activities	0	0	0	0	0	0	0
Renting M & Eq	1	0	0	1	0	1	3
Public admin	−1	0	0	0	0	1	0
Education	0	0	0	0	0	1	1
Health	0	0	0	0	0	0	0
Personal services	−1	−1	0	−1	0	2	0
Private HH	0	0	0	0	0	0	0
Total	−180	−55	18	55	55	889	781

Source: Calculated by the authors

Table 11.6 Decomposition of change in CO_2 emissions (in Mt) between 1995 and 2009 by industry: Russia

Sector	Emissions intensity	Industrial structure	Industrial sourcing	Consumer preferences	Final demand sourcing	Consumption level	Total emissions
Agriculture	−28	−2	−1	−5	−4	19	−22
Mining	−24	−27	9	−9	−2	52	−2
Food	−10	0	0	0	−1	4	−6
Textiles	−1	0	0	0	−1	0	−1
Leather	0	0	0	0	0	0	0
Wood	0	−1	0	0	0	1	0
Paper	−1	0	0	0	0	1	0
Ref. petroleum	20	−7	4	−9	4	31	41
Chemicals	23	4	−9	−1	−10	24	32
Rubber	0	0	0	0	0	0	0
Non-metallic	24	−42	−6	−7	−1	43	12
Metals	−32	20	−22	−9	−23	94	28
Machinery	−4	1	0	0	−2	2	−3
Electrical	−2	0	0	0	−1	1	−1
Transport	2	0	−1	0	−1	1	1
Manufacturing	0	0	0	0	0	0	0
Electricity	−200	−220	−8	−92	−46	458	−108

Construction	−12	1	0	−1	0	5	−7
Maintenance	−1	0	0	0	0	1	1
Wholesale trade	−1	1	0	0	0	3	3
Retail trade	−1	0	0	0	0	2	2
Hotels	−1	0	0	0	0	1	0
Inland transport	−11	−6	−8	−18	0	50	7
Water transport	0	−1	0	−1	0	2	−1
Air transport	7	4	0	2	0	6	19
Other transport	−4	1	0	0	0	3	0
Telecommunications	−2	1	0	0	0	1	1
Financial intermediation	−2	0	0	0	0	1	−1
Real estate activities	−8	1	0	1	0	3	−2
Renting M & Eq	−2	0	0	0	0	1	0
Public admin	−1	0	0	−1	0	3	1
Education	0	0	0	−3	0	2	0
Health	0	0	0	−1	0	2	0
Personal services	5	−4	0	−10	0	10	1
Private HH	0	0	0	0	0	0	0
Total	−268	−272	−41	−163	−90	831	−2

Source: Calculated by the authors

Table 11.7 Decomposition of change in CO_2 emissions (in Mt) between 1995 and 2009 by industry: Japan

Sector	Emissions intensity	Industrial structure	Industrial sourcing	Consumer preferences	Final demand sourcing	Consumption level	Total emissions
Agriculture	−11	−1	0	−3	0	2	−13
Mining	15	0	−2	−5	−4	3	6
Food	−3	0	0	−2	0	1	−4
Textiles	2	−1	−1	−2	−2	1	−3
Leather	0	0	0	0	0	0	0
Wood	1	−1	0	−1	0	0	−2
Paper	−3	−5	−1	0	0	2	−7
Ref. petroleum	2	−7	−2	−1	−1	3	−5
Chemicals	−3	−6	−5	1	−3	11	−6
Rubber	−2	0	0	0	0	1	−2
Non-metallic	4	−19	−6	−20	−2	11	−31
Metals	20	−28	−14	−21	−7	30	−21
Machinery	−5	0	0	0	0	1	−5
Electrical	−10	3	−1	2	−1	2	−6
Transport	−2	0	−1	0	0	3	0
Manufacturing	0	−1	0	−1	−1	1	−2
Electricity	71	−16	−10	20	−7	24	81

Construction	1	0	0	−15	0	2	−13
Maintenance	0	0	0	0	0	0	−1
Wholesale trade	−7	−3	0	−2	0	3	−10
Retail trade	−5	−2	0	−4	0	1	−10
Hotels	−1	−2	0	0	0	1	−2
Inland transport	−1	−6	−1	−2	0	4	−8
Water transport	−8	27	−24	3	−7	24	15
Air transport	−19	−3	−1	0	0	4	−19
Other transport	1	0	0	0	0	0	0
Telecommunications	−2	1	0	1	0	0	0
Financial intermediation	−2	−1	0	0	0	0	−2
Real estate activities	−1	0	0	1	0	0	−1
Renting M & Eq	−9	7	0	3	0	1	2
Public admin	−5	0	0	8	0	1	4
Education	−2	0	0	−1	0	0	−2
Health	−6	0	0	3	0	1	−2
Personal services	−5	−1	−1	2	−1	2	−3
Private HH	0	0	0	0	0	0	0
Total	3	−65	−72	−37	−41	141	−71

Source: Calculated by the authors

Table 11.8 Decomposition of change in CO_2 emissions (in Mt) between 1995 and 2009 by industry: United States

Sector	Emissions intensity	Industrial structure	Industrial sourcing	Consumer preferences	Final demand sourcing	Consumption level	Total emissions
Agriculture	−23	−7	0	−4	−2	23	−12
Mining	−18	−20	−34	11	−3	51	−13
Food	4	−7	−1	−7	−3	22	8
Textiles	2	−9	−2	−3	−9	7	−13
Leather	0	0	0	0	0	0	−1
Wood	0	−2	0	−4	0	6	−1
Paper	9	−30	−5	−4	−2	26	−5
Ref. petroleum	−58	−19	−20	−1	−7	82	−23
Chemicals	−37	−19	−19	6	−14	64	−21
Rubber	−2	−2	−1	0	0	3	−2
Non-metallic	14	−30	−14	−27	−1	50	−8
Metals	−88	−27	−21	−12	−12	71	−89
Machinery	2	−3	−2	−4	−3	8	−2
Electrical	−22	4	−2	5	−1	8	−9
Transport	−7	−2	−2	−4	−2	11	−5
Manufacturing	−4	−1	−1	0	−2	3	−4
Electricity	293	−580	−66	−215	−38	805	199

Construction	−16	−3	0	−17	0	23	−14
Maintenance	−5	0	0	0	0	3	−3
Wholesale trade	−37	1	−2	7	−1	17	−14
Retail trade	−72	−4	−1	3	0	43	−31
Hotels	−24	−3	0	−5	0	28	−5
Inland transport	33	−35	−7	−15	−3	66	39
Water transport	0	1	−34	24	−9	21	3
Air transport	−6	−16	−17	−24	−6	66	−3
Other transport	19	1	−2	1	−1	14	33
Telecommunications	−6	2	−1	6	0	11	11
Financial intermediation	−37	10	−1	4	0	16	−8
Real estate activities	−9	0	0	0	0	5	−4
Renting M & Eq	−84	19	−3	13	−2	49	−8
Public admin	−186	−4	0	−40	0	133	−98
Education	−4	−2	0	−1	0	6	0
Health	−48	−1	0	4	0	38	−7
Personal services	−66	−2	−1	−3	−1	30	−42
Private HH	0	0	0	0	0	0	0
Total	−486	−789	−260	−306	−122	1809	−153

Source: Calculated by the authors

Table 11.9 Decomposition of change in CO_2 emissions (in Mt) between 1995 and 2009 by industry: Europe

Sector	Emissions intensity	Industrial structure	Industrial sourcing	Consumer preferences	Final demand sourcing	Consumption level	Total emissions
Agriculture	−33	−11	1	−10	1	35	−17
Mining	5	−20	−21	12	−13	22	−15
Food	−30	−2	−1	−9	0	30	−12
Textiles	−11	−1	−3	−4	−5	8	−15
Leather	−1	0	0	−1	0	1	−2
Wood	−4	0	1	−1	0	3	−2
Paper	−19	−5	−1	−4	0	17	−12
Ref. petroleum	−70	14	2	−10	4	54	−6
Chemicals	−101	−6	−9	8	3	59	−46
Rubber	−12	2	−1	0	0	5	−6
Non-metallic	−85	−14	−9	−19	−1	87	−40
Metals	−161	−11	−18	−9	−2	97	−105
Machinery	−13	0	−1	0	0	7	−7
Electrical	−13	3	−2	3	−2	5	−6
Transport	−17	2	0	3	−2	8	−7
Manufacturing	−7	0	0	−1	0	5	−3
Electricity	−460	−1	−28	−63	−5	469	−88

Construction	−18	−1	0	−7	0	20	−6
Maintenance	−7	1	0	0	0	6	−1
Wholesale trade	−15	2	0	1	0	10	−3
Retail trade	−15	1	0	−1	0	9	−7
Hotels	−2	0	0	−1	0	4	1
Inland transport	−19	4	0	−6	−1	68	45
Water transport	−29	14	−3	3	1	38	24
Air transport	76	−6	−1	8	−11	39	106
Other transport	−3	3	0	−1	0	5	5
Telecommunications	−8	3	0	3	0	3	2
Financial intermediation	−6	1	0	2	0	3	−1
Real estate activities	−6	1	0	0	0	4	−2
Renting M & Eq	−17	9	0	2	0	12	5
Public admin	−14	−1	0	−3	0	10	−8
Education	−5	1	0	−5	0	7	−2
Health	−13	1	0	3	0	9	−1
Personal services	−2	3	0	−3	0	15	12
Private HH	0	0	0	0	0	0	0
Total	−1136	−16	−96	−109	−36	1175	−217

Source: Calculated by the authors

References

Araújo I, Jackson R, Neto ABF, Perobelli F (2018) Environmental costs of European union membership: a structural decomposition analysis. Working papers working paper 2018-04, Regional Research Institute, West Virginia University

Arto I, Dietzenbacher E (2014) Drivers of the growth in global greenhouse gas emissions. Environ Sci Technol 48(10):5388–5394

Brohan P, Kennedy JJ, Harris I, Tett SFB, Jones PD (2006) Uncertainty estimates in regional and global observed surface temperature changes: a new data set from 1850. J Geophys Res 111(D12106):1–21

Brown MA, Kim G, Smith AM, Southworth K (2017) Exploring the impact of energy efficiency as a carbon mitigation strategy in the U.S. Energy Policy 109:249–259

Chang N, Lahr ML (2016) Changes in China's production-source CO_2 emissions: insights from structural decomposition analysis and linkage analysis. Econ Syst Res 28(2):224–242

Chen X, Wang L, Tong L, Sun S, Yue X, Yin S, Zheng L (2014) Mode selection of China's urban heating and its potential for reducing energy consumption and CO_2 emission. Energy Policy 67:756–764

De Hann M (2001) A structural decomposition analysis of pollution in the Netherlands. Econ Syst Res 13(2):181–196

Dietzenbacher E, Hoen AR (1998) Deflation of input-output tables from the user's point of view: a heuristic approach. Rev Income Wealth 44:111–122

Dietzenbacher E, Los B (1998) Structural decomposition techniques: sense and sensitivity. Econ Syst Res 10(4):307–324

Genty A, Arto I, Neuwahl F (2012) Final database of environmental satellite accounts: technical report on their compilation. WIOD Deliverable 4.6, Documentation

Hallegatte S (2009) Strategies to adapt to an uncertain climate change. Glob Environ Chang Hum Policy Dimens 19(2):240–247

Haynes KE (1984) Environment and coal production. In: Proceedings of the modeling and simulation conference. University of Pittsburgh, Pittsburgh

Haynes KE, Hazleton JE, Kleeman T (1977) Environment and energy on the Texas gulf coast: a short run economic impact model of alternative policies. In: Burkhardt DE, Ittelson WH (eds) Environmental assessment of socio-economic systems. Plenum Press, London, pp 493–518

Haynes KE, Ratick S, Bowen WM, Cummings-Saxton J (1993) Environmental decision models: U.S. experience and a new approach to pollution management. Environ Int 19:261–275

Haynes KE, Ratick S, Cummings-Saxton J (1997) Pollution prevention frontiers: a data envelopment simulation. In: Knapp GJ, Kim TJ (eds) Environmental program evaluation: a primer. University of Illinois Press, Urbana, pp 68–84

Hertwich EG, Peters GP (2009) Carbon footprint of nations: a global trade-linked analysis. Environ Sci Technol 43:6414–6420

Hoekstra R, Michel B, Suh S (2016) The emission cost of international sourcing: using structural decomposition analysis to calculate the contribution of international sourcing to CO_2–emission growth. Econ Syst Res 28(2):151–167

Junius T, Oosterhaven J (2003) The solution of updating or regionalizing a matrix with both positive and negative entries. Econ Syst Res 15:87–96

Kangas HL, Lazarevic D, Kivimaa P (2018) Technical skills, disinterest and non-functional regulation: barriers to building energy efficiency in Finland viewed by energy service companies. Energy Policy 114:63–76

Lenzen M, Wood R, Gallego B (2007) Some comments on the GRAS method. Econ Syst Res 19:461–465

Lenzen M, Kanemoto K, Moran D, Geschke A (2012) Mapping the structure of the world economy. Environ Sci Technol 46(15):8374–8381

Los B, Gouma R, Timmer M, IJtsma P (2014) Note on the construction of wiots in previous years prices. Technical report, WIOD

Malik A, Lan J (2016) The role of outsourcing in driving global carbon emissions. Econ Syst Res 28(2):168–182
Masson-Delmotte V, Zhai P, Pörtner HO, Roberts D, Skea J, Shukla JR, Pirani A, Moufouma-Okia W, Péan C, Pidcock R, Connors S, Matthews JBR, Chen Y, Zhou X, Gomis MI, Lonnoy E, Maycock T, Tignor M, Waterfield T (eds) Intergovernmental Panel on Climate Change (2018) Summary for policymakers. In: Global warming of 1.5°C. An IPCC special report on the impacts of global warming of 1.5°C above pre-industrial levels and related global greenhouse gas emission pathways, in the context of strengthening the global response to the threat of climate change, sustainable development, and efforts to eradicate poverty. World Meteorological Organization, Geneva, Switzerland, 32 pp
Meng L, Crijn-Graus WHJ, Worrell E, Huang B (2018) Impacts of booming economic growth and urbanization on carbon dioxide emissions in Chinese megalopolises over 1985–2010: an index decomposition analysis. Energy Effic 11:203–223
Mi Z, Men J, Guan D, Sham Y, Song M, Wei Y-M, Liu Z, Hubacek K (2017) Chinese CO_2 emission flows have reversed since the global financial crisis. Nat Commun 8:1712
Miller RE, Blair PD (2009) Input–output analysis: foundations and extensions. Cambridge University Press, Cambridge
Minx JC, Lamb WF, Callaghan MW, Fuss S, Hilaire J, Creutzig F, Amann T, Beringer T, de Loiveira Garcia W, Hartmann J, Khanna T, Lenzi D, Luderer G, Nemet GF, Rogelj J, Smith P, Vicente JL, Wilcox J, del Mar Zamora Dominguez M (2018) Negative emissions—part 1: research landscape and synthesis. Environ Res Lett 13:063001
Moss RH, Edmonds JA, Hibbard KA, Manning MR, Rose SK, van Vuuren DP, Carter TR, Emori S, Kainuma M, Kram T, Meehl GA, Mitchell JFB, Nakicenovic N, Riahi K, Smith SJ, Stouffer RJ, Thomson AM, Weyant JP, Wilbanks TJ (2010) The next generation of scenarios for climate change research and assessment. Nature 463(7282):747–756
Oosterhaven J, Van Der Linden J (1997) European technology, trade and income changes for 1975–85: an intercountry input–output decomposition. Econ Syst Res 9(4):393–412
Ozan C, Haldenbilen S, Halim C (2011) Estimating emissions on vehicular traffic based on projected energy and transport demand on rural roads: policies for reducing air pollutant emissions and energy consumption. Energy Policy 39(5):2542–2549
Peters GP, Minx JC, Weber CL, Edenhofer O (2011) Growth in emission transfers via international trade from 1990 to 2008. PNAS 108(21):8903–8908
Petit JR, Jouzel J, Raynaud D, Barkov NI, Barnola JM, Basile I, Bender M, Chappellaz J, Davis M, Delaygue G, Delmotte M, Kotlyakov VM, Legrand M, Lipenkov VY, Lorius C, Pepin L, Ritz C, Saltzman E, Stievenard M (1999) Climate and atmospheric history of the past 420,000 years from the Vostok ice core, Antarctica. Nature 399:429–436. https://doi.org/10.1038/20859
Qu Y, Long H (2018) The economic and environmental effects of land se transitions under rapid urbanization and the implications for land use management. Habitat Int 82:113–121
Ramanathan V (1988) The greenhouse gas theory of climate change: a test by an inadvertent global experiment. Science (April 15: 240, 4850):293–299
Steinberger JK, van Niel J, Bourg D (2009) Profiting from negawatts: reducing absolute consumption and emissions through a performance-based energy economy. Energy Policy 37:361–370
Timmer MP, Dietzenbacher E, Los B, Stehrer R, De Vries GJ (2015) An illustrated user guide to the world input–output database: the case of global automotive production. Rev Int Econ 23(3):575–605
Turner K, Lenzen K, Wiedmann T, Barrett J (2007) Examining the global environmental impact of regional consumption activities – part 1: a technical note on combining input output and ecological footprint analysis. Ecol Econ 62(1):6–10
Vale VA, Perobelli FS, Chimeli AB (2018) International trade, pollution, and economic structure: evidence on CO_2 emissions for the North and the South. Econ Syst Res 30(1):1–17
Wang XR, Hui EC, Choguill CM, Jia SH (2015) The new urbanization in China: which way forward? Habitat Int 47:279–284

Wiedmann T, Lenzen M, Turner K, Barrett T (2007) Examining the global environmental impact of regional consumption activities – Part 2: review of input–output models for the assessment of environmental impacts embodied in trade. Ecol Econ 61(1):37–44

Wier M (1998) Sources of changes in emissions from energy: a structural decomposition analysis. Econ Syst Res 10(2):99–113

Xu S-C, He Z-X, Long R-Y (2014) Factors that influence carbon emissions due to energy consumption in China: decomposition analysis using LMDI. Appl Energy 127:182–193

Yamakawa A, Peters GP (2011) Structural decomposition analysis of greenhouse gas emissions in Norway. Econ Syst Res 23(3):303–318

Yang XJ (2013) China's rapid urbanization. Science 342(6156):310

Zhang H, Lahr ML (2014) Can the carbonizing dragon be domesticated? Insights from a decomposition of energy consumption and intensity in China, 1987–2007. Econ Syst Res 26(2):119–140

Zhang YJ, Liu Z, Qin CX, Tan TD (2017a) The direct and indirect CO_2 rebound effect for private cars in China. Energy Policy 100:149–161

Zhang Z, Zhu K, Hewings GJ (2017b) A multi-regional input-output analysis of the pollution haven hypothesis from the perspective of global production fragmentation. Energy Econ 64:13–23

Chapter 12
Uneven Development in Bangladesh: A Temporal and Regional Analysis

Syed Abu Hasnath

Abstract During the past quarter century, although Bangladesh's economic growth has consistently registered a sustained growth of 6%, its benefits have been highly unevenly distributed across the country's regions—creating leading and lagging areas that laid bare the yawning gaps between economic classes. Based on secondary data, this paper analyzes interhousehold income inequality and the disparities between the northern and southern divisions in Bangladesh. Within a theoretical framework of development, including the notions of equality, we look at some temporal and spatial evidence of income inequality and regional disparities that call for government intervention for inclusive development, as opposed to unregulated market-led economic growth tainted by corruption. Our analysis suggests that mobilization and allocation of resources for industries, infrastructure, and social overheads in lagging regions will help grow income levels and alleviate peoples' suffering due to poor linkages with two metropolitan cores of the country—the capital city of Dhaka and the port city of Chittagong. Accordingly, we put forward an approach that emphasizes redistribution with growth in public-sector resource allocation—in particular, division-wise separate development budget with a priority to Rangpur, Barisal, and Mymensingh division, the most deprived regions of the country. In this allocation process, emphasis should be given to poor groups of the people as well as to poor regions of the country.

Keywords Bangladesh · Chittagong · Dhaka · Development · Economic core · Inequalities · Infrastructure · Regional · Spatial-temporal · Uneven

---

S. A. Hasnath (✉)
Center for Urban Studies, Dhaka, Bangladesh

Z. Chen et al. (eds.), *Development Studies in Regional Science*,
New Frontiers in Regional Science: Asian Perspectives 42,
https://doi.org/10.1007/978-981-15-1435-7_12

12.1 Introduction and the Issues

It is common practice in the economic development literature to categorize uneven development in terms of *regional* development challenges, whereas regional development is actually an economic mosaic superimposed on a piece of national geography. In this essay, we define uneven development as "the condition of an economy of the *country* which has not benefited equally from development either in a spatial sense (economic geography) or within *classes* in society" (macroeconomic sense). Accordingly, the discussion below falls into two parts—economic inequality (i.e., unequal distribution of income and wealth of the country) followed by regional disparity in the level of development in Bangladesh.

Bangladesh embarked on the path toward industrialization and has achieved notable success with an impressive rate of economic growth—6 plus percent annual average gross domestic product—over the last two and a half decades. Steady economic growth has catapulted the country to the 42nd ranking largest economy in the world. With the introduction of democracy in 1991, Bangladesh GDP started growing at double the rate and began surpassing the paltry rate of 3% growth rate of the previous decade. The growth was accompanied by a considerable progress in poverty reduction, gender equality, and several other indicators of socioeconomic development. In terms of the human development index, Bangladesh outshines neighboring countries, India and Pakistan (Sen 2013).

Given limited resources in the country, there has been a substantial increase in public investment in infrastructure—including power generation, building roads and bridges, and telecommunications. Progress in electricity generation was considerable along with additional major projects in the pipeline to accelerate infrastructure growth and development in the country. Foreign Direct Investment (FDI) into the country has consistently increased year over year during the last decade. Bangladesh will continue to need additional investment—domestic and foreign—to continue the present rate of economic growth of 7% and beyond. From the welfare perspective, economic growth in Bangladesh is working well, and added social security net programs—including health and age-related allowances—have driven down overall levels of extreme poverty.

While the growth is projected to rise at a higher rate (8%)—and the country is striving for the middle-income status by 2021—the distribution of the economic benefits of growth is highly uneven among households and across regions, widening the gap between rich and poor. The Gini coefficient for Bangladesh in 1990 was reasonable at 0.320; by 2016, the Gini coefficient for household incomes had increased to 0.483, representing high inequality at the national level. A regional perspective of income inequality in Bangladesh indicates that monthly household income of Rangpur division is less than 60% income of households in Chittagong division. The incidence of poverty in Rangpur and Rajshahi divisions is four times than that of Dhaka and Chittagong divisions (BBS 2016).

As such this paper deals with an apparently paradoxical case of development where despite an accelerating rate of economic growth—accompanied by substantial progress on eradicating extreme poverty—income inequality and regional disparity are nonetheless simultaneously on the rise as well. In this case economic growth benefits only the select few and is enjoyed by a small group of families; this type of growth does not really help the poor. Section 12.2 discusses the importance of region in the context of uneven development. It covers why uneven regional development matters for the economic implications of development and summarizes the thoughts of various scholars of development studies on the issue. Section 12.3 is a selective literature review to illuminate two sets of opposing views: (1) is inequality good or bad and what kind of inequality matters and (2) balanced versus imbalanced regional development. Section 12.4 is the core of the paper. It is divided into two parts: a temporal analysis of unequal income distribution and spatial inequality in regional development in Bangladesh—what are the causes of uneven development in recent years, why it is getting worse so rapidly, and consequences of the phenomenon. The causes of unequal distribution have been considered from an economic perspective (Kuznets hypothesis), financial perspective (endemic corruption), administrative perspective (rent seeking), and political perspective (democracy deficit). The final Sect. 12.5 draws conclusions and presents a number of policy recommendations for achieving sustainable development in Bangladesh.

12.2 Uneven Regional Development Matters

In this section, we focus on uneven regional development of historical importance. Marx wrote extensively about inequality that results from capitalism. The concept of uneven development originates in Marxist thought—with seminal contributions of Lenin and Trotsky to the political economy of capitalism that creates and sustains rising inequality between the rich and the poor and between developed (core) and (underdeveloped) periphery or lagging regions. Ironically uneven regional development was attributed as one of the major causes of the dissolution of the former Soviet Union (Bradshaw and Lynn 1994).

In the context of Bangladesh, a brief recapitulation of the history of uneven political and economic development between the two wings of former Pakistan has an important lesson of experience. Although there were many causes of the failure of national integration in Pakistan, the economic disparity between the two wings—West Pakistan and East Pakistan—had been a major source of discontent and a driving force behind the movement for independence. GDP growth per annum for the period between 1949–1950 and 1959–1960 was 3.1% in West Pakistan and 1.9% in East Pakistan. For the next decade (1961–1970) West Pakistan's economy grew at an annual rate of 6.7%, while East Pakistan's economy expanded by 4% annually. As a result, per capita income difference between West and East Pakistan increased from Rs. 51 in 1949–1950 to Rs. 206 in 1961–1970 (in 1969–1970 price in Rupees) or more than fourfold over the two decades. Social development in East Pakistan was also neglected (Hasnath 2011: 58). The emergence of Bangladesh as a separate nation-state was the product of people's movement that challenged the persistent denial of economic rights to the people of East Pakistan, now Bangladesh.

12.3 Review of Contested Approaches to Uneven Development

Evidence-based discussion of income inequality began with the seminal work of Kuznets' inverted U-hypothesis (1954). His hypothesis points that the first stages of development tend to have inequality, followed by improvements in income distribution later because of structural change in the economy. The merit of structural change lies in empowering economic productivity. The situation is reconsidered by Birdsall (2007) and some other economist as *constructive* (or good) *inequality* for developing countries (Aizeman et al. 2012), provided the tip of the U-shaped inequality curve tapers off sooner rather than later.

The empirical validity of the Kuznets hypothesis has been investigated extensively to mixed results. The experience of economic growth during the peak of the industrial revolution (1820–1880) tends to support the Kuznets curve, but the East Asian Miracle (1960–1990) with low inequality and high economic growth provides a different account.

Authors who approve of and encourage capitalism argue that income inequality is not a *bad* thing: capitalism functions—and flourishes—on the basis of inequality. Capitalists have money, entrepreneurship, talent, and drive to achieve. They work hard, innovate, and take risk and thereby generate employment and raise economic growth through reinvestment of their accumulated capital. While income from total output is distributed among factors of production (land, labor, and capital) and the benefits of growth trickles down to everyone, a rising tide lifts all boats[1] (Okun 1975; Rashid 1991).

There is a plethora of criticism against the above statement. We will put forth only a few of those challenging the so-called "meritocracy" arguments. First, "the tendency of returns on capital is to exceed the rate of economic growth [r>g] which means those with capital are able to accumulate wealth quicker than the rest of the population" (Piketty 2014). Second, accumulated capital from business is not always reinvested and used for job creation. There are several leakages, including offshore savings, tax avoidance, flight of capital, and investment in assets abroad. The process helps the capitalists, not the economy. Third, as the business grows, the tendency of entrepreneurs to substitute capital results in jobless growth and inequality due to unemployment increases. Fourth, a successful business needs more than

[1]The phrase is commonly attributed to President John F. Kennedy who used it in a 1963 speech to combat criticisms at a large investment in mega projects. He argued that although there are policies where the initial beneficiaries are high-income earners, eventually the benefits are accrued by all people.

meritocracy: it also needs political patronage and spoils system behind the scenes. Finally, the concept of trickle-down effect is controversial: the poorest gain a marginal increase, while the rich gain a large percentage, thus transforming inequality toward a case of *destructive* inequality (Pettinger 2016).

Instead of praising capitalism and tax breaks for the rich in the United States, President Obama believed "the middle class grows the US economy, not the rich."

Consider that in 1947 to 1979, when the middle class received 54% of the nation's total income on average, the economy grew at a steady clip of 3.7% per year. That was 1% higher than the 2.7% rate it grew from 1980 to 2010, when the middle class started weakening to its current share of only 46% (Madland 2011).

President Obama explained this negative impact on growth using a rationale that is close to the substance of the *General Theory of Employment, Interest and Money of 1936* by Keynes. The assertion of Keynesian Economics is that aggregate demand—measured as the sum of *spending* by households, businesses, and the government—is the driving force in an economy. An initial change in aggregate demand for goods and services can lead to a bigger eventual final effect on output and employment. This is known as the multiplier effect. The spread of income among a large number of average households helps accelerate economic growth and social development. If national income is concentrated in the hands of few, it deprives the economy of consumer demand, the main engine of growth.

Economist Jean Tirole says that economic inequality itself is a "form of market failure." A higher level of inequality impedes economic growth and dampens educational opportunities and social mobility. Professor Gary Becker argues in his *Theory of Intergenerational Mobility* that wealthy families stay rich because they pass down not just money to their children but human capital, including the access to education and skills, and that this allows them to maintain their privileged position in the society. The argument is further elaborated by Piketty in *Capital* by evaluating "wealth inheritance and inequality."[2]

Professor Amartya Sen (2000) looks into the evolution of income distribution and related features of economic inequality from the perspective of *social justice*—a combination of reasoning and policy. Against the background of India's 1990s onward economic boom and widening of income inequality, Amartya Sen with Jean Drèze (2013) argue in *An Uncertain Glory: India and Its Contradictions* that in the absence of "participatory growth and to make good use of the public resources generated by economic growth to enhance people's living condition, including shelter and services, the future of development in India is uncertain (unsustainable)."

In the same year, *An Uncertain Glory* was published; another book—*Why Growth Matters*—from the Harrod-Domar school of economic thought is written by two Columbia University professors, Jagdish Bhagwati and Arvind Panagariya (2013). They emphasized growth over distribution—a triumph of the free market

[2]Piketty revealed that since 1980, the real income growth of the bottom 50% population has been virtually zero in in the United States, while in 1980, the average income of top 1% was 27 times higher than the bottom 50%. In 2014, this gap widened 81 times (Alam 2018).

liberalization that took place in India in the 1990s. Their favorite model of economic growth is overwhelmingly dominated by "how much you saved (and invested) and how much you get out of that investment (capital-output ratio)."[3]

Issues in growing income inequality among the newly independent less developed countries in Asia and Africa surfaced in the late 1960s. In the mid-1970s, a large number of economists became disillusioned with growth-oriented viewpoints of national economic growth that resulted in inequalities of income and the virtual exclusion of a large segment of the national population (Lakshmanan 1981).

During the same period, the *basic needs* approach to development was introduced by ILO's World Employment Program. The approach puts the needs of the poor at the center of development strategy, and many developing countries endorsed the approach. The two approaches—redistribution with growth and basic needs—provide a springboard for the introduction to the UN Millennium Development Goals (MDGs), followed by the Sustainable Development Goals (SDGs) 2015–2030.

The above authors and institutions mainly focused on macroeconomic aspects of inequality (poverty, income, wealth, and Gini coefficient), not the plural conception of development—housing, transportation, water supply, sanitation, of people, particularly life and living of the urban poor. It was not until the seminal work by a Marxist Geographer, David Harvey—in his book *Social Justice and the City* (1973)—that the normative issues in the geography of difference and distribution were addressed.

12.4 Aspects of Income Inequality and Regional Disparity

Since the publication of the Bangladesh Bureau of Statistics [BBS] *Report of the Household Income and Expenditure Survey* [HIES] *2010*, income inequality gained prominence as a major concern in civil society. We present empirical evidence of unequal income distribution over two consecutive periods: 2010 and 2016 with occasional mention of the year 2005. The distribution of household income is located between production and consumption and hence plays an important role in productivity and economic growth of a country (Oshima 1992). The data on this temporal variation was taken from the two reports on HIES and other statistics published by (BBS), as well as some additional published data.

[3]Amartya Sen, however, never downplayed economic growth for redistribution but sees the interconnection of democracy, distribution, and economic growth. He had tried to stress the importance of education and investment in social infrastructure to attain and sustain growth.

Table 12.1 Percentage distribution of income accruing to household in groups (decile) and Gini Coefficient 2010 and HIES 2016

Household	2010			2016		
Income decile	National	Rural	Urban	National	Rural	Urban
Total decile	100.00	100.00	100.00	100.00	100.00	100.00
Lower 5%	0.78	0.88	0.76	0.23	0.25	0.27
Decile 1	2.0	2.23	1.98	1.01	1.06	1.16
Decile 2	3.22	3.53	3.09	2.83	3.00	2.99
Decile 3	4.10	4.49	3.95	4.04	4.33	4.18
Decile 4	5.00	5.43	5.01	5.13	5.47	4.09
Decile 5	6.1	6.43	6.31	6.23	6.63	5.91
Decile 6	7.32	7.65	7.64	7.51	7.95	7.17
Decile 7	9.06	9.31	9.30	9.12	9.44	8.35
Decile 8	11.50	11.50	11.87	11.33	11.78	10.49
Decile 9	15.94	15.54	16.08	14.84	15.49	13.31
Decile 10	35.84	33.89	34.77	38.16	34.84	41.44
Top 5%	24.61	23.93	23.39	27.89	24.25	32.12
Gini coefficient	0.458	0.430	0.452	0.483	0.454	0.498

Source: Preliminary Report on Household Income and Expenditure Survey 2016. Bangladesh Bureau of Statistics (BBS). Government of Bangladesh. Table 7, pp. 27–28

12.4.1 Household Economic (Income and Wealth) Inequality

The BBS-HIES reports are reasonably exhaustive nationwide surveys. They provide reliable data on household income and expenditure showing distribution and change from 2010 to 2016. Following is a concise statement of what the reports tell us (Table 12.1).

The findings indicate that the highest 10% of households owned 38.16% of the national income in 2016. Their share was 35.84 in 2010; they captured 2.32% more of the national income in only 5 years. On the contrary, the lowest 10% of households' income shares have halved: from 2% in 2010 to just 1% in 2016. The contrast is enhanced with the share of income with the lowest 5% households that reduced from 0.78% in 2010 to a meager 0.23% in 2016, while the income share of the top 5% increased from 24.61% in 2010 to 27.89% in 2016.

It is obvious that there is an overall downward trend in decile 1–decile 3 income groups (the poorer section of the society), but income share has increased in decile 5–decile 10 income groups (the richer section). The gain in the income share of the household groups in the decile 10 was high (6.5%), and the gain of top 5% was disproportionately high—13.5%. A few other examples of inequality are given below.

Reliable data on wealth distribution in Bangladesh depicts the growing phenomenon of ultra-wealth in Bangladesh. The uneven distribution of wealth is conspicuously evident: more than half of national wealth is concentrated in the top 5% of households, while the bottom 5% of households possess a virtually non-existent 0.05%.

The Swiss National Bank Annual Report 2016 disclosed that deposits by Bangladeshi citizens have gone up remarkably—19% increase from 2015 to 2016. The amount of deposit was close to $7 billion. The Washington-based Global Financial Integrity study (2017) revealed the total amount of illicit capital outflow between 2005 and 2016 was $81.74 billion. The money siphoned off the country in 11 years is equal to one-third of the country's GDP in 2017 [*New Age* (Dhaka) January 29, 2019].

12.4.2 Poverty Profile and the and Sources of Prosperity

The Household Income and Expenditure Survey (HIES) 2016 reports 24.3% of the population (or almost 1 in 4 Bangladeshis) live in poverty, following the international poverty line at $1.90 (per person per day). In the poverty reduction literature, however, it is commonplace to discuss more about "extreme poverty" line at $1.25 per person per day. Then people who live in conditions of extreme poverty are about 22 million (13% of total population). The Survey shows that the rate of overall poverty reduction is sustained, but the pace of poverty reduction among the ultra-poor has declined from 1.7%, between 2005 and 2010, to 1.2%, between 2010 and 2016. A similar trend is observed in population living in upper poverty line. The pace of poverty reduction was faster during the previous 5 years (2005–2010) than the following 6 years (2010–2016).

The reasons for slowing down the pace of poverty reduction can be seen from following interrelated perspectives:

1. *Jobless growth*: This is a situation where the economy grows but generates few jobs. In Bangladesh, during the last 5 years (2012–2017), the economy grew at an average rate of 6.5%, while employment grew at an anemic 1%, leaving one-third of the able-bodied population unemployed. In 2018, among university graduates, more than 4o% were unemployed. "Besides the low quality of education, there are serious gaps between demand and supply of skills" (Quibria 2019: 107).
2. *Inadequate income of farmers and people belonging to urban informal sector*: "Farmers celebrate bumper yields but cry for fair price" (December 14, 2014 *Daily Star*, Dhaka). Another poverty-stricken group is the urban informal sector people—their number is large and growing bigger, living in *mega cites* of Dhaka and Chittagong. They play a significant role in the urban economy but live an unstable life in slums with inadequate income and extremely limited access to basic sanitation, urban amenities, and social institutions (Morshed 2018).
3. *Limited social security*: Although the government has introduced statutory social safety net programs that involve spending more than 2% of GDP yearly, it covers only 30% of the nation's poor, with the rest having to go completely without. Critics say "the social assistance for the needy is far from requirement. . .payments of allowances are not regular, rather nebulous, while such programs deserve high priority to ensure the entitlements of the poor,

including the urban poor who are most neglected and marginalized in the society" (Rashid 2019).

4. *Low wage for the poor and high income earning and non-earning income opportunity for the rich*: The minimum wage in Bangladesh is one of the lowest in the world. During the last 7 years (2011–2018) the minimum wage increased only 3%, while cost of living, particularly house rent, utility price, transport, and medical expenses, has risen manifold.

As with monopolies and oligopolies, in Bangladesh a very small group of families own and control the greater share of industries (manufacturing and construction), banks, real estates, power supply, private universities, high-end hospitals, telecommunication service, television stations, and enormous political capital. Besides private ownership of the means of production to produce new output of goods and services, there is another small but well-connected and powerful group that conducts business through corruption and rent seeking. Four major sources of making this abundance of *unearned* money in Bangladesh are as follows.

The banking sector in Bangladesh is severely plagued by loan defaults also known as nonperforming loans (NPL). As of September 2018, NPLs accounted for 11% of total banking loans and $12 billion USD. Out of this, $10 billion has already been written off as unrecoverable. The NPL volume swells in latter months.

Power generation by Quick Rental Power Plant. Over the last two decades (1990–2010), there have been serious, frequent power shortages in Bangladesh. The economic cost of power outage in the industrial sector and load shedding at the domestic level compelled the government to enter into a contractual agreement for an exorbitantly high-cost temporary solution with private sector companies under the Quick Rental Power Plant (QRPP) umbrella. This alternative was chosen against what would otherwise have been the normal process of going through the public sector and expanding the capacity-building of the public utility Power Development Board. The main points of criticism leveled on the project include:

(a) The privatization of a critical public good in the name of public-private partnership.
(b) The deal was commissioned and negotiated between the government and the private companies and bypassed provisions of normal tender process.
(c) The QRPP Indemnity Bill (2012) was passed in the Parliament to give immunity from legal action to the companies involved in irregularities.

As a result, electricity price increased more than seven times in 7 years in Bangladesh (2012–2018) during the period when at the global level energy prices were steeply falling.

Another sector displaying the signs of deep corruption in Bangladesh is its *construction sector*. During the last 7 years (2011–2018), the cost of construction in Bangladesh has increased 25 times; that means each year increases by more than double (2.3 times). The cost of construction of road depends on many factors, including the type of road, the width of the road (or number of lanes), and design of the road. In general, the cost of road construction per kilometer in China is $1.2 million; in India, $1.25 million; in Europe, $3.5 million; and in Bangladesh, $6.5 million. Road construction is primarily a labor-intensive public works project, and the wage of construction workers in Bangladesh is one of the lowest in the world. It is difficult to justify by any valid ground that the construction cost in Bangladesh could be five times higher than India. Professor Jamilur Reza Choudhury, highly respected academic and a civil engineer, believes this is due to the *unholy nexus* between the bureaucrats and the politicians. Others say it is due to the lack of accountability and integrity in public service breeding corruption (*bdnews.com* April 28, 2018, Dhaka).

The incidence of buying goods and services by the government (for instance, procurement of food from international market) and posting of public and semi-public positions (for instance, the position of managing director of a commercial bank) often involve favor, bribes, and kickbacks at the decision-making level. The process is known as state-crafted (political) corruption (Gardizi et al. 2010). In this process of financial irregularities and favor distribution, some people get rich overnight creating further inequality in the society. The incidence of both types of corruption and rent seeking by non-development actors is ubiquitous in Bangladesh (Quibria 2019: 97).

Many experts believe that while corruption is a serious impediment to socioeconomic development and consolidation of the country, without consolidated and stable democracy the vice cannot be uprooted. "The histories of countries where once-high levels of corruption have fallen, in the course of the evolution of more open and competitive politics, support this view" (Johnston 1991). However, in the case of Bangladesh, democracy still has not taken root in politics after nearly half a century of independence.

Democracy Deficit. The raison d'être of the liberation war, following the independence of the country, was to establish a democratic peoples' Republic of Bangladesh where fundamental rights of the people and freedom of the press are granted. Although Bangladesh is going to celebrate its golden jubilee of independence in 2021, the country has failed to establish democracy (and thus limit corruption) as an institution. From the early years of independence, the country has been facing problems to institutionalize democracy with free, fair, and transparent elections that create a vibrant parliament with credible opposition. Press freedom in Bangladesh is the lowest in South Asia (*New Age*, 18 April 2019).

During the present decade (2009–2019), there were two general elections—one in 2014 and other in 2018. The 2014 election was held "amid boycott and violence, leaving the ruling party unopposed in over half the seats." The 2018 election is also marred by major irregularities: the ruling coalition won with 96% of all seats. The opposition rejected the outcome, and the impasse of one-party rule continues (*Economist*: January 3, 2019). The net result is democracy in Bangladesh without political pluralism and participation. According to a Freedom House Report, Bangladesh is partly free; its civil liberty score is half of India (Table 12.2).

Table 12.2 Freedom in the world 2016 (country scores)

	Freedom status	Political right	Civil liberties	Freedom rating	Aggregate score
Bangladesh	Partly free	4	4	4.0	49
India	Free	2	2	2.75	77
Indian Kashmir	Partly free	4	4	4.0	51

Source: https://freedomhouse.org/report/freedom-world-2016/table-scores
PR political rights, *CL* civil liberties
CL, PR, and freedom rating score explanation: *(1 = most free and 7 = least free)*
Aggregate score explanation: *(0 = WORST, 100 = BEST)*

12.4.3 Unequal Growth Between Sectors and Within a Sector

During the early stage of growth in developing countries, the ideas of size of investment and its determinants were dominated by two popular—but seemingly conflicting—arguments in the 1950s and 1960s economic development literature.

The idea of Big Push theory by Rosenstein-Rodan (1943) is that a large and comprehensive package of coordinated public investment in overhead capital—and simultaneous installation of many mutually supportive industries in different regions of the country—are required for taking the low-income economies off the ground before the economy is self-generating (Kumar 1974).

The potential and viability of adopting a "Big Push" approach to development in Bangladesh is constrained by many factors, including large development fund, aid absorption capacity, and corruption-free governance.

The liberation war of Bangladesh ended in December 1971, leaving the country in unprecedented destruction and hardship. The most acute problems in post-liberation Bangladesh were food supply and transport. Bangladesh did not receive any massive economic support from the outside world for the reconstruction of the country. Even today most of the development projects are funded from its own resources: the self-funding Padma Bridge project is a case in point. Policymakers out of necessity selectively pick up projects and allocate resources on a priority basis, thus disqualifying Bangladesh as a good candidate for Big Push model.

Albert Hirschman (1958) presented an opposing view of Big Push in which unbalanced growth of sectors and regions is a better development strategy. Limited resources in developing countries should be invested in the industries and regions with the most potential to accrue external economies and increasing return to scale.

Bangladesh development priorities are reflected in the Perspective Plan 2010–2021. The first propriety is a drastic reduction in poverty. To achieve this goal, economic growth—with productive employment for large labor force—is a key aim of the plan.

The Plan envisages the role of the public sector as a facilitator for attracting private sector investment. Accordingly, the resource is allocated to selected sectors with priorities given as follows:

- *Agriculture including fisheries*: This sector enjoys a larger share in the national budget (6%) with generous subsidies to input supply and extension services. Agriculture provides sustaining food self-sufficiency of the nation and plays key role in reducing poverty.
- *Energy sector*: Energy is a crucial input to modern production system, and it is non-substitutable. The use of energy has increased over time in association with GDP growth all over the world. As the economic activities grow, the demand for energy equally increases, and the government must set clear priorities in the energy sector.
- *Transport infrastructure* permits and promotes productive activities. The network contributes to market integration and social interaction of the country and while vital to economic activities is costly due to difficult terrain (Haynes et al. 1990). Accordingly, the sector is one of the three priority areas for national action and gets a substantial portion (12.5%) of the national budget (2017–2018).

This selective approach with priority to certain sectors bears some resemblance to Hirschman's approach to imbalance development strategy. However, the priority of one sector at the negligence of other sectors—such as industrial services and housing—may not be an efficient allocation of resources.

The small share of industrial and economic services (1% of the national budget) could be one reason for the stagnant level of investment as percentage of GDP. The investment GDP ratio accounts for around 30%—23% from private sector and 7% from the government.

The share of housing sector in the national budget is also minuscule (1% in 2017–2018), and there is no specific expenditure heading for urban development. It is included in housing and gets approximately 2% from local government and rural development head. Urban areas contribute 70% to GDP; Dhaka city alone contributes close to 40%. But its contribution is not counted. The role of cities in economic development is not much appreciated in the context on national economic policies. The problems of urban areas are treated more as welfare problems and sectors of residual investment rather than as issues of national economic importance (Hasnath and Ameen 2018: 97). This is a major cause of poor living condition in urban areas. While the overall living condition in the four metropolitan cities of the country is depressing, the condition of urban poor is palpable—and inequality between the rich and poor within cities is a stark reality.

Let us look at the situation in Dhaka. The level of congestion, pollution, and waterlogging is so high in Dhaka metropolitan area that the very existence of the metropolis seems threatened. Both high rise residential development and slums and squatters are ubiquitous and growing fast. Whatever small amount of fund (1% of the national budget) is allocated to housing sector is utilized for government and semi-government—employees. They also get subsidized land and house-building loans. The well-off buy (or build) their own house; less well-off rent their accommodation. Shortage of owner-occupied housing and apartments for rent loom large. Housing is a huge problem of urban life in Dhaka. The urban poor live in slums and semi-slum shelters with inadequate or no municipal services. Nearly half a million street children work on the street and sleep on the pavement or in rail station. Most of them live on meager income and suffer from malnutrition and weak health; some of them use drugs.

Another example of inequality is the over-occupancy of circulation space in the city. Private cars occupy more than 60% of road space in Dhaka yet carrying only 8% of total commuters, while public transportation, which carries 3 million passengers a day—takes up only about 7% road space. According to a World Bank Report (2017), in the last 10 years the average traffic speed in Dhaka has dropped from 21 kmph to 7 kmph. Another study (BRAC) says traffic congestion in Dhaka eats up around 5 million working hours yearly and costs the country 12 billion USD every year. The financial loss is a calculation of the cost of time lost in traffic congestion and the money spent on operating vehicles for the extra hours, not the cost of life lost due to pollution and accident [*Daily Star* (Dhaka) May 13, 2018].

It is a commonplace to observe housing shortage, traffic congestion, pollution, and slum dwelling as externalities of the precarious rise of megacities in developing countries. But it is also a common practice in most of those countries to address the problem squarely. For example, the government of India renamed the Ministry of Housing as the Ministry of *Housing and Urban Poverty Alleviation*. The Modi government has unveiled an unprecedented focus on cities: 84 new projects on urban development and urban renewal have been launched with an allocation of 100,000 crore Rupees [1 crore = ten million].

The Kolkata Municipal Corporation has taken up slum improvement projects under schemes such as Kolkata Urban Services for the Poor and Kolkata Environment. The success of these projects directly conveys one message: "government intent," columnist Subrata Niyogi said.

By comparison in Bangladesh over the last four decades, there has been no substantial investment for either slum rehabilitation or urban renewal. In 2012, the government took the initiative to build some 7560 flats at the outskirt of Dhaka city. The venture failed on two counts: (1) the constructed flats meant for slum dwellers were being sold off at a higher price to those outside the target group and (2) the developer could not maintain the terms and conditions set by the government and as such the project ended in a fiasco. The urban real estate as a whole is in disarray [*Financial Express* (Dhaka) March 31, 2018].

12.4.4 Regional Disparity in Levels of Development

A region is not simply a division of a territory demarcated by administrative boundary but a piece of geography with natural or man-made social characteristics "which mark it off as being different from the areas around it." Examples are urban and rural, periurban and urban core, and urban middle- and high-income residential areas versus slums and squatters and dilapidated neighborhoods in old towns.

The divisions and sub-divisions of geography experiences, issues in regional disparity, and the role of geography in development—density, distance, urbanization, scale economies, and agglomeration—play an important role to increase inequality, between urban and rural areas, between urban areas, and within the urban area (World Bank 2009).

Since the early 1980s, Bangladesh has been pursuing industrialization as a strategy aimed at promoting rapid economic growth and social progress. During the last quarter century (1991–2017), the contribution of the industrial sector doubled—from 16% to 32%. Industrialization is one of the major causes of urbanization creating economic growth and employment opportunity followed by service sector development. Other causes of urbanization are public administration, education, business, and social functions. Let us see where the major industries, business, government offices, educational institutions, and cultural centers are located.

Bangladesh is divided into eight divisions: Dhaka, Mymensingh, Chittagong, Khulna, Rajshahi, Rangpur, Sylhet, and Barisal. In our analysis we consider each administrative division as a region. Mymensingh division was created in 2015; before that it was part of Dhaka division. As separate data for many indicators of development (underdevelopment) in Mymensingh is not available, we have considered Dhaka and Mymensingh together as Dhaka division; however, where data for Mymensingh is available, we have used it (Map 12.1).

Readymade garment (RMG) industry makes up 80% of the country's total exports, followed by pharmaceutical products and leather goods. About 90% of RMG factories are located in and around Dhaka Metropolitan Region. After readymade garments, the pharmaceutical industry is the second largest contributor—with net worth of $2 billion—to the national exchequer. The top 20 pharmaceutical companies with their manufacturing plants are located in Dhaka. Another major industry is leather and leather products. This industry too is in Dhaka. As is evident, the major industries that boost the Bangladesh economy are all located in Dhaka and its surrounding urban centers—within 20 miles radius of the city.

Dhaka is the center of national government, trade, education, and culture. Out of 115 universities in the country, about 50 (14 public and 36 private) universities are located in and around Dhaka Metropolitan Region, another 30 university in Chittagong. Out of 42 television stations, 40 are in Dhaka and 2 in Chittagong.

Chittagong division is the second largest economy of the country. Located along the Bay of Bengal, the division is endowed with the number one seaport known as the Gateway of Bangladesh for foreign trade. There are a number of beaches along the bay, including the most popular tourist attraction, Cox's Bazar Beach.

Khulna is the third largest city and the fourth largest economy of Bangladesh. The country's second largest seaport (Mongla) is located in this division. The city is an important hub of industry, business, and commerce. The major economic sector includes jute, chemicals, fish and seafood packaging, food processing, sugar mills, power generation, and shipbuilding.

All the three divisions—Dhaka, Chittagong, and Khulna—belong to the southern half of the country. In the northern half—including Rajshahi and Rangpur—there is no seaport, no major industry, nor any major center of trade and commerce. Only a few medium cities are there growing with agriculture, education, and health

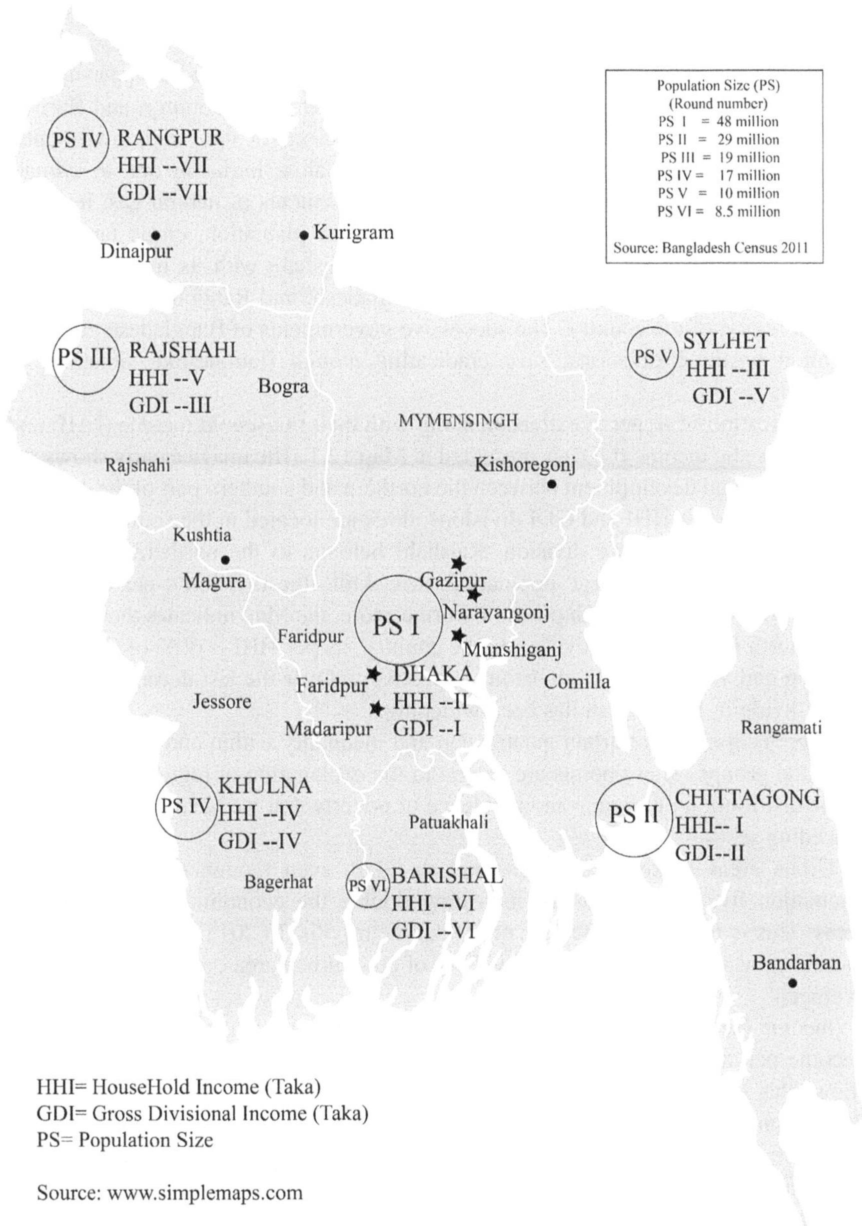

Map 12.1 Regional development in Bangladesh

institutions. There is a north-south divide: the south being more developed and the north lacking that opportunity.

There are two main exceptions to the trend: Sylhet, the third upper-income household division located in the north-eastern corner of the country, and Barisal, the second lowest household income division located in the deep-down south, surrounded by river all around and suffer from saline intrusion due to climate change. Sylhet is a resourceful division with endowments of natural gas, fertilizer plants, cement factories, rice, rubber, palm oil, tea plantation, citrus farms, and diaspora remittance from the United Kingdom. Rajshahi with its modest level of development is a virtual capital of north Bangladesh, and Rangpur division is the poorest region of the country. The successive governments of Bangladesh gave less attention to these divisions, save eradicating *monga* (famine-like situation) in Rangpur.

The location of respective division along with their household income (HHI) and gross domestic income (GDI) is presented in Map 12.1. The image clearly shows the uneven regional development between the northern and southern part of the country. Out of four higher HHI and GDI divisions, three are located in the southern region. Although a lone-growing division, Rajshahi belongs to the northern part of the country because of its large population size, while the division's per household income exists in the low fifth position. Furthermore, the Map indicates that Rangpur in the north is the poorest division in the country: its per HHI is 60% of Chittagong division and 70% of Dhaka division, respectively. Over the last decade, the north-south divide in Bangladesh has been widening.

There is also a rural urban income gap and inequality within and between urban and rural groups. These points are central to the explanation of regional differences in the distribution of income and incidence of poverty that we have discussed in the preceding section.

Urban areas make 70% of Bangladesh GDP, even though only 35% of the population live in urban areas, indicating double the economic power of urban areas. This is more so in the case of Dhaka metropolis. In 2015, per capita income in rural areas was 27% of Dhaka city, 75% of other urban areas, and 54% of national average.

Income inequality in Bangladesh has been growing since the early 1990s. It has become pervasive in the current decade (2009–2019). The last row of Table 12.1 shows that Gini coefficients of two periods (2010 and 2016) have increased in all three columns—national, rural, and urban; inequality is worst in urban area (Gini 0.498), to be more specific, in metropolitan areas, because per capita income of rural areas was 25% less than other urban areas. So, the real difference is made by the two metropolitan regions that contribute approximately 50% to GDP (Mujeri 2018). The evidence from Table 12.1 indicates that between 2010 and 2016, the income of lower income group declined in urban and areas rural areas, while during the same period, the income of upper income group increased substantially. The conclusion is the lower income group lost out to higher income group.

Although Bangladesh has made considerable progress in three major indicators of social development—namely, education, health, and gender equality—facilities for

Table 12.3 Poverty and income inequality (in %) 2019

Top 5 districts with highest poverty HCR (%)	Top 5 districts with lowest poverty HCR (%)
Kurigram (70.8)	Narayanganj (2.6)
Dinajpur (64.3)	Munshiganj (3.1)
Bandarban (63.2)	Madaripur (3.7)
Magura (56.7)	Gazipur (6.9)
Kishoreganj (53.5)	Faridpur (7.7)

Source: Bangladesh Bureau of Statistics Report 2016
Dhaka: Government of Bangladesh
HCR headcount ratio

education and health are asymmetric between urban and rural areas. For education, there is a rural-urban gap between schooling and learning; for health services, in rural areas, there is more building and less doctors, nurses, and medicines. There exists inequality between the genders, and discrimination against women and girls looms large due to structural and social institutions and lack of explicit policy initiatives by the government (Ferdaush and Rahman 2011).

As we have mentioned before, a driving force behind the independence movement was regional disparity, i.e., disparity in economic development against former East Pakistan, today's Bangladesh. Surprisingly, this bitter experience with uneven regional development was not at all reflected in the Five-Year Plans of the country. One reason for the absence of "region" in the Plan document may be that the Planning Commission is composed of economists who trained in the arithmetic of macroeconomics, not in the geometry of regional science.

This trend has continued to this day. The results are obvious. The inter-regional disparity in development shows wide unevenness. For example, the incidence of poverty in Dhaka division is 7.2% in division level and only 3% in urban level, whereas the comparable figure for Rajshahi division is 14.2% in division level and 10.7% in urban level. The situation in Rangpur division is even worse: 30.5% in divisional level and 26.3% in urban level (BBS 2016).

In Bangladesh, 8 divisions are subdivided into 64 districts, each division having minimum of 4 and maximum of 16 districts. BBS statistics shows that all five districts that have the lowest incidence of poverty belong to Dhaka division and the districts are located nearby Dhaka city. While other five districts with the highest incidence of poverty are distributed across the following locations—two in Rangpur, one Chittagong, one Khulna, and one Dhaka—all are far away from their respective divisional headquarter city (Table 12.3 and Map 12.1). This may be an example of place prosperity and neighborhood effect development (Bolton 1992).

The difference in poverty rates (headcount ratio) between two sets of districts is so big that it indicates an absence of effective poverty alleviation programs in those regions. The aggregate data on the decline in poverty rate (12.5%) are also misleading, as is the case of per capita income of $1750 and the net worth of ultra-wealthy $30 million and above.

So far, we have discussed economic context and political background of economic inequality and regional disparity. There is also a physical context for the issues in uneven development.

Bangladesh is a riverine country crisscrossed by three mighty rivers of the world—the Ganges (Padma), Brahmaputra (Jamuna), and Meghna. These are all in an area of 148 thousand square kilometers.

An important geographical reason for regional disparity is lack of convenient access to two growth poles—the metropolitan cores of the country—capital city Dhaka and port Chittagong; both are located in southern region of the country. There are competing demands for budget allocations in other sectors. Nevertheless, investment in physical infrastructure—building roads, bridges, railway stations, and airport—is a compelling need for balanced development and national integration. The government is earnestly pursuing those projects. With the opening up of the Jamuna Bridge (1998) that connects northern region with Dhaka and the rest of the country, the position of two northern divisions has started improving. Another road-rail bridge across the Padma River (the Padma Bridge) is under construction, likely to be completed by 2020, and will further improve transport connectivity between south-west and north-east regions. In addition to the ongoing construction of Padma Bridge, a number of other infrastructure projects, including Meghna-Gumti River Bridge, the expansion of Dhaka-Chittagong Highway, newly built Ishwardi-Pabna Railway line (in northern region), are cases in point.

12.5 Conclusion and Policy

During the period (1991–2019) of fast economic growth in Bangladesh—fed by prosperous agriculture, a burgeoning garment industry, and growth in manpower export—income inequality and regional disparity have increased at a faster rate, and it is getting worse. The lowest 10% household income in Bangladesh has reduced to half, and the situation of the lowest 5% household is even more pitiable. Contrarily, the income shares of the highest 10% household in 2010 have increased in 2016, and the income share of highest 5% has more than doubled.

One part of this inequality is expected at the initial stage of growth due to structural change in the economy. The labor moves from low-productivity (egalitarian) agriculture sector to high-productivity (less egalitarian) manufacturing contribution to rising inequality (the Kuznets effect). But this explains only in part about the harsh truth about income and wealth inequality in Bangladesh.

The influence of corruption and rent seeking in the top incomes dominates the economy, renders inequality, and overshadows the rule of law. It also undermines the popular argument in favor of free market economy—the trickle-down effect. The accumulation of capital in most cases has actually advanced the economic and social well-being of the rich and drives a large-scale change in their more wealth accumulation. The Wealth-X High Net Worth Report 2018 on income distribution in

Bangladesh bears testimony of the fact: Bangladesh ranked third top most country of ultra-rich (*New Age*: January 20, 2019).

The trickle-down economics—through a set of public policy, including time to revising wages of laborer and low-income employees, investing in social overheads, progressive taxation, and transfer payments to poor and needy—has not happened in Bangladesh. Instead income and wealth are poured into the rich and wealthy. Another argument in favor of capital accumulation that it generates employment and raises economic growth through reinvestment of capital was also not definitely proven. We have discussed before the sources of rent seeking entrenched in public sector corruption—a phenomenon closely related to the neoliberal power structure. Those who are outside the power structure, without political patronage, have limited scope to accrue much benefit from the economic growth.

Based on the above discussion, a few unambiguous conclusions can be drawn. First, the rich are getting richer, while the poor are getting poorer—and remain stagnant—in Bangladesh. Second, inequality is rooted in power imbalance—and that power stems from two sources: financial capital and political capital (functional relation with power structure). Finally, in the absence of a functional democracy with credible opposition, "a class of oligarch has emerged in Bangladesh, controlling the economy—and to a large extent the politics" (Hye 2018).

Under these circumstances, unless the mass people are more organized and engaged in constructive politics to create pressure on the government for policy interference in favor of the poor through redistribution, the present situation will not improve but deteriorate, more rapidly afterward. In case of regional disparity, the cumulative causation effects will be intensified (Myrdal 1957).

What Is the Way Forward?

Our analysis suggests two areas of policy formulation as attempts to reduce inequality in household income and regional disparity.

1. *Redistribution* of income among various social groups. It is generally accepted that minimum distribution is required because some people cannot make a living on their own. How much help to be given to them—as transfer payment—depends on ethical judgement of the society. More important part of redistribution is progressive taxation system—that is, tax on income, wealth, capital gains, and inheritance—and the gain from Keynesian multiplier effect. Economy grows as the government provides benefits to people without much spending power. Neoliberal critics argue that higher tax hinders capital formation, dampens investment climate, reduces employment, and slows down economic growth.

The following examples disconfirm the validity of the argument. In India, tax-GDP ratio is 20%; its economic growth was 7.2% in 2018. In Tanzania, the ratio is 14%, and economic growth was 7.1%. In Bangladesh, the ratio is 10%, and economic growth is 7% in 2018. Tax-GDP ratio in Bangladesh is the lowest in South Asia. Moreover, the larger proportion of tax revenue in Bangladesh comes from indirect tax, including value added tax (VAT) while government cuts source tax for export items, including textile and garments. So, the tax burden is disproportionately borne by the poor and makes their well-being lower.

2. How to resolve regional differences in levels of development? First, we need disaggregated data broken down into smaller subpopulations and smaller geographical units to reveal patterns which otherwise remain invisible. In Bangladesh there are no disaggregated up-to-date regional socioeconomic data. It is the responsibility of the Bangladesh Bureau of Statistics (BBS) to develop such a database. Second, we recommend a division by division separate development budget with priority given to Rangpur, Barisal, and Mymensingh, the most deprived regions of the country. Third, we recommend the creation of a new growth pole in Rajshahi as the city in the image of people as the capital of northern Bangladesh. Fourth, a policy pointer is the idea of *spatial Keynesianism* that involves improvement of infrastructure, provision of incentive to mobile investors, employment generation, and an elaborate welfare programs in lagging regions. In case of severe regional disparity, the government may impose short-term restraint on growth in two exciting core regions—Dhaka and Chittagong—to bring convergence in lagging region (Canaleta et al. 2004). Fifth is to employ, at urban scale, *Right to City* approach developed by David Harvey, that is, instead of the forced eviction of slums and squatters, the government should make provision for their resettlement in the city and formalize employment with living wages.

Finally, our analysis suggests that mobilizing resources for improving transport infrastructure, making investment in infrastructure and social overheads in lagging regions as part of larger land-use and transportation network, will significantly alleviate people's suffering from poor linkages with metropolitan cores of the country. These integrated developments—with social inclusion and sustainable environment—are likely to transform the lagging northern regions, metropolitan peripheries, non-metropolitan regions, and rural areas—and, indeed, Bangladesh itself.

References

Alam S (2018) Addressing inequality in the era of sustainable development agenda. The Financial Express, May 09

BBS (Bangladesh Bureau of Statistics) (2016) Household income and expenditure survey 2016. Planning Division, Ministry of Planning, Dhaka

Bhagwati J, Panagariya A (2013) Why growth matters: how economic growth in India reduced poverty and the lessons for other developing countries. Public Affairs, New York

Birdsall N (2007) Inequality matters. Boston review of books. May. http://bostonreview.net/nancy-birdsall-inequality-matters

Bolton R (1992) Place prosperity vs people prosperity' revisited: an old issue with a new angle. Urban Stud 29(2):185–203

Bradshaw M, Lyn N (1994) After the Soviet Union: the post-Soviet States in the world system. Prof Geogr 46(4):438–449

Canaleta C, Arzoz PP, Gárate MR (2004) Regional economic disparities and decentralization. Urban Stud 41(1):71–94
Dreze J, Sen A (2013) An uncertain glory: India and its contradictions. Princeton University Press, Princeton
Ferdaush J, Rahman M (2011) Gender Inequality in Bangladesh. Unnayan Onneshan. https://archive.nyu.edu/bitstream/2451/33900/2/gender_inequality_in_bangladesh.pdf
Gardizi M, Hussmann K, Torbi Y (2010) Corrupting the state or state-crafted corruption? Exploring the Nexus between corruption and subnational governance. Afghanistan Research and Evaluation Unit, Kabul. https://www.refworld.org/pdfid/4c21cd102.pdf
Hasnath S (2011) Bangladesh: from basket case to showcase—an essay on the geography of development. Arab World Geogr 14(1):49–71
Hasnath S, Amin S (2018) Issues in urban livability and public policy in Bangladesh. In: Sengupta U, Shaw A (eds) Trends and issues in housing in Asia: coming of an age. Routledge, New York
Haynes KE, Stough RR, Lakshmanan TR, Hasnath SA (1990) Paper presented at First Summer Institute of the Pacific Regional Science Conference Organization, Bandung, Indonesia (Session: Public-Private Partnership for Economic Development in the Southeast Asian Pacific Rim)
Hirschman A (1958) The strategy of economic development. Yale University Press, New Haven
Hye HA (2018) The nouveau riche of Bangladesh. The Financial Express Dhaka, September 15
Johnston M (1991) Corruption and democratic consolidation. http://www1.worldbank.org/publicsector/anticorrupt/Princeton.pdf
Kumar D (1974) Changes in income distribution and poverty in India: a review of the literature. World Dev 2(1):31–41
Lakshmanan TR (1981) Technological change and income distribution in regional development. Reg Dev Dialogue 2(1):1–21
Madland D (2011) The middle class grows the economy, not the rich: President's speech hints at alternative model of growth. https://www.americanprogress.org/issues/economy/news/2011/12/07/10773/the-middle-class-grows-the-economy-not-the-rich-2/
Morshed A (2018) Is housing for the urban poor a mere dream? The Daily Star, December 3
Mujeri M (2018, 18 September) Rising inequality I Bangladesh. The Financial Express, Dhaka
Myrdal G (1957) Chapter 2: The principle of circular and cumulative causation. In: Rich lands and poor: the road to world prosperity. Harper, New York, pp 11–22
Okun A (1975) Equality and efficient: the big trade-off. Brookings Institution Press, New York
Oshima HT (1992) Kuznets curve and Asian income distribution trends. Hitotsubashi J Econ 33 (1):95–111
Pettinger T (2016) Efficiency vs equity. https://www.economicshelp.org/blog/2473/economics/efficiency-vs-equity/
Piketty T (2014) Capital in the twenty-first century. The Belknap Press, Cambridge, MA
Quibria MG (2019) Bangladesh road to long-term economic prosperity: risk and challenges. Palgrave Macmillan, London
Rashid S (1991) The choice of an economic system. Bangladesh Observer, April 21
Rashid SM (2019) Data versus gathered information. The Financial Express, Dhaka, February 3
Rosenstein-Rodan PN (1943) Problems of industrialisation of eastern and South-Eastern Europe. Econ J 53(210/211):202
Sen A (2000) Development as freedom. Alfred Knopf
Sen A (2013) The Hindu, January 6. National Section
World Bank (2009) Reshaping economic geography. World development report 2009. Washington, DC
World Bank (2017) Towards Great Dhaka: a new urban development paradigm eastward. https://openknowledge.worldbank.org/handle/10986/29925?locale-attribute=es

Chapter 13
Infrastructure and Regional Economic Growth in the One Belt and One Road Regions: A Dynamic Shift-Share Approach

Kailai Wang and Zhenhua Chen

Abstract The One Belt and One Road (OBOR) Initiative was introduced by the Chinese government in 2013 with the purpose of promoting regional economic cooperation and integration among more than 65 Eurasian countries. One of the objectives is to promote infrastructure development in order to facilitate international trade and promote economic growth among OBOR countries. Although the Chinese government has committed to increase infrastructure investment over the next decade, it remains unclear how regional economic growth may be affected by infrastructure investment given that such an initiative targets a wide range of diverse economies. In addition, it is unclear whether the OBOR Initiative is effective in achieving the goal of regional economic integration. This study intends to address these questions through an examination of the linkages between infrastructure and regional economic growth, with a focus on OBOR countries. Through a regional comparative analysis, we confirm that the infrastructure conditions and regional economic growth manifested by the change of employment vary substantially among different sectors and different countries. Specifically, rapid growth in the tertiary sector in some regions, such as the East and South Asia, was confirmed to have benefited from strong local competitiveness due to developed infrastructure. Conversely, regional growth in the Commonwealth of Independent States (CIS), Mid Asia, and Eastern Europe was found to lag due to the lack of local advantages. The research results suggest infrastructure development strategies need to be implemented more cautiously, with a consideration of regional competitiveness in different countries.

Keywords Infrastructure · Regional economic growth · One Belt and One Road · Shift-share analysis

K. Wang
Institute of Transportation Studies, University of California, Davis, CA, USA

Z. Chen (✉)
Knowlton School of Architecture, City and Regional Planning, The Ohio State University, Columbus, OH, USA
e-mail: chen.7172@osu.edu

Z. Chen et al. (eds.), *Development Studies in Regional Science*,
New Frontiers in Regional Science: Asian Perspectives 42,
https://doi.org/10.1007/978-981-15-1435-7_13

13.1 Introduction

The One Belt and One Road (OBOR) Initiative was announced in 2013 with the aim of promoting infrastructure development, in order to facilitate international trade and promote economic growth among 65 Eurasian countries. This initiative is considered to be China's strategy to enhance regional cooperation and promote regional growth at a larger scale (Fukuyama 2016; Huang 2016; Liu and Dunford 2016), making it an infrastructure-led economic plan (Johnston 2018; Yu 2018). Since its implementation, a large number of infrastructure projects have been constructed and developed. These projects cover a wide range of investments, such as in transportation, oil and gas pipelines, telecommunication, and electricity links (China Global Investment Tracker 2018). Table 13.1 summarizes the Chinese infrastructure investments and construction in OBOR regions from 2008 to 2017 in four sectors. The amount of Chinese investments has been much larger in recent years as compared to that in earlier years. A critical question then arises: how infrastructure investments could be allocated more effectively among the OBOR countries? The needs of these countries largely depend on national-level economic development. The variety of national infrastructure systems across these countries has a strong influence in achieving regional cooperation and integration (Turner 2018, p. 70–107). Given the linkage between infrastructure and economic growth, this chapter analyzes regional economic disparities over the last decade among the OBOR countries. The investigation may shed light on the understanding of the effectiveness and efficiency of the existing infrastructure projects.

Infrastructure plays a critical role in promoting regional economic development. Investment in public infrastructure, such as roads, ports, railways, and airport infrastructure has been widely implemented by decision-makers as a policy instrument to reduce regional disparities and promote regional growth (Button 1998; Shenggen and Zhang 2004; Sahoo and Dash 2009). In the past four decades, the improvement of transportation infrastructure has largely facilitated China's

Table 13.1 Chinese infrastructure investments and construction (US dollars in millions) in the OBOR regions (2008–2017)

Year	Energy	Transport	Utilities	Logistics
2008	15,730	2730	140	
2009	28,600	4070	110	
2010	26,870	2770	290	160
2011	21,940	7720	330	810
2012	15,820	4480	1430	
2013	29,820	7720	1060	660
2014	38,240	10,950	890	930
2015	35,540	18,750	3890	290
2016	43,220	19,480	3290	190
2017	30,250	25,000	780	10,090

Source: http://www.aei.org/china-global-investment-tracker/

economic growth and regional integration (Démurger 2001; Yu et al. 2012). With a rising global power, the Chinese central government is eager to strengthen China's political influence and promote closer economic integration with its neighboring Asian nations. This desire is likely to be realized through the improvement of physical interregional connectivity (Fukuyama 2016). Despite the economic contributions to China's Asian neighbors some Western observers have critizited the OBOR Initiatve as "*intrusive surveillance, a potential debt trap, and a self-serving way to address domestic overcapacity*" (Dorsey 2019). This study aims to show the regional economic disparities in OBOR regions and then suggest the possible benefits of Chinese infrastructure investments.

Regional economic disparities can induce numerous concerns about regional stability and economic sustainability (Chen and Haynes 2017). On one hand, the World Bank data suggest that the East and South Asian countries have experienced a rapid development, with an average annual GDP per capita growth rate of 7.4% in the period 2007–2017. On the other hand, economic growth in other countries was much slower. For example, the average annual GDP per capita growth rate of the 16 Central and Eastern European countries was only 2.2%. Analyzing the dramatic changes in economic structure across OBOR subregions may have important implications in achieving a coordinated development and regional stability. The understanding of the economic disparities in OBOR regions would provide important implication to prioritize infrastructure investments with respect to balancing economic development proactively.

This study employs a dynamic shift-share analysis to address the driving force of regional disparity from the viewpoint of sectoral structure across OBOR subregions (Li and Haynes 2011; Mitchell and Carlson 2005). Using the data from the World Bank, this study analyzes employment patterns for primary, secondary, and tertiary industry separately. This study differs from previous research in two aspects. Firstly, this is the first study to investigate the role of sectoral structure change in regional disparity under the OBOR Initiative. Secondly, this study monitors the changes in employment patterns in OBOR subregions on a yearly basis from 2008 to 2017. The change in employment patterns for each industrial sector was decomposed as the OBOR regional effect, the industry mix effect, and the local competitive effect, which allows us to further understand the driving factors of employment growth at both national and regional levels. The rest of the paper is organized as follows. Section 13.2 summarizes the literature, with focuses on the role of infrastructure on regional economic development and regional disparity. Section 13.3 discusses the linkages between infrastructure and regional economic growth in the context of the OBOR region, and introduces the data source and methodologies. Section 13.4 presents the research findings, whereas Section 13.5 summarizes and concludes.

13.2 Background and Economic Theories

Transportation infrastructure has been widely adopted as a policy instrument to reduce regional disparities and promote regional economic growth (e.g., Haynes and Chen 2017; Elburz et al. 2017). Transportation infrastructure generates positive effects on economic growth in two aspects. First, infrastructure investment increases the demand for goods and services. Second, improved transportation infrastructure reduces travel time. Passenger and freight transporters may benefit directly from time and cost saving (Gunasekera et al. 2008). The reduced mobility and communication costs eventually would facilitate economic activities. In other words, the impact of infrastructure on regional development can be achieved through spatial spillover effects (Haynes and Chen 2017). Lower transportation and trade costs may accelerate industrial agglomeration (Baldwin and Forslid 2000; Krugman 1991), and the concentration of economic activities increases labor productivity (Banister and Berechman 2001; Ciccone and Hall 1993).

There is plentiful empirical evidence of the positive effects of public infrastructure on regional economic performance (e.g., Aschauer 1989; Munnell and Cook 1990). After World War II, the US-led and US-funded Marshall Plan provided reconstruction aid to European nations through large-scale infrastructure investments. The plan promoted economic growth and regional integration among the European nations with an exception of pro-Soviet countries (Swaine 2015). Another example is that, since the implementation of the US Interstate Highway Act in 1956, highway infrastructure investment exported a positive and significant effect on industrial productivity in the United States (Fernald 1999). The Chinese government introduced the ambitious OBOR Initiative in 2013. Under this initiative, the Chinese government committed to increase infrastructure investment with the purpose of promoting regional economic cooperation and integration among 65 Eurasian countries (Huang 2016; Swaine 2015). The China Global Investment Tracker (CGIT) reveals that during 2008–2017, China invested more than 42 billion dollars in OBOR regions on transport, energy, utilities, and logistic infrastructure. Through an in-depth investigation of data from CGIT, Du and Zhang (2018) found that the number of Chinese oversea investments increased continually among the OBOR countries from 2005 to 2015, especially among the Eurasian counrties. However, it remains unclear how regional economic growth across OBOR countries may have been influenced by infrastructure investment (Yii et al. 2018).

Recent studies show great interest in investigating which factors are related to economic activities in OBOR countries. Shi et al. (2018) explored the spatiotemporal patterns of electric power consumption (EPC) in these countries between 1992 and 2013. One of the primary motivations of this study was that many OBOR countries' economic structures are mainly energy-based. The results show that GDP is a more powerful predictor than population size of EPC growth. Using social network analysis, Liu et al. (2018) illustrated the structure and evolution of trade relationships among the countries along OBOR regions from 2000 to 2016. The overall results suggest that China has become a leader in the trade networks of OBOR regions since the initiative's implementation in 2013. The authors argued that neither countries with stable and high centrality indices nor other countries with weak trade links should be overlooked. In another study, Chen and Yip (2018) investigated the population dynamics of 65 countries in OBOR regions. They found that the aging population is a potential challenge for countries in Eastern Europe, East, and Southeast Asia. Even though the scope of these studies varies, the results consistently indicate that an understanding the regional economic disparity among OBOR subregions is a timely and important research theme.

The classical economic literature indicates that, as time goes by, the change in regional disparities exposes an inverted U-curve. This trend is known as "Kuznets curve" (Kuznets 1955). Regional differentials (e.g., household income per person or GDP per capita) are expected to increase in the early stage of development. When experiencing a stable period, those differentials will diminish during a mature period of growth (Williamson 1965). The process of increasing regional disparity could attribute to the agglomeration effects of economic activities (Fujita and Thisse 1996; Fujita and Hu 2001). Firms or production activities tend to be located together, resulting from positive externalities such as technology, factor endowments, and information sharing. The positive feedback mechanisms make the agglomerated regions experience higher growth rates than others. The decline in regional disparity is well documented by the conditional convergence theory (Barro and Sala-i-Martin 1995). That is, poor economies are more likely to experience faster growth in per capita units than rich ones. However, a fast-growing country may eventually grow more slowly because of the narrowing gap between human capital investments and productivity, especially when it reaches a stable state.

Structural changes in employment patterns can largely drive economic growth at both the local and national levels (Li and Haynes 2011; Mitchell and Carlson 2005). Since World War II, major Asian economies such as Japan, the Republic of Korea, and the People's Republic of China (PRC) have undergone spectacular economic transformations – fast economic growth and major employment shifts from the agriculture sector toward the manufacturing sector (Lee and McKibbin 2018). Those economies also experienced a change in regional disparity within the era of industrialization (e.g., Chen and Haynes 2017; Li and Haynes 2011). Infrastructure investment as an exogenous factor is assumed to influence both the dynamics of employment patterns and the rates of economic growth. For instance, countries with sufficient infrastructure support may attract more foreign direct investments (FDI) than other countries (Du and Zhang 2018). Deficiencies in infrastructure can further enlarge the disparity of regional economic growth (Anyanwu and Yameogo 2015).

The utilization of shift-share analysis to analyze the role of sectoral structure in the convergence of regional disparity is well documented in literature. Following this approach, Ezcurra et al. (2005, 2007) revealed that, across European Union countries, industry mix played a relatively minor role in regional dispersion and average productivity compared with regional components. Another study focusing on analyzing aggregate and sectoral convergence among Irish regions shows that structural change among agriculture, manufacturing, and distribution has contributed to regional convergence (O'leary 2003). Dinc and Haynes (1999, 2005) used an extended shift-share approach to look at sources of regional manufacturing disparities in the United States. Some scholars have argued that regional disparity in the secondary sector can account for about half of overall inequality (Fan and Zhu 2002).

This study aims to fill two gaps in literature. Firstly, attention is explicitly given to the relationship between infrastructure quality and economic development among OBOR countries. Secondly, this study offers a spatiotemporal comparative analysis on structural changes in employment patterns across OBOR subregions.

13.3 Data and Methodology

This study draws on data from the website World Bank Open Data.[1] Two factors were adopted to reflect current infrastructure development: (1) cost to exports (US dollars per container) and (2) infrastructure quality index (1 = low to 5 = high). Cost to exports refers to all the fees associated with completing procedures to export a 20-foot container in US dollars. Infrastructure quality index is an average score across all logistics professionals' perceptions of a country's quality of trade and transport-related infrastructure (e.g., ports, railroads, roads, and information technology). The index ranges from 1 (very low) to 5 (very high). As the data related to cost to exports and infrastructure quality index are not available for all periods, data are analyzed from three different years: 2010, 2012, and 2014. A country's overall economic performance is measured using per capita GDP in constant 2010 US dollars.

To show the dramatic changes in economic structure, we focus on the period 2008–2017. We studied employment data from the three sectors defined by the World Bank: the primary sector, secondary sector, and tertiary sector. The primary sector contains all activities in agriculture, hunting, forestry, and fishing. The secondary sector consists of mining and quarrying, manufacturing, construction, and public utilities (electricity, gas, and water). All other industries belong to the tertiary sector, such as transportation, business services, and communications.

13.3.1 *Infrastructure and Economic Growth in the OBOR Regions*

This study begins by visualizing the relationship between infrastructure and economic growth. In Fig. 13.1, each dot represents one OBOR country in a selected year. Figure 13.1a demonstrates that cost to export is negatively associated with GDP per capita for the economies in OBOR regions in the selected years.

[1]Data source: https://data.worldbank.org/

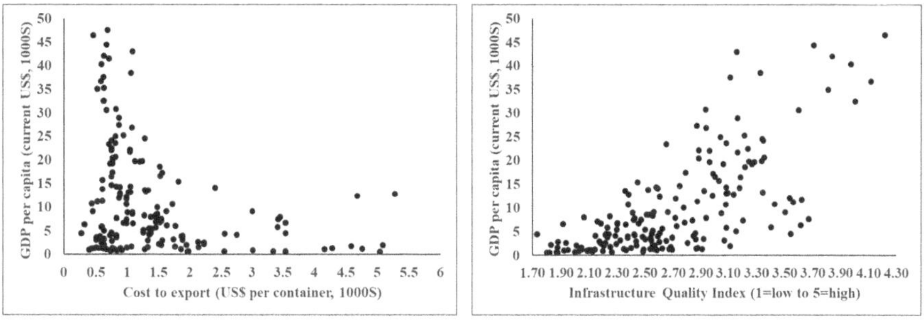

(a) (b)

Fig. 13.1 Infrastructure and economic development across the OBOR countries

Figure 13.1b shows that the higher the infrastructure quality index is, the higher the GDP per capita is. The results indicate that reducing the cost to exports and improving the performance of infrastructure would have substantial effects on local economic growth among the countries in OBOR regions.

13.3.2 Changes in Employment Structure in the OBOR Regions

To provide a comparative analysis for policy makers and stakeholders, we categorized OBOR countries into five subregions (as shown in Table 13.2 and Fig. 13.2). The classification is based on the distance to China and interconnections between these countries. This is because the OBOR Initiative emphasizes China's dominant role as a central trading network in promoting regional economic cooperation and integration among 65 Eurasian countries. Table 13.2 lists the countries of five subregions and summarizes their infrastructure and economic performance in the study period. The preliminary observation suggests that China and East and South Asia experienced faster growth in GDP per capita than the other three subregions. One of the primary drivers of growth could be the interconnections between members belonging to the Association of South East Asian Nations (ASEAN) group. These connections include trade flows and a vast number of infrastructure projects (Turner 2018, p. 75–79). As the leading economy among OBOR countries, China's economic growth and infrastructure quality are much higher than the average levels of other subregions. It is noteworthy that the overall GDP per capita declined during the study period 2008–2017 among West Asian and Eastern European countries. Enhancing the connections between these countries and other OBOR countries through different economic activities may be effective in reducing regional disparity in OBOR regions.

Table 13.2 OBOR countries in subregions

Subregions[a]	Cost to exports (US dollars per container)			Infrastructure quality index			Per capita GDP during 2008–2017 (in 2017 constant dollars)		
	2010	2012	2014	2010	2012	2014	2008	2017	Average growth rate
China	275	319	823	3.54	3.61	3.67	3471	8827	154.29%
East and South Asia	1093	1115	1315	2.50	2.69	2.73	7287	9546	73.20%
CIS and Mid Asia	2450	3203	3467	2.28	2.49	2.39	4294	4439	13.05%
West Asia	1022	1081	1150	2.88	2.89	2.90	25,323	20,909	−4.59%
East Europe	1078	1110	1110	2.62	2.82	3.00	13,117	12,654	−0.97%

We adopt the list countries in OBOR Initiative as the website of ChinaGoAbroad (link: https://www.topchinatravel.com/silk-road/one-belt-one-road.htm). We exclude Palestine from our analysis since the data availability issue

[a]Countries included in the subregions:

East and South Asia: Afghanistan, Bangladesh, Bhutan, Brunei Darussalam, Cambodia, Hong Kong SAR, China, India, Indonesia, Lao PDR, Malaysia, Maldives, Mongolia, Myanmar, Nepal, Pakistan, the Philippines, Singapore, Sri Lanka, Thailand, Vietnam

Commonwealth of Independent States (CIS) and Mid Asia, Armenia, Azerbaijan, Belarus, Georgia, Moldova, the Russian Federation, Ukraine, Kazakhstan, Kyrgyz Republic, Tajikistan, Turkmenistan, and Uzbekistan;

West Asia, Bahrain, Cyprus, Egypt, Greece, Iran, Iraq, Israel, Jordan, Kuwait, Lebanon, Oman, Qatar, Saudi Arabia, Syrian Arab Republic, Turkey, the United Arab Emirates, and Yemen, Rep.;

East Europe, Albania, Bosnia and Herzegovina, Bulgaria, Croatia, the Czech Republic, Estonia, Hungary, Latvia, Lithuania, Macedonia, Montenegro, Poland, Romania, Serbia, Slovak Republic, and Slovenia

Data source: https://data.worldbank.org/

Table 13.3 presents the amount, share, and growth rate of employment in three sectors from 2008–2017 for China and other OBOR countries. In China, the percentages of employment in the primary and secondary sectors decreased constantly during this period. A stable increase in the amount and share of tertiary employment is also observed. The main difference between China and other OBOR countries is that the share in secondary employment in other OBOR countries increased yearly during the entire study period. As an economy's GDP per capita increases agriculture's share falls, and service employment always rises (Schettkat and Yocarini 2006). The observed difference suggests China has local advantages in economic growth and should be the pillar in the OBOR Initiative regarding the promotion of regional economic cooperation and integration. Below, we analyze how employment patterns vary across the five subregions.

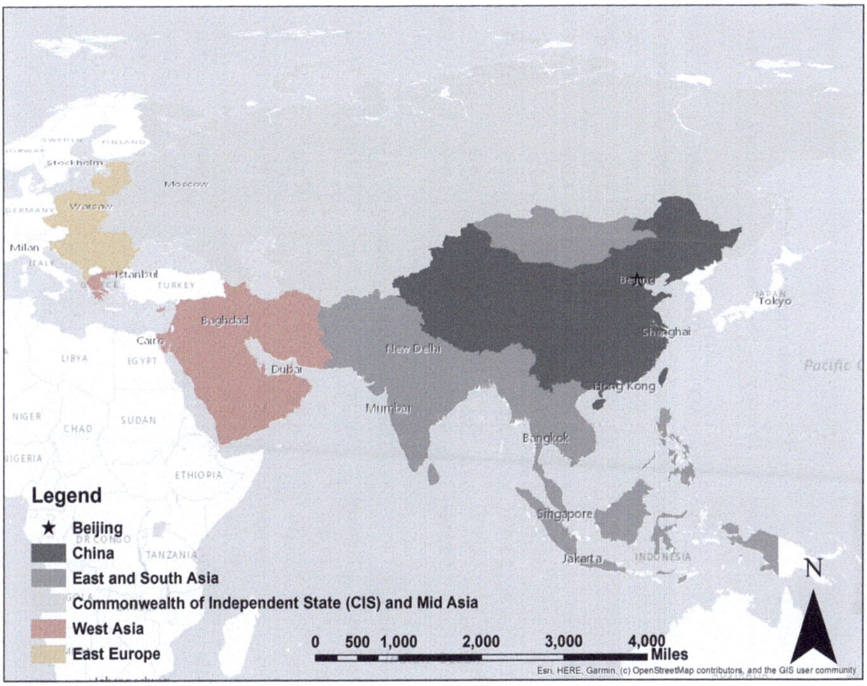

Fig. 13.2 Five subregions of the One Belt One Road (OBOR) Initiative

13.3.3 Dynamic Shift-Share Approach

Shift-share analysis is a descriptive approach that allows for the decomposition of the net change of regional output or employment over a specified period into three elements. To examine the trends in employment patterns by three sectors across OBOR countries from 2008 to 2017, we adopted a dynamic shift-share approach (Barff & Knight 1988). This approach has two major advantages over static analysis. Firstly, it measures the extent to which industrial mix influences total employment growth annually. Utilizing this approach can monitor the sharply changing industrial mix over a specific period. Secondly, the dynamic approach updates the region's total employment on a yearly basis, which allows for the effects of the three components to be assessed accurately. For example, the regional growth effect may be underestimated by the static approach during periods when local growth rate exceeds the regional rate.

In this case, the change of employment in a given OBOR subregion is decomposed into three components:

- Regional share (RS): the component caused by the change in total employment in OBOR regions
- Industry mix (IM): the component caused by the change in employment in a given industry in OBOR regions

Table 13.3 Employment by sector of activity from 2008 to 2017

China											
Year	The number of employed workers (million)				The shares across sectors			The growth rate by sector (%)			
	Primary	Secondary	Tertiary	Total	Primary	Secondary	Tertiary	Primary	Secondary	Tertiary	Total
2008	229.7	233.8	314	777.4	29.5%	30.1%	40.4%				
2009	217	234.6	327.8	779.4	27.8%	30.1%	42.1%	−5.5%	0.4%	4.4%	0.3%
2010	204.6	235.2	340.2	780	26.2%	30.2%	43.6%	−5.7%	0.3%	3.8%	0.1%
2011	191.8	234.5	356.3	782.6	24.5%	30.0%	45.5%	−6.3%	−0.3%	4.7%	0.3%
2012	181.8	231.3	371.4	784.5	23.2%	29.5%	47.3%	−5.2%	−1.4%	4.2%	0.2%
2013	172.3	226.6	386.9	785.7	21.9%	28.8%	49.2%	−5.2%	−2.0%	4.2%	0.2%
2014	163.1	220.7	402.8	786.6	20.7%	28.1%	51.2%	−5.4%	−2.6%	4.1%	0.1%
2015	153.9	213.3	419.9	787.1	19.6%	27.1%	53.4%	−5.6%	−3.4%	4.2%	0.1%
2016	144.5	210.9	431.7	787.1	18.4%	26.8%	54.9%	−6.1%	−1.2%	2.8%	0.0%
2017	137.5	209.1	438.8	785.4	17.5%	26.6%	55.9%	−4.8%	−0.8%	1.6%	−0.2%
The sum of other countries in the OBOR regions											
Year	The number of employed workers (million)				The shares across sectors			The growth rate by sector (%)			
	Primary	Secondary	Tertiary	Total	Primary	Secondary	Tertiary	Primary	Secondary	Tertiary	Total
2008	501.5	262.4	457.1	1221.1	41.1%	21.5%	37.4%				
2009	497.7	268	470.2	1236	40.3%	21.7%	38.0%	−0.8%	2.1%	2.9%	1.2%
2010	491.2	275.2	480.9	1247.3	39.4%	22.1%	38.6%	−1.3%	2.7%	2.3%	0.9%
2011	481.6	287.3	494.6	1263.6	38.1%	22.7%	39.1%	−1.9%	4.4%	2.9%	1.3%
2012	471.9	299.3	507.1	1278.3	36.9%	23.4%	39.7%	−2.0%	4.2%	2.5%	1.2%
2013	473	303	523.4	1299.4	36.4%	23.3%	40.3%	0.2%	1.2%	3.2%	1.7%
2014	467.5	310.2	541.4	1319.1	35.4%	23.5%	41.0%	−1.2%	2.4%	3.4%	1.5%
2015	461.4	316.8	560.1	1338.3	34.5%	23.7%	41.9%	−1.3%	2.1%	3.4%	1.5%
2016	460.2	321.8	579.5	1361.5	33.8%	23.6%	42.6%	−0.2%	1.6%	3.5%	1.7%
2017	459.3	326.7	592.7	1378.7	33.3%	23.7%	43.0%	−0.2%	1.5%	2.3%	1.3%

Source: Authors' calculation

- Local shift (LS): the component caused by specific local characteristics leading to local competitive advantage, including local infrastructure, policy, productivity, human capital, and other characteristics

The total employment change for industry i and any country r is the sum of the three effects:

$$\Delta e_{ir} = RS_{ir} + IM_{ir} + LS_{ir} \tag{13.1}$$

where Δe_{ir} is the change of employment in industry i and in country r during a specific period. Because measuring the relative importance of each component through percentages can provide a more straightforward understanding of dynamic changes, the proportion of Δe_{ir} attributes to each component is calculated. Below is an example for the tertiary sector:

$$\%\text{of RS effect} = \frac{RS_{ir}}{e_{ir,t-1}} = \frac{E_t - E_{t-1}}{E_{t-1}} \tag{13.2}$$

$$\%\text{of IM effect} = \frac{IM_{ir}}{e_{ir,t-1}} = \frac{E_{i,t} - E_{i,t-1}}{E_{i,t-1}} - \frac{E_t - E_{t-1}}{E_{t-1}} \tag{13.3}$$

$$\%\text{of LS effect} = \frac{LS_{ir}}{e_{ir,t-1}} = \frac{e_{ir,t} - e_{ir,t-1}}{e_{ir,t-1}} - \frac{E_{i,t} - E_{i,t-1}}{E_{i,t-1}} \tag{13.4}$$

where $e_{ir,\ t-1}$ represents the amount of employment in the tertiary sector in country r in the initial time t−1 and $e_{ir,\ t}$ represents that of the final time t. $E_{i,\ t-1}$ represents the amount of employment in the tertiary sector in OBOR regions in the initial time t−1, and $E_{i,\ t}$ represents that of the final time t. E_{t-1} represents the amount of employment in all three sectors in OBOR regions in the initial time t-1, and E_t represents that of the final time t. Given Eq. (13.2), the calculated RS effects at a given time period are identical in the three sectors for all countries in OBOR regions. For example, the RS effects contributed to a 0.84% growth in the amount of employment for each sector in each OBOR country from 2008 to 2009 (as shown in Table 13.5). Equation (13.3) shows the IM effects are identical in all countries in OBOR regions during a given period. Table 13.5 exhibits that the IM effects of the primary industry were − 3.10% for all OBOR countries during 2008–2009.

As one of the main objectives is to compare the differences in economic performance between OBOR subregions, we then calculate the amount of total shift (TS) of each industrial sector i for each subregion r, as follows:

$$TS = IM_{ir} + LS_{ir} \tag{13.6}$$

Table 13.4 Total shift groups, classification criteria, and policy implications

Group	TS	Condition	Interpretation
1	Positive	Both IM and LS positive	Local growing faster than OBOR regional average with industry composition and local factors providing advantages
2	Positive	Positive IM > |negative LS|	Local growing faster than OBOR regional average due to a favorable composition of employment offsetting unfavorable local factors. Policy provisions could focus on improving local infrastructure
3	Positive	Positive LS > |negative IM|	Local growing faster than OBOR regional average with local factors offsetting the unfavorable industry mix. Policy provisions should focus on developing growth industries to offset the concentration of industries that are either static or in decline
4	Negative	Positive LS < |negative IM|	Local growing slower than OBOR regional average, due to unfavorable industry mix but offset by advantageous local factors. Policy provisions should focus on developing growth industries to offset the concentration of industries that are either static or in decline
5	Negative	Positive IM < |negative LS|	Local growing slower than OBOR regional average due to disadvantageous local factors but offset by favorable industry mix. Policy provisions could focus on improving local infrastructure
6	Negative	Both IM and LS negative	Local growing slower than OBOR regional average with local factors and industry mix providing disadvantage. Needs attentions to both industry composition and local infrastructure

Source: Mitchell et al. (2005)

The calculated TSs represent trends that cannot be predicted by the RS effects in OBOR regions. Following Mitchell et al. (2005), we categorized the TSs by six groups. Each group has its special policy implications as illustrated in Table 13.4.

13.4 Results and Discussion

13.4.1 The Effects of OBOR Regional Share and Industry Mix

Table 13.5 presents the percentage change in employment among OBOR countries due to the effects of regional share and industry mix. The first column shows the yearly percentage change in employment in three industry sectors across all countries due to overall employment growth in OBOR regions. From 2008 to 2017, the regional share effect led to an approximately 1% growth in employment per year for each of the three sectors in all countries.

Table 13.5 Effects of regional share and industry mix in OBOR regions (including China) from 2008 to 2017

		Percentage (%) of industry mix		
Period	Percentage (%) of regional share	Agriculture	Industry	Service
2008–2009	0.84%	−3.10%	0.46%	2.65%
2009–2010	0.59%	−3.25%	0.96%	2.31%
2010–2011	0.93%	−4.15%	1.31%	2.70%
2011–2012	0.81%	−3.75%	0.87%	2.43%
2012–2013	1.09%	−2.36%	−1.29%	2.53%
2013–2014	0.99%	−3.27%	−0.72%	2.74%
2014–2015	0.93%	−3.37%	−1.09%	2.86%
2015–2016	1.09%	−2.80%	−0.62%	2.09%
2016–2017	0.72%	−2.03%	−0.13%	1.28%

Source: Authors' calculation

The remaining columns present the percent changes in employment in the three sectors due to industrial growth. It has been observed that the primary sector experienced a sweeping decline among the 65 Eurasian countries. From 2008 to 2012, the development of manufacturing industries in OBOR regions exerted positive effects on local employment growth in this sector. Those effects become negative in 2013. The change was driven by increased labor productivity and reduced share of employees of the secondary industry in OBOR regions (Baumol 1967; Freeman 1995). The tertiary sector growth in OBOR regions has a positive and constant influence on the number of employees in this sector for local economies. The annual rate was about 2.5% from 2008 to 2015 regarding the change in employment in the tertiary sector in a given country, due to regional growth of the service sector.

13.4.2 The Effects of Local-Specific Characteristics

Table 13.6 summarizes the effects of local features on employment changes in five subregions. From 2008 to 2017, local characteristics in China had negative effects on the number of employees in the primary and secondary sectors. This could be because the productivity of both sectors allowed for a reduction in the number of workers. Local polices and resources in China have positive effects on the growth of the tertiary industry during 2008–2015. It is also worth mentioning that the signs have been negative since 2016. One potential reason is that the size of the working-age population in China has been declining since 2015 (Holodny 2016).

Regarding East and South Asia, local features had a positive effect on employment growth in the primary and secondary sectors. However, local factors negatively influenced employment levels in the tertiary sector of these subregions. This is likely because most East and South Asian countries have export-led development (Stubbs

Table 13.6 The effects of local shift in three sectors by subregions during 2008–2017

Year	East Europe	West Asia	CIS and Mid Asia	East and South Asia	China
Primary sector					
2008–2009	−0.21%	1.38%	4.50%	1.38%	−3.26%
2009–2010	4.12%	3.08%	0.59%	1.23%	−3.06%
2010–2011	−0.13%	5.16%	2.86%	1.00%	−3.06%
2011–2012	2.97%	0.86%	0.46%	0.90%	−2.29%
2012–2013	−1.82%	5.34%	−0.14%	1.44%	−3.93%
2013–2014	−0.81%	1.42%	−5.99%	1.52%	−3.08%
2014–2015	−1.66%	3.77%	1.48%	0.99%	−3.21%
2015–2016	−5.55%	2.87%	0.59%	1.54%	−4.38%
2016–2017	−0.10%	3.65%	1.64%	0.93%	−3.51%
Secondary sector					
2008–2009	−5.42%	2.53%	−3.76%	2.23%	−0.94%
2009–2010	−5.12%	3.53%	−0.55%	1.66%	−1.29%
2010–2011	−1.44%	−0.93%	−1.90%	3.91%	−2.54%
2011–2012	−2.33%	2.87%	−0.68%	3.46%	−3.05%
2012–2013	−0.18%	2.10%	−0.14%	1.73%	−1.84%
2013–2014	0.61%	2.52%	0.30%	2.51%	−2.83%
2014–2015	0.54%	2.49%	−0.79%	2.94%	−3.21%
2015–2016	0.99%	2.12%	−0.61%	1.22%	−1.63%
2016–2017	−2.10%	1.85%	−0.90%	1.33%	−1.44%
Tertiary sector					
2008–2009	−0.30%	1.54%	−1.89%	−0.83%	0.92%
2009–2010	−0.77%	0.45%	−1.83%	−0.52%	0.88%
2010–2011	−4.21%	−0.48%	−2.25%	−0.10%	1.11%
2011–2012	−1.89%	−0.82%	−2.76%	−0.05%	1.01%
2012–2013	−2.61%	−1.41%	−2.51%	0.61%	0.54%
2013–2014	−2.40%	−1.50%	−2.00%	0.64%	0.38%
2014–2015	−3.25%	−0.46%	−2.36%	0.45%	0.46%
2015–2016	−2.33%	0.17%	−2.57%	1.21%	−0.37%
2016–2017	−2.12%	−0.64%	−2.63%	1.35%	−0.36%

Source: Authors' calculation

1999), so they were largely influenced by the global economic crisis in 2008–2009. As the economy recovered, local factors began to influence employment levels positively in the tertiary sector in 2013. Perhaps, countries in this subregion took some local actions to speed up the transition to the service economy.

Local-specific features positively influenced employment levels of the agriculture sector in CIS and Mid Asia at most of the times during 2008–2017. On the other hand, local features exhibited adverse effects on the size of the labor force in the secondary and tertiary sectors. This may be due to the fact that most economies in the CIS and Mid Asia depend on exporting agricultural products largely.

In the study period, local characteristics were found to have a positive effect on the number of employees in the primary and secondary sectors in West Asia. This is unsurprising since the main export commodities of these countries are petroleum, natural gas, and other agricultural and industrial products. Therefore, local policies and infrastructure provisions might have given priority to increasing the size of the labor force in those sectors. It is still inconclusive for West Asia economies when it comes to the effect of local-specific factors on the employment levels of the service sector. The overall trends suggest that local-specific features may influence employment levels in the subregion of Eastern Europe across three sectors negatively. The empirical results offer clear evidence that development in Eastern Europe lagged behind other countries in OBOR regions from 2008 to 2017.

13.4.3 The Effects of Total Shift

The total number of employment changes due to industry mix, and local shift effects are summarized in Table 13.7. Since the overall trends (regional share effect) cannot exactly predict these changes among the 65 Eurasian countries in the OBOR regions, the calculated total shifts may provide further insight into regional development disparities from 2008 to 2017. We classify the net effects of the industry mix and local shift into six groups (as shown in Table 13.4) and focus on discussing the policy implications of each group as follows.

Group 1 is composed of the subregions growing faster than the OBOR regional average, due to the effects of both industry mix and local factors. For example, the service sector in China was categorized as Group 1 during the period of 2008–2015. These results may be due to the rise of the service economy across the whole OBOR region and local competitive effects. Therefore, local improvements have not been identified based on our findings. Interestingly, the growth of the tertiary sector in China since 2016 is categorized as Group 2. That means that China's service sector grew faster than the OBOR regional average due to a favorable industry mix that offset unfavorable local factors. The results imply that Chinese investors should pay more attention to promoting local policy and infrastructure provisions, thus stimulating the sustainable development of the service economy.

In line with Groups 1 and 2, subregions in Group 3 had a positive total effect of the industry mix and local-specific feature. Group 3 indicates that the subregions grew faster than the OBOR regional average, with local factors offsetting the unfavorable industry mix. For instance, from 2012 to 2017, the growth of the secondary sector in the subregions of East and South Asia belonged to Group 3. The results imply that more OBOR regional cooperation in developing the manufacturing sector may benefit these countries in maintaining the employment level of the secondary sector. The primary sector in the East and South Asia subregion was classified into Group 4 from 2008 to 2017. This may be because the agriculture sector in East and South Asia is growing slower than the OBOR regional average, due to an unfavorable industry mix that is offset by advantageous

Table 13.7 Total shift in three sectors by subregions during 2008–2017 (unit: thousand)

	East Europe			West Asia			CIS and Mid Asia			East and South Asia			China		
Year	IM	RS	Group	IM	RS	Group	IM	RS	Group	IM	RS	Group	IM	RS	Group
Primary sector															
2008–2009	−259.6	−17.4	6	−760.9	338.0	4	−713.0	1035.3	3	−13807.9	6132.5	4	−7117.4	−7488.4	6
2009–2010	−265.3	336.6	3	−790.2	749.2	4	−763.7	139.0	4	−14338.6	5420.7	4	−7045.2	−6645.5	6
2010–2011	−343.9	−10.9	6	−1013.6	1261.3	3	−955.4	659.8	4	−18053.8	4346.2	4	−8484.7	−6256.4	6
2011–2012	−300.3	237.8	4	−933.8	214.7	4	−860.3	106.3	4	−15953.3	3834.8	4	−7186.5	−4393.5	6
2012–2013	−189.0	−145.8	6	−575.1	1303.1	3	−527.7	−30.4	6	−9829.4	6019.4	4	−4283.6	−7146.3	6
2013–2014	−254.1	−62.9	6	−830.4	359.6	4	−721.9	−1321.7	6	−13661.9	6334.2	4	−5634.4	−5309.2	6
2014–2015	−253.4	−124.7	6	−847.3	948.4	3	−681.5	298.7	4	−13953.5	4110.1	4	−5488.0	−5232.5	6
2015–2016	−202.5	−400.5	6	−715.2	732.9	3	−562.3	118.9	4	−11455.2	6293.3	4	−4313.4	−6744.6	6
2016–2017	−135.9	−6.6	6	−523.6	942.9	3	−402.4	325.7	4	−8275.9	3807.0	4	−2931.3	−5069.0	6
Secondary sector															
2008–2009	83.5	−994.4	5	143.1	793.8	1	177.3	−1462.9	5	790.9	3865.9	1	1064.3	−2202.4	5
2009–2010	167.9	−900.1	5	311.7	1151.5	1	363.0	−208.1	2	1718.3	2985.9	1	2241.4	−3029.2	5
2010–2011	221.5	−244.3	5	448.1	−320.1	2	501.6	−727.4	5	2426.2	7254.6	1	3074.3	−5962.7	5

2011–2012	149.3	−397.9	5	303.6	996.0	1	336.6	−261.7	2	1722.2	6811.7	1	2049.8	−7148.2	5
2012–2013	−219.5	−30.6	6	−469.5	762.8	3	−502.9	−55.2	6	−2678.6	3575.8	3	−2990.8	−4252.9	6
2013–2014	−122 2	102.7	4	−267.4	931.7	3	−280.2	115.7	4	−1520.2	5268.0	3	−1637.8	−6418.1	6
2014–2015	−185.4	91.8	4	−413.3	947.5	3	−423.6	−308.6	6	−2349.0	6360.5	3	−2399.2	−7091.1	6
2015–2016	−105.5	168.7	4	−239.8	823.9	3	−237.9	−234.8	6	−1369.1	2710.4	3	−1314.6	−3468.2	6
2016–2017	−22.6	−364.5	6	−52.1	739.6	3	−50.3	−345.8	6	−294.6	2998.6	3	−274.9	−3027.9	6
Tertiary sector															
2008–2009	780.2	−88.0	2	1760.9	1028.0	1	2073.5	−1478.1	2	7479.5	−2336.5	2	8306.5	2874.7	1
2009–2010	701.9	−234.2	2	1612.5	316.3	1	1836.7	−1460.6	2	6694.2	−1504.7	2	7560.5	2883.2	1
2010–2011	839.3	−1309.0	5	1951.0	−344.2	2	2173.1	−1808.1	2	8023.7	−300.4	2	9185.8	3761.8	1
2011–2012	751.0	−584.8	2	1811.4	−611.6	2	1983.0	−2250.9	5	7476.6	−157.7	2	8659.3	3605.0	1
2012–2013	793.3	−818.9	5	1933.6	−1076.6	2	2076.7	−2057.2	2	8041.0	1941.7	1	9408.9	2010.9	1
2013–2014	866.6	−758.4	2	2137.5	−1168.8	2	2271.0	−1653.8	2	9064.6	2114.8	1	10599.5	1466.2	1
2014–2015	916.4	−1041.3	5	2280.6	−369.0	2	2411.2	−1993.5	2	9873.5	1538.6	1	11516.6	1865.3	1
2015–2016	674.1	−750.4	5	1724.1	141.3	1	1789.3	−2196.4	5	7529.8	4372.9	1	8784.3	−1567.4	2
2016–2017	417.0	−689.2	5	1093.0	−546.4	2	1104.3	−2264.6	5	4822.1	5073.6	1	5539.9	−1573.5	2

Source: Authors' calculation

local factors. The results imply that if the OBOR Initiative aims to keep the rate of employment in the agriculture sector static, formulating effective cooperation projects between the subregions may be useful.

Group 5 shows that the subregions grew slower than the OBOR regional average due to disadvantageous local factors that were offset by a favorable industry mix. For example, the secondary sector in the subregion of East Europe was categorized as Group 5 from 2008 to 2012. This can be attributed to the fact that the manufacturing industry in Eastern European countries lagged behind the average level of others in the OBOR region. Local policy provisions are needed among those countries to promote local infrastructure with the purpose of increasing the amount of employment in the secondary sector. Besides, Group 6 illustrates that the subregion grew slower than the OBOR regional average, with local factors and the industry mix creating disadvantages.

13.5 Conclusion

The One Belt and One Road (OBOR) Initiative is one of the major international economic strategies initiated by Chinese President Xi Jinping. The strategy was devised to foster regional connectivity in order to share China's economic prosperity with various Eurasian countries (Fukuyama 2016). This study contributes to the literature by investigating the linkage between regional disparities in infrastructure and economic performance across subregions under the OBOR Initiative. The empirical evidence reveals that reducing the cost to exports and improving infrastructure quality may stimulate economic growth across OBOR countries. As an infrastructure-led economic plan, the implementation of the OBOR Initiative is expected to promote a coordinated and balanced regional development.

The dynamic shift-share analysis confirms that a substantial regional economic disparity does exist among OBOR countries. During the period 2008–2017, local features were found to have positive effects on the employment of the tertiary sector in China. However, such features lead to negative impacts on employment in the tertiary sector among Eastern European and CIS and Mid Asian countries. The dynamics of the total shift effects reveal that regional factors play a key role in promoting economic growth in OBOR countries. The analysis also shows that other factors, such as the changes of industry structure and unspecified local factors, can also play significant roles in employment growth. The change of the total shift effect during the study period implies that future policy provisions and investment strategies need to be designed more cautiously, with a consideration of promoting regional competitiveness at different spatial and temporal contexts.

The research findings may help policy makers and practitioners better understand the linkages between infrastructure development and economic growth in the OBOR regions. Future research can be pursued in three directions. First, since variations do exist across OBOR subregions, a more specific analysis among the different subregions is desirable as it would enable us to better develop policies to reduce regional economic disparity. Second, a further investigation of the direct link between local infrastructure and employment structures among OBOR countries could be valuable to identify effective strategies for infrastructure investment. Third, future research could also be extended to investigate the dynamic interactions among OBOR countries and non-OBOR countries to allow for a better understanding of the broader economic impact of the OBOR Initiative.

References

Anyanwu JC, Yameogo ND (2015) What drives foreign direct investments into West Africa? An empirical investigation. Afr Dev Rev 27(3):199–215

Aschauer DA (1989) Public investment and productivity growth in the Group of Seven. Econ Perspect 13(5):17–25

Banister D, Berechman Y (2001) Transport investment and the promotion of economic growth. J Transp Geogr 9(3):209–218

Baldwin RE, Forslid R (2000) The core–periphery model and endogenous growth: stabilizing and destabilizing integration. Economica 67(267):307–324

Barff RA, Knight PL (1988) Dynamic shift-share analysis. Growth Chang 19(2):1–10

Barro RJ, Sala-i-Martin X (1995) Economic growth, advanced series in economics. McGraw-Hill, New York/London/Montreal

Baumol WJ (1967) Macroeconomics of unbalanced growth: the anatomy of urban crisis. Am Econ Rev 57(3):415–426

Button K (1998) Infrastructure investment, endogenous growth and economic convergence. Ann Reg Sci 32(1):145–162

Chen Z, Haynes KE (2017) Impact of high-speed rail on regional economic disparity in China. J Transp Geogr 65:80–91

Chen M, Yip PS (2018) A study on population dynamics in "Belt & Road" countries and their implications. China Popul Dev Stud 2(2):158–172

China Global Investment Tracker (2018) American Enterprise Institute. http://www.aei.org/china-global-investment-tracker/

Ciccone A, Hall RE (1993) Productivity and the density of economic activity (No. w4313). National Bureau of Economic Research

Démurger S (2001) Infrastructure development and economic growth: an explanation for regional disparities in China? J Comp Econ 29(1):95–117

Dinc M, Haynes KE (1999) Sources of regional inefficiency: an integrated shift-share, data envelopment analysis and input-output approach. Ann Reg Sci 33(4):469–489

Dinc M, Haynes K (2005) Productivity, international trade and reference area interactions in shift-share analysis: some operational notes. Growth Chang 36(3):374–394

Dorsey J M (2019) A China wins twice proposition: the belt and road initiative, SSRN Electron J

Du J, Zhang Y (2018) Does One Belt One Road initiative promote Chinese overseas direct investment? China Econ Rev 47:189–205

Elburz Z, Nijkamp P, Pels E (2017) Public infrastructure and regional growth: lessons from meta-analysis. J Transp Geogr 58:1–8

Ezcurra R, Gil C, Pascual P, Rapún M (2005) Regional inequality in the European Union: does industry mix matter? Reg Stud 39(6):679–697

Ezcurra R, Pascual P, Rapún M (2007) Spatial inequality in productivity in the European union: sectoral and regional factors. Int Reg Sci Rev 30(4):384–407

Fan J, Zhu G (2002) The evolution of China's regional disparity and structural decomposition. Manage World 7:37–44. (in Chinese)

Fernald JG (1999) Roads to prosperity? Assessing the link between public capital and productivity. Am Econ Rev 89(3):619–638
Freeman RB (1995) Are your wages set in Beijing? J Econ Perspect 9(3):15–32
Fujita M, Hu D (2001) Regional disparity in China 1985–1994: the effects of globalization and economic liberalization. Ann Reg Sci 35(1):3–37
Fujita M, Thisse JF (1996) Economics of agglomeration. J Jpn Int Econ 10(4):339–378
Fukuyama F (2016) One Belt, One Road: exporting the Chinese model to Eurasia. The Australian 4
Gunasekera K, Anderson W, Lakshmanan TR (2008) Highway-induced development: evidence from Sri Lanka. World Dev 36(11):2371–2389
Haynes KE, Chen Z (2017). Infrastructure and Regional Development. International Encyclopedia of Geography: People, the Earth, Environment and Technology, 1–8
Holodny E (2016) This chart is an ominous sign for China's future. Available online: https://www.businessinsider.com/chinas-working-age-population-peaked-2016-4
Huang Y (2016) Understanding China's Belt & Road initiative: motivation, framework and assessment. China Econ Rev 40:314–321
Johnston LA (2018) The belt and road initiative: what is in it for China? Asia & the Pacific Policy Studies
Krugman P (1991) Increasing returns and economic geography. J Polit Econ 99(3):483–499
Kuznets S (1955) Economic growth and income inequality. Am Econ Rev 45(1):1–28
Lee JW, McKibbin WJ (2018) Service sector productivity and economic growth in Asia. Econ Model 74:247–263
Li H, Haynes KE (2011) Economic structure and regional disparity in China: beyond the Kuznets transition. Int Reg Sci Rev 34(2):157–190
Liu W, Dunford M (2016) Inclusive globalization: unpacking China's belt and road initiative. Area Dev Policy 1(3):323–340
Liu Z, Wang T, Sonn JW, Chen W (2018) The structure and evolution of trade relations between countries along the Belt and Road. J Geogr Sci 28(9):1233–1248
Mitchell W, Carlson E (2005) Exploring employment growth disparities across metropolitan and regional Australia. Australas J Reg Stud 11(1):25
Mitchell W, Myers J, Juniper J (2005) Extending shift-share analysis to account for spatial effects: a study using Australian census data, Centre of full employment and equity. Coffee, Newcastle, Australia, pp 05–19
Munnell A, Cook LM (1990, September) How does public infrastructure affect regional economic performance? N Engl Econ Rev, 11–33
O'leary E (2003) Aggregate and sectoral convergence among Irish regions: the role of structural change, 1960–96. Int Reg Sci Rev 26(4):483–501
Sahoo P, Dash RK (2009) Infrastructure development and economic growth in India. J Asia Pac Econ 14(4):351–365
Schettkat R, Yocarini L (2006) The shift to services employment: a review of the literature. Struct Chang Econ Dyn 17(2):127–147
Shenggen FAN, Zhang X (2004) Infrastructure and regional economic development in rural China. China Econ Rev 15(2):203–214
Shi K, Yu B, Huang C, Wu J, Sun X (2018) Exploring spatiotemporal patterns of electric power consumption in countries along the Belt and Road. Energy 150:847–859
Stubbs R (1999) War and economic development: export-oriented industrialization in East and Southeast Asia. Comp Polit 31:337–355
Swaine MD (2015) Chinese views and commentary on the 'One Belt, One Road' initiative. China Leadersh Monit 47(2):3
Turner C (2018) Regional infrastructure systems: the political economy of regional infrastructure. Edward Elgar Publishing, Cheltenham
Williamson JG (1965) Regional inequality and the process of national development: a description of the patterns. Econ Dev Cult Chang 13(4, Part 2):1–84

Yii KJ, Bee KY, Cheam WY, Chong YL, Lee CM (2018) Is transportation infrastructure important to the One Belt One Road (OBOR) initiative? Empirical evidence from the selected Asian countries. Sustainability 10(11):4131

Yu S (2018) Belt and road initiative: defining China's grand strategy and the future world order (Doctoral dissertation)

Yu N, De Jong M, Storm S, Mi J (2012) Transport infrastructure, spatial clusters and regional economic growth in China. Transp Rev 32(1):3–28

Chapter 14
Chinese and Western Approaches to Infrastructure Development

Francis Fukuyama, Michael Bennon, and Bushra Bataineh

Abstract Particularly since the announcement in 2013 of China's ambitious Belt and Road Initiative (BRI), infrastructure development has become one of the chief axes of competition between China and the West. Chinese infrastructure finance has gone from about 25% of total lending by international development institutions in 2002 to nearly 75% in 2016. The respective approaches reflect the broader development models of the two sides: China's is heavily state-centric and draws upon the huge domestic construction industry that has fueled its own rise; Western approaches tend to be market-oriented and embedded in legal constraints designed to mitigate a host of environmental, social, safety, and other types of risks. There are systematic biases in both approaches. We find that Chinese project developers tend to overestimate the positive externalities and underestimate negative ones, reflecting their own domestic experience. This leads, on the one hand, to problems with fiscal sustainability, as well as negative environmental and social consequences. One of the consequences is a high level of non-performing loans, whose aggregate size may be approximated by the bailouts provided by the Chinese central bank to its development banks, the China Exim Bank and the China Development Bank. Western developers, by contrast, focus on internal rates of return, and place great emphasis on mitigating risk. This tends to lengthen the time to complete projects and increases their costs. This often makes their projects non-competitive when faced with Chinese competition. Efforts by the World Bank to revise its safeguards regime over the past decade do not appear to have mitigated this problem. The ideal approach to needed infrastructure projects lies somewhere between the Chinese and Western models: China needs to become more compliant with international standards, while Western development agencies need to adopt more realistic standards to meet a newly competitive infrastructure world.

Keywords China · World Bank · Infrastructure · Safeguards · Belt and road

F. Fukuyama (✉) · M. Bennon · B. Bataineh
Stanford University, Stanford, CA, USA
e-mail: ffukuyam@stanford.edu

Z. Chen et al. (eds.), *Development Studies in Regional Science*,
New Frontiers in Regional Science: Asian Perspectives 42,
https://doi.org/10.1007/978-981-15-1435-7_14

China's rise from an impoverished developing country to a global superpower with the world's second largest economy has occasioned great concern in the United States and other Western countries over the projection of Chinese power and influence throughout the world (Walker and Ludwig 2017; Walker 2018; Diamond and Schell 2018). Among the most important sources of so-called Chinese "sharp power" is its support for infrastructure projects around the world, extending from developing countries into the heart of Europe itself. These projects are part of the Belt and Road Initiative (BRI) first announced by President and Party General Secretary Xi Jinping in 2013. This tremendously ambitious project sought to shift the center of the entire global economy away from the existing trans-Atlantic/trans-Pacific one centered on the United States to a Eurasian one centered on China.

There were several concerns raised by Western observers of BRI. The first and most longstanding critique lay in relation to Chinese approaches to infrastructure development in general: Chinese projects tended not to observe the same level of environmental, social, and other safeguards that Western-backed ones did, leading over the long-run to a "race to the bottom" in terms of safeguard compliance. This it was felt ran counter to the interests of the receiving countries, much as they needed new infrastructure. A second concern regards spreading Chinese foreign policy influence. For example, Chinese sponsorship of infrastructure projects in Eastern Europe and the Balkans under the so-called Sixteen Plus One initiative have led individual members of the European Union to veto efforts to criticize China over human rights violations, Tibet, or other traditional areas of Western concern. Abusive regimes like that of Nicolás Maduro in Venezuela have benefitted from Chinese lending and investment; indeed, the Maduro regime has been willing to see its own population literally starve rather than default on its Chinese debt. Finally, there are strategic concerns about the inability of Chinese client countries to exit from their relationships with China: Sri Lanka, for example, found it impossible to end a large Chinese port project due to the large amount of outstanding debt it owed Beijing and instead granted China the rights to that port on a 99-year lease.

There is no question that Chinese influence around the world has grown massively and that BRI and related infrastructure projects are perhaps the chief instrument that Beijing has used to support its broader economic and foreign policy goals. It is our view, however, that there are certain intrinsic limits to Chinese influence using the infrastructure lever. Moreover, the blame for this increase in Chinese presence lies as much with the United States, the EU, and Western-backed international institutions like the World Bank as it does with China. The developing world needs infrastructure, but a combination of factors has prevented Western institutions from providing it on a timely and cost-effective basis.

14.1 Roots of Chinese Policy

China has its own development model. It bears many similarities to those of other East Asian "development states," like Japan, South Korea, Taiwan, and Singapore, while retaining its own unique characteristics.

In general, East Asian developmental states have instituted export-led growth strategies that relied far more heavily on state direction than the more market-oriented approach taken by the United States, Britain, and other Western countries (Haggard 2018). Individual countries in East Asia practiced somewhat different versions of industrial policy, however: South Korea, for example, used directed credits to promote individual national champions, while Singapore and Taiwan encouraged broader sectors through bank policy and the building of intellectual infrastructure.

China's model also relied heavily on the state, but emphasized physical infrastructure investment as the primary engine for growth. Since the early 1990s, Chinese gross capital formation has ranged between 35% and 45% of GDP (World Bank) – a level unprecedented in other developed and developing economies alike. This was particularly true after the US subprime crisis in 2008 that triggered a global slowdown, which Beijing countered through promotion of huge increases in lending by provincial banks. China's infrastructure buildout happened surprisingly fast and, as the Chinese economy matured, showed little sign of letting up. Chinese policy banks, specifically for the China Development Bank (CDB), participated in this public investment strategy, since 70% of its loan portfolio is directed toward domestic Chinese projects.

An example of this approach was China's creation of a massive high-speed rail (HSR) network domestically (Haynes and Chen 2015). Between 2003 and 2016, China built 22,000 km of HSR, compared to existing networks of 2647 km in France, 3164 km in Japan, and zero in the United States. Total investment as of this writing has reached approximately $850 billion, based on equally massive borrowing of $746 billion.[1]

By the beginning of the second decade of the twenty-first century, it was becoming clear that China's export-led growth model centering on domestic infrastructure investment was running out of steam (World Bank and Central Bank of China 2016). Export markets were becoming saturated, and political opposition to Chinese imports in developed countries was growing; new demand would have to come from domestic spending within China and from new markets in developing countries. China's rapid development generated the largest and fastest domestic infrastructure buildout in history, creating a massive infrastructure stock and, correspondingly, a large domestic infrastructure and construction industrial complex. China faced excess capacity in real estate, manufacturing, and infrastructure (Dollar 2016). This rapid industrial start-and-stop created an industry with a sudden lack of projects to build. Local and regional leaders began to invest in domestic projects that destroyed rather than created economic value, contributing to China's widespread problems with domestic non-performing loans (NPLs) (Ansar et al. 2016). These conditions made lending support for international development projects an attractive way to export its excess domestic capacity for construction and infrastructure

[1]Updated estimates for aggregate spending on HSR provided by Zhenhua Chen; we are grateful to the author for this information.

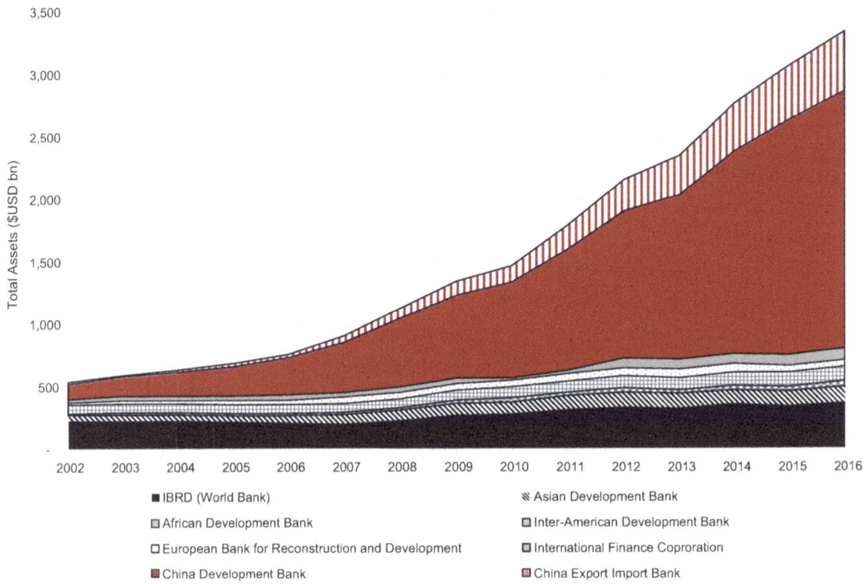

Fig. 14.1 Total assets of select development lending institutions (USDbn)

development and almost certainly contributed to pressure on China's policy banks to finance international infrastructure projects.

The rapid growth of Chinese bilateral lending has coincided with the emergence of Chinese construction firms in the global infrastructure development sector. In 2007, four of the top ten global construction firms were from China. By 2016, seven of the top ten global construction firms by revenue (from both domestic and international contracts) were from China, including four of the top five (ENR 2016). There are two French contractors and one Spanish contractor on the 2016 list and no US contractors. Even when controlling for China's domestic infrastructure boom, China's role in international development has dramatically increased over the last decade. In 2005, nine Chinese construction firms ranked in the top 100 global contractors in international (outside of their home country) revenue. By 2016 there were 20 in the top 100 by international revenue, more than double that of any other nation (ENR 2016).

The expansion of China's state-owned construction firms in infrastructure development both domestically and internationally was largely financed by China's policy banks, notably the CDB and the China Export-Import Bank (CEXIM). The expansion of these two development lenders over the last two decades has dwarfed that of traditional Western development lenders. Figure 14.1 shows the total assets of these two institutions as well as a basket of other multilateral lenders, including the International Bank for Reconstruction and Development, the Asian Development Bank, the African Development Bank, the Inter-American Development Bank, the European Bank for Reconstruction and Development, and the International Finance Corporation.

Like other bilateral lending programs, loans from China's policy banks come with strings attached. They can entail requirements to utilize Chinese construction companies for certain project tasks or import core equipment from Chinese manufacturers. Chinese infrastructure lending has been unique in that a significant portion of its infrastructure lending, at least initially, came in exchange for rights to extract natural resources. More than 50% of Chinese finance in Africa and Latin America is in the form of commodity-backed loans, often with oil or copper (Bräutigam 2015). Projects financed by Chinese policy banks and delivered by state-owned Chinese companies have also been unique in that they have not only tended to utilize Chinese companies as construction contractors but have also used imported Chinese labor for a significant portion of construction. By 2014, there were large numbers of Chinese workers in Africa for both services and contracted projects, with estimates ranging from 250,000 to over a million (John Hopkins 2017; Dollar 2016).[2]

14.2 The Chinese Approach to Development

Infrastructure development is inherently risky. There are a number of risks that have to be evaluated prior to the start of a project, having to do with project execution, natural contingencies like weather and geography, competition, market forces including exchange rates and interest rates, the political and regulatory environment, and geopolitical issues. The value added provided by the organizers of such projects and the financiers backing them has to do with the accurate evaluation of these risks. Nonetheless, developers often get things wrong: a very high percentage of projects are completed over the original budget and behind schedule, the latter of which also affects total project costs.

What makes due diligence even more difficult is the question of externalities. Positive externalities usually center around the extra degree of economic growth that infrastructure is expected to promote, which is why projects are undertaken in the first place. Negative externalities have to do with consequences like environmental damage, displacement of local populations, health and safety issues in project execution and operation, political corruption, and the like. While some projects (e.g., wireless telecoms) can be justified on the basis of their internal rate of return (IRR), many projects require some form of subsidy because many of the benefits accrue to people other than the original investors. This is why infrastructure often needs a public agency to back it. There is often a misalignment between the incentives facing developers and contractors, on the one hand, and public interest on the other: the former have an interest in understating costs and risks, knowing that

[2]These numbers are contested; there is consensus that there needs to be better data produced on migration and the number for Chinese workers in these infrastructure developments and more transparency regarding the terms of loans for infrastructure to guard against mounting unsustainable debt (Dollar 2016).

taxpayers will ultimately pick up the bill for unanticipated problems, producing a systematic bias toward undue optimism. Public-private partnerships have come into vogue in many countries as a way of reallocating risks back to the private sector actors responsible for organizing and implementing projects. In any case, both positive and negative externalities are very hard to measure in retrospect and even more difficult to predict.[3]

When a Western private investor evaluates a potential infrastructure project, that investor focuses primarily on the project's IRR. If that rate is commensurate with the risks of the investment, the project may go ahead. If the rate is not high enough to justify project risks, it may still go ahead if a public agency or international financial institution like the International Finance Corporation (IFC) or World Bank provides backing. Public agencies or donors will also estimate a project's economic returns, but will take into consideration both the positive and negative externalities entailed by the project as well. The due diligence needed to provide these estimates is why Western-backed projects often spend considerable time and resources in early stage planning.

It would appear that Chinese infrastructure projects outside of China suffer from their own systematic biases: Chinese investors tend to overestimate the positive externalities arising from a given project and to underestimate the negative ones. We assert this based both on a large number of comparative cases we commissioned comparing Chinese and Western infrastructure projects and on the aggregate performance of the Chinese overseas loan portfolio. Given the lack of transparency surrounding most Chinese projects, it is virtually impossible to find reliable data on outcomes an individual project-by-project basis, so our judgments are informed by the sources that are available.

Chinese lenders, it would appear, take IRRs seriously, but are much more focused on potential positive externalities. This attitude arises, it would appear, out of China's own experience with its domestic development. China after all invested massively in its own infrastructure, without worrying excessively about the economic returns of individual projects. An example of this is the HSR system noted earlier. While individual lines like the Beijing-Shanghai or Shanghai-Shenzhen routes may well be profitable, it is extremely unlikely that the IRRs come anywhere close to justifying the $850 billion total investment. Chinese policy in rate-setting would seem to be determined more by political than by economic considerations. The payoff that policymakers expect from the system lies in the extra degree of economic growth they believe the system as a whole will encourage. Moreover, they also anticipate political and social benefits from HSR links between metropolitan

[3]China now tops the list of developing countries with the most public-private partnerships at 1,488 projects between 1990 and 2018 (World Bank PPI 2018). The top sponsors of these public-private partnerships include Beijing Sound Environment Industry Group in water and sewerage and Xinao Gas Holdings Limited in natural gas (PPI World Bank 2018). However, given the fact that Chinese SOEs and development banks are likely to be bailed out of bad investments, it is hard to know how what it means when the Chinese call something a "public-private partnership" how risks are being reallocated to project implementors.

centers in coastal China and distant underdeveloped regions in the hinterland (Haynes and Chen 2015). Chinese domestic investment policy has thus been characterized by a "build it and they will come" attitude toward growth.

Chinese policymakers also see advantages to scale and scope. Individual Western-backed projects often fail because of a lack of complementary infrastructure. The Chinese, by contrast, see that a port needs to be connected to a rail system, an electrical grid, and a road network and proceed to invest in all of these projects simultaneously. In the process, they hope to build a relationship of trust with the local authorities who stand to benefit and capitalize ono each project's beneficial economic externalities for the other projects.

Chinese policymakers also appear to underestimate negative externalities in their own country. China's massive investments have led to huge social disruptions, like the more than 1.35 million people who had to be relocated from their homes to make way for the Three Gorges Dam, in addition to the 17,200 hectares of land and 1500 enterprises that had been displaced or inundated (Wilmsen et al. 2011). China's environmental record is terrible (though not necessarily in comparison with other countries at a similar level of development); the country's own Ministry of Natural Resources reported a decline in the total arable land for the fourth consecutive year in 2017, and China's official news agency Xinhua reported that 40% of China's arable land suffers from degradation (Reuters 2018, 2014).

Investment decisions were not based upon appropriate assessment of risks and returns, but upon government instructions from the "Big Four" Chinese state-owned banks (Li 2008). Ansar et al. (2016) suggest that poor project-level outcomes translate into substantial macroeconomic risks: accumulating debt and non-performing loans, distortionary monetary expansion, and lost alternative investment opportunities.

14.3 Chinese Infrastructure Investment in Practice

Many of these same attitudes, both Western and Chinese, are carried over into overseas investments. We can illustrate this through several individual cases.

In Jamaica, the Highway 2000 Project is a USD $1.3bn transportation public-private partnership, the largest project in the country. It was initiated in 1999 after extensive assessment and reviews and was structured as two phases, the first phase is the East-West Highway and the second phase is the North-South Link. Phase 1 is a $324 mm project under an international tender and awarded to French contractor Bouygues after a competitive bidding process. It is a 35-year concession that started in 2001. The financing for the project initially only involved commercial banks, but due to cost overruns during construction, the project was refinanced in 2011 by a consortium of development banks including the IFC, IDB, EIB, and PROPARCO. This refinancing involved revisiting and adding environmental and social safeguards.

Phase 1 was dominated by the Western approach. The North-South Link or phase 2 of the project is a $610 mm project and was abandoned by Bouygues after exercising a first right of refusal citing that it was not economic to continue beyond phase 1. Construction costs for phase 2 were simply forecast to be too high relative to the income the project would generate from tolls. However, Chinese contractor China Harbour Engineering Company (CHEC), a subsidiary of state-owned enterprise China Communications Construction Company, submitted an unsolicited bid to the Government of Jamaica and was awarded phase 2. It is a 50-year concession that began in 2012. The terms of the project included a loan from the China Development Bank as well as rights to develop the land contiguous to the highway project, including a reimbursement to the Government of Jamaica from CDB for $120 mm – the cost overruns incurred on phase 1 due to geotechnical issues. Thus the project could finally proceed, with the added caveat that CHEC would be able to develop the land on parts of the corridor.

Phase 2 has run into some significant challenges. Jamaica's Office of the Contractor General issued a statement that phase 2 of the project cannot be implemented on a commercial basis and highlighted issues with the deal struck with CHEC and the CDB. There have also been some unresolved environmental impacts after receiving a notice from Jamaica's National Environmental Protection Agency regarding excessive sedimentation of the coastal ecosystem as a result of the silt, solid waste, and debris from the construction along the Jamaica North South Highway (Caribbean Development Bank 2017).

In the Democratic Republic of the Congo, China's $6 billion "minerals for infrastructure" deal, signed in 2007, raised concerns among Western countries regarding China's quest for securing natural resources and the impact with regard to political influence in Africa. It also raised much concern on the spread of an unsustainable debt bubble. Chinese firms Sinohydro and China Railway Group Limited are building roads and hospitals in exchange for a 68% stake in the Sicomines copper and cobalt mine, one of the largest in Africa. CEXIM and other Chinese banks lent a further $3 billion to develop Sicomines, with the loans to be repaid with mining profits. The resource-backed infrastructure deal in the Democratic Republic of the Congo brought up many issues of corruption and bureaucracy (Reuters 2015).

Another project in the DR Congo is the Inga 3 hydropower project: a $12 to $14bn project along the Congo River with a 4800 megawatt power plant. The project involved the potential displacement of 35,000 people in its first phase (International Rivers 2016). The World Bank had been involved in the earlier stages and approved a $73 mm technical assistance grant in 2014 aimed at supporting a government-led process for the development of the project as a public-private partnership. The United States had abstained from the initial World Bank grant decision noting "significant implementation risks" and expressed concerns that "at least one of the three pre-qualified consortia includes a company that is debarred from participating in World Bank Projects" (US Treasury 2014). The World Bank funding was suspended in 2016 following "the Government of DRC's decision to take the project in a different strategic direction to that agreed between the World Bank and the

Government in 2014." This was after the project was transferred from the prime minister's office to the president's office. The correspondence between the World Bank and the Government of the DR Congo "proved unsatisfactory and confirmed the Government of the DRC's deviation from agreed-upon strategy for the Inga 3 BC development" per the World Bank's 2018 report. The cancellation of the agreement was based on the failure to provide any evidence of the DRC government taking actions required for lifting the suspension. The total IDA disbursements under the project amounted to $3.11 million, or 4% of the total grant. The African Development Bank (AfDB), through parallel financing, continued with the implementation of its support for the Inga 3 BC project through their Agency for the Development and Promotion of the Inga Project and is currently financing the Government's Transaction advisers (World Bank 2018).

Following an international tender, three consortia bid for the project: a South Korean-led consortium that withdrew in March 2016, the Pro-Inga Consortium led by Spain's Actividades de Construccion y Servicios SA (ACS), and the Three Gorges consortium led by Sinohydro (part of the consortium that built China's Three Gorges Dam) (World Bank 2018).

There are requests from the government to combine the remaining Chinese and Spanish bids, and the financing remains unclear. Given China's heavy involvement in the DRC with the aforementioned "minerals for infrastructure" deal, the speculation is that the Chinese-led consortium may be selected. The head of the Grand Inga Project, Bruno Kapandji, has stated that the Chinese companies could complete the project in a "maximum of five years and if they're free to do whatever they want to do they can even do it in four years" (ESI Africa 2016; International Rivers 2016).

The Western approach toward this project, and more specifically that of the United States, has been quite fragmented, with no lead agency designated to take responsibility for a go-ahead decision. The World Bank has tended to avoid hydropower projects as its internal structure encourages lower-risk clean energy projects. In the US government, President Barack Obama's Power Africa Initiative and the Electrify Africa Act of 2014 focused on access to electricity in sub-Saharan Africa and received bipartisan support. However, the initiative lacked the resources and backbone and essentially had no funds allocated (see below).

In Uganda, the Ministry of Energy and Mineral Development signed loan agreements with CEXIM, part of which is for subsidized loans for the construction of the Karuma and Isimba hydropower projects. CEXIM would lend 85% of estimated project costs, and the remainder would come from the Government of Uganda. The conditions associated with that loan were to use a Chinese contractor to deliver the project as a turnkey project, i.e., without continued operations and maintenance services. The estimated construction time was 6 years. Karuma is being delivered by Sinohydro and Isimba by the China International Water and Electric Corporation. There have been numerous quality issues and corruption claims including structural defects reportedly at 2 billion USD in both hydropower projects.

These project-level results are emblematic of broader trends in developing economy infrastructure lending. In the Jamaica case, China took over part of a project that the Western consortium abandoned because it was forecast to be uneconomic. This judgment proved true, and it is not clear whether China will recoup its investment. In the case of the DRC, Western investors, while interested, in the end decided that the political risks of the project precluded going ahead. Finally, the dam projects in Uganda simply would not have been supported by an international agency, given the environmental opposition from Western NGOs to any large hydroelectric project. They were financed by China instead.

Evidence from these cases is of course anecdotal and meant to illustrate some of the problems associated with Chinese projects, as well as why so many developing nations have turned to China to finance their infrastructure projects. Testing our hypotheses against broader sets of project data remains difficult, however, in part due to a lack of aggregate reporting on individual project lending data by China's policy banks.

One of our expectations of the Chinese approach to infrastructure development is that initial investments in a host nation would naturally lead to follow-on projects within the nation, irrespective as to whether the initial project proved beneficial for either the host nation or the bilateral lender. There would be an expectation of an accelerating string of projects over time that could produce synergies with one another. The downside would be a parallel increase in the debt servicing burden of the projects and growing dependence by the host nation on China. In China's internal buildout of infrastructure, the externalities are captured internally. In their exporting of this approach, the extent to which the externalities (both positive and negative), as well as follow-on projects, are captured by China and its state-owned enterprises is fundamentally different and poses a key risk moving forward.

The case of infrastructure investment in Sri Lanka provides a glimpse of this trend at the national level and across multiple administrations. Major infrastructure investments financed by Chinese policy banks began soon after President Mahindra Rajapaksa took power in 2005, including multiple investments in a large coal-fired power plant in Norocholai and more than $1.3bn in total financing. This was followed by more than $4bn in highway projects across the country over the following decade and major port investments at Hambantota and Colombo between 2008 and 2015. In 2014, the Colombo Port City project began construction, which will develop a $1.5bn industrial city near the Port of Colombo. All of the projects in this rapid buildout were financed by Chinese policy banks – predominantly CEXIM – and all were constructed by Chinese state-owned enterprises. Even this understates the extent to which supporting projects were pursued. Other Chinese investments included cricket stadiums, industrial projects, and an international airport near the Hambantota port.

The rapid series of projects financed and developed in Sri Lanka is illustrative of the focus on speed of implementation in the Chinese paradigm, the pressure that exists to support concessional or under-performing projects with follow-on investments until the system is profitable. While some economic benefits have been cited from the string of infrastructure projects, there is also ample evidence that some of the projects have destroyed economic value or created friction between partners. While there are reports in Chinese media of the economic benefits of the Norocholai power plant, for instance, local media has reported more than 20 breakdowns and other plant failures, leading to significant losses by the national utility (Wijedasa 2014). The massive container port projects, airport, and highway projects in the Hambantota region are particularly problematic given that they were built in a largely unpopulated part of the country (which also happened to be the region President Rajapaksa was from). The airport that was financed in the region has been cited as perhaps the least-trafficked airport in the world (Shepard 2016), and the regional roads were reported to have greater elephant traffic than automobiles (Larmer 2017).

When President Maithripala Sirisena took office in 2015, problems with Sri Lanka's program of Chinese investment were brought out into the open and investigated. Sirisena at that point was seen as a more pro-Western leader who sought to roll back many of Rajapaksa's increasingly authoritarian and corrupt tendencies. Among these was the high degree of dependence Sri Lanka had on China. None of the projects developed and financed by Chinese policy banks under Rajapaksa hand undergone a competitive procurement, and little public information was available on the loan terms and the extent of Sri Lanka's indebtedness. It further surfaced that many of the infrastructure loans had recourse not only to the cash flows of the projects themselves, but were under a sovereign guarantee by the Sri Lankan government. In total, Sri Lanka's debt to Chinese policy banks totaled more than $8bn (Moramudali 2017).

Thus, despite some efforts to disengage from China following the change of regime, the Sri Lankan government is continuing to invest in the relationship with Chinese state-owned firms and policy banks. The Colombo Port City project was originally halted for environmental reasons, but the Sirisena Administration agreed to move the project forward under a new development agreement in 2016 (Mooney 2016). In 2017 the Sri Lankan government, unable to service the debt on the struggling Hambantota port project, agreed to sign over operations of the port to a state-owned Chinese firm under a 99-year lease in exchange for debt restructuring. The Sri Lanka case has prompted discussion on China's use of sovereign debt for geopolitical purposes. Now dubbed "debt-trap diplomacy" – collateralizing loans by strategically important assets, particularly those associated with the Belt and Road Initiative, have raised concerns (Chellaney 2017).

14.4 Chinese Finance in the Aggregate

Taken in aggregate, China's approach to infrastructure development has resulted in the astonishing growth in the lending portfolios of China's policy banks. Here the CEXIM serves as a good example given that their lending portfolio is oriented exclusively to projects and industrial lending outside of China. Between 2005 and 2016, the balance of loans outstanding increased at a combined annual growth rate of more than 26% (China EXIM 2006–2016) (see Fig. 14.2). Between 2014 and 2015, the CEXIM's total assets surpassed that of the World Bank's main development lending arm – the International Bank for Reconstruction and Development (IBRD) (World Bank).

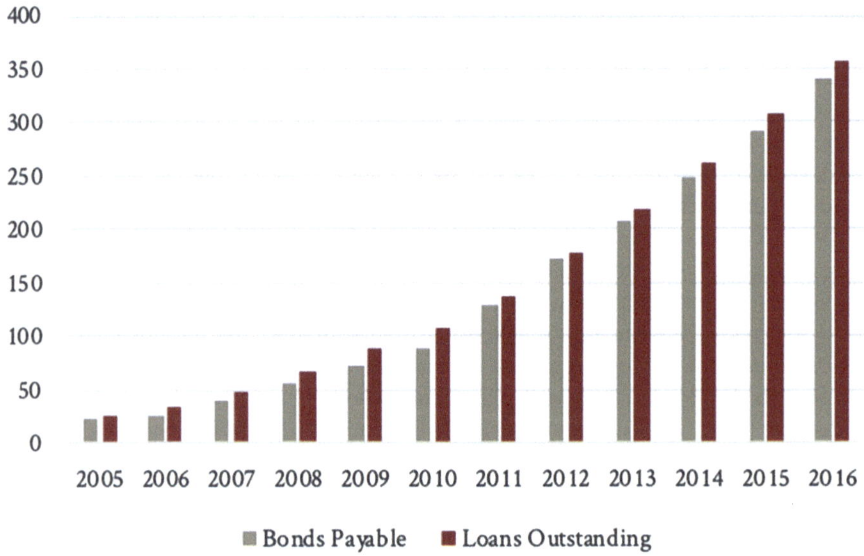

Fig. 14.2 CEXIM loans outstanding and bonds payable (USDbn)

Other metrics further differentiate the practices of the CEXIM and the IBRD and other Western lending institutions for infrastructure. For example, net loans outstanding is a much larger component of the total assets for CEXIM when compared to the IBRD, averaging 74% of total assets between 2012 and 2016, compared to 43% at the IBRD (World Bank). Illustrative measures of transaction costs provide an even starker contrast between the two institutions. Taken as a percentage of loans outstanding, administrative costs at the IBRD were more than *ten times* the administrative costs to loans outstanding of CEXIM in 2016. If some of that differential is accounted for in the fact that the IBRD is a multilateral institution, the comparison also largely holds for Western bilateral lenders. The US Export-Import Bank, which manages a miniscule lending program in comparison to CEXIM, still reported more than five times the administrative costs per loans outstanding when compared to CEXIM that same year (China EXIM). This indicates that the Chinese lenders either are vastly more efficient in making lending decisions or are simply devoting fewer resources to due diligence and other administrative activities.

Booming infrastructure investment is often reported as a major component of China's domestic economic growth (see Fig. 14.3), but many studies of regional infrastructure investment have also produced decidedly mixed results regarding the question of whether higher levels of infrastructure investment help or hinder long-term growth (Shi et al. 2017). Other microeconomic studies of project outcomes for Chinese domestic infrastructure have further indicated that overinvestment could be destroying economic value, rather than creating it (Ansar et al. 2016). China's domestic infrastructure binge began in earnest in 2000, as gross fixed capital formation began outpacing GDP growth and increasing steadily as a component of

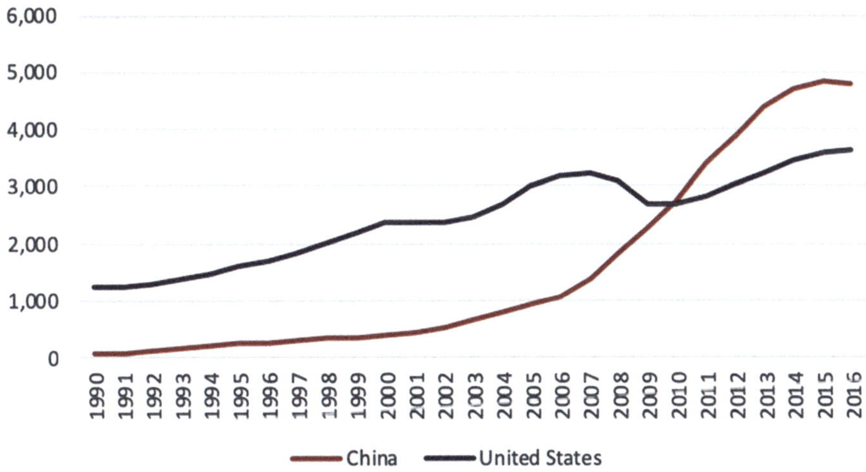

Fig. 14.3 Gross fixed capital formation (current USD$bn)

the Chinese economy. By 2010, gross fixed capital formation within China surpassed that of the world's largest economy, the United States, and continued climbing through 2015. Between 2010 and 2015, gross fixed capital formation climbed from approximately 35% of the Chinese GDP to more than 45% (World Bank 2017a, b).

This massive buildout in domestic infrastructure coincided with a significant increase in debt for local governments within China. Some reports indicate that China's total debt increased from approximately \$2.1tn in 2000 to more than \$28.2tn by 2014 or 282% of GDP – levels higher than other developed economies like the United States and Germany (McKinsey Global Institute 2015). While much of this debt growth was attributable to households or state-owned enterprises, the period since the global recession saw a marked rise in Chinese local government debt, which, according to the National Audit Office, more than doubled between 2010 and 2014 from RMB 10.79 trillion to more than RMB 24 trillion (Wu 2016). By 2014, the need for reforms to reign in local borrowing and avoid a string of defaults was clear.

The Chinese government would spend 2014 and 2015 reforming local government borrowing for infrastructure and refinancing bad debt. The national government's first attempt came in 2014 and included three broad initiatives: (1) requiring an audit by each province to account for the extent of their indebtedness due at the end of 2014; (2) capping local government borrowing from banks and cease Chinese local government financing vehicle (LGFV) borrowing completely, gradually converting it to clearly government or enterprise-related debt; and (3) swapping a significant portion of local government debt coming due to long-term general obligation bonds.

In the spring of 2015, the Ministry of Finance changed its approach to mandate that the local banks that held most of the local government debt refinance it at "negotiated" very low interest rates. To further incentivize the banks to cooperate, the national government made it clear that further government deposits would be tied to participation in the refinancing program, and the central bank further declared that it would recognize any refinanced debt as collateral in future lending or debt restructuring. On the surface, the reforms worked. Local governments were able to refinance into long-term, low interest loans with an implicit guarantee from the national government (Naughton 2015).

If China's reforms in 2015 were successful in averting a catastrophe, it should also be noted that they did not provide an incentive against excessive borrowing to finance infrastructure stimulus. In 2017, infrastructure investment was continuing to grow as a percentage of overall fixed-asset investment and as a component of the Chinese economy (Wildau 2017), and concerns over the use of various forms of off-balance sheet borrowing and other loopholes by local governments continued to mount (Jia 2017).

China's experience with infrastructure development and deleveraging at home provides an important parallel in assessing its international investment, with a few critical distinctions. The first lies in the capture of infrastructure's externalities. One of the motivations for China's approach to infrastructure is to create a portfolio of beneficial projects, even when the individual projects do not create net economic benefits. China's policymakers assume that infrastructure projects will generate beneficial externalities which can be captured by other projects or the local economy generally. Investments in a port project are serviced by the roads and rail projects linking to them, which are serviced by manufacturing from industrial parks in regions made livable by water treatment facilities and access to airports or HSR. Each of these investments generates positive externalities captured by the others. In the end, these network externalities all benefit the local economy and government for infrastructure networks built within China.

The situation outside of China is very different. China's policy banks may finance multiple projects in a region, but the reliance on externalities to create a "rising tide" is less straightforward. Externalities may be captured by the Chinese state-owned firms or policy banks investing in projects in the region, or they may be captured by the nation hosting the projects. Alternatively, China may feel that the externalities are not economic, but rather political, and lie in foreign policy influence that their projects generate. In either case, the dynamics of the relationship between the investor and investee are fundamentally different than China's national investment programs.

The second key difference is that the counterparties receiving China's investments abroad are not provinces operating in a semi-controlled hierarchy under the Chinese national government. They are sovereign nations. When bad debt for infrastructure piled up at home, the Chinese government was able to work out a solution between banks and local governments in part because it controlled all of the parties. That is simply not the case abroad, and China's options will be limited should bad debts accumulate for the projects and host nations that its policy banks finance. We are past the age in which great powers can send gunboats to collect on bad sovereign debts.

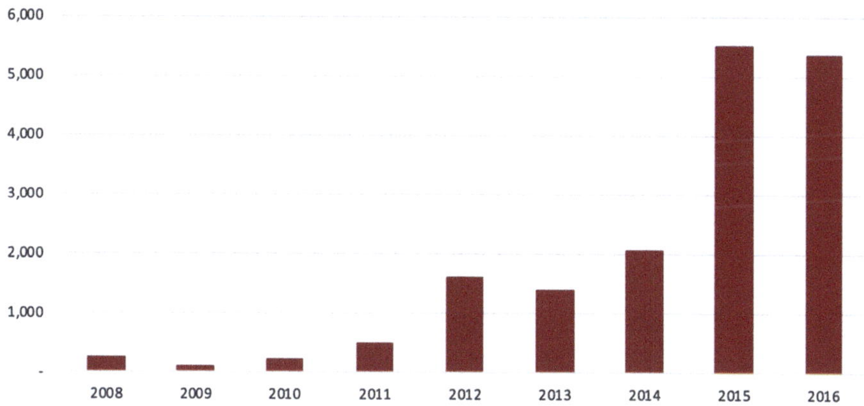

Fig. 14.4 CEXIM loan impairments (USD$bn)

The implications of these differences extend beyond the anecdotal conflicts with host nations highlighted in the investments discussed above. Despite a lack of performance data for individual loans and projects, signs of problems with China's investment programs are emerging in aggregate. Figure 14.4 shows CEXIM's reported loan impairments, which were negligible in 2008 and jumped to more than $5bn per year in 2015 and 2016 (China EXIM 2006–2016). In 2015, China's Ministry of Finance made a cash infusion of more than $90bn split roughly evenly between its two policy banks – the CDB and CEXIM (Jia 2015). The injection was billed as part of a broader reform package for China's policy banks, but it also illustrated the differential performance between the banks' investments at home and abroad. The injection reportedly improved both banks' capital adequacy ratios, but the CDB, which focuses the majority of its lending within China, had a ratio of just under 9% prior to the injection. The CEXIM, which lends exclusively outside of China, had a capital adequacy ratio of just 2.26% prior to the injection – a level well below the Basel requirements for lending institutions.

The problems highlighted above and the difficulty China's policy banks and host nations have in quantifying the extent of bad debt illustrate one of the most significant flaws of the Chinese approach to infrastructure investment, at least in how it has been practiced to date – a lack of transparency. While China's approach reduces transaction costs and promotes projects significantly faster, the lack of transparency significantly increases the potential for negative project outcomes. The vast majority of infrastructure projects financed by China's policy banks have been implemented via a direct negotiation between the banks, Chinese state-owned enterprises, and the host nation. Often it is unclear what the terms and requirements of the loans actually are and, most importantly, whether or not they are recourse to only to the projects themselves or come with a sovereign guarantee from the host nation. This renders it difficult for host nations to even quantify the extent of their indebtedness and possibly too for China's policy banks to accurately assess their risk-weighted liabilities.

14.5 Western Failures

In pointing to the weaknesses of the Chinese approach to infrastructure investment, we do not mean to imply that the Western approach constitutes a gold standard to which all international development institutions should aspire. The Chinese have claimed a very large share of global investment due as much to weaknesses in Western approaches as to their own virtues.

The World Bank's environmental review and safeguard processes provide a good proxy for the rate by which well-meaning reviews and procedures can grow increasingly cumbersome and prohibitive over time. While the World Bank first created modest environmental review and mitigation procedures in the 1980s, the programs evolved considerably in the 1990s and early 2000s. In 1991, the Bank began mandating institutional capacity strengthening for borrowers to meet the Bank's Environmental Assessment (EA) requirements for every project it lends to. Still, throughout the 1990s, the Bank faced difficulty in getting "buy-in" and ownership from host nations in completing EAs and, more importantly, compliance with environmental mitigation measures once projects were in operation.

Despite these challenges, the Bank's internal assessments during this period largely framed difficulty in implementing its environmental procedures as a problem that needed to be addressed by its borrowers, rather than the bank itself. "Accordingly, it is profoundly unsettling if a project proponent questions the need for an EA. When it comes to the crunch proponents may 'accept' to get an EA done if they want international finance. But 'acceptance' is not enough. It shows lack of political will, which suggests there will be problems in effective mitigation after the loan has been signed or after the project has been built" (Goodland and Mercier 1999).

By the early 1990s, the Bank was experimenting with policies that would further ingrain environmental and social reviews into its project assessment procedures by adding "environmental valuation" into the cost-benefit analysis (CBA) completed by the Bank for its projects. Bank staff and prospective borrowers would attempt to quantify environmental factors and translate them into dollar terms in analyzing an individual project. This practice proliferated in the late 1990s. While a 1995 review found that only 1 project in a sample of 162 attempted an environmental valuation, a 2003 review of the practice found that more than a third of the projects sampled included an environmental valuation, a rate "still in many ways disappointingly low" (Silva and Pagiola 2003). While the Bank's environmental review procedures continued to grow, an industry of Western nongovernmental organizations (NGOs) developed in parallel to advocate for the cancellation of or changes to potential Bank projects. Advocacy groups lobbied the Bank itself and, perhaps more importantly, the governments of its Western donor nations, with the Bank left to navigate between interest groups in local politics in host nations at back at home for the projects it aimed to finance (Mallaby 2009).

The World Bank's increasingly cumbersome environmental review programs over time had a measurable negative effect on the bank's lending programs. The Bank reported a marked decrease in lending to middle-income countries throughout the 1990s and, despite a brief surge following the 1997 Asian Financial Crisis, dropped even further in the early 2000s. Throughout the 1990s the Bank markedly shifted away from infrastructure project lending into social sectors and further underwent an "institutional culture shift" from a focus on the "business of lending" to an institution that functions as a "knowledge bank." While there were several factors that contributed to this trend, one was clearly "excessively rigorous and demanding fiduciary and social/environmental safeguards attached to Bank projects" which "slowed down bank lending and increased its effective cost to borrowers" (Linn 2004).

By 2010, and despite a second lending surge following the Global Financial Crisis, the world's largest infrastructure lending institution had largely exited the business of infrastructure lending. In real terms, lending commitments from the IBRD declined from an annual average of more than $25bn in the 1980s and 1990s to $16.6bn between 2000 and 2009 (Currey 2014). By then, other infrastructure finance institutions (such as the Chinese policy banks) were actively replacing and competing with the World Bank in financing developing economy infrastructure. The World Bank's impediments to lending were, in fact, becoming an existential threat to the institution itself – Operating Income, which the Bank largely derived from loans and which it used to fund its staffing requirements, was dwindling. By 2013 the IBRD's loan income, for instance, was less than a third of its levels in 1990 adjusted for inflation (Currey 2014).

A 2010 review of the World Bank's environmental and social safeguard policies highlighted the need for change. The report called for a new, comprehensive environmental and social policy to replace the piecemeal policies that had developed at the bank over time. This would be accompanied by lending reforms proposed for more "programmatic lending" in which host nation assessments received increasing emphasis when compared to individual project assessment. The Bank was also implementing a pilot program that would use host nation systems of environmental safeguards for projects rather than applying the Bank's top-down policies. The review also highlighted some important trends in the Bank's environmental review practices and costs. For example, from 1999 to 2008, the Bank's projects underwent significant classification-creep in determining the level of environmental impacts and thus the necessary scope of the environmental review. During that period, the percentage of "very-high-impact" projects, which require the highest level of environmental review, increased from 5% to 11% of the Bank's project evaluations. "Substantial-impact" projects increased from 37% to 51% of evaluations, while "low-impact" projects decreased from 40% to 18% of projects. The report estimated that, in aggregate, the Bank's client costs in meeting safeguard policies averaged at about 5% of World Bank financing. The vast majority of these costs were borne by the project sponsors, rather than the Bank. The study further found that 38% of Bank clients avoided projects or dropped components to avoid the Bank's safeguards and 18% reported revising a project's scope to avoid classification as a "very-high-impact" project (Independent Evaluation Group 2010).

Following the 2010 report, the World Bank worked to implement reforms to its environmental and social safeguards programs and increase its lending to infrastructure projects. These reforms have been successful by some metrics – infrastructure lending by the bank has increased markedly over the last few years. The environmental policy reforms, though, have become a bit of a metaphor for the Bank's difficulties in implementing and approving new initiatives. The new Environmental and Social Framework has been more than 6 years in development, for what is effectively a review of the environmental and social review policies. According to the Bank, the new framework underwent "the most extensive consultation the World Bank has ever had." The Bank developed a series of draft guidance notes for the implementation of the new framework, and the comment period for Bank stakeholders and NGOs ended in late 2017. The new framework launched in October 2018 now applies to all new World Bank investment projects (World Bank ESF 2018).

In addition to the broad Western emphasis on safeguards and safeguard compliance, there are other weaknesses in specifically in American politics and policy that prevent it from effectively competing with China in the provision of infrastructure to developing countries. An example of this is the Obama Administration's signature infrastructure initiative, Power Africa.

Following on a visit to Africa in 2013, President Obama announced a new energy initiative that he hoped would lead to the investment of $7 billion in US government resources and $9 billion from the private sector (Olorunnipa and Alake 2016). The original goal was to provide 10,000 MW of power and to electrify 20 million new households in sub-Saharan Africa in 5 years, with even more ambitious goals set for 2030. This was followed in 2015 by a complementary Electrify Africa Act passed by Congress that promised 20,000 MW and 50 million connections by 2020 (Leo and Moss 2017). The idea behind Power Africa was that the government would use its resources to mobilize private sector investment through loan guarantees provided by institutions like the Overseas Private Investment Corporation (OPIC) and the US ExIm Bank.

There were numerous obstacles to the implementation of Power Africa, however. The first had to do with the structure of the US government. While the initiative had presidential backing, authority was spread over nearly a dozen US government agencies. While USAID was in theory the lead agency, it had no power to force interagency compliance; its administrator did not even hold Cabinet rank. Secondly, the initiative got caught up in the broad partisan gridlock affecting the US Congress as a whole. The conservative wing of the Republican Party was trying to defund OPIC and the ExIm Bank altogether and was opposed to any new spending on foreign assistance. As a result, the Electrify Africa Act, though passed with bipartisan support, did not allocate any new resources to the initiative. The Administration hoped it could encourage public-private partnerships, and while it did perform a coordinating function that led to some small new projects like the Corbetti Geothermal Project in Ethiopia or the Lake Turkana Wind Power project in Kenya, these efforts had achieved only 5% of the promised 30,000 MW by 2016 (Gasparro 2018). The Trump Administration has not, needless to say, made Power Africa one of its own priorities.

14.6 Conclusions

Is the newly dominant Chinese model a better approach to infrastructure development, for host nation borrowers or even China, for that matter? It is true that China is actually doing what Western governments have promised and, in the past, delivered on: the provision of roads, electricity, railways, ports, and other facilities necessary for economic growth. The US Power Africa initiative identified a clear development need and then failed to deliver significant tangible results. Over the same period, China invested some tens of billions of dollars in infrastructure in sub-Saharan Africa.

On the other hand, this infrastructure has come at a significant price. Loans by China's policy banks generally incorporate a lack of transparency as a feature; the vast majority of their projects have been implemented via a direct negotiation. Often it is unclear what the terms and requirements of the loans actually are and, most important, whether they come with sovereign guarantees or are "nonrecourse," which would mean the loan is secured only by the project itself and the lender would be on the hook if it defaults. This ambiguity renders it difficult for host nations to even quantify the extent of their indebtedness and possibly for China's policy banks to accurately assess their risk-weighted liabilities.

If the actual objective of China's lending programs is to build influence internationally, it has arguably been largely ineffective on that front as well. Today many of the nations that are the largest recipients of Chinese lending have the poorest bilateral relations with China, not the best. High levels of Chinese investment in Sri Lanka, Myanmar, and Ecuador provide the starkest example, as local agencies mired in debt have generated a substantial backlash. Many nations in South Asia that are among the largest recipients of Chinese Belt and Road lending have shifted to realign strategically with India, Japan, or the United States.

Western lending institutions should do more than simply wait for China's lending programs to run their course. Multilateral infrastructure lending institutions must be restructured to account for the fact that they are no longer the only viable alternative for borrowers. The next iteration of Western development lending should promote transparent, competitive procurement, nonrecourse financing without hidden sovereign guarantees, and streamlined safeguard processes, without imposing overly onerous requirements on host nations eager to move their projects forward. The alternative to their participation may be the very same project but without the safeguards and analysis that Western institutions are trying to promote. The onus of enforcing those requirements should lie with the host nations themselves. In order to actively move projects forward abroad, Western lending institutions must be protected from politics at home.

The United States, for its part, is crippled by its own budget deficits and partisan gridlock. In late 2018, the US Congress passed the BUILD Act, which reforms OPIC and parts of USAID to create the US International Development Finance Corporation (USIDFC), which is a direct response to China's emerging dominance of international infrastructure lending. The new institution will have new programs to support private market solutions in international development and more than doubles the funding cap allotted to OPIC to $60bn. While a welcome step toward the reforms necessary to support developing economies with options aside from China and, for that matter, US companies competing with Chinese state-backed financing overseas, US programs still pale in comparison with China's international lending institutions. While Japan, India, and other countries competing with China have sought to promote their own infrastructure projects, they too face resource constraints and bureaucratic obstacles.

This would not necessitate a "race to the bottom" by development institutions for infrastructure. Today Western development institutions are hamstrung to the point at which they can no longer further the goals for which they were created. China is simply filling the gap.

References

Ansar A, Flyvbjerg B, Budzier A, Lunn D (2016) Does infrastructure investment lead to economic growth or economic fragility? Evidence from China. Oxf Rev Econ Policy 32(3):360–390

Bräutigam D (2015) 5 Myths about Chinese investment in Africa. Retrieved from Foreign Policy: http://foreignpolicy.com/2015/12/04/5-myths-about-chinese-investment-in-africa/

Caribbean Development Bank (2017) The Caribbean public private partnership toolkit – environmental and social impact of highway 2000, Jamaica

Chellaney B (2017) China's creditor imperialism. Retrieved from Project Syndicate: https://www.project-syndicate.org/commentary/china-sri-lanka-hambantota-port-debt-by-brahma-chellaney-2017-12

China EXIM (2006–2016) Annual reports. Export Import Bank of China, Beijing

Currey K (2014) Some evolving trends at the World Bank: lending, funding, staffing. Ford Foundation

David, Stanway. Reuters (2018) China's total arable land falls for Fourth Year in 2018: resources ministry. Accessed 2018: https://www.reuters.com/article/us-china-agriculture-land/chinas-total-arable-land-falls-for-fourth-year-in-2017-resources-ministry-idUSKCN1IK059

Diamond L, Schell O (2018) Chinese influence and American interests: promoting constructive vigilance. Hoover Institution Press, Stanford

Dollar D (2016) China's engagement with Africa. John L. Thornton China Center at Brookings, Washington, DC

ENR (2016) Engineering news-record. Retrieved from Engineering News-Record: http://www.enr.com/toplists/2016-Top-250-Global-Contractors1

ESI Africa (2016) DRC: Inga 3 to proceed without EIA, says international rivers. Retrieved from ESI Africa - Africa's Power Journal: https://www.esi-africa.com/news/drc-inga-3-proceed-without-eia-says-international-rivers/

Gasparro K (2018) Power Africa (Leadership Academy for Development Case Study, 2018)

Goodland R, Mercier J-R (1999) The evolution of environmental assessment in the World Bank: from "Approval" to results. Environment Department Paper Series

Haggard S (2018) Developmental states. Cambridge University Press, Cambridge/New York

Haynes K, Chen Z (2015) Chinese railways in the era of high speed. Emerald Group Publishing, Bingley

Independent Evaluation Group (2010) Safeguards and sustainability in a changing world. Washington, DC, The World Bank Group

International Rivers (2016) The Inga 3 hydropower project. Retrieved from International Rivers Web site: https://www.internationalrivers.org/campaigns/the-inga-3-hydropower-project
Jia C (2015) Policy banks get $90bn cash infusion. China Daily
Jia C (2017) Ministry plans rules to curb PPP misuse. China Daily
John Hopkins SAIS (2017) China Africa research initiative – John Hopkins school of advanced international studies. Retrieved from Data: Chinese Workers in Africa: http://www.sais-cari.org/data-chinese-workers-in-africa/
Larmer B (2017) What the world's emptiest international airport says about China's influence. The New York Times Magazine
Leo B, Moss T (2017) Congress passes the electrify Africa act...finally. Center for Global Development. 29 September 2017. https://www.cgdev.org/blog/congress-passes-electrify-africa-act-finally
Li T (2008) China's nonperforming loans: A $540 Billion problem unsolved. SSRN. https://doi.org/10.2139/ssrn.1278235
Linn J (2004) The role of World Bank lending in middle income countries. The OED conference on the effectiveness of policies and reforms. Brookings Institution, Washington
Mallaby S (2009) NGOs: fighting poverty, hurting the poor. Foreign Policy
McKinsey Global Institute (2015) Debt and (Not Much) Deleveraging. McKinsey
Mooney T (2016) Work on Colombo port city project to restart. IHS Fairplay
Moramudali U (2017) Sri Lanka's debt and China's money. The Diplomat
Naughton B (2015) Local debt restructuring: a case of ongoing authoritarian reform. China Leadership Monitor No. 47
Olorunnipa T, Alake T (2016) Obama's Africa power plan falls short, leaving continent in dark. Bloomberg Politics. 29 September 2017. https://www.bloomberg.com/news/articles/2016-09-21/africa-left-in-dark-as-9-7-billion-obama-power-plan-falls-short
Patton, Dominique. Reuters (2014) More than 40 percent of China's arable land degraded: Xinhua. Accessed 2018: https://www.reuters.com/article/us-china-soil/more-than-40-percent-of-chinas-arable-land-degraded-xinhua-idUSKBN0IO0Y720141104
Ross A (2015) China's 'infrastructure for minerals' deal gets reality-check in Congo. Reuters. Accessed 2019: https://www.reuters.com/article/us-congodemocratic-mining-china-insight-idUSKCN0PI1UB20150709
Shepard W (2016) The story behind the world's emptiest international airport. Forbes
Shi Y, Guo S, Sun P (2017) The role of infrastructure in China's regional economic growth. J Asian Econ:26–41
Silva P, Pagiola S (2003) A review of the valuation of environmental costs and benefits in World Bank projects. Environmental economics series
United States Treasury (2014) World Bank Inga 3 Bass Chute (BC) and Midsized Hydropower Development Technical Assistance (TA) Project U.S. Position. https://www.treasury.gov/resource-center/international/development-banks/Documents/Inga.pdf
Walker C (2018) What is "sharp power"? J Democr 29:9–23
Walker C, Ludwig J (2017) From "soft power" to "sharp power": rising authoritarian influence in the democratic world. Intl Forum for Democratic Studies, Washington, DC
Wijedasa N (2014) Coal power chaos: Chinese firm fumes. The Sunday Times of Sri Lanka
Wildau G (2017) China's reliance on infrastructure stimulus at record high. Financial Times
Wilmsen B, Michael Webber M, Yuefang D (2011) Development for whom? Rural to urban resettlement at the three gorges dam, China. Asian Stud Rev 35(1):21–42. https://doi.org/10.1080/10357823.2011.552707
World Bank (2002–2016) Annual reports. World Bank, Washington, DC
World Bank (2017a) World Bank development indicators. Retrieved from Gross Fixed Capital Formation (%GDP) and (current US$): https://data.worldbank.org/indicator/NE.GDI.FTOT.CD
World Bank (2017b) World Bank open data. Retrieved from The World Bank: https://data.worldbank.org/

World Bank (2018) Implementation completion and results report for a DRC Inga 3 and Mid-Size Hydropower Development Technical Assistance: http://documents.worldbank.org/curated/en/266481521472063648/pdf/ICR00004325-03142018.pdf
World Bank Environmental and Social Framework (ESF) (2018) https://www.worldbank.org/en/projects-operations/environmental-and-social-framework
World Bank Private Participation in Infrastructure (PPI) Database (2018) Featured rankings 1990 to H1 2018: http://ppi.worldbank.org/snapshots/rankings
Wu X (2016) China's growing local government debt levels. MIT Center for Finance and Policy, Cambridge, MA

Chapter 15
Subnational Government, Infrastructure, and the Role of Borrowing and Debt

Serdar Yilmaz and Robert D. Ebel

Abstract This chapter addresses the role of subnational government (SNG) borrowing and debt management as the financing conduit for the provision of a nation's investment in its public infrastructure. It begins with a brief review of recent literature on infrastructure deficit and the link between infrastructure services, economic growth, and development. It then describes intergovernmental organizational and institutional arrangements to promote efficiency in the allocation of scarce resources as well as satisfy the equity goal of matching the cost of using those resources to those who pay for them. Spatial considerations lead to the conclusion that SNGs must play a key role in infrastructure financing. And to play this role, the subnational sector must develop the capacity to take on and manage long-term debt. Having established this normative framework, the discussion turns to organizational and institutional arrangements that must be in place to enable a subnational government to carry out its capital financing and spending role. From there the chapter moves on to address financial risks related to SNG debt finance. Two appendices provide a summary of the intergovernmental fiscal rules for nine East Asian countries and the role of subnational borrowing and debt in China.

Keywords Infrastructure finance · Subnational debt · Subnational borrowing · Local economic development

S. Yilmaz (✉)
World Bank, Washington, DC, USA
e-mail: syilmaz@worldbank.org

R. D. Ebel
Andrew Young School of Public Policy, Georgia State University, Washington, DC, USA

Z. Chen et al. (eds.), *Development Studies in Regional Science*,
New Frontiers in Regional Science: Asian Perspectives 42,
https://doi.org/10.1007/978-981-15-1435-7_15

15.1 Introduction

A necessary condition for a nation to grow and develop is to direct economic resources of land, labor and capital away from current consumption to investment on the physical infrastructure.[1] In order to have sustainable growth, an economy needs constant improvements in infrastructure to ensure that the production and exchange of goods and services happen as efficiently as possible. By directing resources to capital goods, tomorrow's generations will not only be able to enjoy a higher level of current consumption than at present but also have in place a capital stock for sustaining growth and development. Therefore, it is important to acquire physical assets with a long life and to prolong that service life with adequate level of maintenance (Bahl and Bird 2018; Fox and Murray 2016).

Globally, the supply of new infrastructure has not kept up with demand, creating an infrastructure deficit. The infrastructure deficit and how to pay for it are now major economic development challenges in developed and developing countries alike. Examples of infrastructure deficit range from an undersupplied often badly maintained transportation and communications networks to the lack of reliable water supply and distribution systems and energy-generating systems.

The numbers attest to a coming demographic-led demand for an expanding infrastructure for development. The United Nations projects that between 2015 and 2025, the world's population will increase from 7.2 billion to 8.1 billion. That is a 12.5% increase in just 10 years. The population further increases to 9.6 billion in 2050 (a third higher than today). And, nearly all of this will occur in the urban areas of the developing world.[2]

The resulting price tag to provide for a stock of infrastructure to keep pace with these changing demographics will run into billions of spending over the next decade and a half. Estache and Fay (2010) estimate that just to keep pace with the trends in population and urbanization, low-income countries must spend 12.5% of GDP on investment and maintenance and that lower–middle-income countries and upper–middle-income countries should spend 8.2% and 2.3%, respectively.[3] In another study, McKinsey (2016) estimates that the worldwide total infrastructure spending as a share of gross domestic product needs to increase to 5.6% by 2020 to cope with the service delivery needs.

---

[1]Infrastructure is defined as publicly provided physical capital assets used in economic production and by households with a useful life of more than 1 year. Within that definition, what counts as "core" infrastructure varies across countries and sectors. Thus, for rural areas, local roads, irrigation networks, and community water boreholes are core infrastructure investments. For urban systems, facilities such as inter-connector roads and highways, tram systems, power and telecom, supply-to-point-of-distribution water systems, wastewater collection and treatment (sewerage and storm water), and street lighting dominate. In both rural and urban areas, physical assets such as schools, health clinics, general government office buildings, post offices, sports and entertainment facilities, fire and police stations, and prisons are needed.

[2]United Nations Department of Economic and Social Affairs (April 2014)

[3]Estache and Fay (2010)

The Asian Development Bank estimates that East Asia needs to invest $1.5 trillion per year in infrastructure to maintain economic growth.[4] South Asia presents a similar infrastructure gap challenge: Andres et al. (2014) estimate that the region needs to invest between US$ 1.7 trillion and US$ 2.5 trillion (in 2014 prices).

As a result, financing for infrastructure provision remains inadequate in all countries except the wealthiest.[5] In many countries, until the changes over the last two decades, the major share of infrastructure services was delivered through national- or subnational-owned enterprises, governed by inefficient economic model and administrative structure coupled with perverse political incentives. The results were disappointing as the inefficient public sector monopolies failed to provide an adequate level of quality infrastructure services. Today there remain many technically viable projects in many countries which public budgets cannot cover, regardless of the prevailing financial and economic analysis of them. A considerable amount of responsibility for infrastructure service provision is being shifted to subnational governments without corresponding changes in the intergovernmental architecture.[6] In many countries, intergovernmental transfers to subnational governments or their own source revenues are insufficient to finance infrastructure investments. In addition, intergovernmental fiscal arrangements are not well designed to provide assurances for responsible borrowing. Borrowing is for short term to cover shortages in cash flow and restricted to banks that are government owned, creating incentive problems for repayment obligations.

After this brief introduction, the paper provides a brief review of recent literature on infrastructure deficit and economic growth. It then delves into the role of subnational governments in providing infrastructure services. Then, the chapter focuses on the financing of infrastructure investments and the role of financial markets for subnational governments to engage in long-term borrowing. After establishing a normative framework, the various organizational and institutional arrangements must be in place to enable a subnational government to carry out its capital spending role, and the discussion moves on to address financial risks related to debt finance and how, in order to minimize those risks, different countries have

[4]Yoshino, Helbe, and Abidhadjaev (2018)

[5]The focus of this paper is the role of subnational borrowing and debt management for the purpose of *financing* of the putting in place the *stock* of capital investments that have a medium- to long-term life. There are other capital financing strategies that are not discussed but that have adequately examined elsewhere. These include special assessments that come in the form of compulsory contributions collected from owners of property benefited by special improvements to defray the cost of improvements (e.g., street paving, sidewalks, sewer lines); developer fees, exactions, and in-kind investments (infrastructure that may be "on-site" such as a sewer hook-up or an off-ramp to a developer's facility or an "offsite" linkage such as requiring a developer to build and transfer a facility such as a fire station or school proximate to the development project); and even payments for the right to name sports stadiums, transit stops, and the use of public utility air rights (Kim 2016; De Mello and Sutherland 2016; Bird and Slack 2017).

[6]Vinuela (2016) reports that SNGs account for an average of 63% of fixed capital formation in OECD countries and 40% in developing countries.

responded by creating a set of ex ante regulations and ex post measures for managing the borrowing and debt.

15.2 Infrastructure: Why It Matters

The literature on infrastructure and economic growth encompasses two primary themes: (i) direct impact of infrastructure investment to GDP formation and as an additional input in the production process of other sectors and (ii), indirectly, raising total factor productivity by reducing transaction and other costs (Escribano et al. 2008; Kappeler and Valila 2008). In a seminal paper, Aschauer (1989a) examines the relationship between infrastructure spending after World War II and variations in economic growth in the United States.

Although the empirical literature is not unanimous about the nature of the relationship between infrastructure and economic growth, there is a general agreement on a positive effect of infrastructure on output and productivity that, in turn, leads to an increase in long-term growth rates. Infrastructure investment is complementary to other investments in the sense that insufficient infrastructure investment constrains other investments, while excessive infrastructure investment has no added value. In other words, if infrastructure is a constraint in production, it has a high marginal productivity; however, with optimal amount of infrastructure provision, the marginal productivity of infrastructure falls dramatically.[7]

Economic benefits of infrastructure investments depend on the source of financing and the geographic benefit area of infrastructure network (Haynes 2010). If the benefits of infrastructure investments are fully localized, central financing fails both efficiency and equity tests (Young 2005; Bird and Slack 2017). From an efficiency perspective, for a fixed amount of total investment spending, the multiplier effects of local projects centrally financed would be offset by the multiplier effects of foregone alternative public investment elsewhere (Young 2005). From an equity perspective, the principle of matching who benefits and who pays is violated (Bird 1994; Bahl and Bird 2018).

[7]Empirical studies have found that high returns to infrastructure investments include Aschauer (1989a, b), Easterly and Rebelo (1993), Eisner (1994), Haynes (1997a, b), World Bank (1994), Sanchez-Robles (1998), Esfahani and Ramirez (2003), and Escribano et al. (2008).

15.3 Intergovernmental Arrangements: Efficiency and Equity

High demand for infrastructure investments and scarcity of financial resources force policy makers to use the available resources wisely. In this context, the question is which type of government is better positioned to provide infrastructure services more effectively and efficiently. Theory tells us that decentralization of infrastructure provision may lead to higher levels of services than central provision (Oates 1972). From an economic perspective, decentralization is a policy instrument to match public good service levels to local preferences and costs (Oates 1972). The implications of decentralizing infrastructure service provision are far-reaching. The way public resources and responsibilities are allocated among different levels of government affects a nation's overall economic and fiscal performance. Thus, the challenge is organizing intergovernmental arrangements in a way that provides incentives to subnational governments for improving the delivery of infrastructure services without endangering economic and fiscal stability.

The pillars of an intergovernmental fiscal system include service delivery responsibilities (expenditure assignment), revenue mobilization powers (tax assignment), intergovernmental transfer system, and borrowing restrictions and practices (Bahl and Bird 2018). Designing an intergovernmental system that can best achieve national policy objectives in the provision of infrastructure service is a challenging task. Such objectives may include not only efficiency, transparency, and accountability but also achieving equity among people and places and maintaining national integrity and political stability.[8] The challenge is to design an intergovernmental system that will (i) improve the efficiency with which public resources can be mobilized and utilized, (ii) achieve fiscal equity, and (iii) promote macroeconomic stability.

The design of an intergovernmental system for the financing of infrastructure sector is also closely linked to the answers on questions of who benefits from the service and who pays the cost of service.[9] For most infrastructure services, it is not easy to give a clean-cut answer to the questions of who benefits and who pays (Bird and Slack 2017). Even when the benefits of an infrastructure activity, such as sewerage system, appear to be local, there may be overriding public health concerns that provide justification for higher-level government interventions. Therefore, economic analysis of the impact of an intergovernmental system on infrastructure services entails both the design of functional responsibilities and the system of financing services.

---

[8] Yilmaz, Vaillancourt, and Dafflon et al. (2012)

[9] At one extreme, all national residents benefit from infrastructure services equally, and there is no diversity in individual preferences for service quality and/or quantity; therefore, it is provided nationally and financed by national taxes. At the other extreme, the public goods aspects of the service (non-excludability) are small, and there are wide differences in desired levels and/or quality of service among various jurisdictions; thus, it is provided locally and financed by local taxes.

There is a robust, growing literature analyzing the polycentric nature of the delivery of infrastructure services that attests to the role of subnational governments in facilitating growth and developing investments (Aschauer 1989b; Bahl and Bird 2014, 2018; Bird et al. 1995; World Bank 1994, 2000). The lessons learned from this literature suggests that a well-designed intergovernmental system is the one that (i) accommodates regional variation in preferences, (ii) addresses spatial externalities, (iii) relies as far as possible on pricing mechanisms, and (iv) creates institutions for efficient delivery of infrastructure services.

15.3.1 Cost and Production Efficiency: Resource Allocation

Regional and local variations in preferences and costs suggest that there are potential efficiency gains from assigning responsibility for infrastructure service provision to the type of government that is "closest to the people" and that also has the administrative capacity to govern (Yilmaz, Villancourt, Dafflon, et al. 2012). However, assignment to the "lowest level" of government would not lead to welfare gains in the case of economies of scale and the presence of externalities.

15.3.1.1 Production Efficiency

In the case of economies of scale, the average cost of infrastructure service provision decreases with the increase in the scale of production (Nicholson 1994).[10] When average costs decline as output increases, it means that it becomes cheaper to produce the average unit as the scale of production rises, hence economies of scale. A cost function reflecting increasing returns to scale is depicted in Fig. 15.1; average cost is decreasing by more production.[11]

In most of the infrastructure sectors, fixed costs are high, as these sectors require large investments to set up the system.[12] Large fixed costs, hence economies of scale, are prevalent in highly capital-intensive infrastructure sectors such as sewerage, electricity, and piped water. In these infrastructure sectors, once the system is set

[10]Another way to characterize economies of scale is with a decreasing average cost curve. Average costs, AC, are calculated as the total costs to produce output Q, TC (Q), divided by total output. Thus, AC (Q) = TC (Q)/Q. Total Cost (TC) = Fixed Cost (FC) + Variable Cost (VC).

[11]At Q_1, marginal cost is less than the average which suggests that in producing one more additional unit, the producer can decrease the average cost (larger output allows costs to be spread over more units).

[12]Fixed costs arise when substantial amounts of capital equipment must be put into place even if only one unit is to be produced and if the costs of this equipment must still be paid even with zero output. In this case the larger the output, the more the costs of this equipment can be spread out among more units of the good.

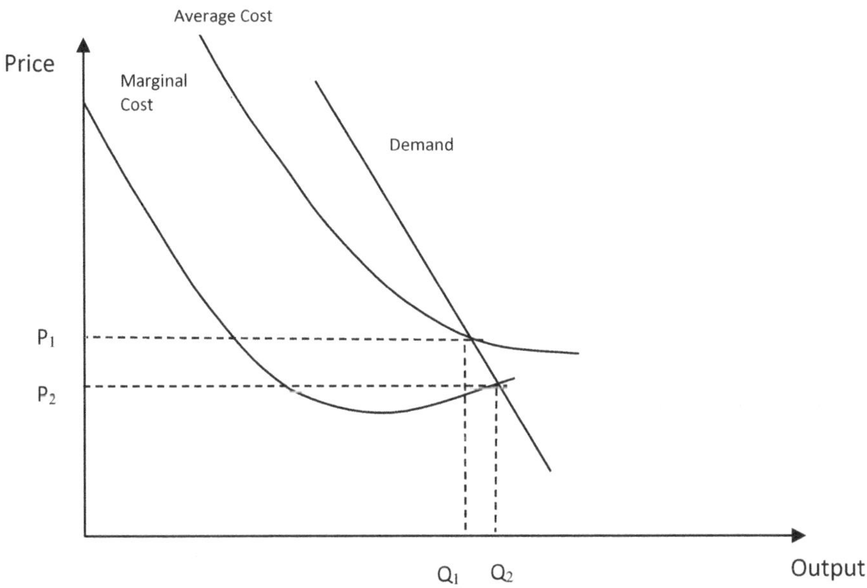

Fig. 15.1 Economies of scale. (Source: Adapted from Nicholson 1994)

up, with the inclusion of more households into the network, the average cost of service declines until the capacity constraint becomes binding.

Allocative Efficiency: Spatial Considerations (Externalities). Recognizing the polycentric nature of infrastructure, spillovers (externalities) occur when the spatial distribution of the costs or benefits of infrastructure services is not confined to the jurisdiction boundaries of the service provider. In the case of spatial spillovers, non-residents either pay part of the costs or enjoy part of the benefits of an infrastructure service. In the case of benefit spillovers, there is a positive externality of infrastructure services, whereas cost spillovers refer to negative externalities. If there is a spillover of costs, residents underestimate the true social cost and demand too much of the service, whereas a spillover of benefits causes residents to underestimate the true social benefit and demand too little.

General-purpose subnational governments often have little incentive to take spatial externalities into consideration if many benefits/harms of the investment "spill over" to non-residents. For example, a well-designed public transportation system can have positive environmental effects and also promotes social equity, which are positive externalities.[13] Similarly, piped-water and sewerage services have positive benefits on public health. On the other hand, emissions from fossil fuel power generation have negative environmental impacts that could lead to excess power being produced with the wrong mix of fuels if the costs are not internalized.

[13]In the United States, special-purpose districts, which are subnational governments, account for the largest type of local governments in 2012 (US Bureau of the Census 2013).

Thus, the role of the intergovernmental system is to make sure spillover externalities are taken into account.

If intergovernmental arrangements are poorly designed, if institutions are weak or incentives misaligned, and/or if there is poor vertical and horizontal coordination among governments (in some cases even intentionally so), then decentralizing infrastructure can lead to an over- or undersupply due to such things as overlooking of potential economies of scales in the production of infrastructure and internalization of costs and benefits that may (or may not) have spillovers across jurisdictions.[14] Thus, getting the prices "right" matters.[15]

15.3.2 *Pricing Equity: Who Pays?*

According to the public finance theory, the major role assigned to subnational governments is to provide goods and services within a geographical area to people who are going to benefit from them and are willing to pay for them. If the benefits/costs of particular services are not confined to local jurisdictions (the services provided in one subnational government jurisdiction have positive/negative effect on other jurisdictions), the resource allocation may not be efficient. The classic economic solution to any externality problem is to internalize the externality—that is, to force the decision-maker to consider the true social costs and benefits. In theory, if all consumers who benefit from service pay the cost of service, then there is no externality. In practice it is not easy to design such a system that would internalize such externalities. The optimal jurisdiction size that would internalize the externalities would differ for each infrastructure service. Furthermore, the optimal jurisdiction size that would internalize externalities might be in conflict with the optimal size required to achieve economies of scale. Therefore, the existence of spatial externalities of infrastructure services can be addressed by designing intergovernmental grants system and/or establishing special districts.

Some of the infrastructure services have public good characteristics where competitive markets fall short of allocating resources efficiently. The most common definitions of public goods stress two attributes of such goods: non-excludability and non-rivalry. The first property that distinguishes public goods concerns whether individuals may be excluded from the benefits of consuming the good. A good is excludable if it is relatively easy to exclude individuals from benefiting from the good once it is produced. A good is non-excludable if it is impossible, or prohibitively expensive, to exclude individuals from benefiting from the good. A second property that characterizes some public goods is non-rivalry. A non-rival good is one for which additional units can be consumed at zero marginal cost.

---

[14]Vinuela (2016), Andres et al. (2014), and Martinez-Vazquez and Vaillancourt (2011)

[15]Bird and Slack (2017), Martinez-Vazquez and Timofeev (2016), and Bird et al. (1995)

Fig. 15.2 Excludability and rivalry

The concepts of non-excludability and non-rivalry are in some ways related. Many infrastructure services that are non-excludable are also non-rival. Street lighting and access road services are two examples of infrastructure services for which exclusion is prohibitively expensive and additional consumption takes place at very low marginal cost. Many other instances might be suggested. The concepts, however, are not identical: some infrastructure services may possess one property, but not the other (see Fig. 15.2). It is, for example, very costly to exclude drivers from congested urban roads, yet having one more car on a congested urban road clearly imposes social costs in the form of pollution and road maintenance. Figure 15.2 presents a cross-classification of infrastructure services by their possibilities for exclusion and rivalry.

The potential for government involvement in providing non-rival and non-excludable goods is obvious. If an infrastructure exhibits the non-exclusion property, it is not feasible to charge a price for consumption, and the taxing power of government is needed to finance provision of this service. In local public finance theory, an attractive and feasible tool to finance local infrastructure is benefit taxation and user charges, with consumers' charge depending on both benefit (use) and cost of service provision. However, if a service has non-excludability characteristics, then individual consumers have no incentive to reveal their true demand for that good. The interdependence of benefit (demand) and the quantity of service provided deserves careful consideration when it comes to efficient provision of infrastructure services (by local or central government).

It is worth noting that non-rivalry property may be thought of as a special case of spillovers (externalities). A non-rival service for which an additional individual may be added at no cost to others can simply be considered as a service with benefit externalities. Everyone can benefit from the service as long as one person pays for the service. This argument applies to some of the local services, such as fire protection. This service is, to a large extent, non-rival and, to a lesser extent, non-excludable. There are substantial interjurisdictional externalities in the provision of this service, especially for contiguous jurisdictions. Transportation infrastructure provides another example. If uncrowded, transportation facilities such as streets, highways, and public transit systems are non-rival, requiring zero marginal price for an additional user (for efficiency). As in the case of other economic characteristics of infrastructure services, excludability and rivalry characteristics require some coordinating mechanism in decentralized provision of services.

15.4 SNG Borrowing and Debt: Infrastructure Financing

Subnational borrowing has become an important source of infrastructure financing in developing countries, owing to decentralization of service delivery responsibilities. There are several sources of long-term subnational borrowing for infrastructure investments. Each of these may take one of several forms, with a country's practice shaped by its history, fiscal architecture, and degree of intergovernmental organizational, institutional, and individual capacity development.[16]

15.4.1 Central Government-Assisted Lending

For most emerging economies, the dominant source of subnational lending is associated with an arrangement whereby an "upper-tier" government financial institution (GFI) provides loans to a "lower-tier" government (SNG).[17] While in principle an intergovernmental loan arrangement has merit in that it reflects a cooperative decentralization, there are three practices that lead some analysts to warn that this form may not be effective in promoting optimal use of borrowed funds (Swianiewicz 2004). The first occurs when loans are made on the basis of political rather than economic criteria (e.g., central credit allocations are directed to governments from the same political party), and, thus the lender does not make the required effort to assess the risk and feasibility of financed projects. A second problem arises when loans are used to support local governments to service their debt (or, at the

[16]Please see Appendix 2 for the Chinese experience with Local Investment Corporations.

[17]GFIs include development banks, specialized instrumentalities for sectorial lending, and municipal development funds.

extreme, may be converted into a gap-filling transfer). This is the case, for example, in Mexico where lenders have little incentive to exert discipline over subcentral borrowing due to the significant role of guaranteed transfers being used as collateral (Sutherland, Price and Joumgard, 2005; Iorio, 2019).

The third practice is related to subnational bailout. When there is a "soft budget constraint" that creates a moral hazard problem: subnational governments are not accountable for the financial risk which leads borrower and lenders alike to underestimate the risk related to borrowing. That a lack of a hard budget constraint will be recognized by the financial markets is evidenced by similar yields (risk premiums) for central and subnational government borrowings irrespective of the financial state of the subnational government. The lack of a spread between the central and subnational risk premium should also be taken as evidence of an implicit subnational "bailout" policy.

15.4.2 Intercepts

One approach that some central government lenders have used to reduce the moral hazard described above is to establish a debt service "intercept." In the case of India, for example, the intercept is structured as an automatic debit whereby the borrowing subnational government must place a deposit in an account with the central bank to cover projected debt service payments. One can think of this arrangement the central government's establishment of a subnational debt service reserve.

Another approach, which is used by the Philippines, is to intercept intergovernmental transfers. The Philippines *Local Government Code of 1991* established the Internal Revenue Allotment (IRA), which is a central transfer that is distributed to local governments on a formula-driven basis. Embedded in the 1991 Code is a provision that the IRA can serve as a tool for securing the payment for local servicing the debt service that has been provided through a central government-supported fund for infrastructure investment.[18] That is, some part of the IRA-to-be-distributed funds can be "intercepted" by the GFI to pay debt (interest + principal). Therefore, Philippine local governments "have nearly a perfect record of paying their obligations."[19] If, as in the Philippines, the intergovernmental grant that is coupled with an intercept is a truly formula-driven grant, *that* is, there is no element of a negotiated ad hoc soft budget constraint, then subnational governments have the incentive to use the intergovernmental grant for general purpose. This is also an incentive for the

[18]The Philippines intercept can be used only by loans made through the Philippines Municipal Development Fund Office, MDFO. Otherwise, government policy does not allow direct use of the intercept government or private banks (Liu, Llanto, Petersen, 426).

[19]Liu et al. (2013, 437)

borrowing subnational to include a line item for debt service in its annual operating budget.[20,21]

15.4.3 Credit Lines and Communal Banks

Another source of central government-assisted lending to subnational governments is to establish special centrally supported financial institutions (e.g., communal banks) that focus predominantly or exclusively on financing low interest rate loans for local government in support of national expenditure objectives. Thus, in some European countries, special environmental protection funds were established in the 1990s to subsidize loans by drawing on own revenues from fees and fines imposed for polluting the environment. The record of such lending is mixed. Due to the suboptimal nature of the arrangement, which tends to supplant a higher return on a limited pool of loanable funds, the recent trend in Europe has been to withdraw from such programs and instead rely on the commercial credit market. However, there has been a positive outcome in that the experience of some East European countries is that not only have special environment funds played a positive role in promoting desired investments but also have served as a tool for teaching local governments about how capital markets function.[22]

15.4.4 Municipal Development Funds

Municipal development funds (MDFs) are another kind of government-assisted lending practice. At present more than 60 developing countries have established wholly or partially owned municipal development funds, which are financial intermediaries that pool funds from a variety of sources and, with the objective to create a safe environment for local governments to learn to borrow, then on-lend to local

[20]However, there are two features of the Philippines intercept that are problematic. The first is that because the intercept applies only loans from a government instrumentality, the Private Financial Institutions, which as a group want to be in the local lending markets, are put at a comparative disadvantage since only the GFI can utilize the intercept. This factor combined with the fact that a PFI cannot use public assets (e.g., land) as collateral has made difficult private sector lending to local governments. A second problem is that "there are continuing concerns about the ability and willingness of local government units to pay on their debt given the three-year election cycle." Liu et al. (2013) in Canuto and Liu, Eds. (2013) 420; 424–425; 436–437

[21]A moral suasion-type variant of the intercept has been applied in Mexico by the state-owned National Works and Public Services Bank, Banobras, whereby a Banobras contract with a client local government would identify revenue line items from where there would be a first call to service the local government's debt. Correspondence with Victor Vergara, Lead Urban Specialist, World Bank, May 7, 2014

[22]Swianiewicz (2004) and Barati-Stec (2015) address the Central and Eastern European experience.

government to (i) finance development projects and (ii) serve as a bridge to the private domestic (e.g., commercial banks) or international credit markets. The source of funds may come from the central- or intermediate-tier government, international financial institutions (IFIs), and/or other international groups. Subnational jurisdictions may also voluntarily set up their own multi-jurisdictional MDF infrastructure bank arrangements.[23] By assembling such funds and providing a guarantee for on-lending, the borrowing government receives a subsidy in the form of a lower cost of capital that it could not find on its own (Freire 2014). Under this arrangement the central government typically bears the ultimate risk of default, though in some countries, such as Colombia's Findeter program, private banks originate municipal loans and bear the risk of default with the central government in the role of second-tier bank providing liquidity. As a result, the central government is exposed only to the risk that the loan-originating bank will fail.

The dual objective of providing credit and paving the way for self-sustaining credit system can be difficult to reconcile, and, indeed, not all MDFs have been successful. MDFs have their "best result" once municipalities graduate from a reliance on an MDF to the credit markets. However, with each such success, an MDF may see its role diminished as a major player in the local infrastructure finance and planning process, thus giving it an incentive to hang on to its clients. That said, there are several cases where MDFs have been successful in providing local governments borrowing access to the credit markets. These include the South African Finance Corporation, Senegal Local Communities Fund, the Tamil Nadu (India) Urban Development Fund, the Bangladesh MDF, and the Brazilian state of Parana's Urban Development Fund (Freire 2014).

15.4.5 Direct Access to the Credit Markets

There are two primary linkages to private investors, each of which became increasingly important in the developing world as governmental systems become more decentralized. The first is *commercial bank* lending, which is of growing importance. Indeed, in some central European countries, there is a growing competition among different banks that offer products and services to local governments (Swianiewicz 2004, 2007).

The second is to go directly to the *bond market* which is the common practice in many OECD countries that have well-developed private capital markets, but which is also of growing in importance in the transition and developing country world.

Due to the need for a high level of institutional and organizational capacity that can entail a long process (and initial high costs) to make a subnational government

[23]The World Bank and Inter-American Development Bank have been particularly active in the establishment of municipal development funds (Freire 2014).

creditworthy, the bond markets tend to be largely utilized by intermediate tiers of government and large municipalities rather than by small and/or emerging subnational governments. When bonds are issued, the vast majority of issues are purchased by a small number of investors such as banks and pension and investment funds.[24] The role of individual private investors tends to be limited.

There are two forms of long-term bond market debt:

(i) General obligation debt, which is typically backed by a pledge of the SNG's taxing powers for timely and full payment of the debt service. While the concept of "full faith and credit" seems quite straightforward, the investor and/or, as discussed below, the credit rating agency will take care to be clear on the exact legal structure of SNG general obligation debt by delving into the detail of matters such as the degree of higher-level government backing (e.g., to what extent can one rely on a guarantee, explicit, or implicit?) and whether the SNG is chronically underfunded. Petersen (2010) warns that expressions such as "general obligation" or "balance sheet debt" can mask an unresolved question of ultimate security; that is, just what remedies are available to a lender in case the borrower fails to pay on time and in full?

(ii) With limited obligation debt, as in the case of revenue bonds, the borrowing enterprise (e.g., a SNG-owned utility, local toll facilities, public markets, local ports, and terminals) generates revenues through charges and fees that are used to defray much or all of the costs of operation and debt service. Again, at a glance this is conceptually clear; but before lending, creditors will want to know not only where the money for payment is coming from and, especially in the case of non-recourse debt, the remedies in case of default.[25] As is the case for general obligation bonds, if there is deemed to uncertainty of payment, the debt

---

[24]Bonds can be sold to investors in a number of ways, ranging from (i) the competitive auctioning of bonds to the highest bidder to (ii) a direct placement with final investors. This is done through a process negotiation in which the issuing SNG procures the services of (one or more) financial services firms such as an investment banking firm that advises the bond-issuing SNG on the bond offering price and agrees to sell the bond issue to the final investors. This firm will either (i) buy (underwrite) the bonds at negotiated price (and here, as will be discussed below, the credit rating agency role comes into play) and then resell them to investors or (ii) act as the placement agent in which it does not agree to buy the bonds but, rather, makes a best effort to sell the bonds. As an underwriter the firm may charge fees as well as make profits on its buy/sell spread. A placement agent will receive a commission. The financial firm (or firms) doing the underwriting or placement will likely to have gone through a Request for Proposal (RFP) process in which they may be asked to not only state their qualifications but also critique a draft of the SNG's bond offering (Petersen 2010).

[25]It can get even more complex. A feature associated with revenue (but not general obligation) bonds is the trust indenture whereby protective covenants may be part of the bond issue. Thus, a rate covenant may assure bond holders that user fees may be raised as necessary to cover payment. Then there is the need to be explicit as whether bond payments will be first in line for payment out of gross revenues or "net" of payment for general operations and expenses. www.investopedia.com/articles/professionaleducation

will come with a risk premium, that is, an interest rate higher than would be paid on what the market considers a risk-free bond.

15.5 Fiscal Risks

So far, we have discussed the various types of borrowing and debt that are defined by lender-borrower structure and the type of security given by the borrowing SNG (general government, special purposes, or instrumentality). There are three key messages:

- Taking on debt is a key strategy for growth and development as well as a strategy that meets the tests of resource efficiency and intergenerational equity.
- The proceeds from borrowing are *not* revenues. Issuing debt carries with it an obligation to make payment. The debt issuer must "service" the debt by paying off the debt principal plus the cost of using the money (interest rate).
- And, since to invest and consume through capital infrastructure is location specific, a country can gain from a financially strong and subnational governmental sector.

This all said, borrowing has its risks—risks that can lead to default, insolvency, and bankruptcy proceedings and a SNG debt crisis. This can happen for a number of (not mutually exclusive) reasons: (i) borrowing from the international markets in a currency other than that of the subnational borrower; (ii) the adverse selection that arises when misaligned incentives and poor information cause SNGs to hide information about their finances; (iii) a "business-as-usual" practice by a "higher-level" government that enables subnational governments' soft budget constraints through practices such as central take-over ("bailouts") of subnational debt; (iv) a failure to prepare a debt sustainability analysis and develop a debt management strategy prior to the onset of an external macroeconomic shock such as occurred in many countries in 2007–2009; (v) lack of political accountability that may result from a term nature of serving in the subnational office (terms can be either too short or too open-ended); (vi) an unwillingness to make tough budgetary choices (for instance, in light of forthcoming elections, refusal to cut back popular spending programs' fiscal imbalances); and (viii) the failure of a SNG to develop a capacity of local own source taxation using a mix of revenue sources.[26]

So, what can be done to balance the need to promote SNG borrowing and minimize the fiscal risk? In addition to "getting decentralization right," there are two paradigms, which are not mutually exclusive:

[26]Subnational governments that do not have or use the authority to increase taxes or users fees and, thus, are reliant on tax transfers have difficulty in entering the credit markets (Ahmad et al. 2005; Ebel and Wang 2017).

(i) Market Discipline Prevails; May Even Suffice. The first occurs when the subnational sector is sufficiently developed and managed that it is the discipline of the private credit markets rather than the existence of a "higher-level" control (and, in the extreme, a promise of central bailouts that makes private investors willing to make the long-term financial commitments that infrastructure investment requires). It is not easy to get to this point, but it can be accomplished. Among the pre-conditions that must be met are a history of macroeconomic stability; a rule of law system that gives investor confidence in the laws and procedures regarding defaults, insolvencies, and public disclosure guidelines; an independent central bank; and well-established private market intermediaries (such as credit rating agencies). Canada and the United States are the most cited of such cases (Bird and Slack 2017).

(ii) Fiscal Rules. The second is for the establishment of a set of ex ante fiscal rules and regulations that lay out the conditions and constraints relating to subnational government borrowing. A fiscal policy rule is a permanent constraint on fiscal policy, expressed in terms of a summary indicator of fiscal performance, such as the government budget deficit, borrowing, debt, or a major component thereof (Kopits and Symansky 1998). Typically established by the "higher-level" central- and/or intermediate-tier government authority, such rules may be accompanied by enforcement mechanisms and sanctions.[27] A centrally imposed regulatory framework is appropriate especially for unitary governments for which it is clear that subnational debt can become a contingent liability; however, there are also such fiscal rules well-established in many federal systems.

Regulatory frameworks place limits on key fiscal variables, such as operating deficit, stock of debt, debt service ratios, and own revenues. Fiscal rules impose a long-lasting constraint on fiscal policy through numerical limits on budgetary aggregates (Schaechter et al. 2012; Liu and Pradelli 2012). Other fiscal rules can take various forms and can range from practices mandated by law and accompanied by enforcement mechanisms including sanctions for non-compliance (Brazil, Denmark, Iceland, Ireland, Japan, Luxembourg, Portugal, and Slovak Republic). Different regulations may also apply whether the SNG is borrowing domestically or from foreign sources and whether the subnational debt is denominated in local or a foreign currency.

Some states temper their fiscal rules with a process for central-subnational coordination in setting a national debt policy. Thus, in Australia, federal and state borrowing is coordinated by the Australian Loan Council, taking into account each jurisdiction's fiscal position and infrastructure needs as well as the center's macroeconomic objectives. Other countries coordinate agreements to balance SNG budgets over a medium (rather than annual)-term period, as in Finland and Norway. And

[27]Ter-Minassian and Craig (1997), Joumard and Kongsrud (2003), and Sutherland et al. (2005)

some countries establish coordinating bodies that meet regularly on matters of budget practice and preparation (Germany, the Netherlands, and Switzerland).[28]

Most frameworks, mandatory or cooperative, that require subnational governments to balance the operating budget may also provide for "escape clauses" when there is major external economic shock such as the fiscal crisis of 2007–2010 (Austria, Germany, and the Canadian provinces with their local governments) or natural disaster (Austria, Canadian Provinces, the Czech Republic, Japan, the Republic of Korea, Poland, Portugal). In the United States, the federal government may respond to such external shocks with short-term non-matching categorical grants (e.g., natural disaster-related aid), but such aid falls short of being designed as general budget support.

In the 1990s subnational debt crises contributed to macroeconomic deterioration in Argentina, Brazil, India, Mexico, and Russia, all major countries. Since then, drawing lessons, various developing countries across the globe strengthened their subnational finances via their regulatory frameworks and fiscal consolidation. As a result, when the financial crisis of 2008–2009 broke out, many SNGs had stronger fiscal and liquidity positions. As reported in Canuto and Liu (2010), in Brazil, SNGs' net debt as a percent of GDP decreased from 18% in 2003 to 14% in 2007. In India, the fiscal deficit of states declined from 4.0% of GDP on average in 2000–2005 to 1.5% in 2007–2008; and states achieved positive operating balances. In Peru and Poland, the governments have emphasized the importance of fiscal sustainability at the start of decentralization.

15.6 Concluding Comments

Much of the empirical case for subnational government's involvement in infrastructure service provision hinges on efficiency gains. As decision-making and implementation arrangements are moved to a government level closer to people, there are production and allocation efficiencies to be gained. Production efficiency argument suggests that subnational governments can build and operate an infrastructure system less expensively. According to Peterson and Muzzini (2005) "[c]ost savings may derive from cheaper local building materials, less expensive local labor, more efficient project design, fewer layers if bureaucratic oversight, and less corruption, among other sources." Allocative efficiency argument suggests that local governments have better information about citizens' preferences and needs because of proximity. Therefore, infrastructure investment decisions of local governments would better reflect citizens' preferences than central government's decisions.

---

[28]For further detail see World Bank (2000, Chapter 5), Joumard and Kongsrud (2003), Sutherland et al. (2005), and the Appendix to this paper providing a summary of the fiscal rules relating for selected countries in Asia.

The involvement of subnational governments in infrastructure service provision raises distinctive issues regarding infrastructure policy and planning as well as implementation and maintenance. As infrastructure investment is a capital-intensive endeavor, it requires decision-making at several various stages (Peterson and Muzzini 2005): (i) preparing capital investment plans and setting priorities for individual capital projects, (ii) operating a network system to provide services and maintaining facilities to sustain the physical capital, and (iii) financing the system by both mobilizing capital to pay for the initial investment and generating revenues to cover operations and maintenance—that is, ensuring financial sustainability.

Appendices

Appendix 1: Fiscal Rules for Central Government Enforcement and Monitoring Mechanisms SNGs

Country	Fiscal framework	Enforcement mechanisms
Australia	*A cooperative approach.* The Australian Loan Council, established in 1923, is a Commonwealth-state ministerial council that coordinates public sector borrowing. The Loan Council considers each jurisdiction's borrowing for the forthcoming year with regard to each jurisdiction's fiscal position and the macroeconomic implications of aggregate borrowing. State participation in the Council was initially voluntary. In 1927, the six states and the Commonwealth signed a financial agreement that granted the Council the authority to determine the amounts, conditions, and timing of all loans of the Commonwealth and the states.[a]	*Market discipline.* States may borrow on their own account; the Loan Council provides information to the financial market on public sector borrowing plans. *Peer pressure.* State borrowings do not have to be approved. However, the Loan Council places a high emphasis on the transparency of public sector finances, through financial market scrutiny of proposed borrowing to restrict borrowing to prudent levels.
China, People's Republic	*Limited fiscal autonomy.* The 2015 Budget Law (Article 35) of the People's Republic of China states that the provincial governments are authorized and allowed to issue bonds for the province and on behalf of municipal governments within the limits determined by the State Council. Debt incurred shall be accompanied by repayment plans and only used for expenditures under capital accounts. Unless otherwise explicitly stated in the law, no local government or department may provide guarantee for debt of any	*Central enforcement rules.* SNGs may not borrow from a financial institution such as a commercial bank. Nor, is an SNG authorized to go directly to the international capital markets. The MOF has the responsibility to establish accountability enforcement rules for SNGs and supervise local government debt but does not set budgetary assumptions. Bonds are issued subject to quotas approved by the State Council. The quotas are the amount of money in Renminbi (RMB)

(continued)

Country	Fiscal framework	Enforcement mechanisms
	entity or individual in any form. Additionally, SNG does not have any repayment obligations to Local Investment Corporations, which are treated like SOEs. (Also refer to Appendix 2).[b]	*Administrative controls.* All governments above the county level are to establish institutions to monitor and evaluate different kinds of debt risks including local government bonds and the contingent liabliities. Debt risks are defined by four levels, I–IV, with level IV most high risk.
Indonesia	*Limited autonomy.* Subnational governments in Indonesia can borrow from (i) the central government, (ii) other subnational governments, (iii) banks/ financial institutions, (iv) non-bank financial institutions, and (v) the public (through the capital market, in the form of regional bonds). They may not, however, borrow directly from overseas sources. However, the central government may on-lend foreign loan (e.g., from international financial institution) to subnational governments via an agreement signed by the Minister of Finance and the respective Head of Region.	*Administrative rules and regulations.* Indonesian law stipulates three types of SNG debt (short, medium, and long term), each associated with an allowable source (type of lending) and stipulated use funds. Thus, an SNG can turn to banks, non-bank institutions, and other SNGS for short-term finance to cover cash flow shortages. Medium and long-term loans for financing non-revenue-generating public facilities may be sourced from banks, non-bank financial institutions, and the central government. To qualify for loans SNGs must meet several requirements such as consistence with regional government plans and debt service coverage ratios.
		Sanctions. Sanctions may apply if the form of postponement and/or cuts the Central Allocation Fund (CAF) grant and/or a CAF intercept for payment of debt service.
Japan	*Limited SNG fiscal autonomy.* The Local Autonomy Law authorizes borrowing by prefectures, cities, towns, and villages, Tokyo special wards, and local government cooperatives. The Prefecture is a central government administrative area (though with the prefect governor elected to a 4-year term). The local government (LG) debt is called *chihousai*, which is usually translated as local government bonds (LGB). There are four types of LG borrowing: private placement funds (commercial banks and non-bank	*Administrative procedures.* An LG can issue bonds in its name, but the conditions of bond issuance are strictly controlled by the Central Ministry of Internal Affairs and Communications or the prefectural governor.
		Central/sovereign guarantee. The central government fully guarantees revenue sources to pay for the principal and interest of LGBs whereby payment is guaranteed through the Local Allocation Tax (grant) system. As such, LG debt has a history of

(continued)

Country	Fiscal framework	Enforcement mechanisms
	institutions such as insurance companies); public (LG); borrowing from Japan Finance Organization for Municipalities (a quasi-public non--profit organization wholly owned by Japanese local governments), and national government funds (a source that has been of decreasing importance since the Treasury Investment and System Reforms of 2001).	creditworthiness and, with that, strong high ratings.[c]
Republic of Korea	*Limited fiscal autonomy.* Subnational governments must run balanced budgets. These are monitored and controlled by the Ministry of Government Administration and Home Affairs.	*Peer pressure.* Because all borrowing must be approved by the central government, the Ministry of Government Administration and Home Affairs has the responsibility of monitoring SNGs to ensure balanced budgets.
	Borrowing. All local borrowing must be approved by the central government.	*Limitation.* A debt ceiling is specified for each SNG; however, the central government may permit additional borrowing for specific projects even if they do not meet the criteria if it finds the additional debt can be serviced. However, debt repayment is one important factor considered by the central government before approval is granted.[d]
Malaysia	*Asymmetry.* The federal (central) government consults the National Finance Council in respect to the exercise of the states' borrowing powers. Article 111 (2) of the Federal Constitution states that "A State shall not borrow except under the authority of State law, and State law shall not authorize a State to borrow except from the Federation or, for a period not exceeding 5 years, from a bank or other financial source approved for that purpose by the Federal Government." Local governments borrow for special purposes relating to residential, commercial, and industrial undertakings, according to Section 46 of the LGA 1976.	*Sanctions.* If a local government defaults in paying back a loan, after 3 months of written demand by the lender, the affected lender may apply to the High Court to seek redress. Subsequently, the Court may order a levy on property in the local government area (which is to be enforced in like manner as any rate imposed by the local authority) and the proceeds paid to the Court for the lender. [(This is provided by Section 45(1) of the Local Government Act (LGA) 1976].
	However, Article 112b states that Article 111 (2) "shall not restrict the power of the Borneo states of Sabah or Sarawak (which are accorded higher degree of autonomy compared to the other	

(continued)

Country	Fiscal framework	Enforcement mechanisms
	11 peninsular states) to borrow under the authority of State law within the State, if the borrowing has the approval of the Central Bank for the time being of the Federation"	
New Zealand	*Autonomy.* Local authorities are required by law to set operating revenues at a level sufficient to cover operating expenses in any financial year (with a relatively narrow exception to run deficits). Local authorities are largely self-funded, and the central government has no formal role in reviewing or approving the budgets of local authorities	*Market discipline.* Subnational loans are not guaranteed by the central government
	Borrowing. No restrictions on borrowing	
Thailand	*Central permission.* According to the Public Debt Management law (PDM 2005), local government organizations include Provincial Organization, Municipality, *Tambon* Organization, Bangkok Metropolitan Administration (BMA), Pattaya City, and other local government organizations established by the law	*Administrative constraints.* Unlike other local government organizations, the PDM law permits Bangkok Metropolitan Assembly and Pattaya City to issue bonds subject to clearance from the Ministry of the Interior. In practice, however, the clearance from the Ministry of the Interior is seldom granted as a way of limiting the degree of moral hazard which may arise if local government determine that they can borrow and easily receive support from the central government in the event of a default
	Source of funds. All tiers of local administration are permitted to borrow from "public and corporate agencies" subject to the approval of the Ministry of the Interior (MOI). (Vu 2019) A traditional source of borrowing for local governments is an MOI fund. A fund committee is chaired by MOI's permanent secretary and is authorized to determine rules and criteria on the fund's management and administration in respect to loan approval. Local governments are permitted to make applications to borrow for a 15-year term maximum below market interest rates from a central pool (Vu 2019).	*Sanctions.* There is a lack of clarity regarding punitive measures imposed on a local government that has a financial emergency.
	Purpose. Local government units (LGUs) can borrow for specific purposes including (i) investment, (ii) debt	

(continued)

Country	Fiscal framework	Enforcement mechanisms
	restructuring, and (iii) revolving fund. The borrowing must not create debt service of more than 10% of the LGU income. The law related to LGU borrowing is the Public Debt Management and Policy Committee's regulation on LGU borrowing B.E.2561 (2018). They borrow mainly from SFIs such as Krung Thai Bank, Government Saving Bank, and Government Housing Bank.	
Vietnam	*Fiscal practice.* In general, borrowing is restricted for financing capital spending at the provincial level as a golden rule. More particularly, however, the State Budget Law (SBL) provides for debt stock limits against decentralized revenue.	*Administrative controls.* The central government imposes a debt service limit of 10% against annual decentralized revenue (Decree 52, 2017).
	Sources of funds. Provinces can borrow from the following sources: (a) the State Treasury for short-term loans not exceeding 1 year; (b) on-lending from the central government of ODA funding; (c) the Vietnam Development Bank (VDB); (d) state-owned and commercial banks; and (e) bond issues to tap the capital markets. A large proportion is from the VDB, from the State Treasury, and from on-lending by the central government, with a small part (i.e., about 27%) supplied through the issue of municipal bonds and other sources[e] (World Bank 2014).	The 2015 SBL and its guiding legislation as well as the Law on Public Debt Management are silent on recourse to ensure that, if a provincial government defaults on borrowings from other sources (such as commercial banks or capital markets), the lenders or financiers could recover them from the provincial budget. However, the Ministry of Finance has an informal recourse mechanism, which involves subtracting the amount of arrearages from the provincial government's future budget allocations. It should be noted that advances from the state treasury are not legally regarded as borrowing or loans provided by the central government (i.e., the MOF) to the provincial government.[f]
		Escape clause. The SBL provides a formal enforcement procedure of the rules as well as possibility to violate the rules in special cases such as serious natural disasters or catastrophes.

[a]Hulbert and Vammalle (2016)

[b]Email correspondence with Baoyun Qiao (4.2019), Quanshe Yang (4.2019), and Xu and Yang (2015)

[c]Email correspondence with Natsuko Kikutake, World Bank Country Team, January 18, 2019

[d]Choi, Choe and Kim (2013)

[e]World Bank (2014), Correspondence with Quyen Hoang Vu, World Bank Country Team. January 17, 2019

[f]Campanarom and Dang (2018)

Appendix 2: The Evolving Role of China Local Investment Corporations and SNG Borrowing and Debt

- The People's Republic of China is structured as a hierarchy of five tiers: (i) central; (ii) 28 provinces (the 28 include 5 autonomous regions and Taiwan) plus, in this same second tier, 4 provincial-level municipalities and the Hong Kong Special Administrative Region (HKSAR) and Macao Special Administrative Region; (iii) 334 prefecture subordinate to the 22 provinces; (iv) 2851 counties, county-level cities, and urban districts that are subordinate to both the prefectures or the provincial municipalities; and (v) 39,888 townships/town/street communities subordinate to the counties. The four provincial-level municipalities are Beijing, Shanghai, Tianjin, and Chongqing.
- The 1994 Budget Law prohibited all subnational government (SNG) borrowing without explicit permission from the State Council. To circumvent this rule, starting in the 1980s, SNGs, mostly provincial, began setting up Local Investment Corporations (LICs). These first LICs were limited in scope as their revenues were restricted to generating monies from operating toll roads and utilities.
- At first the LICs were limited scope. Then, in 1992, Shanghai created a broad-based investment corporation, the General Corporation of Shanghai Municipal Property (SMPC), assigning a variety of fiscal funds to the SMPC from the municipal budget and then authorizing the SMPC to borrow.
- Other SNGs (provinces, prefectures, counties) quickly followed the SMPC approach to finance universities, schools, hospitals, airport subways, museums, and sports facilities and, too, support for private development. At first, it all looked promising.
- But, concerns were growing: (i) the collateral for the LIC debt is that of SNG-owned and SNG-managed land; thus, (ii) to increase their borrowing collateral, the SNGs began exercising their power of rezoning rural to urban land and reaping the appreciation due to the rezoning; and (iii) much of all of this is off-budget.
- Then came the fiscal crisis of 2009–2011, and as part of a national fiscal stimulus policy, the People's Bank of China and the China Banking Regulatory Commission (CBRC) encouraged SNGs to borrow for infrastructure (job, growth creating) spending. And, with that, LICs proliferated. As of the end of December 2017, there were 9185 LICs nationwide. Before 2009 the LICs had accumulated ¥5trillion in bank loans; and, in 2009 alone, they took on another ¥3trillion. As of June 2013, the National Audit Office (NAO) estimate is ¥17.9 trillion (a 70% increase from between 2010 and 2012). More than 40% of local government borrowing has been through non-bank institutions (e.g., securities, firms, insurance and leasing companies).
- All this occurred with little supervision, prompting the National Development and Reform Commission (formerly the State Planning Commission) to issue a warning that the system was one that had "no funding framework, no limit, and no accountability" (NDRC 2010 as cited in Xu and Yang, 2015).

- The central government turned to the National Audit Office (NAO) to audit all SNGs (five levels). The key findings of the NAO audit were released in December 2013 with the NAO conclusion that the rapid increase of local government debt levels is "under control" but that there are "potential risks in some places" (Thomas Mitchell, Financial Times, 12.30.2013). The NDRC and NAO reports led to an overhaul of borrowing and debt risk management policies.
- The 2015 Budget Law (approved by the National People's Congress in, August 2014) newly permits "provincial governments the authority to issue bonds, subject to central government approval for financing only capital projects." Provincial governments can borrow for themselves, and also on behalf of local governments and municipal governments (Xu and Yang 2015). The province may also deny the local government to issue debt (bonds).
- The *Opinions on Strengthening Management of the Local Government Debts* (Document No. 43, October 2014) dictated local governments to separate the LICs from the Council. The LICs were *un*authorized to borrow for the government; hence only governments and its departments are authorized to borrow. ("Close the back door.")
- In May 2017, the *Notice on Further Regulating the Borrowing of the Local Government* enacted by the Ministry of Finance stated that the reserve land are not allowed to be injected into the LICs as asset and the LICs were forced to change their roles they have been taking as the financing platform for local government. By the end of 2017, 2549 LICs had been removed by CBRC from the management and no longer serve as investment financing vehicles for local governments.

Sources: Yang, Quanshe Yang, Capital University of Economics and Business, emails of April and May 2019; Yang, Quanshe, Dong Zhang, and Hang Qi (January 2019), China's Fiscal Rules. Working Paper, Capital University of Economics and Business; Lam and Wang (2018); Wong (2013) in Bahl et al. (2013), WB 2012; Mitchell (*Financial Times*, 12.30.13). Note: The CBRC was transformed to the China Banking and Insurance Regulatory Commission (CBIRC) in March 2018.

References

Ahmad J, Devarajan S, Khemani S, Shah S (2005) Decentralization and service delivery. World Bank Policy Research Working Paper 3603

Andres L, Biller D, Dappe MH (2014) Infrastructure gap in South Asia: infrastructure needs, prioritization, and financing, Policy research working paper 7032. World Bank Sustainable Development Department, Washington, DC

Aschauer DA (1989a) Is public expenditure productive. J Monet Econ 23:177–200

Aschauer DA (1989b) Does public capital crowd out private capital? J Monet Econ 24:171–188

Bahl RW, Bird RM (2014). Decentralization and infrastructure: principles and practice. Georgia State University International Center for Public Policy Working Paper 14-08

Bahl RW, Bird RM (2018) Fiscal decentralization and local finance in developing countries. Edward Elgar, Cheltenham/Northampton

Bahl RW, Linn J, Wetzel DL (2013) Financing metropolitan governments in developing countries. Lincoln Institute of Land Policy, Cambridge

Bahl R, Goh C-C, Qiao B (2014) Reforming the public finance system to fit a more urbanized China. China Financial and Economic Publishing House, Beijing

Barati-Stec I (2015) Destined to be defaulted – local insolvency and bailout in post-transition Hungary. Int J Fin Bank 1–17

Bird R (1994) Decentralizing infrastructure: for good or for ill? World Bank Policy Research Working Paper 1258, Discussion Papers No. 290

Bird RM, Slack E (eds) (2017) Financing infrastructure: who should pay? McGill-Queen's University Press, Kingston/Montreal

Bird RM, Ebel RD, Wallich CE (1995) Decentralization of the socialist state: intergovernmental finance in transition economies. World Bank, Washington, DC

Campanarom A, Dang CD (2018) Mobilizing finance for local infrastructure development in Vietnam, a city infrastructure financing facility. World Bank, Washington, DC

Canuto O, Liu L (2010) Subnational debt finance: make it sustainable. In: Canuto O, Giugale M (eds) The day after tomorrow: a handbook on the future of economic policy in the developing world. World Bank, Washington, DC

Choi JW, Chang SC Jaehoon K (2013) Local Government and Pubic Administration in Korea, Jeonbuk Innovation City, Local Government Officials Development Institute/Ministry of Interior and Local Safety 158

De Mello L, Sutherland D (2016) Financing infrastructure. In: Frank J, Martinez-Vazquez J (eds) Decentralization and infrastructure in the global economy: from gaps to solutions. Routledge, London/New York. Ch 5

Easterly W, Rebelo S (1993) Fiscal policy and economic growth: an empirical investigation. J Monet Econ 32:417–458

Ebel RD, Wang Y (2017) The role of user charges in funding the flow of US infrastructure services. In: Bird RM, Slack E (eds) Financing infrastructure: who should pay? McGill-Queen's University Press, Kingston/Montreal. Ch. 6

Eisner R (1994) Real government saving and the future. J Econ Behav Organ 23:111–126

Escribano A, Guasch JL, Pena J (2008) Assessing the impact of infrastructure quality on firm productivity in Africa. World Bank Policy Research Working Paper 5191

Esfahani HS, Ramirez MT (2003) Institutions, infrastructure and economic growth. J Dev Econ 70:443–477

Estache A, Fay M (2010) Current debates on infrastructure policy. In: Spence M, Leipziger D (eds) Globalization and growth: implications for a post crisis world. World Bank, Washington, DC

Fox WF, Murray M (2016) The challenge of operating and maintaining infrastructure. In: Frank J, Martinez-Vazquez J (eds) Decentralization and infrastructure in the global economy. Edward Elgar, Cheltenham/Northampton

Freire ME (2014) Managing external resources. In: Farvacque-Vitkovic C, Kopanyi M (eds) Municipal finances. World Bank, Washington, DC

Haynes KE (1997a) Infrastructure. J Transp Geogr 5(1):23–24

Haynes KE (1997b) Labor markets and regional transportation improvements: the case of high-speed trains. Ann Reg Sci 31:57–76

Haynes KE (2010) Governance of infrastructure. In: Buijs S, Tan W, Tumas D (eds) Megacities: exploring as sustainable future. OIO Publishers, Rotterdam, pp 254–272

Hulbert C, Vammalle C (2016) Monitoring sib-central governments' debts practices and challenges in OECD countries. Organisation for Economic Cooperation and Development, Paris

Iorio F (2019) Mexico: equity, efficiency and politics. Dissertation Submitted to the George Washington University School of Public Policy and Administration, March 2019

Joumard I, Kongsrud PM (2003) Fiscal relations across government levels. OECD Economics Department Working Papers, No. 375. OECD Publishing, Paris. https://doi.org/10.1787/455513871742

Kappeler A, Valila T (2008) Fiscal federalism and the composition of public investment in Europe. Eur J Polit Econ 24(3):562–570
Kim J (2016) Handbook on urban infrastructure finance. New Cities Foundation, Paris
Kopits G, Symansky S. (1998) Fiscal policy rules. IMF Occasional Paper, No. 162
Lam WR, Wang J (2018) China's local government bond market. International Monetary Fund Working Paper 19/219
Liu L, Pradelli J (2012) Financing infrastructure and monitoring fiscal risks at the subnational level. World Bank Policy Research Working Paper No. 6069
Liu L, Qiao B (2013) Restructuring of legacy debt for financing rural schools in China. In: Canuto O, Liu L (eds) Until debt do us part. World Bank, Washington, DC
Liu L, Llanto G, Petersen J (2013) The Philippines: recent developments in the subnational debt markets. In: Canuto O, Liu L (eds) Until debt do us part. World Bank, Washington, DC
Martinez-Vazquez J, Timofeev A (2016) Capital infrastructure and equity objectives in decentralized systems. In: Frank J, Martinez-Vazquez J (eds) In decentralization and infrastructure in the global economy: from gaps to solutions. Routledge, London/New York. Ch. 6
Martinez-Vazquez J, Vaillancourt F (eds) (2011) Decentralization in developing countries: global perspectives on obstacles to fiscal devolution. Edgar Elgar, Cheltenham/Northampton
McKinsey & Company (2016) Bridging global infrastructure gaps. McKinsey Global Institute, Brussels
Nicholson W (1994) Microeconomic theory basic principles and extensions, 6th edn. The Dryden Press, Fort Worth
Oates WE (1972) Fiscal federalism. Harcourt, Brace Jovanovich, New York
Organization for Economic Cooperation and Development/OECD/DAC (2010) Capacity development. OECD, Paris. https://www.oecd.org/dac/conflict-fragility-resilience/governance/docs/46682429.pdf
Petersen J (2010) Notes on capital budgeting. Presentation to the World Bank Finance Thematic Group, Washington, DC, November 16
Peterson GE, Muzzini E (2005) Decentralizing basic infrastructure services. In: East Asia decentralizes: making local government work. World Bank, Washington DC
Sanchez-Robles B (1998) Infrastructure investment and growth: some empirical evidence. Contemp Econ Policy 16:98–108
Schaechter A, Kinda T, Budina N, Weber A (2012) Fiscal rules in response to crisis. International Monetary Fund WP/12/18, Washington, DC
Sutherland D, Price R, Joumard I (2005) Sub-central government fiscal rules. OECD Econ Stud 2005(2):141–181
Swianiewicz P (ed) (2004) Local government borrowing: risks and rewards. OSI/Local Government and Public Service Reform Initiative, Budapest
Swianiewicz P (2007) Local borrowing and municipal debt. In: Ebel RD, Peteri G (eds) The Kosovo decentralization briefing book. Kosovo Foundation Open Society, Prishtine/Budapest. Ch. 13. https://kfos.org/
Ter-Minassian T, Craig J (1997) Control of subnational government borrowing. In: Ter-Minassian T (ed) Fiscal federalism in theory and practice. International Monetary Fund, Washington, DC
United Nations Department of Economic and Social Affairs, Population Division (2014) World urbanization prospects: The 2012 revision. United Nations, New York, April. www.unpopulation.org
United States Bureau of the Census (2013) Individual state descriptions. www.census.gov
Vinuela L (2016) Trends and quality of decentralized public investment. In: Frank J, Martinez-Vazquez J (eds) Decentralization and infrastructure in the global economy. Routledge, Abington/New York
Vu Q (2019) Subnational fiscal risk management. World Bank Staff Presentation, Hanoi, January 10

Wong C (2013) Paying for Urbanization in China, challenges of municipal finance in the twenty-first century. In: Bahl RW, Roy W, Linn J, Wetzel DL (eds) Financing metropolitan governments in developing countries. Cambridge, MA, Lincoln Institute of Land Policy

World Bank (2014) Ho Chi Minh City investment fund for urban development project, 2007–12, Implementation completion report review. World Bank, Washington, DC

World Bank Development Report (1994) Infrastructure for development. World Bank, Washington, DC

World Bank Development Report (2000) Entering the 21st century. World Bank, Washington, DC

Xu Y, Yang Q (2015) New development: China's budget law and local debt. Public Money Manag 35(6):447–450

Yang Q, Zhang D, Qi H (2019) China's fiscal rules. Working Paper, January. Capital University of Economics and Business, Beijing

Yilmaz S, Vaillancourt F, Dafflon B (2012) State and local government finance: why it matters. In: Ebel RD, Petersen JE (eds) The Oxford handbook on state and local government finance. Oxford University Press, Oxford/New York

Yoshino N, Helble M, Abidhadjaev U (2018) Introduction. In: Yoshino N, Helble M, Abidhadjaev U (eds) Financing infrastructure in Asia and the Pacific capturing impacts and new sources. Asian Development Bank Institute, Tokyo

Young RA (2005) Economics of water resources: a survey. In: Kneese AV, Sweeney JL (eds) Handbook of natural resources and energy economics, vol II. Elsevier Science, Amsterdam

Chapter 16
Urban Nodal Regions Through Communities of Functionally Critical Locations in the Transportation Network

Yang Zhou and Jean-Claude Thill

Abstract The ease of mobility across the urban environment is known to be a major factor of the spatial organization of the city. It is commonplace to look at accessibility in this space as a structuring element of urban functional areas. In this tradition, the urban space is segmented into nodal regions or communities on the basis of trip origins and destinations recorded to uniformly sized grid cells or Voronoi polygons. However, this approach ignores the role of the layout of the transportation network in forming the regionalization of the urban structure. In this article, we argue that an effective approach to identify socioeconomic communities in an urban area is by means of its functionally critical elements. The proposed approach starts with the identification of functionally critical nodal points in the city's transportation system, which allow us to capture people's activity spaces on the aggregate. Then we construct a weighted directed graph based on these functionally critical locations, where each node in the graph denotes a functionally critical location and each edge denotes the presence of travel trajectories between pairs of critical locations; the weight of edges denotes the travel intensity. We introduce recent methods of network science to identify the socioeconomic communities of the urban region, and we examine and discuss interesting socioeconomic clusters. As a use case, we use a big data set that contains all the trajectories of over 11,000 taxis over a month in Wuhan, China. The results of the analysis suggest that (1) characteristics of socioeconomic clusters are very different from the administrative subdivisions of the city of Wuhan; (2) compared to regionalizations that account only for trip ends, the functional criticality approach provides us better ways to understand the regionalization structure of a city, especially how activity spaces are shaped by civil infrastructures such as bridges across major waterways; and (3) the functional criticality

Y. Zhou
College of Urban and Environmental Sciences, Central China Normal University, Wuhan, People's Republic of China
e-mail: yzhou2017@mail.ccnu.edu.cn

J.-C. Thill (✉)
Department of Geography & Earth Sciences and Public Policy Program, University of North Carolina at Charlotte, Charlotte, NC, USA
e-mail: Jean-Claude.Thill@uncc.edu

Z. Chen et al. (eds.), *Development Studies in Regional Science*, New Frontiers in Regional Science: Asian Perspectives 42,
https://doi.org/10.1007/978-981-15-1435-7_16

approach enhances urban communities outlined solely on the basis of physical transportation network topologies.

Keywords Community clustering · Critical locations · Taxi trips · Urban structure · Urban activity spaces · Urban regionalization

16.1 Introduction

The modalities of spatial interaction between different land-use regions are important for understanding the spatial structure of an urban region (Damasc and Timpf 2015; Jiang et al. 2012). The spatial structure/organization of a city or region based on flows has been well studied in the form of commuting (Roth et al. 2011), shopping or traveling (Hu et al. 2015), vehicular traffic (Long et al. 2015), public transportation (Long and Thill 2015), and others. This idea can be traced back to Ed Ullman's "Flow as Geography" (Ullman 1980) and complements other perspectives in geography and regional science aimed at establishing the international structure of cities, either cross-sectionally or longitudinally (e.g., Haynes 1971; Jones and Haynes 1972).

More recently, functional regionalization as communities extracted from mobile phone data, taxi trajectories, smart card data, and other novel sources of flow data has helped to uncover the inherent socioeconomic connections of functional regions inside the urban region. Traditionally, the urban space is segmented into nodal regions or communities on the basis of trip origins and destinations recorded to uniformly sized grid cells (Liu et al. 2015) or Voronoi polygons (Chi et al. 2016). These communities represent the regions located in different urban spaces that bind together places via people's daily activities and travel patterns. However, with the only consideration of recorded trip origins and destinations, the existing methodology to identify communities in an urban area ignores the role of the layout of the transportation network in forming territorial regionalizations of the urban structure. Without taking the transportation network under consideration, the definition of community boundaries could also be influenced in a rather arbitrary fashion by grid cell size or polygon definition. This approach would therefore not represent the real environmental details of the urban region. Finally, full account for the geometry of the transport network and for the path followed by users of the urban environment on their way from an origin to a destination permit to apprehend the portion of the urban environment that is actually used by people. This delineated space is also the territory that urban agents (users) may have some familiarity. In other words, such regionalization would be in line with the concept of activity space, which is a fundamental construct of behavioral geography (Hanson and Hanson 1980; Golledge and Stimson 1997; Rai et al. 2007). In a standard way, the activity space is set to encompass the local areas within which people move or travel during the course of their activities during a certain period of time. Our contention here is that our approach to urban regionalization is richer than conventional methods and preserves the essence of geographic accessibility. It is also closer to the deep behavioral semantics of activity spaces by relying on functionally critical network locations extracted from whole travel trajectories.

Furthermore, many travel activities (e.g., vehicle trajectories) taken inside the city are strictly constrained to the road network or rail tracks. Thus, only focusing on origin-destination information ignores the importance of the layout of the transportation network. Additionally, the comprehensive flow information of interaction patterns inside each community cannot be well described only by locations of the origin and destination points. In order to overcome these shortcomings of existing approaches, we argue the accessibility information based on the transportation network should be considered as part of the evidence to identify a city's socioeconomic communities.

Accessibility is an important concept to help evaluate the performance of transport networks and the geographic distribution of activities/opportunities. Accessibility in an urban environment is highly related to city transportation network distribution and to the costs of traveling between different locations, which are derived from real-time traffic information. Spatial organization and geographic accessibility are mutually interconnected. High accessibility between two regions shows more potential opportunities of frequent connections, which leads to a high probability for the two to be clustered in a same community. Conversely, low accessibility between regions indicates that separate logical communities exist. From this point of view, integrating accessibility with transportation network helps to identify the boundary of the socioeconomic communities in an urban environment in a more comprehensive way.

In this article, we argue that an effective approach to identify the boundary of socioeconomic communities in an urban area is by means of functional criticality based on the city transportation network while integrating elements of geographic accessibility. A big data set that contains all the trajectories of over 11,000 taxis over a month in Wuhan, China, is used as data source to uncovering urban communities articulated around critical locations in the transportation network and demonstrate the distinctive features of the proposed approach. Path information recorded in large numbers of travel trajectories can provide a great opportunity to quantify the accessibility measurement of each community and the comprehensive information of interactions inside of communities. The main contributions of this study are as follows:

- Proposing a method to identify the functional socioeconomic communities by considering the city's transportation system and actual usage of the urban space consistent with the concept of activity space
- Comparing and contrasting the patterns of human interactions supported by the urban transportation network and derived from functional criticality with other possible forms of regionalization patterns

The remainder of this article is organized as follows. Section 16.2 reviews bodies of literature on accessibility and community structures in urban regions. Section 16.3 describes the study area and representation of taxi trip data, as well as the network constructed from the functionally critical intersections in the transportation network. Section 16.4 discusses the regional patterns that this network reflects and compares them with the clusters derived on the basis of a grid network, a TAZ-based network, and a physical road network. Section 16.5 draws the conclusions of this research and discusses future work.

16.2 Background

16.2.1 Spatial Accessibility

Accessibility can be considered as one of the joint results of a transport network and the geographical distribution of activities, which shows the potential for reaching spatially distributed opportunities such as social activities, shopping, employment, and others (Páez et al. 2012). In early studies, the application of accessibility analysis has been more focused on the effect of urban facility and infrastructures (Apparicio et al. 2008), potential regions influenced by city expansion and growth (Chen et al. 2014; Hansen 1959), examination of infrastructure vulnerability and resilience (Kwan et al. 2003; Taylor and Susilawati 2012; Martin et al. 2018), the evaluation of public transit (Murray 2003), or destination choice and trip making (Thill and Kim 2005). These applications provide fundamental information for urban and regional planning and urban regional science.

As pointed by Kwan et al. (2003), the definition of accessibility has two distinct but related directions. On the one hand, Hansen (1959) defined the accessibility to be the potential opportunities for some type of interaction between geographically defined entities (i.e., places). Measures of accessibility derived from spatial interaction models have been quite extensively used across spatial sciences in urban and regional contexts. For example, Horner (2004) used locational accessibility to explore the relationship between jobs/housing locations, urban form, and urban structure. Other forms like potential measures and competition measures of accessibility can be found in Sánchez-Mateos et al. (2014), Wang et al. (2015), and many others. On the other hand, as a measure of the ease of movement, accessibility emphasizes the spatial connectivity of the transport network on which people engage in travel. In the framework of time geography, accessibility is influenced by the individual space-time constraints. Shaw et al. (2014) computed the distance, time, and travel cost forms of accessibility. Cui et al. (2016) employed a contour measure, which is defined as the total number of activity locations that could be reached within each contour region by a certain transport mode within a specific travel time. Reviews of different metrics and formulations of accessibility can be found in Kwan et al. (2003), Curtis and Scheurer (2010), Páez et al. (2012), and others.

16.2.2 Urban Structure Based on Community

In network science, a community is defined as a group of intensely connected nodes that share common properties while being more sparsely linked to the rest of the network (Fortunato 2010). With community detection, it is possible to partition a network into several tightly connected sub-networks that constitute mesoscale structures within the overall network. Focusing on the patterns of the physical urban road network, Duan and Lu (2013) studied the road network robustness through a community structure approach; specifically, they sought to identify densely connected subsets of nodes that are also sparsely connected to the rest of the network.

Big geospatial data, which have drawn the attention of urban planners and geographers and regional scientists (Schintler and Chen 2017), have been widely used to study the mobility patterns and the urban functional structure. Using human interaction data (e.g., mobile phone calls, taxi rides, smart card data), it is possible to capture the regional structure of a study area and detect the influence of social behavior in structuring a territory by identifying the most integrated clusters. At the country level, Ratti et al. (2010) yield geographically cohesive regions of Great Britain by using a large telephone data set. Similar work is reported by Blondel et al. (2010) in Belgium, with evidence that cultural cleavages may be much less powerful than pragmatic economic considerations in structuring geographic spaces. At the urban and regional level, Chi et al. (2016) partitioned the urban space into Thiessen polygons to detected multilevel communities based on millions of mobile phone calls, which revealed how administrative divisions of different levels affect the modalities of human spatial interactions. Gao et al. (2013) adopted an agglomerative clustering algorithm to discover the mesoscale structures of spatial interaction communities using a mobile phone data set from 1 week in a city.

Unlike mobile phone data which are based on cell stations, the taxi trip or smart card data are strictly constrained to the physical fabric of the transportation network. Rinzivillo et al. (2012) explore the geographical borders of human mobility with vehicle GPS tracks for 5 weeks around Pisa. Liu et al. (2015) studied the two-level hierarchical structure in Shanghai by building a spatially embedded network on the basis of taxi trip data over 4 days. Kang et al. (2013) compared the different communities generated from mobile phones and from taxi trips in Singapore and found that taxicab trips generate larger spatial communities and reflect interactions between further separating locations than mobile phone connections. They found that the community regions derived from the taxi trips matched the urban planning subdivisions well. Also focusing in Singapore, Zhong et al. (2014) generated the graph community clusters using smart card data and found that the derived geographical borders are different from existing administrative ones. Indeed, as stated in Kang et al. (2013), "the constraint of urban structure is different for different transport modes." The urban structure constrains the trips by means of different types of transportation networks, which implies that the role of the travel flow network could not be readily ignored. However, in the literature, it has also been common practice to partition the urban space into regular rectangular grids (Liu et al. 2015), traffic analysis zones (TAZ) (Demšar et al. 2014), or census tracts (Rinzivillo et al. 2012) and then seek to identify mesoscale structures around nodal regions in the spatial network formed by the partition. More work is necessary to investigate how the physical transport networks and the modalities of their use for travel by urban residents and visitors impact the regionalization of the human interactions.

16.3 Data and Critical Location Network

16.3.1 Study Area and Taxi Data

Wuhan is the most populous city in central China. The metropolitan area of Wuhan encompasses more than 8000 km^2, spread across 13 districts. The nine districts inside the third ring of expressways shown in Fig. 16.1 form the core urban areas of Wuhan and constitute our study area. Since only a very small part of the Caidian district is located inside the third ring, we take it as part of Hanyang for the purpose of this study.

Taxicabs are one of the most important and frequently used forms of public transportation in many large cities. The distribution of taxi trips has been found to be positively correlated with population density in the city space (Liu et al. 2012);

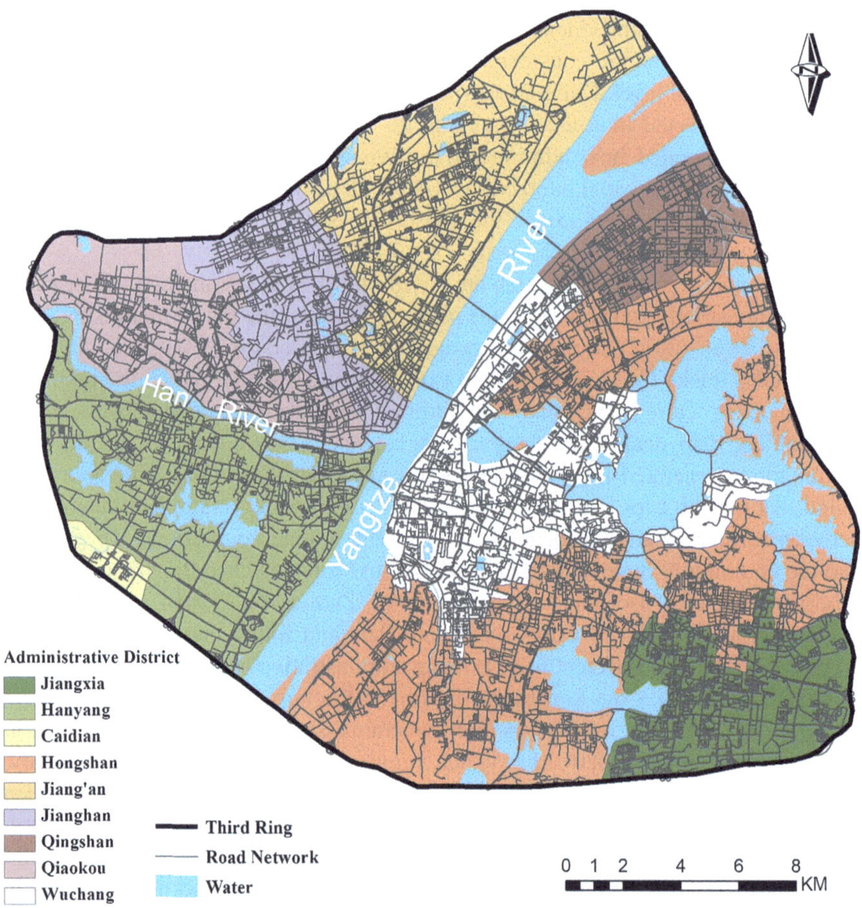

Fig. 16.1 The study area of Wuhan

Table 16.1 The taxi GPS trajectory format

Data item	Description	Example
TaxiID	The unique anonymous ID of each taxi	11,201
TrajectoryID	The ID created after the map matching and trajectory construction process, through which the GPS points are mapped onto the road network and each trip trajectory is created according to the service status	25
ServiceStatus	The service status of the taxi trip: 1 stands for occupied and 0 stands for unoccupied	1
Date	The date when the trajectory starts	2009-09-01
Original point	The trajectory starting point has a form of (x, y, t), in which x, y stands for the point location and t stands for the GPS sampling time	(114.123, 30.456, 0:00:08)
Destination point	The destination of the trajectory. Same as the original point	(114.334, 30.578, 0:10:25)
RoadID_seq	The sequence of road links that compose the trajectory	(6551, 6552, 6555, ...)

meanwhile, the local prevalence of taxis reflects the social functions across the city region and urban mobility patterns in this space (Qi et al. 2011; Yuan et al. 2012). In cities served by a large fleet of taxis such as Wuhan, taxi trajectories offer a representative portrayal of the pulse of the city from the perspective of city users. The source data used in the study contain all the GPS trajectories of approximately 11,000 taxis collected over a 1-month period (August 31–September 29, 2009). The GPS devices that equip each taxi collect the location and time stamp about every 40~60 s. After data preprocessing, we build all the trajectories of each taxi via the occupied or unoccupied status of each point. The trajectory format and description of each data item are shown in Table 16.1. Only occupied trajectories are used in this study.

16.3.2 Critical Location Network

Before searching for mesoscale structures in the taxi trajectories through community detection, we first create a single network that encompasses the functional relationships between places scattered across the urban area, as captured by vehicular trajectories. The resulting network is a synthesis of all trajectories. Given the large number of trajectories, this functional network is generalized and simplified as a Critical Location Network (CLN) on the basis of the so-called functionally critical network locations (FCNL) of the data set. FCNLs are defined as "intersections of the urban road network that have the distinctive properties of having good connectivity, serving a high density of trip trajectories, and exhibiting a variety of patterns of trip trajectories" (Zhou et al. 2015). To operationalize this definition, several data processing steps are taken, as detailed in Zhou et al. (2015). The approach uses kernel density estimation to extract the functionally critical intersections in the urban transport network. The methodology can be described as follows. First, three indices are used to identify the transport network nodes that have high trip frequency and good connectivity and exhibit high diverse patterns among traversing travel trajectories. Then, a kernel density map and a contour map are created to extract the spatial clusters of network nodes. Finally, a buffer area is formed, based on the focal point of each spatial cluster to be the final FCNL.

The concept of the functionally critical intersection proposed by Zhou et al. (2015) to define the nodes to constitute a backbone network has the distinctive property to account for the awareness and the usage of space by humans in their movements within the city. As an extension of the previous work, we focus on the network community patterns of the identified FCNLs. We construct a weighted directed graph based on these FCNLs, where each node in the graph denotes an FCNL and each edge denotes the presence of travel trajectories between critical locations taken pairwise; in this graph, the weight of edges denotes the accessibility, which is calculated in form of travel intensity. Let us assume the resulting CLN is denoted as (F_i, L_{ij}), where F_i is an FCNL and L_{ij} is the link connecting F_i and F_j. We define a trajectory balance index to investigate the differences of trajectory intensity in two directions of a link.

$$\Delta = \left|L_{ij} - L_{ji}\right| \tag{16.1}$$

The result of FCNL extraction is presented in Fig. 16.2. The CLN is a directed and weighted network that contains 110 FCNLs and 1411 links. The mean weight of all the links is 13,785. The log-log plot of Δ in the CLN is plotted as Fig. 16.3, which denotes that the distribution of Δ is highly skewed to the right; many links exhibit a large difference between the two directions. Therefore, the CLN could not be treated as an undirected network in the subsequent processing. Additionally, there are many low frequency links in the CLN, which makes the network extremely large.

16.4 Regionalization of the Urban Space

16.4.1 Community Detection in CLN

In this study, we adopt a widely used community detection algorithm called Infomap, which has been shown to produce stable and quick results on weighted and directed networks (Rosvall and Bergstrom 2008; Fortunato 2010). We use the igraph package in R (Csárdi and Nepusz 2006) to implement the algorithm for this study.

The communities detected in the CLN comprised of 110 FCNLs are shown in Fig. 16.4. At the first level, we obtain 16 communities in total; the modularity equals 0.611, which implies that there is a dense connection among the FCNLs within each

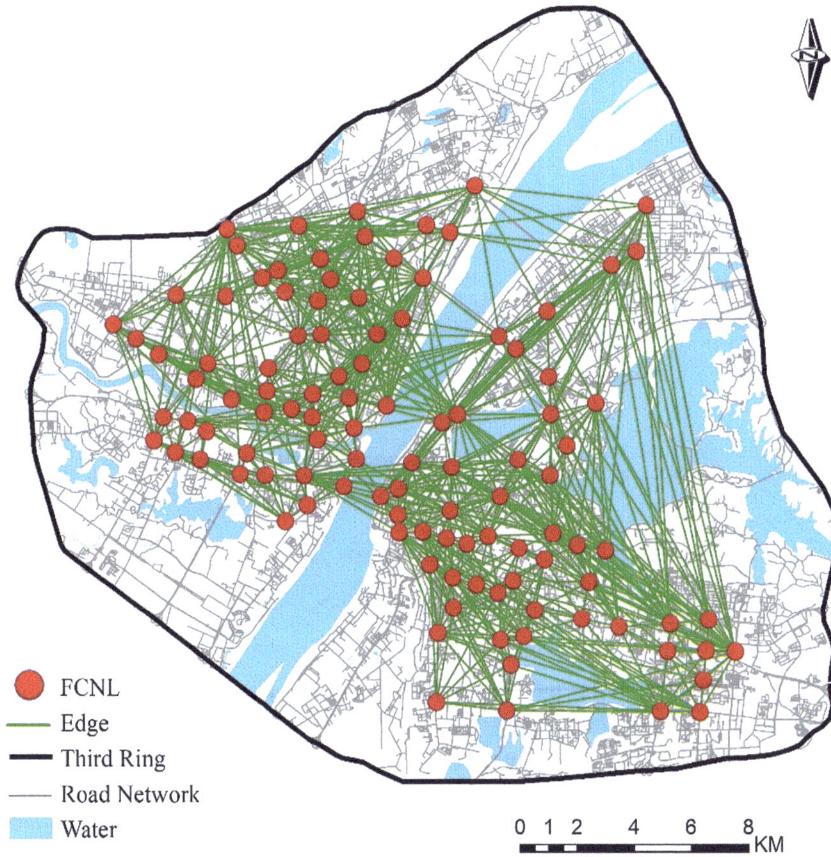

Fig. 16.2 The CLNs constructed by 110 FCNLs using taxi trips

community. When mapped onto the geographic space of the city of Wuhan, all 16 communities delineate territories that are contiguous and fairly compact. Given that no constraint of geographic contiguity is imposed in the process of detecting communities, this remarkable property is a true reflection of the structure of functional relationships embedded in vehicle trajectories. In other words, it stems from the strong structuring effect of geographic proximity and accessibility on personal activity spaces and thence on their aggregation in the form of communities.

It can readily be noticed that the spatial characteristics of socioeconomic clusters extracted from the CLN are very different from the administrative divisions of Wuhan shown in Fig. 16.1. Wuhan is a typical polycentric city. Although Wuhan is physically divided into three large parts by the Yangtze River and its branch, the Han River, the regional structures exhibited by human movements within the urban region are pretty much unaffected by the run of the two rivers. In fact, three communities span the banks of the two rivers. Conversely, the large lakes inside

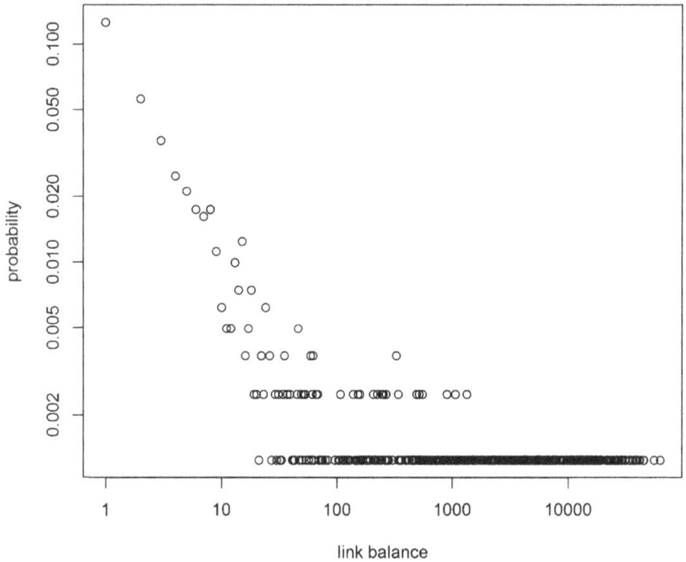

Fig. 16.3 The log-log plot of the link balance Δ in the CLN

the city limits are found to be effective barriers to the spread of the communities. This highlights the role of bridges across the rivers in connecting the activity centers in different parts of the city and in enabling people to expand their activity spaces in spite of physical obstacles. On the other hand, roads are built along the lake shores rather than across the lakes, which leads to the communities of FCNLs located around each lake.

To underscore the hierarchical structure in the city's functional organization, we create a new network based on the community results of the first level. Each community is represented by a new node in this network. We apply the Infomap algorithm again to generate communities of communities of the CLN. As shown in Fig. 16.4b, only two communities are formed at this upper level. Like communities at the lower level, these two large communities are not confined to the opposite banks of the Yangtze and Han Rivers. All the FCNLs of the left bank of the Yangtze River (Jiang'an, Jianghan, Qiaokou, and Hanyang districts) form one large community, while the FNCLs in Wuchang and to the south of it form another community. The lower-level community of Qingshan in the northeastern corner (Fig. 16.4a) of the study area is the only portion of the right bank of the Yangtze River (former city of Wuchang) that has stronger connection with the left bank and belongs to that community at the upper level. Here again, we find that a major bridge over the Yangtze River is instrumental in shaping functional relationships across an urban region. Both banks of the Han River belong to the same upper-level community.

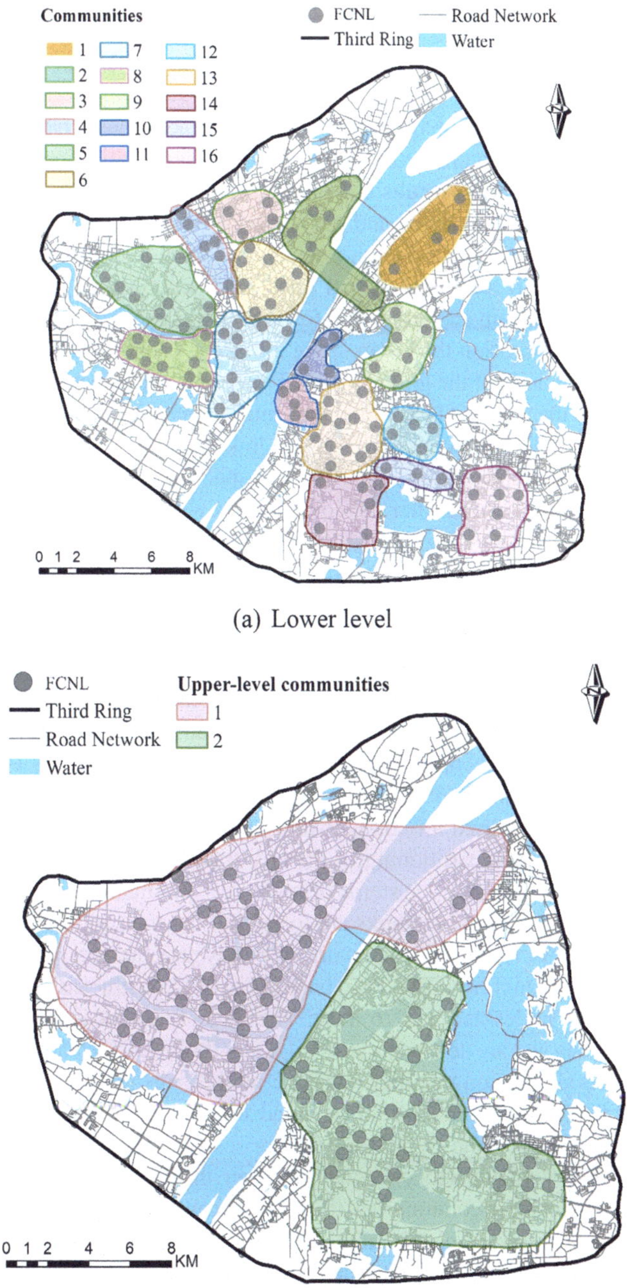

(a) Lower level

(b) Upper level

Fig. 16.4 Hierarchy of communities detected in the CLN: (**a**) lower level; (**b**) upper level

16.4.2 Urban Communities Based on Trip Origins and Destinations Only

To determine whether functionally critical locations make a meaningful difference in the geography of urban communities, we compare the regionalization results formed on the CLN with two sets of results that do not account for the detailed geometry of travel trajectories besides origins and destinations. To this end, we construct two alternative networks and extracted communities based on trips using Infomap as for the CLN. They are, respectively, based on a grid network and on a TAZ-based network using the pick-up and drop-off information of passengers in the trip data set. For the former, we partition the urban space into a 0.5 km∗0.5 km grid, where each cell constitutes the node of the grid network. The amount of trajectories between two nodes is taken as the weight of each link in the non-planar directed network. The grid network contains 1872 grid cells and 558,900 links.

The results of regional clustering on the grid space are shown in Fig. 16.5. Only nine communities are formed after the communities with less than ten grid cells are removed. Except for Hanyang district, the community boundaries are once again different from the administrative districts of Wuhan. Gridded communities show little spatial concordance with the CLN communities, and in particular we see that both the Yangtze River and the Han River are influential in shaping the gridded communities. Since the grid network only encompasses the origin and destination information of each trip and the route followed on each trajectory is ignored, the structure of the transport system has been left out, and the comparison underscores the distinctiveness of the proposed approach that incorporates the FCNLs over traditional regionalization approaches.

The second network used for comparison is constructed on traffic analysis zones (TAZ), which reflect the partitioning of the city space into zones of travel demand and supply based on the city's systems of highways and main roads. This network takes TAZs are nodes, while the links are formed of the trajectories originating and ending at TAZs. As for the grid network, we only use the pick-up and drop-off information of each taxi trip. The TAZ-based network constructed on these principles contains 219 nodes and 41,076 links. The three TAZs located in the Yangtze River have no data and are deleted as isolated nodes during the network construction. Infomap detects six big communities in this network, as displayed in Fig. 16.6a. The left bank of the Yangtze River is all included in the same community, while the former of Wuchang (on the right bank) comprises four large communities. If we remove the links with trajectory frequency lower than 100, a sparser network is obtained, and seven large communities (Fig. 16.6b) can be detected, along with three very small ones. In this case, the tributary Han River splits the left bank into two communities, while communities on the right bank are only slightly affected.

To sum up, the urban communities identified in the network of trajectories can be sharply different from each other. While the three sets of communities based on grid cells and TAZs share certain properties such as relative compactness and alignment

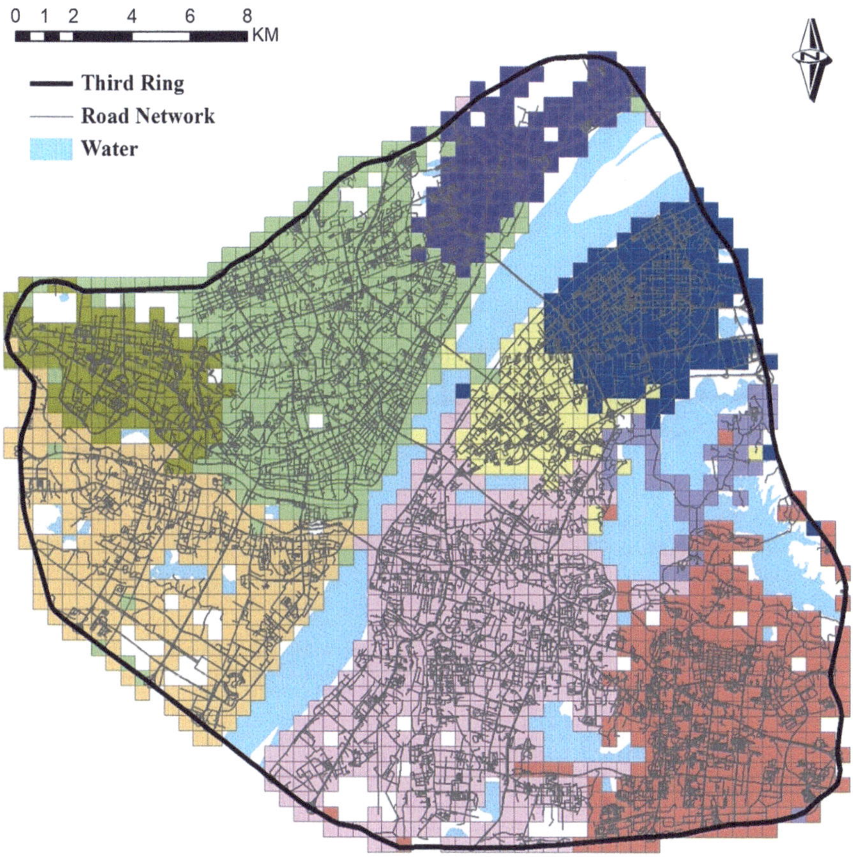

Fig. 16.5 Communities detected on the grid network

with river barriers, communities based on the CLN exhibit a sharp contrast. As they capture the experiences of activity spaces, they align more readily along corridors of vehicular movements in the city and are less affected by the barrier effect of rivers.

16.4.3 Urban Communities Based on the Physical Road Network

Since by design the nodes of the CLN are FCNLs, they are a by-product of the road system that serves the urban region. Hence, the topology of the physical road network may have preponderant influence on connectivity properties of the CLN and therefore on the communities detected in this network. To ascertain whether this

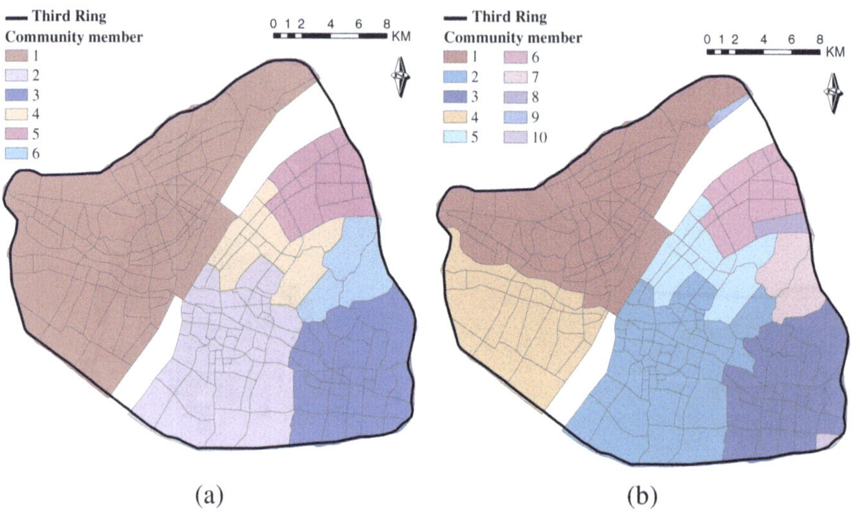

Fig. 16.6 Community detection results of the TAZ-based network: (**a**) whole network; (**b**) simplified network

Table 16.2 The information about the topological road network of three hierarchical levels

Level	Nodes	Edges	Number of communities	Modularity
1	20,320	47,413	1937	0.84
2	1929	5817	184	0.78
3	184	785	17	0.66

is the case, we evaluate communities based on the CLN against communities detected in the topological road network of the city. To this end, we directly input the city's road network as a graph to detect the community clusters and successively build super-networks based on the communities of each level until the modularity falls under 0.5. Communities are once again detected with Infomap.

Through this process, three levels of hierarchical road network structures are formed, and information about the corresponding networks is reported in Table 16.2. The first level has 1937 communities and shows only very localized spatial clusters, as depicted in Fig. 16.7a. The network of the second level only has 1929 network nodes because several communities formed in first level are disconnected (e.g., communities reside on the islands in the Yangtze River) and removed from further consideration. At this level, 184 communities are formed (Fig. 16.7b) and show spatial clusters of road network nodes at a coarse granularity. At the third level, 17 community clusters are detected (Fig. 16.7c).

Given the great disparities in the number of communities, the level-3 communities based on the road network (Fig. 16.7c) are the most directly comparable to the CLN communities (Fig. 16.4a). While the CLN communities bunch up in and around business districts where shopping and social and professional trips abound,

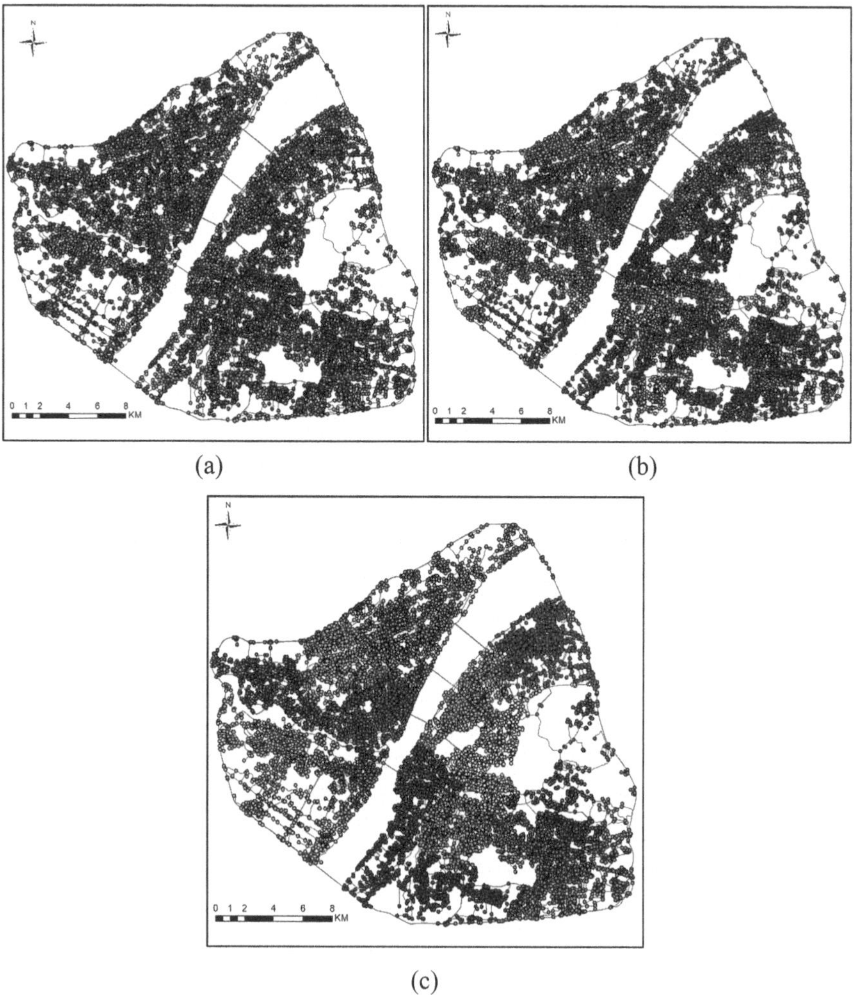

Fig. 16.7 Community patterns of the road network: (**a**) level 1; (**b**) level 2; (**c**) level 3. Nodes in the road network are color-coded according to their community

the level-3 road communities form a pretty even and balanced partition of the urban space. Also, we find that the latter are strongly influenced by the physical geography of the area, such as rivers and lakes. Almost no road community crosses the rivers, except for the pink cluster near the confluence of the Han and Yangtze Rivers. Conversely, three CLN communities straddle the rivers in a meaningful way. These differences between the two sets of communities give us confidence that the regional patterns formed by the CLN network are influenced by both the human activity flows across the urban region and the road network.

16.4.4 Discussions and Policy Implications

The findings of this study underscore the differences of socioeconomic regions derived from flows of human activity and urban infrastructure layout. Since the socioeconomic regions derived on this basis could be very different from the administrative districts, functional regions derived from actual human interactions should be taken into account as part of the regular activities conducted in the city for city management and urban planning. These constructs based on behavioral considerations encapsulate the rich detail of human behaviors. They reveal the collective lived experiences of users of the urban space, instead of the structures assumed by administrative decisions or hypothesized by urban scholars on the basis homogeneity considerations of social areas. It is out of contention that these mesoscale structures of the city should be the basis on which city management and urban planning are conducted in order to achieve greater efficiency and effectiveness in public services and foster communities that operate harmoniously with the built environment that surrounds them. Physical planning may benefit from better information on activity centers that may struggle to establish and maintain themselves and whose attractiveness can be strategically enhanced through land-use rezoning and service infrastructure buildup. In short, the proposed approach to define mesoscale urban structures is in tune with the ambient and changing structure of modern and post-modern urban environments.

Furthermore, the underlying connections within a functional region have a potential to entice citizens to participate in some administrative events, which may lead to the reshaping of administrative management units. In a large and polycentric city, the management of the city should be balanced between encouraging connections and enhancing higher-level management that enables greater-scale economies in private and public service provision, on the one hand, and discouraging connections, on the other. Greater connections enhance city interactions but bring new pressures in traffic and more long-distance travel. Discouraging connections will bring more localized physical and social activities, but might deepen the segregation among regions. Functional regionalization based on the concept of FCLN brings to light the frictions between these two sets of considerations and, because of their dynamic nature, trace patterns of dynamic change of the urban fabric and how urban agents (users) adjust to it. Thus the concept serves to evaluate past urban interventions and to design better ones for the future.

16.5 Conclusions

This study focused on the identification of the functional regionalization pattern of an urban region based on its transportation network via functional critical elements. We argued that this approach better reflects the shared lived experiences of urban residents and visitors, commonly referred to as their activity space. By constructing a directed and weighted network with critical intersections in the road network, we employed a community detection algorithm to generate socioeconomic clusters and compared the results with the several alternative regionalization approaches that have traditionally been used, including a grid-based network, the TAZ-based network, and the physical road network.

The main conclusions of our analysis are as follows. (1) Characteristics of socioeconomic clusters generated on functional critical elements are quite distinct from the administrative districts of the city of Wuhan. (2) Compared to conventional regionalizations that account only for trip ends, the functional criticality approach enables us to better construct the regionalization structure of a city, especially how collective activity spaces are shaped by civil infrastructures aimed at enhancing connectivity across the urban space, such as bridges across major waterways. (3) The functional criticality approach enhances urban communities delineated solely on the basis of physical transportation network topologies owing to their behavioral semantic among the population or urban residents and visitors.

This study has argued that an approach to urban regionalization that rests on functional critical elements effectively reflects the behavioral semantics of urban spaces that can be identified through big spatial data assembled in an era of widespread mobility sensing technologies. Thanks to the rich spatial and temporal indexing of these data streams, the behavioral pulse of the urban environment can be traced. Future work will focus on how human travel patterns within the city change through time and how much repetitiveness is exhibited on an hourly, daily, weekly, and monthly basis. CLN communities are convenient constructs to synthesize functional ties across an urban population. Also, it would be interesting to find those connections between FCNLs that are sensitive to temporal changes. We would additionally argue that other types of mobility data (such as cell phone data or bus and subway smart card data) should be studied to assess the behavioral stability across modal segments and better characterize the mutual interdependence between personal mobility and urban land-use options.

Acknowledgments The authors thank Dr. Zhixiang Fang and Dr. Qingquan Li for making the taxi trip data available. Discussions with Dr. Fang contributed to the formulation of the core ideas of this research project. This work is partly supported by the Fundamental Research Funds for the Central Universities (CCNU18QN006, CCNU19TD002).

References

Apparicio P, Abdelmajid M, Riva M, Shearmur R (2008) Comparing alternative approaches to measuring the geographical accessibility of urban health services: distance types and aggregation-error issues. Int J Health Geogr 7:1–14. https://doi.org/10.1186/1476-072X-7-7.

Blondel V, Krings G, Thomas I (2010) Regions and borders of mobile telephony in Belgium and in the Brussels metropolitan zone. Bruss Stud 42:1–12

Chen S, Claramunt C, Ray C (2014) A spatio-temporal modelling approach for the study of the connectivity and accessibility of the Guangzhou metropolitan network. J Transp Geogr 36:12–23. http://www.sciencedirect.com/science/article/pii/S0966692314000301

Chi G, Thill J-C, Tong D, Shi L, Yu L (2016) Uncovering regional characteristics from mobile phone data: a network science approach. Pap Reg Sci 41271386:1–19. https://doi.org/10.1111/pirs.12149

Csárdi G, Nepusz T (2006) The igraph software package for complex network research. InterJ Complex Syst 1695(5):1–9

Cui J, Liu F, Janssens D, An S, Wets G, Cools M (2016) Detecting urban road network accessibility problems using taxi GPS data. J Transp Geogr 51:147–157. https://doi.org/10.1016/j.jtrangeo.2015.12.007

Curtis C, Scheurer J (2010) Planning for sustainable accessibility: developing tools to aid discussion and decision-making. Prog Plan 74:53–106. https://doi.org/10.1016/j.progress.2010.05.001

Damasc J, Timpf S (2015) Exploring the potential of combining taxi GPS and Flickr data for discovering functional regions Flickr photos functional regions. AGILE 2015:3–18. https://doi.org/10.1007/978-3-319-16787-9

Demšar U, Reades J, Manley E, Batty M (2014) Edge-based communities for identification of functional regions in a taxi flow network. In: Stewart K, Pebesma E, Navratil G, Fogliaroni P, Duckham M (eds) Extended abstract proceedings of the 8th international conference on geographic information science, Vienna, Austria, 24–26 September 2014. Department of geodesy and geoinformation, Vienna University of Technology: Vienna, Austria, pp 55–60

Duan Y, Lu F (2013) Structural robustness of city road networks based on community. Comput Environ Urban Syst 41:75–87. https://doi.org/10.1016/j.compenvurbsys.2013.03.002

Fortunato S (2010) Community detection in graphs. Phys Rep 486:75–174

Gao S, Liu Y, Wang Y, Ma X (2013) Discovering spatial interaction communities from mobile phone data. Trans GIS 17(3):463–481. https://doi.org/10.1111/tgis.12042

Golledge RG, Stimson RJ (1997) Spatial behavior: a geographic perspective. Guilford, New York

Hansen WG (1959) How accessibility shapes land use. J Am Inst Plann 25:73–76. https://doi.org/10.1080/01944365908978307

Hanson S, Hanson P (1980) Gender and urban activity patterns in Uppsala, Sweden. Geogr Rev 70(3):291–299

Haynes KE (1971) Spatial change in urban structure: alternative approaches to ecological dynamics. Econ Geogr 47(Supplement):324–335

Horner MW (2004) Exploring metropolitan accessibility and urban structure. Urban Geogr 25(3):264–284. https://doi.org/10.2747/0272-3638.25.3.264

Hu Y, Gao S, Janowicz K, Yu B, Li W, Prasad S (2015) Extracting and understanding urban areas of interest using geotagged photos. Comput Environ Urban Syst 54:240–254. https://doi.org/10.1016/j.compenvurbsys.2015.09.001

Jiang S, Joseph F Jr, Gonzalez MC (2012) Discovering urban spatial-temporal structure from human activity patterns. The ACM SIGKDD international workshop, p 95. https://doi.org/10.1145/2346496.2346512

Jones DW, Haynes KE (1972) The structure and spacing of intra-urban retailing. Ann Reg Sci 6:117–138

Kang C, Sobolevsky S, Ratti C, Liu Y (2013) Exploring human movements in Singapore: a comparative analysis based on mobile phone and taxicab usages. In: UrbComp'13, Chicago, IL, USA

Kwan MP, Murray AT, O'Kelly ME, Tiefelsdorf M (2003) Recent advances in accessibility research: representation, methodology and applications. J Geogr Syst 5:129–138. https://doi.org/10.1007/s101090300107

Liu Y, Kang C, Gao S, Xiao Y, Tian Y (2012) Understanding intra-urban trip patterns from taxi trajectory data. J Geogr Syst 14:463–483. http://link.springer.com/article/10.1007/s10109-012-0166-z

Liu X, Gong L, Gong Y, Liu Y (2015) Revealing travel patterns and city structure with taxi trip data. J Transp Geogr 43:78–90. https://doi.org/10.1016/j.jtrangeo.2015.01.016

Long Y, Thill J-C (2015) Combining smart card data and household travel survey to analyze jobs–housing relationships in Beijing. Comput Environ Urban Syst 53:19–35. https://doi.org/10.1016/j.compenvurbsys.2015.02.005

Long Y, Han H, Tu Y, Shu X (2015) Evaluating the effectiveness of urban growth boundaries using human mobility and activity records. Cities 46:76–84. https://doi.org/10.1016/j.cities.2015.05.001

Martin JC, Reggiani A, Thill J-C (2018) Editorial introduction for the special issue on accessibility, resilience and vulnerability. Transportation 45(4):1003–1007. https://doi.org/10.1007/s11116-018-9909-0

Murray AT (2003) A coverage model for improving public transit system. Ann Oper Res 123:143–156

Páez A, Scott DM, Morency C (2012) Measuring accessibility: positive and normative implementations of various accessibility indicators. J Transp Geogr 25:141–153. https://doi.org/10.1016/j.jtrangeo.2012.03.016

Qi G, Li X, Li S, Pan G, Wang Z, Zhang D (2011) Measuring social functions of city regions from large-scale taxi behaviors. In: Proceedings of the 9th IEEE international conference on pervasive computing and communications, Seattle, WA, USA

Rai RK, Balmer M, Marcel R, Vaze VS, Schönfelder S, Axhausen KW (2007) Capturing human activity spaces: new geometries. Transp Res Rec 2021:70–80

Ratti C, Sobolevsky S, Calabrese F, Andris C, Reades J, Martino M, Claxton R, Strogatz SH (2010) Redrawing the map of Great Britain from a network of human interactions. PLoS One 5(12):1–6. https://doi.org/10.1371/journal.pone.0014248

Rinzivillo S, Mainardi S, Pezzoni F, Coscia M, Pedreschi D, Giannotti F (2012) Discovering the geographical borders of human mobility. Künstl Intell 26:253–260. https://doi.org/10.1007/s13218-012-0181-8

Rosvall M, Bergstrom CT (2008) Maps of random walks on complex networks reveal community structure. PNAS 105(4):1118–1123

Roth C, Kang SM, Batty M, Barthe M (2011) Structure of urban movements: polycentric activity and entangled hierarchical flows. PLoS One 6(1):2–9. https://doi.org/10.1371/journal.pone.0015923

Sánchez-Mateos HSM, Mohíno I, José M, Francés U (2014) Road accessibility and articulation of metropolitan spatial structures: the case of Madrid (Spain). J Transp Geogr 37:61–73. https://doi.org/10.1016/j.jtrangeo.2014.04.003

Schintler LA, Chen Z (2017) Big data for regional science, 1st edn. Routledge, London

Shaw S-L, Fang Z, Lu S, Tao R (2014) Impacts of high speed rail on railroad network accessibility in China. J Transp Geogr 40:112–122. https://doi.org/10.1016/j.jtrangeo.2014.03.010

Taylor MAP, Susilawati (2012) Remoteness and accessibility in the vulnerability analysis of regional road networks. Transp Res A 46(5):761–771. https://doi.org/10.1016/j.tra.2012.02.008

Thill J-C, Kim M (2005) Trip making, induced travel demand, and accessibility. J Geogr Syst 7:229–248. https://doi.org/10.1007/s10109-005-0158-3

Ullman EL (1980) Geography as spatial interaction. In: Boyce RR (ed) Geography as spatial interaction. University of Washington Press, Washington, DC, pp 13–27

Wang Y, Monzon A, Di Ciommo F (2015) Assessing the accessibility impact of transport policy by a land-use and transport interaction model – the case of Madrid. Comput Environ Urban Syst 49:126–135. https://doi.org/10.1016/j.compenvurbsys.2014.03.005

Yuan J, Zheng Y, Xie X (2012) Discovering regions of different functions in a City using human mobility and POIs categories and subject descriptors. In: Proceedings of the 18th ACM SIGKDD international conference on knowledge discover and data mining. ACM, New York, NY, pp 186–194. https://doi.org/10.1145/2339530.2339561

Zhong C, Arisona SM, Huang X, Batty M, Schmitt G (2014) Detecting the dynamics of urban structure through spatial network analysis. Int J Geogr Inf Sci 28(11):2178–2199. https://doi.org/10.1080/13658816.2014.914521

Zhou Y, Fang Z, Thill J-C, Li Q, Li Y (2015) Functionally critical locations in an urban transportation network: identification and space–time analysis using taxi trajectories. Comput Environ Urban Syst 52:34–47. https://doi.org/10.1016/j.compenvurbsys.2015.03.001

Part III
Global Perspective

Chapter 17
A Global Assessment of Nontariff Customer Assistance Programs in Water Supply and Sanitation

Joseph Cook, David Fuente, Mike Matichich, and Dale Whittington

Abstract A key strategy for adapting to changing water availability and rapid urbanization is a move toward full cost recovery tariffs for water and sanitation services. Because these services are substantially underpriced in most places, this strategy implies that careful attention must be directed at programs to help the poor manage water affordability. In this paper, we describe the types of "customer assistance programs" (CAPs) available and develop a typology that highlights the connection between CAPs and water scarcity. We then present a broad review of evaluations and case studies of CAPs from both industrialized countries and low- and middle-income countries (LMICs). Although several researchers have documented that increasing block tariffs are a poor targeting mechanism for directing subsidies to the poor, there are relatively few careful evaluations of "nontariff" CAPs, including subsidies to connect households to the network.

Keywords Affordability · Pro-poor · Subsidies · Targeting · Water tariffs

---

J. Cook
Washington State University, Pullman, WA, USA

D. Fuente
University of South Carolina, Columbia, SC, USA

M. Matichich
Jacobs Engineering Group Inc., Dallas, TX, USA

D. Whittington (✉)
University of North Carolina at Chapel Hill, Chapel Hill, NC, USA

University of Manchester, Manchester, UK
e-mail: dale_whittington@unc.edu

Z. Chen et al. (eds.), *Development Studies in Regional Science*,
New Frontiers in Regional Science: Asian Perspectives 42,
https://doi.org/10.1007/978-981-15-1435-7_17

17.1 Introduction

The issue of protecting the poor in providing water supply and sanitation services has been of interest in low-income countries for several decades. These settings are often characterized by a significant fraction of households that may have difficulty paying full cost recovery tariffs and customers who are not connected to the network services. These households are unconnected because they cannot afford the connection, they live in informal settlements without land tenure, or they cannot procure a connection because of bureaucratic obstacles or corruption. Unconnected households rely on public taps, water vendors, or tanker trucks or buy water from connected neighbors, in many cases paying higher volumetric prices than those with piped connections. Households unconnected to the piped sewer network rely on private pit latrines, public toilets, or open defecation.

The task for water utility regulators and managers in many cities in low and middle income countries (LMICs) is to move the piped water and sanitation network toward one which provides all households with ready access to a high-quality, 24/7 potable water. They might prioritize connecting households quickly, improving the quality and reliability of the system, or some combination. The choice of which of these alternative "water development paths" to pursue is particularly important in areas where increasing water scarcity could constrain economic growth and where the tariff must send the right economic signal to water consumers. Although the ability of users to pay for these improvements will increase as the economy grows, these paths inevitably require the provision of subsidies to some customers. A key question is therefore finding the right policy mix of (a) improved tariffs to finance movement along the water development path and to ensure water is used efficiently, and (b) targeted, well-designed pro-poor policies that deploy subsidies and assistance in a way that makes poor households better off. Although concerns about affordability and protecting the poor in low-income countries have been raised in relation to private sector participation (PSP) contracts, nearly all existing evaluation studies have focused on the targeting properties of subsidy programs – whether benefits intended to reach the poor actually do – rather than how the subsidies are funded and delivered.

The issue of protecting the poor has received less attention in industrialized countries until relatively recently. There the issue goes by the "affordability challenge" label, but many of the underlying dynamics are becoming similar to situations found in low-income countries. Water and sanitation service providers need to raise tariffs to replace aging capital stock, improve service levels, improve environmental and drinking water quality, and send an economic signal of water scarcity to consumers, if water is indeed scarce. (See Haynes et al. 1984 for an early discussion of planning for capacity expansion and pricing.) Public support for such tariff increases can be jeopardized, however, if a portion of the population would need to pay a substantial fraction of their income for water and sewer services. Compounding this problem is regional inequality: cities and towns in parts of the US that are economically stagnant find themselves struggling to maintain revenue and systems in the face of a dwindling customer base and flat income growth. Because of these problems, a number of utilities in industrialized countries have adopted programs to help the poor and maintain good relations with struggling customers. Throughout this chapter, we will use the term by which these subsidy programs are referred to in the US literature: customer assistance programs (CAPs).

One widely used approach for attempting to help the poor is a tariff structure with increasing blocks – i.e., increasing block tariffs (IBTs) (Fuente and Bartram 2018). Proponents of IBTs believe that (a) if poor households consume less water than rich households and (b) if the lowest blocks of the IBT structure are set below full cost and the highest blocks are set above full cost, then rich households cross-subsidize poor households "through the tariff." In practice, however, a number of studies have shown that IBTs are a poor mechanism for redistribution, particularly in low-income countries (see Fuente et al. 2016 for a review). This is because (a) all blocks of the tariff are typically set below full cost, so all households with a piped connection are being subsidized, (b) poor households are less likely to be connected to the system, (c) poor households are more likely to share meters and thus find themselves in the most expensive volumetric blocks, and (d) the empirical relationship between income and water use is much weaker than many believe. Because of this, we focus our attention on "nontariff" CAPs or subsidy programs that do not involve manipulating the tariff structure that *all* households face in order to help the poor.

The paper is organized as follows. We begin by defining four major elements of CAPs: subsidy administration, funding, targeting, and delivery mechanism. Using these definitions, we describe a typology of subsidies that links the targeting properties of the CAP with the economic signal of water scarcity. We then review experiences with CAPs in the USA, Europe, and Australia before describing a broad overview of subsidy programs in low- and middle-income countries (LMICs) and highlighting two cases from Chile and Singapore. We next discuss the existing evaluation literature on CAPs. We conclude with four lessons from our review of the global experience with nontariff CAPs.

17.2 Elements of Customer Assistance Programs

There are four facets of programs that assist the poor in the water sector: who administers subsidies, how subsidies are funded, how subsidies are targeted, and how subsidies are delivered.

17.2.1 Administration

First, who administers subsidies? This includes determining eligibility criteria for subsidy programs (if those programs are targeted), verifying that eligibility, and deciding how subsidies will be delivered (see "CAP policies" below). By this definition, most CAPs in LMICs are administered by the utility, though donors often play an important role in deciding how subsidies will be delivered (i.e., the

Global Partnership on Output-Based Aid (GPOBA) program to subsidize connections to the piped system). Most CAPs in the USA are administered by utilities, though most use existing poverty criteria to determine eligibility and some partner with local social service agencies to verify eligibility criteria. For example, the US government has a federally funded home heating assistance program (LIHEAP). The water utility in Cleveland, Ohio, contracts with a local nonprofit (Cleveland Housing Network) responsible for verifying LIHEAP eligibility, receiving in turn a list of their LIHEAP-eligible customers. Coordinating CAPs and eligibility is in fact a current focus in many US and European utilities to reduce the administrative burden on utilities and customers.

17.2.2 Funding

Second, how are subsidies funded (Table 17.1)? In the USA, many CAPs are funded by the utility through a financial cross-subsidy in which some users pay slightly higher prices to generate revenue used for the subsidy programs. In many instances in low-income countries, utilities and analysts may describe their subsidy programs as being funded by cross-subsidies when in fact all users are paying prices that are lower than full cost recovery: utilities are often relying on capital or operating subsidies from higher levels of government. Furthermore, true cross-subsidy funding schemes may be infeasible in low-income countries because the percentage of customers needing support is a substantial fraction of the customer base.

In many parts of the USA, such cross-subsidies are expressly forbidden by state law or state-level public service commissions (Berahzer et al. 2017). In those cases, programs are funded with voluntary "round up your bill" options[1] or partnerships with charitable organizations. Voluntary contribution programs typically produce less revenue than would be required to support all identified needs of eligible poor

Table 17.1 Funding types

Funding types	Description
Utility-funded	No significant involvement of any other municipal, county, or federal agency in providing subsidies targeted to the poor (rather than general operations subsidies to the utility as a whole). Subsidies contribute to operating deficit of utility in most places, since overall tariff structure does not reflect costs
State-funded	Other government agency directly involved in delivery or funding of water subsidies to poor households, even if utility still interfaces with clients
Voluntary, charities, donors	A third party is involved in subsidizing households to connect or pay their bills

[1]For example, if a bill is $43.11, the bill statement might ask if you would like to pay $44 and donate $0.89 to the low-income fund.

customers. We also include in this voluntary category donor support programs that explicitly fund subsidies targeted to the poor (e.g., GPOBA).

A third type of financing comes from local, state, or federal government funding. These programs generally do not exist in the USA or Europe and are rare in LMICs. In most countries government financing assistance comes in the form of direct support to the water utility through capital investments, preferential lending, etc., rather than support tied directly to serving the poor. In the USA, however, a bill was introduced in 2018 to provide federal funding to support customer assistance for poor customers of water and wastewater systems on a pilot basis, and California is in the process of implementing a state-wide low-income rate assistance (LIRA) program mandated by the State Assembly in 2015.[2]

17.2.3 Targeting

Means-testing is by far the most common approach in industrialized-country CAPs and typically uses earned income as reported to the federal tax agency (Table 17.2). A poor household may bring paperwork proving economic status either to the utility or a partner agency in order to qualify for the CAP. In areas where income varies substantially through the year, is rarely reported (large informal economies), or is difficult to verify, proxy characteristics can be used to characterize poverty. Common proxy measures include characteristics of the home, durable asset ownership, or

Table 17.2 Targeting types

Targeting type	Description
Means-tested (income and/or proxy measures)	Threshold could be based solely on all-source income. Can be self-reported in an interview, often requiring documentation such as a pay stub to confirm income level; in other cases, it is based on information reported to a tax agency based on employer records. Where income data are unavailable or unreliable, may be combined with proxies such as dwelling type, durable asset ownership, and number of people in the household
Geographic targeting	The household's location determines poverty status; maps areas of a city into poor and nonpoor areas based on observable characteristics of areas
Demographic targeting	Targeting by age, gender, or some other demographic characteristic
Self-targeting	Only poor households would want to use this service (usually public taps or shared connections). Sometimes referred to as "service-level" targeting

[2]The federal bill is Senate Bill 3564 (Sen. Cardin); see https://www.congress.gov/bill/115th-congress/senate-bill/3564. For more information on California's LIRA program, see https://www.waterboards.ca.gov/water_issues/programs/conservation_portal/assistance/.

education levels. Proxy-based poverty measures can also be prone to gaming by the households, e.g., households move durable assets to friends' apartments during interviews. There is also the administrative issue of how frequently eligibility must be rechecked. Geographic targeting relies on a strong spatial pattern of poverty. In the absence of centrally reported income information, it is likely to have lower administrative costs than proxy-based means-testing but typically has worse targeting properties, as discussed below.

Demographic targeting uses age, disability status, or other characteristic of the individual. For example, Ukraine offers bill reductions of 15–100% for pensioners, the disabled, students, the unemployed, war veterans, and victims of Chernobyl (Smets 2008). As discussed below, senior citizens are often eligible for CAPs in the USA.

Finally, self-targeting relies on the assumption that only poor households will opt for the service being offered. In water, this often entails a service-level targeting by subsidizing public taps or shared connections. Untargeted IBTs are sometimes described as being self-targeting under the assumption that only the poor will choose to consume water within the first lifeline block, though this is not true for reasons described above.

17.2.4 Delivery: CAP Policies

Earlier studies (Komives et al. 2005; Banerjee and Morella (2011)) broadly characterize subsidies in LMICs as either connection or consumption subsidies. In the USA, the EPA (2016) classified CAPs as "bill discount," "flexible terms," "temporary assistance," "water efficiency," and "lifeline rates." Since this chapter covers CAPs in both types of settings, we require a common typology.

Furthermore, relatively little attention has been paid to the intersection of CAPs and water scarcity. In settings where water is plentiful or the fraction of customers eligible for CAPs is relatively small, this intersection will not be important. In areas where water scarcity is a concern but where most of the poor are unconnected, the retail water price these unconnected households face at kiosks plus the associated time cost of collection (for themselves or vendors) may approximate the long-run marginal cost. In other words, there is probably little concern that households carrying water home are wasting it. This intersection may be more important in places (like Cape Town) where water resources planning, including demand management, is paramount. Here the fraction of low-income customers is substantial and most have piped connections. In other places, like water-scarce parts of the USA, aging infrastructure will need to be replaced with ratepayer funds. Increasing inequality and stagnating incomes could lead to a larger fraction of customers eligible for CAPs and thus more attention on the incentive properties of CAPs. In the typology below, we have subdivided these CAPs by whether we believe the CAP preserves incentives to use water wisely.

In our typology (Table 17.3), the first policy is a connection subsidy. This can be in the form of a free connection to the water or sewer network or partly subsidized

Table 17.3 Customer assistance policies

	Customer assistance policy	Description
Unlikely to affect monthly consumption	Connection	Free or subsidized cost of connection to the water or sewer network; also includes financing cost of connection through microloan or repayment through the normal bill
	Payment flexibility	Allows customers to pay more frequently than normal billing schedule, use prepaid meters, or pay via innovative billing mechanism. Can also include help with arrears management and repayment assistance
	Water efficiency/conservation assistance	Assists customers in reducing their bill by reducing water consumption: rebates for low-flow appliances (sometimes including Installation), leak detection, etc.
	Temporary/crisis assistance	One-time credits for those episodically in need
Consumption subsidies; More likely to affect consumption	Fixed rebate	A set amount is given to the customer each payment cycle, typically through a bill credit. The rebate is unrelated to the customer's water usage
	Fractional price/bill	The customer pays a certain percentage of the normal water tariff/ bill each payment cycle (i.e. customer pays 25% of bill, 75% discount), which will be tied to consumption if the tariff has a volumetric component
	Volumetric allowance or "lifeline blocks"	Customers are allowed a certain amount of water free or at reduced cost each payment cycle (e.g., 5 m^3 per month); smaller allowances less likely to affect overall consumption, larger "lifeline blocks" more likely to affect consumption
	Free water	Customers are allowed unlimited water free of charge
	Fixed bill	The customer pays a set amount for water each payment cycle, no matter their consumption. Includes bill based solely on customer's income (e.g., Philadelphia's Tiered Assistance Program)

connections. It could involve no- or low-interest financing of the connection fee. A CAP might also charge the full cost of connecting the household but spread the charges over time in the bill. If the utility passes along the full financing costs (i.e., its own borrowing costs), there would be no financial subsidy to the household per se, but the household may have an easier time affording a connection. The utility might finance these connection fees with a dedicated connection fee revolving fund, where more connections can be extended as original connection loans are paid off.

Payment flexibility programs give customers the option to make payments in ways that best suit them. Examples include programs that allow customers to pay more frequently than a monthly or bimonthly billing cycle or to pay using prepaid meters rather than postpaid bills. In the USA these can include programs to help customers deal with past unpaid debts to the utility.

A common CAP in the USA is a water efficiency/conservation program. These include partially or fully subsidized assistance in detecting and fixing leaks that are the homeowners' responsibility, installing low-flow appliances or irrigation timers, repairing appliances, home audits, and education/outreach programs.

Temporary or emergency assistance programs are tailored not to customers who are considered "poor" but to those who may have episodic difficulty paying water bills. This has also been a prominent feature of affordability discussions in the UK (OfWat 2016).

Consumption subsidies have the potential to influence a household's decision about how much water to consume. These can take the form of a fixed rebate, where a set amount of money is credited to the customer, regardless of water consumption. A fixed rebate policy is well suited for two-part tariffs, so that poor households could be credited for the fixed portion of the bill, thereby reducing their average cost while maintaining the marginal cost of water. The rebate could be any fixed amount; however, a policy of charging a uniform volumetric price at marginal cost with a targeted or untargeted rebate has long been advocated in the sector (Boland and Whittington 2000). We include fixed rebates as a consumption subsidy, however, because there is now substantial evidence that consumers respond to complex nonlinear price structures by implicitly calculating average price rather than identifying the relevant marginal price in the block structure (Ito 2014; Wichman 2014). Because of this, any fixed rebate that is tied in a salient way to the water bill may reduce average price in the consumer's mind and dampen marginal incentives to conserve. Although there are no empirical tests, one might expect that marginal incentives will be stronger if fixed rebates are delivered further away in time from the bill (i.e., pay the bill at the end of each month, but subsidy arrives in the middle) or if the subsidy is lumped with other subsidy or transfer payments (as in Singapore's U-Save program that includes electricity).

At the other end of the spectrum of incentives to conserve are programs that provide free water (no bill for use) or fixed bills, where the bill has no volumetric component and the customer pays the same amount each month. Both equally provide no incentive to conserve. Philadelphia's new tariff structure is a variant of the latter.[3] This program became operational only in July 2017, so there is very little discussion or evaluation of the program as implemented. The basic outline of the program is that customers whose income is between 0% and 50% of the federal poverty line (FPL) will pay 2% of their monthly income, those earning between 51% and 100% will pay 2.5%, and those earning between 101% and 150% will pay 3%. The minimum bill was set at $12. The bill for qualifying customers is in no way tied to water consumption.

[3]See http://www.circleofblue.org/2017/world/philadelphia-water-rate-experiment-aims-help-struggling-residents-pay-bills/ or https://beta.phila.gov/services/water-gas-utilities/water-bill-customer-assistance/.

Providing free water from public taps is an example of the former (with type-of-service targeting). In both cases, the program eliminates any financial incentive for the customer to fix leaks or conserve water. In a fractional cost/bill approach, households pay a certain percentage of their bill calculated according to the normal tariff schedule. Because the size of the rebate changes with consumption, one might expect that fractional bill approaches would weaken marginal incentives to conserve compared to a fixed rebate, though this is an empirical question.

The final type of consumption subsidy is a volumetric allowance or "lifeline rate" in which customers are allotted a set amount of water free or at reduced cost each payment cycle. The size of this block may be designed to ensure that the poor receive enough water for basic hygiene, typically given as 40–100 l per person per day (LCD) multiplied by an assumption about average household size. In the discussion below, we consider only *targeted* volumetric allowances as CAPs. Untargeted lifeline rates, or an IBT structure where the price for the first block of consumption is set low for *all* customers, are the most common approach that utilities in low-income countries use in an attempt to direct subsidies to the poor.

Finally, although not necessarily a delivery mechanism for subsidies, prepaid water meters (PPMs) may have a role in ensuring a minimum level of service for poor customers while minimizing administrative nonrevenue water. They empower households to monitor their consumption while protecting the utility from nonpayment (Murrar 2017). PPMs may also encourage conscientious water use; the installation of PPMs in Palmas, Brazil, resulted in a 38% reduction in water consumption (Ruiters 2007). A utility could also install PPMs on public standposts, as in Uganda (Berg and Mugisha 2010). However, the installation of PPMs can also be controversial, as in Cape Town (Calfucoy et al. 2009). In Nairobi, more than half of customers were qualified to be disconnected from the network due to outstanding water and sanitation debt, resulting in poor cost recovery for the utility. In response, the utility installed PPMs with a goal of reducing nonrevenue water to less than 40%. The installation of PPMs resulted in a public outcry, vandalism, and wasted investment due to technological malfunction (Heymans et al. 2014). Ruiters (2007), however, found that PPMs can improve the public image of a utility by requiring customers to "self-disconnect" instead of being directly cut off by the utility.

17.2.5 A Typology of CAP Programs

We developed the typology in Table 17.4 to better identify the CAPs that are most effective at the intersection of helping the poor and preserving incentives to use water wisely (Table 17.4). Type 1, where the CAP does not attempt to target the poor and does not preserve incentives, is the worst case: all of the water the utility provides is subsidized and benefits mainly middle- and upper-income groups. Type 1 policies include free water (for all) and large volumetric allowances (more than 15 m^3 per month) for everyone. One could argue that untargeted IBTs with large first blocks are attempting to target the poor but failing.

Table 17.4 Types of water CAPs

	Policy does not attempt to target poor households	Policy attempts to target the poor
Policy does not maintain economic scarcity signal	*Type 1* (e.g., most IBTs with large first blocks or those where all blocks are below marginal cost)	*Type 2* (e.g., Chile's subsidy policy, Philadelphia's fixed bill program)
Policy attempts to maintain economic scarcity signal	*Type 3* (e.g., IBTs not in Type 1, untargeted connection subsidies, untargeted crisis assistance)	*Type 4* (e.g., Portland targeted fixed rebate program; GPOBA targeted connection subsidies)

In our review of CAP programs below, we deliberately excluded untargeted IBTs as pro-poor policies, though we should note these policies are more common by far than any other CAP program (Fuente and Bartram 2018). According to the 2017 global tariff survey conducted by Global Water Intelligence, the majority (60%) of utilities that responded to the GWI survey use IBTs. They are especially popular with utilities in Latin America (94%), the Middle East and North Africa (92%), and sub-Saharan Africa (88%).[4]

Type 2 limits allocative inefficiency to the poor's water use, as long as the targeting works. Targeted free water and fixed bills are Type 2 policies. We would also consider Chile's well-known program to be Type 2, since the program allows a relatively large discounted consumption block of 15 m^3 for eligible customers. Type 3 provides some help to poor households, but because it is untargeted, it is an inefficient way to direct subsidies: a substantial fraction of the subsidies goes to the nonpoor. IBTs with smaller volumetric allowances[5], early payment discounts, and water at reduced prices for institutions are Type 3 policies. Type 4 is the best-case scenario; subsidies are targeted to those who need them but maintain the price signal. Small volumetric allowances with a normal tariff thereafter, targeted connection subsidies, payment flexibility and/or financing, and targeted fixed rebates, fractional rebates, and fractional bills are Type 4 schemes.

[4]The annual tariff survey conducted by Global Water Intelligence is the most comprehensive tariff survey conducted globally (http://www.globalwaterintel.com). However, the survey does not contain a representative sample of utilities across the globe, in particular regions, or in particular countries. Many utilities that use an IBT also deploy a lifeline block with free water (i.e., the price of water in the lifeline block is zero). Forty-one percent of the utilities in Latin America that use an IBT have a free lifeline block, compared with 33% in South Asia and 15% in sub-Saharan Africa. For utilities that used an IBT, the average size of the lifeline block was typically quite large (global average of 13.6 m^3). However, in the Middle East and North Africa, the average size of the lifeline block was 18 m^3 per month, equivalent to 150 l per capita per day for a household with four members. In South Asia the average size of the lifeline block was 15 m^3 per month (125 l per capita per day). Only in sub-Saharan Africa was the average size of the lifeline block significantly lower (7 m^3 per month, or 58 l per capita per day).

[5]We used a cutoff of 6 m^3, equivalent to 40 l per capita per day for 30 days in a household with five members. This is also the level of free basic water provision in South Africa.

17.3 Overview of CAPs in Industrialized Countries

In this section, we describe a range of CAP programs currently deployed in the USA, Europe, and Australia.

17.3.1 USA

The US Environmental Protection Agency (EPA) published a compendium in 2016 that reviewed 795 utilities across the USA. Of the 795, nearly 30% (228 utilities) were found to offer one or more CAPs, for a total of 365 active programs. Although low-income customers are most frequently the targeted customer type, some CAPs offer assistance to those experiencing a temporary hardship (divorce, death of relative, loss of employment), senior citizens, permanently disabled persons, and military veterans. The EPA review also reveals the number of utilities using each of the delivery/subsidy types. Bill discounts are the most common type (42% of active programs), followed by flexible terms programs (27% of programs), which include payment plans, connection loans, managing arrears, moving from bimonthly to monthly billing, and allowing customers to set up a "levelized" bill that is estimated annually but gives customers the same bill amount each month. Temporary assistance programs were also common (24%), and 9% of programs were aimed at water efficiency, such as subsidized leak repair and rebates for high-efficiency appliances. Targeted volumetric allowances were found in only 5 of 365 active programs (1%).

Table 17.5 reports information from five city case studies we examined in more detail: Portland, Detroit, Cleveland, San Antonio, and Pittsburgh. We chose the cities purposively to broadly represent what we felt was the experience of US utilities, rather than a random sample of the EPA compendium. The table shows that (a) in all five cities, the utility is employing multiple CAP policies; (b) nearly all programs are funded with utility revenue; (c) the percent of customers participating is small (generally <5%); (d) the CAP program costs, though substantial in absolute terms, are a small percentage of utility revenue; and (e) many programs are Type 4 programs in our typology because they use means-tested targeting and generally preserve economic incentives to use water efficiently.

17.3.2 Europe and Australia

WAREG, a network of European Water Regulators, published a study in 2017 regarding the affordability of water, in which utilities in 17 WAREG member countries were surveyed (WAREG 2017). Fixed bills (a cap on the bill as a

Table 17.5 Summary of cases from the USA, Europe, and Australia

Location/ administration	Type	Program elements	Targeting	Source of financing	Approximate % of customers served	Cost as percent of utility revenue
United States						
Portland						
Utility + local agency	4	Fixed rebate; crisis assistance; conservation assistance	Means-tested; partner w/ local social service. Single-family homes only. Reapply every 2 years	Utility revenue	6% (9602/ 153,500)	1% ($4.9 m/ $498 m)
Utility	3	Payment flexibility: more frequent billing; payment extension	None; all customers	Little/no revenue implication	15% (22,743/ 153,500)	Little/no revenue implication
Utility	3	Crisis assistance	Not means-tested; show temporary crisis	Utility revenue	NA	Much less than 1%
Detroit						
Utility	4	Payment flexibility (freeze arrearages; bill credit; past due bill forgiveness); conservation assistance	Means-tested	Utility revenue	NA	0.5%
Utility	3	Payment flexibility (payment plan)	Not means-tested; past-due/delinquent accounts	Little/no revenue implication	13% (25,000/ 200,000)	Little/no revenue implication
Cleveland						
Utility + local agency	2	Different tariff	Means-tested; elderly and disabled; annual application	Utility revenue	8% (24,000/ 313,000)	0.5%
Utility + local agency	4	Bill discount (fractional cost)	Means-tested; partner w/ local social service (LIHEAP)	Utility revenue	1% (2500/ 313,000)	0.5%
Utility + local agency	3	Crisis assistance	Not means-tested; show temporary crisis	Utility revenue	Less than 1% (1135/ 313,000)	0.5%

Pittsburgh						
Utility w/ local nonprofit	4	Fixed rebate/grant	Means-tested; partner w/ local social service	Customer, corporate, employee donations	Less than 1% (1187/ 666,436)	Much less than 1%
Utility w/ local nonprofit	4	Fractional cost (80% discount water, 15% sewerage)	Means-tested; partner w/ local social service	Utility revenue	2% (14,629/ 666,436)	NA
Utility w/ local nonprofit	4	Conservation assistance	Means-tested; partner w/ local social service	Utility revenue	NA	NA
San Antonio						
Utility	4	Fixed rebate	Means-tested; cap on water consumption	Utility revenue	4% (18,000/ 500,000)	0.5%
Utility + local agency	4	Crisis assistance	Means-tested	Voluntary contributions	Less than 1% (2000/ 500,000)	0.5%
Utility	4	Payment flexibility (late fee waiver)	Elderly; disabled on social security	Little/no revenue implication	6% (30,000/ 500,000)	Little/no revenue implication
Utility + local agency	4	Conservation assistance	Means-tested; water and sewer customers	Utility revenue	NA	0.5%
Belgium						
Wallonia (region)						
Utility	4	Bill discount; conservation assistance	Financially vulnerable customers	Utility revenue	0.5%	NA (€4 m)
Flanders						
Utility	4	Bill discount (fractional cost); payment flexibility (payment plan); conservation assistance	Means-tested; social welfare beneficiaries	Utility revenue	10%	NA

(continued)

Table 17.5 (continued)

Location/ administration	Type	Program elements	Targeting	Source of financing	Approximate % of customers served	Cost as percent of utility revenue
Brussels						
Utility + local agency	4	Conservation assistance; payment flexibility (payment plan)	Financially vulnerable customers	Utility revenue	NA	NA (€2 m)
France						
Utility	4	Bill discount; payment flexibility (payment plan)	Financially vulnerable customers	Utility revenue; voluntary contributions	0.25%	NA
Utility	2/4	Lifeline rate	Social welfare assistance beneficiaries	Utility revenue	16% (15,000/ 94,000)	NA
Italy						
Utility	4	Tariff reduction	Means-tested; physical inabilities	Government	Less than 1% (20,000/ 4,500,000)	Less than 1% (€1,100,000/ €550,000,000)
Utility	4	Bill discount	Means-tested	Utility revenue	1% (30,000/ 2,300,000)	NA (€1 m)
Scotland						
Local authority	4	Bill discount	Students; low-income households; disabled persons	Tax revenue	NA	NA
Spain						
Utility	4	Tariff reduction	Means-tested	Utility revenue	1.3%	NA
Utility	4	Bill discount; lifeline rate	Means-tested	Utility revenue	NA	NA

England						
Utility	2	Fixed bill	Means-tested and three or more children or medical condition	Utility revenue	Less than 1% (130,500/ 56,073,000)	NA
Utility	4	Debt advice; conservation assistance	Means-tested	Utility revenue	4% (199,626/ 4,600,000)	NA
Australia, Victoria State						
Govt agency	4	Bill discount	Means-tested	Government	33% eligible	NA; estimated costs 148m AUD

Note: *AUD* Australian dollar(s), *NA* not applicable

percentage of average annual income) are more common than in the USA: 10 of 17 countries have utilities that use these programs. Two of 17 countries use targeted volumetric allowances, and 7 charge lower value-added taxes on water and sewer bills. Six of 17 offered either fixed rebates or bill discounts. European governments have also been more active than Americans in regulating the procedure for disconnecting customers for nonpayment. Nine of 17 countries have compulsory procedures before disconnection, and disconnecting is explicitly forbidden in some. The Italian government passed a decree in October 2016 protecting economically disadvantaged households from being completely disconnected from water service. France passed the Brottes law in 2013, which prohibits any disconnection of water service. Water providers are not able to shut off water no matter the financial situation of the non-paying customer (Aqua Publica Europea 2016).

As part of a 10-year national strategy on energy and water efficiency, Australian utilities operating in areas with customer hardship policy frameworks must provide water efficiency advice and free home water audits. However, there is no national water customer policy framework or guidelines, and as such, customer assistance policies are administered by the individual water utilities. The State of Victoria also offers a utility relief grant scheme for paying overdue water bills of low-income Victoria residents experiencing unexpected hardship due to a temporary financial crisis.

Table 17.5 summarizes case studies from Europe and Australia. Again, because of the use of means-testing, we consider most of the cases Type 4 subsidies that preserve economic signals of scarcity. Utility revenue again predominates as the funding source, though programs in Australia, Italy, and Scotland rely on local- or state-level financing. Unlike in the USA, some of these programs enroll a larger percentage of customers: 10% in Flanders (Belgium) and 16% in France.

17.4 Overview of Nontariff CAPs in Low- and Middle-Income Countries (LMICs)

In this section we review and categorize 77 water CAPs in 45 low- and middle-income countries (LMICs). These CAPs were identified through a search of the published peer-reviewed literature, gray literature, and news items. We know of no global dataset tracking CAPs or affordability programs; Global Water Intelligence (GWI) tracks tariffs but not assistance programs. We thus caution readers that our list of CAPs may not be representative of assistance programs globally in LMICs. Also, although we attempted to determine whether the CAPs remained current and in place, it is possible some programs may have changed or been terminated since our source documents were written. Appendix Table A1 compiles these programs according to the typology and definitions above.

Of the 77 CAPs, 27 are from sub-Saharan Africa, 20 from Latin America and the Caribbean, 9 from East Asia, 8 from the Middle East and North Africa, 7 from South Asia, and 6 from Eastern Europe, the Caucasus, and Central Asia. The vast majority (76%) of cases are based on information in the gray literature. In 24% of cases, at least one article describing the program was published in a peer-reviewed journal.

17.4.1 Administration

In most cases (48%), we could not find an explicit statement about application procedures or who verified eligibility, so it is unclear who administered CAPs. Most of the remaining programs (40% of the total) are administered by the utility, and decisions about how to target subsidies and the levels at which they should be funded are made by the utility. In 9% of cases, the program was administered by a city government (as in Chile) and in only two cases by the state or central government (as in Singapore). In some cases like South Africa, Bangladesh, and Chile, utilities partner with government statistical agencies in verifying eligibility or using existing definitions of poverty.

17.4.2 Financing

Again, the most common classification was missing information: we could not find information on how programs were financed in 56% of cases. Five cases described CAPs as being funded from utility revenue, including programs in Bolivia, Peru, and China (Smets 2008; Komives 1999; Oxford Business Group 2012; Zhong et al. 2008), though it is very likely in these cases that all customers are charged prices that are below full cost recovery rates. These programs are therefore likely funded at least in part by subsidies from other levels of government or implicitly by running down the capital stock. We found state-funded subsidies programs in 12 cases, including Chile (Gomez-Lobo and Contreras 2003; Contreras et al. 2018), Singapore (Chang and Fang 2017), and Iran (Attari and van Dijk 2016). In these cases, the local or central government funds the subsidy, but relies on the utility to deliver water service. The World Bank's connection subsidy grants through the Global Output-Based Aid (GPOBA) program in Cameroon, Kenya, the Philippines, Brazil, and Indonesia are common (9%) examples of third-party donor financing (World Bank 2014; World Bank 2016; Jagannathan et al. 2009; Ehrhardt et al. 2007; Menzies and Suardi 2009). We know of no program asking for voluntary contributions from utility customers themselves, as is common in the USA.

17.4.3 Targeting

Means-tested programs are common (32% of programs), including a third of these that used proxies for income. Examples include Cameroon (World Bank 2014; Banerjee and Morella 2011); South Africa (Department of Water Affairs and Forestry 2002; Brown 2005; Calfucoy et al. 2009; Tissington et al. 2008; Szabo 2015); Kazakhstan, Russia, and Ukraine (OECD 2003); Argentina (Vagliasindi 2012); Uruguay (Komives et al. 2006); and Cambodia (Berg 2013). The most common proxy measures for income found in water CAPs are assets, household size, and type of residence. Another proxy measure commonly used is dwelling type, as in Bangladesh (Lahiri 2009), Singapore (Chang and Fang 2017), Indonesia (Ehrhardt et al. 2007), Mexico (Smets 2008), Paraguay (Foster and Yepes 2006), Mongolia (Smets 2008), and India (Asian Development Bank 2013).

Geographically targeted water CAPs are used in 22% of programs, including in Colombia (Gomez-Lobo and Contreras 2003); Kenya (Mwangi et al. 2015); Mozambique (Jimenez-Redal et al. 2014); Senegal (Lauria et al. 2005); Uganda (Mason 2009); Tajikistan (Jepbarov and Sommer 2012); Morocco (Jagannathan et al. 2009); Bolivia (Komives 1999); Mexico, Nicaragua, Panama, and Venezuela (Komives et al. 2005); the Philippines (Menzies and Suardi 2009); and India (Davis and Tanka 2006). The Colombian subsidy had very high errors of inclusion in this scheme; 83% of all households are in one of the three pro-poor subsidy levels. Gomez-Lobo and Contreras (2003) found Colombia's water CAP to be more poorly targeted but less expensive to administer than Chile's means-tested policy.[6] In Panama, where households were individually interviewed to establish eligibility, Foster et al. (2000) estimated administrative costs of approximately US$10 per beneficiary, which would represent almost 40% of the value of a simulated consumption subsidy of $1.50 per month. Demographic targeting is used in 9% of cases, including Mexico (Smets 2008), Panama (Komives et al. 2005), and China (Warford and Xie 2007; Zhong et al. 2008).

Subsidized or free public standpipes are the most common type of self-targeting (or level-of-service targeting), used in 17% of cases, including Ethiopia (Banerjee and Morella 2011); Lesotho, Madagascar, Namibia, Niger, Nigeria, Tanzania, Uganda, Morocco, and China (Zhong et al. 2008); India (The Hindu 2003); and Nepal (Bardasi and Wodon 2008; Mason 2009; Komives et al. 2005). Banerjee and Morella (2011) found that Ethiopia, Lesotho, and Zambia have issues with third-party operators selling water from public standpipes at prices 3–5 times higher than the formal price, implying that the poor still faced higher prices and operators pocketed what could have been utility revenue. Similarly, in Lusaka, independent operators resold subsidized utility tokens Bardasi and Wodon (2008) found a similar

[6]Coady et al. (2004) found that data on the administrative costs of targeting was difficult to find. They estimated that means and proxy have comparably high administrative costs, while geographic, demographic, and self-targeting were cheaper to administer.

phenomenon in Niger, resulting in nonrevenue water for the utility and errors of exclusion as the subsidy did not benefit its intended beneficiaries. Komives et al. (2005) analyzed public taps in Bangalore, India, and Kathmandu, Nepal. Both suffered from relatively high errors of exclusion, 61% and 72%, respectively. They also found that 10% of the nonpoor used the taps in Bangalore, while 25% of the nonpoor used the taps in Kathmandu. Subsidized shared connections are used in Côte d'Ivoire (Lauria et al. 2005), Gabon and Kenya (Mwangi et al. 2015), Senegal (Lauria et al. 2005), and India (Davis and Tanka 2006). Lauria et al. (2005) found that these group connection subsidies excluded many of the poorest families in Côte d'Ivoire and Senegal because they required household to have tenure to the land the connection would be installed on or live within 12 meters of the main.

17.4.4 Delivery Policies

Besides subsidizing public taps (above, 18% of delivery policies), connection subsidies make up 27% of the CAPs in our survey. In Jakarta, Indonesia, the government paid for all new connections with the assistance of the World Bank's GPOBA (Ehrhardt et al. 2007). Jimenez-Redal et al. (2014) found there was a low uptake of connections after a network expansion in a low-income neighborhood in Maputo, Mozambique; in one neighborhood, only 25% of households purchased connections and only 11% in another. They found households were more likely to purchase connections if they could finance it over several months.

Means-tested fractional bills (18%) are used in Kazakhstan, Russia, and Ukraine; the government provides compensation for households' housing and utility expenditures, including water, which exceed 30% of income in Kazakhstan, 22% in Russia, and 20% in Ukraine. There are relatively high errors of exclusion in these schemes; in Kazakhstan, 28% of the population is poor, but only 8% receive the subsidy; in Russia, 29% is poor, and 9% receive the subsidy; in Ukraine 27% is poor, but 13% receive the subsidy (OECD 2003; United Nations Centre for Human Settlements 2001). In the Ukraine Housing Subsidy Program, the rebate is administered on a monthly basis and paid directly to the utility (Davis and Whittington 2004). Fractional bill schemes were also used in Argentina and Panama City, Panama (Vagliasindi 2012; Foster et al. 2000).

Free or discounted volumetric allowances were used in 23% of cases. (Again, note that we excluded any "discounted" volumetric allowances that were untargeted and available to all customers: these are the common IBT programs described above.) Many municipalities in South Africa use volumetric allowances (of 6 m^3) as a part of the free basic water program for indigent customers, including Douglas, KwaZulu-Natal, Lichtenburg, Mbombela, Polokwane, Pretoria, Rustenburg, Volksrust, and Cape Town (Smith 2010; Calfucoy et al. 2009; Brown 2005;

Szabo 2015; City of Cape Town 2015; Department of Water Affairs and Forestry 2002). In Pretoria, Szabo (2015) found that the subsidy has minimal impacts on household consumption and acts as a lump-sum subsidy for the 12% of households that are indigent.

We found only two cases of payment flexibility. In Palestine, customers are given a bill discount for an early payment. Murrar (2017) found the policy did not successfully incentivize customers to pay their bills on time. Another example of a financing policy comes from the government of Yerevan, Armenia; customers with water and sanitation debt accumulated prior to 2000 had their arrears forgiven as long as 15–20% of it had been paid. As a result, 90% of customers used the subsidy, and the financial situations of the utilities eventually stabilized (United Cities and Local Governments 2014).

Fixed bills, or a set charge for water no matter a household's consumption, are used to help customers in Macau, China. A proxy measure of household size is used to set the price of water; a household of four people pays $12USD per month for water, which is about 3% of the minimum wage (Smets 2008). Some of the literature referenced households having subsidized bills for water; it is unclear if these were fixed bill or fractional cost schemes.

We found no examples of targeted programs offering poor customers conservation assistance in reducing bills through leak detection and repair or incentivizing efficient appliances. This is unsurprising since prices are already so low that conservation measures are unlikely to impact affordability very much, and per capita water use from piped connections is low by global standards in part because of the unreliability of the water supply network.

Overall, the CAPs we examined are split between Type 2 (43%) and Type 4 (43%), both of which attempt to target the poor. We classify 13% as Type 3 that preserve economic scarcity signals but do not attempt to target the poor (mainly connection subsidy programs). We classified none as Type 1, largely because we excluded the most common Type 1 policy: untargeted lifeline blocks.

17.5 Case Studies: Chile and Singapore

17.5.1 Chile

The most well-known example of an innovative CAP in low- and middle-income countries is Chile's program, introduced in 1990. The program was analyzed in a number of papers, notably the comparison of targeting properties with Colombia's geographic targeting scheme in Gomez-Lobo and Contreras (2003). Contreras et al. (2018) recently updated their analysis and described how the program has evolved since 2003, which we briefly summarize here.

The program is administered by a federal agency (the Ministry of Social Development, or MDS in Spanish), which makes decisions about the total subsidy budget as well as how that budget will be distributed to the regions, discussed more below.

Eligible customers pay a reduced percentage of their water and sewer bill for amounts up to 15 m^3 (125 LCD for a four-person family), but the 16th and subsequent units are charged at the full tariff. This is a volumetric allowance program in our typology, where the first block is subsidized.

There are currently three groups that benefit from the subsidy. The first group is households who qualify for the Chile Solidario welfare program introduced in 2004. This program is intended to serve the very poor, and participants receive both subsidies for a number of essential services and access to social workers. This group receives a 100% discount on the first consumption block. The second group is elderly households in the first two quintiles of the income distribution. The third and largest group is households who would pay more than 3% of their monthly income on water and sewerage services. Before 2001, this affordability cutoff was 5%. In all three groups, eligible households must live in permanent dwellings, not be in arrears to the utility, and have a piped water connection, including a connection to a rural cooperative water system.

The total number of subsidies designated to a municipality is based on the city's water/sewer bill for 15 m^3 and the distribution of income in the municipality, based on a nationwide survey and information from private and public pension funds. This gives an estimate of the number of households who would be paying more than 3% of income to the water utility. This number is multiplied by the gap between 3% of income and the full tariff for 15 m^3 to determine the subsidies allocated to the municipality. Aggregating these to the regional and then national level and adding subsidies for the Chile Solidario and poor elderly groups gives the total required subsidies, which are funded entirely from general tax revenue and included in the national budget each fiscal year. The water regulator who is responsible for setting tariffs is not involved in the operation of the system or determining overall subsidy levels.

Households must apply for the subsidy at their municipality. If the municipality determines them to be eligible, the service provider is notified and begins crediting the customer's monthly bill. The service provider regularly bills the municipality for all subsidies awarded in the previous billing period. Households must reapply every 3 years.

The targeting approach has evolved over the nearly three decades of the program's existence, as discussed in Contreras et al. (2018). The earliest program used proxy measures as reported by households during an in-person survey. As incomes grew and durable asset ownership increased among all households, it became increasingly difficult for an asset-based measure to distinguish the poor from the nonpoor, and Chile moved to a socioeconomic vulnerability approach. It was replaced by the FPS program, which measured the age, education, disability status, and income-generating capacity of household members, though it included some geographic proxies such as unemployment rates in the municipality. Like the asset-based approach before it, the FPS was subject to manipulation by households during the interview, and a new system took its place in 2016. This new System centralizes administrative information on the household, including its income (reported to various state institutions such as the Internal Revenue Service) and self-reported socioeconomic attributes. Each household is assigned a score based on this information that determines eligibility for a number of social programs.

Subsidy expenditures have grown 138% in real terms between 1998 and 2015, with the number of subsidies awarded growing by 54%. This is despite a 38% increase in real incomes in the same period nationwide among households that received a subsidy. These increases were driven in part by the change in calculation of subsidies from 5% of income to 3%, but primarily by large real increases in tariffs. Contreras et al. (2018) find that tariff increases in municipalities over the period ranged from 34% to 142%, with tariffs more than doubling in 6 of the 17 service operators.

17.5.2 Singapore

Another example of an innovative program is Singapore's U-Save (for Utility-Save) program, first implemented in 1997 (Chang and Fang 2017). The program is funded from general tax revenue and administered by the government. The delivery type is a fixed rebate: eligible households receive a fixed credit deposited directly into their utility accounts (water and electricity) quarterly. Credits can be applied whenever the customer decides to use them, and the credit rolls over and does not expire. U-Save is one of the three voucher programs aimed at offsetting an increased general goods and services tax; the other two are a cash voucher and a health expenses voucher (Medisave).[7]

In our typology, targeting is proxy-based and based on living in public housing (HDB housing). The subsidies are progressive in that smaller 1- and 2-room flats receive larger fixed subsidies than larger flats. The value of the subsidy is such that a 1- or 2-room flat would be able to offset approximately 3–4 months of utility bills. At least one household member must be a Singaporean citizen, and no occupants can own a second property.

The most recent increase in the U-Save subsidy budget in July 2017 was explicitly meant to offset the cost of a water tariff increase. The current estimate of the number of beneficiaries is 880,000 HDB households, at a total cost of $265 million per year (Charles 2018). Residents can sign up to receive mobile phone/short message service (SMS) notifications that their U-Save credits have been deposited to their account. We are unaware of estimates of the program's administrative costs.

[7]https://www.gstvoucher.gov.sg/Pages/index.aspx

17.6 CAP Evaluations

Considerable research was conducted about pro-poor water and sanitation programs in low-income countries from 2000 to 2010. The primary outcome of interest was the performance of competing targeting approaches in delivering subsidies (e.g., errors of inclusion and exclusion). Several publications discussed and compared the effectiveness of Chile's means-tested and Colombia's geographically targeted programs (Gomez-Lobo and Contreras 2003; Serra 2000; Vargas and Heller 2016; Gomez-Lobo 2001). There have also been several comprehensive research efforts aimed at formally assessing the effectiveness of water subsidies on a regional or global level, including Komives et al. (2005), Smets (2008), Banerjee and Morella (2011), and the World Bank's series on Tariffs and Subsidies in South Asia (2001–2003). The data for these studies were usually gathered from a variety of sources, including utility official interviews, household surveys, and country-level demographic data. More recently, South Africa's Free Basic Water policy has been subject to several evaluations since its implementation (Calfucoy et al. 2009; Szabo 2015; Department of Water Affairs and Forestry 2002; Smith 2010; Tissington et al. 2008; Brown 2005). Nevertheless, in over half of the programs we identified, there appears to have been no published evaluation on whether they help intended beneficiaries. Despite policy recommendations to subsidize connections for those who could afford a cost-reflective monthly bill, there are in fact few empirical studies documenting that such programs do better at helping the poor. Geographically targeted subsidies (including connection or volumetric subsidies) may simply be capitalized into rents (Komives 2003; Anselin et al. 2008) and be captured by landlords.

In contrast, in the USA, Europe, and Australia, targeting and subsidy leakage are rarely raised as concern and evaluated only recently in Australia (Chan 2016). Chan (2016) focused on the State of Victoria, where eligible residents receive a 50% discount on their total quarterly water bill, with a cap of 283.90 AUD. In 2012, around 1.3 million residents, about one-fourth of all Victoria residents, were eligible for water subsidies. In 2012, around 0.67 million households received water subsidies with a total cost of 145 million AUD, paid for by the Victoria state government. The evaluation found that in 2007, the water subsidies scheme had a 68% success rate (successfully targeting eligible households or successfully excluding ineligible households).

We were unable to find any independent cross-utility evaluation studies for programs in the USA and Europe. These countries have relatively robust national income reporting to tax agencies and standard poverty definitions (e.g., federal poverty line), so a focus on subsidy leakage may not be the most important research priority. Eligibility criteria may of course be poorly administered, and such confidence in means-testing misplaced. Instead, the focus of existing research has mainly been on low uptake of the programs among the eligible (errors of exclusion), challenges in funding programs, and the possible administrative benefits of coordinating support among other programs. These reports are case studies and descriptions of best practices rather than detailed empirical evaluations in peer-reviewed outlets.

Accordingly, we have found very few studies that look carefully at how CAPs might change the water use behavior of customers who participate. This type of study is very important in a situation where water scarcity means the short-run marginal cost of water is high but where a large number of customers need support to pay ever-increasing tariffs meant to spur conservation (e.g., the current situation in Cape Town, South Africa). Economic theory suggests that CAPs that rebate poor customers a flat amount untied to volumetric use should both preserve the economic signal to conserve and help the poor. If, however, customers react to their average price or total bill rather than marginal price (Ito 2014; Wichman 2014), such a program might lead to less conservation. Providing information to help customers perceive marginal cost and understand tariff structures is an active area of economic research in the USA, particularly in the energy sector, but this research has not yet connected to the discussion of CAPs in water.

17.7 Conclusions

We conclude with four lessons from our global review of nontariff CAPs. First, despite the large literature on targeting evaluations, little is known about whether CAPs "work". This includes connection subsidy programs, which have been recommended for two decades, and the various types of means-tested consumption subsidies used in the USA and Europe. In many settings, we do not understand why participation in CAPs is low. It simply may be that administrative hassles or corruption make the task of applying not worth the relatively small benefit. Devoto et al. (2012) in Morocco found that simplifying the application process of obtaining a private connection by sending staff to the doorstep increased the percent of respondents applying for a connection from 10% to 69%.

Second, targeting subsidies effectively will continue to be a challenge in LMICs. Even in Chile, a growing, middle-income country, the transition from a survey-based proxy measure for household income that could be used for means-testing applicants to reliance on centralized administrative data occurred only in 2016. Means-testing via household surveys will continue to be expensive and unreliable, so there will continue to be a role for service-level targeting by subsidizing public taps and shared connections and geographic targeting, particularly for connection subsidies. But technology is rapidly evolving. Many are watching India's experience with Aadhar ("Foundation"), a nationwide biometric identification system that is being used to accurately target a number of subsidies and social service programs, but is also being criticized as an invasion of privacy and a security risk.[8]

[8]"'Big Brother' requires fingerprint scans for foods, phones, and finances," https://www.nytimes.com/2018/04/07/technology/india-id-aadhaar.html, and "India loves data but fails to protect it" https://www.nytimes.com/2018/04/03/opinion/india-data-privacy-biometric-aadhar.html

Third, there has been little attention paid in the USA and Europe to the intersection of CAPs and water scarcity. Utilities in LMICs can draw from important experiences in the USA around subsidy programs to provide free conservation audits, discounted low-flow appliances, and in some cases free plumbing work. These programs have been framed around helping poor customers lower water bills, rather than conservation goals to match water supply and demand. The majority of cases we reviewed are from cities with relatively abundant raw water supplies. These programs have not been tried in LMICs, but might have an important role in places with water scarcity concerns. Programs to replace fixtures are likely to be too expensive, but programs to provide audits, to quickly detect leaks, and perhaps to subsidize fixing those leaks inside a house may be worth exploring in middle-income countries where scarcity is a concern. Without targeting, however, the value of these programs would surely be quickly captured by the nonpoor. Furthermore, programs that provide fixed rebates that can be spent throughout the year (like Singapore's) are more likely to preserve the economic scarcity signal than volumetric discounts or preferential, targeted "lifeline blocks," though this conclusion is based only on economic theory and has not been empirically tested.

Finally, because of historic and continuing progress in connecting urban populations, the water supply and sanitation sector is likely to face more situations where most households are connected but water tariffs need to rise substantially to maintain the network and associated capital assets, and to finance system expansion needs due to population and economic growth. Some "middle-income" customers may find it episodically difficult to pay. These situations are in fact parallel to many small- and medium-sized cities in the USA, and this makes the political economy of tariff reforms different. The main task in these settings should be on how to convince policymakers to transition from implicit (typically capital) subsidies to utilities to explicit political support for cost-reflective tariffs paired with credible, well-evaluated subsidy programs that do better at helping the poor. In the USA, this discussion is manifesting itself through a conversation about creating a federally funded subsidy program for water and sewer like the existing federal program for low-income heating assistance (LIHEAP). The experiences in the USA about maintaining good relationships with customers (managing arrears, forgiveness, subsidies predicated on continuing good faith payments, flexibility) may also become increasingly relevant to the operations of utilities in LMICs.

Acknowledgments This work was supported through a contract with the Millennium Challenge Corporation (MCC), a development agency of the US government. We thank Dennis Jackson (Jacobs Engineering) and Omar Hopkins (MCC), as well as many other MCC staff members, for helpful comments and discussion on an earlier version of this paper. Brandie Banner and Darren Betts provided excellent research assistance. The opinions and conclusions in this paper are the authors' alone and should not be construed to represent the position of MCC or Jacobs Engineering Group, Inc.

Appendix

Region	Country	City	Targeting typology	Type of subsidy	Customer assistance strategy	Subsidy administration	Financing	Peer review?	Status	Notes	Sources
EAP	**Cambodia**	**Phnom Penh**	Means-testing	Type 4	Connection	Utility	n.s.	No	Current as of 2013	Connection subsidy depends on family income – 30, 50, 70, or 100% of connection fee	Berg (2013)
EAP	**China**	**Chongqing**	Demographic targeting	Type 2	Volumetric allowance	Utility	Utility-funded	No	Current as of 2007	Voucher for unemployed families the basic amount of water needed	Warford and Xie (2007)
EAP	**China**	**Macau**	Means-Testing and demographic	Type 4	Volumetric allowance	Utility	State-funded	Yes	Current as of 2019	"Elderly in needs": eligible for those over 55 who are also holders of the beneficiary card issued by the Social Welfare Department. Since 2001. "Water For All" Program (since 2005); first 5 m^3 water free to "people or families receiving subsidies from the Social Welfare Department (IASM) as single-parent families, or for medical assistance or disabilities." Funded by regional government: "To alleviate the impact of high water costs on the community, the	Smets (2008) and Zhong et al. (2008)

										Macao SAR government has been providing users with water subsidies of different levels on a long-term basis. Ever since the latest tariff adjustment entered into force on November 1, 2016, in order to further promote the idea of 'use more, pay more,' the Macao SAR government has been providing low volume domestic water users with a higher proportion of water subsidies to encourage water conservation."	
EAP	**China**	**Zhangjiakou**	n.s.	Type 4	Volumetric allowance	n.s.	n.s.	No	Current as of 2008	Poor households get a free monthly allowance of 5 m^3 of water	Smets (2008)
EAP	**Indonesia**	**Jakarta**	No targeting	Type 4	Connection	Utility	GPOBA	No	Finished in 2006. \$1.5 million benefiting 5000 new users		Ehrhardt et al. (2007, pg. 22)
EAP	**Indonesia**	**Surabaya**	Proxy measures	Type 4	Connection	Utility	GPOBA	No	Current as of 2009	Proposal document, no evaluation available; project started in	World Bank (2007)

(continued)

Region	Country	City	Targeting typology	Type of subsidy	Customer assistance strategy	Subsidy administration	Financing	Peer review?	Status	Notes	Sources
										2009. $4.8 million project benefiting 15,000 new users (77,500 people in total). Three types of subsidy: (1) in-fill, (2) expansion, (3) bulk/master meters; household paid 42% ($33) of connection subsidy; beneficiaries targeted by three eligibility criteria: (1) building size (less than or equal to 60 m^2), (2) road width (less than or equal to 6 m), and (3) formal electricity capacity less than or equal to 1300 VA. These criteria were created based on a survey of 10,000 households based on what would be verifiable and minimize errors of inclusion. Subsidy payment made to utility 3 months after beneficiary gained access	

EAP	**Mongolia**	**Khovd**	Proxy measures	Type 2	Fixed bill	n.s.	n.s.	No	Current as of 2008	Apartment dwellers tariff is capped at 3.7% of their income; "Ger" (nomadic population that lives in tents) tariff is capped at 3.2%	Smets (2008)
EAP	**Philippines**	**Manila**	Geographic Targeting	Type 4	Connection	Utility	GPOBA	No	Current as of 2009	10,642 connections made within the first year; disbursements were delayed due to difficulties verifying water pressure output. Later fixed from pressure maps. If the majority of households are officially certified (in accordance with national government directives for poverty surveys) as "indigent" by the respective Barangay leader, the community is targeted for subsidized connections	Menzies and Suardi (2009)
EAP	**Singapore**		Proxy measures	Type 4	Fixed rebate	Utility	State-funded; Ministry of Finance Singapore	No	Current as of 2019	GST voucher/U-Save Program – households in 1- and 2-room flats receive support equivalent to about 3–4 months of their utilities bills on	Ministry of Finance – Singapore (2017) and Tortajada and Buurman (2017)

(continued)

Region	Country	City	Targeting typology	Type of subsidy	Customer assistance strategy	Subsidy administration	Financing	Peer review?	Status	Notes	Sources
										average. 3- and 4-room flats receive support equivalent to about 1–2 months of their utilities bills. 880,000 Singaporean households received rebates in April 2017	
ECA	**Armenia**	**Yerevan**	No targeting	Type 2	Payment flexibility/financing	Utility	n.s.	No	Finished in 2002	Debt forgiveness. Law required that user water and sanitation accumulated prior to 2000 was forgiven if at least 15–20% of it had been paid; 90% of users took advantage of this scheme and 42,000 new subscribers registered; stabilized financial situations of water and sanitation companies	United Cities and Local Governments (2014)
ECA	**Kazakhstan**		Means-testing	Type 4	Fractional price/bill	n.s.	State-funded; central government	No	Current as of 2003	Government provides compensation for housing and communal services (including water) that exceeds 30% of HH income. In 2001,	OECD (2003, pg 75) and United Nations Centre for Human Settlements (2001)

										28.4% of population considered poor; 7.5% received housing subsidy (Table 4.3 OECD)	
ECA	**Russia**		Means-testing	Type 4	Fractional price/bill	n.s.	State-funded; central government	No	Current as of 2003	Government provides compensation for housing and communal services (including water) that exceeds 22% of HH income. In 2001, 29.1% of population considered poor; 9.1% received housing subsidy (Table 4.3 OECD 2003)	(OECD (2003, pg 75) and United Nations Centre for Human Settlements (2001)
ECA	**Tajikistan**	**Farkhor**	Geographic targeting	Type 4	Connection	Utility	n.s.	No	Current as of 2012	Household connection subsidy in small towns	Jepbarov and Sommer (2012)
ECA	**Ukraine**	**Odessa**	Demographic targeting	Type 2	Fractional price/bill	n.s.	Municipality	Yes	Current as of 2008	Pensioners, people with disabilities, police, military, students, victims of Chernobyl, unemployed, war veterans get 15–100% reduced bill; 60% of those surveyed qualified for some sort of subsidy. Credit to bill	Komives et al. (2005), Smets (2008), and Davis and Whittington (2004)
ECA	**Ukraine**	**Odessa**	Means-testing	Type 4	Fractional price/bill	Central/state government	State-funded; central government	Yes	Current as of 2003	Government provides compensation for public	(OECD (2003 pg 75), Davis and Whittington

(continued)

Region	Country	City	Targeting typology	Type of subsidy	Customer assistance strategy	Subsidy administration	Financing	Peer review?	Status	Notes	Sources
										services (including water) that exceeds 15–20% of HH income. Subsidy is paid on a monthly basis, directly to the utility.; 27.2% of population is poor; 13.03% receive subsidy	(2004) and United Nations Centre for Human Settlements (2001)
LAC	**Argentina**		Means-testing	Type 2	Fractional price/bill	n.s.	State-funded; province-level	No	Current as of 2012	Paper focused on energy; only one sentence on water program. High error of exclusion	Vagliasindi (2012)
LAC	**Bolivia**	**El Alto**	Geographic targeting	Type 4	Connection	Utility	Utility-funded; Aguas del Illimani	No	Current as of 1999	Subsidized interest for connections – usually 12% interest rate, but only 8% in parts of El Alto	Komives (1999)
LAC	**Brazil**	**Manaus**	No targeting	Type 3	Connection	Utility	GPOBA	No	Finished in 2006	$3.3 million USD benefiting 11,000 new users. Briefly mentioned only in footnote	IDA (2006) (Annex 1)
LAC	**Chile**		Means-testing	Type 2	Volumetric allowance	City	State-funded; water companies reimbursed by central government based on water used	Yes	Current as of 2018	Almost universal connection in urban areas, so focus was on affordability of consumption; household applies to municipality via	Gomez-Lobo (2001), Gomez-Lobo and Contreras (2003), Serra (2000), and Contreras et al (2018)

										CAS scoring system (must not have arrears w/ provider); must reapply every 3 years (25–85% of bill up to **15 cubic meters/** month); cost = $33.6 million (lower than previous universal subsidy) in 1998. 450,000 subsidies dispersed; 52% of benefits accrued to lowest 3 income groups, while 23% leak to highest 5 groups; better able to identify poor households than geographic targeting	
LAC	**Colombia**	**Bogotá**	Geographic targeting	Type 2	Fractional price/bill	n.s.	Miscellaneous; subsidy paid for mostly by surcharge on higher income dwellings, and the difference is paid for by transfers from national and provincial budgets	Yes	Current as of 2003	Adopted in 1994; geographic classification of dwellings and cross-subsidies to determine whether client pays surcharge of up to 20% of water and sewage bill (levels 5 or 6, commercial, industrial) or receives a subsidy; households receive subsidy of 50% in level 1, 40% in level 2, up to 15% in level 3; high	Gomez-Lobo and Contreras (2003) and Vargas and Heller (2016)

(continued)

Region	Country	City	Targeting typology	Type of subsidy	Customer assistance strategy	Subsidy administration	Financing	Peer review?	Status	Notes	Sources
										errors of inclusion; 83% of households are included; less expensive than means-tested scheme to administer	
LAC	**Colombia**	**Bogotá**	Means-testing	Type 4	Volumetric allowance	City	Muncipal	Yes	Current as of 2016	6 m^3/ household/ month for social strata 1 & 2 based on SISBEN (national agency). It applies automatically; 38% of customers are program beneficiaries 2012–2014	Vargas and Heller (2016)
LAC	**Colombia**	**Bucaramanga**	Means-testing	Type 4	Volumetric allowance	City	n.s.	Yes	Current as of 2016	6 m^3 per hh per month for those classified in SISBEN, "priority to the public that is supplied through public water foundations or via communal water meters"	Vargas and Heller (2016)
LAC	**Colombia**	**Cali**	Means-testing	Type 4	Volumetric allowance	City	n.s.	Yes	Current as of 2016	6 m^3 per hh free to social strata 1 and 2 in SISBEN	Vargas and Heller (2016)
LAC	**Colombia**	**Medellin**	Means-testing	Type 4	Volumetric allowance	City	Muncipal	Yes	Current as of 2016	2.5 m^3/person/ month for water and sanitation for individuals classified in the SISBEN	Vargas and Heller (2016)

										(run by other government agency). It applies at the request of individuals to City Hall. Average 4% of program beneficiaries 2012–2014	
LAC	**Mexico**	**Aguascalientes**	Geographic targeting	Type 2	Fixed bill or fractional cost (unclear), "slum discount"	n.s.	n.s.	No	Current as of 2008	Reduced tariff for slum areas, with a medium and high tariff in other residential areas	Smets (2008)
LAC	**Mexico**	**Mexico City**	Demographic targeting	Type 2	Fractional price/bill	n.s.	n.s.	No	Current as of 2008	Poor over 60 years old get 50% reduction	Smets (2008)
LAC	**Mexico**	**Aguascalientes**	Demographic targeting	Type 2	Fractional price/bill	n.s.	n.s.	No	Current as of 2008	Retirees, pensioners, disabled, older people, and households in precarious situations get a 50% tariff reduction	Smets (2008)
LAC	**Mexico**	**Puebla**	Demographic targeting	Type 2	Fractional price/bill	n.s.	n.s	No	Current as of 2008	Widows without income and pensioners get a 50% tariff reduction	Smets (2008)
LAC	**Mexico**	**Puebla**	Proxy measures	Type 2	Fractional price/bill	n.s.	n.s.	No	Current as of 2008	Price of water increases with value home	Smets (2008.)
LAC	**Nicaragua**	**Managua**	Geographic targeting	Type 2 or Type 4 (unclear)	Fixed bill or fractional cost (unclear), "slum discount"	n.s.	n.s.	No	Current as of 2005	Special tariff for slum areas	Komives et al. (2005)

(continued)

Region	Country	City	Targeting typology	Type of subsidy	Customer assistance strategy	Subsidy administration	Financing	Peer review?	Status	Notes	Sources
LAC	**Panama**	**Panama City**	Demographic targeting	Type 2	Fractional price/bill	n.s.	n.s.	No	Current as of 2006	Special tariff for those with pensioner discount	Komives et al. (2005)
LAC	**Panama**	**Panama City**	Geographic targeting	Type 2	Fractional price/bill	Utility	n.s.	No	Current as of 2005	Special tariff (20–85% reduction) for slum areas; high error of exclusion	Komives et al. (2005) and Foster et al. (2000)
LAC	**Paraguay**	**Urban Paraguay**	Proxy measures	Type 2	Volumetric allowance	n.s.	n.s.	No	Current as of 2006	Households must meet four out of five of the following conditions: earth floors, mud or wood walls, straw or zinc roofs, no more than two rooms, no internal tap, and no sewerage; –15 cubic meters at subsidized price; scale of this scheme is very small affecting no more than 5000 beneficiaries and costing less than US$0.1 m	Foster and Yepes (2006) and Komives et al. (2005)
LAC	**Uruguay**		Means-testing	Type 4	Fixed rebate	n.s.	n.s.	No	Current as of 2006	Means-tested exemption of fixed charge	Komives et al. (2006)
LAC	**Venezuela**	**Merida**	Geographic targeting	Type 2	Fixed bill or fractional cost (unclear), "slum discount"	n.s.	n.s.	No	Current as of 2005	Special tariff for slum areas	Komives et al. (2005)

MENA	**Egypt**		No targeting	Type 4	Connection	Utility	State revolving fund	No	Current as of 2010	Loan for connection fee to the "poor." Eligibility criteria not indicated	de Albuquerque (2010)
MENA	**Iran**	**Mashhad**	No targeting	Type 3	Fixed rebate	Central/state government	State-funded; deposit into a specially-created bank account	Yes	Current as of 2016	Water previously subsidized, but in 2011 the government started providing cash transfers (average of about $60/ month/ household) to aid poor households in paying for utilities; the free lifeline block was eliminated and water bills soared; after reform, the average price per block increased 110%; overall water consumption decreased by 6% after reform; 95% of low-income residents find water to be unaffordable. Subsidies reach 90% of the population, so not targeted in practice	Attari and Pieter van Dijk (2016)
MENA	**Israel**		Proxy measures	Type 4	Volumetric allowance	n.s.	n.s.	Yes	Current as of 2011	Based on household size; an HH with more than 4 people get 36 m^3 per person per year	Dahan and Nisan (2011)

(continued)

Region	Country	City	Targeting typology	Type of subsidy	Customer assistance strategy	Subsidy administration	Financing	Peer review?	Status	Notes	Sources
										at a lower rate; household must opt in by submitting a form with names, ID numbers, and birth certificates of all household members (requires no economic data); only 8% of households with 4 members are below the poverty line; 18% of households with 6 members are below the poverty line (high errors of inclusion); low direct administration cost; since there is no economic data required, there is less of a stigma associated and therefore a greater take-up of the subsidy	
MENA	**Morocco**		Geographic targeting	Type 4	Connection	Utility	GPOBA		Finished in 2009.	2000 connections the first year of the program (only 15% of 3 year goal). Poorest neighborhoods in urban Morocco are	Jagannathan et al. (2009) and de Beauchêne (2009)

										targeted (160 of most disadvantaged communities). Prepaid by operators and reimbursed by Global Partnership for Output-Based Aid grant for 7 million USD	
MENA	**Morocco**		Type of service	Type 2	Subsidized public taps	n.s.	n.s	No	Current as of 2008	Free "Public Fountains"	Smets (2008)
MENA	**Morocco**		n.s.	Type 4	Volumetric allowance	n.s.	n.s	No	Current as of 2008	40 L/ person/ day for the poor. Prepaid cards	Smets (2008)
MENA	**Palestine**		No targeting	Type 3	Payment flexibility/ financing	n.s.	n.s.	Yes	Current as of 2017	Discounts for early payments; found to be ineffective in getting customers to pay bills on time, though based on expert opinion not causal impact evaluation	Murrar (2017)
MENA	**Turkey**	**Istanbul**	Type of service	Type 2	Subsidized public taps	n.s.	n.s.	No	Current as of 2008	Free "Public Fountains"	Smets (2008)
SA	**Bangladesh**		Proxy measures	Type 2	Fractional price/bill	n.s.	State-funded; local community/government funds 10%	No	Current as of 2009	Hardcore poor households pay 50% of cost. They are defined as those that meet any of the following criteria: (1) landless households, (2) pavement dwellers/ homeless, (3) main earning person or the head of family is day	Lahiri (2009) and Local Government Division – Unit for Policy Implementation (2005)

(continued)

Region	Country	City	Targeting typology	Type of subsidy	Customer assistance strategy	Subsidy administration	Financing	Peer review?	Status	Notes	Sources
										laborer, owning less than 50 decimal of agriculture land or residing in a rented premise lesser than 200 square feet, and, having no fixed source of income, (4) households headed by disabled or females or old aged (65+ years) persons but are excluded if they meet either of the following criteria: (1) the households owning more than 1 acre of land (cultivable and homestead) will be excluded from the list; (2) the households with income level greater than the income corresponding to the "Poverty-line" definition would be excluded from the list	
SA	**India**	**Hubli-Dharwad**	Demographic targeting	Type 4	Connection	Utility	Utility plus grants	Yes	Current as of 2015	Urban poor (as determined by certain castes) get reduced connection	Jayaramu et al. (2015)

										fee. The average net connection fee for the urban poor and others decreased from 2004 to 2013; revenues from connection fees increased; number of connections increased; percent of urban poor covered with piped water supply increased; number of illegal connections decreased from 30% to 3%. Grants and high-income residents (determined by building floor area) and retail pay higher connection fee to fund poor users' reduced connection fee. Bulk cheaper connection for apartment buildings. Low-income residents qualify to pay for free in four installations	
SA	**India**	**Andhra Pradesh**	Geographic targeting	Type 4	Connection	Utility	State-funded; financed by National Slum Development Programme (NSDP)	No	Current as of 2006	50% group connection subsidy (about $115 USD) for those living in one of the 800 slum neighborhoods.	Davis and Tanka (2006), Water and Sanitation Program (2001), and Franceys (2006)

(continued)

Region	Country	City	Targeting typology	Type of subsidy	Customer assistance strategy	Subsidy administration	Financing	Peer review?	Status	Notes	Sources
										57,000 new connections over 3 years. NSDP pays Rs 3500 and the residents pay about Rs 3000 for a connection for 10 people	
SA	**India**	**Kolkata**	Proxy measures	Type 2	Fixed bill	Utility	Municipality	Yes	Current as of 2017	Water rate 15 Rs/month for those paying rent up to 100 Rs; Rs 25 for those paying 100–300 Rs; Rs 40 for those paying above 300 Rs; potentially funded with help from ADB grant now. Previously the municipality paid 1.55 billion Rs in subsidies, which they could not sustain; revenues doubled from 1992–2002, but spending increased fivefold	The Times of India (2003), Majumdar and Gupta (2009), and Asian Development Bank (2013)
SA	**India**	**Hubli-Dharwad**	Geographic targeting	Type 4	Fractional price/bill	n.s.	n.s.	Yes	Current as of 2015	Urban poor living in slums (as declared by government) get 50% discount on water	Jayaramu et al. (2015)
SA	**India**	**Bangalore**	Type of service	Type 2	Subsidized public taps	n.s.	n.s.	No	Current as of 2003	Via public taps. High error of exclusion – 61%; benefit targeting	Pattanayak and Yang (2002) and Prokopy (2002)

										performance (omega) = 2.14; 24% of population (44% of poor and 10% of non-poor) use free public taps	
SA	**Nepal**	**Kathmandu**	Type of service	Type 2	Subsidized public taps	n.s.	Utility	No	Current as of 2005	Via public taps. High errors of exclusion (72%); 50% of poor use taps and 25% of non-poor use taps	Pattanayak and Yang (2002), Prokopy (2002), and Komives (2005)
SSA	**Cameroon**		No targeting	Type 3	Connection	Utility	GPOBA	No	Finished 2014	90% connection subsidy for 40,000 low income households (240,000 persons). Households making a daily income less than $0.40 were targeted. Those in the 2nd and 3rd income quartiles were the main beneficiaries as those in the first quartile were too poor to afford the subsidized connection cost and subsequent water bills. Many consumers were unwilling to connect to the network due to the poor level of service and delays in the expansion of	World Bank (2014)

(continued)

Region	Country	City	Targeting typology	Type of subsidy	Customer assistance strategy	Subsidy administration	Financing	Peer review?	Status	Notes	Sources
										the network. Only 25,254 were executed (of potential 40,000 households), and only 18,854 were verified and eligible for reimbursement to the utility "The project did not set strict socio-economic eligibility criteria at the design stage. A mid-term review after two years of implementation was set to assess beneficiary profiles and consider, if needed, further targeting to the poor." Targeting by service level (e.g., those without a connection)	
SSA	**Côte d'Ivoire**	**Abidjan**	No targeting	Type 3	Connection	Utility	Utility; surcharges on a few hundred industrial customers; program collapsed as industrial customers exited network	No	Finished in 1980's	1980's Policy; poorly targeted connection subsidy; 90% of all connections qualifying for subsidy; drastically increased number of people who have	Komives et al. (2005), Franceys (2006), and Lauria et al. (2005)

										access. Excludes many of the poorest by either (1) requiring that subsidy recipients have tenure to the land that an existing house be located on the property where service is installed or (2) live outside of reach of net-work; they must live within 12 m of a water main	
SSA	**Côte d'Ivoire**	**Abidjan**	Type of service	Type 2	Subsidized public taps	Utility	Multiple funding sources; gov-ernment funds and private utilities provide service	No	Current as of 2005		Komives et al. (2005), Franceys (2006), and Lauria et al. (2005)
SSA	**Ethiopia**	**Addis Ababa**	Type of service	Type 2	Subsidized public taps	Utility	n.s.	No	Current as of 2011	40% of water from community-man-aged, free stand-pipes; third party pump operators often sell water, resulting in none of the subsidy making it to the poor. Their profit is estimated to be 44% of the utilities' revenue	Banerjee and Morella (2011)
SSA	**Kenya**	**Malindi**	Geographic targeting	Type 4	Connection	Utility	n.s.	No	2015	590 household water connections	Mwangi et al. (2015)

(continued)

Region	Country	City	Targeting typology	Type of subsidy	Customer assistance strategy	Subsidy administration	Financing	Peer review?	Status	Notes	Sources
SSA	**Kenya**	**Mombasa**	Geographic targeting	Type 4	Connection	Utility	n.s.	No	2015	570 household water connections	Mwangi et al. (2015)
SSA	**Kenya**	**Nairobi**	Geographic targeting	Type 4	Connection	Utility	GPOBA	No	Project and evaluation in progress	Each compound has about 6–10 dwellings that are connected on a first come, first serve basis; to sign-up for a connection the household paid $18; 2200 households received a metered connection; as of March 2015, 306 customers had paid off their portion of the loan. 50% of cost covered and the rest is repaid in staggered amounts on the monthly bill; household pays connection fee once	Mwangi et al. (2015)
SSA	**Lesotho**	**Maseru**	Type of service	Type 3	Subsidized public taps	n.s.	n.s.	No	Current as of 2011	Prepaid cards via public standpipes. Covers only 16% of population; in some instances, however, independent "operators" sell tokens, at a higher price, at the standpipes	Banerjee and Morella (2011)

SSA	**Madagascar**	**Antananarivo**	Type of service	Type 2	Subsidized public taps	n.s.	n.s.	No	Current as of 2011	Less than half of public standpipes are free (40%)	Banerjee and Morella (2011)
SSA	**Mozambique**	**Mozambique**	Geographic targeting	Type 4	Connection	Utility	Voluntary, charities, donors; supported by WSUP through municipality	Yes	Current as of 2014	Indirect connection subsidy from network extension in two of the poorest neighborhoods, reduced cost for private connections since the main water pipe was closer; 25% of households in Maxaquene A purchased household connections after expansion and 11% of households in Maxaquene B purchased. Households were more likely to make connections if they could finance the fee over several months	Jimenez-Redal et al. (2014)
SSA	**Namibia**	**Windhoek**	Type of service	Type 2	pubsidized Public taps	n.s.	n.s.	No	Current as of 2011	Electronic payment cards and vending machines via public standpipes	Banerjee and Morella (2011)
SSA	**Niger**	**Niamey**	Type of service	Type 2	Subsidized public taps	n.s.	n.s.	No	Current as of 2008	Fountains face lower prices, but this benefits the operators. Study implies savings not passed onto users	Bardasi and Wodon (2008)

(continued)

Region	Country	City	Targeting typology	Type of subsidy	Customer assistance strategy	Subsidy administration	Financing	Peer review?	Status	Notes	Sources
SSA	**Nigeria**	**Cross River**	No targeting	Type 3	Connection	Utility	n.s.	No	Current as of 2009	Only benefits those within 4 m of mains; for those outside of 4 m of main, there is a surcharge which can be up to 7 months of salary	Mason (2009)
SSA	**Nigeria**	**Kaduna**	Type of service	Type 2	Subsidized public taps	n.s.	n.s.	No	Current as of 2011	Through free public standpipes	Banerjee and Morella (2011)
SSA	**Senegal**	**Dakar**	Geographic targeting	Type 4	Connection	Utility	State-funded; private utilities provide service through government funding	No	Current as of 2005	Connections subsidized in low-income neighborhoods; household had to meet criteria of (1) not wealthy; (2) house cannot have connection; (3) must not be a business; (4) connection cannot cross private property; (5) must have title to house/land; (6) must be within 20m for a single house *or* 100 m for at least 4 houses; (6) must pay security deposit of $19; excludes many of the poorest households by requiring that subsidy	Franceys (2006), Komives et al. (2005), Lauria et al. (2005), and Brocklehurst et al. (2004)

										recipients have tenure to the land and that an existing house be located on the property where service is installed	
SSA	**South Africa**	**Johannesburg**	Means-testing	Type 2	Subsidized public taps	Utility	State-funded	No	Current as of 2017	Indigent (income less than 5308 rand/ month) uses indigent register (Expanded Social Package) to target. Electronic payment tokens through public standpipes	Banerjee and Morella (2011) and Singh (2017)
SSA	**South Africa**	**Douglas**	Means-testing	Type 2	Volumetric allowance	City	n.s.	No	Current as of 2002	10 kL free for the poor; "the municipality assesses the poverty status of households every three months using a local committee." p.38	Department of Water Affairs and Forestry (2002)
SSA	**South Africa**	**Rustenburg**	Means-testing	Type 2	Volumetric allowance	n.s.	Multiple funding sources; User charges, grants, and other subsidies	No	Current as of 2009	Incomes less than 800 rand/ month); household must register as indigent; to register as indigent, a household must have proof of monthly income and a South African identity document. They must reapply every one or two years. First tier 100% rebate of	Calfucoy et al. (2009) and Tissington et al. (2008)

(continued)

Region	Country	City	Targeting typology	Type of subsidy	Customer assistance strategy	Subsidy administration	Financing	Peer review?	Status	Notes	Sources
										water bill; second tier 50% rebate of water bill. Did not help majority of eligible individuals that lived in rural areas without metered connections; requirements for registering as indigent excluded households that did not possess those documents; 35,893,000 rand surplus between revenue and expenditure for 2006/ 2007	
SSA	**South Africa**	**Volksrust**	n.s.	Type 2	Volumetric allowance	n.s.	n.s.	No	Current as of 2002	9 kL rebate to poor within fixed monthly charge tariff	Department of Water Affairs and Forestry (2002)
SSA	**South Africa**	**Lichtenburg**	No targeting	Type 3	Volumetric allowance	n.s.	n.s.	No	Current as of 2002	Untargeted volumetric allowance; 5 kL	Department of Water Affairs and Forestry (2002) – Desk Review
SSA	**South Africa**	**Cape Town**	Means-testing	Type 4	Volumetric allowance	City	n.s.	No	Current as of 2015	6 kL of water/ month/household for incomes less than 3000 rand/ month or home valued at less than	City of Cape Town (2015)

										88,000 rand; must have latest municipal account, and ID book, names, & IDs of everyone who lives at the property over 18, proof of income & expenses including wage and/ or pension receipts, and bank statements for 3 months to register; provided via private connection or communal water supply point within 200 m of dwelling	
SSA	**South Africa**	**KwaZulu-Natal**	Means-testing	Type 4	Volumetric allowance	n.s.	n.s.	Yes	Current as of 2007	6 kL of water/ month/household for indigent households; households were certified as indigent based on (1) income less than 1957 rand/ month; (2) house/ land value. If house/land value was less than 30,000 rand, they were automatically granted indigent status by "computer systems" and charged accordingly – these households then	Smith (2010)

(continued)

Region	Country	City	Targeting typology	Type of subsidy	Customer assistance strategy	Subsidy administration	Financing	Peer review?	Status	Notes	Sources
										had restriction devices installed in their homes; if house/land value exceeded that amount, households have to apply for indigent status and agree to reduction of amperage (20 A or less), a water restriction device (12 kL or less/ month), and a signed acknowledgement of debt. Low error of inclusion; free basic water only benefited 6% of nonindigent customers	
SSA	**South Africa**	**Pretoria suburbs**	Means-testing	Type 4	Volumetric allowance	n.s.	State-funded; subsidized by central government	Yes	Current as of 2015	6 kL at a "lower price"	Szabo (2015)
SSA	**Tanzania**	**Dar es Salaam**	No targeting	Type 3	Connection	Utility	n.s.	No	Current as of 2009	"First time connections"; miscellaneous; financed "from those already connected"; mainly reaches middle class	Mason (2009)

SSA	**Tanzania**	**Dar es Salaam**	Type of service	Type 2	Subsidized public taps	n.s.	n.s.	No	Current as of 2009	Only 15% of Tanzanians have private household water connections; 85% of kiosks connected but not operational, 10% partially functional, 5% fully functioning but tend to be in areas with high percentage of connections	Mason (2009)
SSA	**Uganda**	**Kampala**	Geographic targeting	Type 4	Connection	Utility	n.s.	No	Current as of 2009	Eligible households pay 10% of connection fee	Mason (2009)
SSA	**Uganda**	**Kampala**	Type of service	Type 3	Subsidized public taps	Utility	n.s.	No	Current as of 2009	Public standpipes get a social tariff that is 65% of the usual residential tariff	Mason (2009)

References

Anselin L, Lozano-Gracia N, Deichmann U, Lall S (2008) Valuing access to water – a spatial hedonic approach applied to Indian cities. World Bank Development Research Group Working Paper 4533

Aqua Publica Europea (2016) Water affordability: public operators' views and approaches on tackling water poverty

Asian Development Bank (2013) ADB Loan Aids Kolkata's Push for Better, Wider Water, Sewerage Services. Asian Development Bank. Available at: https://www.adb.org/news/adb-loan-aids-kolkatas-push-better-wider-water-sewerage-services

Attari J, Pieter van Dijk M (2016) Reaching the poor in Mashhad City: from subsidising water to providing cash transfers in Iran. Int J Water 10:213

Banerjee SG, Morella E (2011) Africa's water and sanitation infrastructure access, affordability, and alternatives. The World Bank, Washington, DC

Bardasi E, Wodon Q (2008) Who pays the most for water? Alternative providers and service costs in Niger. Econ Bull 9:1–10

Berahzer SI, Hughes J, Riggs E, Burgess M, Leopard K, Kopaskie A, Keefe S, Sospenzo A, Irvin D, Herndon L, Harvell E, Millonzi K, Clements J, Raucher R, Giangola L, Duckworth M, Rubin S, Colton R (2017) Navigating legal pathways to rate-funded customer assistance programs: a guide for water and wastewater utilities. UNC Environmental Finance Center

Berg SV (2013) Best practices in regulating State-owned and municipal water utilities. United Nations Economic Commission for Latin America and the Caribbean (ECLAC)

Berg SV, Mugisha S (2010) Pro-poor water service strategies in developing countries: promoting justice in Uganda's urban project. Water Policy 12(4):589–601

Boland JJ, Whittington D (2000) The political economy of water tariff design in developing countries: increasing block tariffs versus uniform price with rebate. In: Dinar A (ed) The political economy of water pricing reforms. Oxford University Press on behalf of the World Bank, Oxford, pp 105–120

Brocklehurst C, Janssens JG, Brocklehurst C (2004) Innovative contracts, sound relationships: urban water sector reform in Senegal. Water Supply and Sanitation Sector Board discussion paper series No. 1(1):vii, 51, p. 5, boxes, 20 fig., 1 tab. Available at: http://www.ircwash.org/sites/default/files/Brocklehurst-2004-Innovative.pdf

Brown J (2005) Water service subsidies and the poor: a case study of greater nelspruit utility company, Mbombela Municipality, South Africa. Working Paper Series No. 112. Available at: http://ageconsearch.umn.edu/record/30629

Calfucoy P, Cibulka J, Davison J, Hinds T, Park M (2009) Improving free basic water provision in South Africa prepared for the financial and fiscal commission, Republic of South Africa

Chan WW (2016) Rethinking water and energy affordability in Australia: an analysis of the efficiency, effectiveness and equity of current policy. PhD dissertation. Australian National University. Available at: https://openresearch-repository.anu.edu.au/bitstream/1885/108597/1/Chan Thesis 2016.pdf

Chang Y, Fang Z (2017) Efficient, equitable and sustainable energy policy in a small open economy: concepts and assessments. Energy Policy 105:493–501. Available at: https://doi.org/10.1016/j.enpol.2017.03.031

Charles RN (2018) 880,000 households to get U-Save rebate this month. The Strait Times. Available at: https://www.straitstimes.com/singapore/880000-households-to-get-u-save-rebate-this-month

City of Cape Town (2015) Credit control and debt collection policy 2015/16. (Policy Number 21144D)

Coady D, Grosh M, Hoddinott J (2004) Targeting of transfers in developing countries: review of lessons and experience. World Bank, Washington, DC

Contreras D, Gomez-Lobo A, Palma I (2018) Revisiting the distributional impacts of water subsidy policy in Chile: a historical analysis from 1998–2015. Water Policy 20(6):1208–1226

Dahan M, Nisan U (2011) Explaining non-take-up of water subsidy. Water 3(4):1174–1196

Davis J, Tanka S (2006) The Hyderabad metropolitan water supply and sewerage board. Teaching Case Study, MIT Open Course
Davis J, Whittington D (2004) Challenges for water sector reform in transition economies. Water Policy 6:381–395
de Albuquerque C (2010) Report of the independent expert on the issue of human rights obligations related to access to safe drinking water and sanitation – mission to Egypt. United Nations General Assembly
de Beauchene XC (2009) Output-based aid in Morocco (Part 1): extending water services to the poor in urban areas. OBApproaches (25). Available at: https://openknowledge.worldbank.org/handle/10986/10984
Department of Water Affairs and Forestry (2002) Free basic water implementation strategy. Government of South Africa (2)
Devoto F, Duflo E, Dupas P, Parienté W, Pons V, Pariente W, Pons V (2012) Happiness on tap: piped water adoption in urban Morocco. Am Econ J Econ Pol 4:68–99
Ehrhardt D, Groom E, Halpern J, O'Connor S (2007) Economic regulation of urban water and sanitation services: some practical lessons. Water Sector Board Discussion Series
Foster V, Yepes T (2006). Is cost recovery a feasible objective for water and electricity? The Latin American experience. World Bank Policy Research Working Paper (3943)
Foster V, Gomez-Lobo A, Halpern J (2000) Designing direct subsidies for water and sanitation services. Panama: A Case Study. World Bank Policy Research Working Paper 2344
Franceys R (2006) Charging to enter the water shop? Waterlines 24(2):5–7
Fuente D, Gakii Gatua J, Ikiara M, Kabubo-Mariara J, Whittington D, Mwaura M, Whittington D (2016) Water and sanitation service delivery, pricing, and the poor: an empirical estimate of subsidy incidence in Nairobi, Kenya. Water Resour Res 52:4845–4862. Available at: http://doi.wiley.com/10.1002/2015WR018375
Fuente D, Bartram J (2018) Pro-poor governance in water and sanitation service delivery: evidence from global analysis and assessment of sanitation and drinking water surveys. Perspect Public Health, 175791391878810. https://doi.org/10.1177/1757913918788109
Gomez-Lobo A (2001) Incentive-based subsidies: designing output-based subsidies for water consumption. World Bank Public Policy for the Private Sector, Washington, DC
Gomez-Lobo A, Contreras D (2003) Water subsidy policies: a comparison of Chilean and Colombian schemes. World Bank Econ Rev 17(3):391–407
Haynes KE, Krmenec A, Georgianna TD, Whittington D, Echelberger WF Jr (1984) Planning for water capacity expansion. J Am Plan Assoc 50(3):359–364
Heymans C, Eales K, Franceys R (2014) The limits and possibilities of prepaid water in urban Africa: lessons from the field. The World Bank, Washington, DC
International Development Association (IDA) (2006) A review of the use of output-based aid approaches. IDA 14, October 2006. At http://siteresources.worldbank.org/IDA/Resources/Seminar%20PDFs/73449-1164920192653/IDANETOBA.pdf
Ito K (2014) Do consumers respond to marginal or average price? Evidence from nonlinear electricity pricing. Am Econ Rev 104(2):537–563
Jagannathan NV, Mohamed AS, Kremer A (2009) Water in the Arab world: management perspectives and innovation. The World Bank Middle East and North Africa Region
Jayaramu KP, Devadiga A, Kumar BM (2015) Connecting the last mile: water access policy in action. Waterlines 34(2):156–173. Available at: http://www.developmentbookshelf.com/doi/10.3362/1756-3488.2015.015
Jepbarov S, Sommer Y (2012) Additional financing municipal infrastructure development project. Project Information Document
Jimenez-Redal R, Parker A, Jeffrey P (2014) Factors influencing the uptake of household water connections in peri-urban Maputo, Mozambique. Util Policy 28:22–27
Komives K (1999) Early lessons from Bolivia. World Bank Policy Working Paper

Komives K (2003) Infrastructure, property values, and housing choice: an application of property value models in the developing country context. PhD dissertation. University of North Carolina at Chapel Hill. Department of City and Regional Planning. Chapel Hill, NC, USA
Komives K, Foster V, Halpern J, Wodon Q (2005) Water, electricity, and the poor: who benefits from utility subsidies? The World Bank, Washington, DC
Komives K, Halpern J, Foster V, Wodon Q (2006) The distributional incidence of residential water and electricity subsidies. World Bank Policy Research Working Paper 3878
Lahiri AK (2009) For the urban sector and water supply and sanitation in Bangladesh: an exploratory evaluation of the programs of ADB and other aid agencies. Asian Development Bank: Independent Evaluation Department
Lauria DT, Hopkins OS, Debomy S (2005) Pro-poor subsidies for water connections in West Africa. Water Supply & Sanitation Working Notes 3
Local Government Division – Unit for Policy Implementation (2005) Pro poor strategy for water and sanitation sector. Ministry of Local Government, Rural Development & Cooperatives Government of People's Republic of Bangladesh
Majumdar C, Gupta G (2009) Willingness to pay and municipal water pricing in transition: a case study. J Integr Environ Sci 6(4):247–260
Mason N (2009) Access for the poor and excluded: tariffs and subsidies for urban water supply. WaterAid Discussion Paper
Menzies I, Suardi M (2009) Output-based aid in the Philippines: improved access to water services for poor households in Metro Manila. OBApproaches (28)
Ministry of Finance – Singapore (2017) 880,000 HDB households to receive GST voucher – U-save rebate in April 2017 [online]. Available at: http://www.mof.gov.sg/news-reader/articleid/1807/parentId/59/year/2017. Accessed 27 Nov 2017
Murrar A (2017) The water invoices and customers payment motivational strategies: an empirical study on Palestinian water service providers. Int J Econ Bus Rev 5(1)
Mwangi P, Otiego L, Ndakorerwa C (2015) Innovation in scaling up access to water and sanitation services in Kenya. Water and Sanitation Program of the World Bank
OECD (ed) (2003) Improving water management: recent OECD experience. IWA, Paris
OfWat (UK Office of Water) (2016) Vulnerability focus report. Prepared by London Economics
Oxford Business Group (2012) The report: Peru 2012. Oxford Business Group
Pattanayak S, Yang J-C (2002) Distributional incidence of water tariffs and subsidies in Kathmandu, Nepal. RTI International, Durham
Prokopy L (2002) Distributional incidence of current and potential water tariffs and subsidies in Bangalore, India. Unpublished paper, energy and infrastructure department, South Asia region, World Bank, Washington, DC
Ruiters G (2007) Contradictions in municipal services in contemporary South Africa: disciplinary commodification and self-disconnections. Crit Soc Policy 27(4):487–508
Serra P (2000) Subsidies in Chilean public utilities. World Bank Policy Research Working Paper
Singh K (2017) Free water limited to the indigent – city of Johannesburg [online]. Available at: https://www.news24.com/SouthAfrica/News/free-water-limited-to-the-indigent-city-of-johannesburg-20170704. Accessed 24 Nov 2017
Smets H (2008) De L'Eau Potable A Un Prix Abordable. Academie de l'Eau
Smith JA (2010) How much water is enough? Domestic metered water consumption and free basic water volumes: the case of Eastwood, Pietermaritzburg. Water SA 36(5):595–606
Szabo A (2015) The value of free water: analyzing South Africa's free basic water policy. Econometrica 83(5):1913–1961
The Hindu (2003) Public taps not to be shut down for now [online]. Available at: http://www.thehindu.com/thehindu/2003/05/11/stories/2003051106860300.htm. Accessed 22 Nov 2017
The Times of India (2003) LF okays 50% withdrawals of water subsidy. The Times of India, January 29
Tissington K, Dettmann M, Langford M, Conteh S (2008) Water services fault lines: an assessment of South Africa's water and sanitation provision across 15 municipalities. Centre for Applied

Legal Studies in Johannesburg, the Centre on Housing Rights and Evictions in Geneva, & the Norwegian Centre for Human Rights at the University of Oslo. Retrieved April 15 (2008): 2009
Tortajada C, Buurman J (2017) Water policy in Singapore. Global-is-Asian: 1–8. Available at: http://global-is-asian.nus.edu.sg/index.php/water-policy-singapore/
United Cities and Local Governments (ed) (2014) Basic services for all in an urbanizing world. Revised. Routledge Press
United Nations Centre for Human Settlements (2001) Part III: changes in housing finance and shelter delivery systems. In: Cities in a globalizing world: global report on human settlements 2001, p 91
US EPA (2016) Drinking water and wastewater utility customer assistance programs
Vagliasindi M (2012) Implementing energy subsidy reforms: evidence from developing countries. The World Bank, Washington, DC
Vargas L, Heller L (2016) Determinants in implementing a public policy for an essential volume of free water in Bogotá and Medellín, Colombia. Ciencia & Saude Coletiva 21(3):719–730
Warford J, Xie J (2007) Water supply pricing in China: economic efficiency, environment, and social affordability. World Bank Analytical and Advisory Assistance (AAA)
WAREG (2017) Affordability in European Water Systems. European Water Regulators
Water and Sanitation Program (2001) Tariffs and subsidies in the urban water and sanitation sector. In: Graham-Harrison K (ed) Urban think tank. Write Media
Wichman CJ (2014) Perceived price in residential water demand: evidence from a natural experiment. J Econ Behav Organ 107:1–16
World Bank (2007) GPOBA commitment paper: expanding piped water supply to Surabaya's urban poor. World Bank
World Bank (2014) Implementation completion and results report for the Cameroon water lease — OBA for coverage expansion. World Bank Report
World Bank (2016) Turning Pipe Dreams into Reality: Maximizing the Impact of Sanitation and Water Pipe Infrastructure through Connection Subsidies and Life Skills Training [online]. Available at: http://www.worldbank.org/en/programs/sief-trust-fund/brief/turning-pipe-dreams-into-reality. Accessed 28 Nov 2017
Zhong L, Mol APJ, Fu T (2008) Public-private partnerships in China's urban water sector. Environ Manag 41(6):863–877

Chapter 18
Entrepreneurship and the Economic Geography of Intergenerational Mobility in US Cities

Haifeng Qian

Abstract Recent research on the geography of intergenerational economic mobility shows that young people born in some US cities demonstrate greater probability of moving up along the income ladder than those born in others. Cities with a higher level of economic mobility benefit from being perceived as "lands of opportunity" and accordingly attract young people and families with kids. In this research, we examine factors that predict regional variations in intergenerational mobility. In particular, we are interested in whether entrepreneurship is associated with economic mobility in US cities. We use the business startup rate as a measure of entrepreneurship, analyze its relationship with three proxies for intergenerational mobility, and control for other regional factors based on the literature. Our regression analysis shows a positive and significant association between entrepreneurship and upward mobility. Implications for intergenerational mobility in cities are discussed.

Keywords Economic development · Entrepreneurship · Intergenerational mobility · New firm formation

18.1 Introduction

The research by Chetty et al. (2014) on the geography of intergenerational economic mobility shows that young people born in some US cities have greater probability of moving up along the income ladder relative to their parents than those born in others. Cities with a higher level of economic mobility benefit from being perceived as the "land of opportunity" (Chetty et al. 2014, p.1553) and are accordingly attractive to young people and families with kids. Policymakers at the subnational level therefore have interests in improving the upward mobility potential of their places. To

H. Qian (✉)
The University of Iowa, Iowa City, IA, USA
e-mail: haifeng-qian@uiowa.edu

Z. Chen et al. (eds.), *Development Studies in Regional Science*,
New Frontiers in Regional Science: Asian Perspectives 42,
https://doi.org/10.1007/978-981-15-1435-7_18

understand how they can achieve it requires research studies on the regional factors predicting intergenerational mobility, which is the focus of this study.

To our best knowledge, the relationship between entrepreneurship and intergenerational mobility has not been studied by scholars, but the former appears to be a relevant factor that may predict the latter. The importance of entrepreneurship to regional economic development has been well documented in the literature. Entrepreneurship or new firm formation contributes to job creation, innovation, and better allocation of market resources (Acs et al. 2009; Audretsch et al. 2015; Fritsch and Noseleit 2013; Haltiwanger et al. 2013; Kirzner 1997; Qian and Acs 2013; Qian and Jung 2017), all further leading to economic development. As economic development improves the living standards for all, entrepreneurship is often assumed to play a role in poverty reduction (Alvarez and Barney 2014). Nevertheless, it is unclear whether entrepreneurship is associated with relative mobility when all boats are lifted by the rising tide.

In this chapter, we investigate the associations between entrepreneurship (measured by business startup rates) and intergenerational mobility in US cities. We use the intergenerational mobility measures from Chetty et al. (2014). They gauge children's family income status given their parents' income. Our interests are in metropolitan areas, which are economically functional urban areas (Audretsch et al. 2015; Qian et al. 2013) and home to more than 93% of business establishments in the United States (Plummer and Headd 2008). To accommodate Chetty et al.'s (2014) geographic focus on commuting zones (CZs), which are also economically functional regions but include all urban and rural counties, we use the sample of CZs that are overlapped with the principal cities of metropolitan statistical areas (MSAs) for empirical analysis. Our multivariate regression analysis reports a positive and significant association between entrepreneurship and each of the three measures of intergenerational mobility.

The chapter is organized as follows. Next, we discuss the possible relationships between entrepreneurship and intergenerational mobility, as well as the geographic scales at which these relationships matter. In the third section, we present data, variables, and methods, followed by quantitative results in Sect. 18.4. The last section concludes.

18.2 Theories: Entrepreneurship and Intergenerational Mobility

18.2.1 Entrepreneurship and Upward Mobility

A large body of empirical evidence shows that entrepreneurship supports socioeconomic mobility of entrepreneurs and their children. For instance, using micro data from the US Panel Study of Income Dynamics and the Survey of Consumer Finance,

Quadrini (1999, 2000) finds that entrepreneurs achieve greater upward mobility through higher savings that over time help accumulate more wealth. Using the US National Longitudinal Survey of Youth data, Fairlie (2005) reports higher earnings of self-employed young men from disadvantaged families than wage workers for the same population group. Additionally, Gandelman and Robano (2014) use household survey data and find that entrepreneurship can be a channel for immigrant families to improve child social mobility, measured by educational attainment, in Uruguay.

Besides direct benefits to entrepreneurs and their immediate family members, entrepreneurship may contribute to social mobility through indirect spillover effects. There are several potential mechanisms. First, self-made successful entrepreneurs are role models for low-income individuals or families in the same area (Laney et al. 2013; Scott et al. 2012). A high density of entrepreneurs therefore creates a more encouraging environment for low-income families to work hard and get out of poverty. Second, startups are widely recognized as the primary driving force of job creation (Haltiwanger et al. 2013). The startup rates are also disproportionally high in some high technology industries (Qian 2016), creating not only jobs but better-paid jobs. The new and/or high-quality jobs from new firm formation bring career opportunities to low-income families, helping them move up along the socioeconomic ladder, especially for those well-educated children of low-income parents. Third, the wealth and income directly or indirectly created from entrepreneurship expand tax revenues (Toder 2017) that can be used for public education, health, and infrastructure. These public services provide the poor with basic needs and flexibility for career development. Fourth, entrepreneurship scholars have argued that, beyond wealth creation, entrepreneurship can lead to broad social, cultural, and institutional changes that lead to emancipation and inclusive growth (McMullen 2011; Rindova et al. 2009). This lifts the boats for everyone in the society.

It should be noted that entrepreneurship may also negatively impact intergenerational mobility because of the importance of wealth and family background in the venturing process. Initial capital for startups is heavily dependent on personal or family savings (63.9%) and personal credit cards (10.3%) of entrepreneurs according to the 2016 Annual Survey of Entrepreneurs (Robb and Morelix 2016). Moreover, members or children from wealthy families have no urgency for immediate income and therefore may be more patient and risk-taking (Desai et al. 2013). Lastly, wealthy families' social networks may help gain access to financial and nonfinancial resources that are needed for startups (Belitski and Desai 2018). As a result of all of these, individuals from wealthy families are expected to have higher possibilities to start businesses and further succeed, resulting in less upward mobility. Hurst and Lusardi (2004) report that, above the 95 percentile of wealth distribution, family wealth is positively related to propensity to become entrepreneurs.

Although entrepreneurship can impact intergenerational mobility both positively and negatively, the multiple direct and indirect benefits reviewed above appear to support a positive overall relationship between them. This hypothesis will be tested in the empirical part of this chapter.

18.2.2 Geographic Dimensions

It is worth discussing the geographic dimensions of entrepreneurship and intergenerational mobility. Although startups may have a national or even international market for their products/services, the benefits of entrepreneurship are largely regional, which motivate state and local policymakers to pursue entrepreneurship policy (Fritsch and Storey 2014).

The four positive spillover effects of entrepreneurship on intergenerational mobility discussed above, i.e., role models, job opportunities, tax bases, and broader societal impacts, may matter at different geographic scales. The role model effect is strong at the neighborhood level. As Laney et al. (2013) put, "exposure to examples of ownership in your own immediate reality is imperative to fostering entrepreneurship—you have to see it to believe it" (p.13). The job opportunity effect is taken at the regional labor market level. The labor market boundary can be best defined by commuting-to-work ties; that is, any resident can travel to the job centers in the same region within a reasonable amount of time. In the US context, examples of regional labor markets include commuting zones and metropolitan statistical areas, which will be discussed in detail in the following "Methodology" section. The tax base effect can occur at different geographic levels – local, state, and federal – given the tax federalism in the United States. The social benefits in terms of public education can be largely local due to the way it is publicly financed. Lastly, the broader societal impacts are most likely at the national level.

In a broader context beyond the focus on intergenerational mobility, geographic studies of entrepreneurship are often conducted at the level of a functional region in which the economy is relatively independent and internally integrated in terms of trade, labor market, and information/knowledge spillovers (Qian et al. 2013). Startups rely on consumers, employees, and knowledge that are largely regional in nature. The regional approach adopted by Chetty et al. (2014) is also used in this study.

18.3 Methodology

18.3.1 Geographic Units

We rely heavily on data from Chetty et al. (2014) who use 1990 commuting zones (CZs) for their analysis, which are functional regions consisting of a group of economically connected adjacent counties. For geographic units, MSAs represent economically functional urban areas (Qian et al. 2013) and are widely used in urban economic analysis. Different from MSAs, CZs cover all US counties and some CZs include rural counties that are excluded from MSAs. We use the overlap between CZs and MSAs, and our final sample covers all 1990 CZs that include at least one MSA principal city identified in the 1993 MSA definition. The final sample size is 259, representing 35% of all 741 CZs but covering 88% of the US population in 2000.

18.3.2 Dependent Variables

The dependent variables are indicators for intergenerational mobility at the CZ level ("CZ" hereafter is interchangeably used with "city"). We use the three preferred measures of intergenerational mobility in Chetty et al. (2014), i.e., relative mobility, absolute upward mobility (simplified as absolute mobility hereafter), and the American Dream Index. Relative mobility is measured by the regression coefficient from regressing children's income ranks on their parents' income ranks based on the 1980–1982 birth cohorts. A higher value of relative mobility, therefore, shows that children's income ranks are more in line with their parents' income ranks, signifying lower intergenerational mobility in the city. Absolute mobility is "the mean rank (in the national child income distribution) of children whose parents are at the 25th percentile of the national parent income distribution" (Chetty et al. 2014, p.1562), also based on the 1980–1982 birth cohorts. A higher value represents a higher level of upward mobility in the city. Lastly, the American Dream Index measures the probability that children with parents belonging to the bottom quintile of the national parent income distribution move to the top quintile of the national child income distribution based on the 1980–1985 birth cohorts. Similar to absolute mobility, a higher value of American Dream indicates better upward mobility in the city. For time periods, children's family income is the average value between 2011 and 2012, and parents' income is the average value between 1996 and 2000. Details of these three measures can be found in Chetty et al. (2014).

18.3.3 Primary Explanatory Variable

In this research, we use entrepreneurship as the primarily explanatory variable for intergenerational mobility. Entrepreneurship is measured by business startup rates. More specifically, we divide the number of new single-unit establishments by the total population in a CZ. We did not consider multiunit establishments, as they are mostly new branches of existing businesses. Consistent with the control variable, the year of the data is 2000. We have also tried a 1999–2001 3-year average as a robustness check and the results are similar. New establishment data are obtained from the US Census Bureau's Business Information Tracking Series (BITS).

18.3.4 Control Variables

Chetty et al. (2014) identify five regional factors that are highly associated with intergenerational mobility in CZs: segregation, income inequality, K-12 education, social capital, and single-parent households. Accordingly, we include all these factors as control variables. For segregation, we separately use two measures, racial

Table 18.1 Variables, measures, and data sources

Variable	Measures	Data sources
Relative mobility	"Relative mobility (rank-rank slope) for core sample (1980–1982 birth cohorts) and baseline income definitions"	Chetty et al. (2014)
Absolute mobility	"Absolute upward mobility for core sample (1980–1982 birth cohorts) and baseline income definitions"	Chetty et al. (2014)
American Dream	"Probability child has family income in top quintile of national child income distribution conditional on having parents with family income in bottom quintile of national parent income distribution using 1980–1985 cohorts"	Chetty et al. (2014)
Entrepreneurship	Number of new single-unit establishments per capita (2000)	BITS; Census
Racial segregation	"Multi-group Theil Index calculated at the census-tract level over four groups: White alone, Black alone, Hispanic, and Other" (2000)	Chetty et al. (2014)
Income segregation	"Rank-Order index estimated at the census-tract level" (2000). For details see Chetty et al. (2014) Appendix D.	Chetty et al. (2014)
Income inequality	"Gini coefficient minus top 1% income share" (2000)	Chetty et al. (2014)
K-12 education	"Average expenditures per student in public schools" (1996–1997 school year)	Chetty et al. (2014)
Social capital	"Standardized index combining measures of voter turnout rates, the fraction of people who return their census forms, and measures of participation in community organizations" (1990)	Chetty et al. (2014)
Single-parent households	"Number of single female households with children divided by total number of households with children" (2000)	Chetty et al. (2014)
Household income	"Aggregate household income in the 2000 census divided by the number of people aged 16–64" (logged)	Chetty et al. (2014)
Population size	Population 2000 (logged)	Census

Descriptions of measures with quote marks are quoted directly from the preferred measures table and online data Table 9 of Chetty et al. (2014), available from https://opportunityinsights.org/data/

segregation and income segregation. In addition, we also control for CZs' average household income and population size.

The descriptions of all variables and their measures are shown in Table 18.1. Descriptive statistics of all variables are presented in Table 18.2.

18.3.5 Methods

We run regression analysis to examine how well entrepreneurship predicts intergenerational mobility. In addition, we also use correlation analysis and scatterplots to show preliminary relationships between them.

Table 18.2 Descriptive statistics

Variable	Obs.	Mean	Std. Dev.	Min	Max
Relative mobility	259	0.3398	0.0503	0.1834	0.4375
Absolute mobility	259	41.6621	3.7811	33.7473	54.5628
American Dream	259	0.0787	0.0278	0.0276	0.1867
Entrepreneurship	259	0.0019	0.0004	0.0011	0.0033
Racial segregation	259	0.1885	0.0877	0.0253	0.4742
Income segregation	259	0.0724	0.0275	0.0237	0.1379
Income inequality	259	0.3173	0.0553	0.1748	0.4471
K-12 education	257	5.9971	1.0370	4.0855	9.9488
Social capital	257	−0.2153	1.0112	−2.6873	2.5506
Single-parent households	259	0.2188	0.0388	0.0949	0.3678
Household income	259	10.4829	0.1534	9.9229	10.9309
Population size	259	13.1898	0.9657	11.2719	16.6124

Table 18.3 Correlation matrix

	Relative mobility	Absolute mobility	American dream	Entrepreneurship
Relative mobility	1			
Absolute mobility	−0.6592***	1		
American Dream	−0.7027***	0.9348***	1	
Entrepreneurship	−0.3974***	0.0428	0.1448*	1

$*p < 0.05$, $**p < 0.01$, $***p < 0.001$

18.4 Results

18.4.1 Correlation Analysis

Table 18.3 shows correlation coefficients between entrepreneurship and the three measures of intergenerational mobility. The correlation coefficient between entrepreneurship and relative mobility is −0.40, which is highly significantly at 0.001 level. Remember that the negative sign indicates a positive relationship between entrepreneurship and upward mobility. In addition, the correlation between entrepreneurship and American Dream is positive and significant at the 0.05 level. The correlation coefficient between entrepreneurship and absolute mobility, despite a positive sign, is not significant at the 0.05 level. Overall, we find that entrepreneurship is positively related to upward mobility.

Figures 18.1, 18.2, and 18.3 presents scatterplots between entrepreneurship and each of three measures of intergenerational mobility. The linearly fitted curve between entrepreneurship and relative mobility is clearly downward-sloping, while the two curves for absolute mobility and American Dream are slightly upward-sloping. They scatterplots (unsurprisingly) show similar patterns with the correlation table.

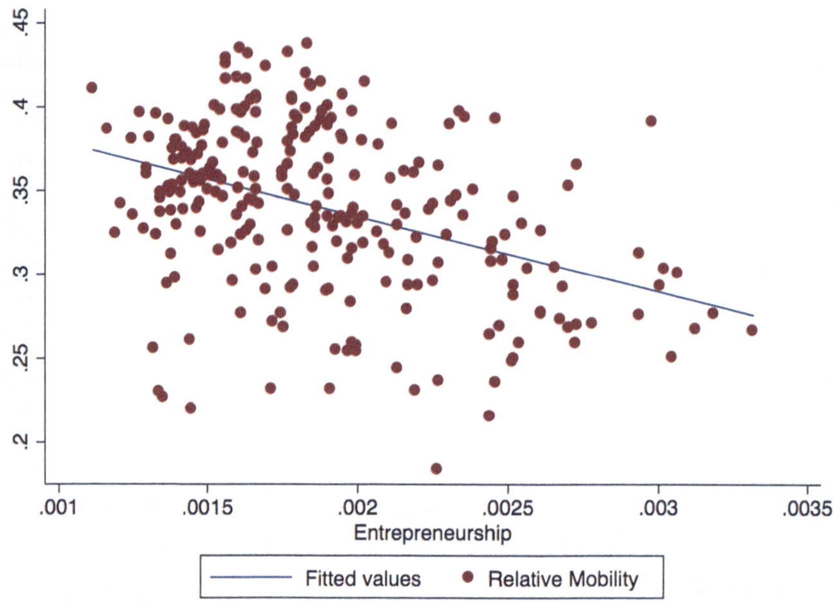

Fig. 18.1 Scatterplot – relative mobility vs. entrepreneurship
Note: A high value of "relative mobility" means a lower chance of moving upward

18.4.2 Regression Results

Table 18.4 shows the OLS regression results using the three measures of intergenerational mobility separately as the dependent variable. We also separately put racial segregation and income segregation into the regressions, therefore leading to six columns of results. Following Chetty et al. (2014), we report standard beta coefficients, which are interpreted through changes in standard deviations of independent and dependent variables.

As the key variable of our focus, entrepreneurship is consistently found to be a positive and significant predictor of upward mobility across all models. When relative mobility is the dependent variable, the negative coefficient of entrepreneurship is highly significant at the 0.001 level. Again, because relative mobility represents the inverse of upward mobility, the negative sign actually indicates a positive relationship between entrepreneurship and upward mobility, a finding consistent with other columns where absolute mobility or American Dream is used as the dependent variable. The coefficient of entrepreneurship is significant at least at the 0.01 level across all models, providing robust evidence.

Based on our sample of CZs that are overlapped with the core part of MSAs, regression results from the five factors highlighted in Chetty et al. (2014) – segregation, income inequality, K-12 education, social capital, and single-parent

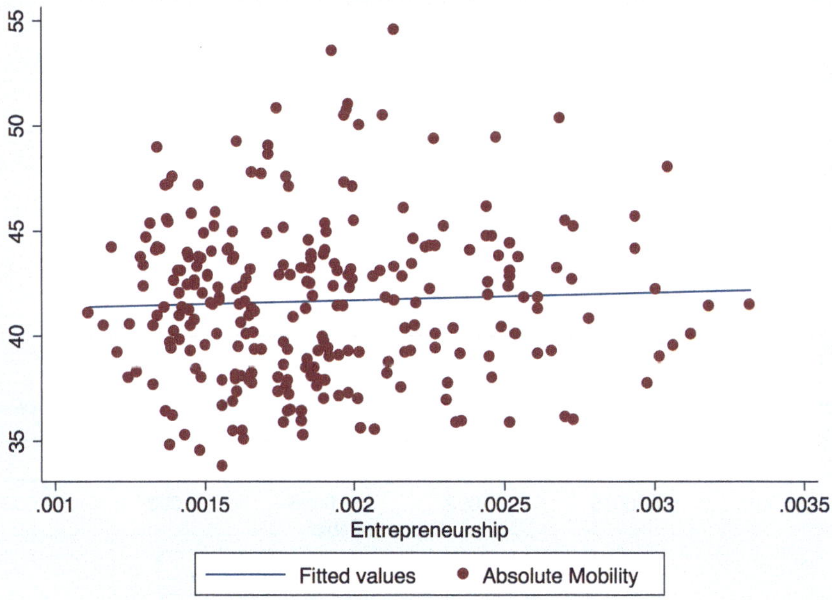

Fig. 18.2 Scatterplot – absolute mobility vs. entrepreneurship

households – are largely consistent with findings from Chetty et al.'s multivariate analysis that uses all CZs and does not consider entrepreneurship.[1] When other competing factors are controlled for, racial segregation is a significant factor only when relative mobility is used as the dependent variable. The positive sign indicates that a higher level of racial segregation in the city predicts a lower level of upward mobility, which is not surprising. Income segregation is not significantly associated with any of the three mobility measures. Neither is income inequality significant in any of the regressions, consistent with Chetty et al. (2014) in their multivariate context. Social capital presents conflicting significant results, similar to Chetty et al. (2014) as well, as it is positively associated with both relative mobility and absolute mobility. Among Chetty et al.'s five factors, the most consistent results across all regression models come from K-12 education and single-parent households. K-12 education is found to be a significant and positive predictor of upward mobility. As the most powerful explanatory variable, the fraction of single-parent households exhibits a significant and negative relationship with upward mobility.

[1]Chetty et al. (2014) used different measures of segregation (short commuting fraction) and K-12 education (high school drop-off rate) in their multivariate regressions. We use racial/income segregation and K-12 public spending instead because of greater interests from planners and policymakers.

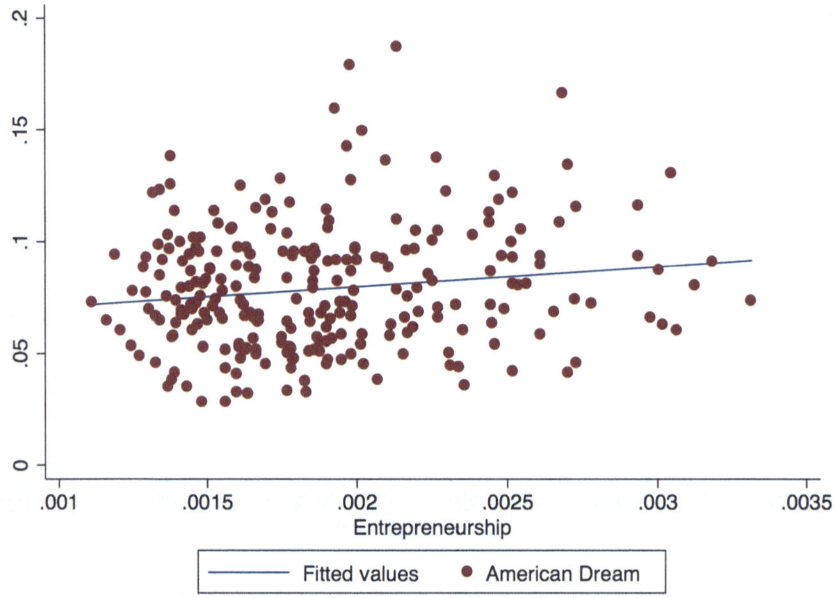

Fig. 18.3 Scatterplot – American Dream vs. entrepreneurship

Among other control variables, wealthier cities show less upward mobility, as supported by the significant coefficients of average household income across all models. City size exhibits no significant relationship with intergenerational mobility in five of the six models.

18.5 Summary and Discussion

Since the seminal work of Chetty et al. (2014), the geography of intergenerational upward mobility has attracted lots of attention. Cities ranked low in upward mobility have started to take actions, such as Charlotte (NPR News 2018). To better address this problem, it is important to understand local or regional factors that may be associated with intergenerational mobility.

This research focuses on the association between the entrepreneurial environment and upward mobility. Our empirical analysis based on urban CZs reports entrepreneurship or startup activity as a positive and significant predictor of upward mobility across different measures of the latter. While the economic impacts of entrepreneurship in terms of job creation, innovation, and productivity growth have been widely studied in the literature, we find another potential benefit of entrepreneurship, i.e., its possible positive contribution to intergenerational

Table 18.4 Regression results

	(1)	(2)	(3)	(4)	(5)	(6)
	Relative mobility	Relative mobility	Absolute mobility	Absolute mobility	American Dream	American Dream
Entrepreneurship	−0.390***	−0.466***	0.177**	0.160**	0.199**	0.212***
	[−6.42]	[−8.52]	[3.08]	[3.14]	[3.11]	[3.72]
Racial segregation	0.215**		0.023		−0.035	
	[3.15]		[0.36]		[−0.49]	
Income segregation		−0.113		0.05		0.016
		[−1.78]		[0.84]		[0.24]
Income inequality	0.086	0.168	−0.076	−0.075	−0.051	−0.064
	[0.97]	[1.92]	[−0.90]	[−0.91]	[−0.55]	[−0.70]
K-12 education	−0.131**	−0.159**	0.148**	0.149**	0.124*	0.128*
	[−2.63]	[−3.15]	[3.15]	[3.19]	[2.35]	[2.44]
Social capital	0.206**	0.284***	0.243***	0.240***	0.089	0.077
	[2.92]	[4.07]	[3.64]	[3.70]	[1.20]	[1.06]
Single-parent households	0.510***	0.593***	−0.568***	−0.570***	−0.585***	−0.598***
	[7.75]	[9.16]	[−9.14]	[−9.47]	[−8.43]	[−8.86]
Household income	0.248**	0.322***	−0.347***	−0.341***	−0.243**	−0.255**
	[3.22]	[4.30]	[−4.77]	[−4.91]	[−2.99]	[−3.27]
Population size	−0.142*	0.036	−0.035	−0.056	−0.036	−0.063
	[−1.99]	[0.47]	[−0.52]	[−0.79]	[−0.47]	[−0.79]
Observations	255	255	255	255	255	255
Adjusted R^2	0.557	0.545	0.605	0.606	0.506	0.506

Standardized beta coefficients; t statistics in brackets
$*p < 0.05$, $**p < 0.01$, $***p < 0.001$

upward mobility. Therefore, cities could benefit socially from their efforts to build a strong entrepreneurial ecosystem or facilitate startup activity.

It should be noted that our analysis reveals only associations, but not causalities, between entrepreneurship and intergenerational mobility because of the cross-sectional nature of this study. As Chetty et al. (2014) point out, unfortunately, the data allow for measuring upward mobility only for one generation at this point. Therefore, we are cautious in recommending entrepreneurship as a policy solution. Policymakers will benefit from future research that tackles the causal relationship between the two.

It should also be noted that the relationship between entrepreneurship and intergenerational mobility may not be the same with findings in this chapter when empirical analysis is conducted for other countries. For instance, Japan is quite different from the United States in terms of both entrepreneurial culture and family intergenerational connections. It would be interesting to see findings of future research on this topic in the Asian context.

Acknowledgment The author would like to thank Sameeksha Desai for her help in framing this chapter and recommending relevant literature.

References

Acs Z, Braunerhjelm P, Audretsch D, Carlsson B (2009) The knowledge spillover theory of entrepreneurship. Small Bus Econ 32:15–30

Alvarez S, Barney J (2014) Entrepreneurial opportunities and poverty alleviation. Entrep Theory Pract 38(1):159–184

Audretsch D, Belitski M, Desai S (2015) Entrepreneurship and economic development in cities. Ann Reg Sci 55(1):33–60

Belitski M, Desai S (2018) Does small business reduce poverty? Evidence from post-Soviet cities. working paper

Chetty R, Hendren N, Kline P, Saez E (2014) Where is the land of opportunity? The geography of intergenerational mobility in the United States. Q J Econ 129(4):1553–1623

Desai S, Acs Z, Weitzel U (2013) A model of destructive entrepreneurship. J Confl Resolut 57 (1):20–40

Fairlie R (2005) Entrepreneurship and earnings among young adults from disadvantaged families. Small Bus Econ 25(3):223–236

Fritsch M, Noseleit F (2013) Investigating the anatomy of the employment effect of new business formation. Camb J Econ 37:349–377

Fritsch M, Storey D (2014) Entrepreneurship in a regional context: historical roots, recent developments, and future challenges. Reg Stud 48(6):939–954

Gandelman N, Robano V (2014) Intergenerational mobility and entrepreneurship in Uruguay. Lat Am J Econ 51(2):195–226

Haltiwanger J, Jarmin R, Miranda J (2013) Who creates jobs? Small versus large versus young. Rev Econ Stat 95(2):347–361

Hurst E, Lusardi A (2004) Liquidity constraints, household wealth, and entrepreneurship. J Polit Econ 112(2):319–347

Kirzner IM (1997) Entrepreneurial discovery and the competitive market process: an Austrian approach. J Econ Lit 35(1):60–85

Laney K, Bowles J, Hilliard T (2013) Launching low-income entrepreneurs. Center for an Urban Future, New York

McMullen J (2011) Delineating the domain of development entrepreneurship: a market-based approach to facilitating inclusive growth. J Bus Ventur 35(1):185–193

NPR News (2018) The American dream is harder to find in some neighborhoods. October 1. Available from: https://www.npr.org/2018/10/01/649701669/the-american-dream-is-harder-to-find-in-some-neighborhoods

Plummer LA, Headd B (2008) Rural and urban establishment births and deaths using the US Census Bureau's business information tracking series. US Small Business Administration Office of Advocacy Working Paper

Qian H (2016) Sectoral variations in startup activity. Paper presented at the North American annual meetings of the regional science association international. Minneapolis, MN, November 9–12, 2016

Qian H, Acs Z (2013) An absorptive capacity theory of knowledge spillover entrepreneurship. Small Bus Econ 40(2):185–197

Qian H, Jung H (2017) Solving the knowledge filter puzzle: absorptive capacity, entrepreneurship and regional development. Small Bus Econ 48(1):99–114

Qian H, Acs Z, Stough R (2013) Regional systems of entrepreneurship: the nexus of human capital, knowledge and new firm formation. J Econ Geogr 13(4):559–587

Quadrini V (1999) The importance of entrepreneurship for wealth concentration and mobility. Rev Income Wealth 45(1):1–19

Quadrini V (2000) Entrepreneurship, saving, and social mobility. Rev Econ Dyn 3(1):1–40

Rindova V, Barry D, Ketchen D (2009) Entrepreneurship as emancipation. Acad Manag Rev 34 (3):477–491

Robb A, Morelix A (2016) Startup financing trends by race: how access to capital impacts profitability. Available at SSRN 2859893

Scott L, Dolan C, Johnstone-Louis M, Sugden K, Wu M (2012) Enterprise and inequality: a study of Avon in South Africa. Entrep Theory Pract 36(3):543–568

Toder E (2017) Taxing entrepreneurial income. Urban-Brookings Tax Policy Center, Washington, DC

Chapter 19
The Rise of the Knowledge Economy in the Megalopolis

T. R. Lakshmanan and William P. Anderson

Abstract This chapter described the evolution of the *Megalopolis*, the region of continuous urban development that stretches along the US East Coast from Boston Metropolitan Region in the North to the Washington DC Metropolitan Region in the South and includes New York, Baltimore, and Philadelphia. Economic dynamism in the Megalopolis over recent decades has been propelled in part by new transport and communication systems which have facilitated the emergence of global economy and the arrival of dynamic new knowledge in the form of physical and institutional technologies in the manufacturing and service economies. The chapter reviews the literature on transition to knowledge economy, explores trends in the entire Megalopolis Region, and provides additional detail on the Boston region's evolutionary shift to the knowledge-intensive service economy. Finally, the chapter implements the Spence and Hlatshwayo (The evolving structure of the American economy and the employment challenge. Working paper, Council on Foreign Relations, Maurice R. Greenberg Center for Geoeconomic Studies, 2011) approach to study the evolution of tradable and non-tradable sectors and the progress of income distribution for one Megalopolis metro area, namely, Boston. In its conclusion, the chapter attributes the rise of knowledge economy in the Megalopolis to three kinds of *proximity* among economic agents: physical, relational, and institutional.

Keywords Income distribution · Knowledge economy · Megalopolis · Non-tradable sectors · Services

---

T. R. Lakshmanan
Boston University, Boston, MA, USA
e-mail: laksh@bu.edu

W. P. Anderson (✉)
Cross-Border Institute, University of Windsor, Windsor, ON, Canada
e-mail: bander@uwindsor.ca

Z. Chen et al. (eds.), *Development Studies in Regional Science*,
New Frontiers in Regional Science: Asian Perspectives 42,
https://doi.org/10.1007/978-981-15-1435-7_19

19.1 Introduction and Overview

This chapter describes *the nature and scope of the economic structural evolution* toward a knowledge economy in the *Megalopolis*, which is the dynamic settlement corridor stretching from Boston to Washington, D.C., in the USA.

The Megalopolis, as christened by Jean Gottman, stretches between the Boston Metropolitan Region in the north and the Washington Metropolitan Region in the south and includes some of the country's oldest areas of industrialization and of urbanization. It had become the densest mega-urban region in the USA by the mid-twentieth century. In the quarter century following 1950, the metropolitan regions of the Megalopolis experienced industrial restructuring and decline as industrial enterprises began migrating to other regions in the USA and abroad. However, over the past 40–50 years, there has been a remarkable reversal of regional economic decline. There has occurred indeed a notable economic resurgence in the various metropolitan areas of the Megalopolis. A variety of knowledge-intensive production and service sector enterprises have arrived and continue to grow in the metro areas that comprise the Megalopolis. These revived metropolises represent today large concentrations of high-quality human, cultural, and organizational capital and some vibrant contemporary "knowledge metropolises" (Lakshmanan et al. 2016).

This chapter will argue that this economic dynamism in the Megalopolis over recent decades has been propelled in part by new transport and communication systems which have facilitated the emergence of global economy and the arrival of dynamic new knowledge in the form of physical and institutional technologies in the manufacturing and service economies.

The recent decades of *globalization* have yielded an explosive expansion of cross-country economic interactions, division of labor, complex webs of production chains, a globally distributed production system, and the emergence of corporate central organizational service functions (financial, legal, accounting, and other business and professional services) that support business operation. There is thus a twofold shift to a "knowledge economy," comprising of *first* a relative shift away from production that is dependent on material resources, physical capital, and low skill labor to one which increasingly exploits knowledge and knowledge workers as key ingredients of competitiveness and innovation and, *second, the emergence of* knowledge-intensive business services, which promote a growing shielding of manufacturing products in a "service sheath," which exploit the economies of scale in human capital and which promote knowledge dissemination and productivity effects in other parts of the economy. Thus economic evolutionary effects in the Megalopolis over recent decades are *joint consequences* of changes in transport systems, the emergence of global economy, and the onset of dynamic new knowledge in the form of physical and institutional technologies in the manufacturing and service economies.

Part II describes how the historically modally organized transport system in the Megalopolis has transformed itself into a *multivalent and multimodal transport system*, which in turn unleashes various economic mechanisms and processes underlying the broader economic consequences of transport investments over time.

Part III highlights an analysis of urban development patterns in the I-95 Corridor over six decades and suggests *urban decline and resurgence.* This evolution ranges from the dense and compact *industrial era spatial pattern* (pre-1950s—manufacturing production and working class households concentrated in dense cities) to the *Decentralized Spread City* (1950s to the early 1980s) in an increasingly affluent economy, to the contemporary (post-1985) *trends toward agglomeration and metropolitan clustering of* "knowledge economy" *activities* along the metropolitan regions in the Megalopolis.

Part IV offers a brief survey of (a) the reinvention of major metro areas in the Megalopolis as knowledge economies. Such economic transformation processes are highlighted in terms of (1) current theoretical formulations of the rise of the "knowledge production economy" and (2) the contributions that the growing knowledge-intensive business services make in the form of positive knowledge and productivity spillovers to other industries in the broader economy. The scale and scope of the growth and evolution of such knowledge-intensive production sectors over recent decades in the Megalopolis and its component five large metro areas are presented. Next, the vibrant growth and evolution of knowledge-intensive business sectors and their functioning as knowledge, innovation, and expertise transfer agents in the Megalopolis are highlighted.

Part V highlights the rising income inequalities in the various metropolitan associated with the advent of the new knowledge economy.

Part VI concludes the chapter.[1]

19.2 Transport Networks in the Megalopolis: Their Evolution and Economic Contributions

19.2.1 Network Evolution

Over the last four to five decades, the highways, railroads, waterways, ports, and the aviation system in the Megalopolis have evolved from those serving the dense city-based transport networks of the immediate post-World War industrial era to the contemporary nationally integrated multimodal transport network enabling seamless transportation, serving a nationally integrated production system and more recently a globally distributed, increasingly knowledge-intensive production economy.

This transformation of the transport system in recent decades has been driven by *three* key transport *technological* innovations—*Interstate Highway System, containers, and jet aircraft—and two organizational reforms, pertaining to economic*

[1]Many of the issues addressed in this chapter are considered in more expanded form in Lakshmanan et al. (2016).

governance of transport, physical flows and border controls. The Interstate Highway System vastly enhanced interurban and intraurban mobility and led to steep drops in regional and national passenger and freight travel times and costs. Containers, first introduced in 1966 in the Megalopolis by US shipping lines on the North Atlantic routes, have greatly enhanced shipping efficiency and rapidly grown and spread worldwide, facilitating intermodal transport of freight. The technical evolution of jet aircraft and the aviation sector has led to sharp drops in travel times and air freight prices and to growing volumes of high value-added goods being shipped by air domestically and globally. The institutional innovations in the form of deregulation and privatization of transport have enabled a broad range of transport service and process innovations and logistical improvements. The reform of rules governing transport physical flows (e.g., vehicle size/wt. rules, reinvented inspection processes) has not only enlarged transport capacities on routes and terminals and logistical potential but has stimulated new "service opportunities," which are critical to the operation of a globalized economy (Lakshmanan et al. 2009).

19.2.2 Transport Improvements and Economic Evolution

As transport infrastructure and service improvements lower costs and increase accessibility to various market actors—input suppliers, labor, and customers—market expansion, increased integration, and mutually sustaining economic growth will ensue. The underlying economic mechanisms are:

1. *Gains from trade:* As transport improvements expand markets for firms, there is an increasing specialization and trade, a surge in productivity, and "Smithian" growth. Export expansion will lead to higher levels of output and efficiencies, and increasing imports lower local prices. Firms enjoy a broader labor pool, lower local prices, and improved land and other factor markets, thereby promoting a highly integrated national economy and over time a globalized economy.
2. *Technology diffusion:* Associated with the growth of interregional and cross-country trade, there has been an upsurge in intra-industry trade and the exchange of intermediate goods. Opportunities for adopting new technical knowledge associated with imports, as well the potential for knowledge and technology growth through "learning by doing" and "learning by using."
3. *Gains from agglomerations made possible by transport*: Some urban agglomerations enjoy *increasing returns* in the form of dynamic location advantages, enabling innovation and dynamic competitiveness of these cities. The three broad modeling approaches which try to capture these advantages are:

   (a) *Economic Geography and Location Economics Models*: e.g., Marshall's (1890) focus on agglomeration economies—(a) *input sharing* among firms, (b) *matching* in metro areas of workers' skills and requirements of employers, and (c) *knowledge spillovers or learning* in these dense locations, with workers being the primary vehicles of these transfers—such ideas are further elaborated by Hoover (1948) and Isard (1956) and later by Haynes and Shibusawa (2005).

(b) *New Economic Geography Model*: Krugman (1991) applied a general equilibrium modeling framework to the geography of the economy under conditions of increasing returns to scale and labor mobility, reinterpreting the findings of Marshall on agglomerations. In the resulting "new economic geography" (NEG) model, spatial concentration and dispersion emerge. The NEG model, however, accounts for only pecuniary economies, makes no mention of either human capital or technological spillovers, and has no answers for the contemporary knowledge creation process and innovation-led growth in urban agglomerations.

(c) Innovation-Led Urban Centers: This class of models views the increasing returns associated with regional agglomerations as dynamic location advantages attributable to:

   (i) Physical proximity among economic actors, promoting interactions and access to appropriation and sharing of tacit knowledge, thus promoting innovation
   (ii) Relational proximity of economic agents, facilitating cooperative behavior, collective learning, and socialization of innovation risk
   (iii) Institutional proximity among the firms in the urban agglomeration in terms of shared rules, codes, and norms of behavior which will promote cooperation in interactive learning processes
   (iv) Lowering of adaptive costs among firms competing in an environment of rapid pace of change of knowledge infrastructures

As has been noted widely, a major consequence of such innovations in both transport and ICT infrastructures has been the economic structural change of globalization of the USA and the Megalopolis economies, namely, the ability to decompose and organize production into many value-adding components, many of which are fabricated in a variety of locations around the world.

While growth deriving from interregional and international trade is most associated with freight transportation, the effects of agglomeration and innovation are also driven by public transportation, including passenger rail within megaregions. Results from sophisticated empirical models indicate that this is especially true for the Megalopolis, as Chen and Haynes (2015) find that the economic contribution of public transit including passenger rail infrastructure tends to be much stronger at the US northeast metro level than the national level of analysis.

19.3 Demographic and Economic Evolution of the Megalopolis

The Megalopolis has witnessed a growth of urban population (approximately 75%) and of urbanized area (a 300% increase)—thereby dropping urban density and reflecting the growth of suburbs and exurbs. In the three decades, 1972–2002, the five major metro areas in the Megalopolis had a modest growth in population (Fig. 19.1). But this period actually comprised two different subperiods. The first half (1972–1987) was more or less a stationary period for the four metro areas and one of even population decline (Fig. 19.1). However, the manufacturing employment performance of this region relative to the nation drops sharply since 1990, indicating sharper regional decline of the manufacturing sector. The earnings shares in the manufacturing sector of the Megalopolis stay higher than the employment shares in the entire period (and more so in the last two decades). In the last two decades, the earnings per manufacturing worker in the Megalopolis are higher, suggesting a higher proportion of high value-adding sectors—deriving from the arrival of more knowledge-intensive sectors in the region.

The Megalopolis shares of national total (non-farm) earnings have dropped in the 1970–1990 period but have since held steady, reflecting the faster growth in the knowledge-intensive service sectors. However, the Megalopolis shares of total non-farm earnings remains high—5% higher than population shares in 2010, suggesting that earnings per employee are higher in the region than in the nation.

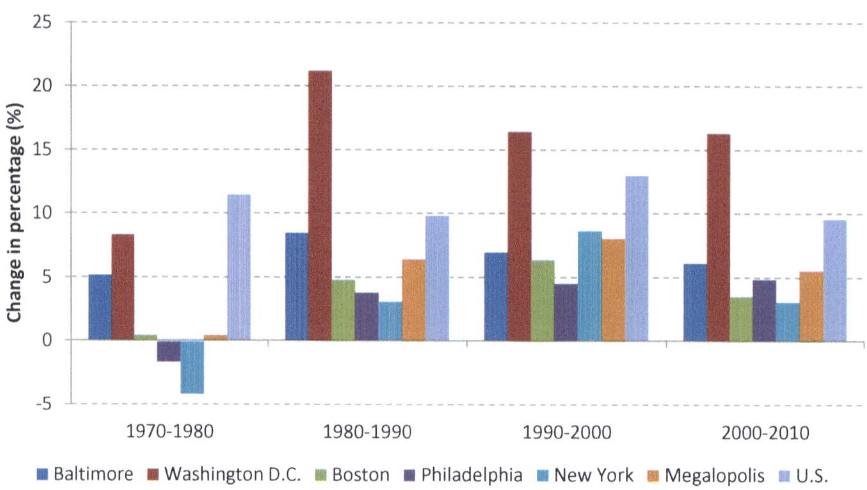

Fig. 19.1 Population growth in Megalopolis metro areas. (Source: Lakshmanan et al. 2016)

19.4 The Transition to Knowledge Economies in the Megalopolis

The major metropolitan areas in the Megalopolis have experienced in the recent past economic decline, as their manufacturing sectors lost their competitive edge in the two decades after World War II. They had to confront the malaise of postindustrial society, unraveling the complexities and dead ends of economic decline.

Yet some of these same urban regions in the Megalopolis have, in the last quarter century, reinvented themselves as hubs of creativity and development, creating jobs utilizing knowledge in technical, economic, social, and cultural fields.[2] These are the "creative regions" or the "knowledge economies." The old industrial metros of Boston and New York are well advanced in this transition to knowledge economies, and Washington, D.C. (with a large public sector), is emerging as a vibrant creative region with economic sectors based on scientific, technical, and cultural knowledge.

How did these metro areas make this transition from a trajectory of decline to "creative regions"? To make such a transition successful, key economic, political, and social actors in the metropolitan region have had to unravel the complexity of change. Such actors should be able to engage in shifting mindsets, changing behavior of various urban agents, evolving and sustaining innovation, and maintaining the dynamics of change. This is a tall order of evolutionary change in the creation of a "creative region." What sorts of processes are at play, and how do they interact in the birth of a "knowledge economy" and its continuing evolution?

Such questions have predictably attracted theoretical interest from a broad range of disciplines: economic geography, business economics, innovation studies, growth theory, evolutionary economics, and urban studies. Two theoretical streams of inquiry on "creative regions" have emerged:

- Models of Nurture and Commercialization of Innovation and Regional Industrial Adaptation
- Evolutionary Processes towards a Knowledge-Intensive Service Economy

This chapter can only highlight the key concepts and the evolutionary processes emphasized in these two classes of models of the rise of knowledge-intensive production and services, in order to set the stage for an empirical review of the economic resurgence of the Megalopolis metros. Further, the empirical part of the analysis is largely limited in this chapter to the Boston metro region, supplemented by some tabular data with reference to other Megalopolis metropolitan areas.

[2]Other examples of such creative regions or knowledge economies are Bay Area and Silicon Valley, Los Angeles, Seattle, London, Tokyo, Milan, Sydney, etc.

19.4.1 The Rise and Evolution of Knowledge-Intensive Production

Most of the literature on the emergence of knowledge-intensive production focuses largely on what may be described as innovation networks which nurture and commercialize innovation and industrial adaptation in various regions (Bathelt 2001; Scott 1998; Best 2000; Cooke et al. 2011). The key idea in this vast literature that has burgeoned over the last two decades or more is that innovation or the creation and commercialization of new knowledge in a dynamic region is based on *multidimensional interactions* among autonomous but interdependent economic agents (Capello 2011).

Such models of innovation-led agglomerations attribute knowledge generation, spillovers, and accumulation in "creative regions" to:

1. *Physical proximity* among economic actors, facilitating interactions and enabling access to appropriation and sharing of tacit knowledge, thus promoting innovation
2. *Relational Proximity* of economic agents, facilitating cooperative behavior, collective learning, and socialization of innovation risk
3. *Institutional Proximity* among the firms in the urban agglomeration in terms of shared rules, codes, and norms of behavior which will promote cooperation in interactive learning processes

These linkages and interactions allow firms and other economic agents to complement their core competencies with requisite knowledge and capacities creatively, speedily, and flexibly. Such linkages are really "embedded in the social network."[3] Firms (often small- and medium-sized) in such regions develop flexible and interdependent relationships with suppliers and competitors and increasingly depend on intangibles, like know-how, synergies, and untraded knowledge (Von Hippel 1988; Storper 1995).

Further, dynamic metro regions also exhibit, from *political and institutional perspectives*, the attributes of "learning systems," such as entrepreneurial ability and relational skills. Such attributes of learning systems reflect the cultures of local entrepreneurial social, economic, and political agents, stimulating them to innovate *institutionally and organizationally* (Lakshmanan and Button 2009). Further, the creation of new "governance systems" in metro regions (e.g., inclusive stakeholder policy decision and implementation processes as in Boston) facilitates, among metropolitan private, public, and civil society actors, new modes of interaction,

[3]Indeed, even the ("autonomous") market relations emphasized by the neoclassical economists' world are socially embedded in the sense that they depend upon assumptions, norms, and institutions shared by the actors and do not themselves derive from economic decisions (Polyanyi 1944; Granovetter 1985). The recent interest in social capital as key supporting asset of productivity has been inspired by the spatial clustering and dynamism in places such as Italy's Emilia-Romagna and California's Santa Clara Region.

decision-making, and implementation of projects and programs. Such governance changes speed up the physical adaptation of the metro region—in the form of rapid generation of new urban infrastructures and land uses appropriate to a knowledge region (Chatterjee and Lakshmanan 2005; Lakshmanan and Chatterjee 2006).

19.4.2 The Rise and Evolution of Knowledge-Intensive Production in Boston Metro Region

Boston, with its near four-century run of impressive innovations—technological, human capital, social, institutional, and financial capital—has a long history of economic growth, decline, resilience, and reinvention at various times.

The two key determinants of the recent upsurge of Boston region as a vibrant knowledge-intensive economy are:

A. *The large and diverse stocks of Human Capital*, derived from its early and continuing large investments on education and public schools[4] and in higher education. This higher education sector is a large regional economic contributor and provides a basis for large stocks of regional human capital in fields as diverse as professional, scientific, technical, computer, legal, financial, and health services.[5]

Table 19.1 sheds light on the high levels of human capital in Boston region. The proportion of knowledge workers in the Boston region's 2011 labor force (as measured by persons over 25 with a Bachelor's degree or higher) is 43.1%—51% higher than the national average and is higher than in other Megalopolis major metros—all of which, in turn, outrank the nation in this measure.

The proportion of labor force in Management in Business, Science and Arts is another measure of knowledge workers (in occupational terms) and is presented in Table 19.1. By this measure also, Boston, Washington, D.C., and other Megalopolis metros evidence richer stocks of human capital.

B. *Tradition of Diverse Innovation Networks*

There has been a tradition of *innovation networks and knowledge creation* in *New England*: This tradition was to set up venues where information about work

[4]Since the nineteenth century, Boston has led globally in its proportion of literate population. Boston created the first school (Latin School in 1635) and the first college (Harvard College in 1636 with a large dose of public funds). Indeed, the states in New England achieved in mid- to late nineteenth century highest levels of education anywhere in the world—followed by Meiji Japan, Scandinavia, Holland, and Prussia.

[5]The scores of colleges and eight major universities in Boston function as major economic engine, enrolling in 2000 over 120,000 students, conducting over $1.5 billion of external research, and reporting total revenues of $5.8 billion.

Table 19.1 Educational attainment and occupation by class of worker in Megalopolis in 2011 (%)

		New York	Philadelphia	Boston	D.C.	Baltimore	Megalopolis	USA
Educational attainment (aged 25 or above)	Less than high school	15.2	11.3	9.4	11.1	11.1	12.7	14.1
	High school graduate	26.5	31.1	24.5	28.3	26.6	27.1	28.4
	Some college/associate	22	24.7	23	27.3	26.6	23.8	29
	Bachelor's degree or higher	36.3	32.9	43.1	33.4	35.8	36.4	28.5
Occupational classes of workers	Management, business, science, arts	39.6	40.9	46.4	50.7	44.6	41.4	36
	Service	19.7	16.9	16.3	16.2	16.1	18.1	18.3
	Sales and office	24.7	25.4	22.9	20.8	23.8	24.1	24.5
	Natural resources, construction, maintenance	6.9	7.3	6.4	6.8	7.5	7.3	9.1
	Production, transportation, material moving	9	9.6	8	5.5	8	9.2	12.1

Source: 2011 American Community Survey, US Census Bureau

techniques can be exchanged among farm workers[6] in the eighteenth century. In the nineteenth century, various firms (e.g., Pratt and Whitney, Browne and Sharpe) created fellowships and networks of skilled machinists, who visited one another, engaged in technical talks and demonstrations (Temin 1999). Such networks and variations thereof have been a potent force in creating and disseminating knowledge-generating high-technology networks in contemporary Boston region, particularly in the generation and commercialization of biotechnology, with the multiplicity of requisite skills—scientific, clinical, manufacturing, legal, financial, legal, sales, regulatory, distribution, etc.—and or to some degree in other creative Megalopolis.

The initial boom in high-technology industries in the Boston region was punctured in the late 1980s by the decline of the minicomputer industry and the falloff in military research budgets. High-technology industries in the Boston region have been, however, able to readjust and rejuvenate their product and process structures in order to sustain further innovation and growth, through *a network model of complementary, vertically disintegrated, open system firms* (Bathelt 1999; Best 2000). Further, Boston's revitalization is based on its technological diversification rather than in an existing trajectory (Best 2000), given its rich and diverse human capital and its dynamic labor markets.[7]

The biotech industry, based on genetic engineering technology, comprises small- and medium-sized research firms and recently multinational pharmaceutical firms, in an ambience of close interactions among small and large firms, university researchers, and public research centers.

The majority of the studies of resurgent regions such as Boston often limit themselves to a discussion of the performance of mostly fabrication sectors, such as military electronics, microcomputer industry, electronic components, instruments, and the biotechnology industry (Bathelt 2001), ignoring the larger knowledge-intensive services.

19.4.3 Evolutionary Shift to the Knowledge-Intensive Service Economy

In the USA where the transition to the service economy is advanced, the share of service employment has progressed from a little over 50% in 1950 to over 75% by year 2000.This long-term evolution toward a service economy—if observed over a century—reflects the drop of consumption on low-income elasticity *goods* (food and

[6]In Connecticut, Massachusetts, and New Hampshire, farmers often shared knowledge about farming techniques and household practices in Unitarian and other churches after Sunday Service in the eighteenth and nineteenth centuries.

[7]Heurmann (2009) suggests that human capital externalities accrue predominantly to growing firms, which benefit from sharing, matching, and learning externalities arising from a large supply of highly qualified workers in skilled labor markets.

clothing—from 75% to 21% of total consumption expenditures) and growing expenditure shares of high-income elastic *services* (health and education) from 3.2% to 42% of total consumption.

A less observed characteristic, over the past two to three decades of the US transition to a service economy, is that the share in the economy of business services has grown monotonically, as the share of the manufacturing sector has been dropping. The share of knowledge-intensive services and products in total output and demand in the USA has steadily increased over time. This "quarternization" of the economies not only points toward the rising shares of services but also stresses the role of knowledge-intensive services and their growing importance as sources of innovation and technology and as inputs into the manufacturing process (Kox and Rubalcaba 2007) and the growing encapsulation of manufacturing products in a "service jacket" (Bryson and Daniels 2007).

This continuing growth of business services reflects a qualitatively new stage in the structure of production and an increasingly complex division of labor between economic sectors (Kox and Rubalcaba 2007). The structure of inter-industry relations is being recast in a new way by the growth and increasing specialization in knowledge-intensive business services (KIBS). KIBS, which include computer and software services, have lowered costs of outsourcing in-house services in firms. A major characteristic of this structural change is that firm-level positive scale economies can occur with regard to knowledge and skill inputs by external deliveries of such inputs. Many knowledge-intensive and nonroutine services in a manufacturing or service enterprise become eligible to outsourcing to independent service firms. Professional specialization in the latter firms can lead to innovations and changes, even in the nature of the service product and potentially toward further innovations.

The argument here is that in recent decades business services (particularly KIBS) have contributed heavily to the US and Megalopolis economic growth, in terms of employment, productivity, and innovation. A direct growth contribution stems from the business services sector's own remarkably fast growth, while an indirect growth contribution was caused by positive knowledge and productivity spillovers from business services to other industries. The spillovers come in three forms: from original innovations, from speeding up knowledge diffusion, and from the reduction of human capital indivisibilities at firm level. The external supply of knowledge and skill inputs exploits positive external scale economies and reduces the role of internal (firm-level)-scale (dis)economies associated with these inputs.

Further, the KIBS sector includes the major corporate central organizational services, such as financial, legal, accounting, and many professional services. Such services permit corporations with headquarters in New York or Boston to coordinate their various value-adding production chains spread across the globe. Thus KIBS sectors play a crucial role in the operation of the global economy and in the American economic structural evolution.

This brief review of the development of knowledge-intensive business services and their role in the generation and evolution of knowledge-intensive components of the US service economy supplements the review (in the earlier section) of various

Table 19.2 Knowledge intensive services, 1997 and 2007

	1997		2007	
	Number of employees (%[a])	Average wage (2007 US dollars)	Number of employees (%[a])	Average wage (2007 US dollars)
New York	381,722 (4.06)	70,141	478,409 (4.37)	82,363
Philadelphia	137,730 (4.50)	66,167	142,742 (4.11)	71,689
Boston	106,292 (3.78)	74,977	163,071 (4.60)	87,860
D.C.	241,800 (7.85)	69,414	374,383 (9.73)	84,319
Baltimore	49,021 (3.41)	57,911	80,521 (4.75)	76,012
Megalopolis	1,091,625 (4.15)	67,921	1,441,850 (4.73)	80,641
USA	4,092,136 (2.65)	57,436	5,696,838 (3.17)	64,675

[a]% of total regional/national employees in the specified sector

models which attempt to explain the rise and evolution of knowledge-intensive production sectors.

The levels of employment and average wages in KIBS sectors in 1995 and 2005 in the nation, Megalopolis, and its five major metros are presented in Table 19.2. While the Megalopolis had 17% of the national employment in 1997 and 2005, it was overrepresented in employment in those years in the knowledge-intensive KIBS sectors, garnering, respectively, 26.7% and 25.3% of the national totals (Table 19.2). Further, the average wages/worker are higher in the Megalopolis and component metros in 1997—with this gap widening in 2007. As noted earlier, these KIBS sectors support the arrival and evolution of knowledge-intensive service economy—by positive knowledge and productivity spillovers to other industries through original innovations and the speedup of knowledge diffusion.

The knowledge-intensive services in the Boston region are financial services, professional services, health-care services, and educational services.

The financial services sector is a large sector that is growing in the region, utilizing highly skilled personnel and offering high wages. New York is a globally dominant region with over 420,800 workers (13% of the national total) with an average wage of $168,800, an average annual wage growth rate of 7.7% in 2004 (Table 19.3). The Boston metro area has the fourth largest employment, the third highest average wage, and the second highest wage growth rate (1990–2004) among US metros in the financial sector in 2004. In Massachusetts, this sector accounts for 10.8% of the gross state product, 5.5% of employment, and 65% of the workers with a postsecondary degree and has a significant multiplier effect on professional and technical services. The annual growth rate of average wage in this sector over a 15-year period in Boston was 7.83, with other Megalopolis metros not far behind. The magnitude and importance of the financial services sector in the Boston region are not surprising given its past history of merchant and industrial capital in earlier times and the region's many *financial innovations* over time (e.g., merchant banking, marine insurance, "Suffolk Bank" notes, venture capital, trust

Table 19.3 Financial services—Megalopolis metropolitan areas by employment, 2004

Metropolitan area (national rank in employment)	Total employment	Share of national employment	CAGR of employment 1990–2004	Average wages	CAGR of average wages 1990–2004
New York-Northern New Jersey-Long Island **(1)**	427,296	13.0	0.44	$168,802	7.66
Boston-Cambridge-Quincy **(4)**	**133,342**	**4.0**	**3.48**	**$114,696**	**7.83**
Philadelphia-Camden-Wilmington **(5)**	113,112	3.4	2.21	$73,158	6.12
Hartford-West Hartford-East Hartford **(9)**	65,219	2.0	1.38	$86,851	6.52
Washington, D.C. **(12)**	58,098	1.8	1.99	$76,880	5.64

The expanded review of the Boston's recent economic evolution in this chapter suggests a robust economic recovery and export capacity across a broad range of knowledge-intensive goods and services. The five key determinants of the Boston region's reinvention as a vibrant knowledge economy are (1) large and diverse human capital, (2) open innovation networks, (3) local entrepreneurship, (4) financial innovations, and (5) innovative models of urban governance to facilitate rapid urban spatial reinvention

bank, mutual funds, etc.).[8] The Megalopolis metro areas of Philadelphia, Hartford, and Washington, D.C., draw respectively, 5th, 9th, and 12th national ranks in employment levels in this sector.

The health services sector is a larger sector in the Boston region, about 2.5 times as large as the financial sector in employment. Table 19.4 offers an employment comparison of the Megalopolis metro areas in 2004. With many major university hospitals and research institutes, Boston region is not only the fifth largest national employer but has registered a 4% annual rate of growth over a recent 15-year period. The elite hospitals and public research institutes in this region also provide a key component of the biotechnology innovation networks.

Higher education plays a major role in the Boston region than in most others. In 2000, Boston metro ranked first in college and university enrollment and first in degrees granted and in per capita spending, per 100,000 people. The eight universities in the metro area, attracting research funds, partnering with firms, generating patents, starting companies, and training large numbers of students are major regional economic contributors.

[8]The "Suffolk system" was developed in Boston by the Suffolk Bank before the Civil War (by the investors who founded the textile industry). This bank issued its own notes which were redeemable at par (along with those issued by any New England bank, provided those banks maintained deposits at the Suffolk Bank—thus rapidly expanding industrial capital in New England).

Table 19.4 Local health services: Megalopolis metropolitan areas by employment, 2004

Metropolitan area (national rank in employment)	Total employment	Share of national employment	CAGR of employment 1990–2004	Average wages	CAGR of average wages 1990–2004
New York-Northern New Jersey-Long Island **(1)**	1,113,374	7.6	1.91	$42,631	3.64
Philadelphia-Camden-Wilmington **(4)**	373,167	2.5	1.71	$38,436	3.17
Boston-Cambridge-Quincy **(5)**	**310,759**	**2.1**	**1.45**	**$42,180**	**3.95**
Washington-Arlington-Alexandria **(9)**	221,485	1.5	2.29	$43,770	3.35
Baltimore-Towson **(16)**	150,055	1.0	1.86	$40,832	3.90

Source: Prof. Michael E. Porter, Cluster Mapping Project, Institute for Strategy and Competitiveness, Harvard Business School; Richard Bryden, Project Direct *Boston Region's Reinvention*

19.5 Rise of "Tradable" and "Non-tradable" Sectors and Income Inequalities in the Megalopolis

Globalization, made possible in recent decades by lowered international trade barriers and technical improvements in transport and information technologies, has restructured the functional and spatial organization of the economy in the Megalopolis and the USA. The production and delivery of goods and services are decomposed into increasing number of value-adding components, and the relevant supply chains of economic activities have been increasingly organized on a global basis. At the same time, innovations in information technologies have created many knowledge-intensive business services (KIBS). KIBS (comprising of financial, legal, accounting, information, and other professional services) enable global corporations, as noted earlier, to develop and support management innovations that make possible the smooth operation of global supply chains and the integration of global corporate operations. Further, KIBS also have become tradable.

In the Megalopolis, as in many highly developed regions, early globalization was marked by corporations moving the lower-wage, lower value-adding components of production to low-income industrializing countries while retaining the more knowledge-intensive components domestically. Thus the activities remaining in the Megalopolis comprise the upstream knowledge-intensive activities (e.g., R&D, product design) and downstream knowledge-intensive activities (e.g., marketing, brand exploitation), while tasks of fabrication of many components (except the more knowledge-intensive components) are outsourced to the newly industrializing countries. At this stage, there is a decline in low- to medium-wage jobs and a growth in higher wage knowledge-intensive jobs in the manufacturing and other tradable sectors in the Megalopolis. Those jobs in manufacturing and other tradable components are relatively devalued and only survive if wages are suppressed. The twofold result of job loss and wage stagnation in manufacturing and other tradable sectors and a rise in value added per job in the more knowledge-intensive value chains of production which remain in the Megalopolis in turn yields *rising income inequality* in the Megalopolis.

The nature of global supply chains is evolving away from this simple low-wage/high-wage dichotomy in recent years, however, due to the rapid pace of economic development in the rapidly industrializing economies of the world. Rapidly industrializing countries (such as China) are accumulating in recent years significant levels of physical, human, and organizational capital, which permit an increasing incorporation of higher value-adding components of global chains into their manufacturing and other tradable sectors, thereby displacing such components of manufacturing and other tradable sectors in the Megalopolis. In this context of globally linked production, the corresponding production chains disappear in the Megalopolis, which increasingly plays host largely to the high value-adding components such as R&D, design, fabrication of some knowledge-intensive components, marketing, and a few post-sales services in such sectors. While overall value added per employee rises in these sectors retained in the Megalopolis, two adverse consequences follow. Powerful market forces operate directly on the tradable sector. More medium wage jobs in these sectors disappear from the Megalopolis locations. There are indirect effects on the non-tradable economic sectors of the Megalopolis and the national economy through wage and price effects and shifting opportunities in labor markets. Income inequalities, as a consequence, widen further in the last two decades in the Megalopolis centers of economic activity.

Spence and Hlatshwayo (2011) have carried out an analysis of the evolution of tradable and non-tradable sectors in the US economy and the progress of income inequalities in the nation during 1990–2007. This part of the chapter implements the Spence-Hlatshwayo approach to study the evolution of tradable and non-tradable sectors and the progress of income distribution in the Megalopolis and component major metros (for a slightly longer period) during 1990–2011.[9] This chapter illustrates this analysis for one Megalopolis metro area, namely, Boston.

Manufacturing was the largest tradable sector in the Boston metropolitan area until fairly recently (Fig. 19.2a). Over a period of 22 years (1999–2011), this sector lost about 150,000 employees (close to 45% of its total). The average earnings per worker in this sector, however, climbed up from $80,000 to over $90,000 (in chained dollars) in that period (Fig. 19.3a). A significant loss of employment accompanied by an upward shift of average wage in that sector in Boston over two decades replicates the pattern of increasing income inequalities predicted earlier for regions engaged in globally organized production and trade. However, two tradable sectors—professional services and finance and insurance—increased in employment

[9]Spence and Hlatshwayo used a methodology developed by Bradford Jensen and Lori Kletzer. Their approach determined the tradability of an industry based on its geographic concentration—the more concentrated the industry, the higher its tradability (and vice versa). For example, take retail trade: its ubiquitous geographic presence implies that it is highly non-tradable.

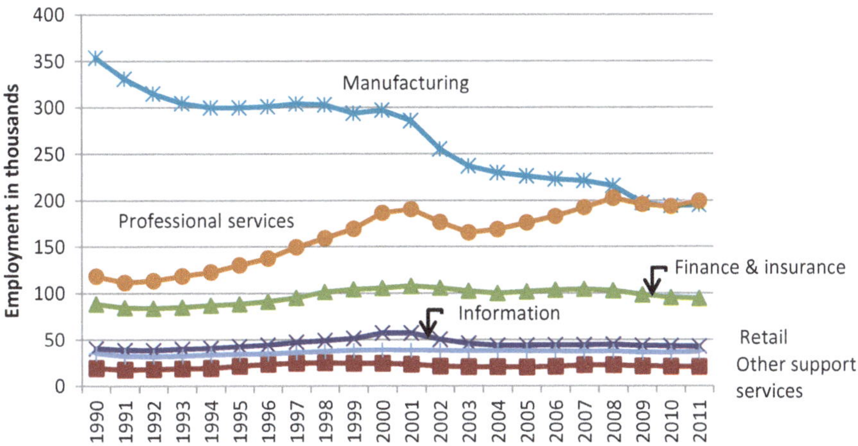

Fig. 19.2a Tradable industrial employment (major sectors) in Boston metro

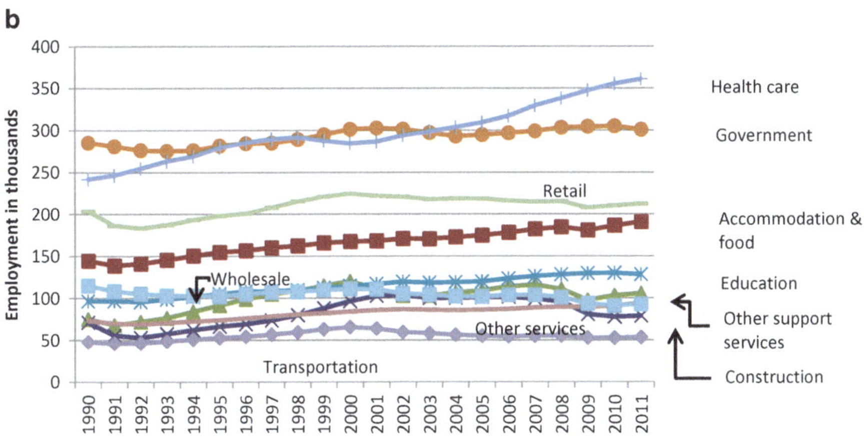

Fig. 19.2b Non-tradable industrial employment (major sectors) in Boston metro. (Source: Lakshmanan et al. 2016)

(about 80,000), and the high average wage per employee, over $140,000 in 2001, climbed up (in chained dollars) 20% and 15%, respectively, in that decade. The overall result is a drop in tradable sector employment and increasing income inequalities in the Boston region.

In contrast to traditional models of regional growth that emphasize the "basic" sector or exported goods and services as driving growth, much of the growth in employment in Boston Metro in these two decades derives from the non-tradable sectors (Fig. 19.2b). Health services sector is the largest contributor to growth. Indeed, the greater part of the employment growth in the Boston metro region by year 2011 derives from the three non-tradable sectors of health services,

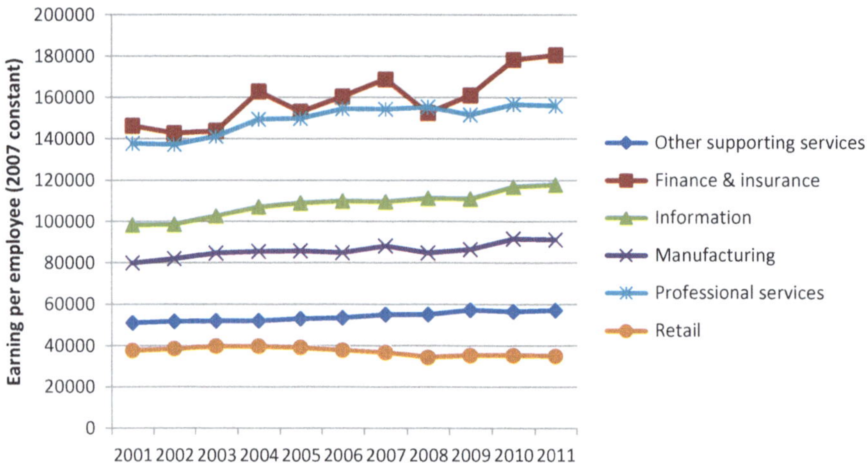

Fig. 19.3a Tradable sectors: earning per employee (in 2007 dollars) in Boston metro. (Source: Lakshmanan et al. 2016)

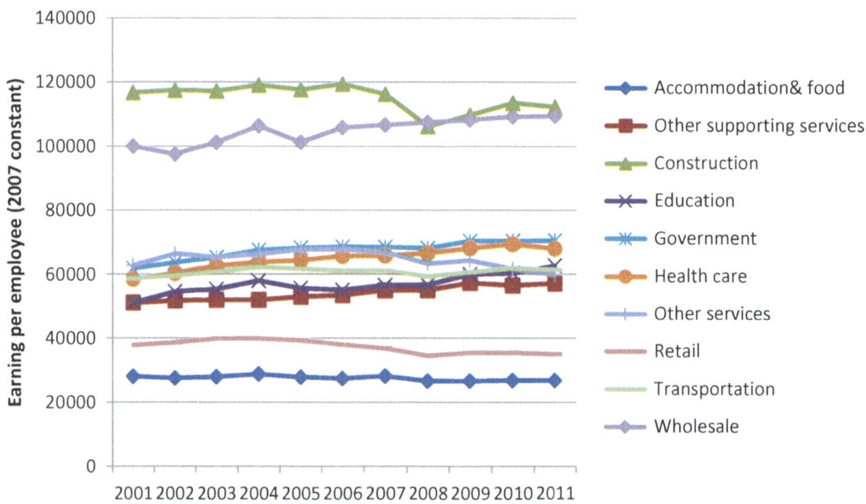

Fig. 19.3b Non-tradable sectors: earnings per employee (in 2007 dollars)in Boston metro. (Source: Lakshmanan et al. 2016)

government, and retail. Health and the government sectors have average earnings per employee of about $70,000, while the earnings per employee in the third employment growth sector of retail are low—less than $40,000 (Fig. 19.3b).

It appears that over the last decade of the twentieth century and the first decade of the twenty-first, employment in the Boston metro region declined in the tradable

Table 19.5 Gini index of household income inequality in the USA and for metropolitan areas of over 1 million population in the Megalopolis

Metropolitan area	1979	1989	1999	2006	2011
New York	0.353	0.385	0.475	0.499	0.507
Boston	0.399	0.449	0.413	0.461	0.477
Philadelphia	0.327	0.341	0.419	0.461	0.472
Providence	0.394	0.427	0.424	0.440	0.463
Baltimore	0.391	0.412	0.405	0.437	0.452
Hartford	0.355	0.421	0.399	0.438	0.456
Washington	0.367	0.380	0.379	0.434	0.438
USA	0.404	0.431	0.458	0.470	0.475

Source: 1979 and 1989 metropolitan Gini indices from Madden, 2000, 1999 metropolitan Gini indices from Lopez, 2004 (data published online, www.diversitydata.org) and 2006 and 2011 metropolitan Gini indices and U.S.'s indices in Table * from US Census Bureau

sectors exposed to global competition. This development combined with a rise in average earnings per remaining employee in those tradable sectors leads to rising income inequalities. Further, the dominant (non-tradable) employment growth sectors of health care, government, and retail evidence moderate to low earnings per employee. Clearly, evolving trends in employment levels and earnings per employee in the globalizing knowledge economy of the Boston region over those two decades led to increasing income inequalities.

We have conducted similar empirical analyses for New York; Washington, D.C.; and other Megalopolis knowledge economies that yield comparable results of recently widening income disparities (Lakshmanan et al. 2016).

19.5.1 Income Inequality in the Megalopolis

Over the same late twentieth-century to early twenty-first-century period, income distribution in the Megalopolis shifted from being more equal than in the USA as a whole to in some cases being more unequal. Table 19.5 shows the progress of the Gini index in the USA and in selected metropolitan areas of the Megalopolis over three decades from 1979 to 2011. In 1979, income inequalities are more pronounced in the nation than in the metro areas of the Megalopolis. By 1989, when globalization has entered a rapid phase, the Gini indices (income inequalities) are climbing in the nation and in the metropolitan areas of the Megalopolis. As global organization of business and a finer differentiation of tradable and non-tradable sectors gather speed in the 1990s and in the decade of 2000s, income inequalities widen faster in the rising knowledge economies of New York and Boston than in the nation.

19.6 Conclusion

This chapter has two major objectives:

First, it offers an understanding of the ongoing structural change and socioeconomic transition underway in the last three decades and more in the Megalopolis, from a mature and declining industrial structure to that of a vibrant "knowledge economy." How has this come to pass? The chapter attributes the rise of knowledge economy to three kinds of *proximity* among economic agents:

Physical proximity promoting appropriation and sharing of tacit knowledge, thus promoting innovation

Relational proximity promoting among economic agents cooperative behavior, collective learning, and socialization of innovation risk

Institutional proximity among the firms in the urban agglomeration in terms of shared rules, codes, and norms of behavior which will promote cooperation in interactive learning processes

These linkages and interactions allow firms and other economic agents to complement their core competencies with requisite knowledge and capacities creatively, speedily, and flexibly.

Second, this chapter applied the above model to the rise and evolution of the knowledge economy in the Megalopolis urban region stretching along the Eastern seaboard in the USA from the Southern New Hampshire to Northern Virginia, including the metropolitan areas of Boston, New York, Philadelphia, Baltimore, and Washington, D.C. Thus, the chapter addresses the evolution of a huge manufacturing and trading economy of the mid-twentieth century—one based on the movement and transformation of materials—to a large, vibrant, and new knowledge economy based on the transformation of new scientific and engineering knowledge into technical innovations, which merged with organizational and institutional innovations generate highly valued novel goods and services for the global market.

References

Bathelt H (1999) Technological change and regional restructuring in Boston's Route 128 area. IWSG Working Papers 10

Bathelt H (2001) Regional competence and economic recovery: divergent growth paths in Boston's high technology economy. Entrep Reg Dev 13:287–314

Best MH (2000) Silicon Valley and the resurgence of route 128: systems integration and regional innovation. In: Dunning J (ed) Regions, globalization and the knowledge-based economy. Oxford University Press, Oxford, pp 459–484

Bryson JR, Daniels PW (2007) The handbook of service industries. Elgar, Northampton

Capello R (2011) Innovation and productivity: local competitiveness and the role of space. In: Cooke P et al (ed) Handbook of regional innovation and growth. Northampton Massachusetts Elgar, pp 107–119

Chatterjee L, Lakshmanan TR (2005) The fashioning of dynamic competitive advantage of entrepreneurial cities: role of social and political entrepreneurship. A chapter of the Festschrift for Borje Johansson (eds) Andersson Å, Karlsson C. 2006

Chen Z, Haynes KE (2015) Multilevel assessment of public transportation infrastructure: a spatial econometric computable general equilibrium approach. Ann Reg Sci 54(3):663–685

Cooke P, Asheim B, Boschama R, Martin R, Schwartz D, Tödtling F (2011) Handbook of regional innovation and growth. Edward Elgar, Northampton, MA

Granovetter M (1985) Economic action and social structure: the problem of embeddedness. Am J Sociol 91:481–510

Haynes K, Shibusawa H (2005) Elements of a knowledge network learning model. In: Johnason I, Dahlberg R (eds) Regions in competition and cooperation. University of Trollhattan, Uddevalla, pp 295–304

Heurmann DF Reinventing the skilled region: human capital externalities and industrial change. Discussion paper series no. 02/2009. Institute for labor law and Industrial Relations in EC (IAEEG) Trier

Hoover E (1948) The location of economic activity. McGraw-Hill, New York

Isard W (1956) Location and space-economy: a general theory relating to industrial location, market areas, land use, trade and urban structure. MIT Press, Cambridge, MA

Kox HLM, Rubalcaba L (2007) Business services and the changing structure of European economic growth. CPB Memorandum 183, CPB Netherlands Bureau for Economic Policy Analysis

Krugman PK (1991) Geography and trade. MIT Press, Cambridge, MA

Lakshmanan TR, Button KJ (2009) Institutions and regional economic development. In: Cappello R, Nijkamp P (eds) Advances in regional economics. Edward Elgar, Cheltenham

Lakshmanan TR, Chatterjee LR (2006) The Entrepreneurial City in the global marketplace. Int J Entrep Innov Manag 6(3):155–172

Lakshmanan TR, Anderson WP, Song Y, Li D (2009) Broader economic consequences of transport infrastructure: the case of economic evolution in dynamic transport corridors, Boston University Center for Transportation Studies Working Paper

Lakshmanan TR, Anderson WP, Song Y (2016) Knowledge economy in the Megalopolis. Routledge, London

Marshall A (1890) Principles of economics. Prometheus Books, New York

Polyanyi K (1944) The great transformation: political and economic origins of our time. Beacon Press, New York, NY

Scott AJ (1998) Regions and the world economy: the coming shape of global production, competition and political order. Oxford University Press, Oxford

Spence M, Hlatshwayo S (2011) The evolving structure of the American economy and the employment challenge. Working Paper, Council on Foreign Relations, Maurice R. Greenberg Center for Geoeconomic Studies

Storper M (1995) The resurgence of regional economies, ten years later; the region as a nexus of untraded interdependencies. Eur Urban Reg Stud 2:191–221

Temin P (1999) The industrialization of New England: 1830–1880. NBER Working Paper Series on Historical Factors in Long Run Growth, Historical Paper 114

Von Hippel E (1988) The sources of innovation. Oxford University Press, Oxford

Chapter 20
Investigating Factors Explaining Spatial Variation in Endogenous Regional Employment Performance Across Australia

Robert J. Stimson and Alistair Robson

Abstract The regional shift component of a shift-share analysis may be used as a proxy indicator of the endogenous regional employment performance of functional economic regions (FERs) in Australia. A model is used to investigate the potential factors that might explain spatial variations in that measure as a dependent variable, modelling that has been undertaken over three overlapping 10-year periods: 1996–2006, 2001–2011 and 2006–2016. The chapter summarises the results of that modelling focusing explicitly on the degree to which explanatory variables in the model remain consistent or not over time as factors that might explain variations in the endogenous regional employment performance of FERs across the nation.

Keywords Endogenous growth · Modelling regional performance · Functional economic regions

20.1 Introduction

For several decades now, regional scientists have been paying increasing attention to the role of *endogenous* factors in regional economic development, a focus that is central to the emergence of the *new growth theory* (NGT) (for a discussion, see Stimson et al. 2011c).

The NGT is typically associated with the writing of theorists such as Romer (1986, 1990), Barro (1990), Rebelo (1991), Grossman and Helpman (1991) and Arthur (1994). There was a focus on technology as an *endogenous* effect generating

R. J. Stimson (✉)
The University of Queensland, Brisbane, QLD, Australia

The University of Melbourne, Melbourne, VIC, Australia
e-mail: rstimson@unimelb.edu.au

A. Robson
The University of New South Wales, Kensington, NSW, Australia

Z. Chen et al. (eds.), *Development Studies in Regional Science*,
New Frontiers in Regional Science: Asian Perspectives 42,
https://doi.org/10.1007/978-981-15-1435-7_20

regional economic development rather than accepting the neo-classical view that long-term growth was due to *exogenous* factors.

Technology as a prime driver in regional economic development had been proposed by Rees (1997) as having an enhancing effect on the competitiveness of regions (Thomas 1975; Erickson 1994). Norton and Rees (1979) and Erickson and Leinbach (1979) showed how the *product cycle*, when incorporated into a spatial setting, may impact differentially on regions through three stages: an innovation stage, a growth stage and a standardisation stage. The roles of innovation and the product cycle were also espoused by Markusen (1985). It is certainly underpinned by R&D and entrepreneurship.

Technological innovation has been linked to *agglomeration* and localisation economies creating an *innovative milieu*, which can lead to the development of new industrial spaces (Scott 1988; Porter 1990; Krugman 1991). Some regions seem to excel as innovative regions surging ahead while others lag.

The NGT approach embracing the notion of endogenous regional growth has evolved to explicitly encompass many factors and processes that are said to be important in enhancing regional economic development. Regional performance may be affected, inter alia, by:

- *Resource endowments* (Stimson and Stough 2009)
- *Population size* or *urban scale* and *agglomeration* (Duranton and Puga 2000; Taylor et al. 2002)
- *Human capital* (Goetz and Rapasingla 2001; Hanushek and Kimko 2000)
- *Industrial structure* (diversity/specialisation) (Henderson et al. 1995; Gordon and McCann 2000)
- *Institutional factors* (Rees 1979; North 1990; Blakely 1994; Vazquez-Barquero 2002; Stimson and Stough 2009; Garlick et al. 2006), including *leadership* (Fairholm 1994; De Santis and Stough 1999; Judd and Parkinson 1990; Rees 2001; Stimson and Stough 2009) and *social capital* and *trust* (Fukuyama 1995)
- *Entrepreneurship* (Jessop 1998; Rees 2001; Stimson and Stough 2009)

However, there are relatively few empirical studies seeking to operationalise models that measure endogenous regional performance and to investigate what factors might be significant in explaining spatial variations in regional economic performance. One modelling approach has been advocated by Stimson et al. (2005) and Stimson and Stough (2009), who proposed the model framework shown in Fig. 20.1.

However, there are typically difficulties in obtaining data sets that relate to some of the factors the NGT literature suggests might influence *endogenous* regional economic performance. There is no explicit metric used to measure endogenous performance that may be used as a dependent variable in modelling regional economic performance. While it is generally easy to develop variables from national date sets, such as the census, to operationalise models of endogenous regional

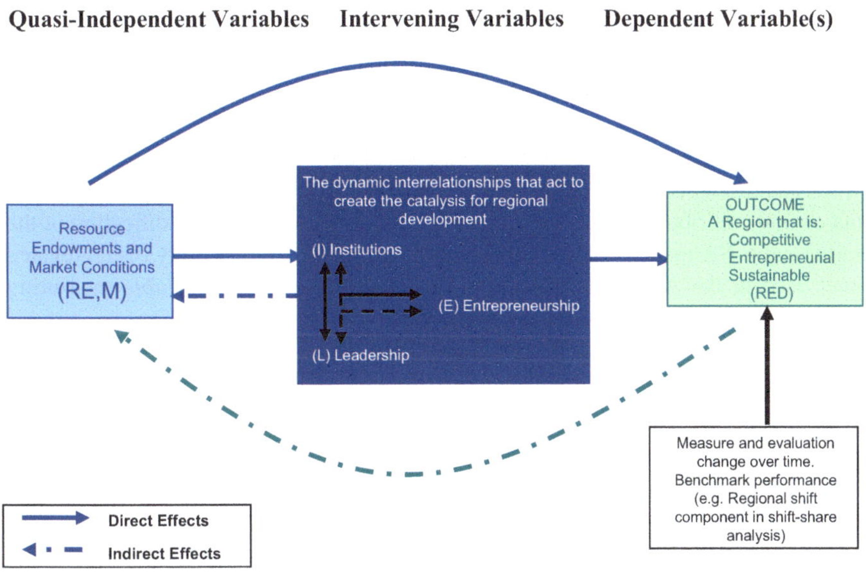

Fig. 20.1 The Stimson and Stough framework for modelling endogenous regional performance

performance – measures relating to factors such as population size, human capital and industrial diversity – there are generally no systematic data sets available that relate to factors such as institutions, leadership and entrepreneurship. As a result, it has proven difficult to fully operationalise the model framework proposed by Stimson and Stough (2009), with attempts to empirically test an endogenous regional performance model being largely restricted to use the aggregate data for regions available in national data sets.

The authors and their collaborators have partially applied the Stimson and Stough model framework to investigate endogenous regional employment performance across Australia over three overlapping 10-year periods: 1996–2006, 2001–2011 and 2006–2016. It has also been used by Plummer et al. (2014) in a study of regional development in the state of Western Australia. And Stough et al. (2009) have applied the model framework to investigate factors that might explain endogenous regional employment performance across metropolitan regions in the United States.

The outcomes of the modelling conducted in Australia are reviewed in this chapter, the explicit focus being on investigating the degree to which the explanatory variables in the model are significant – and may or may not be consistently so over time – as factors that might explain the evident spatial variation in the dependent variable that is used as a surrogate measure of endogenous regional employment performance.

20.2 The Model and Modelling Approaches

20.2.1 Model Variables

The modelling undertaken in Australia has used the traditional shift-share analysis (S-SA) as discussed in Haynes and Dinc (1997), but without separating the labour and capital contribution to productivity growth proposed in their modification of the traditional S-SA model because data are not available at the spatially disaggregated level used in the Australian modelling to derive a *dependent variable* measuring *endogenous regional employment performance*.

As suggested by Stimson and Stough (2009), the surrogate measure used is the *regional* (or *differential*) *shift component* in the S-SA, standardised by the total employment in a region at the beginning of the 10-year time period being investigated. That *dependent variable* (REG_SHIFT) may be either *positive* or *negative*. If that score is *positive*, then that is taken as an indication that the change in a region's employment over the 10-year period over and above that which might be attributed to national and industry mix effects is being positively enhanced through factors that are explicitly *endogenous* to the region. In other words, the region possesses attributes that are important drivers of regional growth. In contrast, a *negative* score on the dependent variable is taken to indicate there are factors and processes endogenous to a region that are a drag on, or are deleterious for, the region's employment performance.

The modelling has used the set of *explanatory variables* set listed in Table 20.1 that might explain the evident variation across regions that occurs in the dependent variable measure of endogenous regional employment performance. Those potential explanatory variables are derived from national census data, and in addition there are a small number of variables that relate to the locational characteristics of a region.

The explanatory variables in the model include both *cross-sectional* and *dynamic* measures relating to:

- Regional industry structure and industry specialisation/diversification and changes over time
- A region's mean individual income and change over time
- The incidence of unemployment in a region and change over time
- A region's population size and change over time
- Location quotients (LQ) for a region's employment in broad industry sectors (manufacturing; information, media and telecommunications; financial and insurance services; professional scientific and technical services) and change in the LQ over time
- A region's human capital (skills and qualifications – post-graduate, bachelor and technical) and change over time
- The incidence of employment in symbolic analyst occupations (managers and professionals) in a region and change over time
- Incidence of employment in creative industries in a region
- A proxy for social capital in a region (the incidence of volunteering)

Table 20.1 Variables used in the model

Variable description	
Dependent variable	
REG_SHIFT	Regional shift (1996 to 2006)/labour force (1996/2006/2016)
Explanatory variables	
Census data derived	
SPEC_96/06/16	Specialisation index for 1996/2001/2006 (Herfindahl-Hirschman Index)
SPEC_CH	Change in specialisation index from 1996–2006/2001–2011/2006–2016 (Herfindahl-Hirschman Index)
SCI	Structural change index (1996–2006/2001–2011/2006–2016)
SCI_CH	Change in the structural change index (from 1996–2006/2001–2011/2006–2016)
L_INC_96/01/06	(Approximate) mean individual income – 1996/2001/2006 annual (log) (real)
L_INC_CH	Change in (approximate) mean individual income – 1996–2006/2001–2011/2006–2016 annual (log) (real)
UNEMP_96/01/06	Unemployment rate in 1996/2001/2006 (%)
UNEMP_CH	Change in unemployment rate from 1996–2006/2001–2011/2006–2016 (percentage points)
L_POP_96/01	Log of population (1996/2001/2006)
L_POP_CH	Change in log of population (1996–2006/2001–2011/2006–2016)
LQ_MAN_96/01/06	Location quotient for the manufacturing industry in 1996/2001/2006
LQ_INF_96/01/06	Location quotient for the information, media and telecommunications industry in 1996/2001/2006
LQ_FIN_96/01/06	Location quotient for the financial and insurance services industry in 1996/2001/2006
LQ_PRO_96/01/06	Location quotient for the professional, scientific and technical services industry in 1996/2001/2006
LQ_MAN_CH	Change in the location quotient for the manufacturing industry, 1996–2006/2001–2011/2006–2016
LQ_INF_CH	Change in the location quotient for the information, media and telecommunications industry, 1996–2006/2001–2011/2006–2016
LQ_FIN_CH	Change in the location quotient for the financial and insurance services industry, 1996–2006/2001–2011/2006–2016
LQ_PRO_CH	Change in the location quotient for the professional, scientific and technical services industry, 1996–2006/2001–2011/2006–2016
POSTGRAD_96/01/06	Proportion of labour force with a postgraduate degree in 1996/2006/2016
BACHELOR_96/01/06	Proportion of labour force with a bachelor degree in 1996/2001/2006
TECHQUALS_96/01/06	Proportion of labour force with technical qualifications in 1996/2001/2006
POSTGRAD_CH	Change in the proportion of labour force with a postgraduate degree in 1996–2006/2001–211/2006–2016
BACHELOR_CH	Change in the proportion of labour force with a bachelor degree in 1996–2006/2001–2011/2006–2016

(continued)

Table 20.1 (continued)

Variable description	
TECHQUALS_CH	Change in the proportion of labour force with technical qualifications, 1996–2006/2001–2011/2006–2016
SYMBA_96/01/06	Proportion of symbolic analysts (managers + professionals) occupations in 1996/2001/2006
SYMBA_CH	Change in the proportion of symbolic analysts (managers + professionals), 1996–2006/2001–2011/2006–2016
VOLUNTEER_06/06/16	Proportion of volunteers in working age population (15–64) in 2006/2011/2016
CREATIVE_06	Proportion of total employment in creative industries in 2006/2011/2016
Locational variables	
A_COAST	FER border is adjacent to coastline (No = 0; Yes = 1)
P_METRO	FER border is adjacent to a metropolitan statistical division (No = 0; Yes = 1)
D_URBAN	Classified as urban under Australian Classification of Local Governments system (1 = Yes, 0 = No)
D_REMOTE	Classified as remote under Australian Classification of Local Governments system (1 = Yes, 0 = No)
W_METRO	FER border within a metropolitan statistical division (No = 0; Yes = 1)

All those variables are derived from census data relating to the beginning and end of a 10-year period. As shown in Table 20.1, the cross-sectional (static) variables are mostly for the beginning year of a 10-year period, except for a small number of variables that are for the end year of the 10-year period, while the dynamic (change-over-time) variables are for change over time across the 10-year period.

In addition, five variables that are locational (spatial) proxies for a region are used, namely, adjacency to coastline, proximity to a metropolitan area, classified as an urban area, classification as a remote area, and being within a major city metropolitan area.

As indicated in Table 20.1, a couple of the variables are not used in all the modelling for all three of the 10-year periods.

20.2.2 Spatial Base Used for the Modelling

The early applications of the model for the 10-year period 1996–2006 were initially applied to local government areas (LGAs) across regional Queensland beyond the capital city metro region (Stimson et al. 2004, 2009a, b) and then to LGAs across all of Australia beyond the capital city metro regions (Stimson et al. 2009a, b, 2011b). Thus, the early modelling used de jure regions as the spatial base.

It is well known that using de jure regions in spatial econometric modelling encounters the modifiable areal unit problem (MAUP) and the associated issue of spatial autocorrelation. In an attempt to help address that problem, subsequent modelling undertaken for the overlapping 10-year periods 1996–2006 (Stimson et al. 2011a), 2001–2011 (Stimson et al. 2018) and 2006–2016 (reported first in this chapter) was undertaken using a new *functional* geography. FERs across all of Australia were derived through applying the Masser and Brown (1975) *Intramax* hierarchical agglomerative methodology in analysing journey-to-work data for statistical local areas[1] (SLAs) available in the national census (for a full explanation, see Mitchell and Watts 2010; Stimson et al. 2016). The outcome using the FER spatial base for the modelling substantially minimised the spatial autocorrelation that had been encountered when the modelling was based on de jure regions (as explained in Mitchell and Flanagan 2009; Stimson et al. 2011a).

That new national geography of FERs was derived from the census journey-to-work data relating to all three of the 10-year periods for which modelling has been undertaken. Because of the nature of the *Intramax* hierarchical procedure used through which SLAs are agglomerated to form the FERs, as expected there may be boundary changes in FERs between the three periods and changes in the number of FERs. That is because commuting patterns evolve over time because of (a) changes in the location of jobs, internal migration and population growth and decline and (b) investments in new transportation infrastructure.

20.2.3 Regression Approaches Used in the Modelling

Various regression models were run for the above referenced applications of the model for the three overlapping 10-year time periods using FERs across Australia as the spatial base for investigating the potential factors that might be significant in explaining spatial variations in FER scores on the dependent variable measuring endogenous regional employment performance.

First, an *ordinary least square (OLS) full model* (a linear model) was used to derive a *general model*. It was run without allowing for spatial effects. For the 2001–2011 modelling, *spatial dependence tests* were run, including the *Lagrange multiplier (LM) tests*, and *Moran's I test* was run on residuals (see Anselin et al. 1996; Anselin 1988). A *multicollinearity test* was also run. It was found that there was no evidence of spatial dependence.

Second, a *backward stepwise regression* (based on AIC) was also run to derive an *OLS-specific model*. Again, for the 2001–2011, modelling spatial dependence tests and a multicollinearity *test* were run. There was no evidence of spatial dependence using the LM test, but there was some significant error on Moran's *I* test.

[1]SLAs were replaced by the Australian Bureau of Statistics in their updated geographical classification system (Australian Statistical Geography Standard) and were last used to report census data in 2011. The equivalent unit of geography used in the 2016 Census of Population is the Statistical Area Level 2.

For completeness, spatial autoregressive models were also looked at – both a *spatial error model* and a *spatial lag model* – the results of which are not discussed here as the authors undertaking the modelling both for 1996–2006 and for 2001–2011 noted that the use of a *functional* geography (namely, FERs) appears to overcome the autocorrelation issued encountered in earlier modelling using de jure regions as the spatial data base (for a full discussion of that, see Stimson et al. 2009a, b, 2011a, 2018). Those studies all recommend that the preferred modelling approach is to focus on the *OLS full model* (a linear model) generating a general solution, the results of which we focus on here. We also consider the results of the modelling conducted for 2006–2016. But we do also take a look at the results of the backward stepwise regression model generating a specific model.

As one would expect, there will be differences in results for different regression models concerning the explanatory variables that are identified as being statistically significant in potentially explaining the spatial differentiation in the performance of FERs on the dependent variable (i.e. endogenous regional employment performance). And one would expect as well for there to be differences between the modelling for the three overlapping 10-year time periods in whether an explanatory variable is or is not significant. It is that consistency or variability over time on which we focus here.

20.3 Macro-context for the 10-Year Time Periods

It is helpful to understand the macro-economic environment in Australia and how that varied over the three overlapping 10-year time periods.

The 10-year period 1996–2006 was part of the long period of continuous economic growth that commenced following the recession of the early 1990s. The latter part of that period also marked the beginning of the remarkable resources boom in Australia. It was also a period of substantial structural shifts in industry sectors employment as manufacturing jobs declined and jobs in the services sectors grew, with rapid growth in producer services jobs. Not surprisingly the outcomes of those not evenly distributed across Australia's cities and regions with some faring well, while others did not.

The 10-year period 2001–2011 was characterised first by the continuation of the boom era and then by the onset of the global financial crisis (GFC) and its aftermath. While Australia as national economy did not experience a technical recession due largely to the resources boom, many regions were, nonetheless, adversely impacted including some parts of the largest cities.

The 10-year period 2006–2016 was characterised by the onset of the GFC and the then abrupt end of the resources boom which badly impacted some regions. That was offset in some regions – including some of the big metropolitan cities – which experienced the benefits of a switch from investment in resources-related construction to investment in infrastructure and housing and the emergence of new services export industries such as education. It was said that Australia was experiencing the

'Dutch disease' (Corden 2011; Stimson 2013). Historically high levels of immigration and record low levels of interest triggered a housing boom cycle, particularly in Sydney and Melbourne. The long-term decline in manufacturing jobs continued with the services sectors growing. The post GFC recovery was characterised by slower growth that had occurred in the long boom years from the mid-1990s to the GFC. Again, the impact of those macro-factors was far from even across regions.

20.4 Modelling Outcomes

20.4.1 Positive and Negative Performance of FERs on the Dependent Variable Scores

Rather than reproducing maps of the pattern of performance of FERs on the endogenous regional employment performance-dependent variable for the modelling for the three overlapping 10-year time periods (1996–2006, 2001–2011 and 2006–2016), here we summarise the findings from that modelling.

As expected, there were considerable variations across FERs in their scores on the dependent variable measuring endogenous regional employment performance for all three time periods. However, as shown in Table 20.2, the incidence of *positive* and of *negative* performance did vary somewhat over time.

Over all three of the time periods modelled, the majority of FERs across Australia have had a *negative* score on the endogenous regional employment performance variable (REG_SHIFT), while the minority of the FERs had a *positive* performance.

The incidence of *positive* performance on the dependent variable had improved from 25% of the FERs for 1996–2001 to 39% for 2006–2016. The incidence of FERs with a *strong positive* performance had remained low at only 8% for 1996–2006 and 2006–2016, while it dipped to 5% for 2001–2011.

The incidence of *negative* performance has decreased from 75% of FERs for 1996–2001 to 61% for 2006–2016. However, the incidence of FERs with a *strong negative* performance had increased substantially from 3% for 1996–2006 to 15% for 2006–2016.

Table 20.2 FER scores on the dependent variable (REG_SHIFT): Number of FERs with positive and negative endogenous regional employment performance

	Strong Negative	Negative	Positive	Strong positive	Number of FERs in the modelling
1996–2006 analysis	20 (*15%*)	65 (*46%*)	44 (*31%*)	11 (*8%*)	$N = 140$
2001–2011 analysis	4 (*3%*)	84 (*63%*)	39 (*29%*)	**7 (5%)**	$N = 134$
2006–2016 analysis	4 (*3%*)	103 (*72%*)	*24 (17%)*	12 (*8%*)	$N = 143$

Over time it is apparent that the incidence of *negative* performance of FERs is consistently widely spread spatially, largely occurring across the inland regional areas, and that would and tend to support the popularly held view that regional Australia is suffering. That is especially evident for inland regions experiencing population decline and for remote regions. But there are inland regions across the wheat-sheep belt with a *positive* performance, and those tend to be FERs with a large regional urban centre that are important regional service centres often with substantial investment in higher education institutions, higher-order regional health services and regional offices of state governments. It is also common for some of the remote mining regions to have a *positive* performance. While some of the coastal non-metropolitan regions that are attracting in-migration have displayed a *positive* performance, for some the performance has been *negative*. And the performance of FERs across the island state of Tasmania has tended to be *negative*.

Meanwhile, for the FERs in the larger city metropolitan areas (in which there are multiple FERs, except for Adelaide), it is apparent that many – but not all – have displayed a *positive* performance on the endogenous regional employment performance variable. But for some there was a *negative* performance, and that was particularly the case for some FERs in Sydney for the period 2001–2011 where the impact of the GFC was marked. Adelaide with a single FER that encompasses the metro region remains across time a *negative* performer.

However, it is not unusual for the performance of a FER on the endogenous regional employment performance-dependent variable to change over time from being positive to negative or from being negative to positive. Indeed, the spatial patterns evident in those performance fluctuations can be quite complex reflecting the socioeconomic structural characteristics of FERs and the degree to which they may have been impacted by *exogenous* factors such as the structural changes occurring in industry sector employment, the impact of the GFC and the resources boom and bust.

20.4.2 The Regression Modelling Results

Detailed statistics for the results from the various regression models used to investigate the performance of FERs on the dependent variable (REG_SHIFT) for all three of the overlapping 10-year periods (1996–2006, 2001–2011 and 2006–2016) are not tabulated here. Rather, tables have been compiled to identify those explanatory variables that are statistically significant in potentially explaining variations in the performance of FERs on the dependent variable. In that way it is obvious whether a variable is significant in either a *positive* or a *negative* way or whether it is not significant for a specific time period and also to see the degree to which that is consistently the case across the three overlapping 10-year time periods. That is explored for the various regression models that have been used.

20.4.2.1 The OLS Full General Regression Model

An ordinary least square (OLS) full regression (a general model) was run for all three time periods. A summary of the results is provided in Table 20.3.

Table 20.3 Summary of results of a full OLS ordinary regression analysis to derive a general model

Explanatory variables	1996–2006 model $R^2 = 0.90$	2001–2011 model $R^2 = 0.94$	2006–2016 model $R^2 = 0.71$
SPEC_96/01/06	P	P∗	P
SPEC_CH	**P∗**	P	P
SCI	**N∗∗∗**	**P∗∗∗**	**N∗∗**
SCI_CH	**P∗∗∗**	P	N
L_INC_96/01/06	N	**N∗∗**	N
L_INC_CH	P	P	N
UNEMP_96/01/06	N	**P∗∗**	P
UNEMP_CH	N	N	N
L_POP_96/01/06	N	P	**N∗∗**
L_POP_CH	**P∗∗∗**	**P∗∗∗**	**P∗∗**
LQ_MAN_96/01/06	P	P	P
LQ_INF_96/01/06	N	P	**N∗**
LQ_FIN_96/01/06	N	P	**N∗∗**
LQ_PRO_96/01/06	P	N	P
LQ_MAN_CH	**P∗**	N	**N∗∗∗**
LQ_INF_CH	N	P	**N∗**
LQ_FIN_CH	P	N	P
LQ_PRO_CH	P	P	P
POSTGRAD_96/01/06	N	P	**N∗∗**
BACHELOR_96/01/06	P	P	P
TECHQUALS_96/01/06	**N∗**	P	P
POSTGRAD_CH	N	N	**P∗∗**
BACHELOR_CH	P	**N∗∗∗**	N
TECHQUALS_CH	P	**N∗∗∗**	N
SYMBA_96/06/16	N	P	N
SYMBA_CH	N	P	N
VOLUNTEER_06/11/16	**P∗∗∗**	P	P
CREATIVE_06	**P∗**	*Not used*	*Not used*
A_COAST	P	N	N
P_METRO	N	P	N
D_URBAN	P	N	N
D_REMOTE	N	**P∗**	N
W_METRO	*Not used*	N	**P∗∗∗**

P positive effect, *N* negative effect
Bold = statistically significant
Significance codes: $p \geq 0.000$ '∗∗∗', 0.001 '∗∗', 0.01 '∗', 0.05 '.', 0.1 ' '

The R^2 for that model is high, but it varies over time from $R^2 = 0.90$ for 1996–2006 to $R^2 = 0.94$ for 2001–2011 and then down to $R^2 = 0.71$ for 2006–2016. The table indicates eight of explanatory variables in the model were identified as having a statistically significant effect on endogenous regional employment performance for 1996–2006 and for 2001–2011, while ten variables were significant for 2006–2016.

The only variable that appears to be statistically significant across all three of the overlapping 10-year periods in having a *positive* effect on explaining spatial variations in FER scores on the dependent variable relates to change over time is the population size of a region [L_POP_CH]. But no variable has had a statistically significant *negative* effect on the endogenous regional employment performance of a FER across all three of the overlapping time periods.

The structural change index [SCI] for a FER constantly has a significant effect on the FER endogenous regional employment performance, but that changed from being *negative* for 1996–2006 to positive for 2001–2011 and then back to being *negative* for 2006–2016.

Some of the industry structure variables had a *significant* effect on the endogenous regional employment performance of FERs, but that was not consistent over time, and it could vary from being *positive* to being *negative*:

- The initial industry employment specialisation [SPEC_01] in a FER had a significant *positive* effect on endogenous regional employment performance for 2001–2011.
- Change in industry employment specialisation [SPEC_CH] had a significant *positive* effect for 1996–2006 as did change in the structural change index [SCI_CH].

Other variables having a significant *positive* effect on the endogenous regional employment performance of a FER were:

- A change in the incidence of employment in manufacturing [LQ_MAN_CH] which had a *positive* effect for 1996–2006 and so too did the incidence of employment in creative industries at the end of the period [CREATIVE_06] and the incidence of volunteering at the end of the period [VOLUNTEER_06].
- The change in the incidence of people with a post-graduate qualification had a *positive* effect [POSTGRAD_CH] for 2006–2016.
- A remote location [D_REMOTE] had a *significant* positive effect on the endogenous regional employment performance of a FER for 2001–2011, reflecting the impact of the rapidly emerging resources boom encompassing remote mining regions.
- Being located within a large and metropolitan region [W_METRO] had a *positive* effect on the endogenous regional employment performance of a FER for 2006–2016.

Variables that had a significant *negative* effect on the endogenous regional employment performance of FERs were:

- The initial level of income [L_INC_06] for 1996–2006
- Initial population size [L_POP_06] for 2006–2016

- The initial incidence of employment in information media and telecommunications industries [LQ_INF_06] for 2006–2016, as did the initial incidence of employment in financial and insurance services [LQ_FIN_06], and the change in the incidence of employment in information media and telecommunications industries [LQ_INF_CH] and in manufacturing [LQ_MAN_CH].

Regarding the variables relating to human capital, there was a mixed impact on FER endogenous regional employment performance:

- For 1996–2006 the initial incidence of workers with a technical qualification [TECHQUALS_96] had a *negative* effect.
- For 2001–2011 the change on the incidence of workers with a bachelor qualification [BACHELOR_CH] *had a negative* effect, as did the change in the incidence of workers with technical qualification over the 10-year period [TECHQUALS_CH].
- For 2006–2016 the initial incidence of workers with a post-graduate qualification [POSTGRAD_06] had a *negative* effect, while (as noted above) the change in the incidence of workers with a post-graduate qualification [POSTGRAD_CH] had a *positive* effect.

Thus, for the OLS full regression general model, there was much inconsistency over the three overlapping 10-year periods in whether or not an explanatory variable might have a significant *positive* effect or a significant *negative* effect on endogenous regional employment performance of FERs across Australia and also in the degree to which that was constant across the three overlapping time periods.

20.4.2.2 The Backward Stepwise Regression to Derive an OLS-Specific Model

A backward stepwise regression was then used to derive an OLS-specific model for all three time periods. A summary of the results are provided in Table 20.4.

The model had a $R^2 = 0.89$ for 1996–2006, and it was higher at $R^2 = 0.94$ for both the 2001–2011 and the 2006–2016 tie periods. For 1996–2006, 16 of the explanatory variables had a statistically significant effect on the endogenous regional employment performance of FERs, while for 2001–2011 and for 2006–2016, 12 of the variables were statistically significant. The results of the specific model are summarised in Table 20.4 where the variables that are significant in explaining variations in the dependent variable [REG_SHIFT] are identified for the three overlapping 10-year periods.

Seven variables were significant across all three of the time periods in explaining variations in the endogenous regional employment performance across FERs. Those variables are:

- Change in the industry specialisation of a region [SPEC_CH] had significant *positive* effect.
- The rate of population change [L_POP_CH] had a *positive* effect.

Table 20.4 Summary of results of a backward step-wise regression analysis to derive a specific linear model

Significant variables	1996–2006 $R^2 = 0.89$	2001–2011 $R^2 = 0.94$	2006–2016 $R^2 = 0.94$
SPEC_01			**P**∗
SPEC_CH	**P**∗∗	**P**∗	**P**∗∗
SCI	**N**∗∗∗	**P**∗∗	**P**∗∗∗
SCI_CH	**P**∗∗∗	**P**∗∗∗	Eliminated
L_INC_96/01/06	**N**∗∗∗	**N**∗∗∗	**N**∗∗∗
UNEMP_96/01/06	**N**∗∗∗	**P**∗∗∗	**P**∗∗∗
UNEMP_CH	**N**∗∗∗	N	N
L_POP_CH	**P**∗∗∗	**P**∗∗∗	P∗∗∗
LQ_FIN_01/06	Eliminated	**P**∗	**P**∗
LQ_PRO_96	P∗	Eliminated	Eliminated
LQ_MAN_CH	P∗∗	N	N
LQ_FIN_CH	Eliminated	**P**∗	Eliminated
LQ_INF_CH	Eliminated	Eliminated	**P**∗
LQ_PRO_CH	P∗	Eliminated	Eliminated
POSTGRAD_96	N∗∗	Eliminated	Eliminated
TECHQUALS_96/01/06	N∗	P	P
BACHELOR_CH	Eliminated	**N**∗∗∗	**P**∗∗∗
TECHQUALS_CH	**P**∗	**N**∗∗∗	**N**∗∗∗
SYMBA_CH	**N**∗	Eliminated	Eliminated
VOLUNTEER_06/11/16	**P**∗∗∗	**P**∗∗	**P**∗
CREATIVE_06	**P**∗∗	*Not used*	*Not used*
D_REMOTE	Eliminated	**P**∗∗	**P**∗∗∗

P positive effect, *N* negative effect
Bold = statistically significant
Significance codes: $p \geq 0.000$'∗∗∗', 0.001 '∗∗', 0.01 '∗', 0.05 '.', 0.1 ' '

- The incidence of volunteering at the end of the time period [VOLUNTEER] had a *positive* effect.
- The initial level of income [L_INC] had a *negative* effect.
- The initial structural change index [SCI] had a significant *negative* effect for 1996–2006, but that changed to a *positive* effect for 2001–2011 and for 2006–2016.
- The initial level of unemployment [UNEMPL] had a *negative* effect for 1996–2006, but that changed to a positive effect for 2001–2011 and for 2006–2016.
- The change in the incidence of workers with technical qualifications [TECHQUALS] had a *positive* effect for 1996–2006, but that changed to a *negative* effect for 2001–2011 and for 2006–2016.
- Change in the structural change index [SCI_CH] had a *positive* effect for 1996–2006 and for 2001–2011, but that variable was eliminated in the backward stepwise model for 2006–2016.

Other variables also had a significant effect on explaining in the endogenous employment performance of FERs, but this was inconsistent across the three time periods:

- The industry specialisation of a FER [SPEC_2006] had a *positive* effect only for 2006–2016.
- The change in the structural change index [SCI_CH] had a *positive* effect both for 1996–2006 and for 2001–2011.
- Initial level of employment [UNEMPL_96] had a *negative* effect for 1996–2006.
- The initial incidence of employment in financial and insurance industries [LQ_FIN_01/06] had a *positive* effect both for 2001–2011 and for 2006–2016.
- The initial incidence of employment in professional, scientific and technical services [LQ_PRO_96] had a *positive* effect for 1996–2006.
- Change in the concentration of employment in manufacturing [LQ_MAN_CH] had a *positive* effect for 2001–2011.
- Change in the concentration of employment in finance and insurance industries [LQ_FIN_CH] had a *positive* effect for 2001–2011.
- Change in the concentration of employment in information, media and telecommunications industries [LQ_INF_CH] had a *positive* effect for 2006–2016.
- Change in the incidence of employment in professional, scientific and technical services [LQ_PROF_CH] had a *positive* effect for 1996–2006.
- The initial incidence of workers with post-graduate qualifications [POSTGAD_CH] and for workers with technical qualifications [TECHQUALS_CH] had a *negative* effect for 1996–2006.
- Change in the concentration of workers with bachelor qualifications [BACHELOR_CH] had a *negative* effect for 2001–2011.
- Change in the incidence of workers in symbolic analyst occupations [SYMBA_CH] had a *negative* effect for 1996–2006.
- The incidence at the end of the period of employment in creative industries [CREATIVE_06] had a *positive* effect or 1996–2006.
- Whether a region was remote in location [D_REMOTE] had a positive effect both for 2001–2011 and for 2006–2016.

20.5 Conclusion

So what might be concluded from the modelling of potential factors that explain variations across FERs in Australia in their endogenous regional employment performance across the overlapping time periods 1996–2006, 2001–2011 and 2006–2016 using the modelling that is a partial application of the framework proposed by Stimson and Stough (2009).

In the results of both the general model using an OLS full regression approach (the general model) and the backward stepwise OLS-specific mode, it is evident that there is some consistency but also some inconsistency across the three time periods in those explanatory variables that are significant in accounting for the endogenous regional employment performance of FERs across Australia, with respect to both whether or not a variable is statistically significant across time and whether that effect is consistently positive or negative across time. That is probably not unexpected.

What might be the implications of the findings of the modelling over the three overlapping time periods 1996–2006, 2001–2011 and 2006–2016?

1. It is clearly evident that population size (scale) of a FER and population growth does certainly have a powerful *positive* effect on endogenous regional employment performance and that is consistent over time. Thus, population size matters.
2. It is also evident that the structural nature of employment in industry sectors of a FER is largely significant with in explaining variation in endogenous regional employment performance with, in general, a more diversified industrial structure having a *positive* effect.
3. The degree of concentration of employment in specific broad industry categories and change in that over time do not seem have particularly powerful impacts on endogenous regional employment performance of FERs. However, some do have a significant *positive* effect, particularly concentration of employment in the producer services industry categories (the knowledge economy) and change in that over time, although that changed to a negative for the 2006–2011 period in which the GFC occurred. Employment in creative industries did have significant a *positive* effect in the 1996–2006 period.
4. For the human capital variables, there was a mixed impact, it being somewhat counter-intuitive. Where it is significant, the effect seems – in general – to be *negative* rather than positive during an era when there was a massive increased investment in higher education and a huge increase in enrolments and generation of graduates. That does not seem to be necessarily generating a positive impact on endogenous regional employment performance.
5. Engagement in work does seem to sometimes have significant effect with levels of unemployment tending to be a *negative*.
6. As a measure of social capital, the incidence of volunteering is seen to have a significant *positive* effect on endogenous regional employment performance.
7. An interesting finding is that the level of income does not seem to have a significant impact on endogenous regional employment performance.
8. Finally, a FER being located within a major metropolitan region has a *positive* effect on endogenous regional employment performance. But counter-intuitively being a remote location can also have a *positive* effect which related to the importance of mining in many such regions and the generation of jobs by the resources boom.

The modelling undertaken by the authors and their collaborators in the studies investigating the potential factors that impact variations in the endogenous regional employment performance of FERs across Australia for the three overlapping 10-year periods 1996–2006, 2001–2011 and 2006–2016 have provided some further understanding of what might be driving variations in regional economic development in Australia which can help regional policy.

The use of a *functional* geography (FERS) as the spatial base for the modelling has been shown to have benefits over the more commonly used de jure (such as LGAs) spatial base as it appears to eliminate the spatial autocorrelation issue.

Finally, it would be instructive for the modelling to be replicated focussing solely on the FERs located beyond the main metropolitan regions to see how the results might differ and to use to identify factors that are having positive and negative effects on endogenous regional employment performance to help inform regional development policy in Australia.

Acknowledgement This chapter draws on research that was funded by the Australian Research Council that was undertaken through its Linkage International Grants programme, project #LX0346785, and its Discovery Grants programme, projects #DP150103437 and #DP150103437.

References

Anselin L (1988) Spatial econometrics: methods and models. Kluwer Academic Publishers, Dordrecht

Anselin L, Bera A, Florax R, Yoon M (1996) Simple diagnostic tests for spatial dependence. Reg Sci Urban Econ 26:77104

Arthur WB (1994) Increasing returns and path dependency in the economy. University of Michigan Press, Ann Arbor

Barro RJ (1990) Government spending in a simple model of endogenous growth. J Polit Econ 98: S103–S125

Blakely EJ (1994) Planning local economic development: theory and practice. Sage, Thousand Oaks

Corden WM (2011) The Dutch disease in Australia: policy options for a three-speed economy, Working papers in trade and development, working paper no. 2011/14, Arndt-Corden Department of Economics, Crawford School of Economics and Government, ANU College of Asia and the Pacific, November

De Santis M, Stough RR (1999) Fast adjusting urban regions, leadership and regional economic development. Region et Development 10:37–56

Duranton G, Puga D (2000) Diversity and specialisation in cities: why, where and when does it matter? Urban Stud 37:533–555

Erickson RA (1994) Technology, industrial restructuring and regional development. Growth Chang 25:353–379

Erickson RA, Leinbach T (1979) Characteristics of branch plants attracted to non-metropolitan areas. In: Lonsdale R, Seyter HL (eds) Non-metropolitan industrialisation. Winston, Washington, DC

Fairholm GW (1994) Leadership and the culture of trust. Praeger, Westport

Fukuyama F (1995) Trust: the social virtues and creation of prosperity. Free Press, New York

Garlick S, Taylor M, Plummer P (2006) An enterprising approach to regional growth: the role of VET in regional development. NCVER (National Council for Vocational Education Research), Australian National Training Authority, Adelaide

Goetz SJ, Rapasingla A (2001) The returns to higher education: estimates for the contiguous states, paper to Regional Science Association International, North American Annual Meeting, Charleston, November

Gordon IR, McCann P (2000) Industrial clusters, complexes, agglomeration and/or social networks. Urban Stud 37:513–532

Grossman GM, Helpman E (1991) Innovation and growth in the global economy. MIT Press, Cambridge, MA
Hanushek EA, Kimko DD (2000) Schooling, labour-force quality, and the growth of nations. Am Econ Rev 90:1884–1208
Haynes KE, Dinc M (1997) Productivity change in manufacturing regions: a multi-factor shift share approach. Growth Chang 28:201–221
Henderson JV, Kuncoro A, Turner M (1995) Industrial development in cities. J Polit Econ 103:1067–1090
Jessop B (1998) The narrative of enterprise and the enterprise of narrative: place marketing and the Entrepreneurial City. In: Hall T, Hubbard P (eds) The Entrepreneurial City. Wiley, Chichester, pp 77–99
Judd D, Parkinson M (eds) (1990) Leadership and urban regeneration. Sage, Newbury Park
Krugman P (1991) Geography and trade. MIT Press, Cambridge, MA
Markusen A (1985) Profit cycles, oligopoly and regional development. MIT Press, Cambridge, MA
Masser I, Brown PJB (1975) Hierarchical aggregation procedures for interaction data. Environ Plan A 7:509–523
Mitchell WF, Flanagan M (2009) The CofFEE functional economic regions: First edition. Centre of Full Employment and Equity, Newcastle
Mitchell WF, Watts MJ (2010) Identifying functional regions in Australia using hierarchical aggregate techniques. Geogr Res 48:24–41
North D (1990) Institutions, institutional change and economic performance. Cambridge University Press, Cambridge
Norton RD, Rees J (1979) The product cycle and the decentralization of North American manufacturing. Reg Stud 13:141–151
Plummer P, Tonts M, Martinus K (2014) Endogenous growth, local competitiveness and regional development: Western Australia's regional cities, 2001–2011. J Econ Soc Policy 16:1–29
Porter ME (1990) The competitive advantage of nations. Macmillan, New York
Rebelo S (1991) Long run policy analysis and long run growth. J Polit Econ 98:S71–S102
Rees J (1979) State technology programs and industry experience in the USA. Rev Urban Reg Dev Stud 3:39–59
Rees J (2001) Technology and regional development: theory revisited. In: Johansson B, Karlsson C, Stough RR (eds) Theories of endogenous regional growth. Springer, Heidelberg, pp 94–110
Scott AJ (1988) New industrial spaces: flexible production organization and regional development in North America and Western Europe. Pion, London
Stimson RJ (2013) Troubling times – the GFC and its implications for regional performance: Part 2, Australia. Roman J Reg Sci 7(1):1–16
Stimson RJ, Stough RR, (with Maria Salazar) (2009) Leadership and, institutions in regional endogenous development. Edward Elgar, Cheltenham
Stimson R, Robson A, Shyy T-K (2004, November) Shift-share analysis and modeling endogenous growth across Queensland's regions, North American Regional Science Council, 52nd annual meeting, Seattle
Stimson R, Stough R, Salazar M (2005) Leadership and institutional factors in endogenous regional economic development. Investig Reg 7:23–52
Stimson RJ, Robson A, Shyy T-K (2009a) Chapter 18: Measuring regional; endogenous growth. In: Capello R, Nijkamp PJ (eds) Regional growth and development theories in the XXI century: theoretical achievements and future challenges. Edward Elgar, Cheltenham, pp 354–372
Stimson RJ, Rohde D, Shyy T-K (2009b, November) Modelling endogenous regional growth in Australia. Paper presented at the 56th North American Regional Science Conference, San Francisco
Stimson RJ, Mitchell W, Rohde D, Shyy T-K (2011a) Using functional economic regions to model endogenous regional performance in Australia: Implications for addressing the spatial autocorrelation problem. Reg Sci Policy Pract 3:131–144

Stimson RJ, Robson A, Shyy T-Y (2011b) Modelling endogenous regional employment performance in non-metropolitan Australia: what is the role of human capital, social capital and creative capital? In: Kourtit K, Nijkamp P, Stough RR (eds) Drivers of innovation, entrepreneurship and regional dynamics. Springer, Berlin, pp 179–204

Stimson RJ, Stough RR, Nijkamp P (eds) (2011c) Endogenous regional development: perspectives, measurement and empirical investigation. Edward Elgar, Cheltenham

Stimson R, Mitchell W, Flanagan M, Baum S, Shyy T-K (2016) Demarcating functional economic regions across Australia differentiated by work participation categories. Australas J Reg Stud 22:27–57

Stimson R, Flanagan M, Mitchell W, Shyy T-K, Baum S (2018) Modelling endogenous employment performance across Australia's functional economic regions over the decade 2001–2011. Australas J Reg Stud:3–34

Stough RR, Song C, Stimson RJ, Shyy T-K (2009) Differentials in endogenous regional employment growth in US metropolitan areas: the explanatory role of entrepreneurship and other leadership and institutional factors, keynote address. 12th Uddevalla symposium, The Geography of Innovation and Entrepreneurship, Bati, Italy

Taylor PJ, Catalano G, Gane N (2002) A geography of global change: services and cities 2000–01. GaWC Res Bull, Globalisation and World Cities Study Group and Network 77:1–9

Thomas MD (1975) Growth pole theory, technological change and regional economic growth. Pap Reg Sci Assoc 34:3–25

Vazquez-Barquero A (2002) Endogenous development. Networking, innovation, institutions and cities. Routledge, London

Chapter 21
Recent Population and Employment Change in US Metropolitan Areas: An Application of the Adjustment Model

Gordon F. Mulligan and Helena A. K. Nilsson

Abstract This chapter uses a 2 by 2 adjustment model to study the changes in population and employment across 381 US metropolitan areas between 1990 and 2015. Population levels depend upon house prices (amenities) and location (climate), while employment levels depend upon wages and industrial specialization (manufacturing, professional services). Important distinctions are drawn between the 100 largest economies (Brookings group) and the 281 smaller ones. Supply-induced growth has dominated change in the larger areas, while demand-induced growth has prevailed in the smaller areas. Utility patents are shown to have had a positive impact on employment, where this impact has been greater in the nation's large metropolitan economies. Estimates are made for four overlapping 10-year intervals and for data pooled across the 25 years.

Keywords Metropolitan areas · Adjustment model · Supply-induced growth · Demand-induced growth

21.1 Introduction

Despite the considerable attention given to studying growth and change in American metropolitan economies, surprisingly little is known about how population and employment interact with one another over extended periods of time (Florida 2002; Glaeser 2011; Moretti 2012; Mulligan et al. 2017; Shearer et al. 2018). At some locations and times, employment shifts precede changes in population levels (either higher or lower, depending on the initial direction) while, at other locations

G. F. Mulligan (✉)
School of Geography and Development, University of Arizona, Tucson, AZ, USA
e-mail: mulligan@email.arizona.edu

H. A. K. Nilsson
Institute of Retail Economics (Stockholm) and Centre for Entrepreneurship and Spatial Economics, Jönköping International Business School, Jönköping, Sweden
e-mail: Helena.Nilsson@ju.se

Z. Chen et al. (eds.), *Development Studies in Regional Science*,
New Frontiers in Regional Science: Asian Perspectives 42,
https://doi.org/10.1007/978-981-15-1435-7_21

and times, population shifts precede changes in employment levels. Analysts sometimes call the first case demand-driven growth and the second case supply-driven growth. The former has been widely studied by urban and regional analysts for decades, but, in recent times, the role of the latter has become increasingly appreciated—especially in those postindustrial societies where mobile households and firms can locate or relocate in places with high levels of natural or human-created amenities. In recent years, this bidirectional relationship existing between population and employment, in part reflecting their inherent spatial interdependence, has been given more and more attention. However, the role of technological change, which is widely recognized as a main contributor to economic growth, has largely been left out of these models. Moreover, the majority of the studies on the topic have either addressed, or have been estimated, over relatively short periods of time. Furthermore, as the mobility of individuals has changed substantially during recent decades, the direction of interdependence between employment and population is likely to have shifted as well. Therefore, it is of great interest to examine the relationship over a period that is sufficiently long to capture these various shifts. Consequently, this chapter analyzes the bidirectional relationship that existed between population and employment change in US metropolitan areas between 1990 and 2015.

The discussion first reviews the growing literature on this perspective and pays special attention to the features of the so-called regional adjustment model, which is the spatial analogue of those partial adjustment models that are seen elsewhere in economics. Then the discussion specifies the actual nature of the adjustments between population and employment that have recently transpired across some 380 US metropolitan economies. Here the analysis, using simple and two-stage linear regression procedures, focuses on the properties of the reduced-form estimates for four overlapping 10-year periods: 1990–2000, 1995–2005, 2000–2010, and 2005–2015. On the one hand, current population is conjectured to be driven by past population and employment as well as current house values and location (total degree days); on the other hand, current employment is conjectured to be driven by past population and employment as well as current average wages, percentage of workers in manufacturing, and percentage of workers in professional, scientific, and technical jobs. A pooled data set is next used to establish more general results, to examine stability conditions, and to shed light on the sustainability of the estimates. Following that, attention turns to other features of the metropolitan economies that might affect population and employment change, including human-created amenities, patents, and proprietary jobs. Distinctions are drawn throughout between the 100 largest metropolitan economies (the so-called Brookings group) and the remaining 281 smaller metropolitan economies (Shearer et al. 2018).

The main advantage of adopting the adjustment model is that it facilitates our understanding of how bidirectional change occurs in a large and complex space economy. So, at some moments, employment might largely be driving population, but, at other moments, population might largely be driving employment. A series of cross-sectional estimates of the adjustment model shows how different contextual conditions, including wages and house prices, can have varied effects on population and employment change; a follow-up pooled estimation shows, over a longer time period, how important these estimates might be in a more general sense. While the current study adopts the simplest 2 by 2 perspective, it lays down a foundation for more complicated 3 by 3 perspectives. Moreover, the current study sheds light on the issue of labor market sustainability, a factor that is not addressed in most spatial or regional adjustment models to date.

21.2 The Regional Adjustment Model

21.2.1 Background

Soon after the 1970 Census, social scientists in the USA noticed that the nation's demographic landscape was changing in a very fundamental way: for the first time in decades, remote rural areas of the country were growing at the expense of central urban areas (Beale 1972). This nonmetropolitan turnaround was explained in several different ways, but, in general, the various arguments were eventually categorized as belonging to one of two camps: the *regional restructuring* explanation or the *population deconcentrating* explanation (Frey 1993). The main difference between the two regards the role of human agency: the former grants agency only to firms, while the latter grants joint agency to households and firms. In other words, one perspective holds that employment is exogenous to the distribution of population, while the other holds that it is endogenous. After a short period of reversal, this counter-urbanization trend reappeared during the 1990s, although by now the underlying processes had widened in geographic scope, extending from the Snowbelt to the Sunbelt, to include the entire spectrum of nonmetropolitan and metropolitan places.

At the same time, in response to the observations made by others, Muth (1971) suggested that household migration in the USA should be studied as a *chicken or egg* problem. For quite some time, the conventional wisdom had been that people followed jobs, both within and between regions, which meant that employment was exogenous to the geographic distribution of population. But slowly a more nuanced account of change in the space economy evolved where jobs were also seen to follow people, meaning that the twin distributions of population and employment must in fact be endogenously determined. Radical as it seemed at the time, this bidirectional hypothesis is now widely accepted in regional science.

Like many difficult problems, solutions to bidirectional growth were slow to emerge and they involved ideas drawn from economists, demographers, planners, geographers, and others. One key stream of ideas arose from the work done on migration where people like Greenwood (1975) and Graves (1976) noted that households often moved from places of high economic opportunity to places of low economic opportunity. This brought key demographic concepts, like the life cycle, to the forefront for consideration and testing (Graves 1979). Another stream of ideas came from the path-breaking work done on hedonic markets by people like Rosen (1979) and Roback (1982), where it was argued that households might trade off higher wages and salaries for valued natural or human-created amenities. Other work continued to demonstrate that heterogeneity exists in mobility and migration choices, where households with very different attributes could make very different choices about where to live and work (Herzog and Schlottman 1986). Finally, other research demonstrated that firms themselves could anticipate the preferences of their workers and locate, or even relocate, to areas that are rich in non-traded amenities (Boarnet 1994). There is now plenty of evidence, at least in the USA, that amenities elicit a steady effect on worker movements over fairly long periods of time, while economic opportunity, typically more localized in space, affects worker movements in different ways at different points in time (Mueser and Graves 1995). In any case, put together, these various insights grant agency to households and firms alike and mean, in support of Muth's claim, that population and employment change should be simultaneously determined. From this perspective, the *spatial equilibrium* framework has become acceptable not only for explaining short-term trends but also those long-term movements of households and firms both within and between regions (Glaeser 2007).

Out of all this debate, two general processes were seen to be operating in the more advanced space economies. Following Bartik (1991) and DiPasquale and Wheaton (1996), these are usually labeled demand- and supply-induced growth:

- *Demand-induced growth* occurs when firms expand employment, causing an increase in the number of *jobs* in the regional labor market.
- *Supply-induced growth* occurs when households relocate for choice, causing an increase in the number of *people* in the regional labor market.

In practice, however, these two forms of growth unfold together where all types of moves, both within and among regions, are made with attention to both economic opportunity and personal preferences.

21.2.2 The 2 by 2 Adjustment Process

Regional adjustment models are spatial analogues to adjustment models that have been used in the various branches of economics. They originate from research focused on the distribution of people and jobs within regions although the application here is between regions (Steinnes and Fisher 1974; Steinnes 1977). These regional adjustment models were really brought to the fore by Carlino and Mills (1987) and then Clark and Murphy (1996), who applied the framework to county-level population and employment change across the entire USA during the 1970s and 1980s, respectively. Later work has addressed diagnostics and has discussed issues like specification, scale, the effects of macroeconomic conditions, and the like (Mulligan et al. 1999; Hoogstra et al. 2017). Especially interesting applications have targeted the role of amenities in regional development (Mulligan and Carruthers 2011); the effects of growth management policies on urban land use (Boarnet et al.

2011); and the role of geographic contiguity in affecting both population and employment change within metropolitan areas (Carruthers and Mulligan 2019).

In all types of partial adjustment models, the variable of interest—in our case, either population or employment—is seen to be constantly in motion but nevertheless moving toward some equilibrium position. Consequently, the current level of this variable is estimated by accounting for its past (lagged) level, the current level of the other variable it is adjusting to, and the lagged values of a number (vector) of other explanatory variables. In the present 2 by 2 case, population adjusts to employment, and, at the same time, employment adjusts to population. In practice, though, this means that estimates must first be made for both current population and current employment based on the lagged values for *both* variables. So, in the end, current population $POPUL_t$ is seen to adjust to an estimate for current employment $EMPLY*_t$, and, alternatively, current employment $EMPLY_t$ is seen to adjust to an estimate for current population $POPUL*_t$. As in Carlino and Mills (1987), this adjustment period is often assumed to be a decade. The two adjustment equations are estimated by two-stage least squares regression procedures where the 2nd-stage results are:

$$POPUL_t = a_1 + b_1 POPUL_{t-1} + c_1 EMPLY*_t + \mathbf{d_1 VECTR_{t-1}} + e_1 \quad (21.1)$$

$$EMPLY_t = a_2 + b_2 POPUL*_t + c_2 EMPLY_{t-1} + \mathbf{d_2 VECTR_{t-1}} + e_2 \quad (21.2)$$

This means that the reduced forms of these two equations can be recovered by substituting for $EMPLY*_t$ in Eq. (21.1) and for $POPUL*_t$ in Eq. (21.2). When making the estimates for current employment and population, using both of their lagged values, it is customary to include all the other explanatory variables in $\mathbf{VECTR_{t-1}}$ else these estimates will likely be biased because the two distributions of errors are correlated. The reduced-form expressions are as follows:

$$POPUL_t = g_1 + h_1 POPUL_{t-1} + i_1 EMPLY_{t-1} + \mathbf{j_1 VECTR_{t-1}} + k_1 \quad (21.3)$$

$$EMPLY_t = g_2 + h_2 POPUL_{t-1} + i_2 EMPLY_{t-1} + \mathbf{j_2 VECTR_{t-1}} + k_2 \quad (21.4)$$

which can, of course, be estimated directly by OLS regression (or a similar technique). The coefficient c_1 (c_2) indicates the rate at which population (employment) is adjusting to employment (population), while both variables supposedly converge toward a spatial equilibrium. In some cases, however, the adjustment process can either under- or overshoot this equilibrium because one, or both, of the two variables continues to change over time. A test for convergence is therefore needed on the reduced-form equations (see below). It is a simple matter to address changes instead of levels on the left-hand sides of Eqs. (21.3) and (21.4), and, in such cases, the estimates h_1 and h_2 become h_1–1 and h_2–1, respectively, while all the other estimates stay the same. Of course, more than two endogenous variables can be considered in the adjustment process, and, in such cases, a third or fourth variable is sometimes chosen from those already included in the list $\mathbf{VECTR_{t-1}}$ of other explanatory variables. A step-by-step example is given below to illustrate the different stages of the estimation using actual population and employment data for 1990–2000.

Stability is a property that is sometimes tested for. It is unclear, though, how important this property really is because so many other factors—including shifts in fertility and mortality, changes in trade policy, and even outright international conflict—can disturb the path of the adjustment process over time. In any case, it is customary to look at the coefficients in the 2 by 2 matrix $\mathbf{M} = (h_1, i_1; h_2, i_2)$, comprised of the lagged elements in the two reduced-form equations (Rogers 1971). If real eigenvalues (characteristics) exist for this matrix, then convergence takes place in the adjustment process. The dominant (larger) eigenvalue indicates the correct specification of the mutual adjustment although the process itself can be replicated by successively powering the original elements of matrix **M** and then examining for convergence in the ratios between the elements of the same column.

Convergence in the adjustment process leads to the specification of the so-called unit vector, which indicates the proportional or fractional importance of the two (or more) variables at the equilibrium. This property of the adjustment process is often overlooked in regional science although it is very informative in demography (Rogers 1968). In the present case, the unit vector proves especially useful because it sheds light on whether the equilibrium solution for the metropolitan labor markets, while being stable, can in fact be sustainable in the long run. Because employment is drawn from the larger population body, population should *at the very least* be equal to employment at the equilibrium. If the population fraction exceeds the employment fraction in the unit vector, then the adjustment process is possibly sustainable; however, if the employment fraction exceeds the population fraction, then the process is clearly unsustainable. This seems a reasonable interpretation of the unit vector when dealing with entire metropolitan areas; however, in those estimations involving smaller spatial units that are contiguous, like census tracts, it is quite possible that this strict rule would have to be relaxed to accommodate cross commuting.

21.3 Variables and Conjectures

The analysis focuses on the 381 metropolitan statistical areas that are now recognized by the Bureau of Economic Analysis (BEA). In 1990 the mean population *POPUL* of these areas was 245,634, but by 2015 this mean figure had risen to 319,464; in 1990 the mean total employment *EMPLY* of these areas was 132,018, but by 2015 this figure had risen to 181,897 (Bureau of Economic Analysis 2018). Of course, many of the current metropolitan areas were nonmetropolitan (but likely micropolitan) in 1990.

Besides prior population and current employment, current population is conjectured to be largely affected by median house values and by location. Expressed in current dollars, in 1990 the median house value averaged \$137,326 across those metropolitan areas, but in 2015 this figure had climbed to \$170,365

(Savageau and Boyer 1993; U.S. Census Bureau 2018). Location is captured by total degree days, whose average is 5765, where climate is known to vary a lot by temperature, humidity, and moisture across the large land mass of the continental USA (Savageau and Boyer 1993; BizEE degree days 2018). The two conjectures are that population is driven lower by *HOUSE* (−) and lower by *DGDAY* (−). The first conjecture is based on the straightforward notion that households prefer to pay less for housing when all else is constant. But in the present case, housing quality and human-created amenities—including local ambience and public goods and services like health and education—are not homogeneous everywhere, and households often are willing to pay more for housing in those areas with high amenities or superior housing quality. This means it is quite possible that higher house prices will instead drive population upward in the 2 by 2 adjustment model. The second conjecture reflects the widely accepted notion that households prefer mild to extreme climates and seek out those locations offering either low heating degree days or low cooling degree days.

Besides prior employment and current population, current employment is conjectured to be significantly affected by average wages and salaries *WAGES* and by certain facets of industrial specialization. Expressed in current dollars, annual wages averaged only $20,731 in 1990, but this figure had risen to $44,645 by 2015 (BEA 2018). On average, manufacturing jobs *PMANU* (classified as NAICS 31-33) comprised 20.94% of all metropolitan jobs in 1990 but only 6.60% of such jobs in 2015; on the other hand, jobs in the professional, scientific, and technical services *PPROF* (classified as NAICS 54) comprised 4.27% of all metropolitan jobs in 1990 and 5.18% in 2015 (BEA 2018). The first conjecture (*WAGES*, −) reflects the fact that firms generally prefer to pay lower wages to their workers, although this tendency varies a lot with industry and with worker productivity. The second conjecture (*PMANU*, −, and *PPROF*, +) recognizes that, with the ongoing transition to a postindustrial society, overall employment levels are expected to climb faster when manufacturing jobs are initially low and when professional service jobs are initially high. In part this relationship should hold because professional service jobs require a lot more human capital than do highly rationalized manufacturing jobs. The possibility also exists that manufacturing activity, when excessive, will act as a disamenity and deter population change, but our analysis does not examine this issue (Carlino and Saiz 2019).

21.4 Some Results

21.4.1 An Example

The estimates in many studies are shown in reduced form because these coefficients are needed to shed light on the issues of stability and sustainability in the adjustment process. However, it is still worthwhile to outline how the adjustment process itself unfolds. To begin, consider all US metropolitan economies during the period

1990–2000. In the first stage, an estimate for current employment *EMPLY*00∗ is made using the lagged values for both population and employment along with the lagged values for all other (seven) explanatory variables (i.e., all endogenous and exogenous variables). Here the estimates for the first-stage regression indicate that:

$$\begin{aligned} EMPLY00* &= 4.270 - 0.001POPUL90 + 1.007EMPLY90 + 0.030HOUSE90 \\ &-0.030DGDAY - 0.430WAGES90 - 0.007PMANU90 + 0.061PPROF90 \end{aligned} \tag{21.5}$$

The estimates for *EMPLY*00∗ are then used in the second stage to estimate the current population equation as follows:

$$\begin{aligned} POPUL00 &= 3.460 + 0.961POPUL90 + 0.042EMPLY00* + 0.068HOUSE90 \\ &-0.068DGDAY - 0.357WAGES90 - 0.008PMANU90 + 0.034PPROF90 \end{aligned} \tag{21.6}$$

Here Eq. (21.6) represents the adjustment equation for current population. Substitution for *EMPLY*00∗ in Eq. (21.5) next leads to:

$$\begin{aligned} POPUL00 &= 3.640 + 0.961POPUL90 + 0.042EMPLY90 + 0.069HOUSE90 \\ &-0.069DGDAY - 0.375WAGES90 - 0.007PMANU90 + 0.037PPROF90 \end{aligned} \tag{21.7}$$

which represents the reduced-form estimation of the TSLS regression. In the tables of the next section, the estimates for *WAGES*90, *PMANU*90, and *PPROF*90 are suppressed only because they are conjectured to affect current employment more than current population.

The entire exercise is then repeated where *POPUL*00∗ is estimated in the first stage (using all other variables), these estimates are next used to estimate *EMPLY*00 in the second stage, thereby specifying the other half of the adjustment process, and then the estimates for *POPUL*00∗ are substituted in order to arrive back at the reduced-form expressions for *EMPLY*00. The reduced-form estimation of current employment, as seen in various tables below, now suppresses the estimates for *HOUSE*90 and *DGDAY* because the emphasis is on modeling employment. In many cases the adjustment coefficients, on either *EMPLOY*∗ or *POPUL*∗, are small (note it is 0.042 above), so the estimates for the vectors of explanatory variables in Eqs. (21.6) and (21.7) turn out to be quite similar.

In this chosen decade, the adjustment process converges because real eigenvalues exist, where the dominant eigenvalue based on the matrix $\mathbf{M} = (0.961, 0.042; -0.001, 1.007)$ is $\lambda = 1.0061$. The unit vector is calculated to be (0.484, 0.516), which means at the equilibrium the population effect (0.484) is exceeded by the employment effect (0.516) in driving the adjustment process. So, from the perspective of a closed metropolitan labor market, the equilibrium is a not a sustainable one.

Table 21.1 All metropolitan areas: reduced-form estimates

	1990–2000	1995–2005	2000–2010	2005–2015
Population				
Constant	3.640**	1.925**	2.123**	2.682**
POPUL	0.961**	1.023**	1.022**	0.938**
EMPLY	0.042	−0.021	−0.014	0.058
HOUSE	0.069**	0.114**	0.062**	−0.013
DGDAY	−0.069**	−0.055**	−0.054**	−0.082**
R^2	0.992	0.993	0.995	0.992
Employment				
Constant	4.720**	2.022**	2.736**	2.106**
POPUL	−0.001	0.154**	0.154**	0.007
EMPLY	1.007**	0.844**	0.838*	0.996**
WAGES	−0.430**	−0.330**	−0.263**	−0.140**
PMANU	−0.007	−0.032**	−0.024*	0.007
PPROF	0.061**	0.065**	0.153**	0.156**
R^2	0.992	0.993	0.988	0.989
Stable	Yes	Yes	Yes	Yes
Sustainable	No	Yes	Yes	No

Note: $n = 381$; * 0.10 level; ** 0.01 level

21.4.2 Decade-by-Decade Findings

The four sets of decade-specific reduced-form results can be viewed in Tables 21.1, 21.2, and 21.3. The first of these tables addresses all 381 metropolitan areas, the second table accounts for the 100 largest areas, and the third table accounts for the other 281 areas. In the results for the current population equations, note that:

- The lagged population effect is higher during the two middle decades in both the large metropolitan areas (0.948 and 0.940 versus 0.873 and 0.827) and the small metropolitan areas (1.026 and 1.036 versus 0.963 and 0.931)
- The lagged population effect is some 8–12% higher in the small metropolitan areas
- The lagged employment effect, while mostly insignificant in both type of metropolitan areas, is higher in the large metropolitan areas
- The positive effect for house prices seen during the first three decades is due entirely to the small economies, but even here the effect steadily declines over time (from 0.105 to −0.012)
- The effect of extreme climate, which reflects location, is significant for all decades in all economies but is clearly more important in the large economies; moreover, this effect is strongest in the final decade

Alternatively, across the current employment equations, it is worth pointing out that:

- The lagged employment effect is lower during the middle decades in both the large and small metropolitan areas

Table 21.2 Large metropolitan areas: reduced-form estimates

	1990–2000	1995–2005	2000–2010	2005–2015
Population				
Constant	4.423**	4.061**	2.545**	3.091**
POPUL	0.873**	0.948**	0.940**	0.827**
EMPLY	0.132	0.049	0.040	0.167*
HOUSE	−0.020	0.014	−0.002	−0.006
DGDAY	−0.127*	−0.116**	−0.103**	−0.112**
R^2	0.985	0.988	0.990	0.993
Employment				
Constant	5.113*	4.205**	2.271*	1.349
POPUL	−0.089	0.163*	0.154*	0.006
EMPLY	1.099**	0.842**	0.841**	1.006**
WAGES	−0.351*	−0.357**	−0.132	−0.057
PMANU	−0.025	−0.071**	−0.084**	−0.039*
PPROF	0.021	0.104*	0.073	0.065
R^2	0.984	0.989	0.993	0.993
Stable	No	Yes	Yes	Yes
Sustainable	No	No	No	No

Note: $n = 100$; * 0.10 level; ** 0.01 level

Table 21.3 Small metropolitan areas: reduced-form estimates

	1990–2000	1995–2005	2000–2010	2005–2015
Population				
Constant	3.215**	1.542**	1.863**	2.869**
POPUL	0.963**	1.026**	1.036**	0.931**
EMPLY	0.010	−0.047	−0.041	0.039
HOUSE	0.105**	0.142**	0.087**	−0.012
DGDAY	−0.056*	−0.038*	−0.035*	−0.076**
R^2	0.969	0.973	0.979	0.962
Employment				
Constant	3.922**	1.683**	3.561**	3.302**
POPUL	−0.001	0.122**	0.109*	−0.029
EMPLY	0.976**	0.842**	0.838**	0.997**
WAGES	−0.415**	−0.309**	−0.297**	−0.162*
PMANU	−0.001	−0.023**	−0.012	0.015
PPROF	0.069**	0.060**	0.164**	0.170**
R^2	0.972	0.974	0.939	0.947
Stable	Yes	Yes	Yes	No
Sustainable	No	Yes	Yes	No

Note: $n = 281$; * 0.10 level; ** 0.01 level

- The lagged population effect is positive and significant across all metropolitan areas during the middle decades but not during 1995–2005 or 2005–2015
- The effect of wages is very important in the first two decades but becomes less so in the last two decades; however, this negative effect remains significant in the small metropolitan areas over the entire 25 years
- Both types of industrial specialization exhibit significant initial effects, but those due to manufacturing are more pervasive (negative) in the large economies, while those due to professional, scientific, and technical services are more pervasive (positive) in the small economies

The various results also expose some dramatic changes that took place in metropolitan America during the recessionary years of 2007–2009. During this time, the traditional argument that *people follow jobs* had little or no effect on the metropolitan economies; instead, the results indicate that the more significant process during that time was that *jobs follow people*. In fact, this nontraditional supply-induced process was very important during both the decades of 1995–2005 and 2000–2010. Nevertheless, the traditional demand-induced process asserted itself at times, and, by 2005–2015, employment was again driving population in the nation's very largest economies. Furthermore, the observation about specialization noted above really suggests that small metropolitan areas competed more on the differential quality of their professional services, while metropolitan areas competed more on other factors (see below).

21.4.3 Effects of Spatial Lags

Current population and employment were re-estimated for each of the four decades using a GS2SLS spatial lag model, where the four observations located in Alaska and Hawaii were removed (Table 21.4). Here an inverse distance matrix was adopted, with a 400-km threshold, so that every metropolitan area had at least one neighbor. Re-estimation was only carried out for all metropolitan areas because the spatial structure would differ so much if separate regressions were run for the large and small areas. Following Kelejian and Prucha (2010), a "minmax" normalized weight matrix (where each element is divided by the smallest of the largest column sum or row sum) is used in order to preserve the internal weighting structure. Both types of spatial lags proved to be negative and significant over all four time periods where the lag effect on employment was always some 50–60% stronger than that on population. However, there was no discernible trend in the strength of either lag effect over the 25-year time period.

Table 21.4 presents the estimates for the total effects. These effects are the sum of the (average) direct and indirect effects that arise within and between neighboring areal units. The direct effects are the impacts from a shift in an independent variable in area i on the dependent variable, also in area i. The indirect effects are the impacts of a shift in an independent variable in area i on the dependent variable in

Table 21.4 All metropolitan areas: total spatial effects for reduced-form estimates

	1990–2000	1995–2005	2000–2010	2005–2015
Population				
POPUL	0.957**	1.026**	1.032**	0.965**
EMPLY	0.039	−0.029	−0.027	0.026
HOUSE	0.075**	0.126**	0.065**	−0.017
DGDAY	−0.073**	−0.060**	−0.059**	−0.083**
Spatial lag	−0.010**	−0.005**	−0.006**	−0.008**
R^2	0.993	0.994	0.995	0.993
Employment				
POPUL	−0.001	0.163**	0.186**	0.052
EMPLY	0.996**	0.828**	0.799**	0.943**
WAGES	−0.306**	−0.261**	−0.189**	−0.053
PMANU	0.016*	−0.020*	−0.002	0.030**
PPROF	0.050**	0.054**	0.149**	0.152**
Spatial lag	−0.014**	−0.008**	−0.011**	−0.012**
R^2	0.993	0.994	0.989	0.990
Stable	Yes	Yes	Yes	Yes
Sustainable	No	Yes	Yes	No

Note: $n = 377$; * 0.10 level; ** 0.01 level

neighboring area *j*. In this case it turns out that the indirect effects, while sometimes significant, were generally very small so that the direct and total effects were always very similar in value. In fact, the only notable differences occurred on the lagged own estimates, and these never exceeded 1%. However, a few shifts were apparent when the spatial coefficients of Table 21.4 were compared to the nonspatial coefficients of Table 21.1. First, in all cases the estimate of the wage elasticity on employment was reduced by some 30% when spatial lags were adopted—for example, shifting from −0.430 to −0.306 in the first decade and from −0.140 to −0.053 in the last decade—thereby indicating that wages did not have as great an effect on employment change as first thought. Second, the spatial lag model elevated the various estimates on manufacturing specialization and in two decades even shifted the anticipated negative direction to a positive one. The message here is that such specialization did not hinder subsequent employment change as much as might be expected. Third, the spatial lag model generally elevated the estimates for lagged population in the current employment equation, suggesting that the jobs-follow-people scenario was even stronger once proximity was accounted for. Negative autocorrelation is somewhat harder to interpret than its positive counterpart, but here the results indicate that spatial spillovers were not all that important in the population-employment adjustment process between 1990 and 2015. In fact, it seems that the metropolitan areas of the USA performed better when they were somewhat isolated from their nearest spatial neighbors, thereby suggesting that inter-metropolitan competition outweighed inter-metropolitan exchange during that period (Haynes and Fotheringham 1984).

21.5 Pooled Results

21.5.1 Existing Variables

Further insights can be gained from Tables 21.5, 21.6, and 21.7 where the four decades of data are pooled together. Model A shows estimates when the time intercepts have been excluded, while Model B shows the various estimates when those intercepts are included. Again, the reduced-form results reflect all seven explanatory variables, but the tables suppress three estimates in the population equation and two estimates in the employment equation. In the current population equations for Models A and B, it is worth pointing out that:

- Lagged population has a somewhat greater effect in the small metropolitan areas (0.972–0.979) compared to the large metropolitan areas (0.922); this not inconsiderable gap of 5% reinforces the findings already noted for the various 10-year periods
- Lagged employment has a noticeably greater effect in the large metropolitan areas (0.066–0.068) compared to the small metropolitan areas (0.002–0.004)
- House values have no significant effect in the large economies but do have a significant, positive effect in the small economies; again, this reinforces the findings noted for the various 10-year time periods

Table 21.5 All metropolitan areas: pooled reduced-form estimates

	Model A	Model B	Model C	Model D
Population				
Constant	2.267**	3.865**	2.422**	3.133**
POPUL	0.978**	0.980**	0.977**	0.979**
EMPLY	0.021	0.024	0.016	0.019
HOUSE	0.025**	0.036**	0.023**	0.033**
DGDAY	−0.079**	−0.071**	−0.083**	−0.076**
R^2	0.993	0.993	0.993	0.993
SEE	0.0911	0.0906	0.0910	0.0905
Employment				
Constant	3.406**	3.086**	3.444**	3.278**
POPUL	0.091**	0.080**	0.091**	0.079**
EMPLY	0.913**	0.922**	0.912**	0.918**
WAGES	−0.322**	−0.299**	−0.323**	−0.308**
PMANU	−0.013**	−0.015**	−0.014**	−0.017**
PPROF	0.120**	0.111**	0.118**	0.107**
PATEN			0.001	0.005
R^2	0.990	0.990	0.990	0.990
SEE	0.1124	0.1097	0.1124	0.1097
Stable	Yes	Yes	Yes	Yes
Sustainable	Yes	Yes	Yes	Yes

Note: $n = 1524$; * 0.10 level; ** 0.01 level; B, D have time intercepts

Table 21.6 Large metropolitan areas: pooled reduced-form estimates

	Model A	Model B	Model C	Model D
Population				
Constant	3.152**	3.587**	3.496**	4.149**
POPUL	0.922**	0.922**	0.920**	0.917**
EMPLY	0.066*	0.068*	0.057	0.061
HOUSE	−0.010	−0.020	−0.012	−0.023
DGDAY	−0.115**	−0.119**	−0.122**	−0.128**
R^2	0.989	0.989	0.989	0.989
SEE	0.0843	0.0843	0.0842	0.0840
Employment				
Constant	3.667**	3.147**	3.759**	3.766**
POPUL	0.101*	0.093*	0.100*	0.087*
EMPLY	0.903**	0.906**	0.901**	0.899**
WAGES	−0.291**	−0.199**	−0.295**	−0.230**
PMANU	−0.044**	−0.051**	−0.046**	−0.061**
PPROF	0.120**	0.109**	0.115**	0.084**
PATEN			0.004	0.018*
R^2	0.988	0.989	0.988	0.990
SEE	0.0928	0.0875	0.0928	0.0871
Stable	Yes	Yes	Yes	Yes
Sustainable	No	No	No	No

Note: $n = 400$; * 0.10 level; ** 0.01 level; B, D have time intercepts

- Extreme climate, reflecting location, has a notably stronger negative effect (at least 65% greater) in the large metropolitan areas

In the counterpart employment equations for Models A and B, it is worthwhile to point out that:

- Lagged population has a somewhat greater effect in the large metropolitan areas (0.093–0.101) compared to the small metropolitan areas (0.047–0.054); however, the differences in the pooled effects are smaller than those for the individual 10-year periods
- Lagged employment, once again, has approximately the same positive effect irrespective of the size of the metropolitan area
- Wages again exhibit a stronger negative effect in the small metropolitan areas, but, as seen before, the pooled effect is somewhat smaller than some of the period-specific effects
- Specialization in manufacturing has a noticeably greater negative effect only in the large metropolitan areas
- Specialization in professional, scientific, and technical services has approximately the same positive effect irrespective of the size of the metropolitan area; this finding differs from that using the 10-year study periods where the effect was notably stronger in the small economies

Table 21.7 Small metropolitan areas: pooled reduced-form estimates

	Model A	Model B	Model C	Model D
Population				
Constant	2.261**	2.728**	2.364**	3.870**
POPUL	0.972**	0.979**	0.972**	0.978**
EMPLY	0.004	0.002	0.002	−0.001
HOUSE	0.039**	0.058**	0.038**	0.057**
DGDAY	−0.069**	−0.058**	−0.072**	−0.061**
R^2	0.969	0.969	0.969	0.969
SEE	0.0908	0.0902	0.0908	0.0902
Employment				
Constant	3.802**	3.355**	3.518**	3.422**
POPUL	0.054*	0.047*	0.055*	0.047*
EMPLY	0.914**	0.919**	0.914**	0.918**
WAGES	−0.330*	−0.309*	−0.330*	−0.312*
PMANU	−0.006	−0.007	−0.006	−0.008
PPROF	0.120**	0.110**	0.119**	0.108**
PATEN			0.001	0.002
R^2	0.954	0.956	0.954	0.956
SEE	0.1162	0.1139	0.1162	0.1139
Stable	Yes	Yes	Yes	Yes
Sustainable	Yes	Yes	Yes	Yes

Note: $n = 1124$; * 0.10 level; ** 0.010 level; B, D have time intercepts

In general, the pooled estimates for Models A and B weakly endorse the case for the people-follow-jobs scenario but strongly endorse the alternative case for the jobs-follow-people scenario. Moreover, the more traditional, demand-induced shift and the less traditional, supply-induced shift both appear to be much stronger in the large economies than in the small economies. This gives yet another perspective on the prospects for those superstar cities that can take great advantage of their knowledge workers and large, diverse labor forces.

21.5.2 Other Variables

The analysis was next extended to consider the effects of two other variables. The first of these was human-created amenities, which was conjectured to have a positive impact on both population and employment levels. The second variable was patents, which was conjectured to have a similar positive effect but only on employment levels.

Human-created amenities, along with public goods and various externalities, have become of considerable interest to regional scientists in recent years (Carruthers and Mundy 2006; Haynes 2006; Mulligan and Carruthers 2011).

Metropolitan areas are known to compete according to their amenities, something that is especially apparent for certain occupations and for certain segments of the working-age population. On the one hand, young, affluent households are drawn to places with both ambience and recreational opportunities; on the other hand, regional offices in the service industries often locate in places enjoying superior accessibility to national or international decision-making centers. Five amenity variables (ordinal rankings of ambience, education, health, recreation, and transportation) were transformed into a single amenity factor using a multivariate technique, and then this variable was added to those considered above (Savageau 2007; Mulligan 2018). Based on data drawn from 349 metropolitan areas (comparable data for 32 of the smaller places were not available), this single factor had no discernible effect on population levels and only a moderate effect on employment levels, so the new estimates are not shown. Quite possibly the results were disappointing because the amenity data were all taken from a single point in time. The other possibility is that these different amenity levels are already capitalized into the different housing prices seen across the various metropolitan areas.

Patent volumes are commonly used to gauge the degree of useful knowledge that is produced in different regions. Patent volumes not only reflect industrial and occupational specialization but indicate whether certain areas enjoy superior amounts of human capital. Areas with high patent volumes are also known to be on the cutting edge of generating new ideas regarding manufacturing processes and both the distribution and marketing of those products. It is now known that utility patents have been concentrating in the larger metropolitan areas of the USA, while design patents continue to show surprising strength in the nation's smaller micropolitan areas (Mulligan 2018; Liu et al. 2018). Although patents are widely believed to affect employment levels, the actual mechanism, and timing, involved is still somewhat unclear (Tsvetkova 2015).

Using the pooled data, Models C and D show the estimates for utility patents *PATEN* across the nation's metropolitan areas in Tables 21.5, 21.6, and 21.7 (U.S. Patent and Trade Office 2018). Surprisingly, the only significant impact (elasticity of 0.018) was found in the large economies when the time intercepts were included (Model D). The various estimates of the employment equation also suggest that patents appear to elevate the negative impact of manufacturing activity but dampen the positive impact of professional, scientific, and technical services. In any case, the results here suggest that patenting is an activity that only the nation's very largest metropolitan economies compete on.

21.6 Conclusions

This chapter has outlined and estimated a 2 by 2 adjustment model for population and employment in order to shed light on the changes seen across US metropolitan areas since 1990. Very clearly, places with higher house prices and milder climates have enjoyed more population growth; likewise, places with lower wages, less manufacturing, and more professional services have enjoyed more employment growth. It is very interesting, though, that the largest metropolitan areas seem to have benefitted substantially more from supply-induced growth, where jobs follow people, than have the smallest metropolitan areas. Furthermore, the evolving economies of these smaller places no longer seem to follow the traditional logic of demand-induced growth, where people follow jobs. This indicates that regional policies to increase growth must be designed differently depending on the size of the targeted metropolitan area. Hence, policies to encourage growth in larger metropolitan areas ought to be focused on increasing the attractiveness of an area, while the same strategy for smaller metropolitan areas may be without effect. This recommendation concurs with that expressed earlier by Carlino and Hunt (2009), who stressed that promoting programs like regional clusters is no substitute for improving human capital and elevating the skill base of the local workforce.

Extensions to the standard models were considered, and the possible roles of both human-created amenities and utility patents were discussed. The results for the former were somewhat disappointing, which could be attributed to the use of median house values, but the results for the latter were not so disappointing in that they suggested large metropolitan areas do compete on patenting activity. Alternative, preliminary estimates suggest that the importance of patenting becomes more evident when population and employment densities are adopted instead of levels. There is also evidence that these positive patenting effects become more pronounced when the time lag adopted for the adjustment process is reduced. Moreover, future work on metropolitan adjustment processes should include consideration of both self-employment levels and the annual volumes seen in the entry and exit of businesses (Parajuli and Haynes 2015). Other models could also experiment with the inclusion of more endogenous variables, especially if those variables (e.g., house prices) were believed to impact both population and employment levels.

Adjustment models can be used to shed light on various aspects of national or regional metropolitan change, and they should certainly be adopted more outside of the USA. These models could prove to be very useful, for instance, in indicating whether growth was becoming too unbalanced in those developing nations where primate cities tend to flourish. Moreover, further attention must be given in all nations to specifying the time frame for the demographic and economic reactions that occur in metropolitan areas in response to changing national or international circumstances.

References

Bartik T (1991) Who benefits from state and local economic development policies? W.E. Upjohn Institute, Kalamazoo

Beale C (1972) Rural and nonmetropolitan population trends of significance to National Population Policy. Economic Research Service. U.S. Department of Agriculture, Washington, DC

BizEE Degree Days (2018) See https://www.degreedays.net. Last accessed 11/01/18

Boarnet M (1994) An empirical model of intrametropolitan population and employment growth. Pap Reg Sci 73:135–152

Boarnet M, McLaughlin R, Carruthers J (2011) Does state growth management change the pattern of urban growth? Evidence from Florida. Reg Sci Urban Econ 41:236–252
Bureau of Economic Analysis (2018) Interactive tables: personal income and employment. See https://www.bea.gov/regional/index/htm. Last accessed 11/01/18
Carlino G, Hunt R (2009) What explains the quantity and quality of local inventive activity? Working paper no. 09–12. Federal Reserve Bank of Philadelphia, Philadelphia
Carlino G, Mills E (1987) The determinants of county growth. J Reg Sci 27:135–152
Carlino G, Saiz A (2019) Beautiful cities: leisure amenities and urban growth, Working paper no. 19–16. Federal Reserve Bank of Philadelphia, Philadelphia
Carruthers J, Mulligan G (2019) The regional adjustment model: an instrument of evidence-based policy. In: Capello R, Nijkamp P (eds) Handbook of regional growth and development theories, 2nd edn. Edward Elgar, Cheltenham
Carruthers J, Mundy B (eds) (2006) Environmental valuation. Ashgate, Burlington
Clark D, Murphy C (1996) Countywide employment and population growth. J Reg Sci 36:235–256
DiPasquale D, Wheaton W (1996) Urban economics and real estate markets. Prentice-Hall, Englewood Cliffs
Florida R (2002) The rise of the creative class. Basic Books, New York
Frey W (1993) The new urban revival in the United States. Urban Stud 30:741–774
Glaeser E (2007) The economics approach to cities, Working paper 13696. National Bureau of Economic Research, Cambridge, MA
Glaeser E (2011) Triumph of the city. Penguin Press, New York
Graves P (1976) A re-examination of migration, economic opportunity, and the quality of life. J Reg Sci 16:107–112
Graves P (1979) A life-cycle empirical analysis of migration and climate, by race. J Urban Econ 6:135–147
Greenwood M (1975) Research on internal migration in the United States: a survey. J Econ Lit 13:397–433
Haynes K (2006) Infrastructure: the glue of megacities. Kenniscentrum Grote Steden, The Hague
Haynes K, Fotheringham AS (1984) Gravity and spatial interaction models. Volume 2, Scientific geography series. Sage, Beverly Hills
Herzog H, Schlottman A (1986) What can be learned from the recent migrants? Growth Chang 17:37–50
Hoogstra G, van Dijk J, Florax R (2017) Do jobs follow people or people follow jobs? A meta-analysis of Carlino-Mills studies. Spat Econ Anal 12(4):357–378
Kelejian H, Prucha I (2010) Specification and estimation of spatial autoregressive models with autoregressive and heteroskedastic disturbances. J Econ 157:53–67
Liu S, Qian H, Haynes K (2018) Entrepreneurship in small cities: evidence from U.S. micropolitan areas. Paper presented at 21st Uddevalla Symposium on Innovation, Entrepreneurship and Industrial Dynamics in Internationalized Regional Economies. June 14–16, Luleå, Sweden
Moretti E (2012) The new geography of jobs. Houghton Mifflin Harcourt, New York
Mueser P, Graves P (1995) Examining the role of economic opportunity and amenities in explaining population redistribution. J Urban Econ 37:176–200
Mulligan G (2018) Patent generation in U.S. metropolitan areas. In: Bernhard I (ed) Uddevalla symposium 2018: diversity, innovation, entrepreneurship—regional, urban, national and international perspectives. University West, Trollhättan, pp 299–313
Mulligan G, Carruthers J (2011) Amenities, quality of life, and regional development. In: Marans R, Stimson R (eds) Investigating quality of urban life. Springer, Dordrecht, pp 107–133
Mulligan G, Vias A, Glavac S (1999) Initial diagnostics of a regional adjustment model. Environ Plan A 31:855–876
Mulligan G, Reid N, Carruthers J, Lehnert M (2017) Exploring innovation gaps in the American space economy. In: Jackson R, Schaeffer P (eds) Regional research frontiers—Vol. 1. Springer, Dordrecht, pp 21–50
Muth R (1971) Migration: chicken or egg? South Econ J 37:295–306

Parajuli J, Haynes K (2015) Broadband internet and new firm formation: a U.S. perspective. In: Karlsson C, Gråsjö U, Wixe S (eds) Innovation and entrepreneurship in the global economy. Edward Elgar, Cheltenham, pp 210–236
Roback J (1982) Wages, rent, and the quality of life. J Polit Econ 90:1257–1278
Rogers A (1968) Matrix analysis of interregional population growth and distribution. University of California Press, Berkeley
Rogers A (1971) Matrix methods in urban and regional analysis. Holden-Day, San Francisco
Rosen S (1979) Wage-based indexes of urban quality of life. In: Mieszkowski P, Straszheim M (eds) Current issues in urban economics. Johns Hopkins University Press, Baltimore, pp 74–104
Savageau D (2007) Places rated almanac, 7th edn. Places Rated Books, Washington, DC
Savageau D, Boyer R (1993) Places rated almanac, 4th edn. Macmillan, New York
Shearer C, Shah I, Friedhoff A, Berube A (2018) Metro Monitor 2018. Brookings Institute. See https://www.brookings.edu/research/metro-monitor-2018. Last accessed 11/01/18
Steinnes D (1977) Causality and intraurban location. J Urban Econ 4:69–79
Steinnes D, Fisher W (1974) An econometric model of intraurban location. J Reg Sci 14:65–80
Tsvetkova A (2015) Innovation, entrepreneurship, and metropolitan economic performance: empirical test of recent theoretical propositions. Econ Dev Q 29:299–316
U.S. Census Bureau (2018) See https://www.census.gov. Last accessed 11/01/18
U.S. Patent and Trade Office (2018) Calendar year patent statistics: listing of all U.S. Metropolitan and Micropolitan Areas, Total Patent Utility Counts, 2000–2015. See https://www.uspto.gov/web/offices/ac/ido/oeip/taf/reports_cbsa.htm. Last accessed 11/01/18

Chapter 22
Estimating US Antidumping/ Countervailing Duty Enforcement Benefits

Adam Rose, Zhenhua Chen, and Dan Wei

Abstract Dumping is the unfair trade practice of a foreign firm exporting its goods at a price below the sales price in its home market or below its production cost plus markup. Dumping displaces production of similar commodities in the importing country, because its domestic producers have difficulty competing with the lower import price. Antidumping (AD) is a major Priority Trade Issue of concern to U.S. Customs and Border Protection (CBP), and its enforcement is undertaken in parallel with that of countervailing duties (CVD), tariffs on imported goods that offset subsidies for these goods in the exporting country.

We present a generalized analytical framework and then apply it to the estimation of the macroeconomic impacts on the US economy of AD/CVD enforcement. We analyze individual markets for commodities that are being dumped to estimate

The authors are, respectively, Research Professor, Price School of Public Policy, and Senior Research Fellow and Interim Director, Center for Risk and Economic Analysis of Terrorism Events (CREATE), University of Southern California (USC); Assistant Professor, Knowlton School of Architecture, The Ohio State University; Research Associate Professor, Price School, and Research Fellow, CREATE, USC. The research contained in this chapter was supported by the United States Department of Homeland Security (DHS) Customs and Border Protection (CBP) under Grant No. BOA HSHQDC-10-A-BOA19 through CREATE. We are grateful to the following people for commenting on the earlier drafts of the study: Bryan Roberts, Katie Foreman, Gia Harrigan, and staff of CBP. We thank an anonymous reviewer and two of the co-editors for their very helpful suggestions to improve the paper. We also thank Brett Shears for his valuable research assistance. However, the views contained in this chapter are solely those of the authors and not necessarily of any of the institutions with which they are affiliated nor the institutions that funded the research.

A. Rose (✉) · D. Wei
Price School of Public Policy, University of Southern California, Los Angeles, CA, USA
e-mail: adam.rose@usc.edu; danwei@usc.edu

Z. Chen
Knowlton School of Architecture, City and Regional Planning, The Ohio State University, Columbus, OH, USA
e-mail: chen.7172@osu.edu

Z. Chen et al. (eds.), *Development Studies in Regional Science*, New Frontiers in Regional Science: Asian Perspectives 42,
https://doi.org/10.1007/978-981-15-1435-7_22

the direct effects, and then use the Global Trade Analysis Project (GTAP) multi-country computable general equilibrium (CGE) model to estimate the total (direct and indirect) impacts.

Our findings indicate an economic welfare gain to the US economy, measured in terms of personal income, of $182.3 million from the $508.8 million AD/CVD duties levied in fiscal year 2014. The duties themselves represent no welfare gain, as they are merely a transfer from importing companies in the USA to the federal government. However, the duties do provide a basis for estimating the macroeconomic benefits of enforcement if we divide them into the economic welfare impacts. They indicate that for every million dollars of AD/CVD duties levied, US personal income is increased by $358 thousand by way of the various direct effects of increased production of domestic substitutes displacing imported goods and the net of various indirect effects relating to resource allocation and the terms of trade.

Keywords Antidumping · International trade · Macroeconomic impacts · Enforcement benefits · Computable general equilibrium analysis

22.1 Introduction

"Dumping" refers to the unfair trade practice of a foreign firm selling its goods imported into another country at a price below its own domestic price or below production cost plus markup. These price/cost bases are referred to as "fair trade value," and the difference between them and the selling price is referred to as the "dumping margin." Dumping displaces US production of similar commodities, which have difficulty competing with the lower import price. US firms who conclude they are being adversely affected by dumping can file a petition with the US Department of Commerce (DOC) and the US International Trade Commission (ITC). If the petition is upheld, a duty (tariff) is imposed on the importer of the foreign shipment and collected by US Customs and Border Protection (CBP) (Czako et al. 2003).

Antidumping (AD) is a major Priority Trade Issue (PTI) of concern to CBP, and its enforcement is undertaken in parallel with the closely related issue of countervailing duties (CVD). CVD refers to offsetting duties imposed by the USA after determination that an exporting country has subsidized those goods, and this has caused injury to at least 25% of US firms in this market (CBP 2015). In general, the benefits of CBP enforcement actions against such anti-competitive and other deleterious behavior are the prevented negative consequences had the violations actually occurred. In this study, we examine the specific case: What are the benefits to the US economy of enforcement to prevent evasion of AD/CVD regulations?

We present a generalized framework for estimating the direct and indirect economic benefits of AD/CVD enforcement by analyzing the macroeconomic impacts of these duties on the US economy. This is performed by analyzing individual markets for commodities that are being dumped or subsidized to estimate the direct effects and then using a computable general equilibrium (CGE) model to estimate the total (direct and indirect) effects. The indirect effects can include not only conventional quantity and price multiplier interactions but also aspects of market distortions and terms of trade effects.

We have identified the Global Trade Analysis Project (GTAP) Model as best suited for our purpose because it is based on a comprehensive dataset that covers more than 120 countries and 57 sectors and is used extensively by trade economists. Nearly every recent study of the macroeconomic impacts of AD/CVD policies to date has used CGE modeling, and the GTAP Model has several attractive features with respect to the analysis of trade policy. We apply the GTAP Model to the case of the addition of AD/CVD duties on a sector by sector basis in order to examine their impacts on the US economy in terms of real GDP and economic welfare (measured in terms of total personal income).[1] All of the simulations are performed under simplifying assumptions of perfect competition and absence of strategic behavior. Thus, they represent an incomplete analysis of the issue, but we are still able to draw reasonable qualitative conclusions about the benefits of AD/CVD duties by comparing results for selective cases of imperfect competition and drawing inferences about the extent of strategic behavior.

Our findings indicate an economic welfare gain to the US economy, measured in terms of personal income, of $182.3 million dollars from the $508.8 million AD/CVD cash deposits in lieu of duties collected in fiscal year (FY) 2014. The cash deposits themselves represent no net gain, as they are merely a transfer from importing companies in the US to the federal government.

22.2 Insights into AD/CVD Enforcement

DOC calculates the dumping margins and ITC ascertains whether domestic producers have incurred material injury. Following an initial determination by both government agencies of a violation, the importer must post a bond or cash within 190 days, with a value corresponding to the preliminary margin calculation multiplied by the stated value of the shipment. CBP assesses the duties (equivalent to the AD margin) and collects these payments at a later date, typically more than a year.[2] They can be adjusted

[1]There are several metrics that are often used to evaluate policies and practices. Two metrics that are widely cited are gross domestic product (GDP) and employment. However, when federal government agencies evaluate the economic impacts of changes in government policies or programs, they are directed by the Office of Management and Budget (OMB) to use different measures, referred to as "economic welfare," that better capture changes in the economic well-being of the US public. These measures are also used by agencies such as the US International Trade Commission (ITC) to evaluate the impacts of trade policies. The measures are always expressed in monetary terms, and they closely correspond to how personal income and profits change after a policy or program change. We provide more details in Sect. 22.3.

[2]Although CBP's major task is revenue collection, it also performs audits, inspections of cargo, processing of entry summary forms, and scrutinizing importers to identify risks or investigate cases of antidumping. All of these functions help detect violations.

through formal administrative review on the basis of the final determination of the AD case by the DOC and ITC, which can take more than a year (Czako et al. 2003).

AD duties are imposed as the percentage differences between the foreign seller's price and its home market price, or, in some cases, especially where markets are not established, of production costs and a reasonable profit margin. These duties can be adjusted annually by the DOC. Ironically, relief from these duties can be obtained by the foreign seller raising its price in US markets. This strategy can, however, generate further losses to the USA. Gallaway et al. (1999) and Blonigen and Prusa (2003) note that this behavior results in the appropriate analysis being more akin to examining a quota, in which the "rents" are transferred to the seller, as opposed to tariffs, where the rents are appropriated by the government of the importing country.

Fischer and Mirman (1994; p. 215) suggest that "the higher the dumping margin, the higher the probability of detecting something." They also note that the larger this margin, the larger the material injury to domestic firms, defined as "harm which is not inconsequential, immaterial, or unimportant" (19 US C. 1677 (7) (A)). Fischer and Mirman (p. 125) also state: "The intensity with which the government pursues dumping investigations depends on political considerations and in turn, the severity of government enforcement affects the probability of detection."[3]

Detection is necessary to prevent several types of evasion of dumping duties, such as illegal transshipping, undervaluation of the shipment, misclassification as a good not subject to duty, and smuggling (GAO 2012). In 2015, 245 duty orders were in effect (ITC 2015) (of the total, 94 AD orders are applied to China and another 58 applied to the next four violating countries: India, Taiwan, South Korea, and Japan). Catching these evasions prevents injury against American firms and adds to the collection of US government revenue.

22.3 Welfare Analysis

Welfare measures are the most frequently used approach to analyze policy impacts on individual markets. They emanate from the sound principles of benefit-cost analysis (see, e.g., Boardman et al. 2001) and focus on net effects in two major ways:

1. Real resource costs, while netting out (subtracting) transfer payments such as taxes paid by one entity to another within a country (e.g., duties paid by US importers to the federal government).

[3]Note that, aside from duties, one could also examine the impacts of any dollar value of penalties or fees, if they are significantly large, on importers and the foreign companies exporting products that are AD violations. These penalties and fees can result from negligence (for failures to exercise reasonable care), gross negligence (for cases with actual knowledge or wanton disregard), or fraud (for voluntary and intentional violation) of the importers. In the context of benefit-cost analysis, the AD duties themselves, since they are paid by US importers, would be considered a transfer payment and would not be included in the calculation of the change in economic welfare. However, any fees paid by the foreign exporter are an infusion into the USA from outside and can be considered a net gain to the economy.

2. Netting out expenditures from value received (the result being measured by consumer surplus) and netting out production costs from revenue received (measured by producer surplus, an approximation of economic profit). The surplus changes represent the "dead-weight" loss from a policy, or the unambiguous change, net of all offsetting factors.

Below, we will measure basic welfare loss with the use of the GTAP Model, in which it is referred to as the "resource allocation" effect. We will also estimate some additional welfare measures related to broader international trade flows.

Note that welfare effects, especially those resulting from supply-chain interactions, are estimated as part of the normal workings of a CGE model, which also estimates an overall net welfare change, in addition to calculating macro indicators such as changes in GDP and employment. The CGE approach is the predominant one when analyzing AD duties or tariffs in general (see, e.g., Gallaway et al. 1999; Dixon and Rimmer 2010; Burfisher 2011). The supply and demand functions necessary to perform the analysis are embedded in the model and need not be extracted and applied separately sector by sector.

22.4 Macroeconomic Indicator Analysis

22.4.1 Direct Effects

AD duties are often characterized as equivalent to tariffs on imports, where a "tariff" is simply a term used in international trade circles in place of the term import tax. As such, AD policies might be considered analogous to correcting one market distortion with another (in the AD case to "level the playing field").[4] This has caused many analysts to refer to AD policy as a restrictive trade practice despite the fact that it is intended to counterbalance an unfair trade practice. We will examine the separate impacts of dumping and antidumping, as well as the net effect.[5]

[4]Another consideration of the effect of the AD duties is the duration that the AD duties are in effect. Based on the AD/CVD data for 2014, a few of the AD/CVD orders have been in place for as long as over 30 years. On average, however, the AD/CVD orders that were active when we conducted this study have been in place for about 10 years. Many economists consider that temporary AD/CVD duties might help correct the market distortion, especially for temporary protection. However, if a foreign country subsidizes a product indefinitely, it worsens its terms of trade relative to the importing country on a long-term basis. In such cases, many economists hold reservations about the strategy of distorting the domestic market by imposing AD/CVD duties when the misallocation effect from the dumping is otherwise felt primarily in the foreign country.

[5]We know from the literature in other contexts that the corrective mechanism does not always have the intended effects. The classic example is placing a pollution tax on the output of a monopoly. While for a competitive firm, this causes the producer to cut back output to the socially optimal level, if the producer is monopolist, the pollution tax further induces the monopolist to restrict its output to garner a higher price in the market. This could either mitigate or exacerbate the dead-weight loss depending on whether the monopolist's private profit maximizing price was above or below the socially optimal price level accounting for the negative externality of the pollution.

We now summarize the direct effects of antidumping policies. The tariff raises the price of the import, which has the following two basic components in the case of final goods, which would be analyzed in the context of a utility or demand function[6]:

- Import-domestic source substitution effect toward demand for the domestic import counterpart, in addition to a reduction in quantity demanded of the imported good
- Domestic market effect associated with the overall reduction in the demand for the good (combined import and domestic) because of its now higher price (in terms of a weighted average of import and domestic prices)

The analysis differs a bit for intermediate goods, which would be analyzed in the context of a production function. The income effect counterpart would be an "output effect" related to the demand for the final commodity in which the intermediate good was used. If the higher price and hence cost of the input (either imported or domestically produced) can be passed along as a higher price to the consumers of the final good, then the output effect will be negative.

Of course, another factor is the price distortion caused by the tariff in the first place and the positive effect of removing it. Removing this inefficiency represents another source of gain in both macro indicators and welfare measures.

However, there are conditions under which the opposite net outcome could take place – when the small country assumption does not hold because of imperfect competition. If the importing country's industries have market power, they can affect the world price through a reduction in its demand and can receive a terms of trade gain that can offset the aforementioned net welfare loss (Blonigen and Prusa 2003, 2015). See also the discussion in the following section of other relevant indirect effects that have a strong bearing on the outcome.

The question arises as to the relative size of these various effects. In imposing an AD duty, the substitution effect would expand overall US production directly and indirectly, except in some instances for intermediate goods (see the discussion below). However, the income effect reflects the decreased purchasing power stemming from the price increase and would lead to an overall dampening of US production and consumption. The distortionary effect also offsets the positive gains from the substitution effect. Several analysts go so far as to suggest that unilateral reductions in a tariff can have a negative effect on an economy (see, e.g., Dixon and Rimmer 2010; Rimmer and Dixon 2015, and the general literature on the "optimal tariff").

Blonigen and Prusa (2003; p. 237) suggest that the findings of a net economic gain from imposing an AD duty are illusory. In point of reference, they state that "workers displaced from import-competing sectors are not lost to the economy and will ultimately relocate to industries that are more competitive." There are two problems with this observation:

First, it implicitly assumes that markets can absorb the unemployed labor – this corresponds to the "neoclassical closure rule" in CGE modeling, the most widely

---

[6]We thank an anonymous reviewer for helping us clarify and rename these effects.

used approach to estimating the macroeconomic and competiveness effects of AD policies (see, e.g., Gallaway et al. 1999). However, in a context in which demand is lagging, their employment is not guaranteed. This situation can be effectively modeled by the counterpart "Keynesian closure rule," which allows for an "under-employment" equilibrium.

Second, there is an asymmetry between the jobs gained and jobs lost situations. If we use as our base the complete absence of AD policies, then our simulations would involve adding the AD duties and potentially stimulating US production on net. Under a full employment economy, this gain would have to come at the expense of other sectors from which workers would have to be drawn. On the other hand, under conditions of less than full employment, the job gains can reasonably be considered to be forthcoming. If we use as our base the reduction in AD duties from our current base, then we would be reducing US production, and the full employment constraint is irrelevant.

Direct effects of AD duties on final goods can be modeled in the context of a utility or consumption function to determine the substitution and income effects. For intermediate goods one would use a production function for the commodity, increasing the price of the import by the amount of the duty to determine its effect on the good it is used to produce (taking into consideration that it is likely only a portion of all of the imports of that commodity is affected, so that a weighted average import price must be calculated).[7] However, if the good is used by a large number of sectors, this could be especially cumbersome to perform separately. The total economy-wide effects (including effects on each sector but with indirect, or general equilibrium, effects factored in) would be the straightforward results from a CGE simulation (see below) and would subsume the direct effects. Note that the analysis should be symmetric. We could examine the benefits of removing AD policies by reducing weighted average prices of current goods to calculate a competitive equilibrium. The differences between model base year values and the competitive values should be equivalent to those in modeling the imputed tariff itself, the full employment issue aside.[8]

22.4.2 Indirect Effects

Indirect effects are of several varieties, ranging from ordinary general equilibrium effects to strategic effects to perverse incentive effects. Our CGE approach relating to AD duties will emulate that of Dixon et al. (2007) in terms of methods and

[7]CGE models are usually thought of as measuring indirect, or general equilibrium, effects. However, given their microeconomic foundations of production and utility functions, they can also be used to estimate direct effects.

[8]Data on CBP detections of violations could be used to check the modeling results in terms of the extent of displaced US domestically produced counterparts generated by the tariff simulation. Any significant difference would necessitate the recalibration of some major production or consumption function parameters.

assumptions, treating them as tariffs. However, rather than use the 50-state USAGE-ITC model, we use the GTAP Model.

The following indirect effects are modeled:

1. Ordinary general equilibrium effects refer to upstream and downstream supply-chain effects in markets in which the good in question is indirectly rather than directly involved. They can be calculated by straightforward application of CGE modeling. Ordinary general equilibrium effects also include changes in the terms of trade, or exchange rate, which also affect the outcome.
2. Indirect effects are important for strategic reasons. Fischer and Mirman (1994) point out the fact that consumers and downstream producers (not the direct competitors but the customers of producers that use the imported goods as inputs) "lobby for more lenient enforcement" because dumping lowers the cost of production in those sectors of the USA using the dumped goods as intermediate inputs (recall the initial discussion in Section IV).[9] Also, domestic firms who seek AD protection might engage in strategic behavior (Blonigen and Prusa 2015). For example, a domestic firm might begin employee layoffs, hoping to gain attention to injury from dumping practices.
3. Perverse incentive effects are best exemplified by the fact that an exporter to the USA facing AD duties might simply raise its price in order to avoid the penalties. In doing so, it obtains more revenue and effectively captures the tariff duties (Gallaway et al. (1999) estimate this effect might be as much as 10 times larger than the ordinary negative distortionary effects of AD policies). This does have the effect of increasing domestic production of the good through the substitution effect but also lowers overall US production directly and indirectly by decreasing purchasing power. Note that foreign firms can also lower the duty by reducing their home market price of the good, though this is rarer than raising its price in the US market (Gallaway et al. 1999).

There are some controversies regarding the macroeconomic impacts of AD duties. For many years, they were viewed simply as a distortion of free trade, and most analysts concluded that the duties would have a negative impact on the country levying the duties, except in cases of imperfect competition in that country, where there would be strong terms of trade (essentially exchange rate) effects in its favor (see Gallaway et al. 1999; Blonigen and Prusa 2003). However, over the past decade, a refined approach has questioned the negative impacts outcome. First, more recent analysts point out that although AD duties and other tariffs lower world economic welfare because the price distortion causes an overall resource misallocation, this does not mean that a given country will be better off if it reduces or eliminates its AD duties unilaterally. This group points out that free trade arguments refer definitively only to improvements if they are multilateral, i.e., if all countries simultaneously

[9]Various other strategic effects relating to expectations of AD policies in relation to importer pricing policies are beyond the scope of this study. Note that these behaviors relate not only to pricing but also to product quality and quantity strategies (see, e.g., Blonigen and Prusa 2015).

reduce their tariffs.[10] Second, terms of trade effects can arise quite apart from imperfect competition or increasing returns to scale. This revisionist position is further supported by the burgeoning literature on "optimal tariffs," which indicates that for any individual country, the optimal import tax is not zero, nor is it some high level (Dixon and Rimmer 2010). The outcome depends on several types of terms of trade and related effects, typically not measured, or not measured properly, by the earlier literature. These effects over and above the allocative efficiency effect ("excess burden") include (Huff and Hertel 2000; MacDougall 2006; Burfisher 2011):

- Commodity terms of trade effect – due to changes in the economy's world (FOB) prices of exported goods and services relative to its world (FOB) prices of imported goods and services
- Investment-savings terms of trade effect – due to a change in the price of domestically produced capital investment goods relative to the price of savings
- Endowment effect – due to changes in the quantities of factors production
- Technology effect – due to changes in the productivity of primary factors and/or intermediate inputs
- Preference change effect – due to changes in the relative shares of consumption, government, and savings

Findlay and Warren (2013) offer an excellent explanation of these factors. They point out that when the price of exports, which is used to derive income, goes up relative to the price of imports, which is used to derive utility, this will yield a positive increase in overall economic welfare. Analogously, for the latter effect, when the price of investment, which is used to derive income, goes up relative to the price savings, which are used to derive utility, this will also yield a positive increase in overall economic welfare.

22.5 AD/CVD Modeling Methodology

22.5.1 CGE Modeling

Many analyses of policies and rules utilize partial equilibrium (PE) approaches, which focus on a single market. The prime example is standard benefit-cost analysis. However, many analysts have noted the limitations of PE approaches in failing to take into account standard indirect, or, in this case, general equilibrium (GE), effects of the price and quantity interactions of markets (see, e.g., Kokoski and Smith 1987; Rose 2015; Farrow and Rose 2018). Moreover, several of the other indirect effects peculiar to AD policies noted above can only be adequately addressed by GE models.

[10]Terms of trade effects simply represent a transfer from one country to another and have zero net impact on world welfare.

CGE models represent the multi-market interactions of producers and consumers in response to price signals and external shocks, and within the limits of available capital, labor, and natural resources (see, e.g., Chen and Haynes 2014). Essentially, CGE models depict the economy as a set of interrelated supply chains. They are the most frequently used models to analyze both international trade and tax policy (see, e.g., Dixon and Jorgenson 2013). The strength of these models is their multi-sector detail, focus on interdependencies, full accounting of all inputs (including intermediate goods and not just primary factors of production), behavioral content, reflection of the actions of prices and markets, nonlinearities, and incorporation of explicit constraints. Also, with regard to analyzing AD categories, it is preferable to have a model with the following features:

- A high level of disaggregation to align with specific HTS product categories
- The latest elasticities of substitution between imports and domestically produced goods of the same type

Because CGE provides a clear linkage between the microeconomic structure and the macroeconomy, this modeling approach is adept at reflecting the interrelationship among multiple industrial sectors and markets. More importantly, CGE can be used to assess both direct and indirect effects from a change of public policy on various economic variables such as output, employment, prices, income, and even economic welfare.

The Global Trade Analysis Project (GTAP 2015) Model is adopted in this analysis. The model consists of 129 country economies, each of which is comprised of 57 industry commodity groupings and incorporates the import/export trade linkages between them. The economic impact of AD enforcement is assessed in a multiregional CGE framework, including other countries into regional groupings relating to the issue at hand – delineating countries or regions that are responsible for the most AD violations. The discussion below builds on the research team's recent experience with the GTAP Model (Avetisyan et al. 2014).

The model consists of four sets of institutions: production, household, government, and foreign trade. Each institution interacts with others while maximizing its utility or profit under relevant constraints.

The production structure is an overall constant elasticity of substitution (CES) form for aggregate factors of production, whereas fixed coefficient relationships are used for intermediate inputs. Value added from primary factors, together with intermediate inputs, generates the final output. The model specifies that goods produced in different countries are imperfect substitutes. Sectoral output is modeled through a constant elasticity of transformation (CET) aggregation of total supply to all export markets and supply to the domestic market by following the approach of Lewis et al. (2003). The allocation of goods between exports and domestic markets is such as to maximize revenue from total sales.

Household consumption in the GTAP Model is represented by constant difference of elasticities (CDE) functional form, whereas the household's preferences over consumption, government spending, and saving are characterized by a Cobb-

Douglas relationship. All the elasticity parameters are based on the most recent estimates collected from the literature.

International trade and transport in the model are represented by merchandise goods and "margin" services (e.g., transport costs), respectively. The rest of the world is treated like any other region in the model, with explicit production, consumption, and trade behavior.

The economic effects of AD enforcement are measured in terms of percent change in ad valorem tariff following the approach by Gallaway et al. (1999). The welfare effects are measured using equivalent variation (EV), consistent with the literature (De Melo and Tarr 1990; Francois et al. 1996). In particular, the utility decomposition function of the GTAP Model allows us to measure the influences of AD duties on the US economy in terms of both resource allocation (efficiency) effects (the "excess burden" of taxes) and various terms of trade effects (Burfisher 2011).

22.5.2 AD/CVD Data

Despite various complications in their application, data on AD duties alone enable us to calculate bottom-line estimates of economic welfare. This is due, to a great extent, to the power of a CGE model. The model itself contains all the necessary information on the mix of intermediate versus final goods by virtue of its industrial classification system. Specific data on antidumping margins is not needed unless we pursue the analysis of strategic behavior. An inspection of available data implies that the extensive behavior of this kind identified by Gallaway and others may no longer be prevalent, or that it is difficult to trace accurately (it is also not applicable for CVD).

Government revenues from AD duties are taken into consideration by the GTAP model. AD penalties paid by foreign firms exporting products into the USA appear to be trivially small.

Our own simulation with the imperfect competition version of the GTAP Model indicates that there is little difference between bottom-line economic welfare estimates and the ones presented below. Moreover, there is a great deal of uncertainty in running the imperfect competition model given the major disagreement about size of price markups in imperfectly competitive industries.

22.6 Aggregate and Sectoral Benefits of AD/CVD Duties

We now apply our methodology to the analysis of the welfare and macroeconomic impacts of antidumping duties and countervailing duties combined. We limit our attention to duties collected on imported goods in a recent year – 2014. All simulations are run with the 56-sector[11] version of the GTAP Model with the invocation of standard neoclassical closure rules. Specifically, the factor endowments (e.g., the total supply of labor, capital, and land) are fixed, whereas factor prices are adjusted to restore full employment. In addition, the saving rate is assumed to be exogenous and constant; hence, the quantity of savings changes as income changes.

One approach to the simulation of AD/CVD duties (cash deposits) is to subtract the duties from the GTAP baseline (in which these duties are imbedded), rerun the model to establish a pure baseline, and then add the duties back in for another simulation to isolate their effects, which is a cumbersome process. As a short-cut, we run the simulations by adding the AD/CVD tariffs to the baseline. Because the tariff rates are relatively small, and the model is reasonably linear over small ranges, the impact of adding or subtracting the duties of the same amounts should be symmetric.

22.6.1 Basic AD/CVD Considerations

Table 22.1 presents a summary of basic data for the analysis. The first column of numbers presents AD/CVD cash deposits collected in 2014, amounting to $508.8 million, collected in 17 of the 57 GTAP sectors.[12,13] There is a large variation in duty collections, ranging from a low of $30 thousand for other animal products to $113.7 million for electronic equipment. Seven of the sectors

[11]The sector known as (imputed value of) owner-occupied dwellings was combined with other services to facilitate CGE simulation accuracy. Since this sector does not have import goods and the associated transport margins are all equal to zero, running the model with this sector included separately causes the "division by zero" error.

[12]CVD duties compose 23.3 percent of this total.

[13]The data on AD/CVD cash deposits were collected at the 10-digit HTS commodity level. We then aggregated the AD/CVD cash deposits to the GTAP-sector level and calculated the AD/CVD tariff rate (in percentage terms) by dividing the total AD/CVD cash deposits of that sector (presented in the second column of Table 22.1) by the sector import volume (in dollar terms) (presented in the last column of Table 22.1). The electronic equipment sector is a typical example of the difference between the calculated AD/CVD tariff rate at the GTAP-sector level and the 10-digit HTS commodity level. In Table 22.1, the AD/CVD tariff rate of the electronic equipment sector is 0.0374%. There are four 10-digit HTS commodities in the electronic equipment sector that were subject to AD/CVD in 2014. The majority of the AD/CVD duty in this sector was imposed on one commodity – HTS 8541406020 Solar Cells Assembled into Modules or Panels – with an implicit AD/CVD tariff rate of 2.763%. Although this is much higher than the weighted average AD/CVD tariff rate (0.0374%) calculated for the electronic equipment sector, it is still a moderate tariff level for the specific commodity. For the other three commodities, the implicit AD/CVD tariff rate is similar to or even lower than the sectoral weighted average level. Our weighting procedure to obtain the sectoral-level AD/CVD tariff rate is likely to ensure the correct terms of trade effect but may fail to capture properly the dead-weight burden of the resource misallocation. However, for future studies, splitting out commodities in the GTAP model that have relatively high AD/CVD tariff rates will help improve the accuracy of the analysis.

Table 22.1 Summary of AD/CVD duty, tariff rates, and import volume

Sector description	AD/CVD cash deposits[a] (thousands of 2014 dollars)	Overall tariff rate[b] (percent)	AD/CVD tariff rate[c] (percent)	Import volume[b] (billions of 2011 dollars)
Vegetables and fruit	3690	0.1429	0.0151	23
Other animal products	30	0.2742	0.0013	2
Sugar	2287	6.0614	0.0570	4
Other food	50,368	2.2670	0.0971	49
Textiles	2471	6.8536	0.0039	60
Lumber	44,114	0.3562	0.0806	52
Paper and paper products	5268	0.0028	0.0028	30
Chemical rubber products	59,692	1.1676	0.0206	276
Nonmetallic minerals	617	2.8854	0.0026	23
Iron and steel	74,138	0.2094	0.1709	41
Nonferrous metals	2337	0.5217	0.0034	66
Fabricated metal products	33,400	1.5607	0.0687	46
Motor vehicles and parts	1365	0.5616	0.0006	225
Other transport equipment	85	0.4514	0.0002	53
Electronic equipment	113,698	0.1826	0.0374	289
Other machinery and equipment	109,539	0.7913	0.0284	367
Other manufacturing	4662	1.0192	0.0052	85
Unassigned	1021			
Total	**508,782**			**1691**

[a]US Customs and Border Protection (2015)
[b]GTAP 9 (2015); Year 2011 base
[c]Calculated by the authors based on the collection of AD/CVD cash deposits on top of the regular tariff rate

contribute AD duties in excess of $33 million. The second column of the table presents overall tariff rates, including AD/CVD duties. These vary considerably as well, from a low of 0.0028% for paper and paper products to a high of 6.85% for textiles. AD/CVD tariff rates are presented in the third column and range from a low of 0.0002% in the other transport equipment sector to a high of 0.1709% in the iron and steel sector. The final column presents the volume of imports by sector coming into the USA and totaling $1.7 trillion. The values range from only a couple of billion dollars for three of the agricultural sectors to a high amount of $367 billion for other machinery and equipment.[14] For our analysis, we simulate the collection of the AD/CVD[15] duties alone in each sector to determine their economic impacts. This amounts to simulating the AD/CVD tariff rate in relation to the regular tariff rate for each sector and running simulations for some of the sectors individually, for a key group of sectors, and for all sectors together. This enables us to examine synergies between sectors and the extent of the linearity or nonlinearity of the results.

Estimates of the benefits of AD duties are presented in Tables 22.2, 22.3, and 22.4. Because of the presence of several subtleties in the analysis, the interpretation of the results requires a combined analysis of all of them.

22.6.2 Sectoral Results

Table 22.2 presents the impacts on total gross output and on total GDP, both in real terms, for AD duties on imports of electronic equipment, chemicals, and fabricated metal products individually and combined, as well as an estimate of the impacts of AD/CVD duties in terms of initial cash deposits on all sectors of the economy. The results vary significantly across sectors. Moreover, there is a sizable disparity between impacts on gross output and on GDP. For the individual sectors presented in the table and for all sectors combined,[16] the gross output impacts are several times larger than the GDP impacts in absolute value terms. For the electronic equipment sector individually and for all AD duties, total output impacts are positive, while, for electronics equipment, total GDP impacts are much less positive. For the economy as a whole, they are positive, though very small. For all AD duties, the total output impacts are a gain of $28 million, though with a negative impact on GDP of $4 million. The variation is due to factors such as relative price changes, domestic demand and supply elasticities, trade elasticities, and the relative competitiveness of sectors, to be discussed further below (see also Adams 2005, and Dixon 2017 for more detailed analyses of underlying factors in CGE analyses relating to exchange rates, factor shares, and consumption-investment shares).

Table 22.3 presents the corresponding impacts of AD duties in terms of initial cash deposits on selected sectors in the economy and in relation to direct changes in imports. The results show that whenever a sector has its AD duties increase, imports

[14]Note that the data reference year of the latest GTAP Model is of 2011. We apply the GDP deflator to transform the data to 2014 values to calculate the AD/CVD tariff rate.

[15]From here on we will simply refer to the combination of AD/CVD duties as "AD" for short.

[16]An inspection of the simulations for the electronic equipment, chemicals, and metal products sectors individually and the three sectors combined shows that the results are almost perfectly additive, indicating the results are essentially linear. This is not surprising given the small changes in AD duties we are simulating.

Table 22.2 Output and GDP changes in the USA from AD/CVD duties (initial cash deposits) on imports of electronic equipment, chemicals, metal products, and all sectors paying duties in FY 2014

		ELE[a]	CRP[b]	FMP[c]	3Sum[d]	All[e]	ELE[a]	CRP[b]	FMP[c]	3Sum[d]	All[e]
Sector	Base outputs	Level (in 2011 billion $)					Percent				
Paddy rice	2	0.0000	0.0000	0.0000	−0.0001	−0.0001	−0.0005	−0.0020	−0.0005	−0.0031	−0.0059
Wheat	21	−0.0002	−0.0005	−0.0001	−0.0008	−0.002	−0.0007	−0.0023	−0.0006	−0.0037	−0.0099
Cereal grains	73	−0.0001	−0.0005	−0.0002	−0.0007	−0.0005	−0.0001	−0.0006	−0.0003	−0.0010	−0.0007
Vegetables	70	−0.0001	−0.0004	−0.0002	−0.0007	0.0031	−0.0002	−0.0005	−0.0002	−0.001	0.0044
Oil seeds	37	−0.0002	−0.0006	−0.0002	−0.0010	−0.0024	−0.0005	−0.0016	−0.0005	−0.0027	−0.0063
Sugar cane	3	0.0000	0.0000	0.0000	0.0000	0.0006	0.0001	−0.0003	−0.0002	−0.0003	0.0195
Plant fibers	10	−0.0001	−0.0002	−0.0001	−0.0004	−0.0010	−0.0008	−0.0023	−0.0005	−0.0036	−0.0093
Crops	19	−0.0001	0.0000	−0.0001	−0.0002	−0.0010	−0.0004	−0.0002	−0.0003	−0.0010	−0.0053
Cattle	50	0.0000	−0.0003	−0.0001	−0.0003	−0.0012	0.0001	−0.0005	−0.0002	−0.0006	−0.0025
Animal products	55	0.0000	−0.0003	−0.0002	−0.0005	−0.0015	0.0000	−0.0006	−0.0003	−0.0009	−0.0027
Raw milk	39	0.0001	−0.0001	0.0000	0.0000	0.0000	0.0003	−0.0002	−0.0001	−0.0001	0.0001
Wool silk	0	0.0000	0.0000	0.0000	0.0000	0.0000	−0.0017	−0.0041	−0.0017	−0.0074	−0.0248
Forestry	23	−0.0003	−0.0001	−0.0002	−0.0006	0.0024	−0.0011	−0.0006	−0.0008	−0.0025	0.0101
Fishing	8	0.0000	0.0000	0.0000	0.0000	0.0001	0.0000	−0.0002	−0.0001	−0.0002	0.0011
Coal	78	0.0000	−0.0002	−0.0001	−0.0003	−0.0013	0.0000	−0.0002	−0.0002	−0.0004	−0.0016
Oil	222	−0.0004	−0.0008	−0.0006	−0.0018	−0.0053	−0.0002	−0.0004	−0.0003	−0.0008	−0.0024
Gas	22	0.0000	−0.0001	−0.0001	−0.0002	−0.0006	−0.0002	−0.0005	−0.0003	−0.001	−0.0028
Minerals	51	−0.0006	−0.0001	−0.0001	−0.0008	−0.0012	−0.0011	−0.0002	−0.0002	−0.0016	−0.0024
Meat	120	0.0002	−0.0005	−0.0002	−0.0005	−0.0021	0.0001	−0.0004	−0.0002	−0.0004	−0.0018
Meat products	98	0.0000	−0.0007	−0.0003	−0.0010	−0.0039	0.0000	−0.0007	−0.0003	−0.0011	−0.0040
Vegetable oils	25	−0.0002	−0.0004	−0.0002	−0.0008	−0.0012	−0.0007	−0.0016	−0.0009	−0.0033	−0.0050
Dairy product	102	0.0002	−0.0003	−0.0001	−0.0002	−0.0006	0.0002	−0.0003	−0.0001	−0.0002	−0.0006
Processed rice	6	0.0000	−0.0002	0.0000	−0.0003	−0.0004	−0.0004	−0.0034	−0.0005	−0.0043	−0.0072

(continued)

Table 22.2 (continued)

Sector	Base outputs	ELE[a]	CRP[b]	FMP[c]	3Sum[d]	All[e]	ELE[a]	CRP[b]	FMP[c]	3Sum[d]	All[e]
		Level (in 2011 billion $)					Percent				
Sugar	15	0.0000	−0.0001	0.0000	−0.0001	0.0033	0.0001	−0.0004	−0.0002	−0.0004	0.0227
Food products	389	0.0006	−0.0014	−0.0006	−0.0014	0.0553	0.0002	−0.0004	−0.0002	−0.0004	0.0142
Beverage and tobacco	156	0.0004	−0.0001	−0.0002	0.0001	−0.0006	0.0003	−0.0001	−0.0001	0.0001	−0.0004
Textiles	172	−0.0019	−0.0067	−0.0020	−0.0106	−0.0130	−0.0011	−0.0039	−0.0012	−0.0062	−0.0075
Wearing apparel	122	−0.0002	−0.0021	−0.0006	−0.0029	−0.0067	−0.0002	−0.0017	−0.0005	−0.0024	−0.0055
Leather products	17	−0.0002	−0.0009	−0.0003	−0.0014	−0.0027	−0.0009	−0.0053	−0.0019	−0.0081	−0.0155
Wood products	295	−0.006	−0.0019	−0.0042	−0.0121	0.0813	−0.002	−0.0006	−0.0014	−0.0041	0.0276
Paper	524	0.0004	−0.0029	−0.0017	−0.0042	−0.0084	0.0001	−0.0006	−0.0003	−0.0008	−0.0016
Petroleum	729	0.0004	0.0029	−0.0006	0.0028	0.0039	0.0001	0.0004	−0.0001	0.0004	0.0005
Chemical	**1086**	**−0.0076**	**0.0781**	**−0.0123**	**0.0584**	**−0.0041**	**−0.0007**	**0.0072**	**−0.0011**	**0.0054**	**−0.0004**
Mineral products	162	−0.0022	−0.0014	−0.0013	−0.0050	−0.0102	−0.0014	−0.0009	−0.0008	−0.0031	−0.0063
Ferrous metals	213	−0.0041	−0.0055	0.0092	−0.0004	0.1555	−0.0019	−0.0026	0.0043	−0.0002	0.073
Metals	180	−0.0019	−0.0078	0.0015	−0.0082	−0.0395	−0.001	−0.0043	0.0008	−0.0046	−0.022
Metal products	**392**	**−0.0009**	**−0.0061**	**0.0968**	**0.0898**	**0.0447**	**−0.0002**	**−0.0016**	**0.0247**	**0.0229**	**0.0114**
Auto parts	618	−0.0185	−0.0106	−0.0133	−0.0424	−0.1167	−0.003	−0.0017	−0.0021	−0.0069	−0.0189
Transport equipment	277	−0.0091	−0.0074	−0.0091	−0.0256	−0.0704	−0.0033	−0.0027	−0.0033	−0.0093	−0.0254
Electronic equipment	**563**	**0.2108**	**−0.0194**	**−0.0146**	**0.1768**	**0.1008**	**0.0374**	**−0.0034**	**−0.0026**	**0.0314**	**0.0179**
Machinery	1158	−0.0496	−0.0334	−0.0314	−0.1145	−0.0390	−0.0043	−0.0029	−0.0027	−0.0099	−0.0034
Other manufactures	119	−0.0029	−0.0034	−0.0022	−0.0084	−0.0160	−0.0024	−0.0028	−0.0019	−0.0071	−0.0134
Electricity	421	0.0021	0.0007	0.0006	0.0033	0.0071	0.0005	0.0002	0.0001	0.0008	0.0017
Gas	74	0.0002	0.0001	0.0001	0.0003	0.0013	0.0002	0.0001	0.0001	0.0005	0.0018
Water	143	0.0005	0.0003	0.0004	0.0011	0.0023	0.0003	0.0002	0.0002	0.0008	0.0016
Construction	1798	−0.0460	0.0061	−0.0139	−0.0538	−0.1645	−0.0026	0.0003	−0.0008	−0.003	−0.0091
Trade	3187	0.0225	0.0008	−0.0033	0.0200	0.0073	0.0007	0.0000	−0.0001	0.0006	0.0002

Transport Nec	692	−0.0014	−0.0002	−0.0004	−0.0020	−0.0030	−0.0002	0.0000	−0.0001	−0.0003	−0.0004
Sea transport	84	0.0002	−0.0002	−0.0003	−0.0002	−0.0013	0.0003	−0.0002	−0.0003	−0.0003	−0.0016
Air transport	266	0.0008	−0.0014	−0.0010	−0.0017	−0.0067	0.0003	−0.0005	−0.0004	−0.0006	−0.0025
Communication	588	−0.0005	0.0004	−0.0004	−0.0004	−0.0005	−0.0001	0.0001	−0.0001	−0.0001	−0.0001
Financial services	1745	0.0036	0.0016	−0.0023	0.0030	−0.0060	0.0002	0.0001	−0.0001	0.0002	−0.0003
Insurance	609	0.0014	0.0003	−0.0003	0.0014	0.0030	0.0002	0.0000	−0.0001	0.0002	0.0005
Business services	2333	0.0015	−0.0048	−0.0055	−0.0088	−0.0350	0.0001	−0.0002	−0.0002	−0.0004	−0.0015
Recreation	1360	0.0055	0.0029	0.0011	0.0095	0.0161	0.0004	0.0002	0.0001	0.0007	0.0012
Public services	6651	0.0260	0.0125	0.0060	0.0445	0.1105	0.0004	0.0002	0.0001	0.0007	0.0017
Total output (Q)	**28,275**	**0.1222**	**−0.0173**	**−0.0091**	**0.0958**	**0.0280**	**0.0004**	**−0.0001**	**0.0000**	**0.0003**	**0.0001**
Total GDP (Q)	**15,534**	**0.0010**	**0.0000**	**−0.0010**	**0.0000**	**−0.0040**	**0.0000**	**0.0000**	**0.0000**	**0.0000**	**0.0000**

[a]Electronic equipment import tariff increases from 0.1516% without AD/CVD duties by 20.47% to 0.1826% with AD/CVD duties
[b]Chemical rubber products import tariff increases from 1.1474% without AD/CVD duties by 1.76% to 1.1676% with AD/CVD duties
[c]Fabricated metal products import tariff increases from 1.4949% without AD/CVD duties by 4.4% to 1.5607% with AD/CVD duties
[d]Simultaneous impact from import tariff increase in electronic equipment, chemicals, and metal products due to AD/CVD duties
[e]Simultaneous impact from import tariff increase in vegetables, other animal products, sugar, other food, textiles, lumbers, paper and paper products, nonmetallic minerals, chemical rubber products, iron and steel, nonferrous metals, fabricated metal products, motor vehicles and parts, other transport equipment, electronic equipment, other machinery and equipment, and other manufacturing due to AD/CVD duties

Table 22.3 Import changes in the USA from AD/CVD duties (initial cash deposits) on imports of electronic equipment, chemicals, metal products, and all sectors paying duties in FY 2014

		ELE[a]	CRP[b]	FMP[c]	3Sum[d]	All[e]	ELE[a]	CRP[b]	FMP[c]	3Sum[d]	All[e]
Sector	Base imports	Level (in 2011 billion $)					Percent				
Paddy rice	0	0.0000	0.0000	0.0000	0.0000	0.0000	0.0009	0.0019	0.0003	0.0031	0.0240
Wheat	1	0.0000	0.0000	0.0000	0.0000	0.0001	0.0007	0.0015	0.0003	0.0025	0.0189
Cereal grains	1	0.0000	0.0000	0.0000	0.0000	0.0001	0.0005	0.0013	0.0002	0.0020	0.0128
Vegetables	23	0.0001	0.0001	0.0000	0.0003	−0.0020	0.0005	0.0006	0.0002	0.0013	−0.0088
Oil seeds	1	0.0000	0.0000	0.0000	0.0000	0.0001	0.0001	0.0005	−0.0003	0.0004	0.0056
Sugar cane	0	0.0000	0.0000	0.0000	0.0000	0.0000	0.0008	0.001	0.0001	0.0019	0.0249
Plant fibers	0	0.0000	0.0000	0.0000	0.0000	0.0000	0.0005	0.0007	0.0002	0.0014	0.0065
Crops	14	0.0000	0.0001	0.0000	0.0001	0.0005	0.0000	0.0005	−0.0001	0.0004	0.0037
Cattle	2	0.0000	0.0000	0.0000	0.0000	0.0001	0.0008	0.0010	0.0004	0.0022	0.0069
Animal products	2	0.0000	0.0000	0.0000	0.0000	0.0002	0.0006	0.0006	0.0002	0.0014	0.0076
Raw Milk	0	0.0000	0.0000	0.0000	0.0000	0.0000	0.0015	0.0025	0.0010	0.0051	0.0169
Wool silk	0	0.0000	0.0000	0.0000	0.0000	0.0000	−0.0001	−0.0005	−0.0002	−0.0008	0.0027
Forestry	1	0.0000	0.0000	0.0000	0.0000	0.0001	−0.0008	0.0046	−0.0009	0.0029	0.0245
Fishing	3	0.0000	0.0000	0.0000	0.0000	0.0004	0.0007	0.0003	0.0002	0.0012	0.0143
Coal	1	0.0000	0.0000	0.0000	0.0000	0.0001	0.0011	0.0013	0.0007	0.0031	0.0085
Oil	324	0.0007	0.0030	0.0001	0.0038	0.0081	0.0002	0.0009	0.0000	0.0012	0.0025
Gas	17	0.0000	0.0004	0.0000	0.0004	0.0004	0.0002	0.0023	−0.0002	0.0023	0.0021
Minerals	11	−0.0001	0.0001	0.0001	0.0000	0.0012	−0.0013	0.0005	0.0008	0.0000	0.0116
Meat	4	0.0001	0.0001	0.0001	0.0003	0.0008	0.0017	0.0034	0.0014	0.0065	0.0185
Meat products	3	0.0000	0.0001	0.0000	0.0002	0.0005	0.0019	0.0034	0.0015	0.0068	0.0206
Vegetable oils	8	0.0001	0.0002	0.0000	0.0003	0.0010	0.0008	0.0025	0.0004	0.0037	0.0131
Dairy product	3	0.0001	0.0001	0.0000	0.0002	0.0006	0.0018	0.0038	0.0017	0.0073	0.0203
Processed rice	1	0.0000	0.0000	0.0000	0.0001	0.0001	0.0009	0.0053	0.0008	0.0070	0.0132
Sugar	4	0.0000	0.0000	0.0000	0.0001	−0.0020	0.0007	0.0008	0.0004	0.0020	−0.0520

Food products	49	0.0006	0.0009	0.0004	0.0019	−0.0772	0.0011	0.0019	0.0009	0.0039	−0.1565
Beverage and tobacco	22	0.0002	0.0002	0.0001	0.0006	0.0015	0.0008	0.0011	0.0006	0.0025	0.0065
Textiles	60	0.0003	0.0023	0.0003	0.0029	0.0007	0.0004	0.0038	0.0005	0.0048	0.0012
Wearing apparel	78	0.0011	0.0022	0.0009	0.0042	0.0101	0.0014	0.0028	0.0012	0.0054	0.0129
Leather products	41	0.0004	0.0007	0.0003	0.0014	0.0032	0.0010	0.0017	0.0008	0.0034	0.0078
Wood products	52	−0.0004	0.0014	0.0008	0.0018	−0.1006	−0.0007	0.0026	0.0016	0.0035	−0.1935
Paper	30	0.0004	0.0009	0.0003	0.0016	0.0017	0.0013	0.0031	0.0012	0.0055	0.0058
Petroleum	91	0.0001	0.0019	−0.0001	0.0020	0.0023	0.0002	0.0021	−0.0001	0.0022	0.0025
Chemical	**276**	**0.0035**	**−0.1178**	**0.0022**	**−0.1121**	**−0.0999**	**0.0013**	**−0.0427**	**0.0008**	**−0.0406**	**−0.0362**
Mineral products	23	0.0003	0.0005	0.0002	0.0010	0.0009	0.0012	0.0024	0.0009	0.0044	0.0039
Ferrous metals	41	−0.0003	0.0000	0.0033	0.0031	−0.1485	−0.0007	0.0001	0.0081	0.0075	−0.3601
Metals	66	0.0015	−0.0004	0.0030	0.0041	0.0031	0.0023	−0.0006	0.0045	0.0062	0.0047
Metal products	**46**	**0.0001**	**0.0011**	**−0.0994**	**−0.0981**	**−0.0857**	**0.0002**	**0.0025**	**−0.2152**	**−0.2126**	**−0.1856**
Auto parts	225	0.0005	0.0046	0.0024	0.0075	0.0159	0.0002	0.0021	0.0011	0.0033	0.0071
Transport equipment	53	−0.0001	0.0010	0.0006	0.0015	0.0039	−0.0002	0.0018	0.0012	0.0028	0.0073
Electronic equipment	**289**	**−0.2152**	**0.0045**	**0.0010**	**−0.2097**	**−0.2028**	**−0.0744**	**0.0016**	**0.0003**	**−0.0726**	**−0.0702**
Machinery	367	0.0043	0.0091	0.0057	0.019	−0.2298	0.0012	0.0025	0.0015	0.0052	−0.0626
Other manufactures	85	0.0015	0.0020	0.0011	0.0047	0.0024	0.0018	0.0024	0.0013	0.0055	0.0029
Electricity	4	0.0001	0.0001	0.0001	0.0002	0.0005	0.0018	0.0025	0.0014	0.0057	0.0140
Gas	1	0.0000	0.0000	0.0000	0.0000	0.0001	0.0017	0.0024	0.0015	0.0056	0.0144
Water	0	0.0000	0.0000	0.0000	0.0000	0.0001	0.0015	0.0026	0.0016	0.0057	0.0149
Construction	4	−0.0001	0.0001	0.0000	0.0000	0.0000	−0.0026	0.0021	0.0009	0.0004	0.0011
Trade	27	0.0004	0.0005	0.0003	0.0013	0.0030	0.0016	0.0020	0.0011	0.0047	0.0108
Transport Nec	51	0.0004	0.0006	0.0003	0.0013	0.0032	0.0007	0.0012	0.0007	0.0026	0.0062
Sea transport	3	0.0000	0.0000	0.0000	0.0001	0.0002	0.0011	0.0010	0.0005	0.0026	0.0054
Air transport	42	0.0003	0.0004	0.0002	0.0009	0.0019	0.0008	0.0009	0.0005	0.0022	0.0046
Communication	13	0.0003	0.0002	0.0001	0.0006	0.0013	0.0021	0.0016	0.0009	0.0046	0.0095

(continued)

Table 22.3 (continued)

Sector	Base imports	ELE[a]	CRP[b]	FMP[c]	3Sum[d]	All[e]	ELE[a]	CRP[b]	FMP[c]	3Sum[d]	All[e]
		Level (in 2011 billion $)					Percent				
Financial services	41	0.0004	0.0007	0.0003	0.0014	0.0027	0.0009	0.0018	0.0007	0.0034	0.0066
Insurance	41	0.0005	0.0007	0.0003	0.0015	0.0034	0.0013	0.0016	0.0008	0.0037	0.0082
Business services	101	0.0025	0.0016	0.0007	0.0049	0.0090	0.0025	0.0016	0.0007	0.0048	0.0089
Recreation	15	0.0004	0.0003	0.0001	0.0008	0.0016	0.0026	0.0017	0.0008	0.0052	0.0108
Public services	47	0.0018	0.0005	0.0001	0.0024	0.0033	0.0038	0.0011	0.0003	0.0052	0.0072
Total import (Q)	**2706**	**−0.1932**	**−0.0745**	**−0.0735**	**−0.3412**	**−0.8580**	**−0.0071**	**−0.0028**	**−0.0027**	**−0.0126**	**−0.0317**

[a]Electronic equipment import tariff increases from 0.1516% without AD/CVD duties by 20.47% to 0.1826% with AD/CVD duties
[b]Chemical rubber products import tariff increases from 1.1474% without AD/CVD duties by 1.76% to 1.1676% with AD/CVD duties
[c]Fabricated metal products import tariff increases from 1.4949% without AD/CVD duties by 4.4% to 1.5607% with AD/CVD duties
[d]Simultaneous impact from import tariff increase in electronic equipment, chemicals, and metal products due to AD/CVD duties
[e]Simultaneous impact from import tariff increase in vegetables, other animal products, sugar, other food, textiles, lumbers, paper and paper products, nonmetallic minerals, chemical rubber products, iron and steel, nonferrous metals, fabricated metal products, motor vehicles and parts, other transport equipment, electronic equipment, other machinery and equipment, and other manufacturing due to AD/CVD duties

into the USA of its products decrease, while typically imports of nearly all other sectors increase, as a result of the substitution effect overcoming any output effect. Changes in imports on net from all AD duties are zero or positive for all sectors, with the exception of food products, sugar, chemicals, ferrous metals, metal products, electronic equipment, and machinery. The variation is due to the factors mentioned in the previous paragraph, with a stronger emphasis on import and export elasticities.

22.6.3 Aggregate Welfare Results

Table 22.4 presents the real bottom line of the analysis in terms of economic welfare, as measured by an equivalent variation approximation of producer and consumer surplus changes. However, the results are more than just an index; they can be translated into changes in disposable personal income (consumption and savings) in billions of 2011 dollars. Examining the total welfare change in the bottom row of the table, we see that AD duties result in a positive impact on this key indicator. This means that AD duties levied in 2014 would yield positive economic benefits, because their presence represents a gain of economic welfare. Of the individual sectors examined, electronics equipment has the largest welfare impact at $32.4 million. The overall benefit of AD duties across all sectors in terms of personal income in the USA is $182.3 million. Again, this is apart from the $508.8 million duties collected. Thus, it appears that our results are in line with the more recent international trade analyses that find decreasing tariffs by a small percentage will decrease economic welfare, while increases in tariffs will do the opposite (see, e.g., Dixon and Rimmer 2010).

The results can be explained by a decomposition of the overall economic welfare effect into its various components. The GTAP Model offers an option of separating six causal factors, though for our analysis three of them would change imperceptibly and thus are held constant. Of the remaining three factors, the first is the allocation

Table 22.4 Welfare decomposition in the USA from AD/CVD duties on imports of electronic equipment imports, chemicals, metal products, and all affected sectors paying duties in FY 2014 (billions of 2011 dollars)

Welfare decomposition	Electronics (ELE)	Chemicals (CRP)	Metal products (FMP)	3 sectors combined	All sectors
Allocation effect	0.0009	0.0004	−0.0014	−0.0001	−0.0037
Endowment effect	0	0	0	0	0
Technical change	0	0	0	0	0
Population growth	0	0	0	0	0
Commodity terms of trade	0.0181	0.0213	0.011	0.0504	0.12
Investment-savings terms of trade	0.0134	0.0054	0.006	0.0248	0.066
Preference change	0	0	0	0	0
Total	**0.0324**	**0.0271**	**0.0156**	**0.0752**	**0.1823**

effect, which pertains to the price distorting effects of the AD duty. The second causal factor is the standard commodity terms of trade effect. The third is an investment-savings terms of trade effect. Both of the two terms of trade effects contribute positively to overall welfare stemming from the imposition of the AD/CVD cash deposits. This is best demonstrated in the last column of Table 22.4, which shows an overall economic welfare gain of $182.3 million for the imposition of AD/CVD duties throughout the economy. The allocation effect is negative, as a result of the price distortion, though at a very small 2% of this total, and it is swamped by the two terms of trade effects. The commodity terms of trade effect is almost twice the size of its counterpart investment-savings effect. Not surprisingly from examination of the previous two tables, there is some variation across sectors in terms of the relative proportion of the terms of trade effects and in the qualitative sign of the allocation effect, but the net effect on economic welfare of all three sectors we have singled out is positive, as it is for all sectors combined that pay AD/CVD duties.

The allocation effect results for the electronics and chemical sectors appear to be anomalous because they are positive. This is difficult to explain because the underlying model parameters for these sectors are not unusual, and the output and import results reported in Tables 22.2 and 22.3 for them have the correct sign. Given that the numerical values of these allocation results are so low, we can only conclude that the results on this score are within the margin of error for the model.

Our findings indicate a gain to the US economy, measured in terms of personal income, of $182.3 million dollars from the $508.8 million AD/CVD cash deposits in 2014.[17] The duties themselves represent no welfare gain, as they are merely a transfer from importing companies in the USA to the federal government. However, the duties do provide a basis for estimating the macroeconomic benefits of enforcement if we divide them into the economic welfare impacts. They indicate that for every million dollars of AD/CVD cash deposits, US personal income is increased by $358 thousand by way of the various direct effects of increased production of domestic substitutes displacing imported goods and the net of various other effects relating to resource allocation and the terms of trade. Actual duties collected are much lower than levied duties, so further analysis is needed to determine the influence this fact has on the effectiveness of AD/CVD enforcement.[18]

[17]After including the economic gains from the collection of $72.46 million of recovered revenues from CBP VA reviews, the total economic welfare gain in terms of personal income is $204.6 million.

[18]In FY 2014, it is estimated that 129 full-time equivalent (FTE) CBP employees were dedicated to the enforcement activities of AD/CVD regulations. This translates to an increase in personal income of $1.4 million dollars per CBP FTE staff member. Furthermore, the per FTE total personal income gain of AD/CVD enforcement corresponding to the full administrative cost of one CBP staff member, on average, is a ratio of $11.4:1 (see Rose et al. 2016 for additional details).

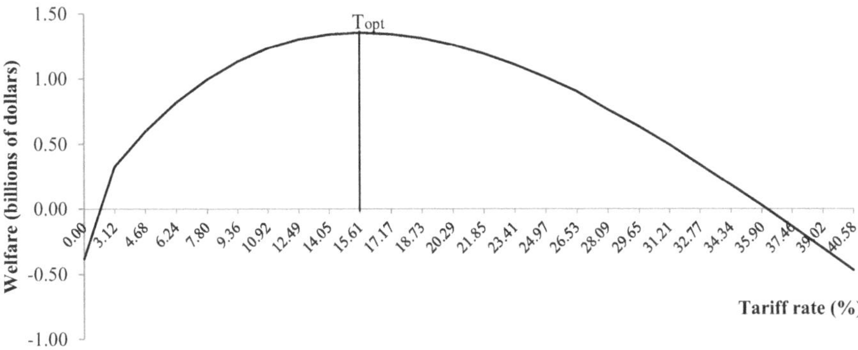

Fig. 22.1 Welfare effects of alternative metal products sector import tariffs

22.7 The Optimal AD/CVD Tariff: A Sensitivity Analysis

Following the approach of Dixon and Rimmer (2010), we tested the optimal tariff rate for the GTAP Model under perfect competition. The analysis was conducted by adjusting the import tariff of the fabricated metal products (FMP) sector away from its base level at 1.56%. The economic welfare effect was calculated at each adjusted level of the tariff rate. The economic welfare level, as illustrated in Fig. 22.1, increases monotonically as the tariff rate rises from 0 to 15.61%, which is the optimal tariff rate. At the optimal tariff level for metal products, the economic welfare gain in the USA reaches its maximum level at approximately $1.35 billion. The welfare level then declines as the tariff rate is further increased.

Note also that economic welfare is negative when the tariff is decreased below 1.56% (as in our analysis above). The tariff also yields a negative welfare effect when it reaches around 37.45%. The welfare decomposition of the increase of tariff on metal products away from its base level is illustrated in Fig. 22.2. The simulation results show that the resource allocation effect reflects efficiency losses due to the distorted imported prices at an increasing rate. Conversely, the terms of trade effects for commodities and for savings and investment increase monotonically but at a decreasing rate as the tariff rate increases. The inverse U-shape of the aggregate economic welfare curve in Fig. 22.2 reflects the combined effect of the changes among the three components, including any synergistic effects.

22.8 Conclusions

We developed a conceptual framework for the study of the economic impacts of antidumping duties and the economic benefits of their enforcement. For the estimation of benefits, we adapted the standard methodology using the latest version of GTAP CGE model. We found that AD/CVD duties have a positive impact on the US

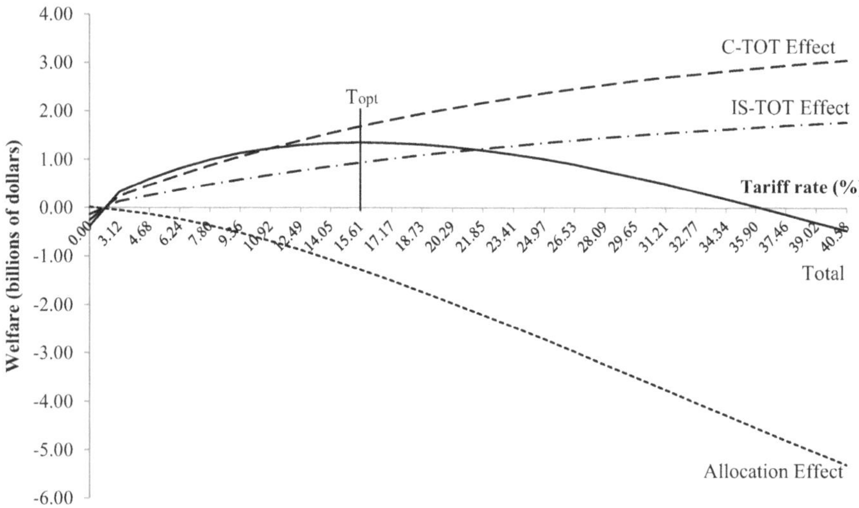

Fig. 22.2 Welfare decomposition of metal products sector alternative import tariffs

economy, and sensitivity tests on the results indicate that strengthening their enforcement will lead to still greater gains. Specifically, our findings indicate an economic welfare gain to the US economy, measured in terms of personal income, of $182.3 million dollars from the $508.8 million AD/CVD cash deposits required in lieu of duties levied in FY 2014.

One dimension of AD policy we have not yet addressed is the distribution of gains and losses. Clearly, customers of final and intermediate goods that incur duties lose, and clearly domestic competitors of the imported goods gain. One issue is whether the gains to domestic producers have broader benefits, such as protecting infant industry or distressed industry status. However, even these claims are controversial and not considered to be worthy of consideration by many analysts, especially those who emphasize the importance of free markets.

One potential motivation for foreign countries dumping commodities in the USA is outright predatory pricing. That is, rather than simply being a tactic to sell more commodities in US markets, the objective might be to cause injury to import-competing US industries, even to the extent of forcing them out of business. For example, the Ball and Roller Bearing industry (part of the broader fabricated metal products sector delineated in this study) has been the focus of much attention regarding dumping in recent years. AD duties (in cash deposits) applied to this commodity have been among the highest of any individual commodity, amounting to over $11 million in FY 2014. But this tariff is very mild compared to the over $10 billion of gross output of this commodity or approximately $6 billion of value added it generates. Even preventing reduction of one-tenth of the production of this industry would exceed the aggregate benefits we estimated for the entirety of AD duties using a standard analysis. The demise of this industry would be a serious blow to the US economy and to our economic security.[19] Thus, the estimates of benefits of AD policy might be considered a lower bound of potential impacts.

Still, AD duties are only one of several policy remedies to address some of the negative impacts of dumping, and that CVDs are only one of several remedies for countering subsidies to foreign importers in their own countries. They have the effect of using one market distortion to offset another and, as in the cases of other areas of public policy discussed above, can have negative side effects. These side effects, at least in terms of aggregate measures of economic welfare, do not appear likely to be forthcoming within the limits of our analysis. They do show up in minor ways in terms of very small negative impacts on customers of import-competing goods. They could also potentially result in even more damaging retaliatory measures by US trade partners. Bilateral or multilateral international trade agreements hold the prospects of avoiding the negative effects of unilateral changes in AD/CVD duties and of minimizing retaliatory responses.

Finally, we note that some of the broader impacts of AD/CVD duties may not show up immediately and instead may take years to develop. One example, short of ultimate predatory pricing, would be a dominant exporter dumping strategy of weakening US competitors and then increasing its prices. Hence, a dynamic CGE model might be needed to fully estimate all important ramifications of this important trade policy issue.

References

Adams P (2005) Interpretation of results from CGE models such as GTAP. J Policy Model 27:941–959

Avetisyan M, Heatwole N, Rose A, Roberts B (2014) Competitiveness and macroeconomic impacts of reduced wait times at US land freight border crossings. Transp Res A 78:84–101

Blonigen B, Prusa T (2003) The cost of antidumping: the devil is in the details. Policy Reform 64:233–245

Blonigen B, Prusa T (2015) Dumping and antidumping duties. National Bureau of Economic Research Working Paper 21573, Cambridge, MA

Boardman H, Greenberg D, Vining A, Weimer D (2001) Cost-benefit analysis: concepts and practice, 2nd edn. Prentice Hall, Upper Saddle River

Burfisher ME (2011) Introduction to computable general equilibrium models. Cambridge University Press, New York

Chen Z, Haynes KE (2014) Transportation capital in the United States: a multimodal general equilibrium analysis. Public Works Manag Policy 19(2):97–117

Czako J, Human J, Miranda J (2003) A handbook on anti-dumping investigations. Cambridge University Press, Cambridge

De Melo J, Tarr DG (1990) Welfare costs of US quotas in textiles, steel and autos. Rev Econ Stat 72:489–497

[19]We also performed an analysis of imports of honey and of coat hangers from China that indicate that AD duties have in fact protected these two relatively smaller US industries from unfair trade practices that might have caused their demise (see Rose et al. 2016).

Dixon J (2017) The impact on Australia of Trump's 45 percent tariff on Chinese imports. Econ Pap 36(3):266–274

Dixon P, Jorgenson D (2013) Handbook of computable general equilibrium modeling. North-Holland, Amsterdam

Dixon P, Rimmer M (2010) Optimal tariffs: should Australia cut automotive tariffs unilaterally? Econ Rec 86(273):143–161

Dixon P, Rimmer M, Tsigas M (2007) Regionalising results from a detailed CGE model: macro, industry and state effects in the U. S. of removing major tariffs and quotas. Pap Reg Sci 86 (1):31–55

Findlay C, Warren T (eds) (2013) Impediments to trade in services: measurements and policy implications. Routledge, Hoboken

Fischer R, Mirman L (1994) Learning about enforcement: a model of dumping. J Econ Integr 9 (2):214–240

Francois JF, Arce HM, Reinert KA, Flynn JE (1996) Commercial policy and the domestic carrying trade. Can J Econ 29:181–198

Gallaway M, Blonigen B, Flynn A (1999) Welfare costs of the US antidumping and countervailing duty Laws. J Int Econ 49:211–244

Global Trade Analysis Project (GTAP) (2015). https://www.gtap.agecon.purdue.edu/models/current.asp

Huff K, Hertel T (2000) Decomposing welfare changes in the GTAP model, GTAP technical papers. Purdue University, West Lafayette

International Trade Commission. (ITC) (2015) Anti-dumping and countervailing duties in place, March 2015

Kokoski M, Smith VK (1987) A general equilibrium analysis of partial equilibrium welfare measures: the case of climate change. Am Econ Rev 77(3):331–341

Lewis JD, Robinson S, Thierfelder K (2003) Free trade agreements and the SADC economies. J Afr Econ 12(2):156–206

Rimmer M, Dixon P (2015) Identifying the effects of NAFTA on the U.S. economy between 1992 and 1998: a decomposition analysis. Paper presented at the GTAP 18th annual conference on global economic analysis, Melbourne, Australia

Rose A (2015) Macroeconomic consequences of terrorist attacks: estimation for the analysis of policies and rules. In: Mansfield C, Smith VK (eds) Benefit transfer for the analysis of DHS policies and rules. Edward Elgar, Cheltenham, pp 172–201

Rose A, Chen Z, Wei D (2016) Chapter 4: Estimating U.S. anti-dumping/countervailing duty enforcement benefits. In: Roberts B et al (eds) Economic analysis of priority trade issues, Final Report to the U.S. Customs and Border Protection, Center for Risk and Economic Analysis of Terrorism Events (CREATE). University of Southern California, Los Angeles, CA

U.S. Customs and Border Protection (CBP) (2015) Priority trade issue: antidumping and countervailing duties. http://www.cbp.gov/trade/priority-issues/adcvd

U.S. Government Accounts and Office (GAO) (2012) Antidumping and countervailing duties: management enhancements needed to improve efforts to detect and deter duty evasion, Washington, DC

Chapter 23
Social Capital, Rurality, and Accessibility: A Comparative Study Between Turkey and Italy

Umut Türk, Martina Dolciotti, John Östh, Aura Reggiani, and Peter Nijkamp

Abstract Over the past years, we have observed a growing interest among social scientists and policy makers in deepening their understanding of the importance of the *social capital* concept, against the background of a broad set of socio-economic experiences in various countries. The concept is popularly defined as a set of individual and societal gains embedded in social ties and networks. The extent to which societies produce and benefit from social capital depends, inter alia, on locational characteristics such as human capital accumulation, segregation, employment rates, the wellbeing of individuals, as well as daily and periodic mobility patterns in relation to the job/housing balance, commuting distances, and in a general sense, rural-urban differences. The aim of this chapter is to examine the impact of job accessibility on social capital at a regional scale, with special attention to rural areas. Job accessibility is considered as an indicator of spatial connectivity, and thus it can

U. Türk (✉)
Department of Economics, Abdullah Gül University, Kayseri, Turkey
e-mail: umut.turk@agu.edu.tr

M. Dolciotti
Department of Statistics, University of Milano-Bicocca, Milan, Italy

J. Östh
Department of Social and Economic Geography, Uppsala University, Uppsala, Sweden
e-mail: john.osth@kultgeog.uu.se

A. Reggiani
Department of Economics, University of Bologna, Bologna, Italy
e-mail: aura.reggiani@unibo.it

P. Nijkamp
Tinbergen Institute, Gustav Mahlerlaan 117, MS, Amsterdam, The Netherlands

Adam Mickiewicz University, Wieniawskiego 1, Poznań, Poland

JADS, 's-Hertogenbosch, The Netherlands

Alexandru Ioan Cuza University, Iasi, Romania
e-mail: p.nijkamp@jads.nl

Z. Chen et al. (eds.), *Development Studies in Regional Science*,
New Frontiers in Regional Science: Asian Perspectives 42,
https://doi.org/10.1007/978-981-15-1435-7_23

strongly relate to social capital. The associated analyses will be done by empirically studying Turkish and Italian provinces (on the basis of the European Union-NUTS3 level regions).

A quantile regression model is employed to examine job accessibility and rurality in relation to social capital in 81 Turkish and 110 Italian provinces. In the analysis, social capital is measured by a community resilience index based on a set of relevant data on civic infrastructure, metropolitan stability, homeownership, and political participation. The empirical analysis is carried out for Italy and Turkey. In the last few decades, both countries have experienced a decline in rural livelihood and now have a similar percentage of rural population. Meanwhile, mainly due to the geographical and socio-economic structure, the two countries show different patterns and development characteristics of accessibility. The findings of this paper highlight these differences and similarities, and show social capital variations in response to accessibility and rurality in both Turkey and Italy.

Keywords Accessibility · Community resilience index · Quantile regression · Rurality · Social capital

23.1 Introduction

Broadly defined, social capital refers to the consequences of personal and community relations that produce advantageous effects for achieving socio-economic goals (Coleman 1988) and improving the efficiency of society (Putnam et al. 1994). Numerous contributions have studied (both empirically and theoretically) the relationship between social capital and economic growth (Whiteley 2000; Temple 2002) and development (Woolcock 1998), health (Kawachi and Berkman 2000), quality of life, and many other concepts that are related to socio-economic characteristics of countries, individuals, and localities. These studies include cross-country comparisons, time series analyses to track social capital accumulation over time in specific countries, and policy recommendations to improve social capital formation for both developed and developing countries. The extensive literature shows that social capital is a context-specific concept and that individual and group differences must be taken into account when investigating it. On the one hand, this fact makes the concept of social capital a more complicated phenomenon with no unique definition and applicability. On the other hand, the differences in how social capital is produced in different contexts make it an attractive subject of research. Contextual differences occur both within countries as a result of population growth and urbanisation processes that generate differential levels of infrastructure and access to opportunities and between countries due to differences in industrialisation experiences.

Since the Industrial Revolution in the eighteenth century, the world has been urbanising (Kourtit and Nijkamp 2013). Although this period has led an overall increase in the GDP per capita (Angel 2012), the West and the world's major cities have accumulated wealth and income at a greater degree than other nations and smaller urban areas (Polese 2014; Storper 2013). The major urban areas have become density populated owing to higher job opportunities and higher wage gains, which have attracted people from rural areas (Glaeser and Maré 2001). Storper (2013) argues that urbanisation is a force of divergence and inequality, as people and economic activities agglomerate in larger cities leaving other areas behind in terms of wealth and income. This implies that as a part of the urbanisation process, rural areas might suffer economically. On the other hand, there is a quantitate evidence that in some countries, rural areas exhibit better living conditions and less crime and unemployment and are characterised by less sparse population and higher accessibility. Therefore, rural areas evolve distinctly in different contexts, achieving, among other factors, different levels of resilience and social capital.

Early studies have argued that interpersonal trust and social capital tend to be higher in rural settlements. For example, Coleman (1988) argues that, compared to closed communities, metropolitan areas lack a normative structure and, therefore, social capital. Similarly, Putnam (2000) argues that Americans who live in small towns enjoy a higher level of trust among them and close social relations. Other empirical studies that have sought to evaluate this relationship provide mixed findings. Hofferth and Iceland (1998) observe a higher likelihood of money exchanges and assistance among rural families. In a comparative study on Australian cities, Onyx and Bullen (2000) show that participation in local communities, feelings of trust, and safety are greater in rural areas. Meanwhile, Glaeser and Sacerdote (2000) find that the residents of big cities who live in apartment buildings have an increased connection between neighbours owing to greater spatial proximity, and less involvement in local politics, as they are less connected to the public space outside the buildings. In a study on cross-national social trust, Delhey and Newton (2005) find that individuals living in rural areas show less general trust compared to urban societies. The studies that compare the social capital generation in rural and urban areas emphasise the impact of spatial proximity. Putnam (2000) argues that communities get apart, as individuals spend longer times on commuting. As the spatial proximity among individuals and various activities decreases, social capital falls (Glaeser et al. 2002), and mobility becomes necessary to maintain social networks (Urry 2002). Therefore, it becomes pertinent to permit individuals to participate in activities and services by providing a basic level of accessibility (Farrington and Farrington 2005; Preston and Rajé 2007). In line with these ideas, Östh et al. (2018) show that a better accessibility of jobs is associated with higher levels of social capital in Sweden.

Departing from the considerations on the dynamic interlinks between social capital and urbanisation/rurality, as well as between social capital and proximity/connectivity, we will, first, focus on the research question whether the geographical distribution of population and distinct urbanisation experiences affect social capital formation. Secondly, we will consider and explore the accessibility as a concept that can embed both proximity and connectivity – and thus impact social capital – in both urban and rural areas.

Having that said, this chapter studies the distinctive association that social capital has with spatial accessibility and rurality/urban concentrations in two Mediterranean countries which have strong similarities in the urbanisation process but also notable differences in how social capital is manifested and spread. In particular, we explore – in these two countries – the links between social capital *stocks* and the state of rurality and spatial accessibility of jobs, from a comparative perspective. This comparison is of interest since both countries have undergone a rapid urbanisation phase resulting in a similar share of the current rural population. However, the urbanisation has impacted the development of social capital differently in the two countries due to variations in socio-economics, geography, and culture.

In summary, in our study, we will give primary attention to the role of accessibility and rurality in social capital from a comparative perspective on Turkey and Italy. In Sect. 23.2, we will discuss urbanisation processes and the likely implications of social capital accumulation for rural and urban areas in both countries. Section 23.3 provides an empirical evaluation of social capital in the two countries with accessibility and rurality as variables of interest and related controls related to socio-economic and demographic characteristics, while Sect. 23.3.2 discusses the findings. Finally, Sect. 23.4 concludes with some retrospective and prospective remarks.

23.2 Rurality and Urbanisation: Comparative Analysis in Turkey and Italy

23.2.1 Rurality and Urbanisation in Turkey

This section will give a brief historical account of the urbanisation process in Turkey: the speed and the nature of internal migration, the characteristics of the remaining population, and the relationships between migrating population and metropolitan areas.

Turkey was a predominantly rural country at the beginning of the young republic; in 1935 only 17% of the population lived in urban areas (Levine 1980). A dramatic/rapid urbanisation followed from 1950 onwards. The urbanisation was related to industrialisation, and as elsewhere big cities and metropolitan areas gained economic advantages, with a growing inequality of wealth between rural and urban regions which drew people to cities. However, the speed of industrialisation did not accord with the urbanisation in Turkey. The latter emerged as an issue before industrialisation could mature, so that the limited resources that the country possessed were used to support the industry and a well-planned urbanisation could not take place (Tekeli 1994). Therefore, much of the urban growth was driven by a rural to urban migration due to socio-economic factors that are common to other nations, such as agglomeration of better services, larger healthcare centres, schools, higher education institutions, and employment opportunities in metropolitan and large regional areas, while limited (often none) services and opportunities in remote and smaller towns. In addition to these – particularly for Turkey – political problems in south-eastern part of the country, the state policy to empty rural settlements in response to separatist movements (Öztürk 2012) and immigration to European countries mostly from small villages in central Turkey and the Black Sea coast (Avci and Kırışçı 2008), chain migration and better transportation means resulted in depopulated rural areas. The migrating population was composed of younger and working aged individuals, who left their villages to seek employment opportunities in metropolitan and commuter areas in coastal cities. They sold the inherited agricultural lands, and hence remaining individuals and concentrations of the elderly population ended up with inadequate land sources and labour to satisfy immediate subsistence needs (Yılmaz 2015). Urban to rural population mobility is still an ongoing process. Even though rural to urban migration is not uncommon especially by individuals who return from Europe and those who retire in cities and return to home, since the 2000s, the population in a few major cities continues to proliferate (Öztürk 2012).

As far as the migrating population is concerned, since the beginning of the urbanisation process, they were expected to become 'true urbanities', in the pursuit of becoming a modern, i.e. Western society, though they were condemned as failure cases (Erman 1998). They mostly lived in *gecekondus* (squatters, literally translated as 'constructed overnight') built by themselves with other migrants, especially from their villages, forming poor and diverse neighbourhoods concentrated in peripheral areas of the major cities. For many years, the *gecekondu* type of settlement and its residents have been at the centre of political debates and numerous studies have been conducted to address the issue (Erman 2001). More recently, these informal houses were demolished, and the residents were relocated to apartments in further peripheral areas following the urban renewal projects. This led to a transition process from informal housing to new formal housing experiences as a result of state interventions aiming at redevelopment (Erman 2018). A similar process has been experienced in terms of accessing employment. At the beginning, the migrant population used their informal networks (family, friends of the same origins) to find a job once they arrived in the city, but in later years townmenship associations ('hemşehri dernekleri') were established to adapt to the city and preserve cultural identities (Özbey 2018).

The recent changes in population mobility, depopulation of rural areas and rising urbanisation, in general, have distinctly restructured the social capital accumulation in rural and urban Turkey. In Anatolia, agricultural activities were carried out by family members and owing to the lack of any formal organisation, corporation and value exchange with neighbours were rather commonplace. Rural settlements have lost these informal networks during the urbanisation process. As mentioned above, the population which migrated to cities brought the rural way of living with them. The majority of migrants identified themselves on the basis of previous links to rural life, and rural origins were emphasised in identity discussions also by subsequent generations. Even today, the relationship with the origin culture is preserved and translated into a degree of participation to associations, mostly organised to bring individuals from similar origins (villages) together. These organisations undertake several events and show a higher political participation and a greater sense of community in the urban context. Therefore, the connection among individuals, social networks, and resulting trustworthiness (Putnam 2000) that was lost in the rural context might have been transported to urban areas by migrants.

23.2.2 *Rurality and Urbanisation in Italy*

In 1861, the year of unification, Italy was a predominantly rural country. Nearly 70% of the total population lived in rural areas, and the percentage decreased only by one percentage point in the following 10 years (Sallmann 1989); according to the World Bank data, it reached about 40% in 1960. In these territories the principal occupations were based on agricultural activities (40% of the total population were employed in agriculture (Federico and Malanima 2004)), leading to a wealth and education selection by the population living in rural areas. As a result of the subsequent development of the industry, people moved to the towns, where they found better facilities. This phenomenon was accompanied after World War II by the internal migration of young and working people who sought employment from the so-called Mezzogiorno to Northern Italy, the more industrialised region with more job opportunities. Putnam et al. (1994) argued that Northern Italy developed faster than Southern Italy due to a higher level of social capital, which resulted with an improvement in the economic activities (de Blasio and Nuzzo 2003). Nevertheless, the process of urbanisation did not follow a constant dynamic pattern across years and areas. The coastal municipalities faced higher urbanisation than those at the regional level. In particular, in the (500-m-wide) coastal belt, urbanisation increased threefold in the second half of the twentieth century (Romano and Zullo 2014). Furthermore, during the 1970s there was a change in the direction of growth of the cities, since suburban areas were not able to compensate for the loss of population in the core of cities. At the beginning of the twenty-first century, urban areas started to grow again (ISTAT 2017). In the last years, this process is promoted by international migration and foreign population (Strozza et al. 2016). Nowadays, one-third of the Italian people lives in highly urbanised areas.[1] On the other hand, 24% of the people lives in the predominantly rural zones. Surprisingly, one-third of the population lives in the four biggest cities: Turin, Milan, Rome, and Naples (ISTAT 2017), where access to such opportunities as higher education is considerably high (Türk 2019).

Today, living in urban areas is not associated with wealth (Anania and Tenuta 2008) and there is an ongoing urban-to-rural migration process. A part of the population prefers to live in a green area with less pollution. Moreover, even not as stronger as in the past, there are still some differences between rural and urban population: Marcellini et al. (2007) show that older people in rural Italy are less educated than those in urban areas and that the size of rural households is larger. Furthermore, there are also individual differences regarding social capital. As Putnam et al. (1994) pointed out, there is a discrepancy in the social capital level among regions, especially between North and South Italy (Carradore 2009). The biggest cities, like Rome, Milan, and Naples are characterised by higher levels of crime and lower participation in voluntary associations with respect to the smallest

[1]According to the Eurostat definition of urbanisation.

towns and Northern Italy. It is argued that voluntary activities might improve social cohesion and increase social capital, encouraging economic growth (Lasagni 2008).

23.2.3 Findings on Turkey and Italy: Synthesis

As our review above suggests, the two countries show a number of similarities as well as significant differences regarding urbanisation. Turkey and Italy have witnessed a decline in the rural population. In both countries, the majority of the population resides in a few metropolitan cities. The speed of urbanisation has been faster in coastal areas in both countries, and the traditional socio-economic divide between south and north Italy is similar to that of in Turkey between west and southeast regions. On the other hand, urbanisation was closely accompanied by industrialisation in Italy (like in other developed countries), while in Turkey urbanisation emerged before industrialisation could develop. Additionally, in Italy, the rural-urban gap in wealth and living standards are less pronounced but account for most of the inequality in Turkey.

Finally, Turkey and Italy show potentially different patterns concerning social capital accumulation. International surveys conducted for Turkey reveal that a lower interpersonal trust characterises the country compared to other nations (viz. 12.30%, where the OECD average is 36.02% [OECD 2016]), despite a relatively higher trust among younger generations. On the contrary, the trust is shown to be much higher between people sharing the same religion or ethnicity (Kayaoğlu 2017). This points out that the bounding type of social capital is potentially high in the country, while bridging type seems to be low. Although below the OECD average, a higher interpersonal trust is recorded for Italy (29.60% [OECD 2016]), and contrary to Turkey, rural settlements might enjoy a higher trust owing to the factors related to wealth distribution and access to goods and services.

The empirical analyses, presented below, aim to exploit the differences in social capital accumulation in relation to population distribution between rural and urban settlements and accessibility patterns in the two counties.

23.3 Empirical Analysis by Means of Quantile Regression

23.3.1 Method and Data

The main focus of the analyses in the present study is the extent to which the composite index of social capital is associated with spatial accessibility and rurality. We use a quantile regression method to conduct empirical analyses. The quantile regression method provides a range of conditional quantile functions, which allow for a comprehensive statistical analysis of the stochastic relationship among random variables, and specifies changes in the quantiles of the response variable (Koenker and Hallock 2001). The method permits us to identify the relationship between predictor variables and specific percentiles of the social capital variable; hence, we are able to estimate the change in a specific quantile of social capital accumulation by one unit change in the predictor variable. We will now describe the empirical model.

The job accessibility index is based on the traditional formula by Hansen (1959) and is interpreted as the highest potential job accessibility within a region. The following index is computed based on a half-life model specification (see Östh et al. 2014, for details on the mathematical formulation):

$$A_i = \sum_i D_j \exp\left(-\beta d_{ij}\right)$$

where A_i is the access from the location i, D_j is the total number of jobs available at j, and d_{ij} is the distance between i and j which discounts further locations by the distance-decay parameter γ. The index uses the exponential decay function, as it is found suitable for modelling commuting behaviour in a number of studies (De Vries et al. 2009; Fotheringham and O'Kelly 1989; Reggiani et al. 2011). In this framework, accessibility captures potential interaction between individuals and job opportunities. In this respect, accessibility embeds spatial connectivity, which points out a strong link to social capital accumulation.

The present chapter uses two primary sources of data: TURKSTAT (Turkish Statistical Institute 2015) and ISTAT (The Italian National Institute of Statistics 2015) to compare social capital responses of accessibility and rurality between Turkey and Italy. We extract data at the province level (NUTS3 regions). There are 81 such regions in Turkey and 110 in Italy. Based on the information provided by the two sources, we are able to construct a composite index of social capital, which brings resilience-related variables together at the province level. Resilience is defined as the ability and readiness of internal mechanisms to respond to external stocks (Reggiani et al. 2002), and the connectivity and interaction among people is seen one of these mechanisms (Foster 2007). In line with this principal approach, we use the community connectivity capacity (CCC) index as the proxy of social capital. The index contains four variables that reflect civic infrastructure, metropolitan stability, homeownership, and voter participation (Östh et al. 2018). The CCC index is a community indicator; therefore, it does not communicate connectivity patterns explicitly. This is why we use accessibility as our variable of interest and the impedance function is expected to reflect connectivity and interaction patterns.

The share of individuals employed or volunteered in NGOs is the first representative element of social capital and proxies the civic infrastructure. The share of the population, which resided in the same province more than 5 years, is a measure of metropolitan stability. The share of individuals who own their homes is included in the index as a measure of potential interaction with neighbours, which might be high when individuals own their homes (Rohe et al. 2013).[2] Finally, the turnout rates[3] in

[2]Note that Rohe et al. 2013 is based on studies in USA.

[3]Source for Italian turnouts: http://elezionistorico.interno.gov.it

the municipal elections show the degree of political engagement. We standardise and aggregate the four variables as a composite index of social capital for each province.

Rurality information is extracted from Eurostat. In predominantly rural areas, the rural population accounts for 50% or more of the total population, whereas in intermediate rural areas the population in rural grid cells accounts for a share between 20% and 50% of the total population (Eurostat 2013). In the study, rurality is defined following the OECD criteria, based on a definition of rural/urban LAU2s, and their population share. However, there are other definitions of rurality. The OECD methodology is affected by two potentially problematic issues, both of them leading to high variability in the area of the NUTS3 regions. Firstly, in the European countries, the considered geographical units (LAU2), on which the classification of the NUTS3 regions is based, vary considerably regarding the area covered. Secondly, in some states, the OECD criterion splits the city centre and its periphery. In this respect, Eurostat provides a different definition, based on a grid of squared cells of the same area equal to 1 Km^2 (ISTAT 2017). Furthermore, since Italy is characterised by an irregular territory, the OECD criterion seems to reflect the distribution of the Italian population and geographical structure inadequately. The MiPAAF (Ministry of Agricultural, Food and Forestry Policies) for its definition of rurality in Italy refers, therefore, to the density of population, the share of agriculture area, and altitude.[4] In order to make a comparison between Turkey and Italy, we use the OECD definition of rurality, despite the issue mentioned above. The accessibility index is constructed by combining data from OSM (Open Street Map) with map data on the geographical distribution of administrative regions.[5]

Other covariates are related to a set of socio-economic and demographic characteristics of provinces. The variable coastal is dummy taking the value 1 for coastal cities. Immigration represents the share of foreign-born individuals and for Turkey includes Syrian refugees[6] along with other immigrants. As a proxy for economic conditions, we include the Gini index (source: Acciari and Mocetti 2013) of inequality, the mean working income, and the share of employed and of unemployed individuals. The variable Internet usage represents the number of Internet subscriptions per hundred people. Human capital accumulation in provinces is proxied by three variables: the share of individuals with at least an undergraduate degree, those with at least high school education, and vocational school. Finally, demographic characteristics are represented by age distribution in each province. Table 23.1 shows descriptive statistics for our measure of social capital, accessibility, rurality, and Gini index for both Italy and Turkey. Social capital is computed higher in Italy, characterised mainly by intermediate rural provinces, and a greater accessibility than in Turkey, where more than one half of provinces are predominantly rural.

---

[4]see www.reterurale.it

[5]Source: GADM.org

[6]Source: http://goc.gov.tr

Table 23.1 Summary statistics of social capital, accessibility, Gini and rurality in Italy and Turkey

	Italy		Turkey	
	mean	sd	mean	sd
Social capital	1.9335	0.3698	1.1229	0.3271
Accessibility	0.1399	0.1561	0.0659	0.1248
Predominantly rural	0.3636	0.4832	0.5926	0.4944
Intermediate rural	0.4545	0.5002	0.3333	0.4743
Gini	0.3905	0.0449	0.3511	0.0295

23.3.2 Quantile Regression: Empirical Results in Turkey and Italy

This section studies social capital accumulation in the two countries with spatial accessibility and rurality as variables of interest. In particular, it presents the findings from a comparative approach based on quantile regressions. The quantile regression results for Turkey and Italy are reported in Tables 23.2 and 23.3, respectively. For both countries, accessibility affects social capital and, for each quantile, similar significant effects are observed (see Östh et al. 2018 for similar findings in Sweden). In comparison to Turkey, accessibility shows a stronger effect in Italy; especially in lower levels (quantiles) of social capital, the difference is more significant. This might be related to longer commuting distances in Turkish cities. While intercity commuting is very rare in Turkey, it is a common activity in most of the Italian regions. As displayed in Fig. 23.1, in Italy the highest values of accessibility are in the northern provinces, while the southern part and the two main islands display (except the provinces of the main cities) lower accessibility. This also reflects the socio-economic gap between north and south. Similarly, in Turkey, accessibility is more advanced in the western and southern provinces, while it is lower in the east part of the country and locations far from the coast. In this respect, the accessibility measures are in line with the urbanisation process, where highly urbanised cities comprise advanced accessibility. In this paper, accessibility is considered as a measure embedding spatial connectivity; hence, higher accessibility might capture a broader and stronger configuration of potential social networks. The regressions results confirm this hypothesis. Worth noting that since in Turkey, commuting is limited to within cities, a part of the potential accessibility remains unused. This explains the relatively lower impact of accessibility on social capital.

Regarding the relationship between rurality and social capital, the findings point out specific differences between Italy and Turkey. The predominantly rural areas are associated with increased levels of social capital in Italy for the lowest and highest quantiles. This means that when social capital is low or relatively high, increasing rurality favours social capital accumulation. Similarly, intermediate rural areas positively affect social capital, especially in lower and higher quantiles. On the other hand, rurality is negatively associated with social capital in Turkey for both predictors of ruralities, predominantly and intermediate rural areas. This might be related to a set of reasons: the reduction in agricultural activities has left a large share

Table 23.2 Quantile regression outputs for Italy, quantiles indicated by tau values

Italy	(1)	(2)	(3)	(4)	(5)	(6)	(7)	(8)
Variables	OLS	tau = 0.05	tau = 0.10	tau = 0.25	tau = 0.40	tau = 0.50	tau = 0.75	tau = 0.95
Accessibility	2.370***	2.496***	2.307***	2.201***	1.884**	2.581***	1.549*	1.939***
	(0.629)	(0.407)	(0.639)	(0.793)	(0.854)	(0.792)	(0.823)	(0.144)
Predominantly rural	0.0510	0.206***	0.0707	0.0457	−0.00263	−0.0689	0.0720	0.0586**
	(0.116)	(0.0748)	(0.117)	(0.146)	(0.157)	(0.146)	(0.151)	(0.0265)
Intermediate rural	0.121	0.407***	0.285***	0.0600	0.0615	0.00459	0.123	0.162***
	(0.0954)	(0.0617)	(0.0968)	(0.120)	(0.129)	(0.120)	(0.125)	(0.0219)
Coastal	0.0116	−0.0356	0.00165	0.0708	0.0615	−0.0269	0.0433	0.106***
	(0.0818)	(0.0529)	(0.0830)	(0.103)	(0.111)	(0.103)	(0.107)	(0.0188)
Immigration	−2.871	−4.519***	−7.284***	−3.330	−0.779	−2.791	−0.0950	−0.117
	(2.001)	(1.293)	(2.030)	(2.520)	(2.715)	(2.517)	(2.616)	(0.459)
Gini	−4.166**	0.0136	1.397	1.059	−2.771	−5.211**	−4.763*	−4.497***
	(1.960)	(1.267)	(1.990)	(2.469)	(2.660)	(2.467)	(2.563)	(0.450)
Working income	0.0704	1.653**	0.239	−0.0137	0.515	−0.701	1.277	2.116***
	(0.976)	(0.631)	(0.991)	(1.229)	(1.325)	(1.228)	(1.276)	(0.224)
Employed	−1.581	−2.238***	0.338	0.984	−0.990	−2.248	−1.527	−1.933***
	(1.284)	(0.830)	(1.303)	(1.617)	(1.742)	(1.615)	(1.679)	(0.295)
Unemployed	−2.573	−8.961***	−6.049***	−4.598*	−3.158	−2.449	−0.758	−0.341
	(1.908)	(1.234)	(1.937)	(2.403)	(2.589)	(2.401)	(2.495)	(0.438)
Internet usage	0.0246*	0.0408***	0.0324**	−0.00212	0.0223	0.0353**	0.0236	0.0345***
	(0.0127)	(0.00823)	(0.0129)	(0.0160)	(0.0173)	(0.0160)	(0.0166)	(0.00292)
Higher education	4.907*	5.354***	2.759	5.565	6.538*	5.588*	5.365	4.217***
	(2.669)	(1.725)	(2.709)	(3.361)	(3.622)	(3.358)	(3.489)	(0.613)
High school	−4.919**	−5.842***	−4.649**	−5.535*	−6.606**	−6.168**	−6.962**	−2.412***
	(2.289)	(1.480)	(2.323)	(2.883)	(3.106)	(2.880)	(2.992)	(0.525)

(continued)

Table 23.2 (continued)

Italy	(1)	(2)	(3)	(4)	(5)	(6)	(7)	(8)
Vocational education	2.123*	3.090***	2.317*	1.480	3.883**	3.748**	3.690**	0.184
	(1.187)	(0.767)	(1.204)	(1.495)	(1.610)	(1.493)	(1.551)	(0.272)
Age 15–29	5.093	10.91***	8.673**	1.489	9.689**	8.519*	8.188*	6.960***
	(3.501)	(2.263)	(3.553)	(4.409)	(4.750)	(4.405)	(4.576)	(0.803)
Age 30–39	−7.504	−10.63***	−2.317	−0.0165	−7.132	−7.448	−8.047	−13.64***
	(5.689)	(3.678)	(5.774)	(7.165)	(7.719)	(7.158)	(7.437)	(1.306)
Age 40–49	−18.73	−33.87***	−42.28***	−32.74*	−38.07**	−39.69**	7.644	15.71***
	(14.04)	(9.075)	(14.25)	(17.68)	(19.05)	(17.66)	(18.35)	(3.222)
Age 50–59	6.427	9.891**	8.314	9.184	10.42	13.79	−9.518	−8.616***
	(7.018)	(4.537)	(7.123)	(8.839)	(9.523)	(8.830)	(9.175)	(1.611)
Constant	3.659***	2.001***	1.052	2.776**	3.000**	3.903***	3.225**	3.023***
	(1.102)	(0.712)	(1.118)	(1.388)	(1.495)	(1.386)	(1.440)	(0.253)
Observations	110	110	110	110	110	110	110	110
R-squared	0.359							

Standard errors in parentheses
***$p < 0.01$; **$p < 0.05$; *$p < 0.1$

Table 23.3 Quantile regression outputs for Turkey, quantiles indicated by tau values

Turkey	(1)	(2)	(3)	(4)	(5)	(6)	(7)	(8)	(9)
Variables	OLS	tau = 0.05	tau = 0.10	tau = 0.25	tau = 0.40	tau = 0.50	tau = 0.75	tau = 0.90	tau = 0.95
Accessibility	1.230***	1.103***	0.947***	1.455***	1.393***	1.412***	1.300*	1.820**	1.386***
	(0.438)	(0.0934)	(0.261)	(0.408)	(0.353)	(0.470)	(0.703)	(0.777)	(0.512)
Predominantly rural	−0.244	−0.175***	−0.250	−0.208	−0.0728	−0.0484	−0.297	−0.197	−0.222
	(0.255)	(0.0543)	(0.152)	(0.237)	(0.206)	(0.273)	(0.409)	(0.452)	(0.298)
Intermediate rural	−0.264	−0.515***	−0.500***	−0.337	−0.169	−0.100	−0.163	0.0262	0.106
	(0.246)	(0.0525)	(0.146)	(0.229)	(0.199)	(0.264)	(0.395)	(0.437)	(0.288)
Coastal	0.268**	0.426***	0.373***	0.297***	0.229***	0.191*	0.123	0.106	0.186
	(0.101)	(0.0215)	(0.0601)	(0.0940)	(0.0815)	(0.108)	(0.162)	(0.179)	(0.118)
Immigration	−1.958	−0.855	−1.986	−1.473	−4.093	−3.728	−2.389	−5.908	7.266**
	(3.108)	(0.662)	(1.847)	(2.891)	(2.506)	(3.330)	(4.986)	(5.510)	(3.630)
Gini	0.0112	−0.139	−0.730	−0.557	0.00747	0.874	0.523	−1.378	−1.172
	(1.406)	(0.299)	(0.836)	(1.308)	(1.134)	(1.506)	(2.256)	(2.493)	(1.642)
Working income	0.276	0.330***	0.226	0.199	0.242	0.420	0.377	1.200**	1.928***
	(0.305)	(0.0650)	(0.181)	(0.284)	(0.246)	(0.327)	(0.489)	(0.541)	(0.356)
Employed	1.664	0.364*	0.708	0.470	0.400	1.217	2.773*	3.543*	4.149***
	(1.008)	(0.215)	(0.599)	(0.938)	(0.813)	(1.080)	(1.617)	(1.787)	(1.177)
Unemployed	−2.408	−2.686***	−2.712***	−4.374***	−4.100***	−3.778**	−2.180	−1.111	−0.740
	(1.640)	(0.349)	(0.975)	(1.526)	(1.322)	(1.757)	(2.631)	(2.908)	(1.916)
Internet usage	−0.0684***	−0.0878***	−0.0777***	−0.0663***	−0.0496**	−0.0514*	−0.0209	−0.116***	−0.127***
	(0.0243)	(0.00517)	(0.0144)	(0.0226)	(0.0196)	(0.0260)	(0.0390)	(0.0431)	(0.0284)
Higher education	0.891	2.841***	2.973**	1.216	1.126	0.660	−0.798	1.882	1.990
	(1.887)	(0.402)	(1.121)	(1.755)	(1.521)	(2.021)	(3.026)	(3.345)	(2.204)
High school	6.586**	2.066***	0.891	7.924***	7.210***	5.814*	5.480	7.899	4.537
	(3.151)	(0.671)	(1.873)	(2.931)	(2.540)	(3.376)	(5.055)	(5.587)	(3.681)

(continued)

Table 23.3 (continued)

Turkey	(1)	(2)	(3)	(4)	(5)	(6)	(7)	(8)	(9)
Vocational education	−0.424	−1.752***	−1.659***	−1.337	0.344	0.464	−0.784	−1.517	−1.884*
	(0.877)	(0.187)	(0.521)	(0.816)	(0.707)	(0.940)	(1.407)	(1.555)	(1.025)
Age 15–29	−10.19***	−3.617***	−2.772	−12.33***	−11.69***	−12.10***	−10.79*	−11.63*	−8.180*
	(3.548)	(0.756)	(2.109)	(3.300)	(2.860)	(3.801)	(5.691)	(6.290)	(4.144)
Age 30–39	−21.57***	−14.12***	−15.99***	−13.52**	−12.82***	−14.82**	−24.75***	−33.10***	−36.23***
	(5.727)	(1.220)	(3.404)	(5.327)	(4.617)	(6.136)	(9.187)	(10.15)	(6.689)
Age 40–49	7.129	8.911***	11.23**	−2.700	−4.177	−3.396	−0.129	13.41	19.86*
	(9.076)	(1.933)	(5.395)	(8.443)	(7.317)	(9.724)	(14.56)	(16.09)	(10.60)
Age 50–59	−19.93***	−9.644***	−9.787**	−19.53***	−17.17***	−16.80**	−19.74*	−19.53	−18.30**
	(6.860)	(1.461)	(4.077)	(6.381)	(5.530)	(7.349)	(11.00)	(12.16)	(8.012)
Constant	6.895***	3.746***	3.799***	7.923***	7.251***	7.127***	8.006***	7.698**	6.300***
	(1.673)	(0.356)	(0.994)	(1.556)	(1.349)	(1.792)	(2.683)	(2.965)	(1.954)
Observations	81	81	81	81	81	81	81	81	81
R-squared	0.465								

Standard errors in parentheses
$***p < 0.01$; $**p < 0.05$; $*p < 0.1$

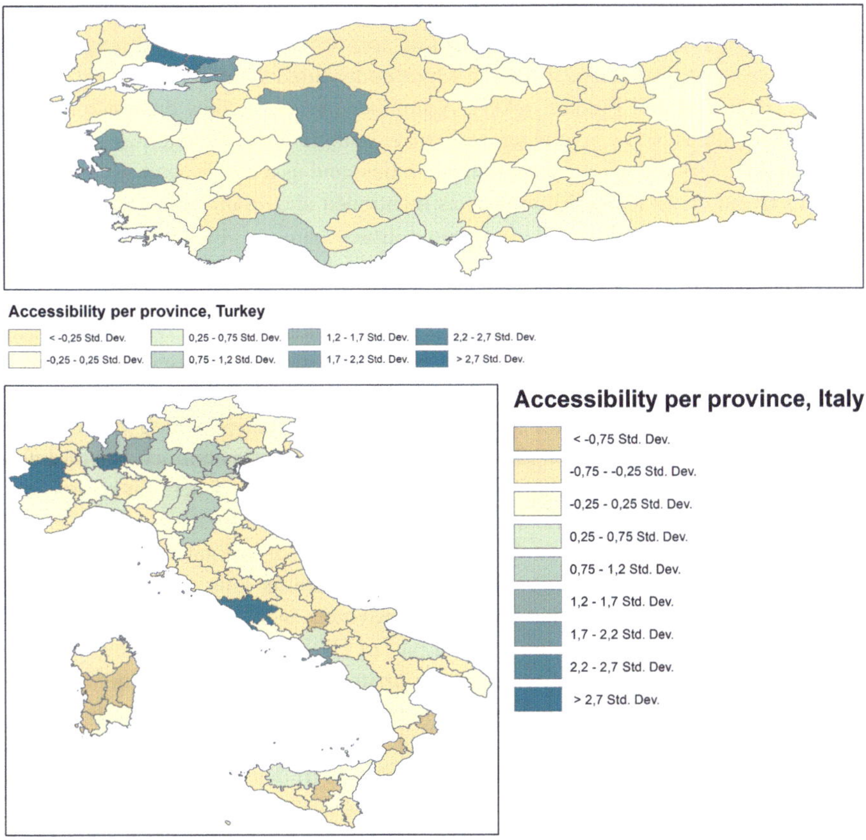

Fig. 23.1 Accessibility per province in Turkey and Italy

of the population unemployed, living in economically distressed villages in Turkey. The former agricultural activities entailed working and producing together in farms and as a result, generated a greater interaction among family members and neighbours. This was lost during the urbanisation process.

Moreover, the speed of internal migration differs in the two countries. The rural population has dropped 30% from the year 1960 to 2015 in Turkey. This is a dramatic change, especially when compared to a 10% drop in Italy in the same period (World Bank). At the same time, the distinct economic activities in Turkey and Italy cause a variation in the degree of internal migration. Italy is traditionally characterised by small family businesses, while informal networks characterised by family ties are the primary source of employment. Hence, younger generations in Italy are more prone to remain in the home or return to it after university education; this is evident from the decreasing trend in internal migration since the 1970s (Bonifazi and Heins 2000). Therefore, Italian rural settlements do not suffer from urbanisation as much as Turkish rural areas. Along similar lines, the work of Putnam et al. (1994) shows that especially northern Italian regions have traditionally benefitted from higher social capital in the form of norms of reciprocity and networks of civic engagement (Putnam et al. 1994), which contributed to the economic growth of regions (Helliwell and Putnam 1995). A number of case studies demonstrate that Italian rural areas show a greater resilience both in case of internal migration (Capello 2015) (bonding social capital, weak ties) and as a buffer against contextual changes (Ruiu et al. 2017). Moreover, as mentioned above, in Turkey, the population which migrated to cities did not become 'true urbanities'; they brought the rural way of living with them, forming subcultures which act collectively and organised (through NGOs established in the name of villages). This is why increasing internal migration (as a result of urbanisation) is associated with a greater civic engagement in urban areas owing to these organisations and in return with increased social capital and resilience. Additionally, as also shown by Kayaoğlu (2017), rural population in Turkey shows relatively less trust compared to urban societies, which supports the findings of Delhey and Newton (2005) for 60 nations. On the contrary, the findings concerning Italy are in line with the work of Putnam (2000), where he argues that American small towns and rural areas show higher levels of trust.

As far as the variable coastal is concerned, Turkish coastal areas contribute significantly to social capital accumulation; meanwhile, in Italy, the relationship is not significant. The reason is that the coastal provinces in Turkey are wealthier with greater employment opportunities; a large part of GDP is produced in coastal areas by industrial, commercial activities and tourism (Kuleli 2015). Furthermore, in Turkey, urbanisation is characterised by internal mass migration from eastern parts to the large western coastal metropolitan areas (Burak et al. 2004). Given the internal employment migration towards coastal cities, the high density of tourism, and the increasing foreign population, the inhabitants of coastal areas might find it easier to interact with different individuals, and hence benefit from bridging social capital to a higher degree with respect to other regions of the country. This idea is supported by the increased 'lifestyle migration' by European retirees in Turkish coastal areas since the early 1990s. Although the general tendency of interpersonal distrust persists among locals, they also consider the foreigners contribute to the economy, multiculturalism, and tolerance. More than half of the European retirees with a university degree prefer to live in neighbourhoods with locals (Balkır and Südaş 2014).

There are a number of differences between the two countries when other covariates are considered. The variable immigration shows a strong negative relationship with social capital in Italy, meanwhile, in Turkey, the effect is not significant. It is interesting to note that only for the highest quantile, immigration has a significant and positive association with social capital. Turkey hosts 3 million Syrian refugees, and in eastern regions, the number of Syrian refugees is close to the number of native population.[7] The studies on the public perception of refugees suggest that Turks see immigrants both as a threat and a benefit, though the latter perception dominates owing to the shared religion and cultural similarities (Topal

[7] https://data2.unhcr.org/en/situations/syria

et al. 2017). This is in line with the study conducted by Kayaoğlu (2017) where she shows that interpersonal trust is at a higher level among individuals with the same religion in Turkey. Although this explains the statistically insignificant coefficients for most quantiles, the negative signs indicate that for the locations of lower social capital level the threat perception might be more prevalent. However, as the regression outputs suggest, at the highest social capital level, the higher population of immigrants enhance the social capital. Municipalities play a crucial role in accommodating and integrating Syrian refugees with newly established migration policy centres and organisations such as the Association for Solidarity with Asylum Seekers and Migrants (ASAM) and many NGOs established by Syrian refugees (Kirişçi et al. 2018). These organisations have been established as a response to Syrian refugee crises in larger cities and contribute to civic engagement and hence to overall social capital in these places where they are active.

As far as economic variables are concerned, in line with previous studies, inequality negatively affects social capital in Italy. The coefficients of the Gini variable show mixed signs with no statistical significance for Turkey, but as the social capital level increases the coefficients indicate an apparent negative relationship between social capital and inequality. Although this trend in Turkey does not confirm previous studies, Östh et al. (2018) also show that increasing the number of wealthy people positively affects the social capital/resilience level of Swedish municipalities. Moreover, for both Turkey and Italy, working income is positively and the share of unemployed individuals is negatively associated with social capital. The variable working people shows a positive impact on social capital in Turkey and a mixed effect is observed in Italy.

The variable Internet usage confirms the previous studies in Italy with a positive association with social capital. However, in Turkey Internet usage negatively affects social capital. The result may indicate that while in Italy Internet users maintain their online contacts in daily interactions and vice versa, in Turkey people do not translate social media friends into real-life networks; the negative and significant coefficients suggest that they also engage in online networks substituting real-life interactions/organisations. This might be related to trust and privacy concerns that Turks have against social networks (Ertan 2010), while the government's control and censorship of the Internet (Akgül and Kırlıdoğ 2015) might have increased this tendency.

As regards human capital and demographic variables, the share of individuals with at least a university degree shows a positive relationship with social capital in both countries. In Turkey, the share of high school graduates affects positively, and the vocational school graduates affect negatively social capital. Conversely, an increased share of vocational school graduates influences positively and high school graduates influence negatively social capital accumulation in Italy. Finally, the accumulation of middle-aged individuals is positively associated with social capital in Turkey, while the opposite is observed for Italy.

Figures 23.2 and 23.3 include maps that display predicted social capital in Italy and Turkey, respectively, for the quantiles 0.25 and 0.75. The areas with high social capital are shown in blue, and those areas with a low level of social capital are coloured red. The maps displayed in Fig. 23.2 confirm previous findings, which

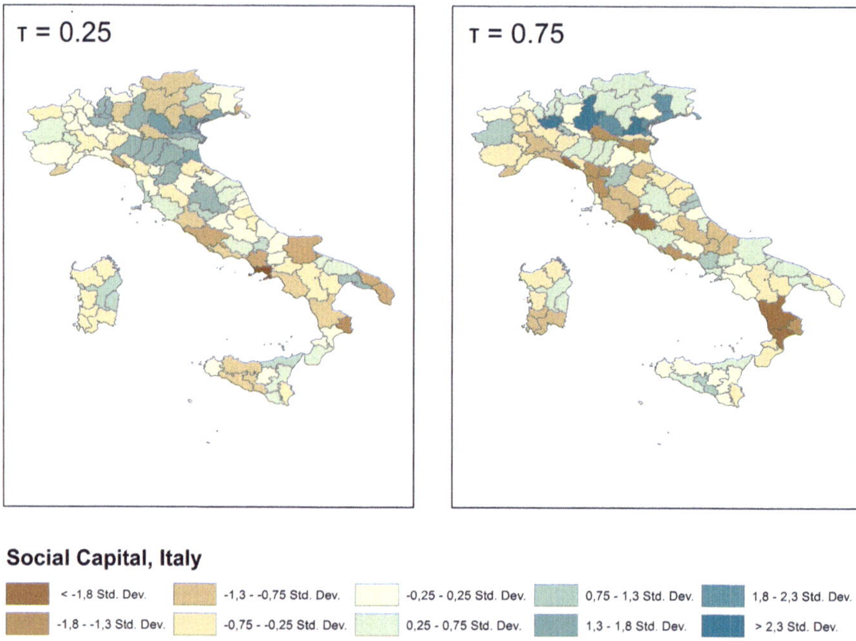

Fig. 23.2 Predicted social capital, Italy

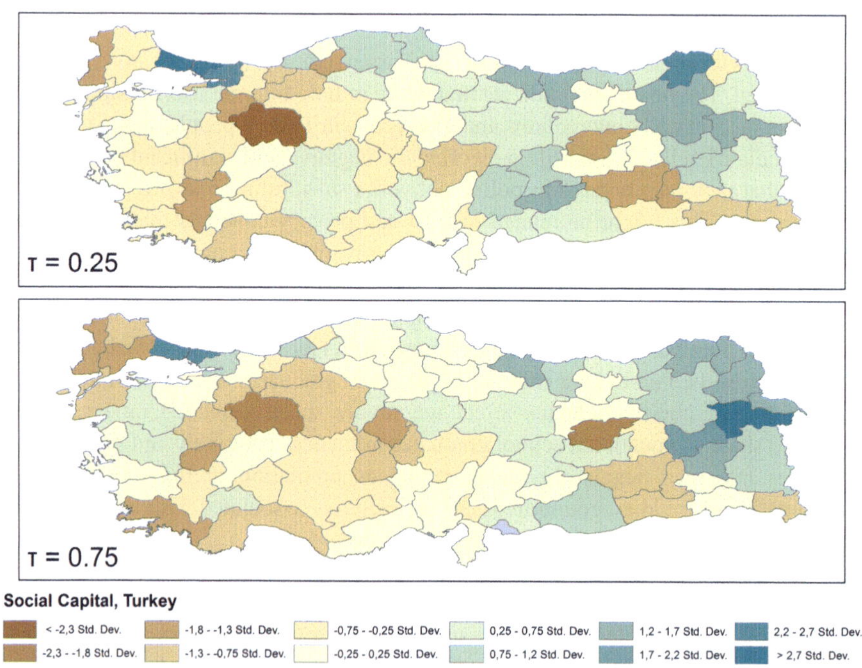

Fig. 23.3 Predicted social capital, Turkey

register a higher social capital in northern regions and a relatively lower social capital in southern regions. Meanwhile, our results do not predict a clear distinction between the two regions. Some southern cities also constitute a higher resilience and social capital. This might be related to urban-to-rural migration that Italy witnesses recently. Figure 23.3 displays a clearer spatial pattern for Turkey. The Black Sea coast, eastern and central Anatolia are characterised by higher social capital. In addition, major metropolitan cities exhibit a considerably high social capital. This is in line with our empirical findings. Figures 23.2 and 23.3 report interesting findings as regards low and high quantiles of social capital distribution. At the first quantile, accessibility is one of the main drivers of social capital. Meanwhile, in the higher quantiles of social capital, socio-economic factors become more effective such as income inequality in Italy and employment rate in Turkey. Therefore, the maps for $\tau = 25$ and $\tau = 75$ show different social capital levels for provinces. For example, locations with higher income inequality depart from the mean downwards at higher quantiles. This means that the areas of low social capital benefit from better spatial connectivity. On the other hand, the highest levels of social capital require more homogenous socio-economic conditions among anyone who share the same built environment.

23.4 Conclusions

This study contributes to the existing literature on social capital and resilience by comparing social capital in Turkey and Italy, and by examining how it varies as a response to rurality and accessibility. As described, Italy and Turkey are characterised by several similarities. Both countries were influenced by a decline in the rural population in the last few decades, ending up with a similar distribution of the population between rural and urban areas. Clearly, the speed and the process of urbanisation have emerged differently.

The study also shows that the urbanisation experiences of countries might lead to a different social capital distribution between rural and urban areas. After a period of urban concentration, Italy has witnessed a geographical deconcentration of settlements and population. Today, in Italy the regional disparities between southern and northern regions are still pronounced but these disparities are less evident between the rural and urban areas in the country. In Turkey, on the other hand, urban population continues to grow with decreasing agricultural activities. Unbalanced spatial structures between Turkish regions are increasingly observed between rural and urban areas in relation to unequal economic and development schemes. These differences cause a variation in the rates of social capital accumulation, which are evident in the empirical findings of the present contribution: Italian rural areas are associated with higher social capital accumulation, whereas, rurality shows a negative impact on social capital in Turkey. However, in accordance with previous studies, accessibility favours social capital in both countries. This is a significant finding, as it implies that despite the differences in structural developments over time, spatial accessibility might be used as a policy tool to enhance social capital and foster socio-economic development of rural areas in Turkey and southern regions in Italy.

Further research might explore the long-run relationship between social capital and accessibility: a study using panel data would enhance our knowledge of social capital in a dynamic impact of cities and regions in transition.

References

Acciari P, Mocetti S (2013) Una Mappa Della Disuguaglianza Del Reddito in Italia (The geography of income inequality in Italy). Bank of Italy Occasional Paper, p 208

Akgül M, Kırlıdoğ M (2015) Internet censorship in Turkey. Internet Policy Rev 4(2):1–22

Anania G, Tenuta A (2008) Ruralità, urbanità e ricchezza dei comuni italiani. QA Rivista dell'Associazione Rossi Doria, pp 71–103

Angel S (2012) Planet of cities. Lincoln Institute of Land Policy, Cambridge

Avci G, Kirişçi K (2008) Turkey's immigration and emigration dilemmas at the gates of the European Union. In: Castles S, Wise RD (eds) Migration and development: perspectives from the south. International Organization for Migration, Geneva

Balkır C, Südaş I (2014) Guests and hosts: European retirees in coastal Turkey. Insight Turkey 16 (4):123

Bonifazi C, Heins F (2000) Long-term trends of internal migration in Italy. Int J Popul Geogr 6 (2):111–131

Burak SA, Dogan E, Gazioglu C (2004) Impact of urbanization and tourism on coastal environment. Ocean Coast Manag 47(9–10):515–527

Capello C (2015) Family, social capital and internal migration in Italy: the case of the people of Tramonti. Hum Aff 25(1):40–57

Carradore M (2009) Social capital in Italian regions: distributions of a resource, according to the Istat Servey. Autonomie Locali e Servizi Sociali 32(1):15–34

Coleman JS (1988) Social capital in the creation of human capital. Am J Sociol 94:S95–S120

de Blasio G, Nuzzo G (2003) Putnam's social capital and the Italian regions: an empirical investigation. mimeo, Bank of Italy, Rome

De Vries JJ, Nijkamp P, Rietveld P (2009) Exponential or power distance-decay for commuting? An alternative specification. Environ Plan A 41(2):461–480

Delhey J, Newton K (2005) Predicting cross-national levels of social trust: global pattern or Nordic exceptionalism? Eur Sociol Rev 21(4):311–327

Erman T (1998) Becoming "urban" or remaining "rural": the views of Turkish rural-to-urban migrants on the "integration" question. Int J Middle East Stud 30(4):541–561

Erman T (2001) The politics of squatter (gecekondu) studies in Turkey: the changing representations of rural migrants in the academic discourse. Urban Stud 38(7):983–1002

Erman T (2018) From informal housing to apartment housing: exploring the 'new social'in a gecekondu rehousing project, Turkey. Hous Stud 34:1–19

Ertan A (2010) The determinants of social capital on facebook. Science and Technology Policies Research Center TEKPOL Working Paper Series STPS-WP-11/08

Eurostat (2013) Eurostat regional yearbook 2013. European Commission, Luxembourg: Publication Office of the European Union

Farrington J, Farrington C (2005) Rural accessibility, social inclusion and social justice: towards conceptualisation. J Transp Geogr 13(1):1–12

Federico G, Malanima P (2004) Progress, decline, growth: product and productivity in Italian agriculture, 1000–2000. Econ Hist Rev 57(3):437–464

Foster KA (2007) A case study approach to understanding regional resilience. http://iurd.berkeley.edu/wp/2007-08.pdf
Fotheringham AS, O'Kelly ME (1989) Spatial interaction models: formulations and applications, vol 1. Kluwer academic publishers, Dordrecht, p 989
Glaeser EL, Maré DC (2001) Cities and skills. J Labor Econ 19(2):316–342
Glaeser EL, Sacerdote B (2000) The social consequences of housing. J Hous Econ 9(1–2):1–23
Glaeser EL, Laibson D, Sacerdote B (2002) An economic approach to social capital. Econ J 112 (483):F437–F458
Hansen WG (1959) How accessibility shapes land use. J Am Inst Plann 25(2):73–76
Helliwell JF, Putnam RD (1995) Economic growth and social capital in Italy. East Econ J 21 (3):295–307
Hofferth SL, Iceland J (1998) Social capital in rural and urban communities 1. Rural Sociol 63 (4):574–598
ISTAT (2017) Forme, livelli e dinamiche dell'urbanizzazione in Italia. Italian National Institute of Statistics
Kawachi I, Berkman L (2000) Social cohesion, social capital, and health. Soc Epidemiol 174:190
Kayaoğlu A (2017) Determinants of trust in Turkey. Eur Soc 19(4):492–516
Kirişçi K, Brandt J, Erdogan MM (2018) Syrian refugees in Turkey: beyond the numbers. The Brookings Institution. June. https://www.brookings.edu/blog/order-from-chaos/2018/06/19/syrian-refugees-in-turkey-beyond-the-numbers
Koenker R, Hallock KF (2001) Quantile regression. J Econ Perspect 15(4):143–156
Kourtit K, Nijkamp P (2013) In praise of megacities in a global world. Reg Sci Policy Pract 5 (2):167–182
Kuleli T (2015) The socio-economic significance of the Turkish coastal environment for sustainable development. Environ Monit Assess 187(5):231
Lasagni A (2008) Volontariato e criminalità in Italia: un'analisi sui dati provinciali. From www.forumsolidarieta.it
Levine N (1980) Antiurbanization: an implicit development policy in Turkey. J Dev Areas 14 (4):513–538
Marcellini F, Giuli C, Gagliardi C, Papa R (2007) Aging in Italy: urban–rural differences. Arch Gerontol Geriatr 44(3):243–260
OECD (2016) Society at a Glance 2016: OECD social indicators. OECD Publishing, Paris. https://doi.org/10.1787/9789264261488-en
Onyx J, Bullen P (2000) Measuring social capital in five communities. J Appl Behav Sci 36 (1):23–42
Östh J, Reggiani A, Galiazzo G (2014) Novel methods for the estimation of cost-distance decay in potential accessibility models. In: Condeço A, Reggiani A, Gutiérrez J (eds) Accessibility and spatial interaction. Edward Elgar (EE), Cheltenham and Northampton, pp 15–37
Östh J, Dolciotti M, Reggiani A, Nijkamp P (2018) Social capital, resilience and accessibility in urban systems: a study on Sweden. Netw Spat Econ 18(2):313–336
Özbey K (2018) Migration and social change: the migration experience of modern Turkey. Modernizing Process Turkey Sociol Views 3:105–122
Öztürk M (2012) Agriculture, peasantry and poverty in Turkey in the neo-liberal age. Wageningen Academic Publishers, Wageningen, p 240
Polese M (2014) The resilient city: On the determinants of successful urban economies. In: Paddison R, Hutton T (eds) Cities and economic change: restructuring and dislocation in the global metropolis. Sage, London, pp 161 145
Preston J, Rajé F (2007) Accessibility, mobility and transport-related social exclusion. J Transp Geogr 15(3):151–160
Putnam RD (2000) Bowling alone: America's declining social capital. In: Culture and politics. Palgrave Macmillan, New York, pp 223–234
Putnam RD, Leonardi R, Nanetti RY (1994) Making democracy work: civic traditions in modern Italy. Princeton university press, Princeton

Reggiani A, De Graaff T, Nijkamp P (2002) Resilience: an evolutionary approach to spatial economic systems. Netw Spat Econ 2(2):211–229
Reggiani A, Bucci P, Russo G (2011) Accessibility and impedance forms: empirical applications to the German community network. Int Reg Sci Rev 34(2):230–252
Rohe WM, Van Zandt S, McCarthy G (2013) The social benefits and costs of homeownership: a critical assessment of the research. Afford Hous Read 40:00-01
Romano B, Zullo F (2014) The urban transformation of Italy's Adriatic coastal strip: fifty years of unsustainability. Land Use Policy 38:26–36
Ruiu ML, Seddaiu G, Roggero PP (2017) Developing adaptive responses to contextual changes for sustainable agricultural management: the role of social capital in the Arborea district (Sardinia, Italy). J Rural Stud 49:162–170
Sallmann JM (1989) Les niveaux d'alphabétisation en Italie au XIXe siècle. Mélanges de l'école française de Rome 101(1):183–337
Storper M (2013) Keys to the city: how economics, institutions, social interaction, and politics shape development. Princeton University Press, Princeton
Strozza S, Benassi F, Ferrara R, Gallo G (2016) Recent demographic trends in the major Italian urban agglomerations: the role of foreigners. Spat Demogr 4(1):39–70
Tekeli I (1994) The patron-client relationship, land-rent economy and the experience of urbanization without citizens. The urban experience: a people–environment perspective, pp 9–17
Temple J (2002) Growth effects of education and social capital in the OECD countries. Hist Soc Res 27:5–46
The Italian National Institute of Statistics (2015) Indicatori Territoriali. The Italian National Institute of Statistics, Rome
Topal MH, Özer U, Dokuzlu E (2017) Public perception of Syrian refugees in Turkey: an empirical explanation using extended integrative threat theory. Problemy Polityki Społecznej
Türk U (2019) Socio-economic determinants of student mobility and inequality of access to higher education in Italy. Netw Spat Econ 19(1):125–148
Turkish Statistical Institute (2015) Indicator values of well-being index for provinces. Turkish Statistical Institute, Ankara
Urry J (2002) Mobility and proximity. Sociology 36(2):255–274
Whiteley PF (2000) Economic growth and social capital. Polit Stud 48(3):443–466
Woolcock M (1998) Social capital and economic development: toward a theoretical synthesis and policy framework. Theory Soc 27(2):151–208
Yılmaz M (2015) Türkiye'de kirsal nüfusun değişimi ve ilere göre dağilimi (1980–2012). Doğu coğrafya dergisi 20(33):161–188

Chapter 24
Second-Degree Price Discrimination and Intergroup Externalities in Airline Routes Between European Cities

Marco Alderighi, Alessandro Cento, Peter Nijkamp, and Piet Rietveld

Abstract This paper presents a model of second-degree price discrimination and intergroup effects. Consumer heterogeneity is assumed on both a horizontal and a vertical dimension, while various distinct market structures, some of which include low-cost carriers (LCCs), are considered. We theoretically show that the rivalry among full-service carriers (FSCs) usually reduces the distance between business and leisure fares. The rivalry with an LCC increases this distance causing a reduction of leisure fares and, possibly, an increase of business fares. We test these implications using data concerning the early stage of low-cost entry in Italy on European routes. The empirical results largely support our theoretical findings.

Keywords Pricing policy · Panel data · Yield management

JEL Classification D22 · L11 · L93

Piet Rietveld passed away on November 1, 2013.

M. Alderighi (✉)
CT-TEM, Università della Valle d'Aosta, Aosta, Italy

GREEN, Università Bocconi, Milan, Italy
e-mail: m.alderighi@univda.it

A. Cento
Etihad Airways, Abu Dhabi, United Arab Emirates

P. Nijkamp
Tinbergen Institute, Gustav Mahlerlaan 117, MS, Amsterdam, The Netherlands

Adam Mickiewicz University, Wieniawskiego 1, Poznań, Poland

JADS, 's-Hertogenbosch, The Netherlands

Alexandru Ioan Cuza University, Iasi, Romania

P. Rietveld
VU University, Amsterdam, The Netherlands

Z. Chen et al. (eds.), *Development Studies in Regional Science*,
New Frontiers in Regional Science: Asian Perspectives 42,
https://doi.org/10.1007/978-981-15-1435-7_24

24.1 Introduction

A notable outcome of a full-service carrier (FSC) pricing policy is that two travellers on the same flight may pay quite different fares in spite of the fact that they both may have acquired the ticket at the same time. This outcome may emerge since an FSC simultaneously offers multiple booking classes, each of them having specific travel restrictions and cabin and ground services, which are designed in order to match various demand segments. Since product characteristics of any booking class rarely change over time, a major concern for an FSC is to define, for any flight, the optimal fare to be assigned to each booking class and, consequently, the optimal fare gap between two consecutive classes.

While fare levels are mainly determined by the competitive environment in the city-pair market, the maximum fare gap between consecutive booking classes reflects the intention of the travellers with higher willingness-to-pay (WTP) to buy more expensive tickets but with better characteristics. If such fare gaps are too large, there is indeed the risk of 'passenger diversion', i.e. a demand switch of business travellers towards less expensive fares. Such a risk corresponds to a situation where a carrier competes against itself: its cheaper tickets divert travellers from buying more expensive tickets, and in this way the carrier ends up losing revenues.

This paper focuses on how the competitive environment and the change in the competitive environment caused by the entry of a low-cost carrier (LCC) affect FSC fare levels and gaps. An LCC has lower operational costs and lower service quality than an FSC; its pricing policy also differs from that of an FSC, at least in the first decade of the new millennium, i.e. during the period to which our analysis refers. As regards this last aspect, an FSC pricing policy usually includes more than ten simultaneous fares (segmented pricing), while that of an LCC tends to be organized around a main fare (unsegmented pricing), although, in addition to this, a few additional services can be sold separately (add-ons) or in a bundle (packages).

Differences in business models and pricing policies have consequences for the way in which different types of carriers compete. In any competing route, two FSCs have similar pricing choices; their travellers have similar characteristics and WTP; and they charge similar fares, implying similar fare gaps between different booking classes. Indeed, when an FSC faces an LCC which uses a different pricing policy, travellers usually differ in characteristics and WTP; fares are different; and also fare gaps are likely to be different.

In our analysis, we focus on two different aspects concerning the asymmetric competition induced by LCCs. First, LCCs may exert strong competitive pressure on FSC fares, especially on the leisure segment. Second, LCCs, by modifying the composition of FSC travellers, may stimulate intergroup effects, i.e. because of a different composition of passengers within the flight, high WTP travellers may attach more value of being in an FSC flight, and, therefore, they would like to pay more for a business ticket. Both aspects generate profound variations in fare levels and gaps.

The rest of the paper is organized as follows. Section 24.2 offers a short review of the related literature. Section 24.3 presents the theoretical model. Section 24.4 provides a description of the data, the estimation procedure, and the main results. Section 24.5 concludes. All proofs are available upon request.

24.2 Related Literature

24.2.1 Second- and Third- Degree Price Discrimination

Carriers pricing behaviour in interurban airline connections has been amply investigated in transport economics research. Among the many theoretical works describing airline pricing policies of FSCs, most are based on the third-degree price discrimination approach (Talluri and van Ryzin 2005).

Third-degree price discrimination models offer two opposite predictions about the relation between price dispersion and market concentration, viz. positive or negative. Competition forces imply that by moving from concentrated to dispersed markets, fares tend to decrease. When fares for business travellers go down less than those for leisure travellers, price dispersion increases; otherwise, price dispersion decreases (Holmes 1989).

Therefore, the sign of the relationship, under third-degree assumption, is not a priori given. Empirical literature equally splits between works finding a negative relation between price dispersion and market concentration in the airline sector (Borenstein and Rose 1994); those finding a positive relation (Gerardi and Shapiro 2009); and, finally, those showing a non-monotonic inverse 'U-shaped' relationship (Dai et al. 2014).

The underlying assumption behind the third-degree price discrimination approach is that the leisure and the business markets are independent, i.e. business travellers do not (or are not allowed to) buy tickets meant for leisure travellers and vice versa. In other words, whatever the gap between leisure and business fares, carriers do not risk 'passenger diversion'.

Under second-degree price discrimination (SPD), indeed, travellers can choose among the full set of offers and can pick up the most preferred one (Obeng and Sakano 2012). Price discrimination is reached thanks to product differentiation and exploiting heterogeneous quality evaluation of passenger segments (Stole 2007). Carriers are, therefore, obliged to satisfy a maximum price differential, called incentive compatibility constraint (ICC) in order to guarantee that each passenger segment will choose the expected product, and to maximize its revenue. Botimer and Belobaba (1999) show that moving towards a SPD approach has many consequences in terms of maximum price differentials and the price dispersion-market structure relationship.

Our approach is based on the seminal works on SPD in oligopolistic markets provided by Rochet and Stole (2002) and Armstrong and Vickers (2001). Here, the authors allow for both horizontal and vertical differentiation between firms, endogenous quality choice, and partial coverage of the weak segment. A main conclusion is that the standard result of 'quality distortion at the bottom' (Mussa and Rosen 1978) disappears and efficient quality is usually provided. Therefore, even if carriers are allowed to choose different quality levels, they do not modify their choice, maintaining the same quality choice in different market structures.

Some recent works also focus on SPD in the airline industry. Dai et al. (2014) present a model of SPD where competition intensity is measured by the transport cost parameter (Villas-Boas and Schmidt-Mohr 1999). They assume that the IIC constraint remains binding in all market structures and that both markets are fully covered. They find that the business-to-leisure price ratio decreases with competition and that there is a U-shaped relation between concentration and price dispersion. In a related paper, Hernandez and Wiggins (2014) also note that competition has a different impact on the various fare classes. In particular, they show that, as markets become more concentrated, the price the ratio of high- to low-type fares decreases (Hernandez 2011), but the ratio of medium- to low-type fares increases.

Finally, our work is also related to the paper by Alderighi et al. (2012), who also analyse the impact of LCCs on the fares charged by FSCs. The focus of the two papers, however, differs. In the present paper, we theoretically and empirically explore the impact of intergroup externalities on fares finding a significant effect. Moreover, we provide a full-fledged analysis of the impact of market structure on pricing behaviour, and we explore the theoretical link between market structure and price differentials.

24.2.2 LCC Entry and FSC Fares and Gaps

Most of the empirical literature on LCC entry has shown that FSC fares tend to decline (Brueckner et al. 2011; Mertens and Vowles 2012; Whinston and Collins 1992). Additional analysis has shown that the fare reductions begin at least some month before LCC entry (Goolsbee and Syverson 2008).

Other works indeed identify an increase to price differentials caused by the entry of a low-cost carrier (LCC). As noted by Forsyth (2002), after the entry of LCCs in Australia: 'In the recent entry period (2000), the spread of fares increased; the incumbents lowered their discount fares but increased their higher fares, on which they were not experiencing much competition. (p. 15)'.

In the early 2000, other analysts reported the increase of business fares in the airline sector due to LCC entry. Jonas (2002) reported that Eclipse Advisors found that 'published airfares in 2003 will be flat to 2% higher, while the average domestic fare paid by corporations will increase between 4 % and 8%' and that American Express predicted 'a 3–4% increase in the typical business fare category'. In our empirical part, we provide some evidence that in this period, this result also occurs in the European airline market.

24.2.3 Intergroup Effects

Interdependent preferences occur 'when an agent's preference ordering over the alternatives in a choice set depends on the actions chosen by other agents' (Manski

2000). When preferences are affected by the passengers belonging to different groups, they are more properly named intergroup preferences.

As far as the airline sector is concerned, empirical evidence suggests that intergroup effects exist. Business travellers, indeed, appreciate more being in flights with their peers than being with leisure passengers: the presence of peers might guarantee a more relaxing and comfortable environment, which can allow them to rest or to work during the flight. Some evidence concerning the annoying behaviour of neighbour passengers is provided, e.g. by Skyscanner, a leading global travel search site, which have conducted a survey over more than 1000 passengers about the most unwelcome neighbour habits (http://www.skyscanner.net).

In addition to this, business passengers can care about the arrangement of passengers during the flight because of the evaluation of the reference group on their buying decision (Childers and Rao 1992). People do not live in isolation, and their choices are observed and criticized by their peers. For example, some luxury goods, such as cars and jewelleries, play a role to indicate status. Similarly, airline flights seem to incorporate a conspicuous component because of their visibility (Heffetz 2012).

24.3 The Model

24.3.1 Setup

The market we are considering is a single route where there are one or two FSCs and, eventually, an LCC.[1] FSCs provide two qualities of flight services (business class and economy class), while low-cost carriers only provide one quality of flight services (economy class). High quality is labelled by q_2 and low quality by q_1, with $q_2 > q_1 > 0$. In our analysis, we employ the simplifying assumption that quality levels are fixed; the aforementioned literature (see footnote 2) has shown that this is not a severe limitation (Moorthy 1984; Katz 1984).

Costs of supplying seats vary in accordance to the cabin class ($1 =$ economy and $2 =$ business) and carriers' type ($L =$ LCC and $F =$ FSC). Traditional firms normally offer a full range of products but at higher cost, while low-cost firms can offer a restricted range of products but at lower cost. Let c_{jl} be the unit cost of firm's type $j = L, F$ for a product of quality $l = 1, 2$. A FSC has higher costs in offering a business class seat than an economy class seat, and a LCC sustains a lower cost than a FSC in providing an economy class seat. Therefore, $c_{F2} \geq c_{F1} \geq c_{L1} \geq 0$. To simplify the notation, let $c_2 = c_{F2}$, $c_1 = c_{F1}$ and $c_0 = c_{L1}$.

Flight services are also horizontally differentiated, either because there are different departure times or because of different departure or arrival airports.

[1]The reader, who is not interested in analytical details can directly continue to Sect. 24.3.7.

Following the Salop (1979) approach, we assume that carriers' supply possibilities are represented by a circumference of unitary length (i.e. the circumference is interpreted as the face of a clock). We will analyse here four main market structures depending on whether there are one or two FSCs and one or no LCCs:

1. Monopoly: one FSC F on the market, located on the circumference at $y_F = 0$.
2. Symmetric duopoly: two FSCs on the market, namely, F_A and F_B, equidistantly located on the circumference, respectively, at $y_A = 0$ and $y_B = \frac{1}{2}$.
3. Asymmetric duopoly: one FSC F and one LCC L equidistantly located, respectively, at $y_F = 0$ and $y_L = \frac{1}{2}$.
4. Oligopoly: two FSCs F_A and F_B, equidistantly located, respectively, at $y_A = 0$ and $y_B = \frac{1}{2}$, and one LCC L in between, located at $y_L = \frac{1}{4}$.

Prospective travellers are both horizontally and vertically heterogeneous. To capture the horizontal dimension, we assume that consumers are also located on the circumference, as they have different ideal departure times or different preferred departure or arrival airports. Travellers who choose a flight which does not fully correspond to their ideal choice are facing a constant unit transport cost. Since business travellers are less flexible (i.e. less prone to modify their departure/arrival time or airport) than leisure travellers, we set the unit transport cost of business travellers σ_2 larger than that of leisure travellers σ_1, i.e. $\sigma_2 > \sigma_1 > 0$.

Vertical heterogeneity stems from a different evaluation of quality and may be related to travel motivations and/or income. There are two types of prospective travellers: businessmen and leisure people. We refer to the business segment as the strong market (labelled 2) and to the leisure segment as the weak market (labelled 1). The willingness-to-pay for quality of travellers belonging to the strong market and the weak market is, respectively, t_2 and t_1, with $t_2 > t_1 > 0$, i.e. both types of consumers appreciate quality, although the consumers belonging to the strong market are more interested in quality than the others.

We assume that both groups of travellers are uniformly distributed around the circumference and have $0 - 1$ demand. The total number of potential travellers is N, which we normalize to one, i.e. $N = 1$; the size of the weak market is $\mu_1 = \mu \in \left(\frac{1}{2}, 1\right)$, and the size of the strong market is $\mu_2 = 1 - \mu$.

The utility that a traveller i located at x who purchases a flight of quality q_l from firm j located in y_j at the price p_{jl} is given by:

$$t_i q_l - \sigma_i D(x, y_j) - p_{jl}, \tag{24.1}$$

where $D(x, y_j)$ is the shortest distance on the circumference from the location of the consumer x to that of firm j. Travellers choose the product that provides the maximum utility. The net utility of the outside option is normalized to zero. Note that we are thus modelling a situation where heterogeneous consumers are free to choose among different qualities and suppliers.

To simplify the notation, let $u_{il} = t_i q_l$. From the assumptions above, we obtain $u_{i2} > u_{i1}$ for $i = 1, 2$; and $u_{22} - u_{21} > u_{12} - u_{11}$. This last inequality is known in the literature as the single crossing property (Mirrlees 1971).

In line with the SPD approach, we suppose that carriers are not able to explicitly segment consumers on the basis of their location on the circumference nor on the basis of their WTP. Implicit segmentation is viable only on the vertical dimension, because the single crossing property does not hold on the horizontal one. Since there are two product qualities and two segments, the models of SPD claim that FSCs offer the product of lower quality q_1 to the weak market, and the product of higher quality $q_2 > q_1$ to the strong market (Stole 2007). Carriers, to avoid *diversion*, i.e. that a type 2 consumer will buy a product designed for type 1 consumers, must choose p_{F1} and p_{F2}, such that the net utility that a type 2 consumer receives when she buys a product of quality q_2 is at least equal to her net utility when she buys a product of quality q_1, i.e. $u_{22} - p_{F2} \geq u_{21} - p_{F1}$. This inequality may also be written as:

$$p_{F2} - p_{F1} \leq u_{22} - u_{21} = r, \tag{24.2}$$

where r is the quality premium (or rent) of travellers belonging to the strong market. This condition is known as the incentive compatibility constraint (ICC) for the strong market. Analogously, a carrier when designing a product for the weak market has to consider how to induce leisure travellers to buy the product designed for them. This can be done by choosing p_{F2} and p_{F1} in such a way that $u_{12} - p_{F2} \leq u_{11} - p_{F1}$. Single crossing property implies that this condition is always satisfied when (2) is binding. We require that the quality premium is larger than cost differences, i.e. $r > c_2 - c_1$. Thus, the FSC has an advantage to sell both qualities.

The simultaneous presence of different firms on the market expands the traveller's choices and makes firm's decisions more complex. We refer to a case where fares are such that, if a consumer decides to fly, she definitely purchases from the closest firms and chooses the fare designed for her type, i.e. all FSCs price schedules satisfy the ICC for the strong and the weak markets, and that fares are such that undercutting does not occur (we are excluding super-competitive market outcomes; see Salop 1979). According to the utility function presented in (24.1), a consumer of type i purchases one unit of product from the firm providing the highest utility.

Consider the arc on the circumference between firm j and firm k.[2] The consumer $\widehat{x}_i$ who is indifferent between purchasing from the two firms is given by:

$$u_{il} - \sigma_i D(\widehat{x}_i, y_j) - p_{jl} = u_{il} - \sigma_i D(\widehat{x}_i, y_k) - p_{kl}. \tag{24.3}$$

A traveller of type i belonging to the arc of circumference jk located in x_i will patronize firm j, if $D(x_i, y_j) < D(\widehat{x}_i, y_j)$, and firm k otherwise. Semi-market demand for firm j by consumers of type i is therefore given by $\mu_i D(\widehat{x}_i, y_j)$, where μ_i is the

[2]When there are two firms, we have to define arcs by considering, for instance, counterclockwise directions.

number of consumers of type i on the market. Let be Q_{ij} the demand for the product of quality i from firm j.

Therefore, the decision problem of an FSC j is given by:

$$\max_{p_{F1}, p_{F2}} (p_{F1} - c_1)Q_{1j} + (p_{F2} - c_2)Q_{2j} \tag{24.4}$$

$$\text{subject to } p_{F2} - p_{F1} \leq r. \tag{24.5}$$

The first equation just states that the firm is profit maximizing. The second equation requires that ICC is satisfied (see: Eq. 24.2). For an LCC the profit maximizing behaviour is simply:

$$\max_{p_L} (p_L - c_0)Q_{1j}. \tag{24.6}$$

We also account for the potential presence of intergroup effects, i.e. that travellers' utility is affected by the characteristics of passengers they travel with and by carrier reputation. In particular, we assume that business travellers and a share $\alpha \in (0, 1)$ of leisure travellers assign a positive value to fly in a comfortable and quiet airplane ($e = 1$), while a given share $(1 - \alpha)$ of leisure travellers does not ($e = 0$).[3] Thus, we arrive at three types of passengers, i.e. 2, 11 and 10. Similar to Corneo and Jeanne (1999), we model the intergroup externalities of a traveller of type i for the flight j as:

$$E_{iej} = \begin{cases} \beta(n_{11} - n_{10}) + (\delta_j - \delta_F) & \text{if } i = 2; \text{or } i = 1 \text{ and } e = 1 \\ 0 & \text{if } i = 1 \text{ and } e = 0 \end{cases} \tag{24.7}$$

where E_{iej} is the intergroup externality of type $ie = 2,11,10$ for the flight j; δ_j captures utility of types 2 and 11 for flying with a carrier $j = F, L$; $\beta \geq 0$ is a measure of the intensity of intergroup externalities; n_{11} and n_{10} are, respectively, the share of leisure travellers on the flight (over the total of potential leisure passengers) who evaluate positively or null being quiet on the plane. In this way we capture two related types of interpersonal effects. The term $\beta(n_{11} - n_{10})$ accounts for the WTP for a comfortable and quiet flight due to passenger arrangement, while the term $\delta_j - \delta_F$ is the WTP for preferential attachment and status signalling by using a FSC. We assume that $\delta_F > 0 = \delta_L$. This specification sets the preferential attachment and status signalling equal to zero when a passenger flies on a FSC and negative for a flight on a LCC. Moreover, we choose $\alpha = 1/2$ so that of types 10 and 11 passengers facing one firm (*Monopoly case*) or two identical firms (*Symmetric duopoly case*), the intergroup effects cancel out, since $n_{11} = n_{10}$, and therefore consumers face null intergroup externalities.

---

[3]For example, some passengers, irrespective from the fact that they are business or leisure travellers, prefer flying without 'wailing baby', 'hyperactive child' or 'screaming kids'. Others, which clearly include parents of these, indeed, do not care about it.

The presence of different types of carriers in the same market, i.e. one FSC and one LCC (asymmetric duopoly case) or two FSC and one LCC (oligopoly case), may yield positive and negative intergroup externalities. Indeed, due to the presence of LCCs, type 11 and type 10 consumers located in the same place may prefer to patronize different carriers. Incorporating the externalities in the utility of travellers, we obtain:

$$\left(t_i + E_{iej}\right)q_l - \sigma_i D\left(x, y_j\right) - p_{jl}, \tag{24.8}$$

To illustrate the point, consider the case of one FSC and one LCC (asymmetric duopoly). The utility of a type 11 traveller located in x when patronizing the FSC is $(t_1 + \beta(x_{11} - x_{10}))q_1 - \sigma_1 D(x, y_F) - p_{F1}$; and the utility she receives when patronizing the LCC is $(t_1 - \beta(x_{11} - x_{10}) - \delta_F)q_1 - \sigma_1 D(x, y_L) - p_L$, where x_{11} and x_{10} are, respectively, the share of type 11 and type 10 passengers travelling with the FSC; δ_F is a measure of the preferential attachment.

Then, type 11 evaluation is affected by the composition of passengers, $\beta(x_{11} - x_{10})$, and by the brand evaluation δ_F, i.e. the traveller prefers to fly on a FSC. For type 10 consumers, there are no intergroup externalities and, therefore, the evaluations for the FSC and LCC offers are, respectively, $t_1 q_1 - \sigma_1 D(x, y_F) - p_{F1}$ and $t_1 q_1 - \sigma_1 D(x, y_L) - p_L$. Let $\widetilde{x}_{11}$ and $\widetilde{x}_{10}$ be the corresponding indifferent consumers for the two types of carriers. Then:

$$\widetilde{\eta} := \widetilde{x}_{11} - \widetilde{x}_{10} = \frac{\delta_F q_1}{2(\sigma_1 - \beta q_1)}. \tag{24.9}$$

The market demand for firm F by consumers of type $1e$, with $e = 0, 1$, is therefore given by $\mu D(\widetilde{x}_{1e}, y_F) = \mu \widetilde{x}_{1e}$; and that of firm L is given by $\mu\left(\frac{1}{2} - \widetilde{x}_{1e}\right)$. From (24.9) it clearly emerges that the FSC has a larger number of passengers of type 11 than of type 10 and that therefore intergroup effects are at work.

24.3.2 Assumptions

Previous literature suggests that in the case of both horizontal and vertical differentiation there is a large set of cases depending on whether the ICC is slack or binding; on the different coverage of the weak and the strong markets; and on the exclusion or not of LCC from the business market (Yang and Ye 2008). To make the analysis manageable, we make the following assumptions:

$$u_{22} \geq \sigma_2 + c_2 \text{ (coverage of the strong market)} \tag{24.10}$$

$$\sigma_1 < u_{11} - c_1 < (M + 1)\sigma_1 \text{ (coverage of the weak market)} \tag{24.11}$$

$$u_{21} \geq 1/2(u_{11} + c_1 + \sigma_2) \text{ (incentive compatibility)} \tag{24.12}$$

$$0 < \beta q_1 < 2/3\sigma_1 \text{ (intergroup effects)}, \tag{24.13}$$

where $M = (1 - \mu)/(2\mu)$.

Equation (24.10) refers to the production costs of an FSC and imposes that, when it supplies to the strong market, the unit transport costs of business travellers are not too large with respect to the WTP of business travellers. It induces hence FSCs to fully cover the strong market.

Equation (24.11) requires that the utility of a leisure travellers is not too small (otherwise the carrier does not provide a service to the weak market), and simultaneously, it is not too high (otherwise the carrier will fully cover the weak market in the monopoly case).

Equation (24.12) requires that the WTP of a business traveller for economy tickets exceeds that of a leisure traveller by a certain amount. This assumption yields a binding ICC in the monopoly case. Indeed, if a carrier tries to increase its fares in the business segment above a certain level, some business travellers will decide to buy a less attractive but much cheaper ticket. This risk is mitigated in other market structures, as rivalry with other carriers induces to set lower fares.

Equation (24.13) requires that intergroup externalities are not very strong. In this way, a single carrier cannot profitably sort travellers belonging to the weak market into two subsegments.

24.3.3 Monopoly

The first market structure we analyse is the monopoly case where we assume that there is one FSC located in zero on the unitary circumference. Proposition 24.1 summarizes the main characteristics of the equilibrium in a monopoly.

Proposition 24.1 Under Assumptions (24.10), (24.11), (24.12) and (24.13), for a monopoly:

(a) In equilibrium, the carrier fully covers the strong market and partially covers the weak market, intergroup effects do not affect the pricing decision, and ICC is binding.
(b) The profit-maximizing prices of a FSC are:

$$p_{F1}^M = 1/2(u_{11} + c_1 + M\sigma_1), \tag{24.14}$$

$$p_{F2}^M = p_{F1}^M + r. \tag{24.15}$$

The results presented at (a) stem directly from the assumptions of the model (see Sect. 24.3.2). Point (b) shows the pricing strategy of the carrier: when the ICC is binding, price differentials, $p_{F2}^M - p_{F1}^M$, are simply given by r. Moreover, since equilibrium prices for the weak segment are increasing in costs, from (1), the participation of the leisure segment is larger, the lower c_1 and σ_1.

24.3.4 Symmetric Duopoly

In the symmetric duopoly case, there are two FSCs, which both offer business and economy class fares. Competitive pressure usually induces carriers to reduce their fares in such a way that both markets are covered. In this market structure, two situations emerge depending on the strength of competition in the strong market. If the level of competition in the strong market is high, fares decline in such a way that ICC is not binding and markets are separate (see Rochet and Stole 2002). If competition in the strong market is lower, two segments remain interdependent and ICC is still binding.

Recall that the quality premium is given by $r = u_{22} - u_{21}$. Let $\Delta = c_2 - c_1 + (\sigma_2 - \sigma_1)/2$ be a measure of the cost differential between the strong and the weak markets.

Proposition 24.2 Under Assumptions (24.10), (24.11), (24.12) and (24.13), in a duopoly:

(a) In equilibrium, carriers fully cover both markets, intergroup effects do not affect the pricing decision, and ICC can be either slack or binding.
(b) When $\Delta < r$, the ICC is slack and the profit-maximizing prices are:

$$p^D_{F1} = c_1 + 1/2\sigma_1, \qquad (24.16)$$

$$p^D_{F2} = c_2 + 1/2\sigma_2. \qquad (24.17)$$

(c) when $\Delta \geq r$, the ICC is binding and the profit-maximizing prices are:

$$p^D_{F1} = \frac{\left(\frac{1}{2} + M\right)\sigma_1\sigma_2 + 2M\sigma_1(c_2 - r) + \sigma_2 c_1}{2M\sigma_1 + \sigma_2}, \qquad (24.18)$$

$$p^D_{F2} = p^D_{F1} + r. \qquad (24.19)$$

We now compare the monopoly case with the symmetric duopoly case.

Proposition 24.3 Under Assumptions (24.10), (24.11), (24.12) and (24.13), moving from monopoly to duopoly, price differences $p_2 - p_1$ decrease when $\Delta < r$ and remain stable when $\Delta \geq r$.

Proposition 24.3 simply states that, by moving from a monopoly to a duopoly, we expect that price differentials decrease or, at least, remain stable. The former implies that, in the symmetric duopoly case, the ICC is slack, while the latter suggests that the ICC remains binding.

24.3.5 Asymmetric Duopoly

The last two sub-sections are devoted to analyse the effect of the entry of a LCC in the monopoly and in the duopoly markets. More specifically, we show that intergroup externalities play a role in affecting the equilibrium outcome. In particular, the entry of an LCC leads to an increase in FSC price differentials, $p_{F2} - p_{F1}$, while in some circumstances, it may induce a FSC to increase their fares in the strong market and to reduce their fares in the weak one. Finally, we also show a reduction in price differentials moving from the asymmetric duopoly to the asymmetric oligopoly case. Here, we focus on the entry of an LCC in a monopolistic market.

As the intergroup externalities are at work, the ICC presented in (24.2) modifies in the following way:

$$p_{F2} - p_{F1} \leq \widetilde{u}_{22} - \widetilde{u}_{21} = \widetilde{r}, \tag{24.20}$$

where $\widetilde{u}_{ij} = (t_j + \beta\widetilde{\eta})q_i$ and $\widetilde{\eta}$ is defined in (24.9). Note that because of intergroup externalities, $r < \widetilde{r}$. Thus, intergroup effects relax the ICC.

Proposition 24.4 Under Assumptions (24.10), (24.11), (24.12) and (24.13), in an asymmetric duopoly:

(a) In equilibrium, carriers fully cover both markets, intergroup externalities affect the pricing decision, and ICC can be either slack or binding.
(b) When $\widetilde{u}_{21} < \frac{1}{3}(c_0 + 2c_1) + \frac{1}{2}(\sigma_1 + \sigma_2) + \frac{1}{3}\widetilde{\eta}\sigma_1$, ICC is slack and the profit-maximizing prices are:

$$p^A_{F2} = \min\{p_L + (t_2 + \beta\widetilde{\eta})(q_2 - q_1) + 2\widetilde{\eta}\sigma_1 - 1/2\sigma_2, \widetilde{u}_{22} - 1/2\sigma_2\} \tag{24.21}$$

$$p^A_{F1} = 1/3(c_0 + 2c_1) + 1/6(3 + 2\widetilde{\eta})\sigma_1 \tag{24.22}$$

$$p^A_L = 1/3(2c_0 + c_1) + 1/6(3 - 2\widetilde{\eta})\sigma_1, \tag{24.23}$$

(c) otherwise, when the ICC is binding and the profit-maximizing prices are:

$$p^A_{F2} = p^A_{F1} + \widetilde{r} \tag{24.24}$$

$$p^A_{F1} = 1/3(c_0 + 2c_1) + 1/6(3 + 2\widetilde{\eta} + 8M)\sigma_1 \tag{24.25}$$

$$p_L^A = 1/3(2c_0 + c_1) + 1/6(3 - 2\tilde{\eta} + 4M)\sigma_1. \quad (24.26)$$

The choice between the first or the second expression on the right-hand side of (24.21) depends upon the fact that in the former case the ICC is slack because the optimal price in the strong market excludes the participation of the LCC in the strong market, while in the latter, the FSC should modify its pricing strategy in the strong market in order to exclude the LCC.

In the weak market, the LCC offers lower prices than the FSC, because $c_0 < c_1$. Moreover, when ICC is binding, the FSC is induced to increase its prices in the weak market, thus relaxing the competition with the LCC in order not to penalize too much its profits in the strong market.

In part (b), although we are considering a situation where LCCs have no direct impact on the strong market, when the ICC is binding, prices in the strong market are clearly affected by two channels. First, due to the ICC, p_{F2} is linked to p_{F1}, and second, p_{F2} is also affected by intergroup effects, $\tilde{x}_{11} - \tilde{x}_{10}$, which depend on the price choice of the LCC.

Proposition 24.5 provides some comparisons between price levels and differentials in various market structures.

Proposition 24.5 Under assumptions (24.10), (24.11), (24.12) and (24.13)

(a) When we are in case (c) of Proposition 24.4, i.e. the ICC is binding:

1. Price differentials between the business segment and the leisure segment are larger in the asymmetric duopoly case than in the monopoly case.
2. Fares are lower in the asymmetric duopoly case than in the monopoly case in the weak market but higher in the strong market, when:

$$\begin{aligned}1/6(3 + 4\tilde{\eta} + 16M)\sigma_1 &< u_{11} - 1/3(2c_0 + c_1)\\ &< 1/6(3 + 4\tilde{\eta} + 16M)\sigma_1 + 2\beta\tilde{\eta}(q_1 - q_2).\end{aligned}$$

(b) When we are in case (b) of Proposition 24.4, i.e. the ICC is slack, then:

1. Price differentials between the business segment and the leisure segment are larger in the asymmetric duopoly case than in the monopoly case, if: $\beta\tilde{\eta}(q_1 - q_2) + 2\tilde{\eta}\sigma_1 + c_0 + c_1 > 1/2\sigma_2$.
2. Fares are lower in the asymmetric duopoly case than in the monopoly case in the weak market but higher in the strong market, when:

$$1/3(2c_0 + c_1) + 1/6(3 + 4\tilde{\eta})\sigma_1 < u_{11} < 1/6(3 + 20\tilde{\eta})\sigma_1 + 2\beta\tilde{\eta}(q_2 - q_1) - \sigma_2.$$

To sum up, the simultaneous presence of an LCC and intergroup effects induces a change in the pricing behaviour of FSCs. Although the SPD assumption limits the ability of carriers to raise prices in the strong market, the presence of a LCC softens this constraint. By diverting a larger share of type 10 passengers with respect to type

11 passengers, the LCC increases the appeal of flying on a FSC, and, therefore, it allows FSC to eventually offer higher fares to type 2 passengers. This means larger price differentials in an asymmetric duopoly than in the other two market structures.

24.3.6 Oligopoly

In this sub-section we analyse the case where there are two FSCs equidistantly located and an LCC positioned between them. This market is characterized by two relevant aspects. First, in the weak market, FSCs sustain quite strong competition, due to the proximity of the LCC, but they also benefit from intergroup externalities. Second, competition in the strong market remains similar to that of the duopoly case, since rivalry among the FSCs eliminates (when δ_2 is sufficiently high) both the possibility to exploit intergroup externalities and the competitive pressure of LCCs. Therefore, prices in the strong market are not affected by the presence of an LCC.

Due to a different market structure, the impact of intergroup externalities on the ICC previously presented in (24.2) and (24.20) modifies in the following way:

$$p_{F2} - p_{F1} \leq \hat{r} = \hat{u}_{22} - \hat{u}_{21}, \tag{24.27}$$

where $\hat{u}_{ij} = \left(t_j + 1/2\beta\hat{\eta}\right)q_i$ and $\hat{\eta} = 2\sigma_1\delta_F/(4\sigma - 3\beta q_1)$.

Proposition 24.6 Under Assumptions (24.10), (24.11), (24.12) and (24.13), in the oligopoly case, we have:

(a) In equilibrium, carriers fully cover both markets, intergroup externalities affect the pricing decision, and ICC can be either slack or binding.
(b) When $\hat{r} > 1/2\sigma_2 + c_2 - 1/5(c_0 + 4c_1) - 1/20(7 + 4\hat{\eta})\sigma_1$, i.e. ICC is slack, equilibrium prices are:

$$p_{F2}^{O} = \min\left\{c_2 + 1/2\sigma_2, 1/5(3c_0 + 2c_1) + 1/10(3 + 16\hat{\eta})\sigma_1 - 1/4\sigma_2 + \hat{r}\right\} \tag{24.28}$$

$$p_{F1}^{O} = 1/5(c_0 + 4c_1) + 1/20(7 + 4\hat{\eta})\sigma_1 \tag{24.29}$$

$$p_{L}^{O} = 1/5(3c_0 + 2c_1) + 1/10(3 - 4\hat{\eta})\sigma_1 \tag{24.30}$$

(c) otherwise, i.e. the ICC is binding, equilibrium prices are:

$$p_{F2}^{O} = p_{F1}^{O} + \hat{r} \tag{24.31}$$

$$p_{F1}^{O} = \frac{1/4(7+2M+4\widehat{\eta})\sigma_1\sigma_2 + (c_0+4c_1)\sigma_2 + c_2M\sigma_1 - rM\sigma_1}{5\sigma_2 + M\sigma_1} \tag{24.32}$$

$$p_{L}^{O} = \frac{1/4(6+M-8\widehat{\eta})\sigma_1\sigma_2 + (3c_0+2c_1)\sigma_2 + 1/2(c_0+c_2-r)M\sigma_1 + 1/8M(1-4\widehat{\eta})\sigma_1^2}{5\sigma_2+M\sigma_1} \tag{24.33}$$

The qualitative results are similar to the asymmetric duopoly case, although the solutions are more complex to obtain. The following proposition compares the outcome of the different market structures.

Proposition 24.7 Under Assumptions (24.10), (24.11), (24.12) and (24.13),

(a) When ICC is binding:

1. Price differentials between the business segment and the leisure segment are larger in the oligopoly case than in the symmetric duopoly case.
2. Price differentials between the business segment and the leisure segment are smaller in the oligopoly case than in the asymmetric duopoly case.

(b) When ICC slack:

1. Price differentials between the business segment and the leisure segment are larger in the oligopoly case than in the symmetric duopoly case.
2. Price differentials between the business segment and the leisure segment are smaller in the oligopoly case than in the asymmetric duopoly case, if:

$$\widehat{u}_{22} > \sigma_2 + c_2 - 2/15(c_1 - c_0) + (3/20 + 1/3\widehat{\eta} - 1/5\widehat{\eta})\sigma_1. \tag{24.34}$$

Note that item b.2 also accommodates a case where price dispersion may become larger, i.e. when (24.34) is not satisfied. This result also comes from the fact that the two FSCs have a different allocation in the two cases. Indeed, the design of the four market structures has been thought to mainly consider the impact of the presence of a new LCC on FSC pricing behaviour.

24.3.7 Summary of the Pricing Behaviour

Propositions (24.3), (24.5) and (24.7) compare the pricing behaviour of FSCs in the four market structures. In Fig. 24.1 we summarize the main theoretical findings. The scheme is organized so that (*i*) moving from the left to the right, the market includes an additional LCC and (*ii*) moving from the top to the bottom, the market includes an additional FSC. We consider the two cases successively.

Case (*i*) In the presence of intergroup effects, the entry of a LCC induces a change in the pricing behaviour of FSCs. Although the SPD assumption limits the ability of FSC to raise prices in the strong market, the presence of a LCC softens this

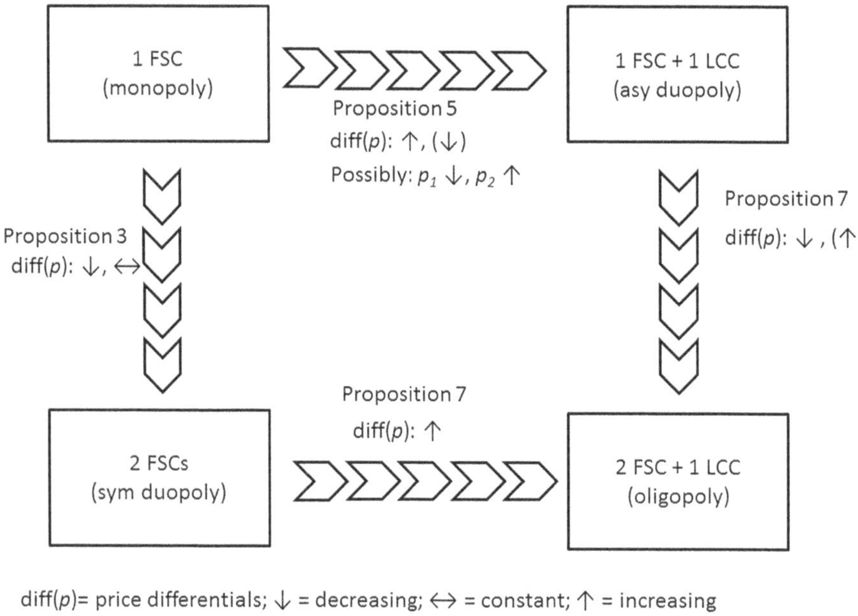

Fig. 24.1 Summary of the main theoretical results

constraint. By diverting a larger share of type 10 passengers with respect to type 11 passengers, the LCC increases the appeal of flying on a FSC and, therefore, it allows FSCs to eventually offer higher fares to type 2 passengers. This effect generally increases price differentials, and in some cases, it may also lead to higher prices for the business segment and lower prices for the leisure one.

A rise in the price differentials always emerges when there are two FSCs and for most of the parameter values also when there is only one FSC. An exception occurs in the latter case, when the ICC of the incumbent becomes slack after the entry of the LCC: the competition between the FSC and the LCC becomes very intense and in order to protect the strong market the FSC will reduce its fares for the business segment.

Case (*ii*) In general, the presence of an additional FSC induces an intensification of the competition in the strong market, and therefore price differentials tend to reduce. This result emerges for most of the parameter values in the model, apart from two minor exceptions. First, we compare two market structures where there are no LCCs and the ICC is binding. In this case price, differentials may remain stable (but they do not increase). Second, we compare two market structures where there is one LCC and the ICC is slack in the two market structures. In that case, under some circumstances, a market structure with two FSCs may have a larger price differential. As mentioned at the end of Sect. 24.3.6, this result also emerges because of the closer position of the LCC to the two FSCs, which induces FSCs to reduce their prices in the weak market much more than competition between FSCs does in the strong market.

These theoretical predictions will be empirically discussed and tested in Sect. 24.4. A summary of the empirical results is provided in Table 24.4.

24.4 Empirical Analysis of European Airfares

24.4.1 Data

We address here the changes in the initial phase of upcoming LCCs challenging the position of flag carries (Button, Haynes and Stough 1998). The main source of data is posted fares retrieved from the computer reservation system Galileo for 40 city-pairs in the period April 2001–July 2003. The fares concern operating non-stop direct flights between Italy and three European countries: UK, Germany and the Netherlands, involving four legacy carriers, viz. Lufthansa (LH), British Airways (BA), Alitalia (AZ) and KLM (KL). The use of city-pairs is usually preferred to that of airport-pairs when the analysis also involves LCCs, as entry often occurs in secondary airports (see, e.g. Nero 1998).

Apart from the limitation concerning the duration of the period under evaluation and the number of destinations, this data has the value of including detailed information on booking class, cabin, ticketing restrictions, etc. An in-depth analysis of fare characteristics was conducted in order to obtain the eight homogeneous booking classes reported in Table 24.1.

The choice of this period of analysis is motivated by data availability. It refers to the first years after the end of the European airline deregulation process (1988–1997), where most of the national carriers were privatized or partially privatized and started adopting sophisticated pricing techniques (Talluri and van Ryzin 2005). Our data have two main characteristics. First, we do not observe entry or exit of FSCs in any city pair for the whole period of analysis. Second, a consistent growth of LCCs is observed even if FSCs still remain dominant at the end of the period.

Table 24.1 Class mapping

Type of fare		AZ	KL	BA	LH	Mean	Std. dev	Min	Max
Promotional	Leisure	O-N	V-T	Q-N	W-V	167	33.9	99	295
Discounted 1	Leisure	W-T	L	V-L	Q-H	276	60.1	165	411
Discounted 2	Leisure	Q	K	M	M	361	58.7	240	494
Economy 1	Intermediate	B	B	K-H	B	454	102.3	300	732
Economy 2	Intermediate	M	S	B-I	B	580	100.3	320	838
Unrestricted 1	Business	Y	Z	Y	Y	815	161	440	1092
Unrestricted 2	Business	I	C	D	D	887	151.7	558	1171
Unrestricted 3	Business	C	J	J	C	898	207.5	574	1459

Usually, carriers label classes with capital letters. For example, the promotional classes of Alitalia are O and N, while those of Lufthansa are V or W. Our classification is obtained by analysing the ticket characteristics of the four FSCs for each of their classes and assigning each original class of each carrier to one of the eight classes valid for all the carriers (Chiou and Liu 2016). The main attributes, that we have taken into account, are ticket characteristics (ticket cancelation, travel date change penalties, purchase time limits, or minimum stay at the travel destination, Sunday rule, etc.) and ground services (flight fast check-in, VIP waiting lounges).[4]

Additional information concerning passengers, flows, frequencies, and seats offered on a biannual basis has been collected from OAG databases and airport authorities. Information on sociodemographics on origin and destination areas has been collected from the Eurostat Euregio database.

Contrary to US data, we do not have information on ticket fares but only on posted fares. Although this is a major shortcoming for the analysis of European markets, in this specific case this is not critical, since we are interested in studying the change in the fare schedule in different market structures and not, for instance, in fare dispersion (where quantities matter). Thus, the change in the posted fares considered in our analysis is the variation of the fares stored in the reservation system.

The construction of the sample begins by converting posted fares into half-yearly information. We take three different steps. First, we exclude one-way fares from the analysis. This is justified because one-way tickets were rarely sold by FSCs in the European market. Second, we transformed the raw data on posted fares into monthly data (obtaining 14,152 different airfares) and added information on the presence or absence of LCCs on the route. In the sample, we have 12 city-pairs with the following LCCs: Ryanair, easyJet, Basiqair, Volare Web, British Midland, Air Berlin, Virgin Express and Hapag Lloyd Express. Finally, to match the data frequency of other sources, as well as to account for pricing practices of carriers, we converted previous observations into biannual data, averaging information by period, route and carrier. To be consistent with OAG practices, the semesters are called winter (which lasts 5 months from November to March) and summer (which lasts 7 months from April to October). The resulting database of 1269 observations concerns 40 routes, 4 carriers, 8 booking classes for 5 periods (semesters).[5]

Summary statistics are presented in Table 24.2.

---

[4]The choice to use a class mapping procedure to classify different fares comes from the observation that high collinearity among fare attributes makes their simultaneous use in the estimation difficult (Stavins 2001).

[5]This is an unbalanced panel since some carriers on specific routes and in specific periods do not post all the class fares. In particular, some promotional fares are often not posted by Alitalia or Lufthansa, and likewise, some other economy and business fares may not be posted by KLM. This is an additional rationale to aggregate the initial 8 booking classes into 3 main classes in the next of the analysis. The list of the routes is available upon request.

Table 24.2 Descriptive statistics

Variable	Short description	Mean	Std. dev	Min	Max
FARE	Logarithm of the fare	6.1173	0.5862	4.7767	7.2855
LCC	Low-cost carrier market share	0.0784	0.1481	0	0.6364
SHARE	Full-service carrier market share	0.7236	0.2768	0.1456	1
FSC	Dummy for the presence of a FSC competitor	0.5145	0.4999	0	1
ENPL	Enplanements at the endpoints	0.5117	0.1409	0.2335	0.8698
DEN	Population density at the endpoints	0.5125	0.3564	0.1638	1.4136

24.4.2 Empirical Model

Our econometric approach is based on the following specification:

$$FARE_{ijtc} = \alpha + \delta_{ij} + \gamma_t + \beta_1 SHARE_{ijt} + \beta_2 LCC_{jt} + \sum_{c=1}^{8} \theta_c CLASS_c + \varepsilon_{ijtc} \quad (24.35)$$

where $FARE_{ijtc}$ is the log fare charged by carrier i on route j in period t for the booking class c; δ_{ij} is the carrier-route fixed effect; γ_t is the period fixed effect; $SHARE_{ijt}$ is the passenger share of carrier i on route j in period t; $CLASS_c$ is dummy variable for booking class c; and LCC_{jt} is the market share of LCCs on route j in period t (sum of frequencies over the total).

The use of carrier-route and time fixed effects help to control for unobserved heterogeneity of the sample. First of all, data on operating costs are difficult to obtain. Jet fuel costs have a time varying component (jet fuel price); a route-specific component (jet fuel consumption, which is positively related with distance); and a carrier-specific component (due to a different level of on board and ground services offered by carriers). The former unobserved component can be controlled by time fixed effects; differences among routes and carriers are limited because during the period of analysis, hedging strategies were not largely employed by FSCs and, in the EU, fuel for commercial aircraft is exempt from taxation (Cobbs and Alex 2004). The latter two components, which are largely time invariant, are managed using carrier-route fixed effects. In addition, demand characteristics, such as average WTP of travellers or their brand preferences along each route and for any carrier, are largely invariant over time and, therefore, are controlled by carrier-route fixed effects. Finally, some residual components of demand, which are usually linked to the economic cycle (e.g. being in a boom or a recession), are mostly captured by time fixed effects, since the routes we were considering belong to European Union countries, whose business cycles are highly correlated.

In addition to the baseline model, we considered some extensions, which include the following dummy variables: TWO^{lei}_{ijt} is a dummy variable for the presence of a second FSC when the fare is intended for leisure travellers (booking classes 1, 2 and 3), and TWO_{ijt}^{bus} is a dummy variable for the presence of a second FSC when the fare is intended for business travellers (booking classes 6, 7 and 8).

The previous literature has emphasized the risk of endogeneity of the variables *SHARE* and *LCC*, which may be potentially correlated with the error term. Standard econometric techniques suggest, therefore, that Eq. (24.35) should be estimated using the method of an instrumental variable (IV). A valid instrument for the variable *SHARE*, proposed by Borenstein (1989) and afterwards utilized by Borenstein and Rose (1994) and Gerardi and Shapiro (2009), is $ENPL_{ijt}$, the ratio between the geometric mean of enplanements of carriers at the two endpoints and the sum across all carriers of the geometric mean of each carrier's enplanement at the endpoints.

The endogeneity issues on the variable *LCC* are more serious, because they concern one of the main variables of interest in our analysis. Endogeneity should derive from the fact that LCCs are attracted by the most profitable markets and FSC fares are also positively related to market profitability. Therefore, if market profitability is not among the explanatory variables, the error term is positively correlated with the low-cost variable, and the estimated fare reduction due to the entry of an LCC is underestimated.

The recent literature suggests that it is difficult to find valid instruments for the entry of LCCs (see Gerardi and Shapiro 2009). Berry (1992) suggested that the presence of an LCC on the two endpoints of a route increases the probability of entry on this route. Goolsbee and Syverson (2008) used this variable in order to capture the potential entry of an LCC and showed that FSCs react to the threat of entry by reducing their prices some months before the entry. However, their analysis is quite different from ours, because they selected only those routes in which entry occurs, and therefore did not account for those routes that were less affected by LCCs entry decision. In our analysis, we cannot rely on this variable since the European market in 2001–2003 has a very different structure from the US market. In our study, since there were no bases of LCCs in Italy, this variable was always zero.

We therefore decided to provide a new instrument for the presence of an LCC: the potential demand on the route. The proposed instrument is clearly correlated with the entry decision of the LCCs (since they want to enter dense markets; see, e.g. Boguslaski et al. 2004; Sinclear 1995) but is marginally correlated with the error term, since FSC profitability is mainly affected by some unmeasurable variable such as the industrial relations among linked areas, etc. We choose to measure the potential demand with DEN_{ijt}, that is, the geometric average of the population density in the regions of the two endpoints (in thousands of inhabitants per square kilometre). This variable is preferred to a measure of the population, which is more affected by the size of the region under consideration.[6]

[6]The European geographical partition of Member States is based on the NUTS (Nomenclature of Territorial Units for Statistics) classification. The size of NUTS territorial areas is quite heterogeneous, since it corresponds to the administrative division of countries which are quite different. We use the NUTS1 classification for the UK, the Netherlands and Germany and NUTS2 for Italy.

24.4.3 Empirical Results

Equation (24.35) is estimated using panel fixed effects, including a carrier-route fixed effect and a time fixed effect. Standard errors are clustered by route in order to control for autocorrelation, as well as for correlation between carriers on the same route. The results are reported in Table 24.3. All models are estimated with a two-stage instrumental variable estimator, apart from Model 1 that presents the ordinary least square estimates.[7]

Models 1–2 show that the market share on a route has a negative impact on FSC fares. In order to measure the impact of the entry of an LCC, we have also estimated the model using a dummy variable for the presence of LCC. The results are quite similar, but the use of the route share of LCCs increases the significance of the coefficient. This reflects that the pricing behaviour of an FSC is more affected when there is a larger involvement of LCCs.

The coefficients of booking classes are statistically significant and have the expected order of magnitude. We choose CLASS4 as the reference class. As expected, the coefficients of the lower classes have a negative sign and those of higher classes a positive one. In those cases, where we split the sample by classes (Models 3–5), the reference class for the leisure segment is CLASS3, for the intermediate segment it is CLASS4, and for the business segment it is CLASS6. The coefficient of SHARE has the expected sign but, in most of the estimates, is not significant (see below, for an explanation).

Our theoretical analysis provided two main arguments concerning the price behaviour of FSCs. One point is that the entry of LCCs reduces fares in the weak market and possibly increases them in the strong one. The other is that fare differentials (between the strong and the weak market) will decrease (or at least remain unchanged), when one moves from one to two FSCs. In Table 24.4 we summarize the main testable predictions of the theoretical model and the corresponding empirical outcomes.

Models 3–5 analyse the impact of the presence of LCCs on the fare structure. We observe a clear pattern indicating a negative and statistically significant impact of *LCC* on fares in the leisure segment and in the intermediate segment and a positive and statistically significant increase for the business segment. This confirms the

[7]The Durbin-Wu-Hausman chi-square test in some estimates rejects the assumption of exogeneity of *LCC* and *SHARE*. We therefore decided to consider these variables as endogenous in line with the current literature. The qualitative results are not affected by this choice. (Estimates where one or both variables are considered exogeneous are available upon request.) Standard tests for the detection of weak instruments are applied. For Model 2, the F-statistics for excluded instruments for *LCC* and *SHARE* are, respectively, 11.83 and 52.79, which are above the value suggested by Staiger and Stock (1997) for identifying weak instruments. We also test the instrument relevance comparing the Shea partial R-squared with the Bound et al. (1995) partial R-squared. Both statistics provide similar values for the two variables suggesting that the model is fully identified (in both cases, the partial R-squared is 0.19 for *LCC* and 0.42 for *SHARE*).

Table 24.3 Main estimations (dependent variable: *FARE*)

	(1)	(2)	(3)	(4)	(5)	(6)	(7)	(8)
	OLS	IV	IV	IV	IV	IV	IV	IV
Variables	Full sample	Full sample	Leisure	Interm.	Business	Full sample	No LCC	Only LCC
LCC	−0.0896**	−0.235**	−0.454**	−0.304**	0.107*	−0.237**		−0.406**
SHARE	0.0267	0.0568	−0.0485	−0.174	0.0894***	0.0746	−0.0141	0.290**
TWO^{lei}						0.0617*	0.119***	0.0563
TWO^{bus}						−0.00465	−0.0164	−0.0671
CLASS1	−0.992***	−0.994***	−0.755***			−1.023***	−0.970***	−1.089***
CLASS2	−0.550***	−0.553***	−0.309***			−0.586***	−0.582***	−0.603***
CLASS3	−0.240***	−0.240***				−0.269***	−0.272***	−0.279***
CLASS5	0.274***	0.271***		0.284***		0.271***	0.267***	0.275***
CLASS6	0.563***	0.560***				0.565***	0.494***	0.649***
CLASS7	0.676***	0.672***			0.119***	0.679***	0.612***	0.752***
CLASS8	0.691***	0.691***			0.247***	0.695***	0.649***	0.801***
Observations	1269	1269	497	375	397	1269	585	684
R-squared	0.96	0.96	0.919	0.798	0.824	0.961	0.966	0.966

Note: Table 24.3 only reports coefficients and significance of the variables of interest. The dependent variable is the log of quoted fare of a return ticket sold in Italy (FARE). All models include carrier-route specific fixed effects and period fixed effect. Robust standard errors are clustered by route. ***, ** and * denote significance at the 1%, 5% and 10% levels, respectively

Table 24.4 Hypothesis testing

Proposition	Model predictions	Test	p-value	Model
5	LCC entry decreases full-service fares in the weak market	$LCC^{lei} < 0$	0.014**	Model 3
5	LCC entry increases full-service fares in the strong market	$LCC^{bus} > 0$	0.036**	Model 5
5 and 7	LCC entry increases fare differentials	$LCC^{lei} < LCC^{bus}$	0.000***	Models 3–5
3 and 7	Fare differences moving from one to two full-service carriers decrease (full sample)	$TWO^{lei} > TWO^{bus}$	0.135	Model 6
3	Fare differences moving from one to two full-service carriers decrease (no low-cost)	$TWO^{lei} > TWO^{bus}$	0.015**	Model 7
7	Fare differences moving from one to two full-service carriers decrease (with low-cost)	$TWO^{lei} > TWO^{bus}$	0.036**	Model 8
	Other relevant results			
	Market shares positively affects high fares, but	$MS^{bus} > 0$	0.002***	Model 5
	Market shares have no significant impact on fares in other classes	$MS^{lei} = 0$	0.728	Model 3
		$MS^{int} = 0$	0.202	Model 4

Note: ***, ** and * denote significance at the 1%, 5%, and 10% levels, respectively

theoretical result that this outcome is likely to emerge, if there is a sufficient cost difference between LCCs and FSCs and intergroup externalities are at work.

Quite interestingly, we also find that *SHARE* has a negative sign for the leisure and the intermediate classes (even though it is not significant) and a positive and highly significant value for the business class. The rationale behind this result is that higher market shares (and therefore higher frequencies and higher quality of the product offered) allow carriers to charge higher fares in the business segment; however, it also induces the FSCs to play more aggressively a role on the leisure segment, when it needs to attract a large number of leisure passengers. These opposite effects may be the reason for the low significance of *SHARE* when we use a single variable for all classes.

The *SHARE* variable may be affected by hub dominance, i.e. the ability of a carrier to charge higher fares at its hubs due to its ability to limit entry and lessen competition, to access better airport services, and to have a high number of frequent-flyer programme members (Borenstein 1989, p. 344). Because of FSC waving system requires that a carrier chooses a high frequency on routes from/to a carrier hub, the positive correlation with *FARE* variable may be partially due to the fact that at hubs, route shares are higher.

Models 6–8 can be used to investigate the relationship between class fares and market structure. Since our database does not include cases where the number of

FSCs change on the same route, the empirical analysis cannot address the question whether fares decline or increase by moving from a case with one FSC to another with two FSCs. However, our data are useful in capturing price differentials. Variables TWO_{ijt}^{lei} and TWO_{ijt}^{bus} are employed for this goal. Equations (24.36) and (24.37) describe FSC fares for the leisure and the business segments when there are one or two FSCs:

$$\begin{aligned} FARE_{ONE}^{lei} &= X_{ONE} + CLASS^{lei} \\ FARE_{TWO}^{lei} &= X_{TWO} + CLASS^{lei} + TWO^{lei} \end{aligned} \tag{24.36}$$

$$\begin{aligned} FARE_{ONE}^{bus} &= X_{ONE} + CLASS^{bus} \\ FARE_{TWO}^{bus} &= X_{TWO} + CLASS^{bus} + TWO^{bus} \end{aligned} \tag{24.37}$$

where X_{ONE} and X_{TWO} summarize all variables of (24.35) that are not present in (24.36) and (24.37), when there are, respectively, one or two FSCs. Then, it follows that:

$$\Delta FARE^{lei} = FARE_{TWO}^{lei} - FARE_{ONE}^{lei} = (X_{TWO} - X_{ONE}) + TWO^{lei} \tag{24.38}$$

$$\Delta FARE^{bus} = FARE_{TWO}^{bus} - FARE_{ONE}^{bus} = (X_{TWO} - X_{ONE}) + TWO^{bus} \tag{24.39}$$

Therefore, the fare differentials are $\Delta FARE^{lei} - \Delta FARE^{bus} = TWO^{lei} - TWO^{bus}$, which can also be interpreted as $\left(FARE_{ONE}^{bus} - FARE_{ONE}^{les}\right) - \left(FARE_{TWO}^{bus} - FARE_{TWO}^{lei}\right)$, i.e. the difference between the fare gap when there is only one FSC and when there are two FSCs. Table 24.4 shows that this gap is positive and statistically significant for Models 7 and 8, in line with the theoretical outcome. Therefore, we find that fare gaps decrease when moving towards more competitive environments and that the ICC is likely to be slack in non-monopolistic markets.

24.5 Conclusions

In this paper we have investigated the pricing behaviour of FSCs by generalizing a simple view of the functioning of the market proposed by Borenstein and Rose (1994). We have relaxed the assumption of market independency, and we have accounted for intergroup effects. The empirical evidence concerning the European market provides external support for our conclusions. We suspect that these findings are not restricted to this specific case, but they emerge worldwide in those markets where legacy carriers are challenged by tough competition, including intermodal competition by high-speed rail as in Asia (Chen and Haynes 2019). When the market structure moves from monopoly to duopoly, the price gap declines suggesting that the quality premium constraint becomes slack. Therefore, in competitive environments, third-degree and second-degree price discrimination approaches give similar results. Nevertheless, the latter provides more stringent conclusions on the effects of the 'peer' competition in the market. Moreover, we have shown how intergroup effects may have an impact on pricing behaviour in a second-degree price discrimination approach through relaxing the quality premium constraint and allowing the FSCs to charge larger price differentials between restricted and unrestricted fares. This aspect is too often neglected in the analysis of markets and deserves to be the subject of future research.

References

Alderighi M, Cento A, Nkjkamp P, Rietveld P (2012) Competition in the European aviation market: the entry of low-cost airlines. J Transp Geogr 24:223–233
Armstrong M, Vickers J (2001) Competitive price discrimination. RAND J Econ 32:579–605
Berry S (1992) Estimation of a model of entry in the airline industry. Econometrica 60(4):889–917
Boguslaski C, Ito H, Lee D (2004) Entry patterns in the southwest airlines rote system. Rev Ind Organ 25:317–350
Borenstein S (1989) Hubs and high fares: dominance and market power in the U.S. airline industry. RAND J Econ 20(3):344–365
Borenstein S, Rose N (1994) Competition and price dispersion in the US airline industry. J Polit Econ 102:653–683
Botimer TC, Belobaba PP (1999) Airline pricing and fare product differentiation: a new theoretical framework. J Oper Res Soc 50:1085–1097
Bound J, Jaeger DA, Baker R (1995) Problems with instrumental variables estimation when the correlation between the instruments and the endogenous explanatory variables is weak. J Am Stat Assoc 90:443–450
Brueckner KJ, Lee D, Singer SE (2011) Airline competition and domestic US airfares: a comprehensive reappraisal. Econ Transp 2:1–17
Button K, Haynes K, Stough R (1998) Flying into the future: air transport policy in the European Union. Edward Elgar Pub, Cheltenham
Chen Z, Haynes K (2019) High speed rail and China's new economic geography. Edward Elgar Pub, Cheltenham
Childers TL, Rao AR (1992) The influence of familial and peer-based reference groups on consumer decisions. J Consum Res 19(2):198–211
Chiou Y-C, Liu C-H (2016) Advance purchase behaviors of air tickets. J Air Transp Manag 57:62–69
Cobbs R, Alex W (2004) Jet fuel hedging strategies: options available for airlines and a survey of industry practices. Unpublished manuscript. Available at http://www.kellogg.northwestern.edu/research/fimrc/papers/jet fuel.pdf
Corneo G, Jeanne O (1999) Segmented communication and fashionable behavior. J Econ Behav Organ 39:371–385
Dai M, Liu Q, Serfes K (2014) Is the effect of competition on Price dispersion non-monotonic? Evidence from the U.S. airline industry. Rev Econ Stat 96(1):161–170
Forsyth P (2002) Low cost carriers in Australia: experiences and impacts, Monash University, Department of Economics. Discussion paper no. 17/02
Gerardi K, Shapiro HA (2009) Does competition reduce price dispersion? new evidence from the Airline industry. J Polit Econ 117:1–37
Goolsbee A, Syverson C (2008) How do incumbents respond to the threat of entry? Evidence from the major airlines. Q J Econ 123(4):1611–1633

Heffetz O (2012) Who sees what? Demographics and the visibility of consumer expenditures. J Econ Psychol 33(4):801–818
Hernandez MA (2011) Nonlinear pricing and competition intensity in a Hotelling-type model with discrete product and consumer types. Econ Lett 110:174–177
Hernandez MA, Wiggins SN (2014) Nonlinear pricing strategies and market competitive conditions in the airline industry. Econ Inq 52(2):539–561
Holmes TJ (1989) The effects of third-degree price discrimination in oligopoly. Am Econ Rev 79(1):244–250
Jonas D (2002) Budget numbers jumbled: airlines are working to reverse their falling fares, business travel news, September 23
Katz ML (1984) Firm-specific differentiation and competition among multiproduct firms. J Bus 57:S149–S166
Manski CF (2000) Economic analysis of social interactions. J Econ Perspect 14(3):115–136
Mertens DP, Vowles TM (2012) "Southwest effect" - decisions and effects of low cost carriers. J Behav Appl Manag 14(1):53–69
Mirrlees J (1971) An exploration in the theory of optimum income taxation. Rev Econ Stud 38(2):175–208
Moorthy KS (1984) Market segmentation, self-selection, and product line design. Mark Sci 3:288–307
Mussa M, Rosen M (1978) Monopoly and product quality. J Econ Theory 18:301–317
Nero G (1998) Spatial multiproduct pricing: empirical evidence on intra-European duopoly airline markets. Appl Econ 30(4):465–475
Obeng K, Sakano R (2012) Airline fare and seat management strategies with demand dependency. J Air Transp Manag 24:42–48
Rochet J-C, Stole LA (2002) Nonlinear pricing with random participation. Rev Econ Stud 69:277–311
Salop SC (1979) Monopolistic competition with outside goods. Bell J Econ 10:141–156
Sinclear RA (1995) An empirical model of entry and exit in airline markets. Rev Ind Organ 10:541–557
Staiger D, Stock JH (1997) Instrumental variables regression with weak instruments. Econometrica 65:557–586
Stavins J (2001) Price discrimination in the airline market: the effect of market concentration. Rev Econ Stat 83:200–202
Stole L (2007) Price discrimination in competitive environments. In Handbook of Industrial Organization III (M. Armstrong, RH Porter, eds), Ch. 34, Elsevier, Amsterdam, pp. 2221–2299
Talluri KT, van Ryzin GJ (2005) The theory and practice of revenue management. Springer, New York
Villas-Boas M, Schmidt-Mohr U (1999) Oligopoly with asymmetric information: differentiation in credit markets. RAND J Econ 30:375–396
Whinston MD, Collins SC (1992) Entry and competitive structure in deregulated airline markets: an event study analysis of people express. RAND J Econ 23(4):445–462
Yang H, Ye L (2008) Nonlinear pricing, market coverage, and competition. Theor Econ 3:123–153

Chapter 25
Business Relocation Incentive Decisions: Opinions of Economic Development Professionals

Fred Young Phillips and Nasir Jamil Sheikh

Abstract Unlike the many surveys of economic development offices' budgets and deal flow, the present survey uncovers the rationales for extending relocation incentives and the criteria city officials consider important for making an incentive offer. Using the STEEP approach (Social, Technological, Economic, Environmental, and Political), we asked a panel of economic development officials to rate the importance of social, technical, economic, environmental, and political considerations in their city's policies regarding relocation incentive offerings. We relate respondents' STEEP importance ratings to their views of the success of their incentive programs. We supplement panel results with cases and news items. Our contribution is to go beyond the usual economic analysis of incentive programs, in order to present a more multidimensional and realistic picture of the decision process. The results indicate that although the economic perspective is significantly important, the other STEEP perspectives are material and deserve attention.

Keywords Business relocation · Relocation incentives · Economic development · Business tax abatement · Tax breaks · Expert judgments · Social · Technical · Economic · Environmental · and Political (STEEP) perspectives

F. Y. Phillips (✉)
Tongji University, Shanghai, People's Republic of China

University of New Mexico, Albuquerque, NM, USA

General Informatics, LLC, Albuquerque, NM, USA
e-mail: phillipsf@unm.edu; fp@generalinformatics.com

N. J. Sheikh
Department of Technology Management, College of Engineering, Business, and Education, University of Bridgeport, Bridgeport, CT, USA
e-mail: nsheikh@bridgeport.edu

Z. Chen et al. (eds.), *Development Studies in Regional Science*,
New Frontiers in Regional Science: Asian Perspectives 42,
https://doi.org/10.1007/978-981-15-1435-7_25

25.1 Introduction

25.1.1 Economic Development Incentives

Many monetary and tax abatement incentives extended by cities to relocating companies are (i) unnecessary as they are irrelevant to the company's location selection; (ii) harmful because they cannibalize the efforts of bordering communities that might offer similar incentives; (iii) unrecoverable due to company non-performance or lax collection procedures; or (iv) not leveraged because the selected company fits no strategic direction for the city. In addition, these incentives can be controversial (Table 25.1) because they appear to funnel tax monies away from other worthy projects or because corruption is suspected.

Migdal (2016) reports that increasing profit pressures drive industrial firms to seek incentives. Economic incentives used to be "icing on the cake," he says, but now they are a "key ingredient" in relocation decisions. Slow job growth in the United States means cities and states are more likely to play the incentive game. Therefore, it becomes more important to try to resolve the items in Table 25.1.

Incentives may include land, cash, subsidies for employee training, or (most commonly in the United States) tax abatements. Incentives may be "front-end," delivered before the company opens its facility, or "back-end," delivered only after the company has performed to the agreed standards (Ham 2014 p. 90). In addition to relocation incentives, cities extend incentives to prevent firms from moving away (Harrell 2012; Martin et al. 2014; Adelman 2016).

The "but for" question – Would the company have come anyway, but for the incentive? – is always prominent and often considered unanswerable. According to Hicks (2014) the but-for question is becoming more problematic, due to changes in the world economy. However, many city officials believe they cannot afford not to continue to offer location incentives.

Table 25.1 and the above discussion show that incentives, and the decision to extend them, affect and are affected by economics, culture, ethics, politics, and still more kinds of considerations. Yet most tools available for analyzing the incentive decision, such as cost benefit analysis, stem primarily from the discipline of economics.

Table 25.1 Relocation incentives: Partial list of controversies

Do they "work," or not?
Would the company have come anyway?
Do they cannibalize nearby communities?
And thus just waste money?
Do companies honor the terms?
Do they create enough jobs?
Are the tax breaks and subsidies worth it?

Table 25.2 Just a few STEEP considerations for economic development incentives

Social	Technological	Economic	Environmental	Political
Alternative needs for incentive funds	Anticipated knowledge spillover	Number, quality of jobs promised	Commuting trips generated	Transparency
Impact on low-income citizens	Fit with industry cluster	Projected tax receipts	Cleanliness of business process	Corruption
Conflicts of interest		"But for"	Water use	Relations with neighboring cities
Educational quality, programs		Cost per job created		Company's reputation for fulfillment of tax agreements
		Payback period		City's history of enforcement
				Bragging rights

25.1.2 Contribution and Organization of This Paper

Existing tools for aiding a locale's incentive decision,[1] e.g., Bolnick (2004), serve only to estimate the financial payback of a relocation incentive. Efforts to be more systematic (Wolkoff 1985) are old and do not go far enough. We structured a survey to determine what other factors city and state/province economic development (ED) officials find pertinent to the decision. In this way the present study differs from the many that measure incentive policies at the national level (Deloitte 2014), that list recent incentives offered (IncentivesMonitor.com; Site Selection 2014), or that attempt to measure the impact of incentives on job growth (Goren 2007; Lester et al. 2014; Chapman 2016).

To affect the survey, we use the STEEP (Social, Technological, Economic, Environmental, and Political) framework, common in multi-criterion decision studies. ED officials rated STEEP considerations including those of Table 25.2, suggested additional considerations and criteria, and assigned weights to these dimensions.

Social criteria may include impacts on disadvantaged populations and opportunities for training. Technological considerations include the opportunity to build innovative clusters or gain leadership in an emerging industry. Environmental criteria cover resource use and minimization of negative externalities. Political considerations include regional image-building and extend even to questions of credit and blame. "After all, if a company moves to Texas just for the business climate, who's going to claim the credit?" (Copelin 2014).

We fill this gap in the economic development toolbox by recruiting and questioning a panel of economic development professionals. Our questionnaire named a number of Social, Technological, Economic, Environmental, and Political

[1]Including some commercial software: For example, http://www.dis1.com and http://www.vgsi.com/Vision/Corporate/SoftwareAssessmentAdministration.aspx

(STEEP) dimensions of the decision. It asked respondents first to assess the importance of several social dimensions and then the same for the remainder of the STEEP perspectives or categories. It then asked respondents to rank the importance of the STEEP categories. A number of questions concerning statistics on the respondents' cities' incentive programs completed the questionnaire. The latter questions enabled us to correlate cities' multifaceted attitudinal approach to incentives to their frequency of offers extended, fraction of offers accepted, and proportion of accepted offers with satisfactory outcomes.

The study is filled out with "demographic" information on the respondents' cities, and case stories of incentive programs, with special focus on the City of Austin and the State of Texas.

25.2 Literature Review

There is extensive research and scholarly literature on economic development; the rationale for business incentive policies by state and local governments for relocating firms; and econometrics for predicting the desired outcomes of such policies. In general, studies were inconclusive as to the correlations of such policies to their assumed or desired outcomes. This brief literature review covers the evolution of the economic development theory and site location and selection by firms. An effort is also made to explain the background of a new approach using multiple STEEP perspectives and expert judgments to influence the decision-making process for incentive policies. This review ends with a conclusion that incentive policies have been largely ineffective and that grandstanding by chief executives of firms may not translate to the community benefits which are the ostensible motivation of the policies.

25.2.1 Economic Development Theory Evolution

In the United States, the motivations and impacts of policy adoption on economic development have been studied extensively. These have been summarized in the literature reviews in multiple doctoral dissertations (Fox 1991; Jain 2012; Rutherford 2012) and are briefly described here.

In his seminal work, Walker studied the regional diffusion of policy innovation by the states in America (Walker 1969). He studied 88 state programs and found that a state was more likely to adopt a new program if the program or idea had been adopted by other states in the region. The likelihood became higher if the state's decision-makers considered the early adopter state as an important point of reference. Essentially, states tend to emulate other states. This implies that the strongest determinate variable for new programs is an external one and is the action of the neighboring state or states.

In the 1990s research shifted to the theory that internal factors such as legislative composition, interest groups, institutional capacity, political culture, and economic crisis influence the adoption of new policy (Fox 1991). However, it was found that this approach was also insufficient, since new policies were impacted by both internal and external factors (Berry and Berry 1992).

Later, a unified theory that included models of internal and external factors also proved insufficient (Fox 1991). New approaches continue to be researched; however studies tend to be narrowly focused on either a type of firm or industry or the impact of specific economic factors, tax incentives (i.e., tax breaks).

25.2.2 Site Location Theory and Methodologies

One aspect of economic development is the policies with respect to business and industrial site locations. There is significant literature that describes factors that determine where companies locate. One set of studies focuses on the factors that impact the firm's location decision, and the other set focuses on a specific industry (Kimelberg and Williams 2013). Initially, location theory was mainly interested in analyzing the location patterns of manufacturers and retailers. In the early and mid-1900s, businesses relied on production and its supply chain. Hence, importance was given to access to raw materials and markets and transportation and labor costs. This would provide a competitive advantage to firms. Around 2000 costs remained an important factor, but studies expanded to include the impact of other factors such as state and local taxes, financial incentives, minimum wage laws, unions, and right-to-work laws. The findings of these studies are inconclusive and mixed. However, there is a common belief that the bottom line drives the decision-making process which means that economic feasibility is paramount.

The research on site selection generally involves two methodologies: econometric models and surveys or interviews (Blair and Premus 1987; Carlson 1999; Kimelberg and Williams 2013). The econometrics approach measures to what extent a place or site-based characteristic (explanatory variable or determinant) can predict the attractiveness of a location for specific firms or industries (dependent variable). Essentially, these are statistical correlations or models. The other methodology of surveys typically involves direct surveys or interviews of firms' decision-makers. Each approach has advantages and disadvantages, but overall the two approaches provide reasonably consistent results. It should be noted that the surveys tend to be of and around the relocating firms, and surveys of state and local economic development professionals are missing.

25.2.2.1 STEEP Analysis, Multiple Perspectives, and Decision-Making

Studies on economic development, industrial recruitment, and location selections tend to take a bottom-up approach of considering a laundry list of variables such as housing costs, public transport, availability of skilled talent, proximity to an airport, state and local taxes, and incentives. For comprehensive studies, an approach known as a "STEEP Analysis" has been used in many fields especially marketing and law. STEEP is an acronym for Social, Technological, Economic, Environmental, and Political. STEEP represents the dimensions or perspectives that should be considered for a comprehensive assessment of the situation or problem. It is sometimes referred to as an environmental scan or PESTLE Analysis (with "L" representing "legal"). It is a top-down approach, starting with the specific perspective (category) and criteria or sub-criteria that make up the perspective are enumerated. The STEEP perspectives may be generally described as (Sheikh and Kocaoglu 2011; Sheikh 2013):

- *Social Perspective.* This perspective includes criteria or sub-criteria that have a significant positive or negative impact on society. As Table 25.2 shows, social criteria may include cultural, quality of life, and health categories such as population growth rate, age distribution, career attitudes, lifestyle conditions, privacy, safety, and security.
- *Technological or Technical Perspective.* This perspective includes criteria or sub-criteria that indicate technical performance and include specific technologies and characteristics such as reliability, durability, and efficiency.
- *Economic Perspective.* This perspective includes criteria or sub-criteria that are related to economic or fiscal feasibility and are indicated by cost of technology diffusion, market adoption, and life cycle costs. This may include the rationale why firms undertake a program for financial gain or wealth.
- *Environmental Perspective.* This perspective includes criteria or sub-criteria that impact environmental sustainability and the earth's natural ecosystems. The environment would be the actual physical surroundings of the project. The project may be a new factory or white-collar office building for knowledge workers. Considerations may include the impact of the project on the environment or ecology. The physical conditions may also have an effect, for example, considering earthquake or flood prone regions.
- *Political Perspective.* This perspective includes criteria or sub-criteria such as policies, regulations, market special interests, compliance, energy security, water security, national priorities, and government incentives. It may also include in-house politics, local, state, or federal conformance to political specifications.

The history of STEEP Analysis is unclear; however it appears that in 1967 Francis J. Aguilar mentioned a related acronym in his book, "Scanning the Business Environment," where he discussed the factors affecting a business (Aguilar 1967). He called it "ETPS" to indicate the four sectors of his taxonomy of the environment: economic, technical, political, and social. (This originated from his 1965 Ph.D. dissertation at Harvard.)

The basic concepts of decision-making using multiple perspectives were introduced by Harold Linstone and can be extended to other areas such as policy assessment, site selection, technology assessment, and ranking of firms (Linstone 1999; Linstone 1981, 1985, 2010). Others, such as Kingsley Haynes (Desai et al. 1991), Dundar Kocaoglu, Thomas Saaty, and Nasir Sheikh, have extended this approach to multi-criteria (hierarchical) decision modeling (Kocaoglu 1987; Saaty 2008; Nasir J Sheikh et al. 2016; Nasir Jamil Sheikh 2013, 2015).

One established approach for decision-making is to elicit the judgment of experts when the data are not available or are inconclusive. Experts have an extended or intense experience through practice, education, and training in a particular field. A study identified detailed characteristics of experts and developed their psychometric measures such as specific education, training, and knowledge; intuition; and self-assurance and confidence in their knowledge (Germain 2006). Expert judgment is the information or data provided by an expert in response to a question or problem. Judgment is defined as an inferential cognitive process by which an individual draws conclusions about unknown quantities or qualities on the basis of available information (Rohrbaugh 1979). Expert judgments are the expression of opinions based on experience and knowledge. By combining the expert judgments of a group of decision-makers, we may arrive at rational decisions. By quantifying the judgments, models can be built to assess the relative importance or rank of the decision elements (perspectives, criteria, and sub-criteria) that underlie the decision (Amer and Daim 2013).

Considering economic development professionals as experts, it may be possible to translate their judgments to criteria that make up business relocation incentive decisions. This may prove more beneficial than surveys of firms and building econometric models for location decisions. A broad range of criteria can be covered in this approach considering STEEP multiple perspectives. Critics of this approach argue that the experts' judgment as a group may be biased if their backgrounds are similar and there is a danger of "groupthink." Hence, expert panels should be well-rounded implying that their backgrounds and experiences should be diverse. To form such panels, economic development experts may be selected from states that are not in the same region; there is a mix of experts from academia, industry, and government; and the number of years of experience of the experts varies from, say 5–20 years. Typically an individual is considered an expert if he or she has more than 10 years of experience in his or her field (Gladwell 2008). However, the experts with fewer years of experience may have exposure to newer types of information including methodologies or technologies which may enrich the decision-making process.

25.2.2.2 The Effectiveness of Business Relocation Incentives

The approach of using STEEP perspectives and multi-criteria expert judgments may prove more effective than the past economics-only approaches of corporate incentives to firms and overblown promises of investments by firms. A 2017 report from the Upjohn Institute for Employment Research presented data on the effectiveness of corporate incentives (Bartik 2017). Economic development incentives for firms are built into state law across the United States. They are designed to attract and retain firms so they can benefit the local communities. The assumption is that the incentives will encourage new or expanding export-based industries. These industries may include manufacturing, technology, media, or any firm that sells its goods or services beyond the local economy.

The Upjohn report (Bartik 2017) is based on the analysis of 26 years of incentives in 33 states. It indicates that the tax breaks have increased threefold since 1990. It affirms the consensus that these tax breaks (called corporate incentives) are not effective in attracting companies. In fact their effect is statistically insignificant. It appears that the main predictor of a state offering an incentive is that they were offered in the prior year. Tax breaks tend to make more political sense than economic sense since the underlying premise is that the firm will create new jobs. The reality is that incentives tend to go to low-wage businesses (Grabar 2017).

Firms also tend to be shopping different locations and making exaggerated pledges to attract publicity and extract benefits but not leading to a viable relocation (Frankel 2017). An example of a firm making big promises and then not following through is Foxconn, a Taiwanese multinational electronics manufacturer. In 2013 Foxconn's chief executive Terry Gou announced that he would invest US $30 million and hire 500 workers for a new high-tech factory in central Pennsylvania. The project never materialized, but new announcements of investment projections continue. In December 2016, Masayoshi Son, the chief executive of SoftBank, a Japanese conglomerate, stood with President-elect Donald Trump to announce plans to invest US $50 billion and create 50,000 new US jobs. To date details are not forthcoming. Such announcements appear to be offered as bait for incentive discussions, rather than as statements of specific intent.

In conclusion, economic development and site location theories have not produced conclusive results for business relocation incentive decisions. It is worthwhile to investigate and research an approach that includes the use of multiple STEEP perspectives and the judgment of economic development government officials as experts. The initial steps of this approach are covered in this paper.

25.3 Methodology

We developed an invitation-only online questionnaire, using Qualtrics. The questionnaire was directed at economic development professionals who work at city or regional ED offices or chambers of commerce and who are active in the process of making relocation incentive decisions.

To assemble the panel of respondents, we posted a solicitation on 6 LinkedIn groups[2] with total (but overlapping) membership of 48,000 and on the University of North Carolina's NCECONDEV listserv. Email solicitations went out to the email lists of World Technopolis Association and General Informatics, LLC. Executives of the Council for Community and Economic Research (C2ER) and the Western Regional Science Association (WRSA) kindly passed the request on to their

[2]Economic Development Professionals, Economic Development 2.0, Economic Development Specialists, High Performance Economic Development, City of Clearwater Economic Development, and Hudson Valley Economic Development Corporation.

membership. Fax requests went to about 40 ED professionals listed in the directory of siteselection.com. Recipients of all messages were asked to respond themselves, if qualified, and to snowball the message to other qualified respondents.

The results below are based on a final panel of 30 professional ED managers. The expert panel methodology justifies only descriptive statistics and cross-tabulations. Therefore, these were the analytic methods used. Quantitative analysis is augmented by qualitative consideration of respondents' free-form comments, case studies assembled from press stories, and certain discussion threads in the LinkedIn groups.

The results were then assessed for conversion rates from inquiries to relocation incentive offers to satisfactory outcomes for the city. This is described in the Variate Relationships section.

25.4 Results of the Survey

25.4.1 Sample Demographics

Figures 25.1 and 25.2 show the nation and the sizes of the city and metro areas where the respondents reside.

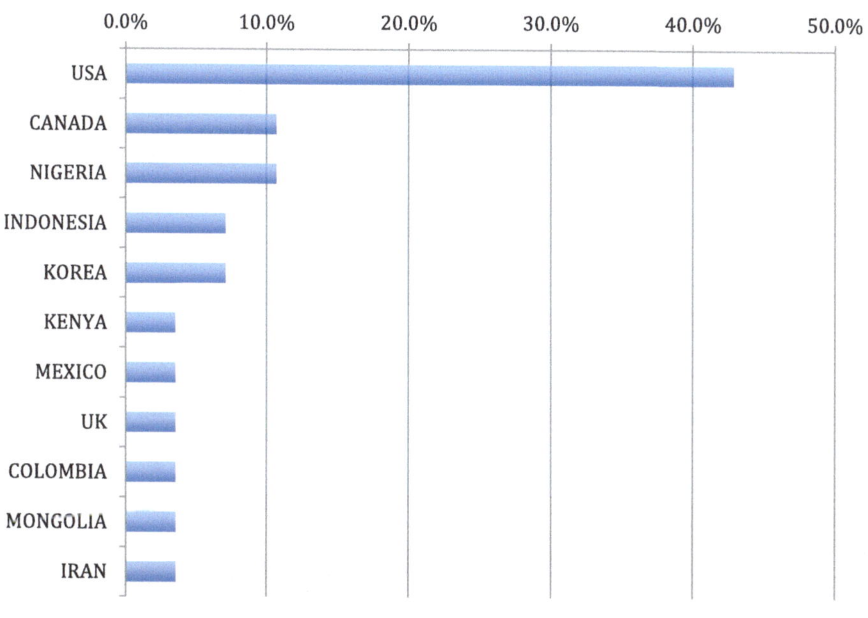

Fig. 25.1 Respondents' countries of residence

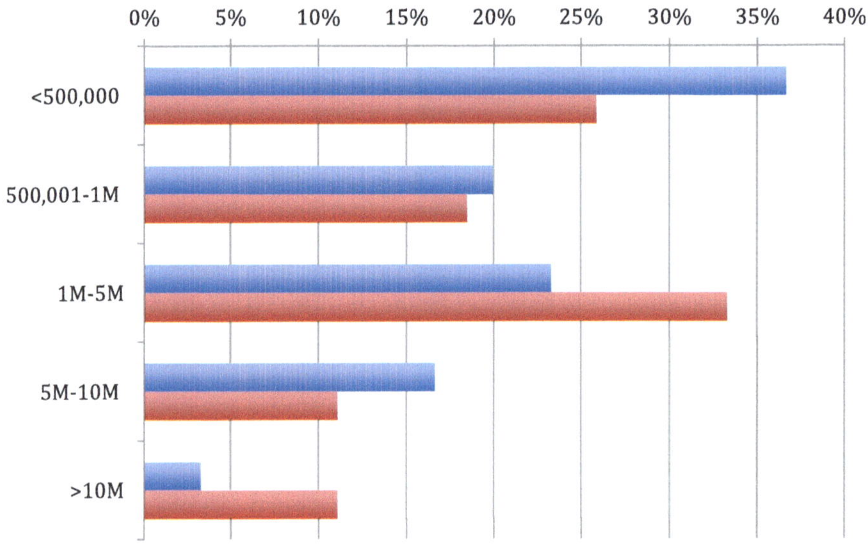

Fig. 25.2 Sizes of cities and metro areas where respondents work. Top bar: City population. Lower bar: Metro area population

25.4.2 Aggregate Statistics

Figures 25.3a, 25.3b, 25.4, 25.5a, 25.5b, 25.6a, 25.6b 25.7a and 25.7b display the relative importance ascribed to each criterion within each of the STEEP categories. The figures show the frequency with which respondents gave each criterion within

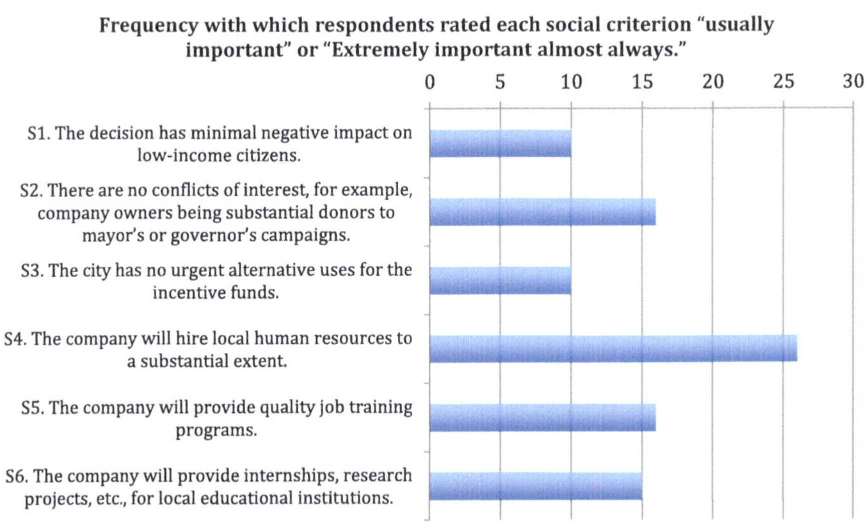

Fig. 25.3a Criteria considered most important from a social perspective

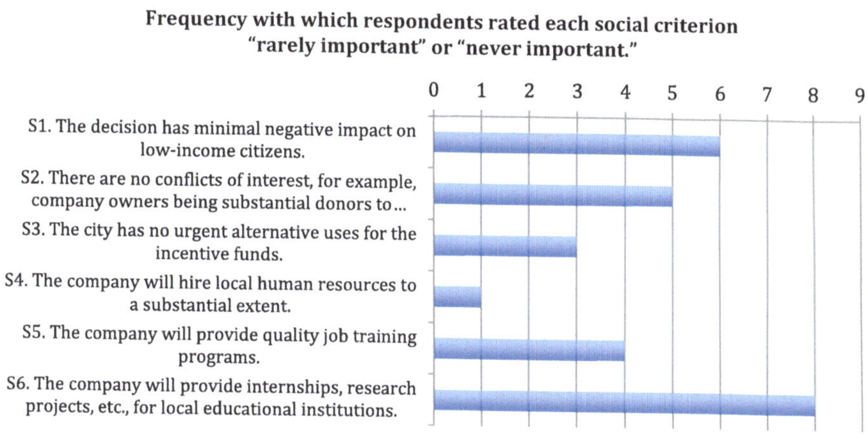

Fig. 25.3b Criteria considered least important from a social perspective

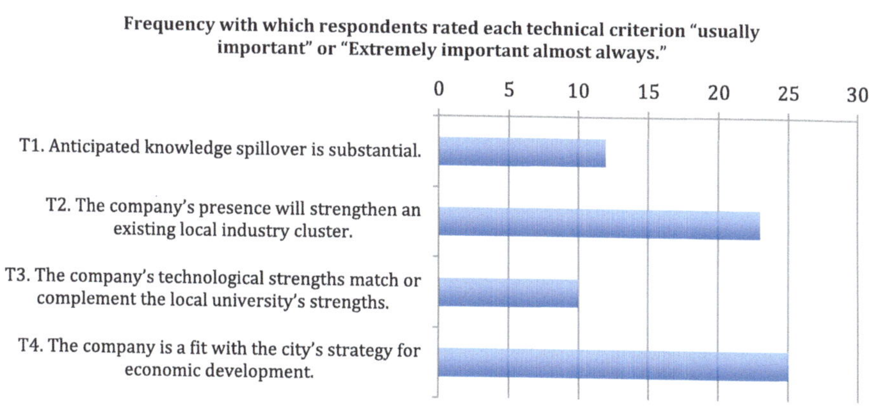

Fig. 25.4 Criteria considered most important from a technological/technical perspective

the five STEEP categories one of the top two importance ratings ("usually important" or "Extremely important almost always") and separately, the bottom two importance ratings, "rarely important" or "never important." In general, the relative importance of the criterion was judged as a matter of cognitive significance by the economic development professionals in their deliberations prior to deciding whether to make an offer to a candidate relocating firm. However, the city's policies and past experiences based on the city's satisfaction of the outcome also influenced the judgments.

Figure 25.3a shows respondents gave greatest social importance to local hiring and training. "No conflicts of interest" was rated of equal importance to training opportunities. This was consistent with Fig. 25.6a, where two measures of transparency and non-corruption were rated highly important.

Respondents did not give a firm's interaction with educational institutions much importance. This accords with Albahari et al.'s (2013) observation that even in

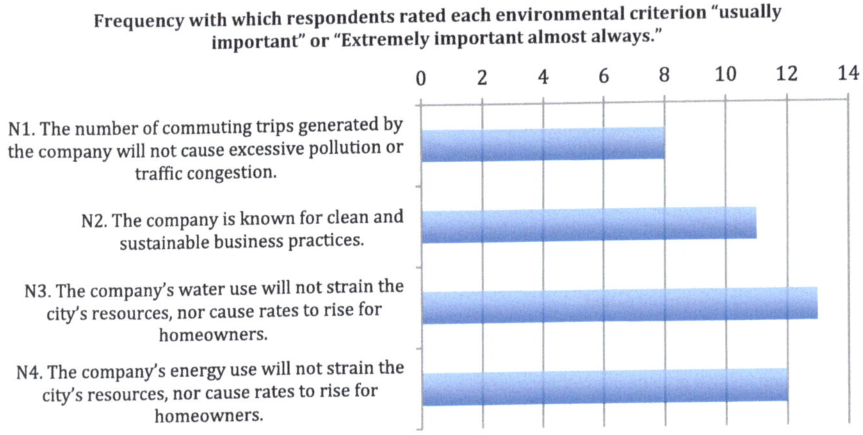

Fig. 25.5a Criteria considered most important from an environmental perspective

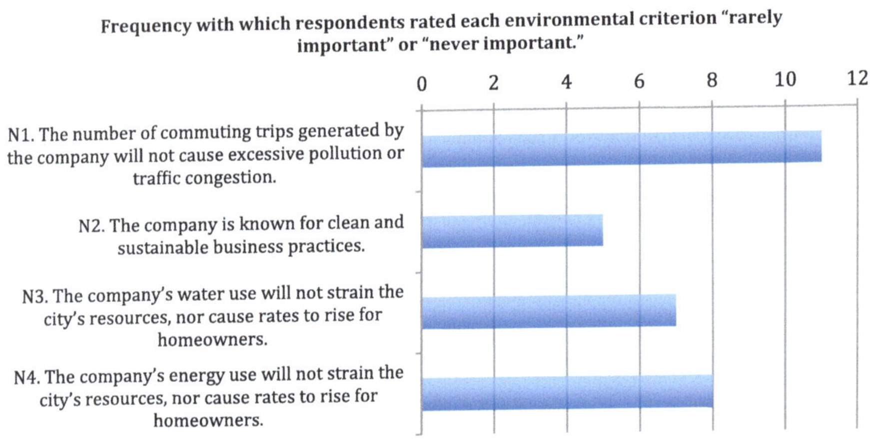

Fig. 25.5b Criteria considered least important from an environmental perspective

university-owned research parks (in Spain), companies do not interact much with the university. But it under-rates the importance of such interaction: Albahari et al. noted that research park tenant firms interacting more with the university won more patents.

Respondents were most concerned that an incoming company's technology focus fit with the city's (possibly cluster-based) growth strategy (Fig. 25.4). They might have under-estimated the importance of knowledge spillover (Item T1) in cluster growth.

Two respondents said technological criterion T3 was rarely or never important. The other technological criteria were rated "rarely important" or "never important" zero times. We do not graph this information.

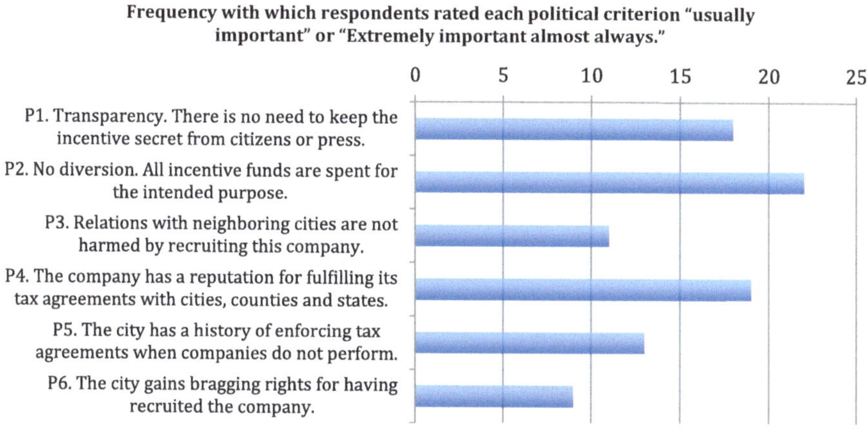

Fig. 25.6a Criteria considered most important from a political perspective

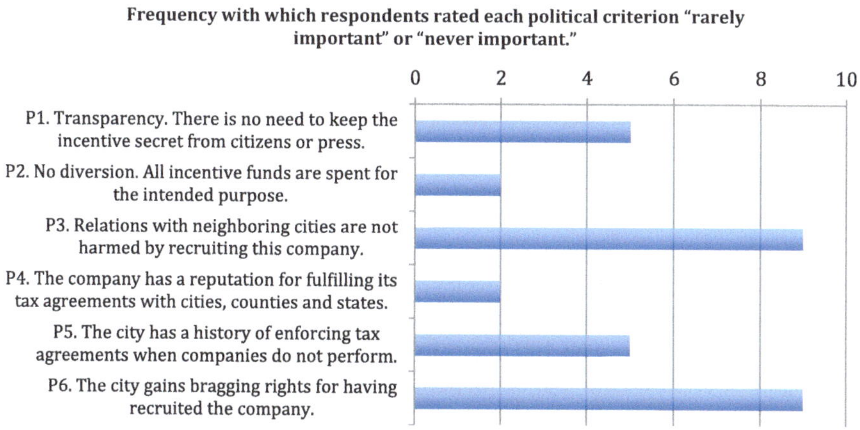

Fig. 25.6b Criteria considered least important from a political perspective

Respondents gave environmental sustainability a nod (Fig. 25.5a) but were much more concerned with a company's prospective water and energy consumption.

Citizens might be chagrined that ED officials gave short shrift to growing congestion. It may be that regions aspiring to growth still see congestion as a sign of success rather than a problem of success.

As noted earlier, transparency and non-corruption were rated highly important.

It is striking that item P3 was given so little importance in this anonymous survey. Contrast the fact with the sermonizing against harming the neighboring city, in the (not anonymous) professional network discussion summarized later in this paper.

Figure 25.7a again shows the importance to respondents of jobs, jobs, jobs. Item E3, an opportunity cost, also gets high importance. Other items were regarded as more or less equal in importance.

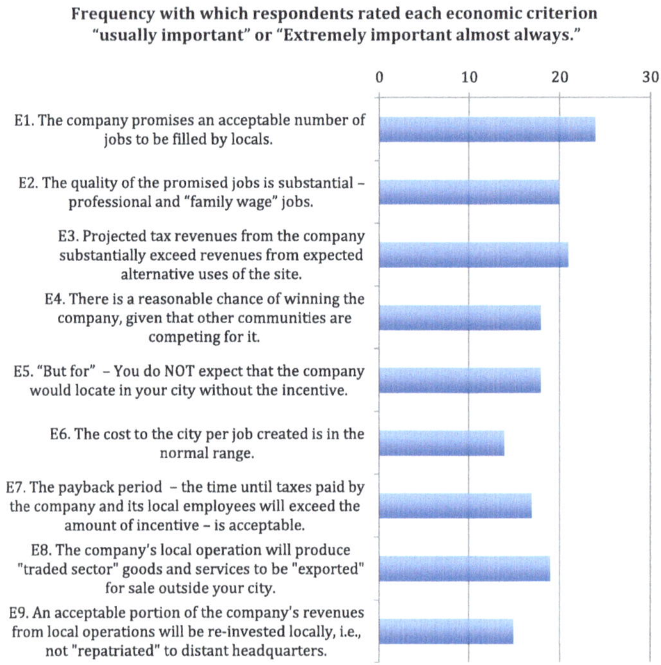

Fig. 25.7a Criteria considered most important from an economic perspective

It seemed odd that respondents most frequently rated item E8 rarely or never important (Fig. 25.7b). Economic development theory holds that producing "traded sector" (export) goods is of paramount importance.

Each respondent allocated 100 points to the five STEEP perspectives or categories. Figure 25.8 shows the sum of "importance points" respondents awarded to the five STEEP categories. Respondents generally value the Economic category of decision criteria quite a bit more than the other STEEP categories. They claim political considerations, while important, are rather less so than the other categories of criteria. Social, Technological, and Environmental categories appear equally important to the responding ED executives.

Only 20% of the respondents did not give the plurality of their points to the Economic category. Except for one mid-sized US city, all of the 20% were from respondents outside the United States and Canada. Each of the 20% either failed to respond or indicated "don't know," to queries about percent of inquiries leading to incentive offers, the percent of offers leading to relocations, or the percent of relos proving satisfactory.

Table 25.3 shows ranges for each of the bars in Fig. 25.8. No respondent gave a zero weight to the Economic category, and none gave it a weight greater than 75.

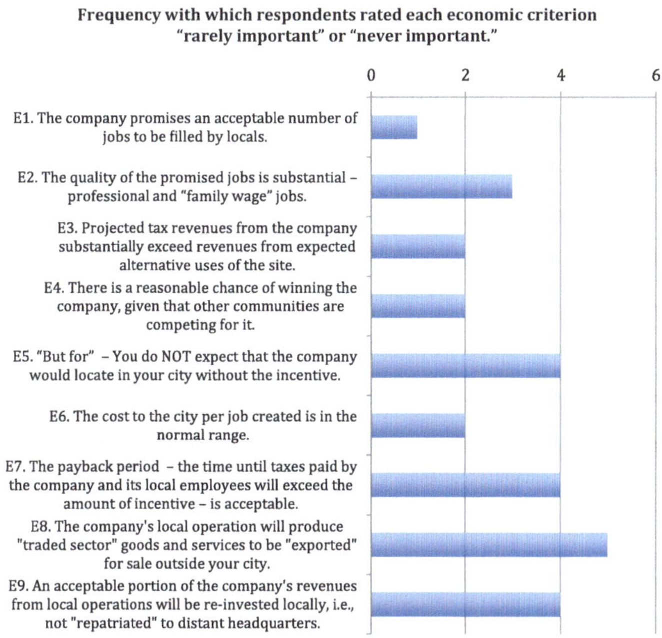

Fig. 25.7b Criteria considered least important from an economic perspective

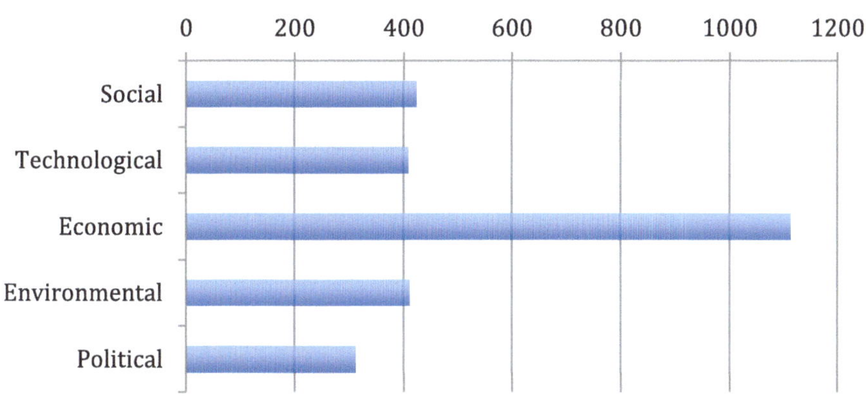

Fig. 25.8 Respondents assess relative importance of the five STEEP categories

Table 25.3 Range of weights respondents gave to each of the STEEP categories

	Min	Median	Max
Social	5	18	30
Technological	5	15	30
Economic	20	40	75
Environmental	5	15	39
Political	0	10	30

25.4.3 Variate Relationships

We now cross-tabulate the event variables against the attitudinal variable shown in Table 25.3. For brevity, and because respondents tended to ascribe equal weight to Technological, Environmental, and Social categories, we show only the weight given to the Economic category as it affects conversion of inquiries to offers (Table 25.4), conversion of offers to relocations (Table 25.5), and conversion of relocations to the city's sense of satisfaction (Table 25.6). It should be noted that the authors did not consider the city and metro sizes and how they are related to the

Table 25.4 Conversion of inquiries to offers

Importance given to economic criteria	Percent of inquiries resulting in an incentive offer					
	Don't know, or blank	0%	Low (1–25%)	Medium (26–50%)	High (51–75%)	V. High (76–100%)
Don't know, or blank	5			1		
Low (20–25)	3	1			1	
Medium (26–50)	6	2	3		2	3
High (51–75)	2		1	1	1	1

Table 25.5 Conversion of offers to relocations

Importance given to economic criteria	Percent of incentive offers resulting in company relocation					
	Don't know, or blank	0%	Low (1–25%)	Medium (26–50%)	High (51–75%)	V. High (76–100%)
Don't know, or blank	5				1	
Low (20–25)	4		2	3	1	1
Medium (26–50)	8		3		1	
High (51–75)	2				1	2

Table 25.6 Incidence of satisfactory incentive relocations by city's view of importance of Economic criteria

Importance given to economic criteria	Percent of incentivized relocations with satisfactory outcomes					
	Don't know, or blank	0%	Low (1–25%)	Medium (26–50%)	High (51–75%)	V. High (76–100%)
Don't know, or blank	5					1
Low (20–25)	4			1		1
Medium (26–50)	8		1	1	1	3
High (51–75)	2		2			3

number of inquiries. This is a limitation of the current study and may need further investigation and may need to be controlled for city/metro size.

Table 25.4 suggests cities placing a relatively low importance on Economic criteria converted more inquiries into incentive offers. Table 25.5 is inconclusive but shows cities placing a high relative importance on Economic concerns were most successful in converting offers to positive company relocation decisions. Cities most successful (80 + %) in converting offers to relocations gave weights between 5 and 20 to Social, Technological, and Environmental categories of criteria and usually less weight to the Political category.

Table 25.6 shows cities with mid to high importance of Economic criteria were more likely to be satisfied with relocated companies, presumably because the companies met their economic obligations to the city. This table shows that cities paying close attention to finances are generally happier with their done deals. However, the cities giving top weight to economic factors suffered a split in satisfaction, racking up a few highly satisfactory outcomes and others much less satisfactory.

25.4.4 *Qualitative Responses*

Respondents had the opportunity to suggest additional decision criteria not covered by the questionnaire. Though in many instances their suggestions duplicated those in the survey, all are listed in Table 25.7. Respondents may have believed repetition conveyed a greater emphasis.

Respondents offered these free-form comments on the purposes of incentives:

> "They are necessary for communities to compete for investment and jobs."
>
> "Expansion projects, new technology development, programs to develop local suppliers."
>
> "To curb social vices [criminality and hoodlums among youths]"

They transmitted these opinions on the value of incentives:

> "Unfortunately, incentives are necessary because every other municipality (city/county/state) offers them. If you have a quality building or land + tax rebates, you're in good shape."
>
> "It was important to create substantial tax base and employment after losing 3 Burlington knitting mills 14 years ago and over 1,200 jobs."
>
> "Frankly I am tired of companies demanding a lot of gimmes when financially they do not need it. Call it corporate welfare. In the long run, most of those companies are not going to make good corporate citizens."

And these views concerning how incentive programs should be managed:

> "In drafting the incentive strategy, I think its necessary to ensure that the terms of the incentives are equally binding yet flexible (strike a balance of sorts) that allows room for periodic review by both parties to extend or adjust them accordingly within agreed timeframes and guidelines. This will enable the city to be more responsive to any changing dynamics to better align with the priorities of its economic development plans."

Table 25.7 Additional decision criteria suggested by survey respondents

"Critical suppliers to key clusters"
"Low skilled labor acceptance"
"The agreement includes stipulations of how the company will invest in the community and students"
"New tax base created"
"Skills required match existing labor force or training is available"
"Quality of jobs to include health benefits"
"Share facilities and infrastructure"
"Culture"
"Also benefits the region"
"Tax abatement cannot exceed the period of the current Council"
"Number of new jobs created"
"Will the new tax revenue pay for the incentives in less than 10 years"
"How well the workforce matches the company's needs"
"Training offered"
"Investment"
"Fit to econ strategy"
"Does not 'steal' jobs from other parts of the region, unless it is the only way to retain jobs in the region"
"Incentives are necessary and appropriate"
"The company also gives back to the community in other ways"
"Incentives must conform to both Alberta Municipal Government Act and the New West Partnership between BC, AB and SK"

> "Any move to provide incentives to a large corporations [that do] not need the money, should provide a report as to how providing a cash incentive that could have gone to community development or small business, is a better choice for the city."
>
> "Truthfully the responses provided here are largely theoretical. Municipalities in Canada are, for all intensive [sic] purposes, forbidden from offering cash or tax incentives to relocating companies. Cash or tax incentives are typically provided by the respective provincial governments. In Alberta the Municipal Government Act makes it clear a sitting Council cannot implicate future Councils in its decision when decided to give any company a tax concession to relocate. In addition, the New West Partnership forbids any municipality in the partnership area from offering any incentive that would be harmful of any other municipality in the partnership."

The survey specified that respondent anonymity was the default option; providing email address was discretionary. A majority of respondents did provide addresses, indicating a high level of interest in the research questions and a desire to see topline survey results.

25.5 Cases and Conversations

In addition to the lengthier accounts in this section of Austin's and Texas' programs, we briefly mention new programs in New York and in Taiwan. Readers may judge how the policies of these programs in opposite hemispheres stack up to the advice given by this study's respondents.

The State of New York's new program is particularly generous.[3] "Companies approved to receive START-UP NY benefits will pay no taxes for 10 years, no income tax, no business tax, no corporate state or local taxes, no sales tax, no property tax and no franchise fees. Employees in participating companies will pay no income taxes for the first 5 years" (Russo 2014).

The nearby State of Rhode Island made headlines with a failed video game development company owned by a former major league pitcher. Loan defaults left Rhode Island taxpayers on the hook for $151 Million (Table 25.8).

Philippidis (2016) relates similar problems plaguing Florida's hopeful biocluster, near Port St. Lucie. He describes the collision between "$1.3 billion showered by Florida's state government and several counties" and "overly optimistic job-creation estimates." The result: "Florida now seeks to take back some of the money" committed to two California research institutes that established Florida branches.

The remainder of this section focuses on the relocation incentive experiences of the City of Austin, the State of Texas, and the island of Taiwan.

25.5.1 *Austin*

> The Austin region has the sixth-most-educated workforce in the U.S., which is why many tech companies look at the Austin region. Quality of life and a fairly predictable state regulatory environment play a key role as well (Harrell 2012).

However, in 2001 the dotcom bust had slowed Austin's economy and raised its unemployment rate (Sayre 2003). City Councilman (and later, Mayor 2003–2009)

Table 25.8 Providence, Rhode Island, pays 38Studios to open facility in Providence

Pros: No apparent pros
Cons
Aimed at stealing jobs from neighboring Massachusetts; a senseless zero-sum game
Risk that this company's business model could not survive without public support
Inadequate transparency: A state official asked 38Studios for a job, weeks after state made the grant

Data from Ladendorf (2012)

[3]The present authors were involved in promoting this program to Korean companies.

Table 25.9 Austin, Texas, pays Apple to open facility in Austin

Pros
Shows a business-friendly policy.
Apple was then the world's most valuable company.
Consistent with Austin's overall tech development strategy.
Austin has strong policies for not rebating taxes until a company has met auditable job-creation targets.
Maybe Apple would create more jobs *more quickly* with the incentive.
Cons
Apple would have come anyway.
Apple didn't need the money.

Data from Ladendorf (2012)

Will Wynn chaired the resulting Mayor's Task Force on the Economy. The task force concluded the City should play a role in revitalizing the economy. Its subcommittee on Retention and Recruitment determined (i) to provide incentives where indicated and (ii) target industries of strategic value to Austin. Strategic value was defined to include "fiscal impact, job creation, links to the local economy, and effect on the quality of life in Austin" (Sayre 2003).

The subcommittee on Cultural Vitality and Creative Economy, recognizing how Austin's prominence as a music mecca had already spurred synergy between the music and tech industries and launched new companies that bridged the two, pledged the city to "establish a cultural review as part of major policy decisions" and to "encourage the development of creativity-based businesses and neighborhoods that support cultural activity" (Sayre 2003).

The City of Austin maintains a sensible incentive policy that has suffered few scandals. Texas, the state in which Austin is located, has not been so lucky; its incentive program has been scandal-prone. Both programs attract criticism from citizens who believe the money given to companies could be better spent in other ways.

Austin has extended 12 tax rebate deals in the last 8 years, including to eBay, Facebook, and Samsung Electronics. This is far fewer incentive deals than Dallas, Houston, San Antonio, or Fort Worth have extended. Austin has offered no incentives to any company promising fewer than 200 new jobs.

Ninety-four percent of companies moving to Austin or expanding since 2004 got no deal. The companies receiving deals brought billions of USD in investment and thousands of jobs. Seven of the deals involved less than \$1 million in rebated tax. Three of those deals were suspended for noncompliance.

Apple received \$8.6 million in tax abatements to create 3600 jobs (Table 25.9). Samsung's investment alone was \$7 billion in factory and equipment. Samsung has become the largest single property taxpayer in Travis County, where Austin is located, and it employs about 2600 people (Ladendorf 2012).

Apple would get more than \$35 million in state, city, and county incentives if it meets its employment goals over the life of its contracts. Its deal with the city is for

10 years, and its deal with Travis County extends to 15 years. The package includes $21 million from the Texas Enterprise Fund, $8.6 million from the City of Austin, and between $6 million and $7 million from Travis County. The deal is the second-largest financial inducement offered in Austin over the past decade, trailing only the package offered to Samsung in 2005 for its massive factory expansion project (Ladendorf 2012).

Tax abatements are agreed upon with formal incentive contracts. The City of Austin hires an outside firm to do detailed compliance reviews. The City holds the money, forcing companies to perform to contract.

In contrast, the State of Texas' incentive program has shown mixed results and flawed design.

25.5.2 Texas

A third-party economic impact assessment, which is paid for by the applying company, is performed by an outside firm. In general, every project must meet certain criteria regarding net job creation. For example, the average wage from those jobs must meet or exceed the average county wage. An economic consumption model is also used to determine the return on investment back to the state. According to state information, the focus for awards based on jobs created is generally in the range of $1000 to $10,000 per job created (Garr 2012).

Businesses are required to submit annual reports, and if the number of jobs created is less than the required amount, a certain percentage of money is withheld. Of the $443 million that has been paid in enterprise fund awards as of Jan. 31, $5.4 million has been clawed back, according to the governor's office. An additional $20.5 million has been repaid by companies that have terminated enterprise fund contracts (Garr 2012; see also Ryan 2017 for an account of incentive clawback from a Warren Buffett-owned firm in Massachusetts).

The Texas Legislature remarked on the State's incentive program: "These incentives have evolved without a comprehensive review of their effectiveness, how they compare with other states' efforts, whether they appropriately target the correct economic activity, how they should be evaluated, or how they can be coordinated with other incentives to be most effective" (Copelin 2013a). See also Copelin (2012).

Copelin (2013b, c) provides further information:

> Amazingly, neither the Enterprise Fund nor the various events trust funds have been audited — ever. And those agreements, granting up to a 90 percent reduction in a company's property tax valuation, haven't undergone a cost-benefit analysis. [One legislator said,] "Taxpayers must be assured that private partners are holding up their end of the bargain in exchange for these grants."
>
> The House version of Senate Bill 149... toughens conflict-of-interest provisions, introduces more checks and balances in awarding grants, and prohibits private foundations from supplementing the salaries of the agency's top leadership.

Garr (2012) adds:

> In total, 43 companies that have received $330 million in enterprise fund awards since 2003 have given almost $7 million to [then Texas Governor] Perry's campaigns and the Republican Governors Association, according to an October report from [Texans for Public Justice]. This is a highly politicized program that has been used to pump up this governor.

25.5.3 Taiwan

In 2016 Taiwan's Executive Yuan resolved to develop the biomedical industry's innovation and exports, using tax incentives (Chen 2016). Even as other locales look favorably toward regulating the practice, the Taiwan project includes relaxation of investment and recruitment regulations, with the aim of attracting foreign capital and brainpower.

The government will appropriate NT$10.94 billion (US$346.32 million) within a year, "to develop 10 large-scale healthcare firms, 20 new drugs and 80 new medical devices to be marketed internationally by 2025 in a bid to boost the annual value of the biomedical industry to NT$1 trillion."

> "The nation's medical service is the best in Asia and the third best in the world, and we want to export the service by completing the infrastructure of the healthcare industry," Tsai Shaw-jenq said (Chen 2016).

The legislation will relieve biomedical start-ups from taxation in the early stages after IPO. There will be a 35–50% tax credit on a company's R&D expense and employee training cost. Shareholders receive a 20% tax credit "on the investment amount, or the purchase price of the stock" (Chen 2016). The program will initially benefit "about 50 medical instrument and 13 regenerative medicine firms in the fields of precision medicine, gene therapy and cell therapy."

The legislation involves more than tax incentives. Regulations on moonlighting professors will be eased. Taiwan firms will be encouraged to acquire overseas companies and build foreign markets.

However, even without special legislation, investment in the biotechnology sector increased to NT$48.4 billion in 2015.

25.5.4 A LinkedIn Conversation

A February 2017 online discussion among economic development professionals dealt with incentives, with special emphasis on "poaching" companies from neighboring or bordering metropolitan areas. There was surprising divergence among the participants' views and depth of argumentation. The conversation revealed additional aspects of a controversial question.

Those opposed to poaching based their positions on logic ("Zero sum game." "If a company can be induced to leave a community for your own, they can be induced to leave yours for another."), on anecdote (a greeting card company moving within the same metro area, with no net benefit to any party), on a wider regional vision ("I am a big proponent of regional collaboration."), on regulations or regional agreements that prohibit it (In New York State, the state government will not allow a local Industrial Development Agency to award a tax exemption "if the business it seeks to help is moving from another location in New York, unless it has been clearly demonstrated the state is at risk of losing the business to another state."), or on professional courtesy and ethics that possibly overrides the obligations given to them by their employer ("If the tables were turned, how would you feel?"). Some offered statements apparently originating in ideology without supporting facts: "There truly is no long term benefit to luring a business from one state to another state."

Other participants noted that poaching happens anyway, regardless of any of the above. "Even governors regularly beat a path to California, Illinois, New Jersey, New York, and other high-cost places, to call on companies, [and offer] lower cost alternatives." One referred to "the dirty little secret that while we never acknowledge poaching, we 'respond' to a business that needs new facilities...".

Still others see value in the practice, though they do not call it poaching. "We work for our community first and while we respect our colleagues, we know where our priority sits." "I see nothing unethical about offering a company lower-cost options." This side has their own anecdote: General Electric moved its headquarters across a state line "largely because of the tax climate." (Chesto (2016) reported that Boston earned a hefty ROI on $25 million in incentives extended to GE.)

Some of the latter participants abdicate responsibility for the practice, saying, "Most businesses, in the end, make their own decisions for their own reasons not ours." "Any company that is truly happy where it is, won't return your phone call anyway."

A few commenters over-simplified. ("Poaching is unprofessional and unethical. Some things should not have to be taught post-kindergarten." "Relocation bad. Expansion good. That simple.")

Some articulated a more nuanced middle ground: "Typically, companies will not move lock, stock and barrel, but open up new satellite operations, looking for new markets and lower cost." "Neither I nor the organizations I have represented actively recruit/poach our neighbors. However, when our phone rings and the industry in a nearby community says they have outgrown where they are, or the tax bill is getting to be too much in that jurisdiction..." "It may not be as clear as many would like it to be but... the leading [ED] professional organization['s] programs and services definitely reflect a disdain for poaching."

Other participants thoughtfully reframed the question: "What does the out-migration of firms mean for the central cities? What is the aggregate cost of continued sprawl? How does this move affect workers, transportation patterns and housing affordability? Poaching leads to abandonment, and as stewards of public dollars we need to be judicious about how and where we offer development incentives." "[Should] we focus our economic development dollars on people or places? In my view we should invest in our citizens, and industry will follow." "If a company comes to you from a neighboring community... contact [its] economic developer and inform him or her what's happening. Give them a chance to 'fix' what might be fixable."

Specifically addressing relocation incentives, a participant wrote, "We would rarely consider a relocation incentive unless it were focused on an expansion, a real net gain for us, our region and state." Another stated that academic research "concludes the supply side incentives are a zero-sum game as well." Another, referring to the "dirty little secret," wrote, "How about we simply prohibit using incentives for a business moving within the region? Not just a non-compete, but a prohibition. . . ."[4]

25.6 Limitations of the Study

Respondents' suggestions showed where the questionnaire could be more clear.

- "Would suggest putting the social part last after the others. I couldn't quite understand them and they made more sense after I had answered the ones for the other sections, i.e., political, economic, environmental."
- "Political decision is not clear."
- "Are you considering how intense the competition is for investment and jobs?"

Future surveys will make it more explicit that we are not asking about poaching neighbors.

The 10-year payback period expected by one city may or may not be typical but will be of interest to other cities. Any repeats of our survey will ask this explicitly.

Our small number of respondents, relative to the large invitation pool, suggests respondents should be incentivized to participate in studies of this sort.

25.7 Discussion

Citing flawed data and implausible proxies, Goren (2007) shows how difficult an economic impact study of business relocation incentives can be. For this reason we attempted a different approach, measuring ED professionals' attitudes on the STEEP dimensions and their (or their officials') feelings of satisfaction with outcomes. Our

[4]The conversation continues at https://www.linkedin.com/groups/3588654/3588654-6247383765795033089?midToken=AQEbOspvaotfuA&trk=eml-b2_anet_digest_of_digests-hero-12-view%7Ediscussion&trkEmail=eml-b2_anet_digest_of_digests-hero-12-view%7Ediscussion-null-3q3s%7Ej0d6nti8%7Eod&lipi=urn%3Ali%3Apage%3Aemail_b2_anet_digest_of_digests%3BP6WK1M%2BIRG6n7h%2FkAFSaAQ%3D%3D. It is open to group members only, but membership is free.

panel of expert professionals, when compared with cases, news items, and professional network discussion threads, uncovered contradictions that merit deeper research. Some were noted in the "Results of the Survey" section above, and others are mentioned here.

Respondents gave "Political" the lowest importance rating of the five STEEP dimensions. This appears to contradict the results of Jansa and Gray (2016), who argue that "the political presence of the business sector within the state is an important determinant of state subsidy spending." The contradiction might be due to most of our respondents representing metro areas rather than states or provinces; state politics are generally bigger than city politics. Indeed, the balance of the news items we found suggests that city incentive programs are less problem-prone than state programs. This is grist for further research.

It was curious and perhaps significant that several respondents knew about the incentive decision process, but not about the results of that process, i.e., could not provide data on conversion of inquiries to offers, etc. If we were to repeat the survey, we would give some weeks advance notice, to allow respondents to think about or research the conversion rates.

It is similarly remarkable that a vocal minority of respondents believed it was a matter of professional courtesy and ethics not to "poach" firms from neighboring cities and regions – despite that doing so might be in their job description and the value proposition might be clear. Others remarked that they do not poach, but "of course" if a firm inquires, they respond... This murky situation becomes clear under the law in New York State and in Canada, where ordinances or regional pacts disallow stealing companies from neighbors. Luring firms from more distant locales appears (to our respondents) to be acceptable.

Many respondents emphasized the importance of training opportunities. Corporate relocation appears to be a game, with municipalities and companies seeking a Nash equilibrium: Companies want to locate where, possibly due to the strengths of local universities, an educated workforce is available (and their education already paid for). Cities want the incoming company to provide, and pay for, additional training for hires and potential hires.

No respondents or discussion participants, however, used the expected phrase "family-wage jobs." It is not just that locales want residents to be able to support families: IncentivesMonitor.com reports that the average incentive cost per job in 2015 was US $34, 364. Thus, any city's hope of a positive ROI rests on the creation of jobs that pay approximately that much or more (with tax revenue, defaults, and desired payback periods complicating the calculation).

The panel results and cases highlight the importance of program audits and performance reviews.

In recent news (late 2018 and early 2019, respectively), Netflix accepted New Mexico's incentives for placing production in Albuquerque, and Amazon rejected New York's generous subsidy offer. Both circumstances illustrate the multidimensional (STEEP and beyond) nature of the incentive process. Reading the ample news coverage of Amazon's warehouse labor practices, neighborhood residents in New York (perhaps most vocally, Representative Alexandra Ocasio-

Cortez) could not see the value to New Yorkers in subsidizing sub-family-wage jobs and opposed the Amazon plan. Two Republican New Mexico State Representatives (Bandy and Anderson 2019) decried the corporate welfare extended to Netflix, remarking, "Imagine the problems that $1 billion[5] could be applied to solving in our State."

Criticism of relocation incentives thus can originate in the political left or the right, sometimes based on facts, sometimes on perceptions[6] – and sometimes, perhaps, on hidden motivations. Bandy and Anderson (2019), for example, call the Netflix deal "the most bloated subsidy offered to Hollywood anywhere in the United States." Is their opposition to it due to distaste for corporate welfare, a rare attitude for conservatives? Is it because Netflix (unlike Amazon) will bring union jobs? Or is their dismissive mention of "Hollywood" a euphemism suggesting a subtle bigotry?[7]

Pew Charitable Trusts (2015) state, "Although every state delivers tax incentives for economic development, there are numerous inconsistencies in how these incentives are evaluated." Pew recommends identifying clear, measurable goals for each incentive, selecting appropriate metrics and a reasonable timeframe for analysis, placing more emphasis on how incentives affect residents (jobs, wages, economic security); and, identifying opportunities for improvement and encouraging lawmakers to regularly review incentives. The research described in this paper helps fulfill these objectives.

Acknowledgments The authors are grateful to the executives of the Council for Community and Economic Research (C2ER), the Western Regional Science Association (WRSA), World Technopolis Association (WTA), and General Informatics, LLC, for assistance in disseminating the data collection instrument. We appreciate the research assistance of Ephraim Patrick Msang'azi. This research was also partially supported by the Ministry of Science, ICT, and Future Planning (MSIP), Republic of Korea, under the "ICT Consilience Creative Program" (reference number IITP-2015-R0346-15-1007) and supervised by the Institute for Information and Communications Technology Promotion (IITP).

---

[5]The New Mexico program is not a tax abatement, but a direct refund of expenses. Bandy and Anderson (2019) claim that media production companies "can be refunded as much as 35% of their qualified expenditures," with an annual cap of $110 million. "New Mexico taxpayers are now on the hook for at least $750 million over the next five years to subsidize the creation of movies and television programs in New Mexico." Though each media job created costs the State $39,000, only slightly above the national average and quite a bit less than many federal government programs, Bandy and Anderson claim the State gets only 40¢ back in taxes on every dollar spent on incentives.

[6]Including perceptions (or posturing) about the other party's negotiating skills. Referring to New York, an Amazon spokesperson remarked, "A number of state and local politicians have made it clear that they oppose our presence and will not work with us to build the type of relationships that are required to go forward. . ." (https://www.cnbc.com/2019/02/15/ny-state-senator-michael-gianaris-defends-stopping-amazon-deal.html). State Sen. Michael Gianaris (D-Queens) said, "Amazon is more interested in shakedowns than constructive dealings with the community. [Their withdrawal] shows they would have been a bad partner. Instead of negotiating, they took their bat and ball and walked away" (https://nypost.com/2019/02/14/politicians-point-fingers-after-amazon-ditches-nyc-headquarters/).

[7]We have no evidence that it is or that it isn't. Yet one cannot read their op-ed without the thought at least occurring.

References

Adelman J (2016) Aramark to keep its world HQ in Philadelphia. Philadelphia Inquirer, April 7

Aguilar FJ (1967) Scanning the business environment. Macmilllan, New York

Albahari A, Pérez-Canto S, Barge-Gil A, Modrego A (2013) Technology Parks versus Science Parks: does the university make the difference? Munich Personal RePEc Archive. https://mpra.ub.uni-muenchen.de/49227/1/MPRA_paper_49227.pdf

Amer M, Daim T (2013) Expert judgment quantification Muhammad Amer and Tugrul Daim Abstract. In: Daim T, Oliver T, Kim J (eds) Research and technology management in the electricity industry. Springer, London, pp 31–65. https://doi.org/10.1007/978-1-4471-5097-8

Bandy P, Anderson P (2019) Lights! Camera! Taxpayer Giveaways! Albuquerque Sunday J, June 30, p A11

Bartik TJ (2017) A new panel database on business incentives for economic development offered by state and local governments in the United States. W.E. Upjohn Institute for Employment Research for Pew Charitable Trusts. Kalamazoo, Michigan. Retrieved from https://research.upjohn.org/reports/225/

Berry FS, Berry WD (1992) Tax innovation in the States: capitalizing on political opportunity. Am J Polit Sci 36(3):715–742. Retrieved from http://www.jstor.org/stable/2111588

Blair JP, Premus R (1987) Major factors in industrial location: a review. Econ Dev Q 1(1):72–85

Bolnick B (2004) Effectiveness and economic impact of tax incentives in the SADC region. Retrieved from http://pdf.usaid.gov/pdf_docs/PNACY929.pdf

Carlson V (1999) Studying firm locations: survey responses vs. Econo Models 2000:1–22

Chapman J (2016, December). Evaluating the effectiveness of State tax incentives, 5–7. Kauffman Foundation Thoughtbook, pp 4–7. http://www.kauffman.org/thoughtbook2015/exploring-and-engaging#entrepreneurshipstartsathome

Chen WH (2016) Biomedical industry development project approved: the government plans to invest NT$10.94 billion in the industry next year to develop large-scale healthcare firms, new drugs and new medical devices. Taipei Times, Nov 11, Page 1. http://www.taipeitimes.com/News/front/archives/2016/11/11/2003659017

Chesto J (2016) General Electric Co. may end up paying Boston tens of millions in property taxes Boston Globe, April 2

Copelin L (2012) Chief of state tech fund panel looking for greater efficiency. Austin American-Statesman, January 15

Copelin L (2013a) Business incentives report too flimsy: released to no fanfare, report leaves key policy questions unanswered. Austin American-Statesman, February 18

Copelin L (2013b) Economic development programs should have to account for spending. Austin American-Statesman, April 22

Copelin L (2013c) CPRIT reform bill nears passage. Austin American-Statesman, May 19

Copelin L (2014) Who gets credit if firms pick Texas? Austin American-Statesman, May 12

Deloitte (2014) 2014 Global survey of R & D tax incentives. Retrieved from http://www2.deloitte.com/content/dam/Deloitte/global/Documents/Tax/dttl-tax-global-rd-survey-aug-2014.pdf

Desai A, Gulledge TR, Haynes KE, Shroff HFE, Storbeck JE (1991) A DEA approach to siting decision sensitivity. Reg Sci Rev 18:71–78

Fox S (1991) The motivations and impacts of business incentive policy adoption in the American states (1970–1989) (Doctoral dissertation). University of Illinois at Chicago

Frankel TC (2017). How Foxconn's broken pledges in Pennsylvania cast doubt on Trump's jobs plan. Retrieved March 22, 2017, from https://www.washingtonpost.com/business/economy/how-foxconns-broken-pledges-in-pennsylvania-cast-doubt-on-trumps-jobs-plan/2017/03/03/0189f3de-ee3a-11e6-9973-c5efb7ccfb0d_story.html?utm_term=.5d2d6b5607e4

Gaar B (2012) Texas Enterprise Fund leaders: 'Process works' on incentive deals. Austin American-Statesman, April 24

Germain ML (2006) Stages of psychometric measure development: the example of the generalized expertise measure (GEM). Academy of Human Resource Development, (1993), pp 893–898.

Retrieved from http://citeseerx.ist.psu.edu/viewdoc/download?doi=10.1.1.107.6379&rep=rep1&type=pdf
Gladwell M (2008) Outliers, 1st edn. Little, Brown and Company, New York
Goren D (2007) Economic development incentives: research approaches and current views. Federal Reserve Bulletin, Volume 93. Retrieved from http://www.federalreserve.gov/pubs/bulletin/2008/articles/econdevelopment/default.htm
Grabar H (2017) Corporate incentives don't work and cost the U.S. $45 billion in 2015. Retrieved March 22, 2017, from http://www.slate.com/blogs/moneybox/2017/03/10/corporate_incentives_don_t_work_and_cost_the_u_s_45_billion_in_2015.html
Ham JJ (2014) Entrepreneurial financing: program review and policy perspective. STI Policy Rev 5 (1):75–97
Harrell B (2012) Key Austin business recruiter: retaining jobs just as important as bringing new ones. Austin American-Statesman, June 11
Hicks MJ (2014) Why tax incentives don' t work: the altered landscape of local economic development. Retrieved from http://projects.cberdata.org/reports/TaxIncentivesDontWork-paper.pdf
Jain RK (2012) A comparison of economic development between Texas cities using the economic development Tax 4a/4b and Texas cities not using the tax (Doctoral dissertation). University of Texas at Arlington
Jansa JM, Gray V (2016) Industry influence and state economic development subsidies in the great recession era. Econ Dev Q 31(1):50–64
Kimelberg SM, Williams E (2013) Evaluating the importance of business location factors: the influence of facility type. Growth Chang 44(1):92–117. https://doi.org/10.1111/grow.12003
Kocaoglu DF (1987) Hierarchical decision modeling. Engineering management program, Portland State University, 1–30
Ladendorf K (2012) City rarely uses tax incentives. Austin American-Statesman, April 24
Lester TW, Lowe NJ, Freyer A (2014) Mediating incentive use: a time-series assessment of economic development deals in North Carolina. Econ Dev Q. https://doi.org/10.1177/0891242413514771
Linstone HA (1981) The multiple perspective concept with applications to technology assessment and other decision areas. Technol Forecast Soc Chang 20(4):275–325. https://doi.org/10.1016/0040-1625(81)90062-7
Linstone HA (1985) Multiple perspectives: overcoming the weaknesses of MS/OR. Interfaces 15 (4):77–85. https://doi.org/10.1287/inte.15.4.77
Linstone H (1999) Decision-making For technology executives using multiple perspectives to improve performance. Artech House, Boston
Linstone HA (2010) Multiple perspectives Redux. Technol Forecast Soc Chang 77(4):696–698. https://doi.org/10.1016/j.techfore.2010.02.009
Martin BR, Muûls M, De Preux LB, Wagner UJ (2014) Industry compensation under relocation risk: a firm-level analysis of the EU emissions trading scheme. Am Econ Rev 104:2482–2508. https://doi.org/10.1257/aer.104.8.2482
Migdal B (2016) Weighing economic incentives in the location decision. Area Development. Q1. http://www.areadevelopment.com/taxesIncentives/Q1-2016/Weighing-Economic-Incentives-Location-Decision-345566.shtml
Pew Charitable Trusts (2015) Tax incentive programs
Philippidis A (2016) Job performance clouds sunshine State Biocluster. Florida Sees promising research, but it has come at a price. Genetic engineering & biotechnology news
Rohrbaugh J (1979) Improving the quality of group judgment Social judgment analysis and the Delphi Technique. Organ Behav Hum Perform 24(1):73–92
Russo J (2014) START-UP NY: a game changer For The 'New' New York. Site Selection Magazine, May. http://siteselection.com/issues/2014/may/sas-empire-state.cfm

Rutherford JW (2012) What are the effects of tax abatements and government incentives on economic development? A study of select Texas cities (Doctoral dissertation). University of Texas at Dallas

Ryan G (2017) In a first, state claws back EDIP job creation tax incentive from Warren Buffett-owned firm. Boston Bus J (1/21/17):1–2

Saaty TL (2008) Decision making with the analytic hierarchy process. Int J Serv Sci 1(1):83. https://doi.org/10.1504/IJSSCI.2008.017590

Sayre K (2003) Task force focuses on companies. The Daily Texan, April 17, p 1

Sheikh NJ (2013) Assessment of solar photovoltaic technologies using multiple perspectives and hierarchical decision modeling (Ph.D. Dissertation). ProQuest/UMI (UMI Number: 3568075), pp 1–238

Sheikh NJ (2015). Dissent and games as a consideration in decision making: case of solar photovoltaic technologies. In: 2015 proceedings of PICMET'15: management of the technology age, pp 374–380

Sheikh N, Kocaoglu DF (2011) A comprehensive assessment of solar photovoltaic technologies: literature review. In: 2011 proceedings of PICMET 11 technology management in the energy smart World PICMET 1–11, IEEE

Sheikh NJ, Kim K, Kocaoglu DF (2016) Use of Hierarchical Decision Modeling to Select Target Markets for a New Personal Healthcare Device. Health Policy Technol 5(2):1–38. https://doi.org/10.1016/j.hlpt.2015.12.001

Site Selection (2014) State incentive programs. November

Walker JL (1969) The diffusion of innovations among the American states. Am Polit Sci Rev 63 (3):880–899. https://doi.org/10.2307/1954434

Wolkoff MJ (1985) Chasing a Dream: The Use of Tax Abatements to Spur Urban Economic Development. Urban Studies 22(4):305–315. https://doi.org/10.1080/00420988520080541

Chapter 26
The Creative Class and National Economic Performance

Richard Florida and Charlotta Mellander

Abstract The role of human capital in shaping cross-national innovative and economic performance is well-understood. But human capital is an indirect measure of skill, based on educational attainment. We introduce and test a more direct measure of skill, based on work that is actually performed, measured by occupation. Empirical studies have shown that such occupational "classes" play an important role in regional economic performance, outperforming human capital in some cases. We employ a measure of occupational skill (the Creative Class) and examine its relation to cross-national innovative and economic performance. We explicitly compare this measure to conventional measures of human capital (based on educational attainment) through formal models of economic performance for 55–78 countries, using 3 measures of innovative and economic performance – innovation (patents), productivity (total factor productivity), and economic output (GDP per capita). The results confirm the hypothesis, indicating that our occupation-based Creative Class measure closely is associated with all three measures of innovative and economic performance and also that it consistently performs better than human capital in these models.

Keywords Creative Class · Education · Innovation · Occupation · Productivity

JEL J24 · J82 · O50

R. Florida
University of Toronto's School of Cities and Rotman School of Management, University of Toronto, Toronto, Canada

New York University's Schack Institute of Real Estate, New York University, New York, NY, USA
e-mail: richard.florida@rotman.utoronto.ca

C. Mellander (✉)
Jönköping International Business School, Jönköping, Sweden
e-mail: charlotta.mellander@ju.se

Z. Chen et al. (eds.), *Development Studies in Regional Science*, New Frontiers in Regional Science: Asian Perspectives 42,
https://doi.org/10.1007/978-981-15-1435-7_26

26.1 Introduction

The role of human capital in shaping economic growth is well-established. Romer (1986) and Lucas (1988) provide compelling theoretical reasons why knowledge accumulation is a central factor in economic growth. Lucas, inspired by Jacobs (1969), argues that knowledge and creative capabilities are key underlying mechanisms of economic growth, human capital externalities, and concentration in cities. Economists and other social scientists have argued that the effect of human capital has to do with a shift in the nature of economies from an industrial or manufacturing base to a postindustrial or knowledge base (Machlup 1962; Bell 1973, 1976; Drucker 1993).

A number of now classic studies (Barro 1991; Becker 1993; Barro and Lee 1993) empirically document the role of human capital for productivity, earnings, and economic growth within and across nations. The role of human capital on economic growth has also been shown in models of regional growth. Several studies (Rauch 1993; Simon and Nardinelli 1996; Simon 1998; Berry and Glaeser 2005) find strong empirical evidence of the role of human capital in the growth of US regions.

But human capital, at bottom, is a proximate measure for skill. Recent research, much of it in urban economics and regional science, contends that occupations provide a more robust measure of skill, by providing a direct measure of the work people actually perform. Several regional-level studies find occupational measures to be closely associated with regional economic performance (Florida 2002; Markusen 2004; Marlet and Van Woerkens 2004; Florida et al. 2008). Marlet and Van Woerkens (2004) provide empirical proof that both human capital and creative occupations (including science, technology, the arts, media, and professions) predict employment growth in Dutch regions, but that the occupational measure is relatively stronger than human capital in explanatory value.

This paper tests a simple hypothesis. It argues that occupation plays a fundamental role, in cross-national innovative and economic performance. Providing a more direct measure of skill than education, we argue that our occupational measure should both predict cross-national variation in innovative and economic performance, and also outperform conventional human capital in doing so.

Our research tests this hypothesis through a series of formal models of innovative and economic performance for 55–78 countries. Our models compare occupations and human capital measures across three standard measures of innovative and economic performance –innovation (patents), productivity (total factor productivity), and economic output (GDP per capita).

The findings of the empirical analysis confirm the hypothesis. Occupation is closely related to cross-national innovative and economic performance; and it consistently outperforms educational measures of human capital in our models.

26.2 Concepts and Theory

The role of human capital in shaping economic growth is well-established. Nelson and Phelps (1966) examined the impact of human capital on the national absorptive capacity of new ideas and new technologies, which they found affects the ability of leading nations to catch up. Becker (1993) revealed a link between education and productivity levels at the individual level, which ultimately affects the wage level. Human capital is included as a variable in many endogenous growth models. Romer (1986, 1990) considers human capital to be a key factor behind innovation and technological progress; a factor that can be influenced through investments in education. Building on Romer's work, Krugman (1991) and Grossman and Helpman (1991) have stressed the role of local knowledge spillovers in economic growth. In detailed cross-national empirical studies, (Barro 1991) found clear evidence of the effect of educational attainment on national growth levels, using data from more than 100 countries from 1965 to 1995.

The importance of human capital has also been a key finding in regional economics. Lucas (1988) examined the impact of investments in human capital on growth and stressed that the accumulation of human capital is a social activity involving group interactions, whereas accumulation of physical capital is not. These group interactions take place in cities, they give rise to human capital externalities, and in the end, they are a key mechanism of economic growth. Lucas draws upon Jacobs (1969), who earlier argued that knowledge and creative capabilities are key mechanisms of economic growth, human capital externalities, and concentration in cities. Extending Lucas' reasoning about human capital as a social good with human capital externalities, Rauch (1993) suggested that human capital should earn higher wages in human capital rich regions than in human capital poor ones. Simon and Nardinelli (1996) focused on the role of cities as arenas for face-to-face interaction for human capital and examined the impact it has on regional economic growth between 1861 and 1961. Their work is rare in that it uses occupational classes as proxies for human capital, rather than the educational levels of the population. Simon (1998) as well as Glaeser et al. (1995) showed the regional human capital effect on employment growth, and Berry and Glaeser (2005) examined the path dependency of the distribution of human capital across cities over time.

Recent research in regional science and urban economics has argued that occupations provide a better, more direct measure of skill than educational human capital. A series of empirical studies have found that occupations can be efficiently grouped into large classes and that these classes tend to outperform standard human capital measures in explaining differences in levels of regional development (Florida, 2002; Marlet and Van Woerkens 2004).

Previous research identifies three broad groupings or "classes" of occupations (Machlup 1962; Bell 1973, 1976; Wright et al. 1982; Wright 1990; Drucker 1993;

Florida 2002; Florida and Martin 2009). The first type is *routine physical work* which includes occupations in manufacturing, production, transportation, and construction. Occupations such as derrick operators, firefighters, electricians, mechanics, and roofers require high levels of physical skills such as dexterity, coordination, and strength, but lower levels of cognitive problem-solving skills. *Routine service occupations* are the second type of work; they include jobs in food preparation and food-service-related occupations, building and grounds cleaning and maintenance, personal care and service, low-end sales, office and administrative support, community and social services, and protective services. These occupations are also more routine and require low levels of analytical, cognitive, or problem-solving skills. The third type of work is work that depends on knowledge, creativity, and cognitive skill. It is referred to variously in previous studies as *knowledge, cognitive, professional, and/or creative work* (Machlup 1962; Bell 1973, 1976; Wright et al. 1982; Wright 1990; Drucker 1993; Brint 1994; Florida 2002).

Based on the work by Florida (2002), we group occupations into three clusters or classes in our analysis; Creative Class, Service Class, and Working Class. This follows the tripartite occupational scheme advanced by Florida (2002) with adaptation and revision based on more recent research and the structure of cross-national data. It is worth noting that while there has been some debate over elements of Florida's work – particularly his findings regarding the relationship between openness, human capital, and economic performance – there is an emerging consensus over this occupational classification system. Glaeser (2004) argued that the Creative Class explains little that is not already explained by human capital measures. However, McGranahan and Wojan (2007) made minor adjustments to the Creative Class measure and evaluated its strength in relation to more traditional human capital and found it more robust in explaining regional employment growth. Marlets and Van Woerkens (2004) found that the Creative Class would explain employment growth more than educational levels in Dutch regions. Florida et al. (2008) systematically tested the role of human capital and creative occupations against several measures of regional economic performance and found that human capital is more closely associated with incomes, while occupations are more closely associated with wages.

Our research is straightforward; this paper aims to examine the role of occupational or occupational skill on cross-national innovative and economic performance. While the importance of educational human capital has been emphasized in economic theory and documented in empirical studies, the role of occupation skill has not been tested in cross-national studies. We argue that occupation provides a more direct measure of skill, and as such it is likely to outperform conventional education-based measures of human capital in predicting cross-national innovative and economic performance.

We test this proposition with formal models of innovative and economic performance for 55–78 countries. We compare the relative strength of the occupational and educational skill (human capital) variables in regressions using three widely used economic performance measures – innovation (patents), productivity (total factor productivity), and economic output (GDP per capita) – as dependent variables.

26.3 Methodology

We focus our analysis on the relationship between Creative Class occupations and cross-national innovative and economic performance. Taking into account Glaeser's (2004) contention that the Creative Class occupations and human capital may reflect the same underlying role of skills, we also include standard human capital measures in our models to control for this. In addition, we also let education explain the share of Creative Class occupations, to examine how much that is left unexplained in a straightforward regression. Our analysis is designed to examine the relative strength of Creative Class occupations and educational human capital in explaining three measures of innovative and economic performance – patents, total factor productivity (TFP), and GDP per capita. We also control for the role of specific countries/continents (OECD, EU15, and Asia), as well as physical capital and investments in R&D.

We utilize data from a number of different data sources across 55–78 countries. Unfortunately, some of the data is not available to all countries for every year, so the number of observations varies to some degree. In order to increase the number of observations, and also to smooth out any extreme values, we use the average values for these variables (as indicated below). We excluded African countries from the data set for two reasons: data scarcity and because they constitute extreme outliers which distort the overall outcome.

26.3.1 *Variables*

Dependent Variables
We employ three dependent variables in our analysis, as noted above: a measure of innovation (patents), productivity (total factor productivity), and economic output per capita (GDP per capita).

Patents Patents are a commonly used measure of technological innovation and innovative performance (e.g., Jaffe 1986; Audretsch and Feldman 1996; Jaffe and Trajtenberg 2002). We employ patent data from two different sources: the US Patent and Trademark Office (USPTO) and the World Intellectual Property Office (WIPO). Inventors from around the world file for patent protection in the United States, and the USPTO tracks the origin of the inventor, we can count the number of *granted* US patents for each nation in the world. This file can undercount (sometimes radically) inventions in other countries due to the fact that not every inventor files for a US patent. Therefore, we also include the number of patents reported to the WIPO by each national patent office. Both variables are expressed as patents per capita. The USPTO data is for year 2001–2008, while the WIPO data is for year 2000–2007.

Total Factor Productivity Ever since Solow (1956), it has been established that long-run economic growth is determined by the "residual factor" or total factor productivity (TFP). Easterly and Levine (2001) have provided compelling evidence that cross-country differences in both the level and growth rate of GDP per capita are explained by TFP, not factor accumulation. Based on work by Gollin (2002) we could expect capital to be approximately 1/3 and labor to account for 2/3. We then calculate the TFP as the residual (log scale): $\ln \text{TFP} = \ln Y - \frac{1}{3}\ln K - \frac{2}{3}\ln L$.

The data is from the World Development Indicators and is for 2006.

GDP per Capita GDP per capita is a standard measure of economic performance. This measure is based on 2005 data from the World Development Indicators.

Independent Variables
We employ several classes of independent variables.

Human Capital We employ two standard measures of human capital.

Barro-Lee Human Capital The first is the well-known Barro and Lee measure of human capital (Barro and Lee 2001), which measures the population's average number of years in education.

WDI Human Capital The second is based on the World Development Indicators Tertiary Education Enrollment data, which is defined as the share of the proper age group enrolled in tertiary education. Tertiary education refers to training at a wide range of post-secondary education institutions, including technical and vocational schools, community colleges, and universities, which normally require as a minimum condition of admission the successful completion of education at the secondary level. Since these data are not reported for each country every year, we calculate an average for the reported numbers for the years 2001–2006.

Occupational Measures We employ the following classification.

Creative Class Occupations Following previous research (Machlup 1962; Drucker 1993; Florida 2002), the Creative Class occupations are those that involve high levels of cognitive skill, complex problem-solving, relatively autonomous decision-making, and independent judgment. The Creative Class occupations include: computer science and mathematics; architecture, engineering; life, physical, and social science; education, training, and library science; arts and design work, entertainment, sports, and media; and professional and knowledge work occupations in management, business and finance, law, sales management, healthcare, and education. The variable is measured as a share of the total employed labor force. The data is from the International Labor Organization. The data this variable is based on is not reported by each country annually; in order to increase the number of observations, we calculate an average for the reported numbers for the years 2001–2007.

Working Class Occupations This group consists of occupations characterized by routine physical skill. It includes occupations in construction and extraction, installation, maintenance and repair, production, transportation, and material moving occupations. The variable is measured as share of the regional labor force. The data is from the International Labor Organization. We calculate an average for the reported numbers for the years 2001–2007, to increase the number of observations.

Service Class Occupations This group consists of traditional and standard services (separate from more knowledge-based services), such as food preparation and food-service-related occupations, building and grounds cleaning and maintenance, personal care and service, low-end sales, office and administrative support, community and social services, and protective services. This variable is measured as share of the total employed labor force. Service Class occupations are based on occupational data from the International Labor Organization. We calculate an average for the reported numbers for the years 2001–2007, to increase the number of observations.

Control Variables We use a variety of control variables in our analysis.

Physical Capital Since GDP, as well as labor productivity, is a function of both capital and labor in the neoclassical context, we include a control variable for physical capital in our regressions for GDP per capita. This measure is based on 2005 data from the World Development Indicators. However, since the number of observations is small, we will run this regression both with and without the physical capital control variable.

R&D Expenditure Innovation, namely, patent production, is a function not only of knowledge levels but also of the capital investments made in R&D (e.g., Jaffe 1989, 2000). We include a control variable for R&D investments – measured as the R&D share of l GDP. This is based on 2005 data from the World Development Indicators. Since the number of observations for this variable is small, we perform regressions with and without this control variable.

We add three additional control (dummy) variables to the above measures, in order to control for continent/country:

OECD This dummy variable indicates if the country is an OECD member. This includes the following nations: Australia, Austria, Belgium, Canada, the Czech Republic, Denmark, Finland, France, Germany, Greece, Hungary, Iceland, Ireland, Italy, Japan, Mexico, the Netherlands, New Zealand, Norway, Portugal, the Republic of Korea, Slovakia, Spain, Sweden, Switzerland, Turkey, the United Kingdom, and the United States.

EU15 This dummy variable indicates if the country is one of the EU15 countries (before the extension of the number of EU member states). This includes Austria, Belgium, Denmark, Finland, France, Germany, Greece, Ireland, Italy, Luxembourg, the Netherlands, Portugal, Spain, Sweden, and the United Kingdom.

Asia This dummy variable indicates if the country is located in Asia, and it includes the following nations: Armenia, Azerbaijan, Bangladesh, Cambodia, China, Georgia, Indonesia, Iran, Israel, Japan, Kazakhstan, Kyrgyzstan, Macau, Malaysia, Maldives, Pakistan, Philippines, the Republic of Korea, Russian Federation, Saudi Arabia, Singapore, Sri Lanka, the Syrian Arab Republic, Thailand, Turkey, and Vietnam. We are well aware of the variance in economic performance of the Asian countries but expect this difference to partly be captured by the OECD variable.

Table 26.1 Descriptive statistics

	N	Minimum	Maximum	Mean	Std. Deviation
USPTO patents	94	0.00	25.35	2.36	4.80
WIPO patents	106	0.00	76.66	7.64	14.98
TFP	78	4.98	8.36	6.82	0.878
GDP per capita	98	326	41,446	10,260	11,631
Creative class	116	3.31	46.57	26.16	10.56
Service class	116	3.13	46.06	24.51	8.50
Working class	116	10.35	74.49	34.95	10.53
Barro-Lee human capital	69	2.58	12.05	7.89	2.16
WDI human capital	97	0.43	86.74	38.11	21.40

Table 26.2 Correlation matrix for occupation and human capital variables (logged relations)

Variables	Creative class	Barro-Lee human capital	WDI human capital
Economic variables			
USPTO patents	0.731***	0.747***	0.593***
WIPO patents	0.774***	0.731***	0.668***
TFP	0.715***	0.733***	0.590***
GDP per capita	0.644***	0.747***	0.516***
Other occupational classes			
Service class	0.423***	0.275**	0.337**
Working class	0.019	−0.250**	−0.105
Continent dummies			
OECD	0.513***	0.556***	0.445***
EU15	0.429***	0.342***	0.361***
ASIA	−0.385***	−0.269**	−0.326***
Capital			
Physical capital	0.204*	0.351***	0.364***
R&D expenditure	0.630***	0.655***	0.652***

***sign at the 0.01 level
** sign at the 0.05 level
* sign at the 0.1 level

Descriptive statistics for the variables are summarized in Table 26.1.

Since the data is not available for all the nations, we used average levels over a number of years for some of the variables as described above. The maximum amount of nations we have is 116 (for the occupational classes) and the minimum is 69 (for the Barro and Lee human capital measure). We do not employ all the variables simultaneously but substitute them where suitable to check for robustness.

Table 26.2 provides a simple correlation matrix for our main variables. The Creative Class measure is significantly correlated with both patent measures, USPTO (0.731) and WIPO (0.774), TFP (0.715), and GDP per capita (0.644). It is also correlated with Barro-Lee human capital (0.690) and WDI human capital (0.558).

Barro-Lee human capital is significantly correlated with innovative performance, 0.731 with USPTO patents and 0.747 with WIPO patents, as well as with economic performance: 0.733 with TFP and 0.747 with GDP per capita. We find significant and positive relationships between WDI human capital and each of the economic performance measures: 0.668 to UPTO patents, 0.593 to WIPO patents, 0.590 to TFP, and 0.516 to GDP per capita. Appendix 1 provides scatterplots which illustrate these relationships.

We conduct two simple regressions to test whether the Creative Class and human capital variables include essentially the same information. In the first, we let Barro-Lee human capital explain the Creative Class; the second does the same for WDI human capital. While the results from the first regression show a strong relationship (coefficient of 1.183 and a t-value of 7.794) between Barro-Lee human capital and the Creative Class, more than half of the variation remains unexplained (R2 is 0.476). While Barro-Lee human capital partly explains the Creative Class, the two variables do clearly not contain exactly the same type of information. In the second regression, when we let WDI human capital explain the Creative Class, the coefficient is 0.332 and significant (t-value of 6.550), but the R2 value remains only 0.311. This means that WDI human capital explains less of the Creative Class than Barro-Lee human capital with almost 70% of the relationship left unexplained.

26.4 Regression Findings

We now turn the results of our innovative and economic performance regressions. We focus on the standardized beta-coefficients to examine the relative strength of the variables. Since we are using a cross-sectional data set, we cannot analyze changes over time. We examine the role of the Creative Class and human capital on three measures of innovative and economic performance: patents per capital, TFP, and GDP per capita. For all regressions, we also control for other occupational groups – Working Class and Service Class – and we include country/continent controls.

26.4.1 Skill and Innovative Performance

We begin with patents as a measure of innovative performance. We use the same regression twice for each of the human capital variables and let them explain patent production. While the Barro-Lee human capital can be expected to be more correlated with the Creative Class, the number of observations is smaller (Table 26.3). To check the robustness of the regression and to increase the number of observations, the second regression (Table 26.4) uses WDI human capital.

Table 26.3 Regression result for USPTO granted patents with Barro-Lee human capital included (logged variables)

Model	Unstandardized coefficients		Standardized coefficients	t	Sig.	Collinearity statistics	
	B	Std. Error	Beta			Tolerance	VIF
(Constant)	−20.402	4.205		−4.852	.000		
Creative class	2.701	.576	.415	4.692	.000	.368	2.715
Barro-Lee human capital	3.251	.788	.330	4.124	.000	.451	2.219
Service class	2.546	.681	.227	3.736	.000	.781	1.281
Working class	−1.472	.710	−.131	−2.073	.043	.721	1.387
OECD	.536	.508	.090	1.055	.297	.394	2.541
EU15	.859	.503	.131	1.708	.094	.492	2.031
ASIA	1.304	.480	.168	2.717	.009	.756	1.323
R2	.859						
Obs	56						

Table 26.4 Regression result for USPTO granted patents with WDI human capital included (logged variables)

Model	Unstandardized coefficients		Standardized coefficients	t	Sig.	Collinearity statistics	
	B	Std. Error	Beta			Tolerance	VIF
(Constant)	−18.591	3.382		−5.498	.000		
Creative class	2.995	.580	.469	5.164	.000	.402	2.486
WDI human capital	.663	.426	.131	1.555	.125	.470	2.128
Service class	2.432	.556	.288	4.376	.000	.765	1.308
Working class	−1.029	.583	−.113	−1.765	.083	.813	1.230
OECD	1.354	.536	.229	2.527	.014	.405	2.469
EU15	.412	.570	.060	.722	.473	.485	2.061
ASIA	.820	.465	.122	1.762	.083	.696	1.436
R2	.798						
Obs	68						

The first two regressions (Tables 26.3 and 26.4) use patents granted in the United States as a dependent variable (USPTO). We also perform the regression, using patents reported by WIPO (Tables 26.5 and 26.6). We also test for the relative importance of occupational skill versus educational human capital.

The results of the regressions (Tables 26.3 and 26.4) show that occupational class explains much of the variation in patents. In the first regression, Barro-Lee human capital has a strong influence (St. β of 0.330, t-value of 4.124), but it is again

Table 26.5 Regression result for WIPO patents with Barro-Lee human capital included (logged variables)

Model	Unstandardized coefficients		Standardized coefficients	t	Sig.	Collinearity statistics	
	B	Std. Error	Beta			Tolerance	VIF
(Constant)	−2.253	4.604		−.489	.627		
Creative class	2.660	.629	.493	4.227	.000	.366	2.730
Barro-Lee human capital	2.088	.859	.255	2.431	.019	.452	2.215
Service class	−.673	.745	−.072	−.904	.371	.783	1.276
Working class	−2.291	.771	−.247	−2.969	.005	.721	1.387
OECD	.603	.562	.122	1.073	.289	.386	2.593
EU15	−.268	.547	−.049	−.490	.626	.496	2.018
ASIA	−.024	.522	−.004	−.046	.964	.757	1.320
R2	.761						
Obs	55						

Table 26.6 Regression result for WIPO patents with WDI human capital included (logged variables)

Model	Unstandardized coefficients		Standardized coefficients	t	Sig.	Collinearity statistics	
	B	Std. Error	Beta			Tolerance	VIF
(Constant)	−4.896	2.726		−1.796	.077		
Creative class	2.252	.551	.458	4.084	.000	.330	3.030
WDI human capital	1.248	.412	.320	3.028	.004	.371	2.699
Service class	−.563	.539	−.080	−1.045	.300	.715	1.399
Working class	−1.421	.533	−.187	−2.664	.010	.842	1.188
OECD	1.181	.523	.228	2.258	.028	.406	2.461
EU15	−.524	.558	−.087	−.940	.351	.486	2.059
ASIA	−.106	.453	−.018	−.233	.816	.675	1.482
R2	.747						
Obs	68						

outperformed by the Creative Class (St. β of 0.415, t-value of 4.692). The Service Class is also positive and significant (St. β of 0.227, t-value of 3.736), while the Working Class is negative and significant at the 0.05 level in this context (St. β of −0.131, t-value of −2.073). The larger the nation's share of Working Class occupations, the less innovative we can expect the nation to be. Among the dummy control variables only EU15 comes out as significant at the 0.1 level. In total the regression generates an R2 value of 0.859.

When we substitute WDI human capital, the Creative Class still has the strongest influence (St. β of 0.469, t-value of 5.164), while WDI human capital loses significance. We also, once more, see a relative increase in strength of the Service Class. Among the dummy control variables, the OECD variable is positive and significant at the 0.05 level, and the Asia variable positive and significant at the 0.1 level and the R2 value is 0.798.

We repeat the regressions controlling for the national share of R&D expenditure (see Appendix 2). This variable is significant in both regressions and increases the R2 value approximately by 0.3–0.5. By including this variable, the human capital variables, particularly the Barro-Lee variable, become relatively weaker and are now only significant at the 0.5 level. The Creative Class variable remains relatively stronger than the human capital variables in both regressions.

The next regressions (Tables 26.5 and 26.6) substitute use WIPO patents as the dependent variable.

The results from these regressions (Table 26.5) are fairly consistent with the results in of USPTO regressions. Barro-Lee human capital remains significant (St. β of 0.255, t-value of 2.431), but it is weaker than the Creative Class variable (St. β of 0.493 and a t-value of 4.227). The variable for Service Class occupations loses significance while that for Working Class occupations becomes even stronger and negatively related to national patenting. None of the dummy variables emerges as significant, and the regression generates an R2 of 0.761, which is somewhat weaker than when we used granted USPTO patents as dependent.

The final regression (Table 26.6) includes the WDI human capital variable. The results are consistent with those in Table 26.5. WDI human capital is now significant, which differs from the GDP per capita, TFP, and USPTO patent regressions. However, the Creative Class still outperforms it (β of 0.458 versus 0.320 and a t-value of 4.084 versus 3.028). The variable for the Service Class is still insignificantly related to patent production, and that for Working Class remains negative and significant (now at the 0.05 level). The OECD variable is the only one of the dummy variables that is significant (at the 0.05 level). The R2 is 0.747, which is approximately at the same level as for the regression in Table 26.5, when average years of education were used instead of tertiary education enrollment.

Once again, when we include the control variable for R&D expenditure, it is highly significant and increases the R2 values with or is this by approximately 0.5 (see Appendix 2). The variables affected the most by this control variable are the human capital measures. The Barro-Lee human capital no longer stays significant, and the WDI human capital only is significant at the 0.1 level. The Creative Class variable stays significant at the 0.01 level in both regressions.

26.4.2 *Skill and Productivity*

We now move on to our regression analysis of productivity performance, letting the same independent variables explain national TFP levels (Tables 26.7 and 26.8).

Table 26.7 Regression result for total factor productivity with Barro-Lee human capital included (logged variables)

Model	Unstandardized coefficients B	Unstandardized coefficients Std. Error	Standardized coefficients Beta	t	Sig.	Collinearity statistics Tolerance	Collinearity statistics VIF
(Constant)	2.957	.900		3.286	.002		
Creative class	.654	.116	.414	5.652	.000	.442	2.262
Barro-Lee human capital	.707	.189	.254	3.740	.000	.516	1.937
Service class	.530	.146	.208	3.630	.001	.725	1.380
Working class	−.370	.166	−.124	−2.233	.030	.772	1.296
OECD	.334	.130	.194	2.561	.014	.416	2.406
EU15	.312	.148	.158	2.105	.041	.423	2.366
ASIA	.005	.119	.003	.044	.965	.619	1.615
R2	.886	.869					
Obs	55						

Table 26.8 Regression result for total factor productivity with WDI human capital included (logged variables)

Model	Unstandardized coefficients B	Unstandardized coefficients Std. Error	Standardized coefficients Beta	t	Sig.	Collinearity statistics Tolerance	Collinearity statistics VIF
(Constant)	2.452	.803		3.052	.003		
Creative class	.677	.136	.434	4.987	.000	.446	2.244
WDI human capital	.092	.097	.080	.950	.346	.475	2.106
Service class	.735	.160	.327	4.600	.000	.668	1.498
Working class	−.153	.161	−.060	−.951	.346	.855	1.170
OECD	.504	.166	.265	3.026	.004	.439	2.279
EU15	.317	.197	.140	1.607	.113	.447	2.237
ASIA	.099	.139	.053	.716	.477	.616	1.624
R2	.798						
Obs	67						

Table 26.9 Regression result for GDP per capita with Barro-Lee human capital included (logged variables)

	Unstandardized coefficients		Standardized coefficients			Collinearity statistics	
	B	Std. Error	Beta	t	Sig.	Tolerance	VIF
(Constant)	2.300	1.362		1.689	.097		
Creative class	.931	.179	.386	5.211	.000	.428	2.334
Barro-Lee human capital	.957	.295	.232	3.245	.002	.460	2.173
Service class	1.120	.215	.287	5.204	.000	.774	1.293
Working class	−.658	.250	−.144	−2.628	.011	.781	1.280
OECD	.503	.193	.196	2.614	.011	.418	2.393
EU15	.343	.201	.117	1.709	.093	.504	1.983
ASIA	.185	.176	.062	1.054	.297	.688	1.454
R2	.869						
Obs	63						

In our first regression (Table 26.7), human capital is represented by the Barro-Lee measure. The results show that the Creative Class is the most important factor in explaining TFP, with a standardized beta value of 0.414 (t-value of 5.652). This is followed by the Barro-Lee variable (St. β of 0.208 and a t-value equal to 3.740). Next is Service Class occupations which is also positive and significant (St. β coefficient of 0.208 and a t-value of 3.630). Both the OECD and EU15 control variables are positive and significant, adding further to the explanatory power of our regression, which generates a R2 of 0.886.

When the WDI human capital measure replaces the Barro-Lee measure (Table 26.8), the human capital measure becomes insignificant, and we get an evaluation of the Service Class variable strength (with a standardized beta coefficient of 0.327 and a t-value of 4.600). Here again, the Creative Class tends to most strongly explain total factor productivity, with a standardized beta value of 0.434 (t-value 4.987). Among the control dummy variables, only the OECD factor is significantly related to the total factor productivity. Taken together, the regression generates a R2 value of 0.798.

Again, the Creative Class measure outperforms both human capital variables in explaining TFP. Also, the low VIF values rule out any collinearity problems between the Creative Class and the human capital variables.

26.4.3 Skill and Economic Output

We now turn to the regressions for economic output. We again use the same regression twice for each of the human capital variables. While the Barro-Lee human capital can be expected to be more correlated with the Creative Class, the

Table 26.10 Regression result for GDP per capita with WDI human capital included (logged variables)

Model	Unstandardized coefficients		Standardized coefficients	t	Sig.	Collinearity statistics	
	B	Std. Error	Beta			Tolerance	VIF
(Constant)	1.386	1.204		1.151	.253		
Creative class	.981	.182	.404	5.383	.000	.536	1.866
WDI human capital	.032	.103	.022	.307	.760	.612	1.633
Service class	1.452	.226	.418	6.429	.000	.716	1.397
Working class	−.263	.240	−.066	−1.096	.277	.845	1.183
OECD	.793	.229	.285	3.454	.001	.444	2.254
EU15	.343	.258	.102	1.333	.187	.515	1.941
ASIA	.248	.199	.085	1.248	.216	.644	1.552
R2	.786						
Obs	78						

number of observations is smaller (Table 26.9). To check the robustness of the regression and to increase the number of observations, the second regression (Table 26.10) uses WDI human capital.

From the regression results (Table 26.9), we can see that two occupational groupings – the Creative Class and the Service Class – are significantly and positively related to GDP per capita. Barro-Lee human capital is also positive and significant in relation to the GDP per capita, but the standardized beta value (St. β) tells us that it has relatively lower strength than either the Creative Class or the Service Class (0.232 versus 0.386 and 0.287). The low VIF values (all below 2.4) exclude that the average years of education and the Creative Class include the same information. The variable for Working Class occupations has a negative and significant relation at the 0.05 level (St. β of −0.144 and a t-value of −2.268). Further, we find a positive and significant relation with the OECD dummy, telling us that if the nation is an OECD country, that will add to the explanatory value of the national GDP per capita value. There is also a positive and significant relation with the EU15 variable at the 0.1 level. Taken together, these variables will explain around 85% of the variation (with a R2 of approximately 0.869).

We now move on to the second regression (Table 26.10) where we use the WDI measure of human capital. Two occupational variables – the Creative Class and the Service Class – are again highly significant and positive (St. β of 0.404 and 0.418). The Working Class variable has now lost significance, and the human capital variable is no longer significant. Among the country or continent dummy variables, only OECD stays significant. Taken together, these variables explain approximately 76% of the variation (the R2 is 0.786). Again, we rule out any collinearity problems, since the VIF values are at an acceptable level.

It is important to note that the both the Creative Class and the Service Class variables outperform each of the human capital measures in explaining GDP per capita. This result leads us to conclude that occupational skill better explains GDP per capita than educational human capital.

Since we normally assume GDP per capita to be a function of both labor and physical capital, we also add a regression controlling for physical capital (see Appendix 2). The variable is insignificant in the regression with Barro-Lee human capital and only significant at the 0.1 level in the regression with WDI human capital variable. The Creative Class and human capital variables stay fairly robust. However, the control for physical capital makes the Service Class coefficient slightly weaker. Including this physical capital variable only marginally increases the R2 value in both regressions.

26.5 Conclusion

Our research has examined the role of occupational skill in cross-national innovative and economic performance. We started from the premise that occupation provides a more direct measure of skill than education. We directly tested the role of occupational skill as compared to human capital in regressions models of innovative and economic performance for a cross-section of countries.

Our findings confirm our hypotheses. Our main occupational variable – the Creative Class – a measure of knowledge, creative, and professional occupations, both is significantly related to cross-national innovative and economic performance and consistently outperforms conventional measures of human capital in our models, using three measures of innovative and economic performance: innovation (patents), productivity (TFP), and economic output (GDP per capita). These findings are in line with earlier work by Marlets and Van Woerkens (2004), McGranahan and Wojan (2007), and Florida et al. (2008). We find that while educational and occupational skills are correlated, our analysis shows they are not the same thing. Our regressions between the Creative Class and the two human capital variables leave much of the variance unexplained, with R2 values of 0.476 and 0.311, respectively. Related work shows that while 88% of college educated workers work in the Creative Class occupations in Sweden, only 26% of Creative Class workers have college educations (Mellander 2009).

A second occupational variable – Service Class occupations – is also related to innovative and economic performance. This is likely to be an artifact of occupational/class structure. Economies with larger Creative Class sectors have greater demand for Service Class workers and thus larger concentrations of those occupations. The two variables are correlated (0.432). This is part and parcel of the general economic development process as more advanced economies move away from traditional industrial sectors and Working Class occupations and toward higher concentrations of Creative Class and Service Class occupations.

Working Class occupations are either insignificant or negatively associated with innovative and economic performance. This again appears to be part and parcel of the more general process of economic development. Nations with large manufacturing and production sectors and large shares of routine physical occupations lag on innovation, productivity, and economic output.

In terms of public policy, our findings suggest that nations which want to improve their innovative and economic performance must do more than simply increase educational attainment and outcomes. They should work to shift their occupational structures from less skilled Service and Working Class occupations to more skilled Creative Class ones. That said, the ongoing shift from an older industrial economy to a more knowledge-based and innovative postindustrial economy is rife with challenges. The shift to postindustrialism generates overlapping class and geographic divides which are generating new political cleavages and a deepening populist backlash which is not only divisive but could threaten the investments in science and human capital and open borders and talent flows on which the postindustrial economy depends. To address and preempt these challenges, care must be taken to ensure that innovation is more inclusive and prosperity is more widely shared. In some cases, it may make more sense to move slowly in building a knowledge-driven and innovation economy to make sure a much broader segment of society is included in it. Redistribution to address inequality may also be effective. In related work (Florida et al. 2015), we find that higher creative performance is positively associated with lower levels of economic inequality. We identify two broad national postures to the inequality-creativity trade-off. Nations like the United States and the United Kingdom define a "low road strategy" where higher rates of creativity and innovation are associated with higher levels of inequality. But the Scandinavian and Northern European nations have taken a "high road strategy" where higher levels of creativity are associated with lower levels of inequality. This seems like the more efficacious path from the point of view of both innovative and economic performance and of social cohesion.

Generally speaking our findings suggest that occupations and occupational skill are important factors in cross-national innovative and economic performance, outperforming the conventional human capital measures in our analyses. We want to encourage future research using occupational measures and further clarifying the relationship between these two measures of skill based on education and work.

Appendices

Appendix 1

Innovation Scatter-Plots

WIPO Patents per Capita | **USPTO Patents per Capita**

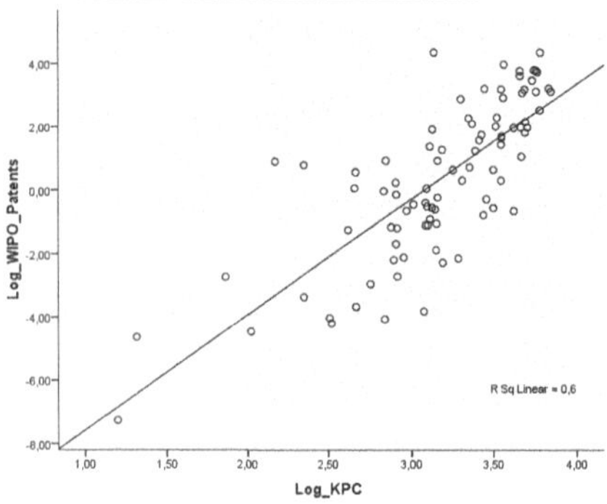

KPC

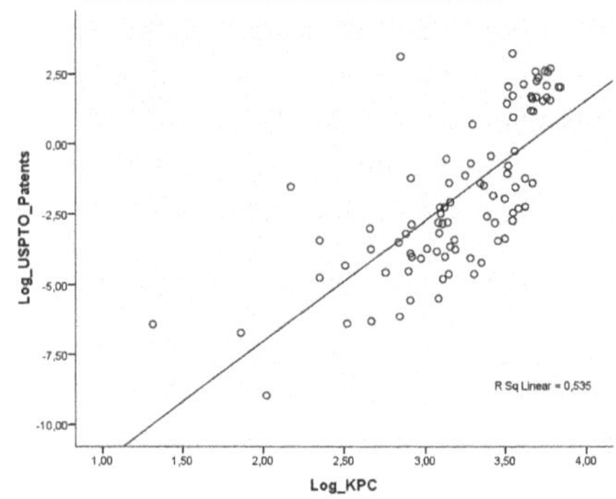

KPC

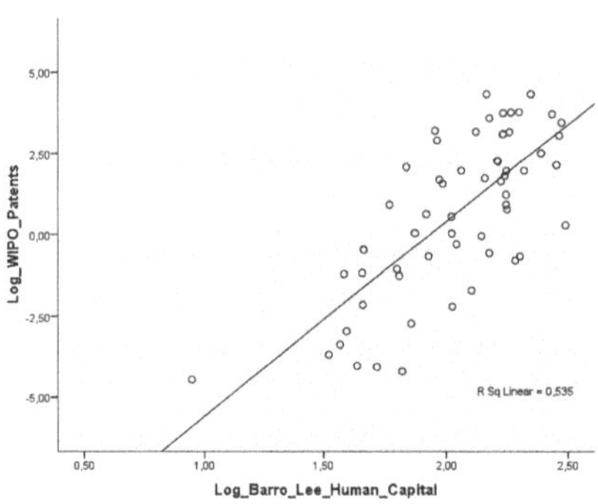

Barro Lee Human Capital

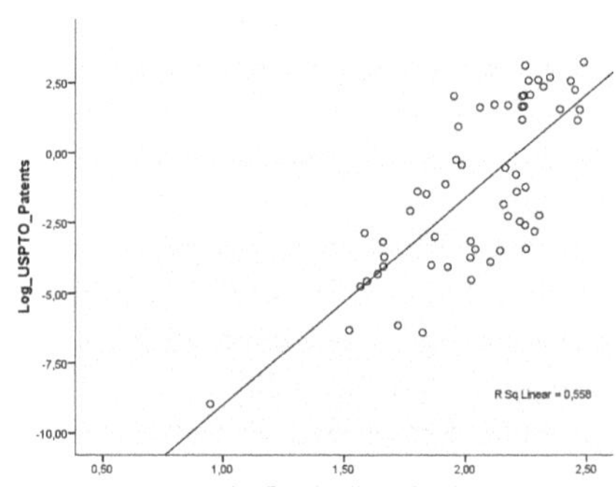

Barro Lee Human Capital

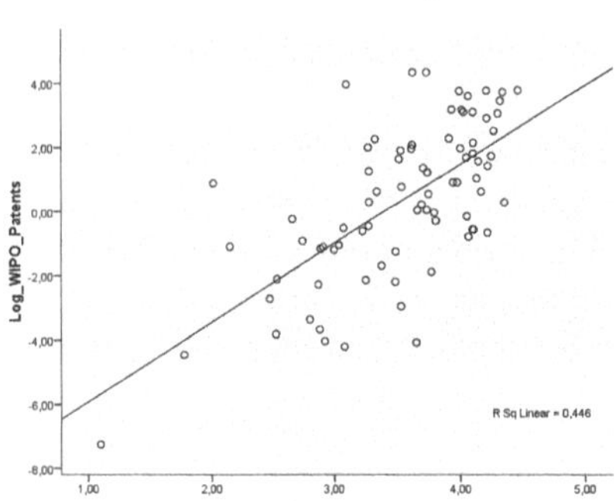

WDI Human Capital

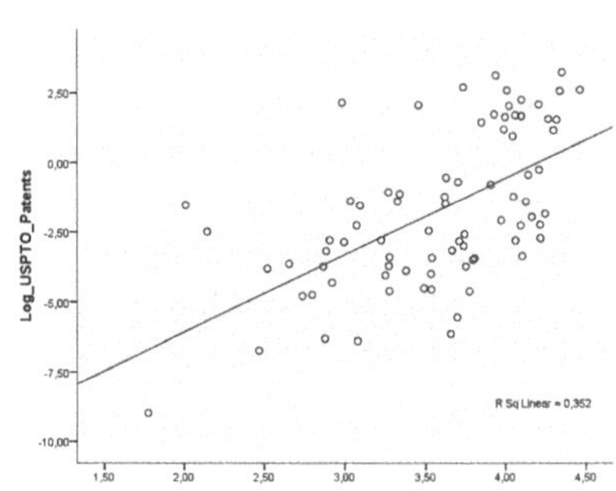

WDI Human Capital

Scatter-Plots for Total Factor Productivity

Scatter-Plots for GDP per Capita

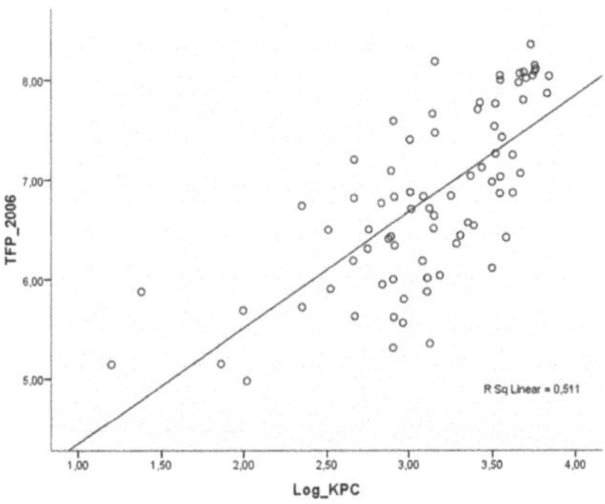

Creative Class

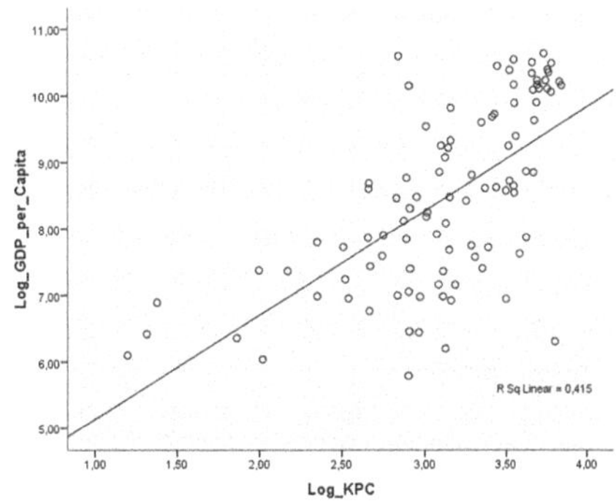

Creative Class

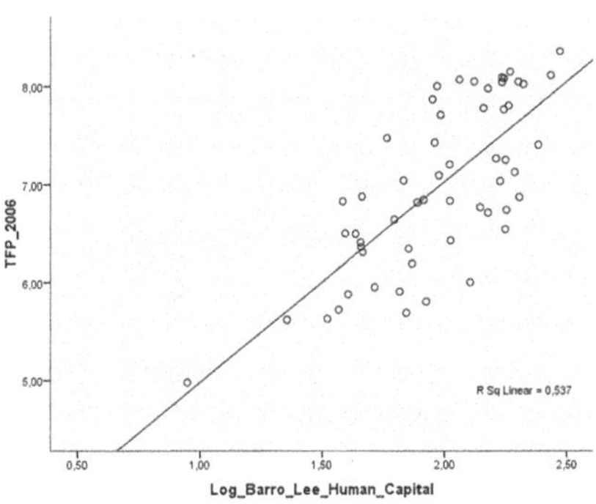

Barro Lee Human Capital

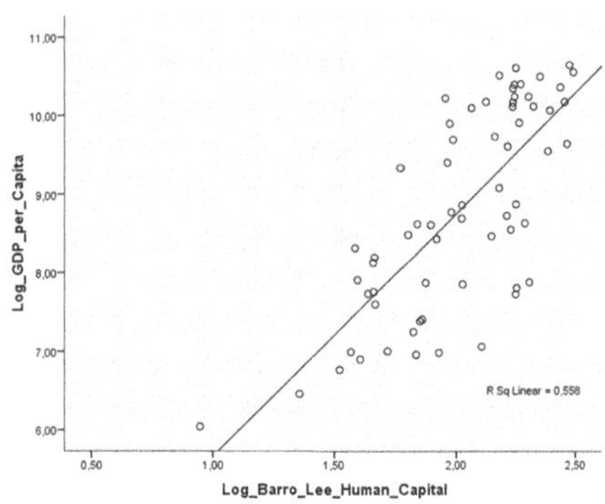

Barro Lee Human Capital

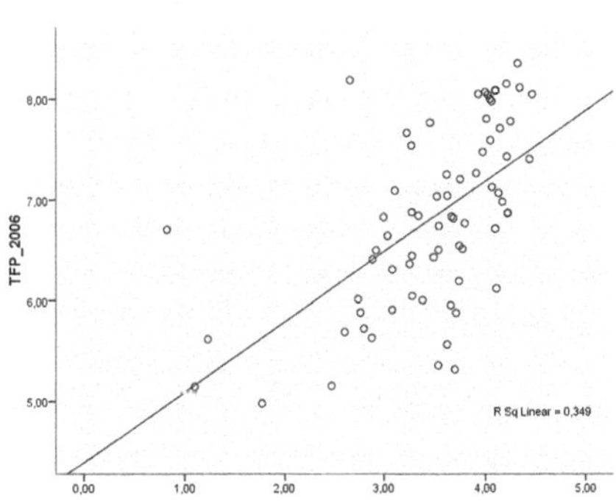

WDI Human Capital

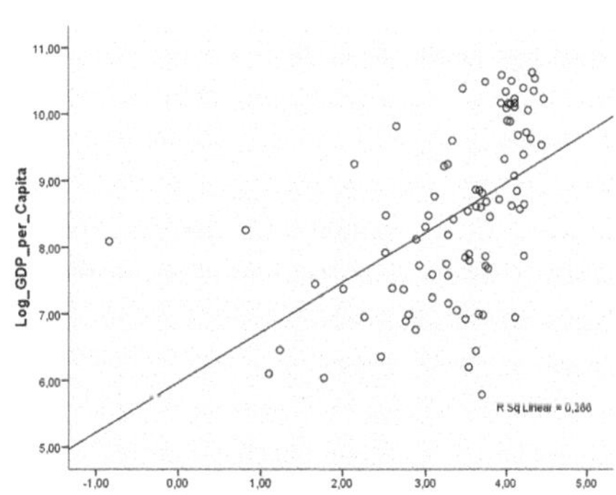

WDI Human Capital

Appendix 2

Tables 26.3 and 26.4 Controlling for national R&D expenditure (USPTO patents per capita)

Model	Unstandardized coefficients		Standardized coefficients	t	Sig.	Collinearity statistics	
	B	Std. Error	Beta			Tolerance	VIF
(Constant)	−10.450	4.523		−2.310	.026		
Creative class	1.966	.548	.294	3.586	.001	.385	2.600
Barro-Lee human capital	1.717	.814	.157	2.110	.041	.465	2.148
Service class	1.542	.640	.149	2.410	.020	.670	1.492
Working class	−1.638	.710	−.148	−2.308	.026	.630	1.587
R&D expenditure	.794	.226	.358	3.505	.001	.247	4.051
OECD	.135	.473	.024	.285	.777	.359	2.788
EU15	.760	.434	.125	1.750	.087	.505	1.979
ASIA	.743	.481	.100	1.543	.130	.615	1.627
R2	.887						
Obs	52						
	Unstandardized coefficients		Standardized coefficients			Collinearity statistics	
Model	B	Std. Error	Beta	t	Sig.	Tolerance	VIF
(Constant)	−9.172	3.424		−2.678	.010		
Creative class	2.075	.540	.320	3.840	.000	.393	2.548
WDI human capital	−.334	.425	−.061	−.785	.436	.454	2.204
Service class	2.121	.492	.263	4.315	.000	.732	1.367
Working class	−1.298	.514	−.147	−2.524	.015	.807	1.239
R&D expenditure	.984	.206	.428	4.782	.000	.340	2.945
OECD	.517	.496	.092	1.043	.302	.353	2.832
EU15	.669	.480	.104	1.395	.169	.494	2.024
ASIA	.616	.423	.093	1.458	.151	.668	1.496
R2	.856						
Obs	61						

Tables 26.5 and 26.6 Controlling for national R&D expenditure (WIPO patents per capita)

Model	Unstandardized coefficients B	Unstandardized coefficients Std. Error	Standardized coefficients Beta	t	Sig.	Collinearity statistics Tolerance	Collinearity statistics VIF
(Constant)	5.128	4.794		1.070	.291		
Creative class	1.848	.577	.345	3.201	.003	.379	2.637
Barro-Lee human capital	.384	.857	.044	.448	.656	.460	2.173
Service class	−1.589	.674	−.192	−2.357	.023	.667	1.499
Working class	−1.655	.741	−.187	−2.234	.031	.630	1.588
R&D expenditure	.826	.237	.467	3.489	.001	.246	4.065
OECD	.384	.502	.085	.765	.448	.354	2.826
EU15	−.326	.453	−.067	−.719	.476	.509	1.963
ASIA	−.672	.503	−.113	−1.337	.188	.617	1.622
R2	.810						
Obs	51						

Model	Unstandardized coefficients B	Unstandardized coefficients Std. Error	Standardized coefficients Beta	t	Sig.	Collinearity statistics Tolerance	Collinearity statistics VIF
(Constant)	−3.273	2.698		−1.213	.230		
Creative class	1.995	.523	.430	3.817	.000	.312	3.204
WDI human capital	.694	.409	.180	1.695	.096	.350	2.861
Service class	−.481	.493	−.075	−.976	.333	.676	1.480
Working class	−1.039	.477	−.148	−2.177	.034	.859	1.164
R&D expenditure	.486	.205	.261	2.368	.022	.326	3.070
OECD	.789	.506	.167	1.560	.125	.346	2.893
EU15	−.351	.484	−.065	−.725	.472	.496	2.015
ASIA	−.108	.425	−.020	−.254	.801	.643	1.555
R2	.791						
Obs	61						

Tables 26.9 and 26.10 Controlling for physical capital (GDP per capita)

Model	Unstandardized coefficients B	Unstandardized coefficients Std. Error	Standardized coefficients Beta	t	Sig.	Collinearity statistics Tolerance	Collinearity statistics VIF
(Constant)	2.590	2.175		1.191	.240		
Creative class	.933	.187	.404	4.985	.000	.440	2.274
Barro-Lee human capital	.892	.310	.219	2.877	.006	.497	2.014
Service class	.895	.243	.232	3.689	.001	.730	1.370
Working class	−.665	.275	−.154	−2.420	.020	.716	1.396
Physical capital	.025	.060	.033	.414	.681	.452	2.213
OECD	.530	.228	.208	2.322	.025	.359	2.787
EU15	.311	.255	.108	1.220	.229	.366	2.732
ASIA	.003	.207	.001	.013	.990	.530	1.888
R2	.873						
Obs	52						

Model	Unstandardized coefficients B	Unstandardized coefficients Std. Error	Standardized coefficients Beta	t	Sig.	Collinearity statistics Tolerance	Collinearity statistics VIF
(Constant)	−.072	1.714		−.042	.967		
Creative class	.930	.228	.397	4.084	.000	.425	2.352
WDI human capital	.065	.157	.039	.414	.680	.448	2.233
Service class	1.258	.269	.365	4.671	.000	.659	1.517
Working class	−.339	.278	−.088	−1.221	.227	.765	1.307
Physical capital	.103	.057	.150	1.806	.076	.584	1.713
OECD	.623	.292	.224	2.132	.037	.363	2.754
EU15	.270	.327	.083	.826	.412	.398	2.511
ASIA	.023	.229	.009	.103	.919	.577	1.732
R2	.779						
Obs	63						

References

Audretsch DB, Feldman MP (1996) R&D spillovers and the geography of innovation and production. Am Econ Rev 86(3):630–640

Barro RJ (1991) Economic growth in a cross section of countries. Q J Econ 106(2):407–443

Barro RJ, Lee J-W (1993) International comparisons of educational attainment. Journal of monetary economics, 32(3):363–394

Barro R, Lee J-W (2001) International data on educational attainment: updates and implications. Oxf Econ Pap 53(3):541–563. Dataset downloadable at: www.klenow.com/Externalities%20and%20Growth%20DATASET.xls

Becker G (1993) Human capital: a theoretical and empirical analysis, with special reference to education. The University Press of Chicago, Chicago

Bell D (1973) The coming of post-industrial society. Basic Books, New York
Bell D (1976) Cultural contradictions of capitalism. Basic Books, New York
Berry CR, Glaeser EL (2005) The divergence of human capital levels across cities. NBER Working Paper No. 11617, September 2005
Brint S (1994) In an age of experts: the changing role of professionals in politics and public life. Princeton University Press, Princeton
Drucker P (1993) Post-capitalist society. Harpers Business, New York
Easterly W, Levine R (2001) It's not factor accumulation: stylized facts and growth models. World Bank Econ Rev 15(2):221–224
Florida R (2002) The rise of the creative class. Basic Books, New York
Florida R, Martin R (2009) Ontario in the creative age. Government of Ontario, Toronto
Florida R, Mellander C, Stolarick K (2008) Inside the black box of regional development. J Econ Geogr 8:615–649
Florida R, Mellander C, King K (2015) The global creativity index. The Martin prosperity institute. Available at: http://www.diva-portal.org/smash/get/diva2:868391/FULLTEXT01.pdf
Glaeser EL (2004) Book review of Richard Florida's "the rise of the creative class". Available at http://post.economics.harvard.edu/faculty/glaeser/papers/Review_Florida.pdf
Glaeser E, Scheinkman J, Shleifer A (1995) Economic growth in a cross-section of cities. J Monet Econ 36:117–143
Gollin D (2002) Getting income shares right. J Polit Econ 110(2):458–474
Grossman G, Helpman E (1991) Comparative advantage and long-run growth. Am Econ Rev 80:796–815
Jacobs J (1969) The economies of cities. Random House, New York
Jaffe AB (1986) Technological opportunity and spillovers of R&D: evidence from firms' patents, profits, and market value. Am Econ Rev 76(5):984–1001
Jaffe AB (1989) Real effects of academic research. Am Econ Rev 79:957–970
Jaffe AB (2000) The U.S. patent system in transition: policy innovation and the innovation process. Res Policy 29:531–557
Jaffe AB, Trajtenberg M (2002) Patents, citations, and innovations: a window on the knowledge economy. MIT Press, Cambridge, MA
Krugman P (1991) Increasing returns and economic geography. J Polit Econ 99(3):483–499
Lucas R (1988) On the mechanics of economic development. J Monet Econ 22(1):3–42
Machlup F (1962) The production and distribution of knowledge in the United States. Princeton University Press, Princeton
Markusen A (2004) Targeting occupations in regional and community economic development. J Am Plan Assoc 70(3):253–268
Marlet G, Van Woerkens C (2004) Skills and creativity in a cross-section of Dutch cities. Discussion Paper Series 04-29, Tjalling C. Koopmans Research Institute
McGranahan D, Wojan T (2007) Recasting the creative class to examine growth processes in rural and urban countries. Reg Stud 41(2):197–216
Mellander C (2009) Creative and knowledge industries – an occupational distribution approach. Econ Dev Q, forthcoming
Nelson R, Phelps E (1966) Investment in Humans, technological diffusion, and economic growth. Am Econ Rev 56(1):69–75
Rauch J (1993) Productivity gains from geographic concentration of human capital: evidence from the cities. J Urban Econ 34:380–400
Romer PM (1986) Increasing returns and long-run growth. J Polit Econ 94(5):1002–1037
Romer PM (1990) Capital, labor and productivity. Brook Pap Econ Act Microecon 21:337–367
Simon C (1998) Human capital and metropolitan employment growth. J Urban Econ 43:223–243
Simon C, Nardinelli C (1996) "The talk of the town: human capital, information and the growth of English cities", 1861–1961. Explor Econ Hist 33(3):384–413
Solow R (1956) A contribution to the theory of economic growth. Q J Econ 70:65–94
Wright EO (1990) The debate on classes. Verso, London
Wright EO, Costello C, Hachen D, Sprague J (1982) The American class structure. Am Sociol Rev 47(6):709–726

The manufacturer's authorised representative in the EU is Springer Nature Customer Service Centre GmbH, Europaplatz 3, 69115 Heidelberg, Germany. If you have any concerns regarding our products, please contact ProductSafety@springernature.com

Printed and bound by CPI Group (UK) Ltd, Croydon, CR0 4YY
25/09/2026
02222886-0010